THE SIMPSONS™

A COMPLETE GUIDE
TO OUR FAVORITE FAMILY

Created By Matt Groening
Edited by Ray Richmond and Antonia Coffman

TED SMART

This edition produced for The Book People Ltd, Hall Wood Avenue
Haydock, St Helens, WA11 9UL

Published by HarperCollins*Publishers* 1997
77-85 Fulham Palace Road, London W6 8JB
3 5 7 9 8 6 4

ISBN 0 583 33809 7

Printed in Great Britain by Scotprint Ltd, Musselburgh

A catalogue record for this book is available from the British Library

Contributing Editor
Scott M. Gimple

Concepts/Art Direction
Mili Smythe

Design
Serban Cristescu and Bill Morrison

Computer Design
Serban Cristescu, Marilyn Frandsen, Binh Phan,
Doug Whaley, Megan Welsh

Contributing Writers
Chip Donnell, Shelly Kale

Contributing Artists
Tim Bavington, Shaun Cashman, Jason Hansen, Bill Morrison,
Phil Ortiz, Cindy Sforza

HarperCollins Editors
Susan Weinberg and Trena Keating

Legal Guardian
Susan M. Grode

Special thanks to
Annette Anderson, Terry Delegeane, Vyolet Diaz, Jason Ho,
Tom Napier, Film Roman, Chris Ungar, and all of the people
who have contributed to *The Simpsons* over the last ten years.

TO THE LOVING MEMORY OF
SNOWBALL I:
WE HOPE THAT
THEY CHANGE YOUR CATBOX
IN KITTY HEAVEN MORE OFTEN
THAN WE DID DOWN HERE.

TABLE OF CONTENTS

CALLING ALL SIMPSONIACS:
AN INTRODUCTION

If "The Simpsons" is a show that rewards you for paying attention (as I've blathered in countless interviews), then this book is for that exalted and/or sorry bunch of you who just can't seem to stop paying attention. It's a jam-packed guide to everything you see on-screen in "The Simpsons," full of sneaky details, hidden jokes, and annoying catchphrases. It's got vital statistics, not-so-vital statistics, and important factoids. It's got the memorable lines, the hard-to-decipher background signs, and even the inside scoop on the notorious freeze-frame jokes. Hell, this thing has so much info in it we could have called it the *Encyclopedia Simpsonica*, except that the marketing people thought that was a stupid title.

And don't worry, this isn't one of those cheapo, cash-in, whip-it-out, crummy guides to popular TV shows—you know the ones: they're printed on lousy paper, they've got about nine words per page, the photos are all gray and washed-out looking. We looked at those books when we started putting this together, and we sneered. We knew we could do better.

So thousands of hours later, after watching each episode over and over and over again, after checking each fact against the scripts and storyboards and original designs, we offer this result. You'll be happy to learn that seventeen people went totally insane in the making of this book, just so that you could know, without doing the counting yourself, that Bart Simpson has nine spikes of hair on his head.

Enjoy!

Your pal,

MATT GROENING

HOMER J. SIMPSON

Age: 36.

Weight: Between 239 and 260 lbs.

Occupation: Worker drone/safety inspector, Sector 7G, Springfield Nuclear Power Plant. (Holds plant record for most years worked at an entry-level position.)

Awards: The C. Montgomery Burns Award for Outstanding Achievement in the Field of Excellence (after Burns found out Homer was sterile due to radiation exposure), Employee of the Month at the Springfield Nuclear Power Plant (after saving the plant from meltdown), Springfield Power Nuclear Power Plant Belching Contest Winner, Grammy Award for "Outstanding Soul, Spoken Word, or Barbershop Album of the Year" for his work with The Be Sharps. High school reunion trophies for most weight gained, most hair lost, most improved odor, and person who travelled least distance.

Favorite foods: Donuts, Pork Rinds Light, Chippos, Krusty Burgers, pork chops, steak, bulk seafood, and honey roasted peanuts.

Favorite beverage: Duff.

Surgeries: A triple bypass operation, resulting from his love of the aforementioned foods.

Favorite pastime: Sitting on the couch while watching TV and drinking beer.

Favorite store: The Kwik-E-Mart.

Says: "D'oh!" when upset, "Mmm..." when tempted.

Extracurricular: Mistaken for Bigfoot. Mascot for Springfield Isotopes. Committed to a mental institution. Manager for country singer Lurleen Lumpkin. Proprietor of the Mr. Plow snowplowing service. Member of The Be Sharps barbershop quartet. Went into space as a NASA astronaut. Charged with sexual harassment for pulling a Gummi Venus de Milo off a babysitter's backside. Neighbor of former President George Bush. Cannonball target with traveling freak show at Hullabalooza. Unknowing assistant to super-terrorist Scorpio in his plot to take over the east coast. Climbed into the ring with the world heavyweight champ. Alcohol bootlegger during short-lived Springfield prohibition. Flirted with homophobia. Voice of the "Itchy & Scratchy" character, "Poochie."

MARGE SIMPSON

Age: 34.

Shoe size: 13AA.

Familial role: Thread that holds Simpson family together.

Famous for: Her marshmallow squares.

Things occasionally found in her hair: Large sums of money, cats, roosters, and Maggie.

Jobs: Strikebreaking teacher at Springfield Elementary, worker at nuclear power plant, carhop waitress, Springfield police officer, pretzel franchisee.

Criminal record: Convicted of misdemeanor shoplifting.

Admirers: Artie Ziff, Mr. Burns, Moe, Springfield Isotopes player Flash Baylor.

Political affiliations: Mary Bailey supporter. Twice voted for Jimmy Carter.

Hair dye: Blue #56.

Favorite singer: Tom Jones.

Turn-ons: Having her elbow nibbled, Homer's "Mr. Plow" jacket.

Quirks: Cooks with less than eight spices. Believes potatoes are neat. Denied having two of Milhouse's teeth, despite the fact that they were actually in her possession. Often sleeps naked. Has webbed feet.

Extracurricular: Lead role in community musical production of "Oh! Streetcar." Considered an affair with kegling pro, Jacques. Came up with the idea for Springfield to host a film festival. Organized town-wide boycott of "Itchy & Scratchy" to eliminate cartoon violence on TV. Developed gambling addiction. Briefly stopped loving son Bart after he shoplifted. Went on lam with criminal neighbor, Ruth Powers. Enjoyed pampering herself after a nervous breakdown at Rancho Relaxo. Conquered a fear of flying after making peace with the fact that her father was a flight attendant. Commissioned by Mr. Burns to paint his portrait. Once encouraged Lisa to smile despite the fact that she was depressed.

SIMPSON

BART SIMPSON

Age: 10.
Personality: Devious, underacheiving, school-hating, irreverent, clever.
Known aliases: Rudiger, El Barto.
Abilities: Possesses a huge repertoire of practical jokes and methods of revenge, with antics ranging from vandalism to international fraud. Prank calls to Moe's Tavern are a specialty.
Discoveries: A comet that nearly destroyed Springfield, Blinky the three-eyed fish.
Idol: Krusty the Clown.
Past loves: Jessica Lovejoy, Laura Powers.
Extracurricular: Sawed off the head of a statue of town founder Jebediah Springfield. Decimated the Australian ecosystem with a bullfrog. Deceived Springfieldians into thinking that a boy named Timmy O'Toole had fallen down one of the town's wells. Made a mockery of a school weather balloon launch by transforming the balloon into an effigy of Principal Skinner. Blew Agnes Skinner off of the commode by throwing a cherry bomb into a toilet in the boy's bathroom. Mistaken for a genius after swapping IQ tests with fourth-grade class brain, Martin Prince. Forced to make antifreeze-laced wine on a student exchange trip to France. Caused marital discord by taking picture of drunken Homer cavorting with belly-dancer, Princess Kashmir. Lead a war against neighborhood bully, Nelson Muntz. Enjoyed brief, injurious career as a daredevil. Nearly disowned by his sister after ruining her Thanksgiving centerpiece. Deadlocked with Todd Flanders in a miniature golf tourney. Saved Mr. Burns's life by donating rare double O-negative blood. Led a rebellion at Kamp Krusty. Helped clear Krusty the Clown's name and finger Sideshow Bob in a Kwik-E-Mart robbery framing. Became famous on Krusty's show as the "I Didn't Do It Boy." Finked on Krusty to the IRS for tax fraud. Won an elephant in a radio contest. Served a brief stint as Mr. Burns's heir. Sold his soul for $5.

LISA SIMPSON

Age: 8.
Role in family: Moral center and middle child.
Once called herself: "The saddest kid in grade number two."
Plays: Saxophone (and, occasionally, the guitar).
First word as baby: "Bart."
Obsession: Ponies.
First crush: Substitute teacher Mr. Bergstrom.
Second crush: Nelson Muntz.
Perpetual crush: Several actors named Corey.
Past addictions: The Corey Hotline, Trucker's Choice Stay-Awake Tablets.
Extracurricular: Mentored by late jazzman Bleeding Gums Murphy. Busted her father for an illegal cable hookup. Won regional *Reading Digest* essay contest, but lost the national competition in Washington, D.C., after losing faith in government. Served brief term as Little Miss Springfield until she became disillusioned by pageant sponsorship by Laramie Cigarettes. Desired by Ralph Wiggum. Disgusted by the talking Malibu Stacey doll's lack of integrity, coinvented poor-selling Lisa Lionheart doll. All-star goalie in pee-wee hockey. Discovered Jebediah Springfield was a pirate. Assisted Mr. Burns in recovering his lost fortune. Passed the second grade as the first female cadet at Rommelwood Military Academy. Refused to participate in "The Simpson Family Smile-Time Variety Hour."

MAGGIE SIMPSON

Age: 1.
Role: Pacifier-sucking youngest Simpson child.
Monetary value: (according to supermarket scanner) $847.63.
Only true enemy: Gerald, the baby with one-eyebrow.
Dexterity: Low. Falls over often.
First word: "Daddy."
Extracurricular: Untied Bart and Lisa after they were bound by notorious Babysitter Bandit. Knows what a credenza is. Can spell out "E=MC2" with her toy blocks and scribble "MAGGIE SIMPSON" on her Etch-A-Sketch. Occasionally drinks from the dog dish. Bonked Homer on head with a mallet and attacked him with a pencil, imitating cartoon violence. Possibly saved her father's life by catching a beer bottle flying at his head. Led a baby rebellion at the Ayn Rand School for Tots. Shot Charles Montgomery Burns.

SCULLY AND MULDER

Occupation:
Agents with the FBI,
Division of Paranormal Activities.

First names:
Dana (Scully) and Fox (Mulder).

Relationship:
Platonic (or so they say).

Favorite letter of the alphabet:
X.

Demeanor:
Truth-seeking (Mulder); skeptical (Scully).

How they view Homer:
As a bumpkin who could stand to lose a few pounds.

AGENTS MULDER AND SCULLY. FBI.

Guest Voice:
Gillian Anderson as Scully,
David Duchovny as Mulder

THE SPRINGFIELD FILES

Episode 3G01 Original Airdate: 1/12/97 Writer: Reid Harrison Director: Steven Dean Moore Guest Voice: Leonard Nimoy as Himself

In a tale hosted by Leonard Nimoy, Homer drinks too much at Moe's Tavern and opts to walk home late one night. He hears something strange and encounters an eerie glowing creature with bulbous eyes and a contorted body emerging from the woods. At home, disheveled and shaken, he wakes up Marge, but the entire family passes off Homer's sighting as a product of his drinking.

The next day, the *Springfield Shopper* prints a story about Homer's UFO encounter. The story finds its way to the Washington bureau of the FBI, where it is read by "X-Files" agents Scully and Mulder. Mulder convinces his skeptical partner to investigate the sighting further. They travel to Springfield to interview Homer and visit the site. Finding Homer's credibility shaky and the people of Springfield annoying, they quickly leave.

Bart and Homer set up camp at the site and videotape the alien during a return visit. The following Friday, hundreds of Springfielders gather to glimpse the alien. When the creature finally appears, Lisa shines her flashlight on it, revealing its true identity. The being is actually Mr. Burns, who has been receiving appearance-altering longevity treatments from Dr. Riviera.

SHOW HIGHLIGHTS

"I saw this in a movie about a bus that had to speed around a city, keeping its speed over fifty, and if its speed dropped, it would explode! I think it was called 'The Bus That Couldn't Slow Down.'"

The horror: After Homer leaves Moe's, he passes through a creepy part of town. He screams in terror when he sees a billboard that reads, "DIE." A gust of wind moves a tree branch, revealing the billboard's complete message: "DIET." Even more terrified, Homer screams again!

"His jiggling is almost hypnotic." Mulder, watching Homer jogging on a treadmill in his underwear.

"All right, they're on to us. Get him back to Sea World!" Moe, spooked by the FBI's visit into unloading the killer whale in the back of his tavern.

"Now, son, you don't want to drink beer. That's for Daddys, and kids with fake I.D.'s."

> **Mulder:** There's been another unsubstantiated UFO sighting in the heartland of America. We've got to get there right away.
> **Scully:** Well, gee, Mulder, there's also this report of a shipment of drugs and illegal weapons coming into New Jersey tonight.
> **Mulder:** I hardly think the FBI's concerned with matters like that.

"Take a look at this, Lisa. You don't see any "Homer Is a Dope" T-shirts, do ya?" Homer, holding up a "Homer Was Right" T-shirt. He later learns that the "Dope" T-shirt sold out in five minutes.

"A lifetime of working in a nuclear power plant has given me a healthy green glow.
And left me as impotent as a Nevada boxing commissioner."

Movie Moments:
Milhouse puts 40 quarters into "Kevin Costner's *Waterworld*" videogame, satirizing the overbudgeting fiasco of *Waterworld*.
The episode also features references to *The Shining*, *E.T.*, and *Close Encounters of the Third Kind*.

> **Mulder:** All right, Homer. We want you to recreate your every move the night you saw this alien.
> **Homer:** Well, the evening began at the Gentleman's Club, where we were discussing Wittgenstein over a game of backgammon.
> **Scully:** Mr. Simpson, it's a felony to lie to the FBI
> **Homer:** We were sitting in Barney's car eating packets of mustard. Ya happy?

THE TRUTH IS NOT OUT THERE
THE TRUTH IS NOT OUT THERE
THE TRUTH IS NOT OUT THERE
THE TRUTH IS NOT OUT THERE
THE TRUTH IS NOT OUT THERE
THE TRUTH IS NOT OUT THERE

> **Homer:** (sipping a Red Tick beer) Hmm, bold, refreshing, and something I can't quite put my finger on. (The scene shifts to the Red Tick Brewery, where dogs are swimming in vats of beer.)
> **Brewery worker:** Needs more dog.

> **Lisa:** All right! It's time for ABC's TGIF lineup!
> **Bart:** Lis, when you get a little older, you'll learn that Friday is just another day between NBC's Must-See Thursday and CBS's Saturday Night Crap-o-rama.

> **Lisa:** Dad, according to Junior Skeptic Magazine, the chances are 175 million to 1 of another life form actually coming in contact with ours.
> **Homer:** So?
> **Lisa:** It's just that the people who claim they've seen aliens are always pathetic low-lifes with boring jobs. Oh, and you, Dad. Heh, heh.

THE STUFF YOU MAY HAVE MISSED

The Simpsons have a *Better Homes Than Yours* magazine on their coffee table.

Leonard Nimoy was last seen in 9F10, "Marge vs. the Monorail."

Moe's Breathalyzer Test's ratings go from "Tipsy" to "Soused" to "Stinkin'" to "Boris Yeltsin."

The official FBI portrait on the wall of FBI headquarters is of J. Edgar Hoover in a sundress.

Springfield Shopper headline regarding Homer's UFO sighting: "Human Blimp Sees Flying Saucer."

The sign at the FBI's Springfield branch: "Invading Your Privacy for 60 Years."

222

THE GUIDE

Color-coded to correspond with the other episodes in the same season, this section features the title of the show and the writer, director, guest voice, and executive producer credits. Also in this section are the episode's original airdate and its production number.

The synopsis of the episode, covering the basic story points.

A brief biography of one of the characters, featuring well-to-little-known facts about them.

Shots from the show.

Notable lines, exchanges, any song lyrics, and memorable moments from the episode.

The icons match the characters with their quotes.

Movie, TV, literary, musical, or historical moments—this box contains the episode's references to various films, television programs, popular culture, and world history.

The signs, the oblique references to previous episodes, the visuals you can only catch by hitting the "pause" button on your VCR—this box contains all that stuff you may have missed.

This episode's blackboard gag.

THE SHORTS
by Matt Groening

FIRST SEASON
#1—"Good Night" (4/19/87)
Story: As Marge and Homer say goodnight to the kids, Bart philosophically ponders the workings of the mind; Lisa hears Marge say, "Don't let the bedbugs bite," and fears that the bedbugs will eat her; Maggie listens to Marge sing "Rock-a-Bye-Baby" and is traumatized by the lyrics.
Noteworthy: Our introduction to the Simpson family.
Look of family members: Extremely crude.
Marge: (singing) *Rock-a-bye-baby, in the tree top/When the wind blows, the cradle will rock/When the bough breaks, the cradle will fall/And down will come baby, cradle and all.*

#2—"Watching TV" (5/3/87)
Story: Bart and Lisa argue over what to watch on TV. They can only agree about stopping Maggie from trying to change the channel.
Lisa: *Change the channel!* **Bart:** *No!* **Lisa:** *Change the channel!* **Bart:** *No!* **Lisa:** *Change the channel!* **Bart:** *No!*

#3—"Jumping Bart" (5/10/87)
Story: Homer always tries to get Bart to jump into his arms, but is never present whenever Bart attempts to do so.
Sign: "No Foolish Horseplay!"
Homer: *Leap like you never–um, leap like you never– what's the past tense of leap? Lept? Leaped? That doesn't sound right.*

#4—"Babysitting Maggie" (5/31/87)
Story: Bart and Lisa are asked to babysit Maggie, but instead they ignore her. Maggie electrocutes herself, falls down the stairs, and chases a butterfly onto the roof and back down again.
Lisa: *I thought I heard a thud.* **Bart:** *You'll hear another one if you don't shut your trap.*

#5—"The Pacifier" (6/21/87)
Story: Bart and Lisa try to get Maggie to stop sucking her pacifier, but Maggie, who has an entire drawerful of them, refuses to give up the habit.
Bart: *You are a depraved little infant.*

#6—"Burping Contest" (6/28/87)
Story: Despite Marge's objections, Bart, Lisa, and even Maggie compete in a contest to see who can make the most disgusting burp.
Look of family members: Often grotesque.
Marge: *What is it with this burping? Why? What's the thrill?*

#7—"Dinnertime" (7/12/87)
Story: Marge serves the family purple goop for dinner, insisting that they say grace first.
Noteworthy: First display of the family's crude eating habits.
You might have missed: News anchor on TV saying, "On tonight's news, bus plunge kills 43, freak rollercoaster accident decapitates family..."
Homer: *Good drink, good meat, good God, let's eat!*

SECOND SEASON
#8—"Making Faces" (9/22/87)
Story: Bart, Lisa, and Maggie make a succession of scary faces at one another despite Marge's warning that their facial positions will be frozen in place forever.
Look of family members: Often frightening.
Marge: *Well, you know, if you keep making those faces you'll freeze that way, and you'll be stuck with a horrible face forever.*

#9—"The Funeral" (10/4/87)
Story: The family attends "Uncle Hubert's" funeral. Bart is excited to see a dead body for the first time but passes out when he glances into the casket.
Bart: *Oh, boy, I never seen a dead body before. Bet his skin'll be all green and clammy and stuff. It'll be just like a zombie movie, only real!*

#10—"What Maggie's Thinking" (10/11/87)
Story: Bart and Lisa hover over Maggie's crib, wondering what she's thinking. Maggie sees them first as demons and then as defenseless infants whom she towers over and tickles.
Bart: *Gooba gooba gabba!* **Lisa:** *You're our little sister!*
Bart: *Gooba gabba! Gooba gabba!* **Lisa:** *One of us, one of us!*

#11—"Football" (10/18/87)
Story: Bart will win a round of frosty chocolate milkshakes if he can catch one of his father's long football passes. Unfortunately, he must stop at the cliff, watching the football, and the milkshakes, disappear...
Homer and Lisa: *Cliff, Bart, cliff!*

#12—"House of Cards" (10/25/87)
Story: Bart's attempts to build a house of cards are constantly interrupted by Lisa and Maggie's sucking sounds.
Bart: *That's one small step for a kid, one giant leap for kidkind.*

#13—"Bart and Homer's Dinner" (11/1/87)
Story: When the girls go out to the ballet, Homer gives Bart a dinner choice of fish nuggets or pork-a-roni.
Bart: *Does eating dog food turn you into a dog?*

#14—"Space Patrol" (11/8/87)
Story: Lisa, Bart, and Maggie role-play a Save-the-Earth game. Lisa is space pilot Lisuey, Maggie is her energetic sidekick Mageena, and Bart is Bartron, the crazed Martian robot who looks like Bart with a vase stuck to his head.
Lisa: *Speak American, Bartron. We Earthlings understand not the Martian tongue.*

#15—"Bart's Haircut" (11/15/87)
Story: Bart goes to a barber who does not know how to trim hair and ends up getting scalped.
Bart: *What the hell did ya do to my head?*

#16—"World War III" (11/22/87)
Story: Obsessed with getting ready for the Apocalypse, Homer repeatedly awakens the family for nuclear-attack drills.
Homer: *Wake up, everybody! It's World War III!*

#17—"The Perfect Crime" (12/13/87)
Story: Bart sets out to steal cookies, figuring that Maggie will take the blame. Instead, he eats too many cookies and lays down among the crumbs to recover, revealing the evidence.
Marge: *I mean it. Don't even think about touching those scrumptious cookies.*

#18—"Scary Stories" (12/20/87)
Story: Bart tells Lisa and Maggie scary stories in the dark that seem to come true.
Bart: *And then they heard it—the sound of the crafty vampire sucking blood from the neck of his latest victim.*

#19—"Grampa and the Kids" (1/10/88)
Story: Grampa tells Bart, Lisa, and Maggie boring stories about the good old days. Realizing that they are not listening, he feigns his own death to recapture their attention.
Noteworthy: Grampa's first appearance.
Grampa: *You know, when I was your age, I had to walk 20 miles just to get to school. And back then we didn't have pacifiers. We had to suck on pieces of wood.*

#20—"Gone Fishin'" (1/24/88)
Story: Bart forgets to pack bologna for his fishing trip with Homer, and secretly substitutes worms in his father's sandwich. Afterwards, father and son take an impromptu ride down the rapids.
Bart: *Boy, for a second there I thought I was up a creek without a paddle.*

#21—"Skateboarding" (2/7/88)
Story: Bart, Lisa, and Maggie ride the local sidewalks on their skateboards, not always with success.
Bart: *Ah, the breeze, the solitude, the wind whistling through your hair...*

#22—"The Pagans" (2/14/88)
Story: While driving to church, Bart, Lisa, and Maggie anger their parents by deciding to convert to paganism.
Lisa: *What a beautiful, paganistic day.*

#23—"Closeted" (2/21/88)
Story: Bart hides in the closet to avoid his chores and ends up outsmarting himself by getting locked in. By the time he escapes, the family has already left to get a round of frosty chocolate milkshakes.
Bart: *I give up! I'll do chores!*

#24—"The Aquarium" (2/28/88)
Story: At the aquarium, Bart foolishly risks his life to do tricks in the shark tank.
Sign: "If You're Here, You're Lost."
Lisa: *Well, the trunks were lucky, even if Bart wasn't.*

#25—"Family Portrait" (3/6/88)
Story: Homer gathers the family for a portrait, but the family continually sabotages his efforts to strike a normal family pose.
Noteworthy: First time Homer strangles Bart.
Homer: *You watch your mouth, you little smart-ass!*

#26—"Bart's Hiccups" (3/13/88)

Story: Lisa and Maggie try to help Bart stop hiccuping, resorting to unorthodox methods to cure their brother of the health nuisance.

Lisa: *Confidentially, Nurse Maggie, this treatment has occasional side effects.*

#27—"The Money Jar" (3/20/88)

Story: Lisa, Bart, and Maggie try to stave off the temptation to steal Marge's money from a cookie jar.

Noteworthy: First time Simpson children consider defying one of the Ten Commandments.

Devil Bart: *Go for it, dude! Get the moolah!*

#28—"The Art Museum" (5/1/88)

Story: Marge and Homer take the kids to an art museum. After Bart ogles a nude painting while Lisa plays with an ancient vase, Marge realizes that the children are not mature enough to appreciate fine art.

Bart: *I have an announcement to make: I'm bored.*

#29—"Zoo Story" (5/8/88)

Story: The Simpsons go to the zoo, where Homer and Bart have a close encounter with a family of monkeys.

Homer: *Now over here, we have the typical monkey family. Just look at their stupid antics.*

THIRD SEASON

#30—"Shut Up, Simpsons" (11/6/88)

Story: Grampa, Homer, and the kids persist in arguing until they formally forgive one another. Bart's forgiveness comes with strings attached: he asks Homer to use a breath mint.

Noteworthy: First time the short plays as a single story instead of a 3- or 4-part episode.

Bart: *(to Homer) I'd forgive you, too, if you'd use a breath mint.*

#31—"Shell Game" (11/13/88)

Story: Bart tries to hide a cookie he stole from the cookie jar. He covers it with one bowl and, finally, to keep his parents guessing, with three bowls.

Homer: *Middle one! Middle one!*

#32—"The Bart Simpson Show" (11/20/88)

Story: Homer demands that the kids stop watching their favorite cartoon, "Itchy & Scratchy." Bart turns off the TV, pulls out the picture tube, gets inside the set, and puts on his own show.

Noteworthy: First appearance of "The Itchy & Scratchy Show."

Bart: *Whoa, gotta run. Goodnight, folks!*

#33—"Punching Bag" (11/27/88)

Story: A punching bag with Homer's picture on it inspires Bart, Lisa, and Marge to new heights of boxing prowess.

Bart: *But you're a mere girl.* **Lisa:** *And you're a sexist pig. Gimme the gloves.*

#34—"Simpson Christmas" (12/18/88)

Story: Bart narrates a holiday tale to the strains of "'Twas the Night before Christmas," which features the Simpson kids sneaking a peek at their Christmas presents.

Homer: *Oh, Maggie, oh, Lisa, oh, little Bartholomew, go upstairs, go right now, before I kill all of you!*

#35—"The Krusty the Clown Show" (1/15/89)

Story: The kids go to see Krusty the Clown's live TV show. To his great disappointment, Bart discovers that his hero is not a real clown but merely some guy in clown makeup.

Noteworthy: Krusty the Clown's first appearance.

Bart: *You know, I base my whole life on Krusty's teachings.*

#36—"Bart the Hero" (1/29/89)

Story: When Bart goes to the candy store for a candy bar, he unwittingly foils a robbery attempt and becomes a hero.

Noteworthy: First time Bart becomes famous for something he did by accident.

You may have missed: The store's name, Chupo's, is an homage to animation executive Gabor Csupo of Klasky/Csupo.

Bart: *Ah, I don't want the money. That's why I've asked for the reward to be paid in candy bars.*

#37—"Bart's Little Fantasy" (2/5/89)

Story: Prompted by his parents' order to clean up his messy room, Bart tells a tale in which children look and sound like the parents and parents look and sound like children.

Child Homer: *I got a plan. You clean up, and I'll tell you a story.* **Child Marge:** *Forget it.*

#38—"Scary Movie" (2/12/89)

Story: Instead of going to see *Return of the Happy Little Elves*, a fearless Bart convinces his sisters to see *Revenge of the Space Mutants*.

Noteworthy: First appearance of the Happy Little Elves and the Space Mutants.

Lisa: *Gee, Bart, you're just like Gloomy, the self-hating elf.*

#39—"Home Hypnotism" (2/19/89)

Story: Marge and Homer use hypnosis to try to make Bart, Lisa, and Maggie behave. The children pretend to act like zombies.

Homer: *From now on you will be good little children.*

#40—"Shoplifting" (2/26/89)

Story: Bart is busted when he tries to steal chocolate from a candy store.

Marge: *The lesson is, ultimately crime hurts the criminal.*

#41—"Echo Canyon" (3/12/89)

Story: During a family vacation, the Simpsons stop at Echo Canyon, where everyone frolics and Bart nearly crunches the family car with a boulder.

Noteworthy: First family vacation.

Bart: *Don't have a cow, Homer!*

#42—"Bathtime" (3/19/89)

Story: To make his bath more exciting, Bart mimics Jacques Cousteau but leaves the water running and the bathroom.

Bart: *(with thick accent) Come with Bart as he dives into ze briney deep searching for the wily and elusive washcloth.*

#43—"Bart's Nightmare" (3/26/89)

Story: After devouring too many cookies, Bart has a nightmare in which Homer catches him stealing cookies and threatens to punish him.

Homer: *Lay off those cookies, boy!*

#44—"Bart of the Jungle" (4/16/89)

Story: Homer is incensed at Bart, Lisa, and Maggie, who are swinging from trees on makeshift vines made from Homer's ties.

Lisa: *This fun, Barzonga!* **Bart:** *Right on, Lisumba!*

#45—"Family Therapy" (4/23/89)

Story: Homer tricks the family into going to a psychologist by pretending to take them out for frosty chocolate milkshakes. He seeks an answer to the family's problems, saying that they don't laugh anymore. The family breaks into a collective chuckle after the psychologist kicks them out of his office.

Psychologist: *(to Lisa) Why, you little borderline psychotic!*

#46—"Maggie in Peril (Chapter One)" (4/30/89)

Story: Bart and Lisa do a poor job babysitting for Maggie. Unsupervised, she hops on Bart's skateboard and rolls through a sewage pipe to a waterfall. As she goes over the falls, the short ends, to be continued the following week.

Maggie: *Suck, suck!*

#47—"Maggie in Peril (The Thrilling Conclusion)" (5/7/89)

Story: Maggie survives her trip over the falls, flies out of the river and into a carnival, grabs onto helium balloons, and lands safely back into her playpen—just as her parents return home.

Maggie: *Whew!*

#48—"TV Simpsons" (5/14/89)

Story: Homer sends Bart outside to fly a kite, but the kite gets tangled in the antenna and distorts the TV picture. Homer is forced to climb up onto the roof to restore it.

Homer: *(to Bart) Why don't you go fly a kite?*

SANTA'S LITTLE HELPER

Current position:
Simpson family dog.

Breed:
Greyhound.

Track record:
Lost continually at Springfield Downs.

Adopted:
After being booted out for the last time.

History:
Returned to dog track once to mate.

Former name:
Previously answered to No. 8.

Favorite beverage:
Toilet-bowl water.

Favorite foods:
Snouts and entrails; most anything Homer eats.

Favorite pasttime:
Shredding newspapers; burying small appliances in the backyard.

Marge asks her children what they would like for Christmas. Lisa requests a pony. Bart asks for a tattoo. Marge takes them to the mall to buy presents. Bart spies a tattoo parlor and lies about his age to get a "Mother" tattoo. With only "Moth" completed, Marge bursts in and drags him out. She spends the family's Christmas money on removing Bart's tattoo and plans to use Homer's Christmas bonus to buy presents. However, Mr. Burns does not give his employees a bonus.

Discovering he has no money for Christmas, Homer gets a job at the mall as a Santa Claus. Bart goes to the mall and harasses Santa, pulling off his beard and exposing his identity. Homer is left without a job and only thirteen dollars. He gets a hot tip from his buddy, Barney Gumble, and takes Bart to the dog track. Homer bets on another dog, "Santa's Little Helper," on a hunch instead. Santa's Little Helper finishes last.

As a dejected Homer and Bart leave the track, Santa's Little Helper gets the boot from his owner for losing another race. Bart is ecstatic when Homer reluctantly agrees to take the dog home. The pair leave with the mutt, ready to tell the family that there will be no Christmas. However, Marge and Lisa assume Santa's Little Helper is the family present and are overjoyed.

SHOW HIGHLIGHTS

"It says it's for dogs, but she can't read." Homer, picking up a squeaking rubber pork chop to buy for baby Maggie at Circus of Values ("Nothing Over $5.00").

Homer at Santa School trying to name the reindeer: "Dasher, Dancer... Prancer... Nixon, Comet, Cupid...Donna Dixon."

"Dad, you must really love us to sink so low." Bart, upon discovering that his father has taken a temporary job as a shopping mall Santa.

"Ah, come on Dad, this can be the miracle that saves the Simpsons' Christmas. If TV has taught me anything, it's that miracles always happen to poor kids at Christmas. It happened to Tiny Tim, it happened to Charlie Brown, it happened to the Smurfs, and it's going to happen to us."

The Spirit Of Taking: Homer is unable to afford a Christmas tree, so he steals one from a forest and is trailed by bloodhounds. When he gets the tree home, the family notices it has a birdhouse in it.

"Now whatever you do boy, don't squirm. You don't want to get this sucker near your eye or your groin." The tattoo removal technician, turning on his laser.

A First and Now Classic Line:

Bart: *Hey Santa, what's shaking?*
Homer: (disguised voice) *What's your name, Bart ...ner? — er — Little partner?*
Bart: *I'm Bart Simpson. Who the hell are you?*

Bart Requests a Tattoo for Christmas:

Marge: *You will not be getting a tattoo for Christmas.*
Homer: *Yeah. If you want one, you'll have to pay for it out of your own allowance.*

ON AN OPEN FIRE

Episode 7G08
Original Airdate: 12/17/89
Writer: Mimi Pond
Director: David Silverman

Created By: Matt Groening
Developed by: James L. Brooks; Matt Groening; Sam Simon
Executive Producers: James L. Brooks; Matt Groening; Sam Simon

Annual Christmas Pageant—The Children's Choir Sings "Jingle Bells":

Marge: (whispering) *Isn't that sweet, Homer? He sings like an angel.*
Bart: (close up, singing) *Jingle bells, Batman smells, Robin laid an egg. The Batmobile broke its wheel, the Joker got away.*

Payday:

Homer: *Thirteen bucks? Hey, wait a minute!*
Clerk: *That's right. One hundred and twenty dollars gross, less social security, less unemployment insurance, less Santa training, less costume purchase, less beard rental, less Christmas club. See you next year.*

THE STUFF YOU MAY HAVE MISSED

The Springfield Elementary School Christmas show receives 3 1/2 stars in a recent review advertised in front of the building.

Lisa requests a pony six times on her Christmas wish list.

Marge pulls her car into parking area "ZZ" at the Springfield Mall.

One tattoo in the Happy Sailor Tattoo Parlor features a knife piercing a heart.

Next door to the tattoo parlor is Dr. Zitsofsky Dermatology Clinic. A sign in the window reads, "Tattoos removed by laser."

Dogs in the race against Santa's Little Helper: Quadruped, Whirlwind, Fido, Dog O' War, Chew My Shoe.

Dear Friends of the Simpson Family,

We had some sadness and some gladness this year. First, the sadness: our little cat Snowball was unexpectedly run over and went to Kitty Heaven. But we bought a new little cat, Snowball II, so I guess life goes on. Speaking of life going on, Grampa is still with us, feisty as ever. Maggie is walking by herself, Lisa got straight A's, and Bart, well, we love Bart. The magic of the season has touched us all. Homer sends his love.

Happy Holidays,
The Simpsons

Bart Simpson on Santa:

Marge: *All right, children. Let me have those letters. I'll send them to Santa's workshop at the North Pole.*
Bart: *Oh, please. There's only one fat guy that brings us presents and his name ain't Santa.*

Marge: *This is the best gift of all, Homer.*
Homer: *It is?*
Marge: *Yes, something to share our love. And frighten prowlers.*

BART THE GENIUS

Episode 7G02 Original Airdate: 1/14/90 Writer: Jon Vitti Director: David Silverman

MARTIN PRINCE

Position:
Brainy fourth-grade class president.

Attracts:
Bullies.

I.Q.:
216.

Insufferable traits:
Squealing on classmates; correcting classmates' grammar; telling the teacher that the class has yet to turn in its homework assignment; kissing up to the principal; baking Raisin Roundees for Mrs. Krabappel.

Positive traits:
Not readily evident.

Injuries:
Once broke his arm in a soapbox derby race while operating a space shuttle mock-up.

Aspirations:
To create a vaccine against cooties.

PICK ME, PICK ME, TEACHER! I'M EVER SO SMART!

Faced with the prospect of flunking an intelligence test, Bart switches exams with brainy Martin Prince. When school psychologist Dr. Pryor studies the results, he identifies Bart as a genius, to the delight of Homer and Marge, who enroll Bart in a new school.

On his first day at the Enriched Learning Center for Gifted Children, Bart feels out of place among other students with advanced academic skills. At home, however, he enjoys the newfound attention Homer shows him. Hoping to stimulate her son with a little culture, Marge buys the family opera tickets.

Ostracized by his genius classmates, Bart visits his old school, where he is rejected by his friends and labeled a "poindexter." When Bart's science project explodes and nearly destroys his new school, he confesses to Dr. Pryor that Martin Prince is the real genius. Bart returns home and tells Homer that he switched tests, and although it was a stupid thing to do, he is glad that they are now closer together. An irate Homer chases Bart through the house.

SHOW HIGHLIGHTS

I WILL NOT WASTE CHALK
I WILL NOT WASTE CHALK
I WILL NOT WASTE CHALK
I WILL NOT WASTE CHALK
I WILL NOT WASTE CHALK
I WILL NOT WASTE CHALK

Mrs. Krabappel, preparing her class for standardized testing:
"Now I don't want you to worry, class. These tests will have no effect on your grades. They merely determine your future social status and financial success. If any."

"Toreador, oh don't spit on the floor. Please use the cuspidor, that's what it's for."

"Well...you're damned if you do and you're damned if you don't."
Bart's contribution to an advanced discussion on paradoxes.

"I bet Einstein turned himself all sorts of colors before he invented the lightbulb." Homer, consoling Bart after his project blows up in class.

"There's nothing wrong with a father kissing his son... I think. Now go on, boy, and pay attention, because if you do, one day you may achieve something that we Simpsons have dreamed about for generations. You may outsmart someone."

"Jeez. No beer...no opera dogs..."
Homer, on the opera.

"I think Bart's stupid again, Mom."
Lisa, explaining to Marge why Homer is chasing Bart through the house.

Kwy•ji•bo: Bart's game-winning Scrabble word. According to Bart, a kwyjibo is a "fat, dumb, balding North American ape with no chin."

"Discover your desks people."
How class is called to order at the Enriched Learning Center for Gifted Children.

The Secret of Bart's Genius:
Homer: *Doc, this is all too much. I mean, my son a genius — how does it happen?*
Dr. Pryor: *Well, genius-level intelligence is usually the result of heredity and environment...*
(Pryor sees Homer staring blankly.)
Uh...although in some cases it's a total mystery.

Bart's First Utterance of a Now-infamous Line:
Martin: *(telling on Bart) I hope you won't bear some sort of simple-minded grudge against me. I was merely trying to fend off the desecration of the school building.*
Bart: *Eat my shorts.*
Martin: *Pardon?*

Martin Brings Bart's Graffiti to Skinner's Attention:
Skinner: *Umm...whoever did this is in very deep trouble.*
Martin: *And a sloppy speller, too. The preferred spelling of wiener is W-I-E-N-E-R, although E-I is an acceptable ethnic variant.*

Marge: *Bart, this is a big day for you; why don't you eat something a little more nutritious?*
Homer: *Nonsense, Marge! Frosted Krusty Flakes are what got him where he is today. It could be one of these chemicals here that makes him so smart. Lisa, maybe you should try some of this.*
Marge: *Homer!*
Homer: *I'm just saying, why not have two geniuses in the family? Sort of a spare in case Bart's brain blows up.*

THE STUFF YOU MAY HAVE MISSED

Maggie spells out EMCSQU (or E=MC2) on her building blocks.

Principal Skinner devotes an entire file drawer to Bart Simpson.

Marcia Wallace's name is misspelled "Masha" in the closing credits.

Books on the shelf in Bart's new advanced school classroom include *Crime & Punishment, Babylonian Myths, Paradise Lost, Moby Dick, Plato, Dante's Inferno,* and *The Illiad.*

The Simpson family attends the opera "Carmen," advertised as "Tonight Only in Russian."

On the opera poster, the conductor is identified as Boris Csuposki, a play on the name of producer and supervising animation director Gabor Csupo.

After he is dubbed a genius, Bart's Principal Skinner graffiti likeness and word balloon is framed and labeled as a work of art entitled "The Principal" by Bart Simpson.

There is a picture of Bart on the wall opposite one of Albert Einstein in Dr. Pryor's office.

HOMER'S ODYSSEY

Episode 7G03   Original Airdate: 1/21/90   Writers: Jay Kogen and Wallace Wolodarsky   Director: Wesley Archer

Mrs. Krabappel takes Bart's class on a trip to the Springfield Nuclear Power Plant. While riding through the plant in an electric cart in an effort to find them, Homer takes his eyes off his driving and crashes into a radioactive pipe, causing the plant to shut down.

Homer is fired for repeated safety violations. Depressed and unable to find a new job, he writes a good-bye note and leaves to jump off a bridge. Lisa finds the note and alerts the family. Rushing across the bridge to stop him, they are almost run down by a speeding truck. Homer pulls them out of the way just in time.

Homer embarks on a public safety crusade to make Springfield a safer place to live. Speed bumps, warning signs, and public awareness posters are placed throughout the city. When he becomes bored with traffic safety, Homer takes on the nuclear power plant, rallying the people of Springfield to his cause. To end the furor Homer is creating, Mr. Burns offers him a position as safety supervisor with a large pay increase. Homer accepts the job, telling the mob to go home and assuring them that he will make their nuclear power plant safe.

> I WILL NOT SKATEBOARD
> IN THE HALLS
> I WILL NOT SKATEBOARD
> IN THE HALLS
> I WILL NOT SKATEBOARD
> IN THE HALLS

SHOW HIGHLIGHTS

"I don't think you're ever going to get another job and be able to pay me back." Moe to Homer, on why he refuses to extend him a bar tab.

Springfield's Age of Consent for Tattoos, According to Otto: 14.

Bart, on Homer's depression. "All he does is lie there like an unemployed whale."

"Dammit, I'm no supervising technician. I'm a technical supervisor. It's too late to teach this old dog new tricks."

"I'll just put it where nobody'll find it for a million years." Smilin' Joe Fission, addressing the nuclear waste problem in a pro-nukes propaganda film.

"There, there, Homer. You've caused plenty of industrial accidents and you've always bounced back."

"You can't depend on me all your lives. You have to learn that there's a little Homer Simpson in all of us."

"Unlike most of you, I am not a nut." Homer, addressing the safety rally outside the power plant.

"Our lives are in the hands of men no smarter than you or I. Many of them incompetent boobs. I know this because I've worked alongside them, gone bowling with them, watched them pass me over for promotions time and again

---

A Few of Homer's New Safety Signs:

"Dip," "Please Drive Friendly," "Speed Bump," "Sign Ahead."

Chip off the Ol' Block:

Sherri: *Hey, Bart. Our dad says your dad is incompetent.*
Bart: *What does "incompetent" mean?*
Terri: *It means he spends more time yakking and scarfing down donuts than doing his job.*
Bart: *Oh, okay. I thought you were putting him down.*

First-ever Appearances:

Wendel; Smilin' Joe Fission; Otto.

Chief Wiggum Addresses the Town Meeting:

Wiggum: *Well, it's no secret. Out city is under siege by a grafitti vandal known as El Barto. Police artist have a composite sketch to go over and if anyone has any information, please contact us immediately.*
(A sketch is passed around; Bart gets it and sees that the drawing is of an older, stubbly, mean-looking version of himself.)
Bart: *Cool, man.*

THE STUFF YOU MAY HAVE MISSED

Springfield Shopper headlines: "Simpson Says Safe!," "Dozens Cheer Homer Simpson," "Homer Simpson Strikes Again!," "Watch Out, Here Comes Homer," and "Enough Already, Homer Simpson!"

A three-eyed fish swims near the nuclear plant in a pond.

A sign at the plant reads, "Our Safety Record: [7] Days Since Last Accident."

Bart's report card includes an F in Social Studies, an F in Math, and a D in Physical Education.

Homer pens his suicide note on "Dumb Things I Gotta Do Today" stationery.

"Hello, Moe's Tavern..."

Moe: *Moe's Tavern.*
Bart: *Is Mr. Freely there?*
Moe: *Who?*
Bart: *Freely. First initials, I.P.*
Moe: *Hold on, I'll check. (calls out) Is I.P. Freely here? I. P. Freely?*

Homer: *You'll get that punk someday, Moe.*
Moe: *I don't know. He's tough to catch. He keeps changing his name.*

Springfield Anti-nuclear Group:

People against People for Nuclear Energy.

TV announcer #1: *Loaftime, the cable network for the unemployed, will be right back with more tips on how to win the lottery right after this.*
TV announcer #2: *Unemployed? Out of work? Sober? You sat around the house all day, but now it's Duff time. Duff, the beer that makes the days fly by.*
Jingle chorus: *(sings) You can't get enough of that wonderful Duff. Duff Beer!*
Homer: *Beer! Now there's a temporary solution.*

MR. BURNS

Occupation:
Rich and ancient owner of the Springfield Nuclear Power Plant; most powerful man in Springfield.

Accomplishments:
Has lived through twelve recessions, eight panics, and five years of McKinleynomics.

Past disguises:
Wavy Gravy; Jimbo Jones.

Favorite lunch:
A pillow of shredded wheat; steamed toast; a dodo egg.

Secret shame:
Physically weaker than an infant.

Favorite non-monetary wager:
Coca-Cola (one can of).

Miscellaneous:
Denture collection includes fangs; once tried to court Marge; once tried to marry Marge's mother.

LOOK AT THEM, SMITHERS. GOLDBRICKERS, LAYABOUTS, SLUGABEDS! LITTLE DO THEY REALIZE THEIR DAYS OF SUCKING AT MY TEAT ARE NUMBERED!

DR. MARVIN MONROE

Occupation:
Media psychotherapist.

Practice:
Dr. Marvin Monroe's Family Therapy Center.

Phone number:
1-800-555-HUGS.

Radio host:
Call-in therapy show — dial 555-PAIN.

Established:
The Marvin Monroe Take-Home Personality Test/ The Monroe Meshuggenah Quotient (or MMQ).

Turn-ons:
Rich people with emotional problems; TV cameras and microphones.

Turn-offs:
Poor people with emotional problems; sanity; patients who take him up on his double-your-money-back guarantee.

OK, YOU .WANT TO KILL EACH OTHER. THAT'S GOOD. THAT'S HEALTHY.

THERE'S NO DISGRACE LIKE HOME

Episode 7G04 Original Airdate: 1/28/90 Writers: Al Jean and Mike Reiss Directors: Gregg Banno and Kent Butterworth

SHOW HIGHLIGHTS

Homer, after watching Dr. Monroe's television commercial:
"When will I learn? The answers to life's problems aren't at the bottom of a bottle. They're on TV!"

 "You know, Moe, my mom once said something that really stuck with me. She said, 'Homer, you're a big disappointment,' and, God bless her soul, she was really onto something."

Marge, on drinking the punch: "I don't want to alarm anyone, but I think there's a li'l al-key-hol in this."

Homer, to God: "You're everywhere. You're omnivorous."

Lisa, on the family receiving double their money back after being kicked out of Monroe's clinic: "It's not the money as much as the feeling we earned it."

"Rub a dub dub, thanks for the grub."

Homer, preparing the family for the company picnic: "As far as anyone knows we're a nice, normal family."

> **Movie Moment:**
> In a scene reminiscent of *A Clockwork Orange* (1971), the Simpson family members are seated in a stark white laboratory, wired with electrodes, fronted by a bank of buttons. Each has the ability to shock everyone else.

> **Mr. Burns:** *And make yourselves at home.*
> **Bart:** *Hear that, Dad? You can lie around in your underwear and scratch yourself.*

> **The Simpsons Go Spying:**
> (The Simpsons peer through a dining room window, watching another family happily eating dinner together.)
> **Homer:** *Look at that, kids! No fighting, no yelling.*
> **Bart:** *No belching.*
> **Lisa:** *The dad has a shirt on!*
> **Marge:** *Look, napkins!*
> **Bart:** *These people are obviously freaks.*

THE STUFF YOU MAY HAVE MISSED

Red, purple, green, blue: The colors of Jell-o molds Marge makes for the picnic.

A sign outside Burns manor reads, "Poachers will be shot."

Smithers wears his plant I. D. even at the picnic.

Dr. Monroe keeps his aggression therapy mallets in a gun cabinet.

> **Homer Needs Money for Dr. Monroe's Therapy:**
> **Lisa:** *No, Dad! Please don't pawn the TV!*
> **Bart:** *Aw, c'mon Dad—anything but that!*
> **Marge:** *Homer, couldn't we pawn my engagement ring instead?*
> **Homer:** *Now, I appreciate that, honey, but we need one hundred and fifty dollars here.*

> **Homer:** *I'm sorry, Marge, but sometimes I think we're the worst family in town.*
> **Marge:** *Maybe we should move to a larger community.*

> **The Lyrics to Marge and the Wives' Musical Salute to Wine:**
> Here we sit, enjoying the shade!
> Hey, brother, pour the wine!
> Drink the drink that I have made!
> Hey, brother, pour the wine!
> He's here at last, my one and only.
> Goodbye friends and don't be lonely.
> Hey, brother, pour the wine.

> **After Burns Sees a Father Kiss His Son:**
> **Burns:** *Awww. That's the kind of family unity I like to see. Smithers, get that man's name. I predict big things for him down at the power plant.*
> **Homer:** *Quick, Bart, give me a kiss.*
> **Bart:** *Kiss you? But, Dad, I'm your kid!*
> **Homer:** *Bart, please. Five bucks for a kiss.*

> **Mr. Burns:** *(greeting guests) ...and this must be (looking down at card) ..."Brat"*
> **Bart:** *Bart.*
> **Homer:** *Don't correct the man, Brat.*

I WILL NOT BURP IN CLASS
I WILL NOT BURP IN CLASS
I WILL NOT BURP IN CLASS
I WILL NOT BURP IN CLASS
I WILL NOT BURP IN CLASS

Homer takes his family to the company picnic given by his boss, Mr. Burns. A cruel and tyrannical employer, Burns fires any employee whose family members are not enjoying themselves. Homer sees that Burns is drawn towards a family that treats one another with love and respect and he wonders why he is cursed with his unloving and disrespectful family.

The Simpsons observe other families on their street. Peeking through living room windows, they see happy families sharing quality time together. Convinced that both he and his family are losers, Homer stops by Moe's Tavern, where he sees a TV commercial for Dr. Marvin Monroe's Family Therapy Center. When he hears that Dr. Monroe guarantees family bliss or "double your money back," Homer pawns his TV set and enrolls the family in the clinic.

When standard methods prove useless in civilizing the family, Dr. Monroe resorts to shock therapy and wires the Simpsons to electrodes. Soon the whole family is sending shocks to one another. Resigned to the fact that the Simpsons are incurable, the doctor gives them double their money back. With $500 in his pocket, Homer takes his blissful family to buy a new television.

BART THE GENERAL

Episode 7G05   Original Airdate: 2/4/90   Writer: John Swartzwelder   Director: David Silverman

Bart gets into a fight with Nelson, the school bully, while protecting the cupcakes that Lisa baked for Miss Hoover. Nelson beats up Bart after school and warns him to expect the same treatment the following day. At home, Homer advises Bart to fight dirty, while Marge suggests that he try to reason with Nelson. Choosing Homer's advice, Bart confronts Nelson, but is beaten up again. This time, he turns to the toughest member of the Simpson family, Grampa Simpson.

Grampa introduces Bart to Herman, a crazed veteran who runs an army surplus store. Herman declares war on Nelson and instructs Bart on a full-assault strategy. Bart gathers other kids at school who have been traumatized by Nelson and enlists them as troops. As Herman commands from the field, Bart leads them into battle. Cornering Nelson and his thugs, they commence firing water balloons.

Terrorized, the thugs surrender. Nelson is taken prisoner, but he threatens to kill Bart as soon as he is untied. Afterwards, Herman drafts an armistice, which Bart and Nelson agree to sign. Marge enters with cupcakes, and

HERMAN

Occupation:
Owner of Herman's Military Antiques.

Past occupation:
Once ran a counterfeit blue jeans operation out of Homer's garage.

Voice:
Bears an uncanny resemblance to that of George Bush.

Pet peeve:
Pacifists.

Prized possession:
An A-bomb built in the 1950s, to be dropped on beatniks.

Springfield lore:
Lost his arm sticking it out of a school bus window, after failing to heed his elementary school teacher's warning.

SHOW HIGHLIGHTS

"Here's one for the road, dude."
Nelson, in Bart's nightmare, punching Bart in the stomach as he lays dead in his funeral casket.

"I am disgusted with the way old people are depicted on television. We are not all vibrant, fun-loving sex maniacs. Many of us are bitter, resentful individuals, who remember the good old days, when entertainment was bland and inoffensive." Excerpt from Grampa's letter to television advertisers.

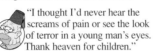
"The key to Springfield has always been Elm Street. The Greeks knew it. The Carthaginians knew it. Now you know it."

"You can push them out of a plane, you can march them off a cliff, you can send them off to die on some God-forsaken rock. But for some reason, you can't slap 'em." Grampa, grabbing Bart after seeing him hit one of his soldiers.

"I thought I'd never hear the screams of pain or see the look of terror in a young man's eyes. Thank heaven for children."

"Contrary to what you've just seen, war is neither glamorous nor fun. There are no winners; only losers. There are no good wars, with the following exceptions: the American Revolution, World War II, and the Star Wars Trilogy. If you'd like to learn more about war, there's lots of books in your local library, many of them with cool gory pictures."

Herman: *When he leaves the Kwik-E-Mart, we start the saturation bombing. You got the water balloons?*
Bart: *Two hundred rounds, sir. Is it okay if they say "Happy Birthday" on the side?*
Herman: *Well, I'd rather they say "Death from Above," but I guess we're stuck.*

Weasel #1: *Nelson, y-you're bleeding.*
Nelson: *Naw, happens all the time; somebody else's blood splatters on me.*
(Nelson realizes his nose is bleeding.)
Nelson: *Hey, wait a minute—you're right! (to Bart) You made me bleed my own blood.*

Bart: *Nelson, it was all a mistake. This is how it happened, man. Listen up; you may get a kick out of it. My sister was baking cupcakes and—*
Nelson: *I'll see you at the flagpole at 3:15.*
Weasel #1: *And you better be prompt!*
Weasel #2: *He has four other beatings scheduled this afternoon.*

The Code of the Schoolyard:
Marge: *Well, Bart, I hope you're going straight to the principal about this!*
Bart: *I guess I could do that.*
Homer: *What, and violate the code of the schoolyard? I'd rather Bart die!*
Marge: *What on earth are you talking about, Homer?*
Homer: *The code of the schoolyard, Marge! The rules that teach a boy to be a man! Let's see; don't tattle, always make fun of those different from you, never say anything unless you're sure everyone feels exactly the same way you do.*

Movie Moment:
While Bart trains his platoon, the trumpets blare the theme from *Patton*.

Bart's Army's Marching Song:
I got a B in arithmetic, woulda got an A, but I was sick/ In English class I did the best, because I cheated on the test/We are happy we are merry, we got a rhyming dictionary.

Principal Skinner: *Uh oh, there's your bell. Come along now, all of you. No dawdling, now.*
Nelson: *(to Bart) I'll get you after school, man.*
Bart: *But–*
Principal Skinner: *Oh, no, no, no. He'll get you after school, son. Now hurry up, it's time for class.*

The Simpson-Muntz Armistice Treaty:
Article IV: Nelson is never again to raise his fists in anger.
Article V: Nelson recognizes Bart's right to exist.
Article VI: Although Nelson shall have no official power he shall remain a figurehead of menace in the neighborhood.

THE STUFF YOU MAY HAVE MISSED

Lisa calls her teacher "Mrs. Hoover" instead of "Miss Hoover."

During their first "fight," Nelson hits Bart twelve times in the face before he knocks Bart out.

In Herman's model of town, he misspells the "Kwik-E-Mart" as "Quick-E-Mart."

There are African shields and spears in Herman's antique shop.

CAN I INTEREST YOU IN SOME AUTHENTIC NAZI UNDERPANTS?

MOANING LISA

Episode 7G06 Original Airdate: 2/11/90 Writers: Al Jean and Mike Reiss Director: Wesley Archer

Lisa awakens one morning with a potent case of the blues. Her teacher notices her sadness and sends a note home to her parents. Homer and Bart, meanwhile, are playing a video boxing game. Undefeated with forty-eight wins, Bart takes only one round to knock off the head of Homer's boxer. While Homer is down for the count, Marge gives him the note from Lisa's teacher. Nothing her parents say can bring Lisa out of her depression.

Hearing distant music, Lisa sneaks out of her room to follow it. She finds a soulful saxophone player, Bleeding Gums Murphy, playing some hard blues. Murphy teaches Lisa how to express her sadness on the sax.

Afterwards, Marge drops off Lisa at school and tells her to smile no matter what she feels inside. She sees Lisa hiding her true feelings and classmates taking advantage of her and tells Lisa that it is best to be herself. When Lisa hears this, she feels happy again.

Meanwhile, Homer takes lessons from a local video game wizard for a rematch with his son. Just as he starts to win, Marge unplugs the TV to announce Lisa's recovery. Seizing the opportunity to maintain his undefeated status as boxing champ, Bart gleefully announces his retirement from the ring. Afterwards, the Simpsons visit a jazz club to hear Bleeding Gums Murphy sing a blues number written by Lisa.

SHOW HIGHLIGHTS

Marge's advice to Lisa: "It doesn't matter how you feel inside, you know. It's what shows up on the surface that counts. Take all your bad feelings and push them down, all the way down, past your knees, until you're almost walking on them. And then you'll fit in, and you'll be invited to parties, and boys will like you...and happiness will follow."

Maggie's choice: Pressured to decide between Bart and Lisa as the one she loves most, Maggie instead chooses the TV set.

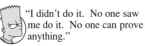 "I didn't do it. No one saw me do it. No one can prove anything."

"Homer 'The Human Punching Bag' Simpson": Bart's nickname for Homer while video boxing.

> **Lisa vs. Mr. Largo**
>
> **Mr. Largo:** Lisa, there's no room for crazy bebop in "My Country 'Tis of Thee!"
> **Lisa:** But, Mr. Largo, that's what my country is all about.
> **Mr. Largo:** What?
> **Lisa:** I'm wailing out for the homeless family living out of its car. The Iowa farmer, whose land has been taken away by unfeeling bureaucrats. The West Virginia coal miner, coughing up his—
> **Mr. Largo:** Well, that's all fine and good, but Lisa, none of those unpleasant people are going to be at the recital next week.

"I Never Had an Italian Suit Blues": The first song Lisa hears Bleeding Gums Murphy play.

"You know you play pretty well for someone with no real problems." Bleeding Gums Murphy, to Lisa.

> **Marge:** (upon finding Lisa jamming with Bleeding Gums Murphy) Lisa, get away from that jazzman! (to Murphy) Nothing personal. I just fear the unfamiliar.

> **Murphy:** My friends call me Bleeding Gums.
> **Lisa:** Ew! How'd you get a name like that?
> **Murphy:** Well, let me put it this way. You ever been to the dentist?
> **Lisa:** Yeah.
> **Murphy:** Not me. I suppose I should go to one, but I got enough pain in my life as it is.

> **Bart:** In the red trunks, with the record of 48 wins and no losses, the undisputed champ of this house, battling Bart Simpson! Whoopee! Woo-woo-woo! And, in the lavender trunks, with a record of zero wins and 48 defeats-oh, correction: humiliating defeats-all of them by knockout—
> **Homer:** Must you do this every time?
> **Bart:** Homer "The Human Punching Bag" Simpson.

> **The Lyrics to Lisa's Blues Number:**
>
> *I got a bratty brother/he bugs me everyday/and this morning my own mother/she gave my last cupcake away/my dad acts like he belongs/he belongs in the zoo/I'm the saddest kid in grade number two.*

> **"Hello, Moe's Tavern..."**
>
> **Bart:** Is Jacques there?
> **Moe:** Who?
> **Bart:** Jacques, Last name Strap.
> **Moe:** Hold on. (Calling out) Jacques Strap! Hey, guys, I'm looking for a Jacques Strap!

I WILL NOT INSTIGATE REVOLUTION
I WILL NOT INSTIGATE REVOLUTION
I WILL NOT INSTIGATE REVOLUTION

THE CALL OF THE SIMPSONS

Episode 7G09 Original Airdate: 2/18/90 Writer: John Swartzwelder Director: Wesley Archer

I'M GONNA GIVE YOU A PRICE FOR YOU, NOT FOR SOMEONE ELSE...SOMEONE ELSE, I'M DOUBLING THIS.

Guest Voice:
A. Brooks as Bob

SHOW HIGHLIGHTS

"Man built this...it's a vehicle." Bob, awed, while introducing the Ultimate Behemoth.

RV salesman Bob, to Homer, on his hopes of buying "The Ultimate Behemoth": "You ever known a siren to be good? No, Mr. Simpson, it's not. It's a bad siren. That's the computer in case I went blind telling me, 'Sell the vehicle to this fella and you're out of business!' That's what the siren says. It seems the Ultimate Behemoth is a wee bit out of you're price range, and 'wee bit' is me being polite. You couldn't afford this thing if you lived to be a million."

Revealed this episode: Ned Flanders makes only $27 a week more than Homer, but Homer makes far better use of his credit.

Birds and bees: While they build a campfire awaiting the return of Bart and Homer, Marge and Lisa discuss the subject of where babies come from. Lisa: "I heard a hideous story about it once in the schoolyard." Marge: "Oh. Well, it's true, I'm afraid."

TV anchorman, making the Bigfoot announcement: "Bigfoot, legendary half-man, half-ape, is no longer a legend. He's very, very real. . . now, the naturalist who took these absolutely extraordinary pictures was most impressed by the creature's uncivilized look, its foul language, and most of all, its indescribable stench. A popular supermarket tabloid has offered a reward of $5,000 to anyone who brings in the creature alive. Naturally, we'll have more on this story as soon as it develops. We now return you to the President's address, already in progress."

The screaming headlines: "I Married Bigfoot," "Bigfoot's Wife Pleads: 'Call Him Homer,'" and "The Bigfoot Diet: 'Pork Chops Aplenty.'"

"And remember not to act afraid. Animals can smell fear. And they don't like it."

"Avenge me, son. Avenge my death." Homer, after being shot with tranquilizer darts by Bigfoot hunters. He begins to snore loudly shortly afterwards.

Homer is envious of neighbor Ned Flanders's new mobile home and goes to Bob's RV Round-Up to buy one of his own. Because of his poor credit, he only qualifies for a dilapidated one. Thrilled with the new RV, Homer takes his family on an excursion. Driving on remote back roads, he loses control of the camper and comes to a halt on the edge of a cliff. The family abandons the vehicle just before it plummets into an abyss.

Stranded in the wilderness, Homer and Bart set out for civilization, unaware that baby Maggie is tagging along. Separated from Homer and Bart, Maggie is soon adopted by a family of bears. Homer and Bart lose their clothes in a fast-moving river and use plants and mud to cover themselves. A nature photographer, mistaking Homer for Bigfoot, takes a picture and flees. Soon the forest is inundated with Bigfoot hunters and souvenir stands. Reporters find Marge and warn her about the hideous creature roaming the woods. When she sees the picture of Homer, Marge identifies the grotesque monster as her husband.

Cold and near exhaustion, Homer is captured by hunters, shot with a tranquilizer gun, and taken to a lab for tests. Scientists observe Homer, but are unsure if he is Bigfoot or a below-average human being. They allow Homer to return to his family until they can determine to what species he belongs.

Into the Woods:
Lisa: Remember, Dad. The handle of the Big Dipper points to the North Star.
Homer: That's nice, Lisa, but we're not in astronomy class. We're in the woods.

THE STUFF YOU MAY HAVE MISSED

The Ultimate Behemoth RV: two-stories high with a fireplace, a full kitchen, four deep fryers—"one for each part of the chicken," a big-screen television set, and its own satellite, The Vanstar I, orbiting the planet.

Signs at Bob's RV-Roundup (formerly RVs R Us): "We give credit to everyone!"; "Bad Credit. Good!"; "Bankruptcy Schmankruptcy."

Signs advertising the Bigfoot cottage industry include "Half-Man, Half-Ape Burgers" and "Get Your Photo Taken with Bigfoot."

The Elusive Truth:
(Scientists from around the world are holding a press conference to announce their findings regarding Homer.)
Marvin Monroe: Ladies and gentlemen, distinguished colleagues, after extensive biological and anatomical testing, I regret to announce that the evidence we have is inconclusive.
Scientist #1: That's what he thinks; I say it's none other than Bigfoot in the flesh.
Scientist #2: Oh no, I disagree. I think it is a man. The eyes have a glimmer of human intelligence.
Scientists #3: Glimmer in the eyes... What about the sloping ape-like forehead?
(Homer and Marge watch the press conference in bed.)
Homer: Oh, the guys at work are going to have a field day with this.

I WILL NOT DRAW NAKED
LADIES IN CLASS
I WILL NOT DRAW NAKED
LADIES IN CLASS
I WILL NOT DRAW NAKED
LADIES IN CLASS

JIMBO JONES

Description:
Shaggy-haired, buck-toothed town lowlife.

Reputation:
Proud to be known as one of the worst kids in school.

Cohorts:
Dolph and Kearny.

Attire:
Never seen wearing anything other than a black skull T-shirt and navy blue watch cap.

Hobbies:
Beating up intimidated classmates; shoplifting from the Kwik-E-Mart; getting kicked out of Space Mutants movies.

Record:
Served time as an abusive counselor at Kamp Krusty.

Secret shames:
Watching soap operas with his mother; the fact that Moe once brought him to his knees.

> I MEAN, THROWING ROCKS AT A STATUE IS ONE THING, BUT I'D NEVER CUT THE HEAD OFF A GUY WHO ICED A BEAR WITH HIS BARE HANDS.

THE TELLTALE HEAD

Episode 7G07   Original Airdate: 2/25/90   Writers: Al Jean, Mike Reiss, Sam Simon and Matt Groening   Director: Rich Moore

Homer and Bart are chased through the streets of Springfield by an angry mob. Someone has sawed off the head of the statue of town founder Jebediah Springfield. Surrounded by the surly crowd, Bart pleads for understanding and relates the events of the previous day.

As the story unfolds, Bart borrows $5.00 from Homer and sneaks away to see *Space Mutants IV* at the local movie theater. On his way, he runs into a gang of troublemakers. One of them, Jimbo, invites Bart to sneak into the movies with him and his buddies. Later, as the boys throw rocks at Jebediah's statue, Jimbo wishes someone would cut off the statue's head. When Bart tries to defend the town's hero, Jimbo and the boys laugh at him. To be cool, Bart sneaks out of the house that night and saws the statue's head off.

The next day, all of Springfield grieves the decapitation of the town founder. Bart finds Jimbo and his pals and discovers they are as distraught as everyone else. Feeling remorse, Bart returns home and confesses to his family. As Homer escorts Bart to the authorities, they are confronted by the angry mob. Bart tells the crowd that his act has united the town and taught people to appreciate their heritage. The townspeople agree, and Bart is forgiven.

SHOW HIGHLIGHTS

Homer, on heaven: "I can understand how they wouldn't let in those wild jungle apes, but what about those really smart ones who live among us who rollerskate and smoke cigars?"

History lesson: A legendary story has it that Jebediah once killed a bear with his bare hands. But modern historians recently uncovered evidence suggesting that the bear probably killed him.

> **Bart:** *Well, I was wondering—how important is it to be popular?*
> **Homer:** *I'm glad you asked son. Being popular is the most important thing in the world.*
> **Bart:** *So, like sometimes you can do stuff that you think is pretty bad so other kids will like you better?*
> **Homer:** *You're not talking about killing anyone, are you?*

> **Movie Moment:**
> The morning after sawing off the head of Jebediah Springfield's statue, Bart wakes up with the head beside him in bed à la the horse's head in *The Godfather*.

I DID NOT SEE ELVIS
I DID NOT SEE ELVIS
I DID NOT SEE ELVIS
I DID NOT SEE ELVIS
I DID NOT SEE ELVIS
I DID NOT SEE ELVIS

> **Literary Moment:**
> Jebediah Springfield's disembodied statue head talks to Bart, representing Bart's conscience in a manner similar to the beating heart in the classic Edgar Allan Poe story, "The Telltale Heart."

> **Sunday School Lesson on Heaven:**
> **Bart:** *Uh, mam, what if you're a really good person but you're in a really, really, really bad fight and your leg gets gangrene and it has to be amputated. Will it be waiting for you in heaven?*
> **Teacher:** *For the last time, Bart, yes!*

 "But that guy founded Springfield. He built our first hospital out of logs and mud. If it weren't for him all the settlers would have died in the great blizzard of '48."

Homer's Wisdom (to Bart): "A boy without mischief is like a bowling ball without a liquid center."

Jebediah Obediah Zachariah Jedediah Springfield: The full name of Springfield's town founder.

> **First-ever Appearances:**
> Dolph, Jimbo, and Kearny.

THE STUFF YOU MAY HAVE MISSED

Marge pulls a Radioactive Man comic book from inside Bart's jacket before leaving the house for church.

Homer has an 8-track tape deck in his car.

A Member of the angry mob carries a sign with the likeness of Jebediah Springfield's head and the words, "Have You Seen Me?"

The football announcer on Homer's car radio says, "This could be the most remarkable comeback since Lazarus rose from the dead."

Announcer: "Wolodarsky takes it at the 5... oh my, he fumbles," reference to show writer-producer Wallace Wolodarsky.

A sign inside church where Rev. Lovejoy has just given a sermon on the evils of gambling reads, "Bingo—Tuesday Night. Monte Carlo Night—Wednesday. Reno Retreat Saturday."

The movie marquee reads, "Space Mutants IV: The Trilogy Continues."

Among the items Jimbo, Dolph, and Kearny steal from the Kwik-E-Mart is a copy of *Playdude* magazine.

Kearney stands on the lawn and leans on a sign that reads "Keep off the Grass."

Sideshow Bob's hair evolves from a huge red afro.

> **The Hammer of Thor:**
> (Homer sits in the kitchen, reading "the Bowl Earth Catalog.")
> **Homer:** *Ooh, look at this one! The Hammer of Thor!* (reading) *"It will send your pins to...Valhalla?"* Lisa?
> **Lisa:** *Valhalla is where vikings go when they die.*
> **Homer:** *Ooh, that's some ball.*

LIFE ON THE FAST LANE

Episode 7G11   Original Airdate: 3/18/90   Writer: John Swartzwelder   Director: David Silverman

For her birthday, Homer presents Marge with a bowling ball with his name engraved on it and drilled to fit his fingers. Feeling unloved and uncared for, Marge takes up bowling so that Homer cannot use her gift. At Barney's Bowl-A-Rama, Marge takes lessons from the local pro and womanizer, Jacques, who shows her the attention she never receives from Homer. Marge bowls every night, leaving Homer alone with the kids, and begins to enjoy Jacques's company.

Homer suspects something is not right, but is unable to tell Marge how he feels. Jacques asks Marge to meet him at his apartment, and she accepts. Before walking out the door for work, Homer tries to tell Marge how much he appreciates and needs her, but cannot find the right words.

On her way to Jacques's apartment, Marge has second thoughts. She encounters a fork in the road. One path leads to Jacques, the other to the nuclear power plant where Homer works. Marge takes the road to the plant. An overjoyed Homer lifts his wife into his arms, and leaves to make love to Marge in his car.

SHOW HIGHLIGHTS

"Hep! Hep! Lisa! My ungue! Hep - stuck in the eater." Bart, after sticking his tongue into the still-moving electric mixer.

Patty, on the phone to Marge: "He never gets you anything you want. He always gets something for himself.... Remember when he got you the tackle box? ... And when he surprised you with the Connie Chung calendar?"

> **Bart:** Great lunches, eh Lis?
> **Lisa:** Oh, Bart, don't you see? This is what psychologists call over-compensation. Mom is racked with guilt because her marriage is failing...
> **Bart:** Hey, don't rock the boat, man. Whatever it is, we're making out like bandits.
> **Lisa:** Bart, I read about what happens to kids whose parents no longer love and cherish each other. They go through eight separate stages. Right now, I'm in Stage 3, fear. You're in Stage 2, denial.

"I couldn't very well chop your hand off and bring it to the store, could I?" Homer, explaining to Marge why he could not get her bowling ball drilled to her finger size.

Jacques, on brunch: "It's not quite breakfast, it's not quite lunch, but it comes with a slice of cantaloupe at the end. You don't get completely what you would at breakfast, but you get a good meal."

Homer makes his feelings known: Homer tells Marge how impressed he is when she makes peanut butter and jelly sandwiches – the jelly never drips over the sides but "stays right in the middle where it's supposed to."

"Let it out, Marge. Laugh loud. Laugh out loud. You'll lose weight."

> **Jacques:** Mimosa?
> **Marge:** (nervous) I'm a married woman. Please don't call me that.

Restaurant Chat at The Singing Sirloin:
> **Patty:** Look at him wolf down that gristle.
> **Selma:** Hmmm, hmmm. It's an accident waiting to happen.
> **Patty:** Do you know the Heimlich maneuver?
> **Selma:** No.
> **Patty:** Good.

Mistaken Identitiy:
> **Jacques:** It is nice to meet you...(looks at her ball) ... Homer.
> **Marge:** (flustered) Oh, no no. Homer is my...ball's name. I'm Marge...
> **Jacques:** Your fingers are so slender, so feminine. They are far too tapered for the ball you are using. You need something lighter, more delicate. Here, use my ball...
> **Marge:** No... no thank you, Mr....uh... (looks at the name on his ball)...Brunswick.
> **Jacques:** Call me Jacques.

> **Marge:** You never intended for me to use that ball.
> **Homer:** Well, if that's how you feel, I'll take it back.
> **Marge:** You can't take it back. You had your name engraved on it.
> **Homer:** So you'd know it's from me!
> **Marge:** Homer, I'm keeping the ball. For myself.
> **Homer:** What? But you don't know how to bowl!...whoops.

Movie Moment:
To the strains of "Up Where We Belong" from *An Officer and a Gentleman*, Marge walks with a purposeful expression into the nuclear power plant and embraces Homer. He picks her up and carries her out of the plant announcing, "I'm going to the back seat of my car with the woman I love and I won't be back for 10 minutes."

THE STUFF YOU MAY HAVE MISSED

At Springfield Mall, Homer parks his car in a spot that warns "Do Not Park Here" and "No Parking."

The stores Homer passes in the mall include: International House of Answering Machines, The Jerky Hut (conducting a "Sausage Sale!"), The Ear Piercery, Girdles 'N Such, Fancy Lingerie, and The Caramel Corn Warehouse.

Sign at The Singing Sirloin restaurant: "Home of Ballads and Salads." The logo is a steak singing with a microphone à la a young Frank Sinatra.

During a moment when Marge and Jacques are outside, the moon behind them has three holes, like a bowling ball.

The nuclear radiation gauge moves from "Okay" to "Danger" as Homer carries Marge out of the plant.

JACQUES

Occupation:
Professional bowling instructor at Barney's new Bowl-A-Rama.

Characteristics:
Tall; thick accent; suave.

Favorite look:
A heavy-lidded lounge lizard expression.

Bowling knowledge:
Knows what the little arrows on the wood floor mean; how to make a 5-7-10 split; which frame is the beer frame.

Fan club:
Apparently the only bowler in all of Springfield to have groupies.

Typical charge:
$40 for a bowling lesson, but only $25 for Marge.

Decor:
Trophies abound for his lovemaking prowess (at least in Marge's dreams).

> TO THE MOST BEAUTIFUL MOMENT IN LIFE... BETTER THAN THE DEED, BETTER THAN THE MEMORY..THE MOMENT OF ANTICIPATION.

Guest Voice:
A. Brooks as Jacques

Occupation:
Belly dancer for hire.

Title:
Queen of the Mysterious East.

Real name:
Shawna Tifton.

Also known as:
April Flowers.

Pet peeve:
Rude people.

Turn-ons:
Silk sheets and a warm fireplace.

Costume:
Occasionally is required to wear birdlike outfits with big wings and a feathery headdress.

GET OUT OF MY CAGE! MY BOSS WILL FREAK OUT.

HOMER'S NIGHT OUT

Episode 7G10   Original Airdate: 3/25/90   Writer: Jon Vitti   Director: Rich Moore   Guest Voice: Sam McMurray as Gulliver Dark

Homer tells Marge that he will be attending a stag party for a co-worker at a restaurant. Meanwhile, Bart receives a mail-order spy camera that has taken six months to arrive. At the stag party, Homer is enticed to dance with a sexy belly dancer named Princess Kashmir.

While Homer is gone, Marge takes the children out for dinner. Unknowingly, they choose the same restaurant where the stag party is well under way–the Rusty Barnacle. On the way to the Buoy's room, Bart stumbles onto the party and sees his father dancing with Kashmir. He takes a photograph with his spy camera and gives the picture to Milhouse, who duplicates it and distributes it to

his classmates. Soon, all of Springfield has a photograph of Homer and the dancer, including Marge, who orders Homer out of the house.

Homer returns home and pleads forgiveness. Marge tells him he needs to show Bart that all women are not sexual objects. Homer and Bart set off to find Kashmir and locate her at a Vegas-type burlesque show. When Homer stumbles onstage during the show, the crowd recognizes him from the picture and applauds. Homer quiets the crowd with a sentimental speech about the importance of women to men. Touched, the men leave to go home to the women they love. Marge, who is also in the audience, runs to Homer and forgives him.

SHOW HIGHLIGHTS

Homer, stepping on the bathroom scale: "Two-hundred-thirty-nine pounds?! I'm a blimp! Why are all the good things so tasty?"

Bart's first spy camera pictures: His eye, Homer exercising in his underwear, Marge shaving her armpits, a run-over squirrel, and his own butt.

New words: Bart rearranges the letters on a sign that says "Cod Platter $4.95" to "Cold Pet Rat $4.95."

Barney, to Homer, spending the night at his apartment after Marge boots him out: "In case you get hungry, there's an open beer in the fridge."

"Animal magnetisme": How Mr. Burns describes Homer's secret to his success with the fair sex.

(Homer walks in the house, only to have Marge shove the photo of him and the belly dancer in his face.)
Marge: *What is the meaning of this?!*
Homer: (stammering) *It's m-meaningless, Marge! Don't even attempt to find meaning in it. There's nothing between me and Princess Kashmir.*
Marge: *Princess who?!*
(Bart walks by, noticing the clamor.)
Bart: *Hey, my photo!*
Homer and Marge: *Your photo?!*
Bart: *Uh oh.*
Homer: *Why you little...!*
Marge: *Why you big...!*
(Marge grabs Homer by the throat.)

Marge: *Homer, is this some kind of stag party?*
Homer: *No, no, Marge. It's going to be very classy, a tea-and-crumpets kind of thing.*
Marge: *Hmmm. Eugene Fisk? Isn't he your assistant?*
Homer: *No!* (quietly) *My supervisor.*
Marge: *Didn't he used to be your assistant?*
Homer: *Hey, what is this? The Spanish Exposition?*

(Bart develops his spy picture in the school darkroom. The photo reveals Homer dancing with Princess Kashmir.)
Martin: *My goodness! Quite exciting!*
Girl: *Extremely sensual.*
Boy: *The subtle grey tones recall the work of Helmut Newton...*
Martin: *Who's the sexy lady, Bart?*
Bart: *Beats me, but the guy dancing with her is my pop.*
All: *Wow!*
Boy: *He brings to mind the later work of Diane Arbus.*

Apu: *You look familiar, sir. Are you on the television or something?*
Homer: *Sorry, buddy. You got me confused with Fred Flintstone.*

"It's an honor to have a real swinging cat with us tonight; Homer Simpson, party guy."
Gulliver Dark, introducing Homer to the crowd.

"You know something folks, as ridiculous as this sounds, I would rather feel the sweet breath of my beautiful wife on the back of my neck as I sleep than stuff dollar bills into some stranger's G-string."

THE STUFF YOU MAY HAVE MISSED

Marge uses an electric razor to shave her armpits.

At the Rusty Barnacle restaurant, Maggie sucks on a piece of fish instead of her pacifier.

When she makes her initial appearance, Princess Kashmir dances out of the dishroom.

The price on the copying machine reads "5 cents" at the front and "10 cents" at the coin slot.

There is a stuffed polar bear in Mr. Burns's office.

A framed copy of the picture of Homer dancing with Princess Kashmir is displayed behind Apu in the Kwik-E-Mart.

Barney's cluttered apartment has a cable spool table and a peeling Farrah Fawcett poster on the wall.

Girlie joints featured in this episode include: Florence of Arabia, Girlesque, Foxy Boxing, Mud City, and the Sapphire Lounge.

I WILL NOT CALL MY TEACHER "HOT CAKES"
I WILL NOT CALL MY TEACHER "HOT CAKES"
I WILL NOT CALL MY TEACHER "HOT CAKES"
I WILL NOT CALL MY TEACHER "HOT CAK

THE CREPES OF WRATH

Episode 7G13 Original Airdate: 4/15/90 Writers: George Meyer, Sam Simon, John Swartzwelder, Jon Vitti Directors: Wesley Archer, Milton Gray

UGOLIN AND CESAR

Occupation:
Evil French winemakers.

How evil:
Very.

Home vineyard:
Chateau Maison.

Their secret ingredient:
Anti-freeze.

Examples of hospitality:
Making guests sleep on the; floor, using them as slaves in their vineyard; testing possibly fatal wines on them.

WHENEVER MY FAITH IN GOD IS SHAKEN, I THINK OF THE MIRACLE OF ANTI-FREEZE.

UNGRATEFUL SWINE!

SHOW HIGHLIGHTS

Homer's food request while laid up: Grilled cheese sandwiches, little wieners in a can, and fruit cocktail in heavy syrup.

Newsweeque: French magazine whose cover features Bart.

Bart, on the people of France: "So basically, I met one nice French person."

"Au revoir, suckers." Bart, to Cesar and Ugolin, as they're taken off to prison.

 "Always remember that you're representing our country. I guess what I'm saying is, don't mess up France the way you messed up your room."

"You may find his accent peculiar. Certain aspects of his culture may seem absurd, perhaps even offensive. But I urge you all to give little Adil the benefit of the doubt. In this way, and only in this way, can we hope to better understand our backward neighbors throughout the world."

"Ah, the life of a frog. That's the life for me."

"See these? American donuts. Glazed, powdered, and raspberry-filled. Now, how's that for freedom of choice?"

"Spanky": Mrs. Skinner's nickname for her boy, Seymour.

Homer: *He makes me crazy twelve months a year. At least you get the summer off.*
Skinner: *Mmm hm.*

Bon Voyage:
Lisa: *What do you know about France?*
Bart: *I know I'm going and you're not.*

Adil: *How can you defend a country where five percent of the people control ninety-five percent of the wealth?*
Lisa: *I'm defending a country where people can think and act and worship any way they want!*
Adil: *Can not!*
Lisa: *Can too!*
Adil: *Can not!*
Lisa: *Can too!*
Homer: *Please, please kids, stop fighting. Maybe Lisa's right about America being the land of opportunity and maybe Adil has a point about the machinery of capitalism being oiled with the blood of the workers.*

Skinner: *Mr. and Mrs. Simpson, we have transcended incorrigible. I don't think suspension or expulsion will do the trick. I think it behooves us all to consider... deportation.*
Marge: *Deportation? You mean kick Bart out of the country?*
Homer: *Hear him out, Marge.*

Cesar: *Drink this.*
Bart: *No thanks.*
Cesar: *Do not worry. This is France. It is customary for children to take a little wine now and then.*
Bart: *Yeah, but it's got anti-freeze in there.*
Cesar: *Drink it!*

Milhouse: *So you're gonna flush it?*
Bart: *What can I say? I got a weakness for the classics.*

(Subtitled from French.)
Bart: *You gotta help me. These two guys work me night and day. They don't feed me. They make me sleep on the floor. They put anti-freeze in the wine, and they gave my red hat to the donkey.*
Policeman: *Anti-freeze in the wine? That is a very serious crime.*

Bart Deported:
Homer: *Wait a minute, Skinner. How do we know some principal over in France isn't pulling the same scam you are?*
Skinner: *Well, for one thing, you wouldn't be getting a French boy. You would be getting an Albanian.*
Homer: *You mean all white with pink eyes?*

THE STUFF YOU MAY HAVE MISSED

Springfield International Airport offers direct flights from Tirana, Albania, and Paris as announced over a PA.

Adil's picture hangs on the wall above Marge's and Homer's bed.

Bart's lower extremities become semi-permanently stained from squishing grapes.

rincipal Skinner encounters Bart and his friends while giving a tour of Springfield Elementary to his mother. When Mrs. Skinner excuses herself to use the ladies room, Bart ignites a cherry bomb and flushes it down a toilet. Mrs. Skinner is blown off the commode.

Exasperated with Bart's demonic behavior, Skinner persuades Homer and Marge to place him in a student exchange program. Expecting the good life, Bart enthusiastically sets off for France as the Simpsons welcome their exchange student, Adil Hoxha, from Albania. Bart arrives in Paris only to discover that his exchange parents, Ugolin and Cesar, intend to use him as their slave. In Springfield, Adil asks Homer to take him to the nuclear power plant. Once inside, he takes pictures of sensitive equipment and secretly relays the information back to Albania.

Ugolin and Cesar force Bart to sample their wine laced with anti-freeze to see if it harms him. When Bart is sent to the store for more anti-freeze, he amazes himself by speaking fluent French and begs a policeman for help. Meanwhile, the FBI detects the satellite signal Adil uses to send his secret material and arrests him. In France, Ugolin and Cesar are arrested and Bart is hailed as a national hero for saving France's precious wine.

GARLIC GUM IS NOT FUNNY
GARLIC GUM IS NOT FUNNY
GARLIC GUM IS NOT FUNNY
GARLIC GUM IS NOT FUNNY
GARLIC GUM IS NOT FUNNY
GARLIC GUM IS NOT FUNNY

Homer stops by the Kwik-E-Mart on the way home from work and witnesses a robbery committed by Krusty the Clown. He positively identifies the clown as the thief, and Krusty is arrested. Krusty is kicked off his show, and Sideshow Bob becomes the new host. Devastated, Bart refuses to believe that his idol is guilty and sets out to prove Krusty's innocence.

Bart returns with Lisa to the scene of the crime to search for clues. They reason that Krusty could not have used the microwave as depicted by the hidden camera footage, because he wears a pacemaker. They also surmise that Krusty would not have been reading at the magazine rack,

SHOW HIGHLIGHTS

Homer, to police sketch artist: "Yeah. Wait a minute. It's the guy from TV. My kid's hero... Cruddy...Crummy...Krusty the Clown!"

"Krusty the Clown, you are under arrest for armed robbery. You have the right to remain silent. Anything you say blah blah blah blah blah blah."

"He's my idol. I've based my whole life on his teachings." Bart, on Krusty.

News headline on TV: "Krusty Gets Busted: The Day the Laughter Died."

"Give a hoot! Read a book!" Semi-original slogan for Krusty's literacy campaign.

"Because these are children's toys the fire will spread quickly... stand back and try not to inhale the toxic fumes." Reverend Lovejoy, leading an anti-Krusty crusade.

"Krusty wore big floppy shoes but he's got little feet like all good-hearted people." Bart, revealing to the world that Bob framed Krusty.

Apu: *What's the matter, sir? Never have I seen you look so unhappy while purchasing such a large quantity of ice cream.*
Homer: *The reason I look unhappy is that tonight I have to see a slide show starring my wife's sisters—or as I call them, "the gruesome twosome."*

Krusty: *Hand over all your money in a paper bag.*
Apu: *Yes, yes, I know the procedure for armed robbery. I do work in a convenience store you know.*
(Krusty takes the money and flees.)
Apu: *(to Homer) You can emerge now from my chips. The opportunity to prove yourself a hero is long gone.*

Marge: *(to Bart) Oh, Bart...maybe it'll turn out he was innocent all along.*
Homer: *Earth to Marge. Earth to Marge. I was there... the clown's (spelling) G-I-L-L-T-Y.*

Judge: *Krusty the Clown, how do you plead?*
Krusty: *I plead guilty, Your Honor...(bewildered, then panicked) Uh...I mean, not guilty. Opening night jitters, Your Honor.*

Bart Asks for Lisa's Help to Prove
Krusty's Innocence:
Bart: *(reluctantly) I'll never forgive you for making me say this, but...you're smarter than me.*

THEY ARE LAUGHING AT
ME, NOT WITH ME.
THEY ARE LAUGHING AT
ME, NOT WITH ME.
THEY ARE LAUGHING AT
ME, NOT WITH ME.
THEY ARE LAUGHING AT
ME, NOT WITH ME.

BUSTED

Episode 7G12
Original Airdate: 4/29/90
Writers: Jay Kogen & Wallace Wolodarsky
Director: Brad Bird
Guest Voice: Kelsey Grammer

because he is illiterate. They conclude that Krusty was framed.

At a live broadcast of "The Sideshow Bob Cavalcade of Whimsy," Bart reveals the impostor. Sideshow Bob had the most to gain by Krusty's downfall. Unlike Krusty, the impostor had feet large enough to completely fill Krusty's clown shoes—that's why he yelled when Homer stepped on his feet. Bart contends that the big feet belong to Sideshow Bob and demonstrates the fact by bashing Bob's feet with a mallet. Sideshow Bob admits that he framed Krusty because he was tired of being the brunt of Krusty's jokes. Krusty is set free. He thanks Bart for his help.

Itchy & Scratchy Theme Music:

Chorus: *"They fight, they bite/they bite and fight and bite/bite, bite, bite/fight, fight, fight/The Itchy and Scratchy Show."*

THE STUFF YOU MAY HAVE MISSED

Sign on Kwik-E-Mart microwave: "People with pacemakers should stay away from this thing."

The Krusty/Elvis connection: Krusty got his start in Tupelo, Mississippi, too.

The cover of *Timely Magazine*: "Krusty—Krook of the Year."

Number of slide carousels Patty and Selma bring from their trip to the Yucatan:
Eight

Krusty's Opening Cheer:

Krusty: *Hey, kids! Who do you love?*
Audience: *Krusty!*
Krusty: *How much do you love me?*
Audience: *With all our hearts!*
Krusty: *What would you do if I went off the air?*
Audience: *We'd kill ourselves!*

IF THIS IS ANYONE BUT STEVE ALLEN, YOU'RE STEALING MY BIT!

MS. BOTZ

Real name:
Lucille Botzcowski.

Known as:
The Babysitter Bandit.

Carries:
Lots of luggage.

Hired from:
The Rubber Baby Buggy Bumper Babysitting Service.

Most revealing physical characteristic:
Her pronounced overbite.

Turn-ons:
Gaining access to homes by posing as a babysitter; tying up and gagging family members before robbing them blind; pickled beets.

Turn-offs:
Being profiled on "America's Most Armed and Dangerous"; children who give her guff; possessions that lack value.

YOU'RE A SMART YOUNG MAN, BART. I HOPE YOU'RE SMART ENOUGH TO KEEP YOUR MOUTH SHUT.

Guest Voice:
Penny Marshall as Ms. Botz

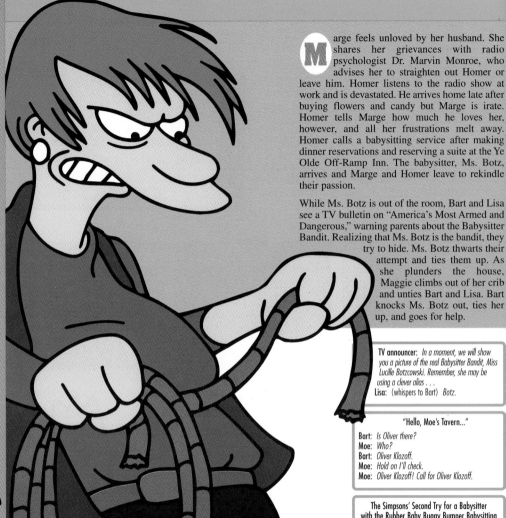

Marge feels unloved by her husband. She shares her grievances with radio psychologist Dr. Marvin Monroe, who advises her to straighten out Homer or leave him. Homer listens to the radio show at work and is devastated. He arrives home late after buying flowers and candy but Marge is irate. Homer tells Marge how much he loves her, however, and all her frustrations melt away. Homer calls a babysitting service after making dinner reservations and reserving a suite at the Ye Olde Off-Ramp Inn. The babysitter, Ms. Botz, arrives and Marge and Homer leave to rekindle their passion.

While Ms. Botz is out of the room, Bart and Lisa see a TV bulletin on "America's Most Armed and Dangerous," warning parents about the Babysitter Bandit. Realizing that Ms. Botz is the bandit, they try to hide. Ms. Botz thwarts their attempt and ties them up. As she plunders the house, Maggie climbs out of her crib and unties Bart and Lisa. Bart knocks Ms. Botz out, ties her up, and goes for help.

TV announcer: *In a moment, we will show you a picture of the real Babysitter Bandit, Miss Lucille Botzcowski. Remember, she may be using a clever alias . . .*
Lisa: *(whispers to Bart) Botz.*

"Hello, Moe's Tavern..."
Bart: *Is Oliver there?*
Moe: *Who?*
Bart: *Oliver Klozoff.*
Moe: *Hold on I'll check.*
Moe: *Oliver Klozoff! Call for Oliver Klozoff.*

The Simpsons' Second Try for a Babysitter with the Rubber Baby Buggy Bumper Babysitting Service:
Homer: *Hello, this is Mr...Sampson.*
Receptionist: *Did your wife just call a second ago?*
Homer: *No. I said Sampson, not Simpson.*

"Hello, Moe's Tavern..."
Bart: *Hello, is Al there?*
Moe: *Al?*
Bart: *Yeah, Al. Last name, Koholic.*
Moe: *Phone call for Al. Al Koholic. Is there an Al Koholic here?*

Radio screener: *First name, age, problem.*
Marge: *I'm Marge, thirty-four, and my problem is my husband. He doesn't listen to me. He doesn't appreciate me. I don't know how much more of this I can —*
Screener: *Hey, lady! Save your whining for when you're on the air, okay?*

SHOW HIGHLIGHTS

"Marge, it's what I call harsh reality time. Your husband sees you as nothing." Radio therapist Dr. Marvin Monroe, counseling Marge on-air.

"You're a pig. Barney's a pig. Larry's a pig. We're all pigs...once in a while, we can crawl out of the slop, hose ourselves off, and act like human beings."

"You're just like Chilly, the elf who cannot love." Lisa, on Bart's distaste for the Happy Little Elves.

The big night out: Dinner at Chez Paree, dancing to The Larry Davis Experience, and a night at Ye Olde Off-Ramp Inn.

Marge's reassurance to Homer: "The way I see it, if you raise three children who can knock out and hog-tie a perfect stranger, you must be doing something right."

"Homer Simpson, Local Boob": Subtitle under Homer's picture on the TV news.

EVENING

Episode 7G01
Original Airdate: 5/13/90
Writers: Matt Groening & Sam Simon
Directors: David Silverman & Kent Butterworth

Meanwhile, Marge and Homer arrive home and find Ms. Botz bound and gagged. Assuming that the kids are playing a prank, Homer frees Ms. Botz and pays her triple her normal fee. He sees her off just before police and reporters arrive. As TV newsmen confront him about helping the Babysitter Bandit escape, Homer learns he has been duped.

THE STUFF YOU MAY HAVE MISSED

Screener cards at Dr. Monroe's radio show say: "Line 1: Marge, 34, Another Unappreciated Housewife" and "Line 2: Paul Hsi, 41, Nail Biter (not his own)."

Bart has a Krusty the Clown lunchbox.

Lisa has a Happy Little Elves lunchbox.

Bart and Lisa watch "The Happy Little Elves Meet the Curious Bear Cub" videos, rated "GGG."

Number of times Maggie fall down in this episode: 19

Babysitter Bandit call-in line: "Vigilant Viewer Hotline: 1-800-U-Squeal."

There is a picture of a Space Mutant (from the *Space Mutants'* film series) on the wall beside the pay phone Bart and Lisa use in the Babysitter Bandit capture.

The painting on the Rubber Baby Buggy Bumper Babysitting Service wall features a dog barking at a burning house.

Homer's clean-shaven look lasts exactly 7 seconds. Then his shadow returns.

Nuclear Power Plant signs: Warning - Radioactive Area, No Smoking, No Eating, No Foolish Horseplay, 7 Days Since Last Accident, In Case of Meltdown, Break Glass (glass is already broken).

Bart vs. Botz:

Botz: *Come, children. Let's go watch the Happy Little Elves.*
Bart: *Look, lady, we've seen the crappy little elves about fourteen billion times. Maybe we can watch some real TV.*
Botz: *I said we're gonna watch the tape.*
Bart: *Aw, that's merely suggested viewing matter, lady. Mom lets us watch whatever the hell we want.*
Botz: *I said, you're gonna watch this tape and you're gonna do what I say or I'm gonna do something to you and I don't know what that is because everybody has always done what I say!*

I WILL NOT YELL 'FIRE!' IN A CROWDED CLASSROOM
I WILL NOT YELL 'FIRE!' IN A CROWDED CLASSROOM
I WILL NOT YELL 'FIRE!' IN A CROWDED CLASSROOM

Homer: *They all look so tasty. But I think I'll eat this one right there.*
Maitre D': *Why don't you pick one that's a little more frisky, sir?*
Homer: *Why?*
Maitre D': *Well, when you choose one that's floating upside down, it somewhat defeats the purpose of selecting a live lobster.*

HOMER SAYS, "D'OH..."

. . . upon discovering that the extension cord for the Christmas lights is tangled. (7G08) . . . after Bart pulls the fake beard off of his Santa suit. (7G08) . . . when he bangs his head on the door frame of Santa's Workshop. (7G08) . . . when Bart says, "You think I'm dumb enough to fall for that?" as he tries to coax Bart out of his room. (7G02) . . . while the kids are misbehaving at the company picnic. (7G04) . . . after a ball hits him in the back of the head. (7G04) . . . upon discovering that he has crushed the flowers around his own house. (7G04) . . . in response to Marge's suggestion that the family move to a larger community, after Homer identifies them as the worst family in town. (7G04) . . . after Lisa snatches a cupcake away from him. (7G05) . . . as he is pelted with water balloons. (twice) (7G05) . . . when, after looking all over the house for his keys, he discovers that they are in the door. (7G06) . . . while getting beat up by Bart in a boxing video game. (7G06) . . . during a nightmare in which Bart beats him up. (7G06) . . . after his own echo tells him to shut up. (7G09) . . . when, after lamenting Bart's death, he finds out that his son is alive. (7G09) . . . after tasting a mouthful of bee-laden honey. (twice) (7G09) . . . as he watches a football game before going to church. (7G07) . . . when a player fumbles. (7G07) . . . when he finds out that Patty and Selma are joining the family for dinner. (7G11) . . . when his lottery numbers are not picked. (7G10) . . . when he discovers that the picture of him dancing with Princess Kashmir is on display at Moe's. (7G10) . . . after he falls and is unable to get back up. (7G13) . . . after Marge tells him that Patty and Selma are coming over. (7G12) . . . after a videotape depicting him as a coward is shown in court. (7G12) . . . when Bart's vision returns and he asks for a TV in his room. (7F03) . . . when he realizes that he's out of tartar sauce. (7F02) . . . after Carl calls him "chrome dome." (7F02) . . . after Smithers tells him that he has to deliver his speech in five minutes. (7F02) . . . when Marge tells him her plans for the evening. (7F01) . . . when Marge says he can't "wave [his] fanny" in public while sitting next to Mr. Burns. (7F05) . . . when he falls into the dugout. (7F05) . . . when he realizes that he's out of Duff. (7F08) . . . as his golf ball bounces out of the park. (7F08) . . . when Bart names his putter, "Mr. Putter." (7F08) . . . when Flanders sees Bart meditating with his putter. (7F08) . . . when Homer's "'fraid not infinity" is beat by Flanders's "'fraid not infinity plus one." (7F08) . . . when he realizes that Flanders is not humiliated by having to wear his wife's best dress. (7F08) . . . when he realizes that Patty and Selma are at the door. (7F07) . . . after Patty and Selma comment that even a caveman could start a fire, as he struggles to light the logs in the fireplace. (7F07) . . . as Lisa plays her saxophone loudly. (7F07) . . . after Skinner announces that the recital he is attending is the first in a series. (7F06) . . . after Bart makes an insincere promise. (7F06) . . . as he falls down Springfield Gorge. (7F06) . . . upon learning that Marge is too busy to make pork chops. (7F09) . . . when Marge testifies that she doesn't think Dr. Nick is a real M.D. (7F10) . . . when he is told that his meatloaf will take eight seconds to cook. (7F11) . . . when the phone rings while he is taping his video message to Maggie. (7F11) . . . when he sees Barney from the prison window. (7F11) . . . after Dr. Hibbert tells Marge that she's pregnant. (7F12) . . . when Principal Skinner calls about Bart. (7F15) . . . after realizing that he has introduced Patty as Selma to Skinner. (7F15) . . . when he is pulled over by a state trooper on the highway. (7F16) . . . when Santa's Little Helper rips up the sports section of the newspaper. (7F14) . . . when he realizes that Santa's Little Helper has run away. (7F14) . . . after Bart tells Marge that his Assassins sneakers cost $125. (7F14) . . . upon seeing that the family has disappeared just as he warns them not to get separated. (7F18) . . . as he is stuck in a waterslide and hit by several kids. (7F18) . . . after all the channels broadcast the story about how he got stuck in the waterslide. (7F18) . . . when his stomach gurgles, just as he promises to start dieting. (7F18) . . . upon viewing Marge's nude painting of Mr. Burns. (7F18) . . .

when he opens his car door after a storm and water rushes out of it. (7F21) . . . when Bart's only reward for donating blood was a thank-you card. (7F22) . . . after finding out that Bart mailed his insulting letter to Mr. Burns. (7F22) . . . after he is unable to think of a fake name. (7F22) . . . upon seeing the giant Olmec Indian head. (7F22) . . . when Lisa tells him that she'll fill out a form for him only if he listens to some of her poetry. (7F24) . . . when he is interrupted by the announcement of a visitor just as he is about to eat his pancakes. (7F24) . . . when the man from the collection agency who is looking for Flanders says he'll be back for Homer. (7F23) . . . after Jimbo and Kearney egg his house. (8F02) . . . when Lisa tells him that he has confused Monaco with Morocco. (8F02) . . . when Maggie uses one of the Simpsons' four wishes to wish for a pacifier delivered by limousine. (8F02) . . . when, after his transformation into a jack-in-the-box, a baseball hits him in the head. (8F02) . . . when he discovers that a surveillance camera is monitoring him. (8F02) . . . while banging his head on Moe's bar top. (four times) (8F06) . . . after realizing that he doesn't know whether Lisa has an alto or a tenor sax. (8F06) . . . when Lisa doesn't forgive him at Phineas Q. Butterfat's 5600 Flavors Ice Cream Parlor. (8F06) . . . when Marge says that horses can live as long as 30 years. (8F06) . . . when he realizes that Lisa heard him say he would do something with her, Bart, and Maggie. (8F07) . . . as Bart, driving Martin's soapbox racer, passes him in his car. (8F07) . . . upon discovering that Patty is drinking the last beer during the Czechoslovakian slide show. (8F08) . . . after catching himself telling Marge that he is going to Moe's. (8F08) . . . when the power plant's vending machine refuses his mangled dollar bill. (twice) (8F09) . . . when he realizes that he's the negligent safety inspector Horst is talking about. (8F09) . . . when Lisa tells him that Germans are "efficient and punctual, with a strong work ethic." (8F09) . . . when Marge's pregnancy test results in an ambiguous pink rather than blue or purple. (8F10) . . . when he finds out that Marge is pregnant with Bart. (8F10) . . . when Bart gives Homer's gift back. (8F11) . . . upon discovering that there is no more chocolate in the Neapolitan ice cream. (twice) (8F11) . . . when Homer says that Bart is an unwanted child on live television. (8F11) . . . while watching football, after his team fumbles. (8F12) . . . when he discovers that the woman on TV who is having a mental breakdown is Marge. (8F14) . . . after failing to think of someone who has gotten rich by doing yo-yo tricks. (8F16) . . . after discovering that he has nailed a piece of his homemade doghouse to himself. (twice) (8F16) . . . after dropping his beer can due to having stubby fingers. (8F15) . . . upon seeing that he is missing the numbers 3 and 17 in the state lottery. (twice) (8F17) . . . after the building on which he has hung all his "Lost Dog" flyers is demolished. (8F17) . . . after consecutively losing two parking spaces at the Springfield Googoplex theaters. (twice) (8F19) . . . when Bart eludes him by grabbing on to the ceiling fan and making a quick 180-degree turn. (8F22) . . . when he's told to report to Mr. Burns's office. (8F23) . . . after hearing that he has the wrong lottery numbers. (four times) (8F24) . . . after roller skates that were left on the lawn get caught in the lawn mower. (8F24) . . . when he finds out that Bart is the leader of the revolt at Kamp Krusty. (8F24) . . . after getting a 7-10 split and a gutterball while playing Bowling 2000. (twice) (8F18) . . . upon realizing that he's forgotten what to do in the event of fire. (9F01) . . . after seeing a raincloud douse the fire on Flanders's roof. (9F01) . . . after his toga snags on a nail and rips off, exposing him in his underwear in front of all the party guests. (9F04) . . . when he realizes that he's forgotten to get Bart's birthday gift. (9F04) . . . after realizing that he's messed up the scary story he was telling. (9F04) . . . in response to Marge, who correctly guesses the number 37, after Homer asks her to think of a number between 1 and 50. (9F03) . . . when, forty years into the future, movie tickets to The Itchy & Scratchy Movie cost $650. (9F03) . . . when he finds out that Surly Joe is the only foundation repair man in town. (9F05) . . . after Maggie steals his cookie. (9F08) . . . after Lisa calls him "Homer" instead of "Daddy." (9F08)

. . . when Mr. Burns cancels the condolence ham after realizing that Homer is alive. (9F09) . . . when he messes up the "Monorail" song. (9F10) . . . when the out-of-control, solar-powered monorail resumes after a solar eclipse has caused it to briefly stop. (9F10) . . . after thinking out loud about the legend of the Dog-Faced Woman while driving to Aunt Gladys's funeral. (9F11) . . . when he discovers that the school pageant is not yet over. (9F13) . . . as he is being arrested for drunk driving. (9F14) . . . when he finds out the union president position is an unpaid one. (9F15) . . . after trading Bart a Danish for a "delicious doorstop." (9F15) . . . when Principal Dondelinger mistakes him for a vagrant. (9F16) . . . when he discovers a plunger stuck on his head at his 50th high school reunion. (9F16) . . . after he almost runs over Bart and Marge. (9F18) . . . when, in response to Mr. Burns's request for his name, he answers, "Mr. Burns." (9F20) . . . when he has a blowout shortly after announcing that he sold his spare tire at the flea market. (9F21) . . . when he can't think of good lyrics for a new song. (9F21) . . . after a bee stings him in the rear. (1F02) . . . after opening his college rejection letters. (four times) (1F02) . . . when Marge figures out that Benjamin, Doug, and Gary changed his grades. (1F02) . . . as he slips on Bart's skateboard and falls down the stairs. (twice) (1F01) . . . when he is ordered to report for "much worse duties" at work. (1F01) . . . when the vampire Mr. Burns returns from the dead to fire him. (1F04) . . . upon learning that a lumber yard burned down while the fire department tried to free his arms from two vending machines. (1F03) . . . as he is pummeled into the ledge of a cliff by a trampoline (à la Wile E. Coyote). (1F05) . . . when, while teasing Bart about making "crappy furniture," the chair he is sitting in breaks. (1F06) . . . after realizing that his use of reverse psycholgy on Bart has backfired. (1F06) . . . upon learning that his relaxed theory on currents has sent his boat drifting away from land. (1F06) . . . when he destroys a rescue plane with a flare gun. (1F06) . . . when the pilot is rescued and Homer's group is not. (1F06) . . . when he discovers that Mindy shares his idea of heaven (drinking beer and watching TV). (1F07) . . . when, while wearing Henry Kissinger's glasses, he confuses an isosceles triangle with a right triangle. (1F08) . . . upon discovering that the cat burglar stole the portable TV. (1F09) . . . when, after he breaks a lamp, he sets off a litany of catchphrases. (1F11) . . . when he is unable to rhyme during Apu's song. (1F10) . . . when he learns that India is 16,000 km. away. (1F10) . . . upon learning that Abe's inheritance (mint condition 1918 liberty head silver dollars) is bequeathed to the whole family instead of just him. (1F12) . . . when he cuts his finger on Sgt. Thug's Mountaintop Command Post. (1F12) . . . when, after stating that the TV respects him, he turns it on and finds a man laughing at him. (1F13) . . . when he is hit on the head by the Fox satellite. (1F13) . . .when he flattens his tires while driving in to the power plant through the exit. (1F14) . . . when he discovers why no one wants to clean the basement. (twice) (1F15) . . . while crashing into a statue of a female deer at the Springfield Tar Pits. (1F15) . . . when he draws three cards during a poker game. (twice) (1F20) . . . when Maggie proves she knows the difference between a monkey and a credenza. (1F21) . . . when he builds a barn rather than a swimming pool ("D'oheth"). (1F22) . . . when the family instantly hits traffic upon entering the on-ramp to the freeway en route to Itchy & Scratchy Land. (2F01) . . . when, on Tuesday, Homer forgets to lock the front door. (2F03) . . . when, on Wednesday, he realizes that he didn't lock the back door. (twice) (2F03) . . . upon introducing himself as Johnny Carson to an empty room. (2F03) . . . upon introducing himself as David Letterman to an empty room. (2F03) . . . upon learning that Ned

Flanders is the unquestioned lord and master of the world. (2F03) . . . as he emerges in an alternate, but seemingly better, world. (2F03) . . . when he realizes that the sexual harrassment protesters are protesting about him. (2F06) . . . during his portrayal of Dr. Smith from "Lost in Space" in Marge's dream. (2F08) . . . after he tells Marge that he is stalking Lenny and Carl. (2F09) . . . upon losing a $100 phone bet on red at Las Vegas. (2F14) . . . when he misses a question on his written test for a limousine license. (2F14) . . . after he writes "Simpson" instead of "Sherman." (twice) (2F31) . . . after mastering Burns's catchphrase. (2F31) . . . upon opening a can of spring snakes labelled "beer nuts." (2F31) . . . as the greyhound puppies eat his potato chips. (eight times) (2F18) . . . when the hanging light bulb he is batting to cheer himself up hits him in the head and breaks. (2F18) . . . after Marge informs him that, while jazz-singing "Mary Had a Little Lamb," he replaced "De's" with "Do's." (2F32) . . . when, à la "I Love Lucy," he separates the house with a line of chalk and corners himself. (2F21) . . . when Burns fails to remember his name, even after Homer attacks him. (2F16) . . . upon his arrest for attempting to murder Mr. Burns. (2F20) . . . when, while driving with his knees, he drops one of his two ice creams. (2F20) . . . just before holding Chief Wiggum's gun to Mr. Burns's head. (2F20) . . . upon realizing that he has invited Ned to a barbecue instead of snubbing him. (3F03) . . . when he finds out that a colossal donut is really just a normal donut. (3F04) . . . after a bucket of bolts misses him, foiling his attempt to injure himself in the hard hat area. (3F05) . . . when he backs the car over tire spikes in a parking lot. (3F08) . . . when his brain tells him, "There it is, Homer, the cleverest thing you'll ever say, and no one heard it." (3F09) . . . upon realizing that George Bush is ahead of him at a fast-food drive-thru. (3F09) . . . when he fails to get the last word in an exchange with Bush. (3F09) . . . when Burns throws a book at his head. (3F14) . . . as Smithers hits him with a phone. (four times) (3F14) . . . when Lisa asks him, "Who do you love most–me, Bart, or Maggie?" during a game of "truth or dare." (3F17) . . . when he accidentally rips off Maggie's clothes while trying to free her from a newspaper vending machine. (3F18) . . . when the fuse on his M-320 burns off. (3F22) . . . when an alien overseer whips him. (4F02) . . . when, during a trust exercise, Scorpio answers a phone call instead of catching Homer's fall. (3F23) . . . when Marge tells him that a competent doctor must approve his boxing career. (4F03) . . . in slow motion, after Drederick Tatum hits him in the head. (4F03) . . . when, while escaping from Moe, his head hits a metal beam. (4F05) . . . while trying to hide in an abandoned warehouse that is bustling with activity. (4F05) . . . when, after eating an insanity pepper and trying to cool down his tongue with ice cream, his hot tongue melts the ice cream. (3F24) . . . after waiting for a very slow tortoise to relay a message. (3F24) . . . when he wakes up in the sandtrap of a golf course and is hit on the head by Kent Brockman's golfball. (3F24) . . . when he discovers that the "Homer Is a Dope" T-shirts are sold out. (3G01) . . . when a second avalanche traps him and Mr. Burns after they escape from a snowed-in cabin. (4F10) . . . after his brain tells him, "Now look sad and say, 'D'oh.'" (4F12)

Episode 7F03 Original Airdate: 10/11/90 Writer: David M. Stern Director: David Silverman
Executive Producers: James L. Brooks; Matt Groening; Sam Simon

EDNA KRABAPPEL

Occupation:
Fourth-grade teacher at Springfield Elementary.

Marital status:
Divorced, but still looking (once tried to pick up Homer and the drummer from Aerosmith at Moe's).

Habits:
Can sometimes be seen smoking inside the school.

On strike:
While leading a teacher's strike, held up a sign that said, "Honk if you like cookies."

Favorite apparel:
Blue skirt, green sweater, blue pumps.

Favorite canned dinner brand:
Chef Lonelyhearts.

Restricted:
Can't go to the library anymore because "everybody stinks."

SEYMOUR, THE CHILDREN ARE PLAYING IN THE HOLE AGAIN.

Bart's teacher, Mrs. Krabappel, warns him that he is in danger of flunking history if he does not do better on his next test. Instead of studying, however, Bart plays video games and watches TV with Homer. Knowing he is going to fail the test, Bart pretends he is sick and is sent home. That night, he calls Milhouse to get the test answers. Without knowing it, Milhouse's answers are wrong, and when Bart takes the exam he gets an F.

Told he is going to be kept back a grade, Bart promises to do better if he is given one more chance. He makes a bargain with Martin: if he helps Martin transform into a regular kid, Martin will help him pass his test. However, Martin plays video games with his new friends instead of helping Bart study. The night before the big test, Bart asks God for one more day. The next morning, a freak blizzard closes all the schools. Heading out the door to play, Lisa reminds Bart that he made a deal with God, and he trudges upstairs to study.

Bart gets another F. In frustration, he blurts out to Mrs. Krabappel a history fact, proving that he really did study. Impressed, she gives him an extra point, changing his F to a D-minus. Homer proudly displays Bart's paper on the refrigerator door.

SHOW HIGHLIGHTS

Bart's antics: Bart squirts condiment packets on the butt of Martin, doubling as Hemingway, and quips, "Little ketchup for your buns, Papa?"

The Simpson ears: When Mrs. Krabappel talks, Bart hears, "Blah, blah, blah, blah, blah, blah." When Dr. Pryor speaks, Homer hears, "Blah, blah, blah, blah, blah, blah."

> **Bart Concludes His "Treasure Island" Book Report:**
> *Mrs. Krabappel: Bart, did you read the book?*
> *Bart: Mrs. Krabappel, I'm insulted. Is this a book report or a witch hunt?*
> *Krabappel: Then perhaps you'd like to tell us the name of the pirate.*
> *Bart: Blackbeard...Captain Nemo...Captain Hook... Long John Silver...Peg Leg Pete...Bluebeard.*

Procrastination: Before studying, Bart plays "Escape from Grandma's House" at Noise Land video arcade, watches an episode of Itchy & Scratchy, "Let Them Eat Scratchy," and then sees the classic film, *Gorilla the Conqueror* on Big Gorilla Week on Million Dollar Movie with Homer.

Twelve: Bart's score on a test of state capitals.

> **Bart's Chalkboard Punishment for Not Reading *Treasure Island*:**
> *I will not fake my way through life.*

> **How Not to Be a Geek:**
> *Bart: Only geeks sit in the front row. From now on you sit in the back row. And that's not just on the bus. It goes for school and church, too.*
> *Martin: Why?*
> *Bart: So no one can see what you're doing.*
> *Martin: Oooh. I think I understand. The potential for mischief varies inversely to one's proximity to the authority figure or MOP 1/PA.*

 "Part of this D-minus belongs to God."

Honors and achievements: Lisa has dozens of "A" papers covering the refrigerator door while Bart's sole contribution is the drawing of a cat he made in the first grade.

 "I heard you last night, Bart. You prayed for this. Now your prayers have been answered. I'm no theologian. I don't know who or what God is exactly. All I know is He's a force more powerful than Mom and Dad put together and you owe him big."

Mayor Quimby, announcing a new holiday: "I hereby declare this day to be 'Snow Day'—the funnest day in the history of Springfield."

> *"Old Red" is the name of Mrs. Krabappel's pen for grading tests.*

> **How Not to Be a Geek:** (see above)

Cram Session:
In order to derail his success on the history exam, Sherri and Terri tell Bart that the Pilgrims came over on the Spirit of St. Louis, landed in sunny Acapulco, and were escaping from giant rats.

THE STUFF YOU MAY HAVE MISSED

Milhouse sits in the front seat of the bus.

There is a poster in the nurse's office that reads: "Give a hoot... Brush."

Bart wears a purple shirt in this episode instead of the usual orange one.

The flag outside Springfield Elementary remains still in the wind.

RV Salesman Bob and Jacques the bowling instructor join the rest of Springfield in singing "Winter Wonderland."

Two kids build an ice sculpture of Jebediah Springfield standing between two bears.

Dr. Pryor, Principal Skinner, Mrs.Krabappel, Moe and a red-haired lady play a game of hockey.

Ben Franklin's new sled has "Don't sled on me" written on it.

I WILL NOT ENCOURAGE OTHERS TO FLY
I WILL NOT ENCOURAGE OTHERS TO FLY
I WILL NOT ENCOURAGE OTHERS TO FLY

SIMPSON AND DELILAH

Episode 7F02 Original Airdate: 10/18/90 Writer: Jon Vitti Director: Rich Moore

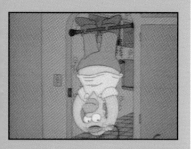

Homer discovers a miracle hair growth formula named Dimoxinil and rushes out to buy it. His visions of robust hair, however, are cut short when he finds out that the formula costs $1,000.00. Homer is persuaded by Lenny to cheat his employer's health insurance policy so that the company will pay for it. Applying the formula overnight, Homer awakens to find a thick mop of hair.

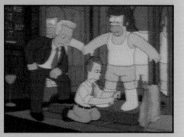

Marge finds the new Homer exciting. Mr. Burns mistakes him for an energetic young go-getter and promotes him. Assuming his new title, Homer hires an assistant named Karl. With Karl's help, Homer so impresses Burns that he is given the key to the executive washroom. Smithers, fuming with jealousy, snoops through Homer's files and finds the bogus insurance claim. He confronts Homer, but Karl takes the blame for doctoring the claim. Karl is fired, leaving Homer to fend for himself.

When Bart breaks the bottle of hair potion, Homer returns to his old, bald self. Karl convinces Homer that it was not his hair that made him a better person, it was believing in himself. Homer gives a speech to his fellow executives on increasing profitability, but without hair, no one takes him seriously and he is demoted to his old position. At home, Homer also expects rejection, but Marge assures him that she loves him just the way he is.

SHOW HIGHLIGHTS

> TAR IS NOT A PLAYTHING
> TAR IS NOT A PLAYTHING
> TAR IS NOT A PLAYTHING
> TAR IS NOT A PLAYTHING
> TAR IS NOT A PLAYTHING
> TAR IS NOT A PLAYTHING

Homer: I'm just a big fool.
Karl: Oh no, you're not!
Homer: How do you know?
Karl: Because my mother taught me never to kiss a fool! (Karl kisses Homer on the mouth.)
Homer: Karl...
Karl: Now go get 'em, tiger. (Karl pats Homer on the rear as he runs out.)

Looking for a miracle: Mr. Burns has his own supply of Dimoxinil that he rubs into his scalp, muttering, "Bah! Snake oil."

Union Regulations:
Smithers: It's in the union contract, sir. One token promotion from within per year.
Burns: Wait. Who is that young go-getter?
Smithers: Well, it sort of looks like Homer Simpson...only more dynamic and resourceful.

"I'm only eighty-one. You may find this hard to believe, but in my salad days, my crowning glory was a bright shock of strawberry blond curls."

Homer's hairstyles: Over the course of this episode, Homer's hair changes from a round, sideburned 1970's semi-afro, to a shorter, 1950's style cut, to a slicked back 1980's look, to a tied-back "Miami Vice" style with a short ponytail, to a moussed, angular 1990's haircut.

On Homer:
Marge: He's much happier at work and, well, just between us girls...well, he hasn't been this frisky in years.
Patty: I don't want to think about it.

THE STUFF YOU MAY HAVE MISSED

Name of hair restoration product Dimoxinil bears more than a coincidental similarity to real-life hair product Minoxidil™.

The contents of Homer's medicine cabinet: "Hair Master," "Gorilla Man," "Hair Chow," "Bald Buster," "NU GRO," "U Wanna B Hair-E," baby powder.

A sign inside the "Royal Majesty for the Obese or Gangly Gentleman" shop reads: "You Rip It, You Buy It."

On his insurance form, Homer accidentally checks off "Female" before partially erasing it and filling in "Male."

Homer reads Playdude magazine in Jake's Unisex Hair Palace.

"Oh, hey ho, men. You know, I was watching the DuMont last night and happened to catch a fascinating documentary on Rommel, the Desert Fox. Now there is a man who could get things done."

"Keep brain from freezing." Homer's fraudulent explanation for requesting insurance coverage on the purchase of Dimoxinil.

Bart's blunder: After Bart breaks Homer's bottle of Dimoxinil, Homer tells him three things that he predicts will haunt him for the rest of his life: "You've ruined your father. You've crippled your family. And baldness is hereditary."

Movie Moment:
Homer runs through the streets celebrating his newfound hair, reminiscent of It's a Wonderful Life.

Karl's Pep Talk to Homer:
Karl: You don't belong here. You're a fraud and a phony and it's only a matter of time until they find you out.
Homer: (gasps) Who told you?
Karl: You did! You told me with the way you slump your shoulders, the way you talk into your chest, the way you smother yourself in bargain basement lime-green polyester. I want you to say to yourself: I deserve this! I love it! I am nature's greatest miracle!

Watching a Game Show:
Host: The capital of North Dakota is named after what German ruler?
Homer: Hitler.
Marge: Hitler, North Dakota?

KARL

Occupation:
Personal assistant to Homer.

Speech:
Gravelly voice belies elegant taste, significant motivational skills.

Specializes in:
Aiding oafish upper managers with low self-esteem through consoling; advising; sending singing telegrams to spouses; and the occasional pat on the buttocks.

Social status:
Friends with many gals in the typing pool.

Enjoys:
Breakfast in bed and shopping for clothes.

Attitude:
Selflessness manifests itself in bearing the full brunt of any malfeasance involving his boss and handing him his own umbrella during a rainstorm.

A MAN'S SUIT SHOULD MAKE HIM FEEL LIKE A PRINCE. IT SHOULD CRY OUT TO THE WORLD, "HERE I AM! DON'T JUDGE ME! LOVE ME!"

Guest Voice:
Harvey Fierstein
as Karl

Marge's warning: "Hello, everyone. You know, Halloween is a very strange holiday. Personally, I don't understand it. Kids worshipping ghosts, pretending to be devils...things on TV that are completely inappropriate for younger viewers. Things like the following half-hour. Nothing seems to bother my kids, but tonight's show—which I totally wash my hands of—is really scary. So, if you have sensitive children, maybe you should tuck them into bed early tonight instead of writing us angry letters tomorrow. Thanks for your attention."

THE STUFF YOU MAY HAVE MISSED

The skeleton that decorates the side of the treehouse has only three fingers—just like the Simpsons.

THE OPENING SEQUENCE

In Springfield Cemetery, there are tombstones for Ishmael Simpson, Ezekiel Simpson, Cornelius V. Simpson (reference to Cornelius Vanderbilt), Garfield, Casper the Friendly Boy, Elvis, Your Name Here, Paul McCartney (a play on the "Paul Is Dead" legend), and Disco.

THE SET-UP

Bart and Lisa tell each other scary stories up in the treehouse, as Homer eavesdrops outside.

BAD DREAM HOUSE

The Simpsons move into an old house and soon learn why the price was so cheap: it is haunted. The walls ooze blood, and a voice tells them to get out while they still can. Marge wants to leave, but Homer convinces her to give the house a chance.

That night, Homer, Lisa, Bart, and Maggie are possessed and chase each other with knives and axes. Marge tells the spirit of the house to find a way they can all live together. After pondering its options, the house blows itself up.

STORY HIGHLIGHTS

"It's a fixer-upper. What's the problem? We get a bunch of priests in here..." Homer, trying to talk Marge into keeping the haunted house.

"Why are you trying to scare us? Are you trying to keep us from getting close to you? Maybe even loving you?" Lisa, to the house.

"This family has had its differences and we've squabbled, but we've never had knife fights before, and I blame this house."

"You will die, you will die slowly. Your stomach will swell, your intestines will writhe and boil, your eyes will burst; and some horrible stuff, possibly your brains, will start coming out through your nose...." The house, to the Simpsons.

THE STUFF YOU MAY HAVE MISSED

Tombstones in the basement of the haunted house: Hiawatha, Crazy Horse, Not-So-Crazy Horse, Pocahontas, Sitting Bull, Cochise, Tonto, Geronimo, Sacajawea, and Mahatma Gandhi.

The bunny doll beside the box that Bart unpacks appears to be the "Life in Hell" character, Binky the rabbit.

Marge wears bunny slippers.

As Bart and Lisa leave the house, their coats fly onto them.

Maggie's pajamas change colors from blue to gray to pink during the story.

A moat encircles the Simpsons' new house.

Movie Moments:
Maggie turns her head all the way around à la *The Exorcist*.
The haunted house's behavior and the Indian graves in the cellar parody *Poltergeist*.
Blood oozes down the walls and the chimney runs up the center of the wall à la *The Amityville Horror*.
The haunted house's shape recalls *Psycho*.
The haunted house implodes à la *The Fall of the House of Usher*.

HOW TO COOK HUMANS

BAD DREAM HOUSE
Writer: John Swartzwelder
Director: Wesley Archer
Guest Voice: James Earl Jones
as the Moving Man

HUNGRY ARE THE DAMNED
Writers: Jay Kogen and Wallace Wolodarsky
Director: Rich Moore
Guest Voice: James Earl Jones as Serak the Preparer

THE RAVEN
Writers: Edgar Allan Poe and Sam Simon
Director: David Silverman
Guest Voice: James Earl Jones as
the Narrator

HUNGRY ARE THE DAMNED

The Simpsons are abducted from their backyard by one-eyed extraterrestrials. En route to another planet, they learn that they are the guests of honor. They are offered an endless feast of food and thoroughly gorge themselves. Lisa accuses the aliens of fattening up the family so that they can be eaten. The aliens' feelings are hurt. They turn the spaceship around and return the Simpsons to their lowly lives. Lisa concludes that it was the Simpsons who were the real monsters.

STORY HIGHLIGHTS

"Look, I know that to you we Simpsons are a lower order of life. We face that prejudice every day of our lives, but we are happy on our little planet."

"Listen, you big, stupid space-creature. Nobody, but nobody, eats the Simpsons!"

Lisa's suspicion: Lisa suspects that the Simpsons will be eaten upon reaching the aliens' planet. She shows the family the book *How to Cook Humans*. Kang blows dust off the book cover, showing the title, *How to Cook for Humans*. When Lisa blows off more dust, the title reads, *How to Cook Forty Humans*. Finally, Kang blows off the last bit of space dust, revealing the title, *How to Cook for Forty Humans*.

Heavy cargo: When the spaceship's tractor-beam grabs Homer, his weight causes the ship to sink to the ground. A second beam is fired, which completes the airlift and brings Homer safely inside.

Kang: Let me get this straight; you thought—
Kodos: They thought we were going to eat them!
Kang: Good god! Is this some kind of joke?
Kodos: No! They're serious!
Lisa: Well, why were you trying to make us eat all the time?
Kodos: Make you eat? We merely provided a sumptuous banquet, and frankly, you people made pigs of yourselves!
Serak: I slaved in the kitchen for days for you people and—
(Serak breaks down into sobs.)
Kodos: Well, if you wanted to make Serak the Preparer cry, mission accomplished.

Kang: And over here is our crowning achievement in amusement technology: an electronic version of what you call table tennis. Your primitive paddles have been replaced by an electronic—
Bart: Hey, that's just Pong. Get with the times, man!
Homer: Me and Marge played that old game before we were married!
Kodos: Well, we did build this spaceship, you know.
Kang: Anyone from a species that has mastered intergalactic travel, raise your hand.
(Kang and Kodos each raise a tentacle. Bart raises his hand, but Homer slaps it down.)
Kang: All right, then.
Marge: Sorry. Your game is very nice.

THE STUFF YOU MAY HAVE MISSED

Homer's cooking apron reads "Mafia Staff Apron."

The TV on the spaceship airs "The Itchy & Scratchy Show."

The angle of the shot that features Homer and Marge discussing the great feast makes it appear that their heads are on platters.

The Simpsons Meet Kang and Kodos:

Kang: Greetings, Earthlings, I am Kang. Do not be frightened. We mean you no harm.
Marge: You speak English?
Kang: I am actually speaking Rigellian. By an astonishing coincidence, both of our languages are exactly the same.
Bart: Well, what are you gonna do with us, man?
Kang: Kodos and I are taking you to Rigel-4, a world of infinite delights to tantalize your senses and challenge your intellectual limitations.

Movie/TV Show Moments:

The cookbook, *How to Cook for Forty Humans*, parodies the "Twilight Zone" episode, "To Serve Man."
The "Ow," heard when the fly hits the bug zapper, parodies the movie *The Fly*.

THE RAVEN

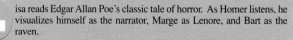

Lisa reads Edgar Allan Poe's classic tale of horror. As Homer listens, he visualizes himself as the narrator, Marge as Lenore, and Bart as the raven.

After telling their stories in the treehouse, the kids return home to go to bed. They doze peacefully, while Homer sleeps with the lights on.

STORY HIGHLIGHTS

"Quoth the Raven...Eat my shorts." Bart, interrupting the narrator with "Eat my shorts!" instead of the standard "Nevermore!"

"Come here, you little raven!"

Bart: Hey, poindexter, it's Halloween! Put the book away!
Lisa: For your information, I'm about to read you a classic tale of terror by Edgar Allan Poe.
Bart: Wait a minute! That's a schoolbook!
Lisa: Don't worry, Bart, you won't learn anything.

Bart: That wasn't scary. Not even for a poem.
Lisa: Well, it was written in 1845. Maybe people were easier to scare back then.
Bart: Oh, yeah—like when you look at Friday the 13th, Part 1; it's pretty tame by today's standards.

THE STUFF YOU MAY HAVE MISSED

The hands of the wisps of smoke that cradle Homer's head have just three fingers and a thumb, like the Simpsons.
The word "Amontillado" appears on Homer's drinking mug, referring to the Poe story, "The Cask of Amontillado."
The Raven/Bart drops "The Pit and the Pendulum," "The Telltale Heart," and "The Purloined Letter,"
all stories by Poe, on Homer's head.

Identity:
Three-eyed fish.

Home:
Stream outside Springfield Nuclear Power Plant.

How third eye formed:
Mutation resulting from water polluted by nuclear waste.

Mr. Burns's theory:
Blinky's the next step on the fish evolutionary scale.

Taste:
Only Mr. Burns knows for sure.

TWO CARS IN EVERY GARAGE AND THREE EYES ON EVERY FISH

Episode 7F01 Original Airdate: 11/1/90 Writers: Sam Simon & John Swartzwelder Director: Wes Archer

While fishing near the Springfield Nuclear Reactor, Bart and Lisa land a three-eyed fish. The event makes headlines and a Washington regulatory committee sends a team to investigate nuclear waste coming from the plant. Despite Mr. Burns's attempts at bribery, the team tells him to clean up his plant or they will shut it down.

Homer tells Burns that if he were governor he could pass laws to keep the plant open. Surprised that something Homer said actually made sense, Burns runs for governor. He hires slick spin doctors and publicists to boost his public image. Slowly, he gains on the incumbent, Mary Bailey, to

whom Marge remains loyal. Questioned by reporters about the three-eyed fish, Burns declares that it is Mother Nature's way of improving her handiwork and that three eyes are better than two.

Burns's public relations people fear he may be losing touch with the common man and arrange a media event: Burns will have dinner with the Simpsons. Homer makes Marge promise she will not say anything to make his boss look bad. With the TV cameras rolling, Marge places the three-eyed fish onto Burns's plate. Prompted by one of his PR men, Burns takes a bite of the radioactive fish. He spits it out in front of the TV cameras, sinking his campaign.

SHOW HIGHLIGHTS

Springfield Nuclear Power Plant safety violations: Gum used to seal crack in coolant tower; plutonium rod used as paperweight; monitoring station unmanned; nuclear waste shin-deep in hallway.

I WILL NOT XEROX MY BUTT
I WILL NOT XEROX MY BUTT
I WILL NOT XEROX MY BUTT
I WILL NOT XEROX MY BUTT
I WILL NOT XEROX MY BUTT
I WILL NOT XEROX MY BUTT

"I'm going to be sore tomorrow." Burns, after a photo shoot where he is forced to smile.

"Oooh, a political discussion at our table. I feel like a Kennedy!"

Bedroom politics: Though Marge supports Mary Bailey for governor, Homer requests she cook an election eve dinner for Mr. Burns. Feeling that Homer is not letting her express herself, Marge refuses to snuggle.

At the Ol' Fishin' Hole :

Dave Shutton: ...What's your name, son?
Bart: I'm Bart Simpson, who the hell are you?
Dave: I'm Dave Shutton. I'm an investigative reporter who's on the road a lot, and I must say that in my day, we didn't talk that way to our elders.
Bart: Well, this is my day and we do, sir.

Observing Artist's Rendering of Burns à la Thomas Hart Benton's Rendering of "The Kentuckian" :

Mr. Burns: Why are my teeth showing like that?
Danielson: Because you're smiling.
Burns: Ah. Excellent. This is exactly the kind of trickery I'm paying you for. But, how do we turn your average Joe Sixpack against Mary Bailey?

A Subtle Bribe :

Chief Inspector: Mr. Burns, in twenty years I have never seen such a shoddy, deplorable ...
Mr. Burns: Oh, look! Some careless person has left thousands and thousands of dollars just lying here on my coffee table. Smithers, why don't we leave the room and hopefully, when we return, the pile of money will be gone.

Youthful encouragement: As Homer leaves for work Lisa tells him, "Try not to spill anything, Dad." Bart adds, "Keep those mutants comin, Homer."

The positions on Burns's political team: Speech Writer, Joke Writer, Spin Doctor, Make-Up Man, Personal Trainer, Muckraker, Character Assassin, Mudslinger, Garbologist.

"Oh. I get your angle. Every Joe Meatball and Sally Housecoat in this God-forsaken state will see me hunkering down for chow with Eddie Punchclock. The media will have a field day!"

"Dear God, we paid for all this stuff ourselves, so thanks for nothing."

Mr. Burns: I'm here to talk to you about my little friend, here. Blinky. Many of you consider him to be a hideous genetic mutation. Well, nothing could be further from the truth. But don't take my word for it, let's ask an actor portraying Charles Darwin what he thinks...
Darwin: Hello, Mr. Burns.
Burns: Oh, hello Charles. Be a good fellow and tell our viewers about your theory of natural selection.
Darwin: Glad to, Mr. Burns. You see, every so often Mother Nature changes her animals, giving them bigger teeth, sharper claws, longer legs, or in this case, a third eye. And if these variations turn out to be an improvement, the new animals thrive and multiply and spread across the face of the earth.
Burns: So you're saying this fish might have an advantage over other fish, that it may in fact be a kind of super-fish?
Darwin: I wouldn't mind having a third eye, would you?

THE STUFF YOU MAY HAVE MISSED

Monty Burns and Mary Bailey are battling to become chief executive of a state whose name is never mentioned.

Bart pastes his new pictures from the newspaper headlines in his scrapbook next to "Vandal Decapitates Town Statue," referring to 7G07, "The Telltale Head."

While on the campaign trail Burns poses atop a tank reminiscent of Michael Dukakis's campaign.

Mary Bailey has the same name as the Donna Reed character in It's a Wonderful Life.

The motto of the state that Springfield is in: "Not Just Another State."

DANCIN' HOMER

Episode 7F05 Original Airdate: 11/8/90 Writers: Ken Levine and David Isaacs Director: Mark Kirkland Guest Voices: Tony Bennett as Himself

While drinking a beer at Moe's Tavern, Homer recounts his adventures during the past few weeks. He begins with the family attending "Nuclear Plant Employee, Spouses, and No More Than Three Children Night" at the local minor league baseball stadium. Homer's hopes of letting loose at the ballpark are ruined when Mr. Burns and Smithers sit next to him. To Homer's surprise, Mr. Burns buys him several rounds of beer to show good company relations.

Soon, Homer is drunk. With the Springfield Isotopes down by three runs, an inebriated Homer excites the crowd with an impromptu dance and rallies the team to victory. The Isotopes owner offers Homer a job as the team mascot and the team goes on a winning streak. Before long, Homer is offered a job with the Capital City Capitals. The Simpsons sell everything and move to the big city.

Homer's break comes when he fills in for the Capitals's mascot, the Capital City Goofball. However, his small-town routine flops before the big-city crowd and he is fired. Back in Springfield, the patrons of Moe's Tavern do not care about Homer's failure, only about his adventure. Homer realizes that, for the first time in his life, he has something to say that people want to hear.

> I WILL NOT TRADE PANTS
> WITH OTHERS
> I WILL NOT TRADE PANTS
> WITH OTHERS
> I WILL NOT TRADE PANTS
> WITH OTHERS

SHOW HIGHLIGHTS

Bart, reading the baseball Marge got autographed for him: "Hmmm, Springfield Kozy Kort Motel, Room 26...How 'bout it? — Flash."

"Kids, look! Street crime!" Homer, pointing to a thug stealing a lady's purse as they arrive in the big city.

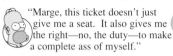
"Marge, this ticket doesn't just give me a seat. It also gives me the right—no, the duty—to make a complete ass of myself."

> **After Hours:**
> Springfield Elementary busdriver, Otto, moonlights as a Springfield Nuclear Power Plant special events busdriver.

Mr. Burns, to a plant employee: "Well, take your mind off contaminants for one night and have a hot dog."

"Ah, Mancini. The mascot's best friend." The Capital City Goofball, appreciating Homer's taste in mascot-antics music.

Homer, relating how it felt to dance for the crowd: "As I got up in front of them, I felt an intoxication that had nothing to do with alcohol. It was the intoxication of being a public spectacle."

"A Simpson on a T-shirt. I never thought I'd see the day." Marge, seeing "Dancin' Homer" shirts on sale at the ballpark.

"Each individual smart-ass remark" Homer hears while dancing for the crowd in Capital City: "Well, this guy doesn't make me want to cheer," "Gee, I really pity him; making a fool of himself in front of so many people," and "These cornball antics may play in the sticks, but this is Capital City."

> **Movie Moments:**
> Homer's farewell speech on "Dancin' Homer Appreciation Night," in which he holds his cap to his heart, parodies Lou Gehrig in *Pride of the Yankees*: "... today, as I leave for Capital City, I consider myself the luckiest mascot on the face of the Earth!"

THE STUFF YOU MAY HAVE MISSED

Signs on the outfield wall at Springfield War Memorial Stadium include: "Royal Majesty—Clothing For the Obese or Gangly Gentleman," "Springfield Savings. Safe from 1890-1986, 1988", "Moe's Tavern—Hit This Sign and Win a Free Well Drink," "Girdles 'N Such—Fancy Lingerie," "The Springfield Mall," and "The Jerky Hut."

Helen, the organist, has a martini atop the organ and pictures of body builders tacked up next to her. One of the pix looks like McBain.

The Simpsons have a Krusty doll stuck to the window of their car when they drive to Capital City.

Capital City has restaurants named The Penny Loafer (shaped like penny loafer shoes) and The 'Original' Frenchies.

Dancin' Homer T-Shirt sell 2 for $24.99.

At the Capital City Dome, one entrance sign reads, "Players and Mascots."

The Lyrics to Capital City as Sung by Tony Bennett:
There's a swingin' town I know called...
Capital City
People stop and scream hello in...
Capital City!
It's the kind of place that makes a bum feel like a king
and it makes a king feel like some nutty coo-coo super king.
It's against the law to frown in
Capital City!
You'll giggle like a stupid clown
when you chance to see 4th street and D!
Once you get a whiff of it, you'll never want to roam,
from Captial City my home sweet swingin' home!

Bonding with Burns:
Mr. Burns: (chanting) *The hitter's off his rocker/ kissing Betty Crocker!*
Homer: Good one, sir.
Burns: Oh, well, I used to rile the late, great Connie Mack with that one at old Shibe Park.
Homer: (chanting) *Little baby batter / can't control his bladder!*
Burns: (to Homer) Mmm...Crude, but I like it. What do you say we freshen up our little drinkie poos?
Homer: Don't mind if I do?
Burns: Well, Simpsie, you up for another wave?
Homer: All right, Burnsie.
(Burns and Homer do a frantic, two-man wave.)

THE CAPITAL CITY GOOFBALL

Profession:
Mascot for the Capital City baseball team.

Nickname:
The Goof.

Idol of:
Homer Simpson.

Uniform Number:
0.

Weight:
197 pounds without costume,
242 pounds with it.

Costume:
Includes a long "wazoo" horn, odd wire antennae coming out of bushy hair atop his head, looney eyes, and a torso that resembles a baseball.

Desires:
Wishes he had a zipper on the front of his costume come the fifth inning.

HEY, CALL ME PLAIN OL' GOOF.

Guest Voice:
Tom Poston
as the Capital City Goofball

TODD FLANDERS

Position in life:
God-fearing son of God-fearing Ned Flanders.

Nicknames:
The Todd-meister; Study Buddy; and Toddsky.

Religion:
Wholeheartedly devoted to Christianity.

Sport:
Miniature golf.

Secret shame:
Was once transformed into a hellion by the sugary power of Pixi-Stix.

> HOW COME WE ONLY GET TO GO TO CHURCH THREE TIMES A WEEK?

DEAD PUTTING SOCIETY

Episode 7F08 Original Airdate: 11/15/90 Writer: Jeff Martin Director: Rich Moore

SHOW HIGHLIGHTS

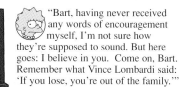

> I AM NOT A
> 32-YEAR-OLD WOMAN
> I AM NOT A
> 32-YEAR-OLD WOMAN
> I AM NOT
> A 32-YEAR-OLD WOMAN

 "Bart, having never received any words of encouragement myself, I'm not sure how they're supposed to sound. But here goes: I believe in you. Come on, Bart. Remember what Vince Lombardi said: 'If you lose, you're out of the family.'"

"You've been rubbing my nose in it since I got here! Your family is better than my family, your beer comes from farther away than my beer, you and your son like each other, your wife's butt is higher than my wife's butt! You make me sick!"

Homer: Hey, Flanders, it's no use praying. I already did the same thing, and we can't both win.
Flanders: Actually, Simpson, we were praying that no one gets hurt.
Homer: Oh...well. Flanders, it doesn't matter. This time tomorrow, you'll be wearing high heels.

At the Library:
Lisa: (loading Bart with books) And, finally, the most important book of all, The Tao Te Ching by Lao Tzu.
Bart: Lisa we can't afford all these books.
Lisa: Bart, we're just going to borrow them.
Bart: (winks; slyly) Oh, heh, heh. Gotcha.

Flanders: Y'know, Simpson, I feel kinda silly, but, uh, you know, what the hay, you know... kinda reminds me of my good ole' fraternity days.
Homer: D'oh! Oh my God! He's enjoying it!

Homer psychology: When Flanders answers Homer's offer to wager on their sons' golf tournament by saying he is not a betting man, Homer begins clucking like a chicken.

Homer and Violins and Putter Names:
Homer: That putter is to you what a bat is to a baseball player, what a violin is to the...ya...guy tha...the violin guy. Now, c'mon give your putter a name.
Bart: What?
Homer: Come on, give it a name.
Bart: (timidly) Mr. Putter.
Homer: Do you wanna try a little harder, son? Come on, give it a girl's name.
Bart: Mom.
Homer: (gruffly) Your putter's name is Charlene!
Bart: Why?
Homer: It just is. That's why.

"Bosom!" Bart, Homer, and Lisa laughing and poking fun at Flanders's heartfelt letter of apology, in which he says, ". . . I feel a great sadness in my bosom."

 "That shot is impossible! Jack Nicholson himself couldn't make it!"

THE STUFF YOU MAY HAVE MISSED

The beer mug at Ned Flanders's house is decorated with the slogan, "Macho Mug."

The top of Ned's note pad reads, "From the 'Noggin' of Ned."

Speed dial numbers on Ned Flanders's telephone: "Reverend-Work," "Reverend-Home," "Recycling Center," "Book Mobile."

When Homer misses a putt, he hops and waves his arms in the same fashion as the mechanical ape he confronts on the miniature golf course.

"To Todd, Love Dad" is engraved on Todd Flanders's putter.

At Sir Putt-a-Lot's Merrie Olde Fun Center, a sign for the golf tournament reads, "**Free Balloon for Everyone Who Enters."

Bart has a trophy from "Everybody Gets a Trophy Day."

At the miniature dinosaur hole, a sign reads, "Do Not Climb on Statuary."

Pet Names:
Ned Flanders: There's my little Popcorn Ball. Kissy, kissy.
Maude Flanders: Hello, Sponge Cake.

Flanders and Homer Mow the Lawn in Their Wives' Dresses:
Marge: (moaning) Oh, my best dress.
Lisa: Why do I get the feeling that someday I'll be describing this to a psychiatrist?

Getting Bart Ready to Compete against Todd in the Miniature Golf Tournament
Bart: But Dad, I've never won anything in my life.
Homer: Son, this is the only time I'm ever gonna say this. It is not okay to lose.

Homer is invited to Flanders's house for a beer. Homer sees Flanders's game room with beer on tap and observes that his son Todd is loving and brilliant in school. He thinks Flanders is bragging about his lifestyle and storms out. When Homer and Bart run into Flanders and Todd at the miniature golf course, Homer boasts that Bart will win the big miniature golf tournament. Flanders advises Homer not to count on Bart, since Todd will also enter.

Despite his most ardent efforts, Bart's putting is lacking. Lisa senses Bart's anguish and shows him an ancient Oriental method of concentration. Using his new Zen approach, Bart's game improves dramatically. Homer challenges Flanders to bet on the tournament, and the two agree that the father of the boy who doesn't win must mow the other's lawn while wearing his wife's best dress.

Both Todd and Bart are pressured to win. The score is tied as they approach the last hole. To avoid the dire consequences if they lose, Bart and Todd quit and call the game a tie. Without a winner, both Homer and Flanders put on their wives' clothes and mow each other's lawn.

BART VS. THANKSGIVING

Episode 7F07 Original Airdate: 11/22/90 Writer: George Meyer Director: David Silverman

KENT BROCKMAN

Occupation:
Local Emmy-winning news anchor.

Hosts:
"Springfield Action News"; "Eye on Springfield"; "Smartline"; "My Two Cents."

Biggest windfall:
Winning the lottery and announcing it on the air (later turning up with a gold medallion around his neck).

Married to:
Stephanie, the Weather Lady.

Turn-ons:
Bikinis; scandals; the warm feeling he gets when he uses a cliché.

Turn-offs:
Being interrupted; being questioned; when his Danish is stolen.

It is Thanksgiving in the Simpsons' house and Lisa assembles a decorative centerpiece for the dinner table. The family sits down to give thanks along with Patty, Selma, Marge's mother, and Grampa. When Lisa sets down her centerpiece, however, she argues with Bart about where it should go. In the ensuing struggle, the creation flies into the fireplace and burns up. Devastated, Lisa runs upstairs sobbing while Marge and Homer send Bart to his room for ruining Thanksgiving.

Bart feels mistreated and runs away. Walking the streets alone, cold and hungry, he finds a homeless shelter that is serving Thanksgiving dinner. A TV crew covering the event interviews Bart, and puts him on the local news.

When Homer and Marge see their son on TV, they tell the police that Bart has run away. Bart eventually wanders back home. Not sure that he wants to give up his life of freedom on the open road, he climbs up on the roof to think things out. Hearing Lisa cry because she misses him, Bart calls her onto the roof. He realizes that what he did was wrong and apologizes to her. Reunited, the family resumes its Thanksgiving dinner.

SHOW HIGHLIGHTS

"Mom, it's broken. Mom, it's broken. Mom, it's broken. Mom, it's broken" Bart, singing about his problem with the can opener as he "helps" Marge prepare the cranberry sauce.

Lisa, describing her centerpiece:
"It's a tribute to the trailblazing women who made our country great...see, there's Georgia O'Keefe... Susan B. Anthony... and this is Marjorie Stoneman Douglas. I'm sure you haven't heard of her, but she worked her whole life to preserve the Florida Everglades."

The Half-Time Show: "Hurray for Everything" performs a salute to the Western Hemisphere, "the dancin'-est hemisphere of all!" Their prop is a giant half-globe.

"...And, Lord, we're especially thankful for nuclear power, the cleanest, safest energy source there is, except for solar, which is just a pipe dream. Anyway, we'd like to thank you for the occasional moments of peace and love our family's experienced...well, not today. You saw what happened. Oh, Lord, be honest. Are we the most pathetic family in the universe, or what?"

> **Grampa:** *Homer was never stubborn. He always folded instantly over anything. It was as if he had no will of his own. Isn't that true, Homer?*
> **Homer:** *Yes, Dad.*

"Howl of the Unappreciated," by Lisa Simpson: (writing) "I saw the best meals of my generation destroyed by the madness of my brother / My soul carved in slices by spiky-haired demons..."

"Alright! Twelve bucks and free grub to boot! Viva Skid Row!"

"I'd say something comforting, but you know... my voice..." Mrs. Bouvier, after Bart is discovered missing.

> **Literary Moments:**
> Lisa's poem is strongly reminiscent of poet Allen Ginsberg's "Howl." She also keeps a book of his work on a shelf next to Jack Kerouac's *On the Road*, and a collection of poems by Edgar Allan Poe.

> (Bart and Homer watch the Thanksgiving Day Parade. Bullwinkle and Underdog balloons float by on the TV.)
> **Bart:** *...it wouldn't hurt 'em to use some cartoons made in the last fifty years.*
> **Homer:** *Son, this is a tradition. If you start building a balloon for every flash-in-the-pan cartoon character, you'd turn the parade into a farce.* (As Homer is saying this, we see a Bart balloon go by on the TV behind him.)

> I WILL NOT DO THAT THING
> WITH MY TONGUE
> I WILL NOT DO THAT THING
> WITH MY TONGUE
> I WILL NOT DO THAT THING
> WITH MY TONGUE

> **Marge:** *Mom! You made it! How are you?*
> **Mom:** (hoarse whisper) *I have laryngitis and it hurts to talk, so I'll just say one thing: You never do anything right.*

THE STUFF YOU MAY HAVE MISSED

Dallas Cowboys players "Jay Kogen" and "Wallace Wolodarsky" are the names of two Simpsons' producers.

A Springfield Retirement Castle sign reads: "Thank you for not discussing the outside world."

Everyone drinks wine with dinner except Homer, who sips a can of Duff.

On his excursion, Bart walks through a large drain pipe upon which a vandal has painted "El Barto."

A member of Burns's security staff reads *Les Miserables* over his dinner.

Electrical outlets in the Simpson house have no hole for the ground plug.

Bart passes a liquor store sign when he's on the bad side of town that reads, "Yes, We Have Rotgut!"

Though the roof of the Simpson house is significantly graded, balls still get stuck on it.

> **Homer Picks Grampa Up from the Retirement Home:**
> **Homer:** *This place is depressing.*
> **Grampa:** *Hey! I live here.*
> **Homer:** *Oh, well, I'm sure it's a blast once you get used to it.*

LADIES AND GENTLEMEN, I'VE BEEN TO VIETNAM, AFGHANISTAN, AND IRAQ, AND I CAN SAY WITHOUT HYPERBOLE THAT THIS IS A MILLION TIMES WORSE THAN ALL OF THEM PUT TOGETHER.

CAPTAIN LANCE MURDOCK

Profession:
World's greatest daredevil.

Affiliated slogans:
No stranger to danger;
If he's not in action, he's in traction.

Number of bad breaks:
Has broken every bone in his body, even the little ones in his ears; one thumb has been broken several dozen times.

Danger level:
Has been known to attempt leaps over water tanks filled with great white sharks, deadly electric eels, ravenous piranhas, bone crushing alligators, and one ferocious lion.

Multilingual:
Can request morphine in over 20 languages.

Comfort level:
Likes being in the hospital because of the sponge baths and tube feedings he gets from nurses.

ON THE CHANCE THAT I DON'T SURVIVE, LET ME JUST SAY, SEAT BELTS SAVE LIVES SO BUCKLE UP.

Episode 7F06 Original Airdate: 12/6/90 Writers: Jay Kogen and Wallace Wolodarsky Director: Wesley Meyer Archer

Homer and Bart learn that Truckasaurus—a giant, fire-breathing mechanical dinosaur made out of trucks—is coming to the Springfield Speedway. Homer proposes that the whole family attend the event, even though it falls on the same night as Lisa's saxophone recital. Homer and Bart anxiously sit through the performance and then rush the family to the rally. Entering the speedway arena by mistake, the Simpsons' car is mauled by Truckasaurus.

At the show, Bart is enthralled with the stunts of fearless daredevil Captain Lance Murdock. When Murdock's stunt goes awry, he is pulled from a shark-and lion-infested tank to a rousing ovation. Bart knows he has found his calling. Performing his first stunt in front of the local kids, Bart flies off

his skateboard and smashes into the pavement. Dr. Hibbert gives him a safety lecture, while Captain Murdock, healing in the hospital, urges Bart to live life on the edge.

With Murdock's encouragement, Bart decides on the greatest stunt of his life: jumping the Springfield Gorge. Homer concludes that the only way he can stop Bart is to do the stunt himself and show Bart how dangerous it is. He mounts Bart's skateboard, but Bart, knowing Homer will surely die if he tries the stunt, agrees to give up his daredevil career. Homer accidentally rolls backwards down the ramp. Airborne, he feels the elation of flight, but runs out of momentum and crashes into the gorge.

SHOW HIGHLIGHTS

"I'll be playing my first solo. If you miss it on Saturday, I'd advise you to start looking for a child therapist on Sunday."

At the Recital:
Principal Skinner: Tonight Sherbert's, heh, heh, Schubert's Unfinished Symphony.
Homer: Oh, good, unfinished. This shouldn't take long.

Truckasaurus fallout: When the Simpson car is snatched in the jaws of Truckasaurus at the Monster Truck Rally, the damage it sustains includes a cracked windshield, melted bumpers, a punctured radiator, and teeth marks in the trunk. But there appears to be no frame damage.

"Oh, cruel fate. Why do you mock me?"

TV voice #1: Plus the amazing...
TV voice #2: The astounding...
TV voice #3: The unbelievable...
All 3 announcers: Truckasaurus!!!
TV voice #2: Twenty tons and four stories of car-crunching, fire-breathing prehistoric insanity!
TV voice #1: One night only!
TV voice #2: One night only!
TV voice #3: One night only at the Springfield Speedway, this Saturday!
TV voice #1: If you miss this, you'd better be dead or in jail.
TV voice #2: And if you're in jail, break out!
TV voice #3: Be there!

The Good Doctor: Dr. Julius Hibbert is introduced in this episode.

The Three Stooges ward: Part of the most horrifying section of the hospital, where care is given to children who have injured themselves imitating stunts they saw "on television, films, and the legitimate stage."

Bart: (meeting Lance) It's an honor, Lance. How you feeling?
(Lance huffs, puffs, sweats and strains to give the "thumbs-up.")
(A loud crack is heard.)
Lance: Ow! Doc, I heard a snap.
Dr. Hibbert: Hmm. I'm afraid the bone's broken. Well, that's all of them.

In traction: Captain Lance Murdock is so banged up following his Monster Truck Rally mishap that he must sign an autograph for Bart by putting the pen in his mouth.

"**It's always good to see young people taking an interest in danger.**" Captain Lance Murdock from his hospital bed, to Bart.

"...if you got hurt or died, despite the extra attention I'd receive, I'd miss you."

"**This is the greatest thrill of my life! I'm king of the world! Wooo, wooo! Wooo, wooo!**" Homer, flying across the gorge on Bart's skateboard.

Marge: Homer, you're his father. You've got to reason with him.
Homer: Oh, that never works. He's a goner!

THE STUFF YOU MAY HAVE MISSED

Lisa reads a book throughout the entire wrestling match being shown on TV.

Nobody in the Simpson car wears seat belts, except Maggie, when Truckasaurus grabs their car in its jaws.

The billboard in front of Springfield Speedway Sports, under the "Truckasaurus" event listing reads, "Sunday: Bear Baiting."

At Springfield General Hospital, a small sign reads, "Cash Only."

When he is poised to jump Springfield Gorge, the skull on Bart's skull-and-crossbones T-shirt is spiked like Bart's head.

Movie Moments:
Bart's emergence through the heat and haze with his skateboard to jump Springfield Gorge is an ode to Lawrence of Arabia.

I WILL NOT DRIVE THE PRINCIPAL'S CAR
I WILL NOT DRIVE THE PRINCIPAL'S CAR
I WILL NOT DRIVE THE PRINCIPAL'S CAR

Episode 7F09 Original Airdate: 12/20/90 Writer: John Swartzwelder Director: Jim Reardon

Maggie attacks Homer in the basement with a mallet. Wondering where Maggie is getting such ideas, Marge joins her children as they watch their favorite TV cat-and-mouse cartoon, "The Itchy & Scratchy Show." Marge is stunned by the show's violence and writes a letter to its creators.

When her letter has no effect, Marge protests in front of the studio where the show is produced. Soon, her protest turns into a nationwide boycott. Marge appears on TV and asks parents to write letters to the producer. A flood of negative mail pours into the show's offices. As ratings plummet, the producer asks Marge to come up with acceptable story ideas.

Itchy & Scratchy soon turns into a tame cat-and-mouse team, and the show's ratings hit rock bottom. Subsequently, Michelangelo's nude "David" is exhibited at a museum, and other crusaders ask Marge to rally to their cause. But Marge finds nothing objectionable about the statue. Caught in a dilemma, she realizes that she was wrong for protesting against one form of free speech while supporting another.

I WILL NOT PLEDGE
ALLEGIANCE TO BART
I WILL NOT PLEDGE
ALLEGIANCE TO BART
I WILL NOT PLEDGE
ALLEGIANCE TO BART

SHOW HIGHLIGHTS

 "But, mom! If you take our cartoons away, we'll grow up without a sense of humor and be robots."

"Dear purveyors of senseless violence: I know this may sound silly at first, but I believe that the cartoons you show to our children are influencing their behavior in a negative way. Please try to tone down the psychotic violence in your otherwise fine programming. Yours truly, Marge Simpson." Marge's letter to the producers of Itchy and Scratchy.

"In regards to your specific comments about the show, our research indicates that one person cannot make a difference, no matter how big a screwball she is..." Roger Myers, dictating a response to Marge.

 "You heard me. I won't be in for the rest of the week. (*listens*) I told you. My baby beat me up. (*listens*) Oh, it is not the worst excuse I ever thought up."

The new "Itchy & Scratchy Show" theme: "They love / they share / they share and love and share / love love love / share share share / The Itchy & Scratchy Showwww!"

"You know, some of these stories are pretty good. I never knew mice lived such interesting lives." Homer, on "The Itchy & Scratchy Show."

 "Hello, I'm Kent Brockman, and welcome to another edition of 'Smartline.' Are cartoons too violent for children? Most people would say 'No. Of course not. What kind of stupid question is that?' But one woman says 'yes'... Marge Simpson."

S.N.U.H.: Springfieldians for Nonviolence, Understanding, and Helping.

S.N.U.H.'s rallying cry: "Substantially-less-violence-in-children's-programming!"

Roger Meyers Jr.: *That screwball Marge Simpson, we've got to stop her. But how?*
Animator: *Drop an anvil on her?*
1st board member: *Hit her on the head with a piano?*
2nd board member: *Stuff her full of TNT, then throw a match down her throat and run?*

The New Itchy & Scratchy in "Porch Pals":
(Itchy and Scratchy sit on a porch.)
Scratchy: *Lemonade?*
Itchy: *Please.*
Scratchy: *I made it just for you.*
Itchy: *You are my best friend. Mmm. This really hits the spot.*
Scratchy: *Doesn't it though?*
Itchy: *You make really good lemonade, Scratchy.*
Scratchy: *Thank you, Itchy.*

Homer and Marge Watch the Cartoons:
Marge: *What kind of warped human being would find that funny?*
Homer: *Heh, heh, heh.*

Marge: *...that's Michelangelo's "David." It's a masterpiece!*
Helen Lovejoy: *It's filth. It graphically portrays parts of the human body which, practical as they may be, are evil!*
Marge: *But I like that statue.*
Maude Flanders: *I told you she was soft on full frontal nudity.*

Marge's Stationery Reads:
From the Mind of Marge.

THE STUFF YOU MAY HAVE MISSED

Homer's hammer still has the pricetag dangling from it.

Itchy & Scratchy International chairman Roger Meyers Jr. has a poster of Itchy & Scratchy endorsing Duff Beer and a bottle of Itchy & Scratchy cologne on his desk office.

Signs at the protest:
"I'm protesting because Itchy & Scratchy are indirectly responsible for my husband being hit on the head with a mallet" — Marge.

"Don't ban Itchy and Scratchy" — Bart.

"Bring Back 'Wagon Train'" — Moe.

"What if they blew up a cat and nobody laughed" — random.

ROGER MYERS

Profession:
Chairman of Itchy & Scratchy International.

Occupation:
Arrogant purveyor of senseless cartoon violence.

Enjoys:
Belittling the writing staff, particularly those who graduated from Harvard.

Beliefs:
One protester cannot make a difference, no matter how big a screwball she is.

Hates:
Being called a sleaze merchant, but does not necessarily deny it, either.

THERE WAS VIOLENCE IN THE PAST, LONG BEFORE CARTOONS WERE INVENTED.

Guest Voice:
Alex Rocco
as Roger Meyers, Jr.

BART GETS HIT BY A CAR

Episode 7F10 Original Airdate: 1/10/91 Writer: John Swartzwelder Director: Mark Kirkland

> WRONG!!! YOU ARE NOT FINE! YOU ARE IN CONSTANT PAIN!

Guest Voice:
Phil Hartman
as Lionel Hutz

SHOW HIGHLIGHTS

"For crying out loud. Just give him a nickel and let's get going." Mr. Burns, angered at being delayed after hitting Bart.

Climbing the escalator to Heaven: Bart passes a cloud with his Aunt Hortense and Great-Grampa Simpson who is strangling a young boy. He also sees his first cat, Snowball, with tire marks across its body.

"I'm Bart Simpson, who the hell are you?" Bart, introducing himself to the Devil.

The Devil, introducing himself and welcoming Bart to Hell: "Ah, please allow me to introduce myself. I'm the Devil! (*evil chuckle*) And you've earned eternal damnation for your lifetime of evil deeds, Bart. Spitting off the escalator just clinched it."

Hell awaits Bart: When Bart wonders if there is anything he can do to avoid returning to hell, the devil informs Bart, "Oh sure, yeah; but eh, you wouldn't like it."

 "Doctors! Pffft! Doctors are idiots...you can ching-ching-ching cash in on this tragedy."

Mr. Burns's side of the story: "Oh, it was a beautiful day. The sun was shining. I was driving to the orphanage to pass out toys...suddenly, that incorrigible Simpson boy darted in front of me."

Bart's side of the story: "It was a beautiful Sunday afternoon. I was playing in my wholesome childlike way, little realizing that I was about to be struck down by the Luxury Car of Death."

"Aw, you're better off. Rich people aren't happy. From the day they're born to the day they die, they think they're happy but, trust me...they ain't."

Mr. Burns hands Homer and Marge another offer: This time it's $500,000. But after eavesdropping on Marge and Homer discussing the figure and subsequently learning that Homer has hired a phony doctor, he rescinds it.

> **Dream Sequence:**
> **Bart:** Hey, cool. I'm dead.
> **Heavenly voice:** Please hold on to the handrail. Do not spit over the side. Por favor, aguantese en la baranda. No escupas en los lados.

> **Movie Moment:**
> When Bart regains consciousness in the hospital he points to everyone who was in his visit to the afterlife à la Dorothy at the end of *The Wizard of Oz*.

> **Dr. Nick Riviera:** Your son is a very sick boy. Just look at these X-rays! (He holds up a large X-ray of Bart's head, spikey hair and all.) You see that dark spot there? Whiplash.
> **Homer:** Whiplash! Oh no!
> **Dr. Nick Riviera:** And this smudge here that looks like my fingerprint? No. That's trauma.

> **Moe's Reuniting Special (after Homer Proclaims His Love for Marge):**
> **Moe:** Okay, everybody! For the next fifteen minutes, one third off on every pitcher . . . one per customer . . . domestic beer only . . . hey, no sharing!

> **Homer:** (admiring diplomas) You sure have got some education, Mr. Hutz.
> **Hutz:** (impressed with himself) Yes...Harvard, Yale, MIT, Oxford, the Sorbonne, the Louvre...

THE STUFF YOU MAY HAVE MISSED

Burns's luxury auto is a 1948 Rolls Royce.

Bart skates by Mort's Deli and Sushi Yes before getting hit.

Hell is a Hieronymous Bosch painting.

The devil's desktop is equipped with a Windows-based program.

Lionel Hutz's office is in the mall next to the Yogurt Nook where two big-nosed, hatted twins sit.

Dr. Nick Riviera's office is two doors down from Hutz's. They are separated by a Gum for Less store.

Herman is moved by Bart's testimony.

While riding his skateboard, Bart is hit by a car driven by Mr. Burns. He has an after-death experience and regains consciousness in the hospital. Attorney Lionel Hutz tells Homer to call if he wants to make a lot of money. When Mr. Burns offers Homer a mere $100 as compensation for Bart's injuries, he turns it down and calls Hutz.

Hutz assures Homer that he can get a million-dollar settlement. But first, Bart must lie about his injuries in court. Hutz also uses the expert testimony of Dr. Nick Riviera. When Burns realizes that he will lose the lawsuit, he offers Homer and Marge a settlement of $500,000. Marge wants to accept the offer, but Homer will not settle.

Burns's lawyers put Marge on the stand. She tells the jury the whole truth. Homer listens in disbelief as his million slips away. Sitting in Moe's Tavern, he wonders if he can still love the woman who cost him a million dollars. Marge enters to apologize. Homer looks her in the eyes and tells her he loves her more than ever.

I WILL NOT SELL SCHOOL PROPERTY
I WILL NOT SELL SCHOOL PROPERTY
I WILL NOT SELL SCHOOL PROPERTY

ONE FISH, TWO FISH, BLOWFISH, BLUE FISH

Episode 7F11 Original Airdate: 1/24/91 Writer: Nell Scovell Director: Wesley M. Archer
Guest Voices: Larry King as Himself, Sab Shimono as the Master Chef

Homer takes the family to the Happy Sumo for sushi. After sampling most of the items on the menu, he tries the blowfish—the dangerous sushi delicacy. One false cut by the chef can make the dish fatal. When the master chef sees that the fish Homer ate was prepared improperly, he directs Homer to the hospital, where Dr. Hibbert tells Homer that he has twenty-four hours to live.

Homer writes a list of "things to do before dying" and attempts to complete it in his last day. He has a heart-to-heart talk with Bart, tries to enjoy an impromptu saxophone recital by Lisa, makes amends with his father, joins Barney for one last beer at Moe's, tells off Mr. Burns, and takes Marge into the bedroom for one last night of passion.

Leaving Marge to sleep, Homer slips away to kiss his children one last time. He then falls asleep in his easy chair, listening to the Bible on tape, expecting never to wake up. The next morning, Marge holds Homer's lifeless body. Homer stirs, discovers he's alive, and celebrates overcoming his brush with death. Soon, he is back in front of the TV set, munching on pork rinds.

SHOW HIGHLIGHTS

"Mr. Simpson-san. I shall be blunt. We have reason to believe that you have eaten poison...no need to panic. There's a map to the hospital on the back of the menu." Toshiro, the apprentice chef at the Happy Sumo, comforting Homer.

Marge's request: Marge asks if they can rise early to watch the sun come up together. When his alarm goes off at six a.m., Homer turns it off and stays asleep for another five and a half hours.

Presumed guilty: When Homer calls Bart for a final man-to-man discussion, Bart drops his pants and lays across Homer's knee.

"I want to share something with you— the three little sentences that will get you through life. Number one, 'cover for me.' Number two, 'oh, good idea, boss.' Number three, 'it was like that when I got here.'"

"Gee, Dad, way to hog my last moments." Homer, to Grampa, crossing him off his list of people to see after Grampa extends their visit.

Final hours: After being intimate with Marge, Homer kisses the kids. He tells Maggie to stay sweet. He tells Lisa he knows she will make him proud. After taking a moment to think about it, he tells Bart he likes his sheets.

"So You're Going to Die": A pamphlet Dr. Hibbert gives to Homer.

"When the Saints Go Over There": Homer's version of "When the Saints Come Marching In." He sings it while Lisa plays her sax one last time for him.

Homer's List of Things to Do before Dying:
(Printed on "Dumb Things I Gotta Do Today" notepaper)

1. Make list (which is crossed out)
2. Eat a hearty breakfast
3. Make videotape for Maggie
4. Have man-to-man with Bart
5. Listen to Lisa play her sax
6. Make funeral arrangement
7. Make peace with Dad
8. Beer with the boys at the bar
9. Tell off the boss
10. Go hang gliding
11. Plant a tree
12. A final dinner with my beloved family
13. Be intamit [sic] with Marge

"Hello, Moe's Tavern..."

Moe: Hello, Moe's Tavern — birthplace of the Rob Roy.
Bart: Is Seymour there? Last name, Butts.
Moe: Just a sec. (calling out) Hey, is there a Butts here? Seymour Butts? Hey, everybody, I wanna Seymour Butts!
Moe: (catching on) Hey, wait a minute. Listen, you little scum-sucking pus-bucket. When I get my hands on you, I'm gonna pull out your eyeballs with a corkscrew.

I WILL NOT CUT CORNERS

THE STUFF YOU MAY HAVE MISSED

The Happy Sumo restaurant is on Elm Street.

Homer drinks a large-sized Duffahama at the Happy Sumo.

Homer eats and eats off his plate of sushi, but he always has two pieces on his plate.

Richie Sakai, who takes to the karaoke stage to do Cher's "Gypsies, Tramps, and Thieves," is named after Richard Sakai, producer of "The Simpsons."

Flanders's doormat reads "Welcome to Flanders Country." A sign by their closet reads "Bless this mess."

Barney's living room table is an empty cable spool

(As Barney and Homer drive by, Homer sees Burns.)
Homer: Hey, Burns! Eat my shorts!
Burns: Who the Sam Hill was that?
Smithers: Why, it's Homer Simpson, sir. One of the schmoes from Sector 7G.
Burns: Simpson, eh? I want him in my office at nine o'clock Monday morning. We'll see who eats whose shorts.

AKIRA

Occupation:
Waiter at the Happy Sumo Japanese restaurant.

Occupation II:
Owner/operator/teacher, Springfield Martial Arts Academy.

Topnotch:
Among the many sufferers of bad hair in Springfield.

Teacher:
Karate — so we need never use it.

Specialty:
Knows when to suggest raw quail egg with a dish.

In search of:
A pair of left-handed nunchucks to make his life complete.

> FIRST YOU MUST FILL YOUR HEAD WITH WISDOM, THEN YOU CAN HIT ICE WITH IT.

Guest Voice:
George Takei as Akira

When the Simpsons' TV set breaks, Marge tells her children how she and Homer met. The year is 1974. A young Homer smokes cigarettes and ditches class, while Marge kindles the women's movement by burning her bra. Both end up in detention hall. When Homer sees Marge, he falls instantly in love.

To impress Marge, Homer signs up for the debate team. Then he asks Marge to tutor him in French so he can sweet-talk her. After accepting his invitation to the prom, Marge finds out that Homer does not care about French or debating but is only interested in her. She tells Homer she hates him and accepts Artie Ziff's invitation to the prom.

Undaunted, Homer goes to the prom alone. Later, when Artie tries to get romantic with Marge in the backseat of his car, she demands to be taken home. On the way, they pass Homer walking on the side of the road. Marge returns in her car to pick Homer up, realizing that he was the man for her all along.

SHOW HIGHLIGHTS

Guess Who: When the Simpsons' television breaks they are watching a movie review show hosted by a chubby guy and a bald guy. They are reviewing McBain's latest picture.

"D'oh! English! Who needs that? I'm never going to England. Come on, let's go smoke." Homer, talking Barney into cutting class.

Extended Sentence: After Homer starts talking to Marge in detention, every word he says to her gets him another day's worth of detention.

"And anyone can be tooted?" Homer, asking Marge about her tutoring.

ReBUTTal: Homer brings a new low to the debate team by mooning Artie Ziff for his final argument.

"I can think of a dozen highly cogent arguments. The first is from *Time* magazine, dated January 8, 1974, 'America's Love Affair with The Prom: Even wallflowers can look forward to one date a year.'" Artie Ziff, on why Marge should accept his offer to go to the prom.

Grandpa's Advice for Life:
Grampa: *Now, this girlfriend of yours. Is she a real looker?*
Homer: *Uh-huh.*
Grampa: *A lot on the ball?*
Homer: *Oh, yeah.*
Grampa: *Ohhh, son, don't overreach. Go for the dented car, the dead-end job, the less attractive girl. Ohh, I blame myself. I should have had this talk a long time ago.*

First Appearance:
Marge's father, Mr. Bouvier. (It seems that Patty and Selma inherited their love of smoking from their father, along with murmuring style.)

Marge's first act of activism:
Marge: *(speaking at a rally) The first step to liberation is to free ourselves from these... (she pulls out a bra) ...male imposed shackles.*
Kim: *I didn't think it would burn so fast.*
Marge: *I guess it's the tissue paper inside.*

Barney: *Hi, Estelle, will you go to the prom with me?*
Estelle: *I wouldn't go to the prom with you if you were Elliot Gould.*

Days Gone By :
Barney: *Boy, you never stop eating and you don't gain a pound.*
Homer *It's my metaba-ma-lism. I guess I'm just one of the lucky ones.*

Principal Dondelinger: *(taking the cigarettes out of their mouths) Allow me, gentlemen. You just bought yourselves three days of detention. You know where and when.*
Homer/Barney: *(sadly) Three o'clock. Old building. Room 106.*

Guidance Counselor McIntyre: *Homer, do you have any plans for after graduation?*
Homer: *Me? Stay out late, drink a lot of beer.*

The Debate:
Mrs. Bloominstein *(the teacher): This year's topic is "Resolved: The national speed limit should be lowered to fifty-five miles per hour.*
Homer: *Fifty-five! That's ridiculous! Sure, they'll save a few lives. But millions will be late!*

Episode 7F12
Original Airdate: 1/31/91
Writers: Al Jean & Mike Reiss and Sam Simon
Director: David Silverman
Guest Voice: Jon Lovitz as Artie Ziff and Mr. Seckofsky

ARTIE ZIFF

Who he is:
Bushy-haired, bespectacled know-it-all;
Marge's date to the senior prom.

Main claim to fame:
Most skilled member of
Springfield High School forensic team.

Private shame:
His busy hands.

Greatest challenge:
Humility.

Greatest achievement:
Being voted Homecoming King
to Marge's Queen.

**His special
name for Homer:**
Ignoramus.

INSTEAD OF VOTING FOR SOME ATHLETIC HERO, OR A PRETTY BOY, YOU HAVE ELECTED ME, YOUR INTELLECTUAL SUPERIOR, AS YOUR KING. GOOD FOR YOU!

I WILL NOT GET VERY FAR
WITH THIS ATTITUDE.
I WILL NOT GET VERY FAR
WITH THIS ATTITUDE.
I WILL NOT GET VERY FAR
WITH THIS ATTITUDE.

Episode Song List:
"Close to You" by The Carpenters, "The Joker" by the Steve Miller Band, "Pick Up the Pieces" by the Average White Band, "Can't Get Enough of Your Love, Baby" by Barry White, "Goodbye, Yellow Brick Road" by Elton John, "Do the Hustle" by Van McCoy.

Selma and Patty's first impression of Homer:
Selma: Marge's dates get homelier all the time.
Patty: Mm-hmm. That's what you get when you don't put out.

After the TV goes fuzzy:
Homer: All right, all right. Time for Dr. TV to perform a little surgery! (He slams his fist down; the picture gets worse).
Bart: Looks like you lost the patient, Doc.

Mrs. Bouvier On Rouge
Marge : (pinching her cheeks) Couldn't we just use rouge for this?
Mrs. Bouvier: Ladies pinch. Whores use rouge.

THE STUFF YOU MAY HAVE MISSED

Rainier Wolfcastle is clearly German (or Austrian, or Swiss), but his McBain character has a Scotch/Irish name.

Homer is a Pink Floyd and Led Zeppelin fan according to the posters on his wall.

In 1974, Marge wore her hair down. She put it up in the current style for the prom.

Mr. Burns visage is on the front of the Springfield Nuclear Power Plant career information pamphlet.

Grampa and Homer dined on a bucket of Shakespeare Fried Chicken.

Shop teacher Mr Seckofsky is missing a finger.

Features on the cover of Marge's Ms. Magazine: -Hating and Dating: Do they mix? - Why all men are bad. -25 reasons not to shave your armpits.

When Selma asks Artie Ziff, "Don't we look handsome" he answers "Yes, indeed we do" actually refering to himself, Patty, and Selma.

The Larry Davis Experience plays the prom (see 7G01 "Some Enchanted Evening," and 7F17, "Old Money").

HOMER VS. LISA AND THE 8TH COMMANDMENT

Episode 7F13 Original Airdate: 2/7/91 Credits: Writer: Steve Pepoon Director: Rich Moore Guest Voice: Phil Hartman as Moses; Cable Guy

REVEREND LOVEJOY

Occupation:
Man of God; motorist; marriage counselor.

Biggest competitors:
The NFL; warm beds on a Sunday morning; cable.

Books/pamphlets:
Hell: It's Not Just for Christians Anymore and *Satan's Boners.*

Hobby:
Toy trains.

Secret shame:
Has his dog do its "dirty business" on Ned Flanders's lawn.

Words of comfort to death-row inmates:
"There there; there, there"; "Well, if that's the worst thing to happen to you today, consider yourself lucky."

> THE CHURCH RECEIVETH AND THE CHURCH TAKETH AWAY.

Homer gets an illegal cable TV hook-up and invites all his friends to the house to watch a major upcoming boxing match. Lisa learns about the eighth commandment at Sunday School and fears her family will really go to hell for stealing the cable.

Lisa seeks advice from Reverend Lovejoy, who tells her to set an example by not watching any cable programs. Marge also worries that cable is a negative influence on the family and suggests that they get rid of it. Homer, however, is determined to keep his cable and watch the big fight with his friends.

On the night of the big fight, Lisa protests and is sent outside by Homer, where Marge joins her. During the fight, Homer's conscience finally wins over and he leaves the gathering to sit with his family. After the match, wire cutters in hand, he climbs the power pole in front of the house and snips the cable line—plunging the neighborhood into total darkness.

SHOW HIGHLIGHTS

The Eighth Commandment: Thou shalt not steal.

Flashback to "Sinai Desert, 1220 B.C.": Homer the Thief (who bears a striking resemblance to Homer Simpson, is talking with his friends Hezron, Carver of Graven Images, and Zohar, the Adulterer. Moses comes down from the mountain to read the ten commandments . . . thus changing their lifestyles forever. Homer awakens.

"I should box your ears you, you, you . . . Sneaky Pete!" Flanders, to the cable man, following an offer to hook up his cable service for free. The cable man's only comeback is, "Easy, tiger."

"So You've Decided to Steal Cable": Pamphlet from the cable man.

From the "So You've Decided to Steal Cable" pamphlet that comes with the Simpsons's illegal cable: "Myth: cable piracy is wrong. Fact: cable companies are big faceless corportations, which makes it okay. Myth: it's only fair to pay for quality first-run movies. Fact: most movies shown on cable get two stars or less and are repeated *ad nauseum*."

"Cable. It's more wonderful than I dared hope."

"Nothing a month? Yeah, I think we can swing that." Homer, to Marge, when she asks if they can afford cable.

"Wouldn't you eventually get used to it, like in a hot tub?" Bart, after the Sunday school teacher explains that in hell you would burn day and night forever and ever.

"Man, I wish I was an adult so I could break the rules."

"Bart, you're no longer in Sunday School. Don't swear." Marge, to Bart, on his use of the word "hell."

"I'm so keen on seeing 'Watson vs. Tatum II,' I'd even go to an employee's house. Oh, I can picture it now: the

screen door rusting off its filthy hinges, mangy dog staggering about, looking vainly for a place to die."

Fight night: As guests file in, Homer must hide objects he has stolen from them, including beer mugs from Moe's and a computer from work. Lisa announces she is on a protest and Homer sends her outside.

Movie Moment:
After finding out the cable man does illegal hookups, Homer chases down his truck and fakes getting hit in order to get him to stop. It is reminiscent of *North by Northwest.*

I WILL NOT MAKE FLATULENT
NOISES IN CLASS
I WILL NOT MAKE FLATULENT
NOISES IN CLASS
I WILL NOT MAKE FLATULENT
NOISES IN CLASS

Homer: *Oh. Look at it this way. When you had breakfast this morning, did you pay for it?*
Lisa: *No.*
Homer: *And did you pay for those clothes you're wearing?*
Lisa: *No, I didn't.*
Homer: *Well, run for the hills, Ma Barker, before I call the feds.*
Lisa: *Dad, I think that's pretty spurious.*
Homer: *Well, thank you, honey.*

Spiritual Guidance:
Lisa: *So, even if a man takes bread to feed his starving family, that would be stealing?*
Reverend Lovejoy: *No. Well, it is if he puts anything on it. Jelly, for example.*

THE STUFF YOU MAY HAVE MISSED

Homer the Thief steals Zohar's money purse when he pats him on the back.

A plant beside the couch grows to maturity and dies as the Simpsons watch hour after hour of cable.

Sign in the showers at the nuclear power plant: "Decontamination Showers. Wash everything!"

Sign outside the church: "God, the Original Love Connection."

Jimbo shows up in the background shoplifting twice—in the grocery store, stuffing produce in his parka and at the Kwik-E-Mart, swiping more merchandise.

The two pugilists are "modeled" after Mike Tyson (Tatum) and Buster Douglas (Watson).

We hear part of a "Davey and Goliath" episode where Goliath warns against using Dad's car.

PRINCIPAL CHARMING

Episode 7F15   Original Airdate: 2/14/91   Writer: David Stern   Director: Mark Kirkland

When Selma confides to Marge her desire to be married, Marge asks Homer to find Selma a man. Homer searches but cannot find anyone suitable or desperate enough to marry Selma. Homer meets with Principal Skinner about Bart's behavior and, learning that Skinner is also single, invites him home to dinner to meet Selma.

Skinner arrives and is introduced first to Patty. He is instantly smitten. As Patty and Skinner start dating, Selma sinks deeper into despair.

Barney learns about Selma's lack of prospects and offers to be fixed up with her. When Skinner asks Patty to marry him, Selma gives up all hope and decides to accept Barney's advances. Patty realizes the effect her relationship is having on her sister and turns down Skinner's proposal. Rescuing Selma from her date with Barney, she takes Selma home.

SHOW HIGHLIGHTS

Gimme four: Homer runs in and tells Marge excitedly, "I've got five words to say to you. (*Counting on his fingers*) Greasy Joe's Bottomless Bar-B-Q (*moving to his next hand*) Pit."

 "I'll get right to the point. I'm getting older, fatter, and uglier... help me find a man before it's too late."

"She has always been the lucky one. Two minutes younger, skin like a China doll, and bosoms 'til Tuesday." Selma, on Patty.

Say when: Even as she explains that sodium tetrasulfate is "highly caustic and can remove your skin," Mrs. Krabappel pours it sloppily into a beaker near Bart and Martin.

"You know, food tastes better when you're revolving." Principal Skinner, on dining at the Springfield Revolving Restaurant.

Hands off: When Skinner tries to put his arm around Patty at the movies while they watch *Space Mutants IV: The Land Down Under*, Patty snaps, "Don't be stupid!"

"Homer, lighten up. You're making 'Happy Hour' bitterly ironic."

Patty's brands: She smokes Lady Laramie 100's; her candy of choice is cherry cordials.

> **First Appearance:**
> Hans Moleman (although his driver's license reads, "Ralph Mellish").

Marge: *Homer, remember you promised you'd try to limit pork to six servings a week?*
Homer: *Marge, I'm only human.*

Selma: *It's time to give away my love like so much cheap wine.*
Homer: *Take it to the hoop, Selma!*

Homer: *Find a husband? Wait, which one's Selma again?*
Marge: *She's the one who likes Police Academy movies and Hummel figurines and walking through the park on clear autumn days.*

"Hello, Moe's Tavern..."
Bart: Hello. Is Homer there?
Moe: Homer who?
Bart: Homer Sexual.
Moe: Wait one second, let me check. (to the bar) Homer Sexual. Ah, come on, come on, one of you guys has gotta to be Homer Sexual.
Moe: Oh no, you rotten little punk! If I ever get a hold of you, I'll sink my teeth into your cheek and rip your face off!

THE STUFF YOU MAY HAVE MISSED

Marge uses the cosmetic cream "Gee, Your Lip Looks Hairless" on sister Patty.

From the Springfield Revolving Restaurant, you can see a prison riot, a man threatening to jump while standing on an apartment ledge, and a garish neon sign reading "House of Tires."

The Moe's Tavern happy hour is 5-5:30 p.m.

A jewelry store in Springfield: "Family Jewels." Another store is called "Discount Meat Hut" (reference from "Life in Hell").

Bart's disciplinary file includes write-ups for vandalism, tardiness, absenteeism, making faces and rude behavior.

The sign in front of the church reads "Peterson Wedding" at 2:00 and "Hayride to Heaven" at 8:00.

Skinner: *So Patty, tell me more about your trip to Egypt.*
Patty: *Nothing more to tell, really. The Nile River smells like cattle rot and they've got horseflies over there the size of your head.*

> **Movie Moments:**
> Homer's futuristic means of analyzing potential suitors for Selma parodies *The Terminator*. Principal Skinner declares that "Tomorrow is another school day!" à la *Gone with the Wind* ("Tomorrow is another day!"). Skinner carries Patty up the steps to the bell tower à la Quasimodo carrying Esmeralda in *The Hunchback of Notre Dame*. Skinner's climb up the stairs at Springfield Elementary recalls the final scene from Hitchcock's *Vertigo*.

Occupation:
Principal of Springfield Elementary School.

Nickname:
Spanky.

Residence:
Still lives with his mother.

Education:
According to the students, he knows everything.

Reputation:
Renowned stuffed shirt.

Top secret:
Rumored to wear a toupee.

Speech:
Uses big words.

Turn-ons:
Orderliness; promptness; respect; good grooming.

Turn-offs:
Chaos; tardiness; disrespect; Bart Simpson.

> HMMM, SAY WHAT YOU WILL ABOUT OUR CAFETERIA. I STILL THINK THEY'RE THE BEST TATER TOTS MONEY CAN BUY.

OH BROTHER, WHERE ART THOU?

Episode 7F16 Original Airdate: 2/21/91 Writer: Jeff Martin Director: W.M. "Bud" Archer

HERB POWELL

Born:
Half-brother of Homer Simpson; put up for adoption shortly after birth.

Son of:
Abraham Simpson and a carnival floozy.

Occupation:
CEO of Powell Motors.

Education:
Worked his way through Harvard by washing dishes and scrubbing toilets.

Motivation:
Exhibits a drive uncommon for anyone with Simpson blood in his veins.

True happiness:
Considers wealth in terms of love and family, not money.

Nickname:
Prefers to be called Unky Herb by nieces and nephews.

I'M JUST A LONELY GUY.

Guest Voice:
Danny DeVito as Herb Powell

SHOW HIGHLIGHTS

Thumbs down: At the McBain movie, Grampa and Jasper want their money back because "the screen was too small, the floor was sticky, and the romantic subplot felt tacked on."

I WILL NOT SELL LAND IN FLORIDA
I WILL NOT SELL LAND IN FLORIDA
I WILL NOT SELL LAND IN FLORIDA

Homer, saying grace before dinner: "...and thank you most of all for nuclear power, which is yet to cause a single proven fatality, at least in this country."

Mild arrhythmia: Dr. Hibbert's diagnosis of Grampa. Grampa disagrees about the mild part and calls Hibbert a quack.

"Wait-wait-wait-wait-wait-wait! Let me see if I got this straight...It's Christmas day, four a.m., there's a rumble in my stomach..." Homer, checking the validity of the promise of pork chops anytime he wants them at Herb's.

Nepo-ma-tism: Powell Motors is losing ground daily to the Japanese. Their cars are too sluggish, too small, and they are named after "hungry old Greek broads." Herb hires Homer to help set the company straight.

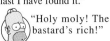

"You know that little ball you put on the aerial so you can find your car in a parking lot? That should be on every car... And some things are so snazzy they never go out of style! Like tail fins! And bubble domes! And shag carpeting!" "I want a horn here, here, and here. You can never find a horn when you're mad. And they should all play 'La Cucaracha.'"

The ad for "The Homer": An arty, ethereal segment featuring Homer driving along a coast, as his voice calls out, "All my life, I have searched for a car that feels a certain way. Powerful like a gorilla, yet soft and yielding like a nerf ball. Now, at last I have found it."

"Holy moly! The bastard's rich!"

Homer the Enforcer:
(Bart and Lisa taunt each other.)
Homer: *Quiet, you kids! If I hear one more word, Bart doesn't get to watch cartoons and Lisa doesn't get to go to college.* (Bart and Lisa silently act out insults to each other. Homer catches them.)
Homer: . . . *no panta-ma-mime, either!*

Herb: *So, Marge, a little about yourself.*
Marge: *Hmm, well, I met Homer in high school. We got married and had three beautiful children.*
Herb: *Wow, we have so much catching up to do.*
Marge: (murmurs) *Actually, I just told you pretty much everything.*

Herb Is Introduced to the Family :
Herb: (aside to Homer) *All born in wedlock?*
Homer: (aside to Herb) *Yeah, though the boy was a close call.*

From the New "McBain" Film:
Female commando: *You certainly broke up that meeting.*
McBain: *Right now I'm thinking about holding another meeting...in bed.*

Herb: *I want you to help me design a car. A car for all the Homer Simpsons out there! And I want to pay you two hundred thousand dollars a year!*
Homer: *And I want to let you!!*

THE STUFF YOU MAY HAVE MISSED

As McBain shoots, men shake and tremble before he even has his gun trained on him.

Grampa grabs the ushers tie as he has a heart attack. Maggie grabs Herb's tie when he holds her for the first time.

Baby Homer has the same hair as full-sized Homer.

Marge wears bunny slippers with her robe.

The Simpsons stop at an ESEO gas station so Homer can relieve himself.

Before he chews out his staff, Herb Powell growls, "D'oh!"

The orphanage director is Dr. Hibbert's first long-lost brother. (Bleeding Gums Murphy is his second.)

Guest List:
The Pope shows up for the unveiling of Homer's new car.

After suffering a mild heart attack, Grampa reveals a secret to Homer: as a young man, he had an illicit affair that produced another son. Homer sets out to find his long-lost half-brother. He learns that his sibling's name is Herb Powell and that he lives in Detroit. Homer makes contact with Herb and takes the family to Detroit. They arrive at Herb's house, discovering that he lives in a huge mansion and runs a multimillion-dollar car company.

Homer is overcome with joy that he has a wealthy half-brother. Recognizing that Homer represents the typical American, Herb hires him to design a car that will appeal to middle America, thus saving his company from foreign competition. Homer sets out to design his dream car, becoming more of a hard-driving businessman like Herb. Meanwhile, Herb spends time with Marge and the kids, becoming more of a family man like Homer.

Homer's car, "The Homer," is a total flop. Herb loses his business and is forced to give up all of his possessions. Loathing the day Homer came into his life, he leaves on a bus. As the Simpsons drive home, dejected, Homer is comforted by Bart, who admits that he thought Homer's car was cool.

BART'S DOG GETS AN F

Episode 7F14 Original Airdate: 3/7/91 Writer: Jon Vitti Director: Jim Reardon

H omer runs out of patience with Santa's Little Helper after he destroys Homer's brand new sneakers. Homer tells Bart that either the dog goes to obedience school or they get rid of him.

Bart takes Santa's Little Helper to Canine College, but he makes no progress. When the dog eats Homer's favorite cookie and ruins the family heirloom quilt, Homer decides it is time for him to go. Bart begs Homer to give Santa's Little Helper one more chance. Homer agrees to let the dog stay if he passes the final exam at obedience school.

Bart works tirelessly to train his dog, but success seems hopeless. Giving up, Bart tells Santa's Little Helper that if he will only learn to sit, roll over, and speak he can stay with the family. Suddenly, Santa's Little Helper sits, rolls over, and barks on cue. Bart gives other commands, which the dog also follows. The next day, Santa's Little Helper passes his final exam as the Simpsons watch with pride.

SHOW HIGHLIGHTS

Bad dog!: Through the hole the dog chewed in his newspaper, Homer sees Santa's Little Helper preparing to scarf down his sausage and eggs on top of the kitchen table.

"You know, they got Velcro straps, a water pump in the tongue, built-in pedometer, reflective sidewalls and little vanity license plates." Flanders, on his "Assassins" sneakers.

When Homer goes to the newsstand to buy Lisa magazines, he sees: *Teen Dream, Teen Scheme, Teen Scream, Teen Steam, Teen Beam,* and *Non-threatening Boys Magazine.*

"Join the Conspiracy." Marketing tag line used to sell "Assassin" sneakers.

Lisa's Sick with the Mumps

Bart: *No way! She's faking! If Lisa stays home, I stay home.*
Lisa: *If Bart stays home, I'm going to school.*
Bart: *Fine. Then...(confusion)...(to himself) Wait a minute. If Lisa goes to school then I go to school, but then Lisa stays home so I stay home, so Lisa goes to school...*
Marge: *Lisa, don't confuse your brother like that.*

Lisa: *Get my homework from Miss Hoover.*
Bart: *Homework? Lisa, you wasted chicken pox! Don't waste the mumps!*

At Home:

Homer: *Here's your magazines. How many of these guys are named Corey?*
Lisa: *Eight. Thanks, Dad.*

"I'm sorry, sir. Our warranty doesn't cover fire, theft, or acts of dog." Shoe store salesperson, to Homer, after he tries to return his chewed "Assassins."

"You son-of-a-bitch—good show!" Ms. Winthrop congratulates Santa's Little Helper upon graduation.

The Bouvier family quilt: Bed covering in progress that has been in Marge's family for five generations. The earliest patch is a human tobacco leaf wearing a crown, with the title "King Tobacco." Others include a woman shooting a buffalo, a World War I dough boy getting shot, a stock market graph with the arrow pointing down and the caption reading "1929,'" and Marge's "Keep on Truckin,'" with yin and yang sign. Lisa adds likenesses of Mr. Largo and Bleeding Gums Murphy.

"Oooh...maca-ma-damia nuts."

"As an actor, my eyeballs need to look their whitest!"

Santa's Little Helper Shreds the Family Quilt:

Marge: *My quilt! Six generations, ruined!*
Homer: *Now Marge, honey, honey, honey. Come on. Come on, don't get upset. It's not the end of the world. We all loved the quilt, but you can't get too attached to...* (He sees his cookie note on the bed, surrounded by crumbs.)
Homer: *Guuaah!! My cookie!!!! This is not happening! This is not happening!* (Homer buries his face in his hands. He finally looks up.)
Homer: *Everybody in the kitchen! We're having a family meeting!*

Movie Moment:
When Lisa finishes the quilt, she and Marge touch sewing fingers à la *E.T.*

Property of Homer J. Simpson:
"Hands off!" Homer's note to potential eaters of his cookie.

THE STUFF YOU MAY HAVE MISSED

D'oh count: 6 (5 from Homer, 1 from Bart).

Homer's sneakers before the "Assassins" are along the lines of Converse All Stars. He wears them at work.

The little license plates on back of Flanders's "Assassins" read, "Ned."

Martin is the proud owner of a Shar-pei.

Jacques, the bowling instructor, has a french poodle.

"Your dog isn't the problem. You are!" Ad for Dr. Marvin Monroe's dog obedience school in the yellow pages.

Criminal/baby-sitter Ms. Botz (7G01, "Some Enchanted Evening"), has escaped from prison, according to Kent Brockman.

The Springfield Mall shoe store carries footwear grouped by sport, including bocci ball, kickboxing, street crime, and night life.

EMILY WINTHROP

Job:
Owner/operator of Emily Winthrop's Canine College.

Nationality:
British.

Experience:
Training dogs since at least 1954, when she graduated Lord Smiley.

Commands:
Believes "choke" and "chain" are the most important words in life.

Specialty:
Humiliating owners of bad dogs.

Favorite magazine:
JOCO (Journal of Canine Obedience).

Kudos:
Rewards dogs and people, equally, for a job well done.

PERHAPS I CLING TO THE OLD WAYS LIKE A WELL-CHEWED SHOE AS THE TRADITIONS I WAS WEANED ON ARE PUT TO SLEEP OR NEUTERED ONE BY ONE.

Guest Voice:
Tracey Ullman as Emily Winthrop

BEA SIMMONS

Identity:
Resident, Springfield Retirement Castle.

Daily medication intake:
Substantial.

Style in which she ingests pills:
Seductively.

Carries a torch for:
Grampa Simpson.

Cause of death:
A burst ventricle—or, as some believe, a broken heart.

How Grampa knew she really cared for him:
Did not make him a pallbearer.

> I'M NOT HERE TO SCARE YOU. THEY'VE GOT ME HAUNTING A FAMILY IN TEXAS.

Guest Voice:
Audrey Meadows as Bea

OLD MONEY

Episode 7F17 Original Airdate: 3/28/91 Writers: Jay Kogen & Wallace Wolodarsky Director: David Silverman

SHOW HIGHLIGHTS

"Embraceable You": Gershwin tune Grampa and Bea sing to each other. They are accompanied by the Larry Davis Dance Kings. (Larry's other band appears in 7G01, "Some Enchanted Evening" and 7F12, "The Way We Was.")

Grandma's World: A store that sells doilies, picture frames, seashell soap, sachets, and potpourri. Grampa buys a wool shawl from the activewear department for Bea. The store's motto reads, "For the Old Lady in All of Us."

> **First:**
> This episode marks the first appearance of Professor Frink, "a thin, sweaty man wearing coke-bottle eyeglasses."

"By the way, old timer, I do wills." Lionel Hutz, to Grampa, after giving him the money he was willed by Bea.

Shakedown: Mr. Hazelwood (retirement home administrator): ". . .let me assure you that here at Springfield Retirement Castle, money does make a difference. I mean, there are rub-downs and then there are rub-downs."

Prize fez: The first thing Grampa buys with his inheritance is a hat Napoleon wore for a week in 1796, just before he defeated the Sardinians.

"Not since this reporter's marriage to Stephanie, the weather lady, has this town been so consumed with rumor and innuendo. . . Today, one Abraham 'Grampa' Simpson announced that he will give away over a hundred thousand dollars to the person–or persons–he finds most deserving . . . Is Grampa Simpson a modern-day saint, a rich nut, or both?"

Waiting in line for Grampa's money: Jacques, Dr. Hibbert, blue-haired stranger, Apu, Mrs. Krabappel, Mr. Largo, Krusty, Nelson, the master sushi chef from the Happy Sumo, Emily Winthrop, Princess Kashmir, Sideshow Mel, Darth Vader, The Lovejoys, Mayor Quimby, the Joker, a trekkie, Ned and Maude Flanders, Principal Skinner, Kent Brockman, and Barney.

Busman: Otto drives the charter bus for the seniors casino junket. To stop his passengers from complaining he threatens, "Hey, mellow out old dudes, or I'll jam this baby into a river."

"Mr. Simpson, I dread the day when a hundred thousand dollars isn't worth groveling for."

Plato's Republic: The Casino, a mammoth structure in the middle of nowhere, where Homer stops Grampa from losing his fortune. It looks like the Parthenon, except it's covered in neon and light bulbs. It claims to have the loosest slots in town.

THE STUFF YOU MAY HAVE MISSED

While stuck in the car at Discount Lion Safari, Bart looks a lion in the eye, violating one of the entry rules.

A sign reads, "Diz-nee-land — Not affiliated with Disneyland, Disney World, or anything else from the Walt Disney Company."

Once Grampa buys his fez from Herman's Military Antiques, he is seen wearing it through the rest of the show.

Selection three on Dr. Marvin Monroe's phone menu is for people who are having trouble "maintaining an er..."

In a scene modeled after Edward Hopper's painting, "The Nighthawks," Grampa has coffee in a diner.

At Discount Lion Safari:
Bart: Hey, did anybody notice this place sucks?
Lisa: It seems that most of the animals are sleeping.
Homer: (angry) Well, let them sleep on their own time! (He honks the horn repeatedly).

Grampa and Beatrice upon Meeting:
Bea: So, tell me about yourself.
Grampa: Widower, one son, one working kidney. And you?
Bea: Widowed, bad hip and liver disorder.

Bart: You know, Grampa kinda smells like that trunk in the garage where the bottom's all wet.
Lisa: Nuh-uh, he smells more like a photo lab.
Homer: Stop it, both of you! Grampa smells like a regular old man, which is more like a hallway in a hospital.

After the Simpsons take Grampa out for their once-a-month family get-together, Grampa feels that there is little left to live for. However, when he meets Beatrice, a beautiful woman at the retirement home where he lives, he finds a new reason to carry on. After a few dates, Beatrice and Grampa fall in love. When he learns that the following Sunday is Beatrice's birthday, Grampa makes plans to celebrate. Homer, however, drags him off against his will to join the family at Discount Lion Safari.

When Grampa returns to the rest home, he finds that Beatrice has died. At the reading of Beatrice's will, he inherits her fortune. Appearing as an angel, Beatrice suggests to Grampa that he help those in need. He interviews hundreds of needy people and realizes that he needs more money than the $100,000 he inherited. He joins a casino junket to gamble with the money.

Homer finds his father at the roulette wheel, steps in, and saves him from losing all his newly acquired money. Unsure of how to spend the fortune, Grampa realizes that the retirement home is in disrepair and needs modernization. He puts his money where his heart is and spends it on refurbishing the home.

I WILL NOT GREASE THE
MONKEY BARS
I WILL NOT GREASE THE
MONKEY BARS
I WILL NOT GREASE THE
MONKEY BARS

BRUSH WITH GREATNESS

Episode 7F18 Original Airdate: 4/11/91 Writer: Brian K. Roberts Director: Jim Reardon Guest Voice: Ringo Starr as Himself

When Homer gets stuck inside the water slide at the Mount Splashmore theme park, he realizes he is overweight and goes on a diet. Rummaging through the attic for his barbells, he comes across an old painting Marge made of Ringo Starr when she was a schoolgirl. After seeing Marge's work, Lisa urges her mother to go back to school and continue her artistic endeavors.

Marge signs up for a class at Springfield Community College and paints a portrait of her rotund husband asleep on the couch in his underwear. Marge's instructor, Professor Lombardo, falls in love with the painting and enters it in the Springfield Art Fair. After Marge wins the competition, Mr. Burns commissions her to do a portrait of him for the grand opening of the Burns Wing at the museum. While immortalizing Burns at her house, Marge accidentally walks in on him as he is getting out of the shower.

After Burns mocks Homer's attempts at weight loss, Marge decides that she does not have enough talent to uncover Burns's inner beauty. But when she gets a thank-you note from Ringo Starr responding to her old portrait of him, Marge decides she can do it. The next day at the unveiling, Marge's portrait depicts a naked, withered Mr. Burns. Burns is outraged at first, but later accepts his new glory with humility.

Occupation:
Art professor at Springfield Community College.

Demeanor:
Rarely has a bad word to say about anything. Is sure to balance any unflattering criticism with a compliment.

Attire:
European: black T-shirt, suit, sunglasses indoors.

Invention:
The Lombardo Method — where everyday objects can be seen as a simple grouping of geometrical shapes.

Achievements:
Once drew a bunny rabbit with two concentric circles; various trapezoids; ellipses; and a rhombus.

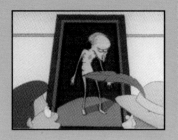

SHOW HIGHLIGHTS

I WILL NOT HIDE BEHIND THE FIFTH AMENDMENT.
I WILL NOT HIDE BEHIND THE FIFTH AMENDMENT.
I WILL NOT HIDE BEHIND THE FIFTH AMENDMENT.

"Bald Adonis": The painting of Homer sleeping on the couch in his underwear that wins Marge first prize at the Springfield Art Exhibition. "Bald Adonis" is chosen over a painting of dogs playing ping pong and a unicorn wondering "why?"

"The Dung Heap": Mr. Burns's closet full of discarded paintings, bronze busts, bas-reliefs, and some weird modern art sculptures — all resembling himself.

Great Burns Lines:

On The Beatles: *Oh, yes. I seem to remember their off-key caterwauling on the old Sullivan Show. What was Ed thinking?*

On Ziggy: *Ah, Ziggy. Will you ever win?*

To one artist: *What matchbook art school did you flunk out of, you ham-fisted, near-sighted house painter?*

On Homer's weight loss: *Why, my good man, you're the fattest thing I've ever seen, and I've been on safari.*

On spending time in the Simpson house: (under breath) *Another day in this suburban nightmare, and I would've needed half a white Valium.*

Dieting, Homer Style:

Marge: (on rice cakes she feeds Homer for dinner) *Well, they're only thirty-five calories apiece.*
Homer: (tasting them) *Hello? Hello? Hello, taste? Where are you?*
Marge: *You can put a little something on top for flavor.*
Homer: (after creating a multi-decker rice cake sandwich consisting of cold cuts, melted cheese and a fried egg) *Mmm. Only thirty-five calories.*

Who's Homer Simpson? When Smithers suggests that the prize winner, Mrs. Homer Simpson, paint Mr. Burns's portrait, Burns responds, "Who?"

"I've just enrolled in a screenwriting class. I yearn to tell the story of an idealistic young Hindu, pushed too far by convenience store bandits. I call it, 'Hands Off My Jerky, Turkey.'"

"Marge! I'm two-thirty-nine and I'm feeling fine!"

Ringo's thank-you note: "Dear Marge. Thanks for the fab painting of yours truly. I hung it on me wall. You're quite an artist. In answer to your question, yes, we do have hamburgers and fries in England, but we call french fries 'chips.' Luv, Ringo. P.S. Forgive the lateness of my reply."

Burns thanks Marge: After acknowledging that he does not hate the painting, Mr. Burns thanks Marge for not making fun of his genitalia (Though Marge thought she had).

THE STUFF YOU MAY HAVE MISSED

Otto is among the animated throngs waiting in line at H2Whoa.

The line for the H2Whoa ride looks like an Escher drawing.

The children sent down the water slide to dislodge Homer are safely extricated by the time the rescuers get to him.

Among the stuff in the Simpson attic are a "Burns for Governor" placard, "Dr. Nick Riviera's Gym in a Jar," a football, a football jersey with the number seventeen on it, and a copy of *Gee, Your Pecs Look Terrific*.

Some of the paintings in the "dung heap" have hung on Mr. Burns's office walls in previous episodes.

There is a painting of a can of soup at the Springfield Art Exhibit.

A sign at Mount Splashmore reads, "This Park Is Not Copless So Please Don't Go Topless."

Another sign with an image of Neptune reads, "Caution. You Will Get Wet."

Movie Moments:

Homer's declaration, "As God is my witness, I'll always be hungry again!" parodies Scarlett O'Hara's in *Gone with the Wind*.

Over a montage of Homer getting fit is an accompaniment similar to the theme from *Rocky*.

BRAVO! WALK AWAY FROM IT. NOW IT BELONGS TO THE AGES.

Guest Voice:
Jon Lovitz as
Professor Lombardo

MR. BERGSTROM

Occupation:
Substitute teacher who cares.

Psychological Profile:
Secure enough to appreciate childish digs at his geekiness.

Noted for:
Praising Ralph Wiggum for who he is.

Talents:
Guitar; storytelling; accents; sensitivity.

Knowledgeable in:
Literature; geology; American Jewish cowboy history; and music.

I'M MR. BERGSTROM. FEEL FREE TO MAKE FUN OF MY NAME IF YOU WANT. TWO SUGGESTIONS ARE MISTER NERDSTROM AND MISTER BOOGERSTROM.

Guest Voice:
Sam Etic
as Mr. Bergstrom

LISA'S SUBSTITUTE

Episode 7F19 Original Airdate: 4/25/91 Writer: Jon Vitti Director: Rich Moore

Lisa's teacher, Miss Hoover, comes down with Lyme Disease and a substitute teacher, Mr. Bergstrom, takes over the class. Bart's class, meanwhile, prepares to elect a president. Mrs. Krabappel nominates Martin Prince. Sherri and Terri nominate Bart. During a Presidential debate with Martin, Bart tells jokes and wins the class's support. Meanwhile, Lisa develops a crush on Mr. Bergstrom.

Lisa runs into Mr. Bergstrom at a museum and is embarrassed when Homer displays his usual oafishness. Sensing that Lisa is missing something in her relationship with her dad, Mr. Bergstrom takes Homer aside to suggest he be a more positive role model. At school on Monday, Lisa is shattered to find Miss Hoover is back and Mr. Bergstrom gone. Certain of Bart's inevitable victory, none of the kids in his class vote except for Martin and his friend, Wendell. Mrs. Krabappel joyously announces Martin as the class president.

Devastated by Mr. Bergstrom's departure, Lisa takes her grief out on Homer, calling him a baboon. With Lisa grief-stricken and Bart reeling from his election loss, Homer decides it is time to act like a father. After he gives Lisa a pep talk, she apologizes. Next, he pays Bart a visit. Pointing out that being class president is a nonpaying job and requires doing extra work, Homer makes Bart glad he lost the election. Although it is still early, he asks Marge if they can just go to bed, saying he is on the biggest roll of his life.

SHOW HIGHLIGHTS

Diagnosis:

Principal Skinner: *Lyme Disease is spread by small parasites, called ticks. When a diseased tick attaches itself to you and begins sucking your blood—*
Miss Hoover: *Oh...*
Principal Skinner: *Malignant spirochetes infect your bloodstream, eventually spreading to your spinal fluid, and on into the brain.*
Miss Hoover: *The brain? Oh, dear God!*

Diagnosis II:

Miss Hoover: *You see, class, my Lyme Disease turned out to be psychosomatic.*
Ralph: *Does that mean you were crazy?*
Janey: *No, that means she was faking it.*
Miss Hoover: *No, actually, it was a little of both. Sometimes when a disease is in all the magazines and all the news shows, it's only natural that you think you have it.*

Show and Tell: Bart grosses out his class with a video featuring the birth of Snowball II, entitled "How Kittens Are Born: The Ugly Story." He holds up the remote and says, "Oh, look, this is really cool. When I hit reverse, I can make them go back in!"

Mr. Bergstrom, correcting Lisa's statement that "...there weren't any Jewish cowboys.": "And for the record, there were a few Jewish cowboys, ladies and gentlemen. Big

guys, who were great shots, and spent money freely."

The chant Bart leads while campaigning in class: "More asbestos! More asbestos! More asbestos!"

Historic moment: When Martin wins the election, he poses with a prematurely printed copy of the *Fourth Gradian*, whose headline, "Simpson Defeats Prince" parodies the famous photograph of Dewey beating Truman.

Homer Embarrasses Lisa at the Museum:
He enthusiastically tells Mr. Bergstrom he doesn't have to pay the suggested donation.
After Mr. Bergstrom explains about mummification, Homer exclaims, "Ooooh. Pretty creepy. Still, I'd rather have him chasing me than the Wolf Man."
Homer acts as though he convinced Mr. Bergstrom to give Lisa an A when Mr. Bergstrom says she really earned it.

Monkey Man:
Lisa: (to Homer) *Yes, you! Baboon, baboon, baboon, baboon!*
Homer: *I don't think you realize what you're saying...*
Bart: *Well, well, somebody was bound to say it one day. I just can't believe it was her.*
Homer: *Did you hear that, Marge? She called me a baboon! The stupidest, ugliest, smelliest ape of them all!*

Next Assignment:
(Mr. Bergstrom is on his way to teach in the projects of Capitol City when Lisa catches up with him.)
Lisa: *But I need you...*
Mr. Bergstrom: *That's the problem with being middle class. Anybody who really cares will abandon you for those who need it more.*

Lisa and Miss Hoover (on Mr. Bergstrom):
Miss Hoover: *He didn't touch my lesson plan. What did he teach you?*
Lisa: *That life is worth living.*

SEX! NOW THAT I'VE GOT YOUR ATTENTION, VOTE FOR BART!

Firsts:
This episode features the first overt antagonism between Homer and his brain.

THE STUFF YOU MAY HAVE MISSED

This episode presumably takes place in April, according to the calendar on the wall in Lisa's classroom.

Also on the walls in the room is one of the posters from Krusty's literacy campaign. It reads, "Give a hoot! Read a book!"

Principal Skinner calls Ms. Hoover by her first name, Elizabeth, while consoling her.

Wendell puts his hand over his mouth as if he is going to vomit when Bart plays his kitten video backwards. We know Wendell gets queasy easily from 7G03, "Homer's Odyssey."

Principal Skinner, a Vietnam veteran, takes immediate cover when Mr. Bergstrom enters the class shooting blanks.

54

Episode 7F20 Original Airdate: 5/2/91 Writer: John Swartzwelder Director: Mark Kirkland

GENERAL SHERMAN

What:
A freakishly big catfish.

Age:
A hundred years old if he's a day.

Weight:
Upwards of five hundred pounds.

Resides:
In Catfish Lake.

Sport:
Competes with wives for their husbands' time.

Marge and Homer throw a party. Homer gets drunk and humiliates himself by leering at Maude Flanders, telling off total strangers, and stumbling over furniture. The next day at church, Marge signs up for a weekend retreat of marriage counseling hosted by Reverend Lovejoy and his wife. She recruits Grampa to babysit the kids for the weekend.

Homer finds out that the retreat will be held at Catfish Lake and packs his fishing pole. On the way there, he learns of the legendary catfish, General Sherman. Meanwhile, at home, left with Grampa's weak authority, Bart and Lisa decide to throw a party. At the lake the next morning, Homer tries to sneak away to go fishing. Marge is upset that he would choose fishing over their marriage. Homer takes a walk instead. On a dock, he picks up an abandoned fishing pole. The pole yanks him and pulls him along the pier, into a rowboat, and out onto the lake. From their cabin window, Marge watches Homer struggle with the fish. Meanwhile, Bart and Lisa's party has ended and the house is a mess. Fearing that Grampa will get into trouble, they frantically clean up.

Marge attends the workshops alone while Homer catches his trophy fish. When he returns, Marge tells him that their marriage is in serious trouble if he values a fish more than her. To prove that he loves her more, Homer lets the fish go. Marge forgives Homer and they return home–house intact.

SHOW HIGHLIGHTS

Party music: Homer puts on "It's Not Unusual" when the party starts. Later, we hear "The Look of Love," and "That's the Way (Uh Huh Uh Huh) I Like It."

The list: ". . . He's so self-centered. He forgets birthdays, anniversaries, holidays–both religious and secular–he chews with his mouth open, he gambles, he hangs out at a seedy bar with bums and lowlifes. He blows his nose on the towels and puts them back in the middle. He drinks out of the carton. He never changes the baby. When he goes to sleep, he makes chewing noises. When he wakes up, he makes honking noises. Oh, oh, and he scratches himself with his keys. I guess that's it. Oh no, wait. He kicks me in his sleep and his toenails are too long. . .and yellow."

Traumatized: The babysitter arrives to watch the kids for the weekend, and remembers that in an earlier experience a diapered Bart chased her down to the car. When Bart meets her at the door and asks, "Come back for more, eh?" she runs off screaming.

Grampa's guidance: Bart and Lisa take complete advantage of Grampa's haplessness as a babysitter. They stockpile sweets and smoke cigars. When Grampa asks Bart if he is sure that they are allowed to drink coffee, a caffeine-addled Bart explodes, "For the last time, yes!"

Homer the Great: Homer becomes legend to the "weirdos" in the bait shop for nearly catching General Sherman. The bait man describes Homer as "Seven feet tall… with arms like tree trunks. And his eyes were like steel, cold and hard. Had a shock of hair, red like the fires of hell."

 "Out at five, catch General Sherman at five-thirty, clean him at six, eat him at six-thirty, back in bed by seven with no incriminating evidence. Heh heh heh. The perfect crime."

Movie Moment:
Flanders quickly makes a drink, mimicking moves from *Cocktail.*

Recipe for Flanders's Planter's Punch:
Three shots of rum, a jigger of bourbon, and just a little dab-a-roo of creme de cassis for flavor.

Literary Moment I:
When Marge asks Homer if he remembers how he acted at the party, he envisions witty conversation and a sophisticated atmosphere akin to the Algonquin Round Table.

Literary Moment II:
John and Gloria are the fourth couple at the retreat. The twosome bait each other à la "Who's Afraid of Virginia Woolf?"

Literary Moment III:
Homer's battle with General Sherman is reminiscent of *Moby Dick* and *The Old Man and the Sea.*

THE STUFF YOU MAY HAVE MISSED

When Marge turns on the radio in the car to mute the conversation between her and Homer, the Mexican Hat Dance is playing. The song is also used for the same purpose when Homer makes plans with a doctor to defraud his company's insurance to pay for a baldness cure (7F02, "Simpson and Delilah").

Marge tells Homer to go easy on the al-key-hol. The last time she uses the term she is half in the bag herself (7G04, "There's No Disgrace Like Home").

Barney's shirt hangs out of his fly at the party.

When Homer arrives in church, Maude Flanders makes sure her blouse is buttoned to the top.

Homer packs his clothes in a Duff Beer duffel bag.

There is a picture of a fisherman with the very large shark he landed in the bait shop. There are also "leaches" (as opposed to "leeches") for sale, according to a sign.

At Bart and Lisa's party, Nelson is in the background dunking kids' faces in brown goop.

I WILL NOT DO ANYTHING BAD EVER AGAIN
I WILL NOT DO ANYTHING BAD EVER AGAIN
I WILL NOT DO ANYTHING BAD EVER AGAIN
I WILL NOT DO ANYTHING BAD EVER AGAIN

COMIC BOOK GUY

Appearance:
Overweight man stuffed into a T-shirt with an Amazon woman on it.

Occupation:
Purveyor of comic collectibles and memorabilia.

Education:
Master's degree in folklore and mythology.

Demeanor:
Sarcastic; surly; insulting; and rude.

Loves:
Eating; profiteering.

Hates:
Getting off his stool for anything other than a cash transaction.

Prized possession:
A rare copy of "Mary Worth," in which Mary advises a friend to commit suicide.

FRIGGIN' KIDS.

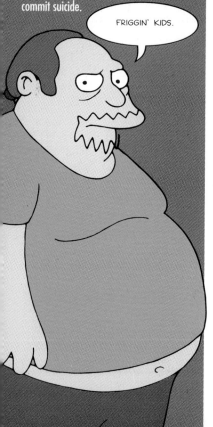

Bart attends a comic book convention and finds the first issue of "Radioactive Man" at the Android's Dungeon sale table for $100. He doesn't have enough money to pay for it, so he gets a job. He does odd jobs for Mrs. Glick, an elderly acquaintance of Marge's, but is given a paltry 50 cents for all his hard work. With only $35, Bart goes to the Android's Dungeon to try to buy the comic book.

At the comic book shop, Bart runs into Milhouse and Martin. He talks them into pooling their money to buy the comic book. None of the three are willing to let the comic book out of his sight, so they spend the night together at Bart's treehouse. When Martin stirs in the middle of the night, Bart thinks he is trying to steal the comic book and ties him up.

A storm moves in. Milhouse tries to alert Marge that Bart has gone crazy, but Bart thinks he is making a move for the comic and tackles him. Milhouse rolls over the side of the treehouse, and Bart holds him precariously by his sleeve. When a gust of wind carries the comic book towards the door, Bart must decide whether to hold onto Milhouse or save the comic book. He saves Milhouse. The comic book is blown out of the treehouse and zapped by lightning. Bart realizes that he and his friends wound up with nothing because they could not share.

SHOW HIGHLIGHTS

"A hundred bucks!? For a comic book? Who drew it, Micha-ma-langelo?" Homer, after Bart asks for the money to buy "Radioactive Man" #1.

"Me? A job? Were they serious? I didn't realize it at the time, but a little piece of my childhood had slipped away forever." Bart's "Wonder Years"-style narration, voiced by Daniel Stern and accompanied by the first few bars of "Turn, Turn, Turn."

The heat: Officers Lou and Eddie bust Bart after he switches from selling lemonade to beer without a license. Bart discourages them from writing him a ticket by offering them one on the house.

Heard it twice: Lisa tells Bart, "I stand corrected" when he proves how witty Radioactive Man is. Moments later, Mayor Quimby says, "I stand corrected" when Jimbo sets him straight on Radioactive Man's name.

Marge: *So maybe a part-time job is the answer.*
Bart: *Aw, Mom, I couldn't ask you to do that. You're already taking care of Maggie, and Lisa is such a handful —*
Lisa: *She means you should get a job, stupid.*

Movie Moment I:
The suspicion that develops between the boys, and Bart's subsequent paranoia is reminiscent of the classic *Treasure of the Sierra Madre.*

Music Moment:
While Bart is searching for money under a sofa cushion, he's humming to the tune "We're In The Money" but he sings "I need some money/ A lot of money..."

A COMIC BOOK

Episode 7F21
Original Airdate: 5/9/91
Writer: Jeff Martin Director: Wes M. Archer
Guest Voices: Cloris Leachman as Mrs. Glick;
Daniel Stern as The Narrator (adult Bart voice)

THE STUFF YOU MAY HAVE MISSED

One kid in line at the comic convention is dressed like Krusty the Clown.

Bart pesters Homer for money the same way he and Lisa pestered Homer to go to Mount Splashmore (7F18, "Brush with Greatness").

A very unanimated worker stands at the Krustyburger register smoking a cigarette.

Patty and Selma have feminine voices until they start smoking.

There are posters for "Beach Blanket Beethoven" and "Private Surfboarder" in young Patty and Selma's room.

Bart exchanges coins from Bolivia for three cents.

Following the nuclear blast, Radioactive Man has five fingers.

In the episode shown at the convention, Fallout Boy wishes he is old enough to smoke. Minutes later, at the Q&A session, Buddy "Fallout Boy" Hodges appears holding a cigarette.

Movie Moment ii:

The scene of Mrs. Glick's shadow looming over Bart's quivering shadow and Bart pleading, "No! No, not the iodine! Burn the germs off with a torch, amputate my arm, but not the — YAAAUUUGGGHHH!" is reminiscent of the scene in *Gone With The Wind*, in which the soldier gets his leg amputated.

An Old Black-and-White Clip from the "Radioactive Man" TV Show:

Radioactive Man: *Aaahh ... These Laramie cigarettes give me the steady nerves I need to combat evil.*
Fallout Boy: *Gee Whillikers, Radioactive Man. Wisht I was old enough to smoke Laramies.*
Radioactive Man: *Sorry, Fallout Boy, not until you're sixteen (winks at the camera).*

Bart: *What do you care about good comics? All you ever buy is "Casper the Wimpy Ghost."*
Lisa: *I think it's sad that you equate friendliness with wimpiness, and I hope it will keep you from ever achieving true popularity.*
Bart: *Well, you know what I think? I think Casper's the ghost of Richie Rich.*
Lisa: *Hey, they do look alike!*
Bart: *Wonder how Richie died.*
Lisa: *Perhaps he realized how hollow the pursuit of money is and took his own life.*

Inside Joke:

(Lisa sees the Springfield Convention Center entrance sign: "Close Encounters of the Comic Book Kind — Admission $8 — $5 if you're dressed like a cartoon character.")
Lisa: *Too bad we didn't come dressed as popular cartoon characters.*
Bart: *This looks like a discount for . . . (steps into phone booth; comes out with cape and cowl) Bartman!*

I will not show off.
I will not show off.
I will not show off.
I will not show off.
I will not show off.

RADIOACTIVE MAN

DR. HIBBERT

Relationship to the Simpsons:
Simpson family doctor, delivered all Simpson children.

Annoying habits:
Laughing at inappropriate times; jokingly telling wives that their husbands are dead; informing patients that their legs will have to come off when he really means their "wet bathing suits."

Fashion sense:
Cosby sweaters; the occasional *Rocky Horror Picture Show* costume; a haircut that changes with the times.

> WE DON'T BELIEVE FUR IS MURDER, BUT PAYING FOR IT SURE IS!

BLOOD FEUD

Mr. Burns is diagnosed with hypohemia, an affliction that leaves a person without enough blood to sustain life. Desperate to save his boss, Smithers issues a plea to the plant's employees for a double-O negative blood donor. No one at the plant comes forward except Homer, who thinks that Burns will reward him richly. However, Homer does not have the right blood type, and instead volunteers Bart, who is the right match.

After the blood transfusion, Burns is more alive than ever and sends Bart a thank-you note. Homer is outraged by Burns's inadequate response. He immediately writes Burns a vindictive letter, but Marge stops him from mailing it. The next morning, however, when Homer goes to tear up the letter, he discovers that Bart has already mailed it.

When Burns receives the letter, he vows to make Homer's life miserable. He orders Smithers to have Homer beaten to a pulp, but Smithers refuses, explaining that he is unable to harm the man who saved his boss's life. Coming to his senses, Burns realizes the good deed the Simpsons have done, and buys them a rare Olmec Indian head statue. Bart thinks it's a cool gift, but Homer insists that it's a cheap reward for saving a man's life.

SHOW HIGHLIGHTS

"Once upon a time there was a big, mean lion who got a thorn in his paw and all the village people tried to pull it out, but nobody was strong enough. So, they got Hercules and Hercules used his mighty strength and bingo! Anyway, the moral is: the lion was so happy, he gave Hercules this big thing of riches."

"Nobody leaves Diamond Joe Quimby holding the bag!" Mayor Quimby, after Burns fails to show up at the warning sign dedication.

Selective memory: When Smithers tells Burns the name of the boy who saved his life, Burns asks, "Who?" When Burns later catches Homer rifling through the mail in his office he asks, "Who are you?"

Xt'Tapalatakettle:
The gift Burns chooses for the Simpsons. It is a $32,000 statue of the Olmec Indian God of War

"As usual, you've been the sober 'yin' to my raging 'yang.'" Mr. Burns, to Smithers's suggestion that he call off Homer Simpson's beating.

Gift impossibilities: At the mall, Burns has trouble finding the right gift. Brushes are "too practical." Tam o'Shanters are "too cutesy-poo." The down-home novelties of the Sweet Home Alabama store are "too cornball."

"Smithers, I'm back in the pink! Full of pith and vinegar!"

"We get the Simpsons a present, an extravagant present! A mad, unthinkable, utterly impossible present! A frabulous, grabulous, zip-zoop-zabulous present!"

I WILL NOT SLEEP THROUGH MY EDUCATION
I WILL NOT SLEEP THROUGH MY EDUCATION
I WILL NOT SLEEP THROUGH MY EDUCATION

Episode 7F22
Original Airdate: 8/11/91
Writer: George Meyer
Director: David Silverman

Homer: *Marge, you're my wife and I love you very much. But you're living in (fairy voice) a world of make-believe. With flowers and bells and leprechauns, and magic frogs with funny little hats ...*
Bart: *Yeah, Mom. We got screwed!*

"Hello, Moe's Tavern..."

Bart: *Uh, hello. Is Mike there? Last name, Rotch.*
Moe: *Hold on, I'll check. Mike Rotch! Mike Rotch! Hey, has anybody seen Mike Rotch lately?*

THE STUFF YOU MAY HAVE MISSED

Otto hums "Iron Man" by Black Sabbath as he washes up for the bloodletting procedure.

The ghostwriter Burns hires (and fires) writes "Like Hell I Can't," a play on Sammy Davis, Jr.'s "Yes I Can." His other credits include, "Up from the Muck" and "The Unsinkable Sadruddin Mahbaradad."

Mr. Burns fumes over the fact that Homer calls him senile, buck-toothed, bony-armed, liver-spotted, and chinless, but Homer never says anything about liver spots, or his chin.

Burns's butt is seen when he leaps to life after the transfusion. It is also seen in 7F18, "Brush with Greatness."

A mural in the post office depicting a gallant mail carrier delivering a parcel in several feet of snow as dogs snarl and lightning strikes him was inspired by Michelangelo's "Creation of Adam."

Snowball II rests on Xt'Tapalatakettle as it sits in the living room at the end of the episode.

Homer: *Marge, what's my blood type?*
Marge: *A-positive.*
Homer: *Aw, nuts. Extremely rare blood and I don't have it!*
Lisa: *You know his blood type? How romantic!*
Marge: *A mother knows everything about her family.*
Lisa: *Oh, yeah, what's my shoe size?*
Marge: *Four B.*
Bart: *How many teeth do I have?*
Marge: *Sixteen permanent, eight baby.*
Homer: *Earmuff?*
Marge: *XM.*
Lisa: *Ring?*
Marge: *I don't want you wearing rings—it looks cheap. But three.*
Bart: *Allergies?*
Marge: *Butterscotch and imitation butterscotch.*
Bart: *And?*
Marge: *Glow-in-the-dark monster make-up.*
Bart: *Impressive.*

Bart: *Whoa, Otto-man! You work here?*
Otto: *Yeah, during the day, all my friends are in school, so I got a job as a certified bloodletting tech-dude!*
Homer: *Now, let's get the show on the road!*
Otto: *Okay, Het me just wash up.*
(Otto takes a moist towelette out of a bucket of chicken and starts to scrub.)

Bart Takes a Letter:

Homer: *(dictating) ". . .You stink!" Could you read that last part back to me?*
Bart: *"You stink."*
Homer: *Heh, heh, heh. Good. "You are a senile, buck-toothed old mummy with bony girl arms ... And you smell like..."*
Bart: *An elephant's butt?*
Homer: *(chuckling) "An elephant's butt."*

HOMER SAYS, "MMM..."

"Mmm...marshmallows"
when he notices marshmallows in Marge's Jell-O™ mold. (7G04)

"Mmm...cupcakes"
after Marge offers cupcakes. (twice) (7G05)

"Mmm...chocolate, ooh... double chocolate, *(gasp)* new flavor...triple chocolate!"
as he selects ice cream from the Kwik-E-Mart freezer. (7G12)

"Mmm...beer"
after taking a last gulp of beer. (7F03)

"Mmm...ooh... maca-ma-damia nuts"
after tasting a free sample at Cookie Colossus. (7F14)

"Mmm...hors d'oeuvers"
at Marge's party. (7F20)

"Mmm...pancakes"
while eating breakfast at the New Bedlam Rest Home for the Emotionally Interesting. (7F24)

"Mmm...money"
as he watches the money-printing process in Washington, D.C. (8F01)

"Mmm...barbecue"
upon catching a scent of Flanders's cookout. (7F23)

"Mmm...purple"
after tasting donut fillings. (8F04)

"Mmm...sprinkles"
in response to eating a donut, after his brain has been implanted in a robot. (8F02)

"Mmm...spaghetti"
upon learning that Lisa's class is holding an all-you-can-eat spaghetti dinner. (8F02)

"Mmm...beer"
after choosing Moe's Tavern over King Toot's Music Store. (8F06)

"Mmm...salty"
upon sampling beef jerky while working at the Kwik-E-Mart. (8F06)

"Mmm...the Land of Chocolate"
while daydreaming in front of the new German owners of Burns's plant. (8F09)

"Mmm...chocolate"
upon anticipating the chocolate in Neapolitan ice cream. (three times) (8F11)

"Mmm...crumbled-up cookie things"
as he compares gambling on football to the topping on a sundae. (8F12)

"Mmm...strained peas"
after sampling Maggie's baby food. (8F14)

"Mmm...donuts"
upon seeing donuts in the break room. (8F13)

"Mmm...potato chips"
while wishing he was eating them as Mr. Burns flashes him the base-running signals. (8F13)

"Mmm...snouts"
preferring Santa's Little Helper's food to his plate of chub. (8F17)

"Mmm...fattening"
while admiring his very own, patented, space-age, out-of-this-world moon waffles wrapped around a stick of butter. (8F17)

"Mmm...burger"
responding to a reference to former Chief Justice of the Supreme Court Warren Burger. (9F03)

"Mmm...Soylent Green"
at the Springfield movie theater candy counter, 40 years in the future. (9F03)

"Mmm...shrimp"
after hearing Marge describe how her throat closed up when she went into convulsions the last time she ate shrimp. (9F06)

"Mmm...hog fat"
upon smelling the stench outside the rendering plant. (9F08)

"Mmm...ham"
after hearing Burns order Smithers to send Marge a condolence ham, as his spirit floats from his body following his heart attack. (9F09)

"Mmm...grapefruit"
during a daydream in which Bart shoves a grapefruit in his face. (9F12)

"Mmm...organized crime"
during a fantasy about being a crime boss lavished with donuts. (9F15)

"Mmm...beer"
upon hearing that excess alcohol can cause liver damage and cancer of the rectum. (9F17)

"Mmm...chocolate"
when he sees a candy machine at the hospital. (9F17)

"Mmm...nuts"
after the candy machine falls on him and chocolate bars fall into his mouth, suffocating him. (9F17)

"Mmm...beer"
upon opening a can of beer just before hearing that Bart has been expelled. (9F18)

"Mmm...pie"
in response to Apu's testimony that he can recite pi (π) to 40,000 places. (9F20)

"Mmm...delicious"
after Krusty hits him in the face with a pie. (9F19)

"Mmm . . . 64 slices of American cheese"
as he eats his midnight-to-dawn snack while Mr. Burns and Smithers, who have snuck in to steal back Bobo, hang from the kitchen ceiling. (1F01)

"Mmm...forbidden donut"
after eating the last bite of his "soul" donut. (1F04)

"Mmm...invisible cola"
while passing a vending machine with new Crystal Buzz Cola. (1F03)

"Mmm...candy"
upon seeing a second vending machine. (1F03)

"Mmm...convenient"
as he dreams of treating everyone to candy and soda on Maggie's wedding day, with two vending machines stuck on his arms. (1F03)

"Mmm...business deal"
upon Mr. Burns's purchase of the Springfield blood bank. (1F04)

"Mmm...free goo"
as he picks at the pile of Toothless Joe's Bubble Gum Flavored Chewing Product that covers Bart and Milhouse. (1F06)

"Mmm...apple"
after tasting the pie that Bart has put in one of his boobytraps as bait. (1F06)

"Mmm...hamburger"
after smelling a Krustyburger restaurant on an offshore oil rig. (1F06)

"Mmm...footlong chili dog"
before he and Mindy Simmons eat the chili dog and share a Lady and the Tramp-style kiss. (1F07)

"Mmm...Marge"
after choosing Marge over a turkey in a Capital City hotel room. (1F07)

"Mmm...mediciney"
after drinking the liquid used in the NASA lung-capacity test. (1F13)

"Mmm...free wig"
while imagining himself with Marge's hair. (1F14)

"Mmm...sacrilicious"
after eating the waffle he had mistaken for God. (1F14)

"Mmm...elephant-fresh"
after getting his own grooming bird, inspired by Stampy. (1F15)

"Mmm...caramel"
when, after Lisa and Bart get stuck to him at the Springfield Tar Pits, Marge reminds him about the trip that the family took to the caramel factory. (1F15)

"Mmm...something"
after a montage of "mmms." (2F33)

"Mmm...bowling fresh"
while smelling freshly sprayed bowling shoes at Barney's Bowl-A-Rama. (2F10)

"Mmm...urinal fresh"
while placing deodorant cakes in the urinals at Barney's Bowl-A-Rama. (2F10)

"Mmm...slanty"
after celebrating by tilting his chair at the dinner table. (2F14)

"Mmm... beer nuts"
after purchasing a can of spring snakes labelled "Beer Nuts." (2F31)

"Mmm... incapacitating"
after tasting Marge's pepper spray on eggs. (2F21)

"Mmm...sprinkles"
after seeing Lard Lad's sign, "Now with Sprinkles." (3F04)

"Mmm...unprocessed fishsticks"
when he sees goldfish swimming in a pool in the third dimension. (3F04)

"Mmm...open-faced club sandwich"
in response to Burns's advice to use an open-faced club, the sand wedge, in a golf game. (3F11)

"Mmm...pointy"
after swallowing the plastic bride and groom from Selma and Troy's wedding cake. (3F15)

MUCH ADO ABOUT STUFFING

STARK RAVING DAD

Episode 7F24 Original Airdate: 9/19/91 Writers: Al Jean and Mike Reiss Director: Rich Moore Executive Producers: Al Jean & Mike Reiss

Occupation:
Michael Jackson: King of Pop from Gary, Indiana.
Leon Kompowsky: Bricklayer from Paterson, New Jersey.

Accomplishments:
Jackson: US Magazine called him the most famous man in the world. Known for his Victory Tour, the songs "Thriller," "Billie Jean," "Beat It"— and who his dates are at the Grammys.

Kompowsky: Very angry all of his life until one day he began talking like Michael Jackson; voluntarily committed himself to the New Bedlam Rest Home for the Emotionally Interesting.

Known as:
Jackson: Creator of the moonwalk.
Kompowsky: Layer of many bricks.

Body type:
Jackson: A vegetarian who does not drink.
Kompowsky: A hulking 300-lb. mental patient.

TO MAKE A TIRED POINT, WHICH ONE OF US IS TRULY CRAZY?

Guest Voice:
John Jay Smith as
Michael Jackson

L isa's eighth birthday is approaching, and to make sure that Bart doesn't forget, she reminds him of the forthcoming event. Meanwhile, Homer is horrified to discover that Bart has tossed his lucky red hat into the washer along with his white dress shirts, turning the shirts pink. When Mr. Burns spots Homer on a video surveillance monitor, he detains him for being a radical, pink-clad troublemaker. Dr. Monroe gives Homer a sanity test to take home, but afraid that he will answer the questions incorrectly, Homer has Bart fill it out. After Monroe scores the test, Homer is placed in the New Bedlam Rest Home for the Emotionally Interesting.

At the institution, Homer meets a big white man who talks like, dances like, and thinks he is Michael Jackson. Not knowing who Michael Jackson is, Homer believes him. Michael telephones Bart to tell him that Homer is in a mental institution and needs the love of his family more than ever. When Marge arrives at the rest home to get Homer released, Homer invites Michael to come home with him.

Lisa's birthday arrives and Bart forgets to buy her a gift. Lisa disowns him as a brother. To bring the siblings back together, Michael helps Bart write a birthday song for Lisa. Lisa forgives Bart and thanks him for giving her the best present ever. Feeling good about himself, Michael admits that his name is really Leon Kompowsky. Talking in his normal deep voice, Leon leaves to help more of his fellow men.

SHOW HIGHLIGHTS

The Marvin Monroe take-home personality test: Twenty simple questions that determine exactly how crazy, or "meshuggenah," someone is.

The diagnosis: When Marge learns that Homer suffers from "a persecution complex, extreme paranoia, and bladder hostility," she tells the nurse that he might improve if she would talk to him for five minutes without mentioning Bart's name. To which the nurse replies, *"You mean there really is a Bart? Good lord!"*

Lisa's Poem (As Read to Homer):
*I had a cat named Snowball.
She died, she died!
Mom said she was sleeping—
She lied, she lied!
Why, oh why is my cat dead? Couldn't
that Chrysler hit me instead?
I had a hamster named Snuffy. He died...*

"Hey, we're just like the Waltons. We're praying for an end to the depression, too." Bart, responding to President George Bush's point in a televised speech that "We need a nation closer to the Waltons than to the Simpsons."

Smithers, instructing security on how to handle Homer: "Careful, men. He wets his pants."

"Oh, my God, Mother was right!" Marge, on hearing that Homer is in a mental institution.

"Joe's Crematorium. You kill 'em, we grill 'em." Bart, answering the phone when Michael Jackson calls. Later, he answers, "Joe's Taxidermy. You snuff 'em, we stuff 'em."

Lisa's Birthday Song:
Lisa, it's your birthday. God bless you this day. You gave me the gift of a little sister, and I'm proud of you today. Lisa, it's your birthday. Happy birthday, Lisa. Lisa, it's your birthday. Happy birthday, Lisa. I wish you love and goodwill. I wish you peace and joy. I wish you better than your heart desires. And your first kiss from a boy. Lisa, it's your birthday. Happy birthday, Lisa. Lisa, it's your birthday. Happy birthday, Lisa.

Michael: Hi. I'm Michael Jackson, from The Jacksons.
Homer: I'm Homer Simpson, from the Simpsons.

Michael's Story: Contractual obligations at the time prevented the show from confirming that the real Michael Jackson supplied the voice of "Michael Jackson." Hence, the mysterious John Jay Smith.

I AM NOT A DENTIST.
I AM NOT A DENTIST.
I AM NOT A DENTIST.
I AM NOT A DENTIST.
I AM NOT A DENTIST.
I AM NOT A DENTIST.
I AM NOT A DENTIST.

THE STUFF YOU MAY HAVE MISSED

When Marge phones up the New Bedlam Wrongly Committed Hotline, she is placed on hold to the Muzak version of "Crazy" by Patsy Cline.

An ad appears on the box of Krusty Flakes for the "Krusty Hotline —1-909-0-U-KLOWN."

Signs at the New Bedlam Rest Home for the Emotionally Interesting include "You Don't Have to Be Crazy to Be Committed Here, but It Helps!" and "Your Mother Isn't Committed Here, So Clean Up after Yourself."

Springfieldians waiting for Michael Jackson: Mayor Quimby, Moe, Dr. Marvin Monroe, Kent Brockman, Chief Wiggum, Helen Lovejoy, Grampa, Patty and Selma, Ned and Todd Flanders, Milhouse, Sherri and Terri, Professor Lombardo, Dr. Hibbert, Apu, Principal Skinner's mother, Princess Kashmir, Jasper, Groundskeeper Willie, Dr. Nick Riviera, Kearny, Wendell, Springfield Isotopes' owner Antoine "Tex" O'Hara, and the man from sporting events with the rainbow hair and "John 3:16" sign who is always trying to get on camera at sporting events (real name: Rockin' Rollen Stewart).

MR. LISA GOES TO WASHINGTON

Episode 8F01 Original Airdate: 9/26/91 Writer: George Meyer Director: Wes Archer
Guest Voices: JoAnn Harris as Truong Van Dinh and Lona Williams as Minnesota Girl

Lisa is chosen as a semi-finalist in the *Reading Digest* "Patriots of Tomorrow" essay contest and receives an all-expense-paid trip to Washington, D.C. There, the Simpsons get special VIP passes and take an historical tour of the city.

The morning of the contest, Lisa wanders off to a little-known memorial, where she witnesses Congressman Bob Arnold taking a bribe from a lobbyist. Her faith in democracy now destroyed, she tears up the essay she had prepared for the final competition.

Deciding that the truth must be told, Lisa writes a new essay that exposes Congressman Arnold and condemns the politicians in Washington. Alarmed that a young citizen has lost faith in her country, one of the judges notifies a senator, who informs the FBI about Arnold's activities. Arnold is immediately put under surveillance and arrested in a sting operation. Although Lisa loses the essay contest, her faith in the democratic process is restored.

SPITWADS ARE NOT
FREE SPEECH
SPITWADS ARE NOT
FREE SPEECH
SPITWADS ARE NOT
FREE SPEECH

SHOW HIGHLIGHTS

"I don't think real checks have exclamation points." Lisa, to her father, who has just mistaken a sweepstakes pitch for an actual $1,000,000 check.

"Oh, Marge, cartoons don't have any deep meaning. They're just stupid drawings that give you a cheap laugh." Homer, as he stands up from the couch and reveals the top of his butt sticking out of his pants.

> **Jerry:** Congressman, this is Springfield National Forest. Now, basically what we want to do is cut 'er down. (He points to a drawing on an easel of a dark, decrepit forest full of rotting trees.)
> **Jerry:** As you can see in our artist's rendition, it's full of old growth just aging and festering away... (He flips the page on the easel, revealing a happy scene of animals dancing and having a tea party among a hillside of tree stumps.)
> **Jerry:** In comes our logging company to thin out the clutter. It's all part of nature's, you know, cycle.
> **Bob Arnold:** Well, Jerry, you're a whale of a lobbyist and I'd like to give you a logging permit, I would, but uh, this isn't like burying toxic waste. People are gonna notice those trees are gone.

"How very strange. His job description clearly specifies an illiterate." Mr. Burns, when told by Smithers that the "bookworm" he has just set eyes on is Homer Simpson.

Dinnertime: Using a tip from *Reading Digest* magazine, Marge makes "meatloaf men" for dinner.

"When America was born on the hot July day in 1776, the trees in Springfield Forest were tiny saplings trembling towards the sun and as they were nourished by Mother Earth, so too did our fledgling nation find strength in the simple ideals of equality and justice. Who would have thought such mighty oaks or such a powerful nation could grow out of something so fragile, so pure?"

"The city of Washington was built on a stagnant swamp some 200 years ago and very little has changed; it stank then and it stinks now. Only today, it is the fetid stench of corruption that hangs in the air."

The conclusion of Nelson Muntz's entry to Springfield's state regional finals of the "Patriots of Tomorrow" essay contest: "So burn the flag if you must, but before you do, you better burn a few other things! You better burn your shirt and your pants! Be sure to burn your TV and car! Oh, yes, and don't forget to burn your house because none of those things could exist without six white stripes, seven red stripes, and a hell of a lot of stars!"

"My back is spineless, my belly is yella. I am the American nonvoter." A portion from an entry to Alabama regionals.

> (Dressed for the contest, Lisa walks into Homer and Marge's hotel room as they are sleeping.)
> **Lisa:** Mom?
> **Marge:** Lisa, the contest isn't for three hours.
> **Lisa:** I'm too excited to sleep. Anyone up for the Winifred Beecher Howe Memorial?
> **Homer:** Who's that?
> **Lisa:** An earlier crusader for women's rights. She led the Floor Mop Rebellion of 1910. Later, she appeared on the highly unpopular seventy-five cent piece.

> **Faith:** Lisa, I'm Faith Crowley, Patriotism Editor of Reading Digest.
> **Homer:** Oh, I love your magazine. My favorite section is "How to Increase Your Word Power." That thing is really, really, really... good.

THE STUFF YOU MAY HAVE MISSED

Home Security Trust's motto is, "We're Not a Savings and Loan."

Some *Reading Digest* features: "Can We Trust Bermuda?," "They Call Me Dr. Soybean," "Motoring Ms.-Haps."

The Springfield regional finals for the "Patriots of Tomorrow" essay contest are held at the Veterans of Popular Wars Hall.

Blinky is seen in the corner of the state map that features Springfield.

Lisa's speech scorecard: "Originality—10"; "Clarity—10"; "Organization—9"; "Jingoism—10." With the five extra points she was awarded after the judge met Homer, her total score was 44 points out of a possible 40.

Bart's tab for room service at the Watergate Hotel includes "2 Shirley Temples, $14.00"; "2 Crab Salads, $28.50"; "Laundry, $8.75"; "2 Pedicures, $75.00"; "2 Massages, $150.00." Bart also writes in a $20 tip.

WHEN FLANDERS FAILED

Episode 7F23 Original Airdate: 10/3/91 Writer: John Vitti Director: Jim Reardon

NED FLANDERS

Occupation:
Left-handed item merchant.

Education:
Ph.D. In mixology.

Prize possessions:
Propane Elaine, his gas grill.

Favorite book:
The Bible.

Pet peeve:
Maude underlining passages in his Bible.

ABSATIVELY POSILUTELY!

SHOW HIGHLIGHTS

Movie Moment:
Elements of the final scene including the way that Ned and Maude are dressed and Homer's toast to the sing along are reminiscent of the end of *It's a Wonderful Life*.

Lisa: Dad, do you know what Schadenfreude is?
Homer: No, I do not know what Schadenfreude is. (sarcastic) Please tell me, because I'm dying to know.
Lisa: It's a German term for "shameful joy," taking pleasure in the suffering of others.
Homer: Oh, come on, Lisa. I'm just glad to see him fall flat on his butt!

 "I don't care if Ned Flanders is the nicest guy in the world. He's a jerk—end of story."

"Yes! Oh, yes! Read it and weep! In your face—I got more chicken bone!" Homer, making a wishbone wish that Flanders's "stupid left-handed store" goes out of business.

 "See Marge, you knock TV and then it helps you out. I think you owe somebody a little apology."

"Hey, Barteleeboobely, care for a steak-a-rooney?" Homer, to Bart as he cooks on the grill that used to belong to Flanders.

"C'mon you lefties, oh, what did I tell ya? It's all here, and it's all backwards!" Homer, rushing the crowd into the Leftorium.

"Well, the worm has turned, has it not, my tin-plated friend? Look out, you—you who were once so proud! Feel the wrath of the left hand of Burns!"

In Karate Class:

Akira: We learn karate, so that we need never use it.
Bart: Um, excuse me, sir. I already know how not to hit a guy. Can we break out the nunchucks?

Ned: I think word of mouth is starting to spread.
Man: Hey, I hear you validate parking tickets without purchase.
Ned: Oh, right as rain! Or, as we say around here, left as rain.
Man: Just stamp the ticket.

Ned Broke:

Ned: At times like these, I used to turn to the Bible and find solace, but even the Good Book can't help me now.
Homer: Why not?
Ned: I sold it to you for seven cents.
Homer: Oh.

Burns: Smithers, I'm licked. You open this can.
Smithers: Okay, but you softened it up for me, sir.
(Burns reads a note from the suggestion box.)
Burns: Hold it, Smithers. I'll open the can.
Smithers: But, sir, how?
Burns: To the mall! I'll explain on the way!

NOBODY LIKES SUNBURN SLAPPERS
NOBODY LIKES SUNBURN SLAPPERS
NOBODY LIKES SUNBURN SLAPPERS

Ned: Homer, affordable tract housing made us neighbors, but you made us friends.
Homer: To Ned Flanders, the richest left-handed man in town.

Ned: Come on over and strap on the feed bag. We're going to fire up old Propane Elaine and put the heat to the meat! Nummy-nummy-num!
Homer: I'll be there! (aside) Notty-notty-not.

Homer: What's the opposite of that "shameful joy" thing of yours?
Lisa: Sour grapes.
Homer: Boy, those Germans have a word for everything.

THE STUFF YOU MAY HAVE MISSED

While Homer watches the Canadian Football League draft, the names of producers Jay Kogen and Wallace Wolodarsky appear on the draft list. They are also mentioned as football players for the Dallas Cowboys in 7F07, "Bart vs. Thanksgiving." John Swartzwelder is on the draft list as well.

Akira's school is in the Springfield Mall next to Shakespeare's Fried Chicken.

After Homer buys most of Ned's possessions, Bart wears a shirt that says, "Maude Loves Ned."

The jingle for Barney's Bowl-A-Rama: "Let's go to Barney's Bowl-A-Rama for entertainment and exercise," plays while Homer watches television just before the bill collector arrives.

Ned Flanders invites the Simpsons to a barbecue. When he announces that he is quitting his job to open a store that sells items for left-handed people, Homer hopes that the business will fail. Marge, meanwhile, worried that Bart is watching too much television and not getting enough exercise, allows him to take karate lessons at the mall. When Homer drops Bart off at his lesson, he visits Flanders's store, the Leftorium, and is pleased to see that Ned is doing poorly. At karate class, Bart discovers that he has to read books and work hard, so he goes to the arcade instead.

Ned's business flounders and he holds a yard sale to make ends meet. Homer buys Ned's best possessions for practically nothing. Although he runs into people who desperately need items made especially for lefties, Homer doesn't tell them about the Leftorium. Meanwhile, Bart continues to ditch karate class. He comes across a gang of hoodlums trying to steal Lisa's saxophone and Lisa calls upon him to use his karate skills to help her. Bart tries to fake his way out of the jam, but the thugs beat him up.

Homer's wish finally comes true: Flanders's business fails. Homer is guilt ridden when Ned loses his home and his family moves into their car. Only two days before Flanders is officially bankrupt, Homer calls all his left-handed friends and tells them about Ned's unique store. As Ned's business starts to boom, the satisfied customers join in a chorus of "Put on a Happy Face."

BART THE MURDERER

Episode 8F03 Original Airdate: 10/10/91 Writer: John Swartzwelder Director: Rich Moore Guest Voice: Neil Patrick Harris as Himself playing Bart

At the end of a particularly bad day, Bart gets caught in a downpour and loses control of his skateboard. He crashes down a flight of stairs into the Legitimate Businessman's Social Club, which is actually a mobster hangout. The mobsters, Fat Tony, Louie, and Joey, are impressed with Bart's spunk and give him a job tending bar. Marge finds out what Bart is doing, and asks Homer to intervene. Homer pays the mobsters a visit and likes them so much, he asks if they can give Lisa a job, too.

When Fat Tony finds out that Principal Skinner is making Bart stay after school, the mobsters pay Skinner a visit. The next day, Skinner is missing. After dreaming that Skinner is killed by the mobsters, Bart confronts Fat Tony. When the police burst in, Fat Tony pins Skinner's disappearance on Bart, who is thrown in jail and put on trial.

As Bart is about to be convicted, Skinner rushes in, telling the court that he has been stuck in his basement since a stack of newspapers crashed down on him the week before. A free man, Bart quits his job, having learned that mobsters make lousy friends.

SHOW HIGHLIGHTS

Laramie spokesman Jack Larson, reassuring Springfield smokers that the truck hijacking will not cause a shortage: "Folks, I'm pleased to announce that a new truckload of Laramies with their smooth good taste and rich tobacco flavor is already heading towards Springfield and the driver has been instructed to ignore all stop signs and crosswalks."

"How long does it take to deliver a pizza?" Marge, asking why a truck labeled "Pizza Delivery Truck" has been sitting outside the house for two weeks. It has a radar dish, periscope and antenna on top of it. Right after Marge's question, the truck zooms off.

A Female Psychic Joins the Search:

Psychic: *I see wedding bells for Vanna White and Teddy Kennedy...*
Wiggum: *Please, Princess Opal, if we could just stick to Principal Skinner.*
Psychic: *Chief Wiggum, I am merely a conduit for the spirits.* (She pauses.) *Willie Nelson will astound his fans by swimming the English Channel.*
Wiggum: *Really? Willie Nelson?*

It's replaced moments later by a new truck that reads Flowers By Irene. The letters (FBI) are big and obvious.

> **Movie Moment:**
> Bart's job as a gofer for Fat Tony and his mobster pals parodies the life of young Henry Hill in *Goodfellas*.

"And how, may I ask, did you get past the hall monitors?" Principal Skinner, wondering how Fat Tony and his fellow mobsters were able to get into his office.

Bart: *Say, are you guys crooks?*
Fat Tony: *Bart, um...is it wrong to steal a loaf of bread to feed your starving family?*
Bart: *No.*
Fat Tony: *Suppose you got a large starving family. Is it wrong to steal a truckload of bread to feed them?*
Bart: (shakes head) *Uh-uh.*
Fat Tony: *And what if your family don't like bread, they like cigarettes?*
Bart: *I guess that's okay.*
Fat Tony: *Now, what if instead of giving them away, you sold them at a price that was practically giving them away. Would that be a crime, Bart?*
Bart: *Hell, no!*
Fat Tony: *Enjoy your gift* (Bart opens a box and pulls out a sharkskin suit).
Bart: *Supoib.*

"People now...Please, please, I can assure you we'll be using the most advanced, scientific techniques in the field of...body finding."

"Blood on the Blackboard: The Bart Simpson Story:" Title of TV mini series about Bart's mob experience, starring Neil Patrick Harris as Bart Simpson.

"...I'm Troy McClure. You probably remember me from such films as *The Revenge of Abe Lincoln* and *The Wackiest Covered Wagon in the West*."

"Fat Tony is a cancer on this fair city. He is the cancer and I am the...uh...what cures cancer?"

> HIGH EXPLOSIVES AND
> SCHOOL DON'T MIX.
> HIGH EXPLOSIVES AND
> SCHOOL DON'T MIX.
> HIGH EXPLOSIVES AND
> SCHOOL DON'T MIX.

THE STUFF YOU MAY HAVE MISSED

When Bart is thrown in jail, his cellmate is a seriously pumped-up Sideshow Bob.

The smiling Aztec in Troy McClure's short film about chocolate is nearly identical to the mascot for the Cleveland Indians baseball team.

Items in the Simpsons' basement include a large barrel of nuclear waste.

The horses in the third race at Shelbyville Downs are all phrases from classic cartoons, including "Yabba-Dabba-Doo," "Sufferin' Succotash," "Ooh Ain't I a Stinker," "That's All, Folks," "I Yam What I Yam," and "Donhavacow."

The cereal Lisa is eating is called Jackie O's, with a box note: "Free Stretch Pants Inside!" Bart's cereal of choice is Chocolate Frosted Frosty Krusty Flakes, which boasts, "Only Sugar Has More Sugar!"

FAT TONY

Occupation:
Mobster.

Hair:
Slicked back.

Hangout:
The Legitimate Businessman's Social Club, with associates Legs, Louie, and Joey.

Transportation:
A limousine.

Favorite literature:
Daily racing news.

Favorite beverage:
Manhattan.

Weapon of choice:
.38 revolver.

Hijacks:
Cigarette trucks.

Plays dumb:
With Chief Wiggum.

WHAT'S A MURDER?

Guest Voice:
Joe Mantegna as Fat Tony (and as himself playing Fat Tony)

THERE WAS MORE DUMB LUCK IN THE NEWS TODAY...

HOMER DEFINED

Episode 8F04 Original Airdate: 10/17/91 Writer: Howard Gewirtz Director: Mark Kirkland
Guest Voices: Earvin Johnson, Jr., as Himself and Chick Hearn as Himself

SHOW HIGHLIGHTS

I WILL NOT SQUEAK CHALK.
I WILL NOT SQUEAK CHALK.
I WILL NOT SQUEAK CHALK.
I WILL NOT SQUEAK CHALK.
I WILL NOT SQUEAK CHALK.
I WILL NOT SQUEAK CHALK.

Milhouse: *Bart, my mom won't let me be your friend anymore. That's why you couldn't come to the party.*
Bart: *What's she got against me?*
Milhouse: *She says you're a bad influence.*
Bart: *Bad influence, my ass! How many times have I told you? Never listen to your mother!*

"Mangy cud-chewing ugly goats": How Amadopolis refers to his employees.

"They called me old-fashioned for teaching the duck-and-cover method. But who's laughing now?"

The party: Milhouse invites Sherri, Terri, Martin, and Otto to his birthday party—but not Bart.

"Dear Lord, if you spare this town from becoming a smoking hole in the ground, I'll try to be a better Christian. I don't know what I can do...ummm, oh, the next time there's a canned food drive I'll give the poor something they'd actually like instead of old lima beans and pumpkin mix."

Smithers: *Sir, there may never be another time to say... I love you, sir.*
Burns: *Oh, hot dog. Thank you for making my last few moments on Earth socially awkward.*

Kent Brockman: *Uh, Mr. Burns, people are calling this a meltdown.*
Mr. Burns: *Oh, meltdown. It's one of those annoying "buzzwords." We prefer to call it an unrequested fission surplus.*

Marge: *Look, I know Bart can be a handful, but I also know what he's like inside. He's got a spark. It's not a bad thing. Of course, it makes him do bad things.*
Mrs. Van Houten: *Well, Marge, the other day, Milhouse told me my meatloaf sucks. He must have gotten that from your little boy because they certainly don't say that on TV!*

"Eenie meenie miney mo: Is Homer a hero? The answer, employees, is... no."

The rug: Burns wears a toupee in his press file photo.

For his bravery and skill: Homer is awarded a ham, a plaque, a coupon book, Burns's personal thumbs up, and his picture on the Wall of Fame.

"Well, you know boys, a nuclear reactor is a lot like a woman. You just have to read the manual and press the right button."

The Alarm Announces a Problem in Sector 7-G:
Burns: *7-G? Good God, who's the safety inspector there?*
Smithers: *Uh, Homer Simpson, sir.*
Burns: *Simpson, eh? Good man? Intelligent?*
Smithers: *Actually, sir, he was hired under "Project Bootstrap."*
Burns: *(bitterly) Thank you, President Ford.*

Moe: *Looks like this is the end.*
Barney: *(takes a swig of beer) Ah, it's all right; I couldn'ta led a richer life.*

Bart: *I had a fight with Milhouse.*
Homer: *That four-eyes with the big nose? You don't need friends like that.*
Lisa: *(looks up glowing) How Zen.*

Milhouse: *(on walkie-talkie) Milhouse to Bart, do you want to come over and play?*
Bart: *Really? We can be friends again? Did your mom die?*

THE STUFF YOU MAY HAVE MISSED

One of Burns's office monitors show that the workers who file by are identical.

The coffee mugs at the Springfield Nuclear Power Plant are shaped like cooling towers.

Otto "sings" the bass line from Edgar Winter's *Frankenstein* as he drives 70 mph to the Kwik-E-Mart.

Burns wears Smithers's radiation suit during the meltdown.

Radioactive waste leaks out of a trash can outside the plant coffee room.

Bart is crushed when he learns that Milhouse did not invite him to his birthday party. Meanwhile, at the plant, Homer falls asleep on the job, unaware that a nuclear meltdown has begun. He is awakened by the sirens and immediately panics. With only seconds left, he randomly presses the right button and saves the city. Homer becomes a local hero, but feels like a fraud after a congratulatory call from Magic Johnson. Aristotle Amadopolis, owner of the Shelbyville Nuclear Power Plant, asks Homer to give a pep-talk to his employees.

Bart finds out that Milhouse is forbidden to play with him because he's a bad influence. After Marge talks to Milhouse's mother, Mrs. Van Houten decides to let Bart play with her son again.

Homer tries to deliver his speech to Amadopolis's employees, but he's at a loss for words. He is saved when the meltdown alarms go off. Everyone turns to Homer to avert disaster, but Homer does not know what to do. Closing his eyes and pointing "eenie, meenie, miney, mo," he again picks the right button. This time, however, everyone realizes that Homer has merely gotten by on dumb luck.

LIKE FATHER LIKE CLOWN

Episode 8F05 Original Airdate: 10/24/91 Writers: Jay Kogen & Wallace Wolodarsky Directors: Jeffrey Lynch with Brad Bird

RABBI KRUSTOFSKI

While eating dinner at the Simpsons' house, Krusty reveals a side of himself that is nothing like the "happy-go-lucky" clown they all know and love. Ever since his father disowned him for not carrying on the rabbinical family tradition, Krusty has been devastated. Bart and Lisa realize that Krusty needs to make amends with his father.

Reverend Lovejoy, who appears with Rabbi Krustofski on a weekly radio show, gives Bart and Lisa the rabbi's address. When they visit him, Krustofski tells them that he has no son and slams the door in their faces. Bart and Lisa try to reason with the rabbi and even search the Talmud, the ancient text of rabbinical wisdom, for a solution. However, nothing can convince Rabbi Krustofski to reunite with his son.

When Bart quotes an inspirational phrase from the entertainer Sammy Davis, Jr., Rabbi Krustofski recognizes his mistake by not acknowledging his offspring. Father and son celebrate their reunion on Krusty's show.

RABBI KRUSTOFSKI

Occupation:
Rabbi; thinker.

Special gift:
Can solve any problem as long as it is posed as an ethical question.

Diversions:
Chess in the park; Talmudic conferences in the Catskills.

Dislikes:
Entertainers as immediate family members; people who call and hang up without saying anything.

Philosophy:
Life is not fun; life is serious.

SHOW HIGHLIGHTS

"He's talking funny talk." Homer, after hearing Krusty's Hebrew prayer.

"Seltzer is for drinking, not for spraying. Pie is for noshing, not for throwing." Krusty's father, explaining to young Krusty why he forbids clowning.

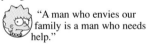

"First of all, my real name isn't Krusty the Clown. It's Herschel Krustofski. My father was a rabbi. His father was a rabbi. His father's fath... Well, you get the idea."

"A man who envies our family is a man who needs help."

"Gabbin' about God": Radio show that Rev. Lovejoy hosts with Rabbi Krustofski.

"Oy, this guy's tough." Bart, unsuccessfully convincing Rabbi Krustofski that he should forgive his son.

Ham, sausage, and bacon with a smidge of mayo on white bread: Izzy's Deli recipe for the Krusty the Clown sandwich.

"Sorry, my friend, I'm still not convinced. And this is hardly the time or place to discuss it." Rabbi

---

No Pressure:

Homer: Boy, you don't have to follow in my footsteps.
Bart: Don't worry, I don't even like using the bathroom after you.
Homer: Why you little—!

Bart's Letter to Krusty:

Dear Krusty,
This is Bart Simpson, Krusty Buddy #16302, respectfully returning his badge. I always suspected that nothing in life mattered. Now I know for sure. Get bent, Bart Simpson

---

Movie Moment:

The theme of a rabbi father rejecting his son's choice of entertainment as a career is reminiscent of the film *The Jazz Singer*.

Bart: We came to talk to you about your son.
Krustofski: I have no son!
Bart: Oh, great, we came all this way and it's the wrong guy.
Krustofski: I didn't mean that literally.

Lovejoy: Rabbi Krustofski? I do a radio call-in show with him every Sunday night!
Bart: Really?
Lisa: I didn't know that.
Lovejoy: Gee, I mention it in my sermon every week.
Bart: Oh, oh, that radio show!
Lisa: Oh, yeah! It's all the kids talk about Monday at school.

Krusty's Sign-Off Lyrics:
We've had lots and lots and lots and lots and lots of fun/ but now the time has come to go/ if this old clown was found dead in his bed tomorrow/ I'd be in heaven still doing this show.

Bart: Krusty, do you think about your father a lot?
Krusty: All the time. Except when I'm at the track. Then it's all business.

Lisa: What's the one thing rabbis prize above everything else?
Bart: Those stupid hats?
Lisa: No, Bart, knowledge. We're gonna hit him where it hurts, right in the Judaica.

THE STUFF YOU MAY HAVE MISSED

During Krusty's singing sign-off, Corporal Punishment holds up a nearly unconscious Sideshow Mel.

Krusty has photos of himself with Alfred Hitchcock and the Beatles in the studio.

Krusty and his father walk down the street past a deli with the sign, "Tannen's Fatty Meats."

As a boy, Krusty stared into Yiddle's, a store that advertises "practical jokes, magic tricks, and medical supplies."

KBBL has a gold album from The Larry Davis Experience and a Bleeding Gums Murphy poster hanging on the wall.

The following movies are playing at the Springfield X theater:
For Your Thighs Only/ Crocodile Done Me/ Dr. Stangepants.

I WILL FINISH WHAT I STA
I WILL FINISH WHAT I STA
I WILL FINISH WHAT I STA
I WILL FINISH WHAT I STA
I WILL FINISH WHAT I STA
I WILL FINISH WHAT I STA

GREAT IS THE CAR WITH POWER STEERING AND DYNA-FLOW SUSPENSION.

Guest Voice:
Jackie Mason as Rabbi Krustofski

TREEHOUSE OF HORROR II

"Hello, everyone. Before last year's Halloween show, I warned you not to let your children watch. But you did anyway. Hmm. Well, this year's episode is even worse; it's scarier and more violent and I think they snuck in some bad language, too. So, please tuck in your children and . . . Well, if you didn't listen to me last time, you're not going to now. Enjoy the show."

OPENING SEQUENCE

As the sky thunders and lightning crackles, we pass a tombstone in Springfield Cemetery reading, "Bambi's Mom." We then see a hippie sitting in front of another tombstone that reads, "Jim Morrison." Another features the words, "Cajun Cooking." Icicles hang from a tombstone that reads, "Walt Disney." The last tombstone in the cemetery reads, "Lose Weight Now. Ask Me How."

THE SET-UP

Against Marge's wishes, Homer and the kids eat too much candy, sending them into nightmare land.

Newspaper Headline:
"Monsters Okay Slavery Plan."

LISA'S NIGHTMARE

Lisa dreams that the family is on vacation in Morocco, where Homer buys a magic monkey's paw that grants four wishes. Upon returning home, Maggie wishes for a brand new pacifier, Bart for fame and fortune, and Lisa for world peace.

Space aliens Kang and Kodos take advantage of Earth's new-found pacifism and invade the planet, making humans their slaves. Homer uses the last wish to get a turkey sandwich and throws out the paw, but Flanders picks it up and wishes the aliens away. He then wishes that his home turn into a castle.

Movie Moment:
The scene in which Homer is caught at the Moroccan airport trying to smuggle tacky souvenirs by taping them to his chest parodies the heroin-smuggling opening scene in *Midnight Express*.

STORY HIGHLIGHTS

"At first they were cute and funny, but now they're just annoying." A woman, remarking about the Simpsons, after Bart wishes wealth and fame for the family.

"I wish for a turkey sandwich on rye bread with lettuce and mustard. And— and I don't want any zombie turkeys, I don't want to turn into a turkey myself, and I don't want any other weird surprises—you got it?"

"Homer, there's something I don't like about that severed hand."

"Before, I was just bored with their antics and their merchandise. Now I wish they were dead." A man, being lead away by Kang and Kodos, after the aliens take over the Earth.

(Homer sees a monkey's paw on an old, haggard merchant's table. The merchant tells Homer that the paw has the power to grant wishes.)
Homer: *Oh, yeah? How much?*
Merchant: *Sir, I must strongly advise you, do not purchase this. Behind every wish lurks grave misfortune. I, myself, was once president of Algeria.*
Homer: *C'mon, pal, I don't want to hear your life story! Paw me.*

THE STUFF YOU MAY HAVE MISSED

Lisa's T-shirt reads "I Kissed the Balmoujeloud," a play on the "I Kissed the Blarney Stone" shirts sold in Ireland.

Homer's fez hat has the price tag attached to it.

Homer's smuggled bounty at the airport includes: an "I [heart] Marrakesh" mug, a "Honk If You're Moroccan" bumper sticker, a camel bank, and a pack of Camel cigarettes.

A store peddles Simpsons merchandise, after they become rich and famous, in a Simpsons Overstock 2-for-1 Sale.

Some stores in downtown Springfield: The Horseradishery, Candy Most Dandy, Semi-Painless Dentistry, and Rags for Less.

"That board with the nail in it may have defeated us. But the humans won't stop there. They'll make bigger boards and bigger nails. Soon, they will make a board with a nail so big it will destroy them all." Kang to Kodos, after they are driven from Earth.

Homer: *What a dump. Why would Princess Grace live in a place like this?*
(Homer, sightseeing in Morocco.)
Lisa: *Dad, that's Monaco.*

HOMER'S NIGHTMARE

Homer dreams that Mr. Burns fires him and cuts out his brain, placing it in a robot that will become the perfect employee. When the experiment goes awry, Burns puts Homer's brain back into his head. The brainless robot falls on top of Burns, injuring him severely. In order for Burns to live, Smithers sews his head onto Homer's body. Homer awakens and is relieved to learn that he was only dreaming. Or was he? When Homer looks in the bathroom mirror, Burns's head is still attached to his.

Episode 8F02
Original Airdate: 1/31/91
Writers: Atrocious Al Jean & Morbid Mike Reiss, Jittery Jeff Martin,
Gasping George Meyer, Slithering Sam Simon, Spooky John Swartzwelder
Director: Jim Rondo Reardon

BART'S NIGHTMARE

Bart dreams that he has the power to both read minds and make things happen just by thinking about them. When the townspeople have bad thoughts, he turns them into something grotesque. Everyone in Springfield lives in fear of Bart. They force themselves not to think anything bad about him. When Homer makes Bart angry, Bart turns him into a jack-in-the-box. Marge takes Bart and Homer to Dr. Marvin Monroe, who suggests that they spend more time with one another. After going out together and bonding, Bart makes Homer human again.

SHOW HIGHLIGHTS

"He gets it from your side of the family, you know. No monsters on my side." Homer, to Marge.

"Well, class, the history of our country has been changed again, to correspond with Bart's answers on yesterday's test. America was now discovered in 1942 by 'some guy.' And our country isn't called America anymore—it's 'Bonerland.'"

Narrator: *Presented for your consideration. Springfield—an average little town with a not-so-average monster. The people of Springfield have to make sure they think happy thoughts and say happy things, because this particular monster can read minds and, if displeased, can turn people into grotesque walking terrors...*
(The scene cuts to Jasper, walking through town.)
Jasper: *Happy thoughts, happy thoughts, boy, I'm gettin' mighty sick of this.*
(Jasper is instantly changed into a doglike creature.)
Narrator: *And did I mention that the monster is a ten-year-old boy? Quite a twist, huh? Bet you didn't see that one coming.*

"Hello, Moe's Tavern..."

Moe: *Moe's Tavern. Hold on, I'll check. . . . Hey everybody! I'm a stupid moron with an ugly face and a big butt, and my butt smells, and I like to kiss my own butt.*

Monroe: *You like attention, don't you, Bart?*
Bart: *Do I ever!*

THE STUFF YOU MAY HAVE MISSED

Bart eats Chocolate Frosted Frosty Krusty Flakes.

A dead rat and three apples sit on Mrs. Krabappel's desk.

Bart writes "Eat My Shorts!" using three of the answer spaces on his history test. He does the same thing in 8F22, "Bart's Friend Falls in Love."

The front door to Dr. Marvin Monroe's office states: "Member of the Bonerland Medical Association."

Bart wears Krusty the Clown pajamas.

Classic TV Show/Cartoon Moments:
The storyline of a boy who can read minds and wreak havoc with his thoughts is taken directly from the "It's a Good Life" episode of "The Twilight Zone" that starred Billy Mumy.

Bart: *You know, these last few days have been really swell. I wish there was something I could do to repay you.*
Homer: *Well, if you wanted to, you could give me my body back.*

STORY HIGHLIGHTS

"You know Smithers, I've always despised the laziness of the common worker. Then I realized his spirit was willing, but the flesh was weak. So I replaced the flesh—which is weak—with steel, which is strong. Behold, the greatest breakthrough in labor relations since the cat o' nine tails!" Mr. Burns, revealing a 10-foot robot that bears a vague resemblance to Homer.

"Damn it, Smithers. This isn't rocket science. It's brain surgery!"

"Look at me, I'm Davy Crockett!" Burns, dancing around with Homer's brain on his head.

THE STUFF YOU MAY HAVE MISSED

A "Watch Your Step" sign is posted on Burns's secret passageway.

(After returning Homer's brain to his head, Burns stitches the top of Homer's skull back on.)
Homer: *(still asleep)* *Ow. Ow. Ow. Ow.*
Burns: *Oh, will you quit your complaining!*
Smithers: *Sir, do you know what this means? He is alive!*
Burns: *Oh, you're right, Smithers. I guess I owe you a Coke.*

TV Moment:
Johnny Carson appears on television at the Simpson home in his Karnac the Great get-up. He holds an envelope to his head and says, "Geraldo Rivera, Madonna, and a diseased yak." No question is heard.

(Burns and Smithers look at employees on surveillance monitors.)
Burns: *Little do they realize their days of suckling at my teat are numbered.*
Smithers: *Oh, in the meantime, sir, may I suggest a random firing? Just to throw the fear of God into them?*

Movie Moments:
Homer's dream of a transplanted brain parodies the old *Frankenstein* films. The end of the story parodies *The Thing with Two Heads.*

Episode 8F06 Original Airdate: 11/7/91 Writers: Al Jean & Mike Reiss Director: Carlos Baeza

MILLICENT

Occupation:
Riding instructor at the Grateful Gelding Stables.

Sounds like:
Katharine Hepburn.

Loves:
Thoroughbred ponies.

Dislikes:
People with little appreciation or know-how in breeding and raising ponies.

Affectations:
I'm-wealthy-so-stop-wasting-my-time routine.

Also teaches:
Highbrow pronunciation, free with riding lessons.

ALTHOUGH THERE IS NO CHANGE IN MY PATRICIAN FACADE, I CAN ASSURE YOU MY HEART IS BREAKING.

L isa calls Homer just before the school talent show to ask him to pick up a reed for her sax. On the way, Homer stops at Moe's Tavern for a quick drink and arrives late to the school. Lisa's performance is a disaster. Homer sincerely feels bad, realizing that he has never paid Lisa enough attention. He decides that the only way to make amends is to buy Lisa the pony she has always wanted.

Despite Marge's warnings that they cannot afford a pony, Homer takes out a loan from the plant's credit union. Already pressed to the limit on bills, Marge tells him that there is no money to pay the rent on a stable. Homer applies for a job at the Kwik-E-Mart. Working both the graveyard shift at the convenience store and his daytime job at the nuclear plant, he is soon a walking zombie.

Marge tells Lisa that Homer is working two jobs so that she can keep the pony. Although she loves her pony very much, Lisa knows that she must give it up. She gives the pony one last hug good-bye and goes to the Kwik-E-Mart to tell Homer that he does not have to keep his second job. Assured that she still loves him, Homer gives Lisa a piggyback ride home.

SHOW HIGHLIGHTS

"This is a whole lotta nothin'."
Lunchlady Doris, judging the talent show.

 "Maybe I should just cut my losses, give up on Lisa, and make a fresh start with Maggie."

"He slept, he stole, he was rude to the customers. Still, there goes the best damned employee a convenience store ever had."
Apu, on Homer's brief tenure at the Kwik-E-Mart.

 "Isn't that cute? Smithers, he's joining the horsey set. That is it, isn't it? You're not planning to eat it?"

"A cherry! Oh, Mr. Homer, what has reduced you to such cheap chicanery?" Apu, after Homer lies about having three Liberty Bells on his "Scratch for Cash" lottery ticket.

 "I won't lie to you. On this job you will be shot at."

"Sounds like someone's angling for a pony of her own." Homer, after Marge expresses displeasure of the pony.

Homer's new schedule: "I'll work from midnight to eight, come home, sleep for five minutes, eat breakfast, sleep six more minutes, shower, then I have ten minutes to bask in Lisa's love, then I'm off to the power plant fresh as a daisy."

> **Movie Moment:**
> In a sci-fi dream, an apefied Homer takes a nap while perching on the monolith from *2001: A Space Odyssey*. While the other apes are discovering tools, Homer invents goofing off.

> **Homer:** Hurry, Moe, hurry! I've only got five minutes till the music store closes.
> **Moe:** Why don't you go there first?
> **Homer:** Hey, do I tell you how to do your job?
> **Moe:** Sorry, Homer.
> **Homer:** You know, if you tip the glass, there won't be so much foam on top.
> **Moe:** Sorry, Homer.

> (A waitress at Phineas Q. Butterfat's 5600 Flavors Ice Cream Parlor rolls a wheelbarrow-sized sundae to Homer and Lisa.)
> **Teenager:** Okay, who ordered the Mount Bellyache?
> **Homer:** I ordered it for my little girl.
> **Lisa:** (after one small bite) I'm done.
> **Homer:** Oh, that cost eighty-eight dollars!

> **Millicent:** Our ponies start at five thousand dollars. Cash.
> **Homer:** Isn't there like a pound where you can pick up cheap ponies that ran away from home?

> **Marge:** We can't afford to buy a pony.
> **Homer:** Marge, with today's gasoline prices, we can't afford not to buy a pony.

> **Bart:** Hey, how come Lisa gets a pony?
> **Homer:** Because she stopped loving me.
> **Bart:** I don't love you either, so give me a moped.
> **Homer:** And I know you love me so you don't get squat.

> **Marge:** We're just going to have to cut down on luxuries.
> **Homer:** Well you know, we're always buying Maggie's vaccinations for diseases she doesn't even have.
> **Marge:** Actually, I was thinking we could cut down on your beer.
> **Homer:** Nah, we're not going to be doing that.

THE STUFF YOU MAY HAVE MISSED

A calendar in the background reads November 7, the original airdate of the episode.

The Simpsons have a Beta tape VCR.

Homer first looks for a pony at a pet store called "All Creatures Great and Cheap."

A sign inside All Creatures Great and Cheap reads, "You pet it, you bought it."

> **Lisa:** Dad, I broke my last saxophone reed, and I need you to get me a new one.
> **Homer:** Uh...isn't this the kind of thing your mother's better at?
> **Lisa:** I called her. She's not home. I also tried Mr. Flanders, Aunt Patty, Aunt Selma, Dr. Hibbert, Rev. Lovejoy, and that nice man who caught the snake in our basement.

"BART BUCKS" ARE NOT LEGAL TENDER. "BART BUCKS" ARE NOT LEGAL TENDER. "BART BUCKS" ARE NOT LEGAL TENDER.

SATURDAYS OF THUNDER

Episode 8F07 Original Airdate: 11/14/91 Writers: Ken Levine & David Isaacs Director: Jim Reardon

Marge gives Homer a test from the National Fatherhood Institute to evaluate his performance as a father. Homer fails the test and concludes that he is not a good father. He signs up for therapy at the Institute and after a confidence-building pep talk, offers to help Bart build his soapbox racer. Bart reluctantly accepts Homer's help and together they build a meager racer.

At the qualifying race, Bart's car does not even cross the finish line. Martin's sleek, aerodynamic model easily wins, but loses control at breakneck speed and crashes. Martin breaks his arm and cannot enter the final race against Nelson. He asks Bart to race for him, and Bart gladly accepts. However, Homer feels betrayed by Bart's choice to drive Martin's car instead of the one he helped Bart to make, and pouts around the house. Despite being behind the wheel of Martin's machine, Bart does not have his heart in the race.

Homer takes the fatherhood test again. This time, his experience helping Bart build a racer enables him to answer all of the questions correctly. He rushes to the track to watch Bart. Bart sees him cheering in the bleachers and, buoyed by his father's support, blasts by Nelson to win the race.

SHOW HIGHLIGHTS

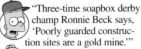

"Three-time soapbox derby champ Ronnie Beck says, 'Poorly guarded construction sites are a gold mine.'"

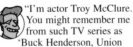

"Thank you, Bill Cosby, you saved the Simpsons!"

"Li'l Lightning": Bart's soapbox racer. According to Bart, "It's slow, it's ugly, it handles like a shopping cart…"

"The Honor Roller": Martin's sleek, aerodynamic soapbox racer. It resembles the space shuttle and even has sponsors: Mensa, General Dynamics, Tang.

"Roadkill 2000": Nelson's soapbox racer. It features a stolen bumper, an intimidating paint job, and it has someone trapped in the trunk.

"I'll just sit here in Li'l Lightnin'—which the Simpsons built— and remember that for one brief shining moment, I had a son."

"I'm actor Troy McClure. You might remember me from such TV series as 'Buck Henderson, Union Buster' and 'Troy and Company's Summertime Smile Factory.'"

Music Moment:
The theme from *The Natural* plays as Bart looks up into the grandstand and sees that his father has shown up to support him in the race.

THE STUFF YOU MAY HAVE MISSED

Patty, Selma, and Marge read *Peephole* and *Idle Chatter* magazines at the beauty salon.

The sign at the video store reads, "VHS Village, Formerly the Beta Barn."

Tapes at the video store include, "Du Du Du," "Border Siesta," "The Bad Football," "Speed Boat Bloopers," "Frisbee," "Super Jock III," "Death By Knockout," "Bench Clearing Brawls," "Blood on the Ice," and "Football's Greatest Injuries."

The head of the National Fatherhood Institute drinks from a Super Dad mug.

Chuck is waiting to have an ice cube tray removed from his tongue in Dr. Hibbert's office.

Scoey: Hey, McBain, you keep eating them hot links you're never gonna make it to a pension.
McBain: C'mon, live a little, Scoey.
Scoey: No, thank you. Got me a future partner; I'm two days away from retirement, my daughter's graduating from college—
McBain: Little Suzie's growing up.
Scoey: —and as soon as we nail Mendoza, my old lady and I are gonna sail around the world like we always wanted.
(Scoey hands McBain a picture of his wife with the boat. It's called the *Live-4-Ever*.)
Scoey: We just christened the boat. Oh, yes sir, everything's gonna be just per—
(A "waiter" reaches into a turkey and pulls out a gun. As Scoey reaches for a condiment, he's shot repeatedly.)

At the Trophy Ceremony:
Bart: I was alone out there, but someone was riding with me in spirit; this is for you, Dad.
Homer: No, son, you earned it.
Martin: I might remind you both I did design that racer, the driver is essentially ballast.

Homer Answers the National Fatherhood Institute Test:
Marge: Name one of your child's friends.
Homer: Uh, let's see, Bart's friends… Well, there's the fat kid with the thing… uh, the little wiener whose always got his hands in his pockets.
Marge: They want a name, Homer, not a vague description.
Homer: Okay… Hank.
Marge: Hank? Hank who?
Homer: Hank… Jones.
Marge: Homer, you made that up. Question two, who is your son's hero?
Homer: Steve McQueen.
Marge: That's your hero. Name another Dad you talk to about parenting.
Homer: Next.
Marge: What are your son's hobbies?
Homer: Kids don't have hobbies.
Marge: Oh, really? Well maybe you should go out to the garage and see.
(Homer goes out to the garage and finds Bart hammering away on his racer.)
Homer: Bart… Bart!
Bart: What?
Homer: You don't have any hobbies, do you boy?
Bart: No, not really.
Homer: Well that's what I—wait a minute, what are you doing?
Bart: Building a soapbox derby racer.
Homer: Ooooooh! That's a hobby!
Bart: Hey, so it is.
Homer: Oh, my God! I don't know jack about my boy!
(Homer starts to sob as Marge, Patty, and Selma stand around him.)
Homer: I'm a bad father!
Selma: You're also fat!
Homer: I'm also fat!

NELSON

HAW! HAW!

Full name:
Nelson Muntz.

Occupation:
Springfield Elementary School Bully.

Favorite pranks:
Hot-footing (putting a lit match between someone's toes); hocking freshly caught fish at cars.

Secret to success:
Cheating.

Companions:
Two weasels who carry out many of his evil whims; Jimbo, Dolph, and Kearney.

Wears:
T-shirt; shorts; vest with ragged hemline.

FLAMING MOE'S

Business is so bad at Moe's Tavern that Moe cannot afford to buy beer for the bar. Homer shows him the "Flaming Homer," a concoction of various liquors mixed with Krusty Non-Narkotik Kough Syrup and then set ablaze. An instant hit, the drink attracts a lot of business. Moe renames it the "Flaming Moe" and takes all the credit.

Soon Moe's is the most popular spot in Springfield. The rock band Aerosmith makes it their official hangout. However, Homer feels that he deserves a piece of the pie and confronts Moe. Moe refuses to cut him in.

Unable to determine the Flaming Moe's secret ingredient, a giant restaurant chain, Tipsy McStagger's, offers to buy the recipe for $1 million. Just as Moe is about to take the money, Homer bursts into a rage and reveals the mystery ingredient before the entire bar. The representative from Tipsy McStagger's tears up the contract. Afterwards, with no hard feelings, Moe makes Homer a "Flaming Homer" on the house.

Classic TV Show Moments:
The character of Collette the waitress and the "Flaming Moe's" theme song are inspired by "Cheers."

UNDERWEAR SHOULD BE
WORN ON THE INSIDE
UNDERWEAR SHOULD BE
WORN ON THE INSIDE
UNDERWEAR SHOULD BE
WORN ON THE INSIDE

(As Moe plans to sign the million-dollar contract with Tipsy McStagger's, Homer appears, cackling and standing in the rafters of Moe's.)
Homer: *Fools! You poor, pathetic misguided creatures choking down your Flaming Moe's, all the time wondering "how does he do it?" Well, I'm going to tell you. The secret ingredient is—*
Moe: *Homer, no!*
Homer: *Cough syrup! Nothing but plain, ordinary, over-the-counter children's cough syrup!*

SHOW HIGHLIGHTS

Krusty's Non-Narkotik Kough Syrup for Kids: The secret ingredient in the Flaming Homer and the Flaming Moe.

"Whoa! Homer, it's like there's a party in my mouth and everyone's invited."
Moe, after his first taste of a Flaming Homer.

"How could you do this to me, Moe? This bar was going under and it was the drink I invented that saved it! If there was any justice, my face would be on a bunch of crappy merchandise!"

"He may have come up with the recipe, but I came up with the idea of charging $6.95 for it."

"Hello, Moe's Tavern..."
Bart: *Uh, yes, I'm looking for a friend of mine. Last name Jass, first name Hugh.*
Moe: *Hold on, I'll check. (To crowd) Hugh Jass, Hey, I wanna Hugh Jass. Oh, somebody check the men's room for a Hugh Jass.*
(A man approaches Moe.)
Hugh: *Uh, I'm Hugh Jass.*
Moe: *Telephone.*
(Moe hands Hugh the receiver.)
Hugh: *Hello, this is Hugh Jass.*
Bart: *Uh, hi.*
Hugh: *Who's this?*
Bart: *Bart Simpson.*
Hugh: *What can I do for you, Bart?*
Bart: *Uh, look, I'll level with you, mister. This is a crank call that sorta backfired and I'd like to bail out right now.*
Hugh: *All right. Better luck next time.*

Episode 8F08 Original Airdate: 1/21/91
Writer: Robert Cohen
Director: Rich Moore & Alan Smart
Special Guest Voices: Aerosmith: Steve Tyler as Himself, Joe Perry as Himself,
Brad Whitford as Himself, Tom Hamilton as Himself, Joey Kramer as Himself;
Catherine O'Hara as Collette the Waitress

MOE SZYSLAK

Occupation:
Surly, two-faced owner
of Moe's Tavern.

Specializes in serving:
Duff Beer.

Cocktail mixing skills:
Virtually nonexistent.

Trusts:
No one.

Serves drinks on the house:
Never.

Bane of his existence:
Bart Simpson and his regular prank calls asking for such fictitious bar patrons as Jacques Strap, I.P. Freely, B.O. Problem and Amanda Hugginkiss.

Heritage:
Claims his forefathers were bartenders to the Czar.

WHEN I GET AHOLD OF YOU, I'M GOING TO USE YOUR HEAD FOR A BUCKET AND PAINT MY HOUSE WITH YOUR BRAINS.

(As Marge reads in bed, Homer paces and mutters to himself.)
Marge: Homer, maybe you can take some consolation in the fact that something you created is making so many people happy.
Homer: Oh, look at me! I'm making people happy! I'm the magical man from Happyland in a gumdrop house on Lollipop Laaane!
(Homer walks out and slams the door. He immediately sticks his head back in the bedroom.)
Homer: Oh, by the way, I was being sarcastic.
(He slams the door again.)
Marge: Well, duh.

Harve: My name is Harve Bannister. I work for Tipsy McStagger's Good Time Drinking and Eating Emporium.
Moe: Oh yeah? Hey, what's Mr. McStagger really like?
Harve: Actually, there is no Tipsy McStagger. He's just a composite of other successful logos.

Homer: What's the matter, Moe?
Moe: Oh, business is slow. People today are healthier and drinking less. You know, if it wasn't for the junior high school next door, no one would even use the cigarette machine.
Homer: Yeah, things are tough all over.
Moe: Increased job satisfaction and family togetherness are poison for a purveyor of mind-numbing intoxicants like myself.

Collette: What do you offer in the way of salary?
Moe: Minimum wage and tips. Of course, there are fringe benefits.
Collette: Such as?
Moe: An unforgettable weekend at Club Moe.
Collette: I'd prefer to take my vacation someplace hot.
Moe: I like your moxie, kid! You're hired.
Collette: You shan't regret this!
Moe: Methinks I shan't.

The "Flaming Moe's" Song Lyrics:

When the weight of the world has got you down/And you want to end your life/Bills to pay, a dead-end job/And problems with the wife/But don't throw in the towel/'Cause there's a place right down the block/Where you can drink your misery away/At Flaming Moe's/Let's all go to Flaming Moe's/Let's all go to Flaming Moe's/When liquor in a mug/Can warm you like a hug/And happiness is just a Flaming Moe away/Happiness is just a Flaming Moe away.

THE STUFF YOU MAY HAVE MISSED

A bowie knife, a glass eye, a troll doll, and Krusty's Non-Narkotik Kough Syrup are in the "Lost and Found" box at Moe's.

Moe cheats at solitaire.

A sign behind the bar reads, "Bartenders do it 'til you barf."

The headlines in various publications touting Moe's success with the Flaming Moe include "Wizard of Walnut Street" (Springfield Shopper), "One Moe for the Road" (Timely) and "Through the Roof!" (Bar and Stool Magazine).

The gang at Flaming Moe's includes Lenny, Carl, Barney, Krusty, Dr. Nick Riviera, Princess Kashmir, Ned and Maude Flanders, Jasper, Otto, Mrs. Krabappel, Kent Brockman and Barney.

King Toot's Music Store is the business next door to Flaming Moe's (first seen in 8F06, "Lisa's Pony").

Under the floorboards at Lisa's slumber party are a pipe that says "Lead," insulation with the label "Asbestos," and a mouse.

The knockoffs of Flaming Moe's that spring up overnight include Flaming Meaux, Flaming Moe's pushcart, and Famous Moe's.

Maggie's utterance of "Moe" may or may not be her first-ever spoken word, depending on whether hallucinations count. She spoke during a Homer freak-out when everyone looked like, and was saying the name, Moe. (Maggie also "spoke" during Bart's nightmare in 7F07, "Bart vs. Thanksgiving." She told Bart, "It's your fault I can't talk!" but her lips did not move.)

FRITZ

Who he is:
One of the wealthy German investors who buys Burns's power plant.

From:
West Germany, where he owned a big company. He partnered with an East German who also had a big company. Together, they have a very big company.

Other plans:
To buy the Cleveland Browns.

Believes:
American beer is like swill.

> GOTT IN HIMMEL! WHO'D'VE THOUGHT A NUCLEAR PLANT COULD BE SUCH A DEATHTRAP!

SHOW HIGHLIGHTS

 "I may just quit my job at the plant to become a full-time stock market guy."

"Oh, thank you. My English is not perfect, but I have to tell you, your beer is like swill to us. Do I have that right? I am saying that only a swine would drink this beer." Fritz, at Moe's, turning down the offer of a free beer from Homer.

"I am Horst. The new owners have elected me to speak with you because I am the most nonthreatening. Perhaps I remind you of the lovable Sergeant Schultz from 'Hogan's Heroes.'" Horst, sitting down to talk with the workers.

The Land of Chocolate: Homer finds common ground during a meeting with the Germans. They talk about candy, sending Homer into a dream in which everything is made of chocolate. Homer takes bites out of a lamppost, a mailbox, and a dog. At the end of the dream, Homer stares into a candy shop advertising chocolate at half price.

"Ich bin ein Springfielder." Diamond Joe Quimby, welcoming foreign investment.

 "What good is money if you can't inspire terror in your fellow man? I've got to get my plant back."

Sycophantic German: Audio tapes Smithers studies to prepare for his new bosses. The tapes teach phrases such as, "You looken sharpen todayen, mein herr."

"We regret to announce the following layoffs, which I will read in alphabetical order. Simpson, Homer. That is all." Horst, retooling the plant staff.

"Ah, the mirthless laugh of the damned. Hold your nose, Smithers—we're going in." Burns, entering Moe's Tavern.

> **Burns:** *Please sell me my plant back. I'll pay anything.*
> **Horst:** *Isn't this a happy coincidence! You are desperate to buy, and we are desperate to sell.*
> **Burns:** *Desperate, eh? Advantage: Burns!*

> **Burns:** *You'll see the Statue of Liberty wearing liederhosen before you see Germans running my plant.*
> **Brockman:** *Well then, sir, why are you meeting with them?*
> **Burns:** *So I can look Uncle Fritz square in the monocle and say nein!*

> **"Hello, Moe's Tavern..."**
> **Moe:** *Moe's Tavern, Moe speaking.*
> **Bart:** *Uh, yes, I'm looking for a Mrs. O'Problem? First name, Bea.*
> **Moe:** *Uh, yeah, just a minute, I'll check. Uh, Bea O'Problem? Bea O'Problem! Come on guys, do I have a Bea O'Problem here?*
> **Barney:** *You sure do!*
> **Moe:** *Oh… It's you, isn't it! Listen, you. When I get a hold of you, I'm going to use your head for a bucket and paint my house with your brains!*

> **Namesake:**
> Burns names the queen of his hive after Smithers.

> **Homer on Thin Ice:**
> **Horst:** *We plan to have some frank discussions with your safety inspector.*
> **Homer:** *Yeah. Sock it to him, Horst!*
> **Lenny:** *Psst, Homer. Aren't you the safety inspector?*
> **Homer:** *D'oh!*

THE STUFF YOU MAY HAVE MISSED

Homer runs his telephone cord through his sandwich.

The barber who appears in Homer's thought balloon while he considers how to spend his windfall appears in 7F02, "Simpson and Delilah."

Smithers visits Burns Manor while his former boss is beekeeping, and is stung by several bees, without having any reaction. In 3F18, "22 Short Films about Springfield," Smithers nearly dies after being stung by a single bee.

The logo for Burns Worldwide features a family holding hands around a mushroom cloud.

Burns and the Germans dine and negotiate at the Hungry Hun.

Homer sells his stock in the nuclear power plant for $25 and spends the money on beer. The same afternoon, rumors about the sale of the plant circulate, and the stock value rises. The next day, all of Homer's co-workers make fortunes, as Mr. Burns sells the plant to a German company for $100 million.

In the aftermath of the takeover, Homer loses his job and slips into a depression. One night, as he is drinking at Moe's, he runs into Burns and Smithers, who have stopped in to have a drink and catch up since Burns's retirement. Homer gives his old boss a piece of his mind, while Bart, who has come to bring Homer home, stomps on Burns's foot. Other customers get surly with Burns and he and Smithers leave.

Burns realizes that because he is no longer in a position of power, he is no longer feared. He decides to buy his plant back. The Germans discover that it will cost another $100 million to bring the plant up to code, and they agree to sell it back to Burns for $50 million. Burns immediately rehires Homer so that someday he can get revenge.

> THE CHRISTMAS PAGEANT DOES NOT STINK.
> THE CHRISTMAS PAGEANT DOES NOT STINK.
> THE CHRISTMAS PAGEANT DOES NOT STINK.

I MARRIED MARGE

Episode 8F10 Original Airdate: 12/26/91 Writer: Jeff Martin Director: Jeffrey Lynch

Marge visits Dr. Hibbert to find out if she is pregnant. While she is gone, Homer recounts to the children how their marriage started...

It is 1980, and Homer is dating Marge. After seeing *The Empire Strikes Back* one night, the two "snuggle." A few weeks later, Marge finds out that she is pregnant. To make her an honest woman, Homer proposes.

Following brief nuptials, Homer sets out to find a decent job. He tries several places, including the power plant, but nothing seems to work out. When the baby clothes and furniture are repossessed, Homer decides that Marge would

be better off without him. Ashamed, he leaves in the middle of the night, but not before writing Marge a letter, telling her that he will send her every cent he makes. Marge tracks him down at the Gulp 'N Blow restaurant and pleads with him to come home.

With renewed determination, Homer returns to the power plant and tells Burns that he will be the perfect spineless employee. Burns hires him.

Homer tells his children what a blessing they have been. When Marge arrives home with the news that she is not pregnant, she and Homer "high-five."

SHOW HIGHLIGHTS

"You're a machine, Homer!" Bart, finding out Marge may be pregnant.

"It all happened at the beginning of that turbulent decade known as the eighties. Those were idealistic days: the candidacy of John Anderson, the rise of Supertramp. It was an exciting time to be young." Homer, setting the scene.

"Homer, maybe it's the Champale talking, but I think you're pretty sexy."

"So You've Ruined Your Life": The name of the pamphlet Dr. Hibbert gives Marge after telling her that she is pregnant.

"Marge, you're as pretty as Princess Leia and as smart as Yoda."

"You deserve all the finest things in the world and although I can give them to you, they will be repossessed and I will be hunted down like a dog." An excerpt from Homer's farewell letter to Marge.

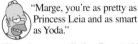

I WILL NOT TORMENT THE EMOTIONALLY FRAIL. I WILL NOT TORMENT THE EMOTIONALLY FRAIL. I WILL NOT TORMENT THE EMOTIONALLY FRAIL.

"Woo hoo! Woo hoo! Yeah! She's gonna marry me! In your face everybody!" Homer, honking his horn and flashing his headlights after Marge accepts his proposal.

Shotgun Pete's: The chapel where Homer and Marge get married just across the state line. Newlyweds get ten dollars in gambling chips for getting married there.

"Pfft. Now you tell me." Homer, finding out that working at a nuclear power plant can make one sterile.

(Homer and Marge stand in the bathroom as Marge reads a small box.)
Marge: *"Barnacle Bill's Home Pregnancy Test?"* Homer, shouldn't we have gone with a better known brand?
Homer: But Marge, this one came with a free corn cob pipe!
Marge: Okay, let's see; *"Ahoy mateys, if the water turns blue, a baby for you. If purple ye see, no baby thar be."*
Homer: Well, what color is it—blue or purple?
Marge: Pink.
Homer: D'oh!
Marge: *"If ye test should fail to a doctor set sail."*

Homer's Resume:
Candle maker at Olde Springfield Towne: *Fired and put in stocks for incompetent candle making.*
Slash-Co knife salesman: *Presumed fired for handing accidentally slicing an elderly woman's hand.*
Attack dog trainer at the Pitiless Pup Attack Dog School: *Quit. Didn't like being attacked.*
Millions for Nothing Seminar attendee: *Seminar dissolved when presenter jumped out of window to escape police.*
Gulp 'N' Blow: *Service Trainee.*

"Shut up with that pen-scratching down there!" Patty, hollering to Homer as he pens his farewell letter to Marge.

Revealed This Episode:
Smithers was once a member of the Alpha Tau fraternity.

(Smithers is testing Homer for a job at the power plant.)
Smithers: *Next. There's a problem with the reactor—what do you do?*
Homer: *There's a problem with the reactor??*
(Homer leaps up from his chair.)
Homer: *We're all going to die!!*
(Homer runs out of the room, screaming.)

THE STUFF YOU MAY HAVE MISSED

Homer has a chain-link steering wheel.

Marge was a carhop at a restaurant called Berger's Burgers.

Barney and Homer watch a tiny television set which is on top of his cable spool table.

In 1980, the height of Marge's hair was not quite to where it is today.

Instead of "Men" and "Women," the restrooms at the Gulp 'N' Blow are labeled "Gulps" and "Blows."

The Gulp 'N' Blow serves beer according to the drive-up menu.

At Shotgun Pete's, weddings cost $20. Photos cost $50.

JUSTICE OF THE PEACE

Occupation:
Bargain minister at Shotgun Pete's Wedding Chapel.

Style:
Insensitive.

Tends to:
Not bother with learning the names of the people he's marrying.

Way he performs ceremonies:
With great speed.

Believes:
A life of wedded bliss begins with $10 worth of chips.

NEXT!

GROUNDSKEEPER WILLIE

Occupation:
Thickly accented Springfield Elementary maintenance man/groundskeeper.

Nationality:
Scottish.

Hair:
Red and shaggy.

Eyebrows:
Red and even shaggier.

Physique:
Muscular; body-builder.

Attitude:
Surly, particularly when confronted by Principal Skinner.

Carries:
A flask of liquid courage.

Favorite problem-solving device:
12-bore shotgun.

THERE'S NARY AN ANIMAL ALIVE THAT CAN OUTRUN A GREASED SCOTSMAN!

or his birthday, Bart gets a Superstar Celebrity microphone that transmits sounds through an AM radio. As a prank, he tosses a small radio down a well in the middle of town and, identifying himself as "Timmy O'Toole," uses the microphone to call out for help. Soon a large crowd gathers. Fears mount when the crowd realizes that rescuers cannot fit down the well's small hole. Krusty and Sting spearhead a video, "We're Sending Our Love down the Well," to raise money for "Timmy's" rescue.

Lisa discovers Bart's ruse and warns him that he will not get away with it. Bart laughs off her warning until he remembers that he put a "Property of Bart Simpson" sticker on the radio. As he climbs down the well to retrieve the radio, the rope breaks, trapping him for real.

Bart admits to Lou and Eddie that he is "Timmy O'Toole" and was only playing a joke. When the townspeople learn

SHOW HIGHLIGHTS

Dance man: As part of his birthday take, Bart receives a coupon for a free tango lesson, which he takes from a woman named Rosarita.

"I used to open for Krusty in '69. In fact, he fired me as I recall... But this isn't about show business, this is about some kid down a hole, or something, and we've all got to do what we can." Sting, explaining his participation in the video project.

Solutions:

Falcon Man: *Grasping the child firmly in his talons, Socrates here will fly him to safety! Just watch.* (his falcon flies away) *I don't think he's coming back.*
Sailor: *With this hook, and this hunk of chocolate, I'll land your boy. And I'll clean him for free.*
Professor Frink: *Although we can't reach the boy, we can freeze him with liquid nitrogen so that future generations can rescue him.*

Homer and Lisa Discuss the Nature of Heroism:

Homer: *That Timmy is a real hero!*
Lisa: *How do you mean, Dad?*
Homer: *Well, he fell down a well, and (pause) he can't get out.*
Lisa: *How does that make him a hero?*
Homer: *Well, that's more than you did!*

During Bart's Birthday Party at Wall E. Weasel's:

Robot Weasel: *Hey there, I hear it's your birthday. How old are you?*
Bart: *Well, I'm—*
Robot Weasel: (cutting him off) *That's great! Would you like us to sing you a special song?*
Bart: *Hell, no.*
Robot Weasel: *You got it! Ready, Signor Beaverotti?*
Signor Beaverotti: (Italian accent) *I'm-a ready. And-a one, and-a two...*
Robot Animals: (singing) *You're the birthday/You're the birthday/You're the birthday boy or girl.*

At the Playground, Jumping Rope:

Janey/Wanda: *One plus one plus three is five/Little Bart Simpson's buried alive/He's so neat/He's so sweet/Now the rats have Bart to eat.*

"I wanted to do something to help the boy. So I called my good friend Sting. He said, 'Krusty, when do you need me?' I said, 'Thursday.' He said, 'I'm busy Thursday.' I said, 'What about Friday?' He said, 'Friday's worse than Thursday.' Then he said, 'How about Saturday?' I said, 'Fine.' *(pause)* True story."

BART

Episode 8F11
Original Airdate: 1/9/92
Writer: Jon Vitti
Director: Carlos Baeza
Guest Voice: Sting as Himself

about Bart's prank, they decide to leave Bart stranded in the well. Homer overhears Bart crying and starts to dig. Soon, others join. Shoveling furiously, the townspeople finally band together to rescue Bart.

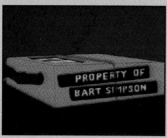

A Partial List of Krusty's Birthday Buddies, Who Were Charged $8 Apiece:

Anna Goodwin, Reagan Gray, Paul Grenville, Jim Greigor, Harriet Hartman, Mike Himes, Julie Hirsh, Janet Hopkins, Cara Hunter, Gracie Jensen, Loretta Kangas, Marilyn Katz, Ken Keeler, John Lanzetta, Lorna Lefever, Marie Lichterman, Iris Lowe, Kim Madrigal, Cammie McGovern, Bill McLain, David Moulton, Mary Myron, Nigel Nelson, J.P. Patches *(actual name of a former kids show host in Seattle)*, Ted Phillips, Randy Plut, Brady Reed, Kevin Reilly, Pete St. George, Casey Sanders, Matthew Schneider, Patrick Semple, Emma Shannon, Bart Simpson, Larry Stone, Beth Summerlin, Kate Sunberg, Dale Thomas, John Travis, Eric Van Buerden, Patric Verrone, Lee Wallace, Jay Weinstein, Chris White, Jay Wiviott, and Henry Yeomans. Several of the buddies once wrote for the *Harvard Lampoon*.

"Well, I'm afraid we've got a budget problem, Mrs. Simpson. Your boy picked a bad time to fall down a well. If he'd done it at the start of the fiscal year, no problemo."

"It's an old-fashioned hole digging! By gar, it's been a while!" Jasper, following the crowd of people heading to the well, shovels and torches in hand.

"The circumference of the well is thirty-four inches. So, unfortunately, not one member of our city's police force is slender enough to rescue the boy." Kent Brockman, reporting on the Timmy O'Toole story.

Children's Emporium Moment:
Wall E. Weasel's, with its frenetic combination of games, pizza, and odd animatronic characters, parodies the Chuck E. Cheese Pizza Time Theater chain.

Record Industry Moment:
"We're Sending Our Love down the Well" was inspired by the celebrity recording, "We Are the World"/USA for Africa.

"I Do Believe We're Naked" by Funky C Funky Do:
The song that replaces "We're Sending Our Love down the Well" as number one.

Marge: *Sting, you look tired. Maybe you should take a rest.*
Sting: *Not while one of my fans needs me.*
Marge: *Actually, I don't know if I've ever heard Bart play one of your albums —*
Homer: *Shhh! Marge, he's a good digger.*

Lyrics to "We're Sending Our Love down the Well":
Sting: *There's a hole in my heart/As deep as a well/For that poor little boy/Who's stuck halfway to hell...*
Sideshow Mel: *...Though we can't get him out/We'll do the next best thing...*
McBain: *...we'll go on TV and sing, sing, sing...*
Choir: *And we're sending our love down the well!*
Krusty: *All the way down!*
Choir: *We're sending our love down the well!*
Krusty: *Down that well!*

THE STUFF YOU MAY HAVE MISSED

McBain wears his gun at the "We're Sending Our Love down the Well" recording session.

The video games at Wall E. Weasel's include: "Larry the Looter" (the player breaks into an electronics store and earns points for each stolen item), "Time Waster," "Coffee Fiend," "Touch of Death," and "Comic Shop."

Lisa reads *Non-Threatening Boys*, a magazine she has read before (7F14, "Bart's Dog Gets an F.")

At the site of the well: a vendor sells "I Survived Timmy O'Toole Getting Trapped in a Well" T-shirts, a man sells "Timmy's Baby Teeth—$6 per bag," a sign on the well reads, "Admission $2.00," and there is a hot dog stand, a "Games" stand, and a Ferris wheel.

Present at the "We're Sending Our Love down the Well" recording session include: (front row) Troy McClure, Scott Christian, Stephanie the Weather Lady, Bleeding Gums Murphy, Mayor Diamond Joe Quimby, Krusty, Princess Kashmir; (second row) Sting, Sideshow Mel, McBain, Dr. Marvin Monroe, Captain Lance Murdock, and the Capital City Goofball.

The TV ad for the Superstar Celebrity Microphone is inspired by the Ronco Mr. Microphone ads of the 1970s.

```
I WILL NOT CARVE GODS
I WILL NOT CARVE GODS
I WILL NOT CARVE GODS
I WILL NOT CARVE GODS
I WILL NOT CARVE GODS
I WILL NOT CARVE GODS
```

SMOOTH JIMMY APOLLO

Occupation:
Professional football prognosticator on TV.

Accuracy rate:
52%.

Chief prop:
A huge padlock that is slapped on the table to illustrate his "Lock of the Week" pick.

"Lock of the Week" accuracy rate:
52%.

Turn-ons:
Being right; not being wrong.

Turn-offs:
Being wrong; compulsive gamblers who take his advice.

OUR FIRST GAME TODAY DENVER AND NEW ENGLAND IS TOO CLOSE TO CALL. BUT IF YOU'RE ONE OF THOSE COMPULSIVE TYPES WHO JUST HAS TO BET...WELL, I DON'T KNOW..UH...DENVER.

Guest Voice:
Phil Hartman as Smooth Jimmy Apollo.

Lisa complains to Marge that Homer never gets involved with her interests. Marge suggests that Lisa take an interest in something her father does. Lisa watches a football game with Homer, who asks her to pick a team for a $50 bet.

Lisa's pick wins and Homer makes every Sunday during football season Daddy-Daughter Day. Lisa studies the game and remains perfect in her picks for eight weeks, earning her father more and more money as the Super Bowl approaches. When Lisa asks Homer if they can go hiking the Sunday following the Super Bowl, he tells her that Daddy-Daughter Days are over until next football season.

Lisa is devastated. Homer feels bad for taking advantage of her and apologizes. Still upset, Lisa makes a Super Bowl bet. If Washington wins, she'll love Homer. If Buffalo wins, she won't. As a nervous Homer watches the game at Moe's Tavern, Washington comes from behind to win. The next Sunday, Homer and Lisa go hiking.

SHOW HIGHLIGHTS

Wee Monsieur: Discount children's clothing outlet in the Springfield Mall where Marge takes Bart.

Call security: While trying on clothes in the surveillance-monitored dressing room at Wee Monsieur, Bart pulls out a piece of cardboard, writes "GET BENT" and holds it up to the camera, setting off a security emergency.

"Let's see...football...football: homo-eroticism in...oddball Canadian rules...Phyllis George and..." Lisa, going through the card catalog at the library.

Making music: Lisa's favorite song is "The Broken Neck Blues," as told to the violinist in The Gilded Truffle.

> **Homer's Parenting Skill:**
> Lisa: *Look, Dad. I'll tell you who's going to win the Super Bowl if you want me to, but it'll just validate my theory that you cared more about winning money than you did about me.*
> Homer: *Okay.*

> Marge: *Ooh, perfume. Meryl Streep's "Versatility."* (The bottle is shaped like an Academy Award.)

Troy McClure premiere: His new sitcom "Handle with Care," in which he plays a retired cop who shares an apartment with a retired criminal, premieres right after the Super Bowl. "We're the original Odd Couple!" he promises.

"Look around you, Malibu Stacy. All this was bought with dirty money. Your penthouse, your Alfa Romeo, your collagen injection clinic..."

> **Ralph Wiggum:** *...when the doctor said I didn't have worms anymore–that was the happiest day of my life.*
> **Miss Hoover:** *Thank you, Ralph. Very graphic. Lisa Simpson, would you like to read your essay?*
> **Lisa:** *The happiest day of my life was three Sundays ago. I was sitting on my daddy's knee when the Saints, who were four and a half point favorites, but only up by three, kicked a meaningless field goal at the last second, to cover the spread.*
> **Miss Hoover:** (shocked) *Dear God!*

> **Homer Explains Gambling:**
> Lisa: *What could be more exciting than the savage ballet that is pro football?*
> Homer: *Well...you know...you like ice cream, don't you?*
> Lisa: *Uh-huh.*
> Homer: *And don't you like ice cream better when it's covered with hot fudge and mounds of whipped cream and chopped nuts and - oh - those crumbled up cookie things they mash up. Mmm...crumbled up cookie things.*
> Lisa: *So gambling makes a good thing even better.*
> Homer: *That's right.* (startled) *My God, it's like there's some kind of bond between us.*

> Homer: *Moe, I'd like to bet twenty dollars on Denver.*
> Moe: (slyly) *I think I can provide that service.* (looking around) *Um, uh, Chief Wiggum, could you hand me that little black book?*
> Wiggum: *Oh, sure thing, Moe. I was just using it as a coaster.*

> **Movie Moment:**
> When Homer says, "I used to hate the smell of your sweaty feet. Now it's the smell of victory," he is mimicking a line from *Apocalypse Now*.

> **Beating Heart:**
> Marge: *All of those fatty, deep-fried, heavily-salted snacks can't be good for your heart.*
> Homer: *Pfft, my heart is just fine.*
> (Fast and extreme zoom into Homer's body. Close-up on his heart pumping wildly. We see a clot build up in an artery which starts to expand like a balloon. Finally, it unclogs itself with a gurgle.)
> Homer: *A little beer will put out that fire.*

> **After Denver Loses:**
> Smooth Jimmy Apollo: *When you're right 52% of the time, you're wrong 48% of the time.*
> Homer: (yelling at the TV) *Why didn't you say that before?*

THE STUFF YOU MAY HAVE MISSED

Inside Moe's black bookie betting book are listed the following entries: "Barney $5 Pittsburgh," "Smitty $12 New Orleans," and "Homer $20 Denver."

Herman is seen at Moe's Tavern holding a pool cue, though with one arm it is unclear how he is able to play the game.

Homer's collection of junk food snacks while watching football include New Bar-B-Q Chips, pork rinds, Salt Doodles, Krunchy Korns, and two bowls of dip—all of it washed down by a can of Duff.

The family's dining at The Gilded Truffle marks a return visit. Their first trip came during 8F02, "Treehouse of Horror II" in the "Monkey's Paw" segment.

HOMER ALONE

Episode 8F14 Original Airdate: 2/6/92 Writer: David Stern Director: Mark Kirkland

A fter a horrendous day of endless chores, errands, and traffic, Marge loses her equanimity. She stops her car on the Springfield Bridge, blocking traffic in both directions. A long stand-off ensues and Homer is brought to the scene to talk to her. Marge emerges from the car and is immediately arrested. Fearful of alienating women voters, Mayor Quimby releases Marge to bring attention to the plight of the overworked housewife.

Marge sees a commercial for Rancho Relaxo resort and decides she needs a vacation alone. Leaving Bart and Lisa with Patty and Selma, she boards a train to relax. Marge lives it up at the resort while Lisa and Bart try to survive the perils of their aunts. At home, Homer's hands are full with baby Maggie.

In the middle of the night, Maggie crawls out of bed to look for her mother. The next morning, Homer searches all over the house, but cannot find her. Just as he leaves to go pick up Marge from the train station, Chief Wiggum shows up with Maggie. When Marge returns, the family vows to be more helpful in the future if she promises never to leave them again.

I WILL NOT SPANK OTHERS.
I WILL NOT SPANK OTHERS.
I WILL NOT SPANK OTHERS.
I WILL NOT SPANK OTHERS.
I WILL NOT SPANK OTHERS.
I WILL NOT SPANK OTHERS.

SHOW HIGHLIGHTS

The events that push Marge over the edge: Homer chases Bart through the house, breaking a lamp. Bart needs her to find his red cap. Lisa requests no pimentos in her lunch. Homer rips his pants and wants double bologna. Homer asks her to have a beer cap removed from his bowling ball. Bart and Lisa miss the bus. Bart and Lisa fight in the car on the way to school. Maggie throws groceries on the floor in the market. No ball flushers are willing to remove Homer's beer cap. As a crank call, Bill and Marty call a man over the radio and tell him his wife is dead after she walked through a plate glass window. Maggie spills her milk all over Homer's newly dry-cleaned bowling uniform.

"I'm Troy McClure. You might remember me from such films as *Today We Kill, Tomorrow We Die*, and *Gladys the Groovy Mule*. But today you'll see me in my greatest role — your video tour guide to Rancho Relaxo!"

(Homer and the workers watch on TV as an angry mother has stopped traffic on the bridge.)
Homer: *Hey sweetheart, what's the matter?! Not getting enough of the good stuff at home?*
(The window of the car on TV rolls down, revealing a wild-eyed Marge.)
Homer: *D'oh!*

Homer, the single parent: He uses a staple gun to fasten Maggie's diaper. He lays on top of her while watching TV from the couch. He prepares her 9 a.m. feeding at 11:45 a.m.

Last hurrah: Before she leaves Rancho Relaxo, Marge orders a hot fudge sundae, chocolate chip cheesecake, and a bottle of tequila from room service.

The official radio station of Rancho Relaxo: D.J. (through the radio): "This is Coma —WKOMA. Restful, easy listening. Coming up next, a super set of songs about clouds."

Clash of the Titans:
Wiggum: *Don't you worry, Mr. Mayor, this little bird will be crackin' rocks by the end of the week.*
Quimby: *Wiggum, you glorified night watchman, let her go!*
Wiggum: *But she broke the law.*
Quimby: *Thanks for the civics lesson. Now listen to me. If Marge Simpson goes to jail, I can kiss the chick vote goodbye. And if I go down, you're gonna break my fall!*
Wiggum: *Word to the wise, Quimby. Don't write checks your butt can't cash.*
Quimby: *Hear me loud and clear, Wiggum. You bite me, I'll bite back.*
Wiggum: *You talk the talk, Quimby. But do you walk the walk?*

Marge: *(to Patty and Selma) Thanks again for taking the children while I'm away.*
Selma: *Don't worry yourself.*
Patty: *Uh-huh. We've got six months of maternity leave we're never going to use anyway.*

Marge: *Homer, I need a vacation...I mean a vacation by myself.*
Homer: *What? You mean we're getting a divorce?*

T.V. announcer: *Many years ago, the Spanish explorers discovered a little piece of heaven nestled in the Springfield Mountains. They called it "Rancho Relaxo," and so do we. Today it's Springfield's only two-star health spa....Swim, play tennis, or just sit and stare at the walls. At Rancho Relaxo, you're the boss. Remember, you can't spell "Relaxo" without "relax."*

THE STUFF YOU MAY HAVE MISSED

The bus on the Springfield Bridge is filled with actors in costume.

The bus driver wears a Skoal tobacco cap.

Krusty's license plate reads: KRUSTY.

Marge's train stops at Shelbyville, Badwater, Cattle Skull, and Testing Grounds before stopping at Rancho Relaxo.

The man who so rudely turns down the lube job ("Don't touch me") is the same man who gets his parking ticket validated by Ned at the Leftorium without making a purchase ("Just stamp the ticket").

The Xt'Tapalatakettle head is still in the Simpsons' basement.

Occupation:
Trained chimp on "The Krusty the Clown Show."

Chief vice:
Chain-smoker.

Chief goal:
Drive Krusty crazy.

Enjoys:
Futzing with things he has no right to futz with.

Aspires to:
Something more.

Tired of being lonely, Mrs. Krabappel takes out a personal ad. When Bart smashes the classroom fish tank with his new yo-yo, she gives him one month's detention. Snooping through her desk for his confiscated yo-yo, Bart discovers Mrs. Krabappel's ad and comes up with a way to get back at her. He sends her a love letter and signs it "Woodrow." Mrs. Krabappel reads it and she thinks she has finally found her true love. She sends a response with a sexy photo.

After writing back and forth and building the romance, Bart writes to Mrs. Krabappel, acknowledging it is time she and Woodrow

meet. He sets up a time and place for the meeting. Mrs. Krabappel arrives at the appointed time, but the man of her dreams never shows.

Feeling bad, Bart tells his family what he has done. Marge suggests that Woodrow write Mrs. Krabappel another letter, letting her down easy and salvaging her remaining self-esteem. Marge, Homer, Bart, and Lisa compose a poetic masterpiece. When Mrs. Krabappel receives the letter, her spirits are lifted.

> WRITE RALPH
>
> 1+1=2 ?
>
> RECENTLY DIVORCED
> 4TH GRADE TEACHER
> WISHES TO MEET MAN
> AGE 18-60
>
> OBJECT :
>
> SAVE

Gordie Howe's Pro-Hockey Career Totals, as Flashed at the End of the Show:

	Games	Goals	Assists	Pts.
National Hockey League	1767	801	1049	1850
World Hockey Association	419	174	334	508
Major League Totals	2186	975	1383	2358

SHOW HIGHLIGHTS

"Thank goodness I still live in a world of telephones, car batteries, handguns, and many things made of zinc!" Jimmy, the teenage protagonist of a 1960s science film shown to Bart's class.

"Damn Flanders." Reverend Lovejoy, hanging up the phone after a talk with Ned Flanders about Todd's swearing.

"Look, Homer, all of us pull a few boners now and then, go off half-cocked, make asses of ourselves. So, I don't want to be hard on you, but I just wish you wouldn't curse in front of my boys."

Bart Is Caught String-Handed:

(Milhouse leans over to Bart in the middle of class.)
Milhouse: *Hey, Bart, got any new tricks for us today?*
Bart: *Just one. A little something I call "Plucking the Pickle." I build up a little steam and—*
(Bart twirls the yo-yo and it smashes into the aquarium. Water and fish pour onto the floor. Mrs. Krabappel looks over to the yo-yo in the aquarium and follows the string to Bart's finger.)
Bart: *I didn't do it.*

(Miss Hoover and Mrs. Krabappel sit in the back row of the Twirl-King Yo-Yo Champions Assembly.)
Miss Hoover: *I question the educational value of this assembly.*
Mrs. Krabappel: *Hey, it'll be one of their few pleasant memories when they're pumping gas for a living.*

LOVER

Episode 8F16
Original Airdate: 2/13/92
Writer: Jon Vitti
Director: Carlos Baeza

WOODROW

Alias:
Bart Simpson.

Reason for deception:
Retaliation at teacher for taking his yo-yo away.

Turn-ons:
Holding hands; dinner by candlelight; writing romantic letters.

Really hates:
Yo-yos.

Carries a fabricated torch for:
Edna Krabappel.

TRULY, YOURS IS A BUTT THAT WON'T QUIT.

(The students of Springfield Elementary are gathered for an assembly. A man walks out on stage, twirling a yo-yo.)
Ted Carpenter: *Kids, this is a yo yo. Kinda dull, huh? Not much competition for a video game... or is it? Presenting the Twirl-King champions! Mr. Amazing!*
(A man in a blue jumpsuit hand-flips onto the stage and twirls out six yo-yos at once.)
Ted Carpenter: *Sparkle!*
(A woman in a blue jumpsuit twirls out two yo-yos and then twirls out another two from her ears.)
Lisa: *She's beautiful!*
Ted Carpenter: *Zero-gravity!*
(Another man moonwalks out onstage and twirls a yo-yo towards the ceiling.)
Ted Carpenter: *The Cooobra!*
(A man pops out of a wicker basket, opens his mouth, and twirls a yo-yo from his tongue.)
Bart: *Those guys must be millionaires!*

The Threat:

Maude Flanders: *Todd, would you like some mixed vegetables?*
Todd: *Hell, no!*
Maude: *What did you say?*
Todd: *I said I don't want any damn vegetables.*
Ned Flanders: *All right, that's it, young man! No Bible stories for you tonight!*
(Todd runs crying out of the room.)
Maude: *Weren't you a little hard on him?*
Ned: *Well, you knew I had a temper when you married me.*

Bart Researches His Role:

Announcer: *(on TV) We return to "Two for Tunisia" on "Colorization Theater."*
Charles Boyer-type: *Ah, my love, a million poets could try for a million years and still describe but three-eighths of your beauty.*
Bart: *(writing on pad) Whoa, slow down, Frenchy! This stuff is gold!*

Bart's First Woodrow Letter:

"Dear Edna, I've never answered a personal ad before, but I found yours irresistible. My name is Woodrow. I like holding hands and dinner by candlelight. And, oh yes, I really hate yo-yos."

Lisa: *Maybe we should write her another letter. One that says goodbye, but lets her feel loved.*
Homer: *Step aside everyone! Sensitive love letters are my speciality.*
(Homer rips off a sheet of paper and starts writing.)
Homer: *Dear Baby, Welcome to Dumpsville. Population: you.*

Woodrow's Farewell Letter:

"Dearest Edna, I must leave you. Why, I cannot say. Where, you cannot know. How I will get there, I haven't decided yet. But one thing I can tell you, any time I hear the wind blow it will whisper the name...Edna. And so, let us part with a love that will echo through the ages. — Woodrow"

THE STUFF YOU MAY HAVE MISSED

At the Yo-Yo Champions Assembly, Miss Hoover and Mrs. Krabappel smoke under a "No Smoking" sign.

At the Kwik-E-Mart, Mrs. Krabappel buys a can of Chef Lonely Hearts' Soup for One Chicken Noodle, which has a picture of the chef with a tear running down his cheek.

The copy of *Springfield Magazine* read by Mrs. Krabappel includes the cover story "Krusty Picks Springfield's Best Chili." Another piece headlines "We Talk with J.D. Salinger"—an impossibility, since he is a known recluse.

Flanders's list of possible bad influences on his son Todd: bumper stickers, comic books, Grandma, television, brother.

Homer sends Marge a postcard from Duff Brewery in Capital City in 1978 that says, "See the World's Biggest Pull-Tab."

ARISTOTLE AMADOPOLIS

Occupation:
Owner/operator of the Shelbyville Nuclear Power Plant.

Native country:
Greece.

Attire:
Double-breasted jacket; shirt open several buttons to reveal numerous gold chains; sunglasses; large ring.

Favored greeting:
Three kisses on the cheek.

Persona:
Moody.

Hangout:
Springfield Heights Millionaire's Club.

> MY GLADIATORS WILL CRUSH YOUR TEAM LIKE NINE FLABBY GRAPES!

Guest Voice:
Jon Lovitz
as Aristotle Amadopolis

HOMER AT THE BAT

Episode 8F13 Original Airdate: 2/20/92 Writer: John Swartzwelder Director: Jim Reardon
Guest Voice: Dan Castellaneta as Aristotle Amadopolis

SHOW HIGHLIGHTS

2 and 28: The Springfield Nuclear Plant team's abysmal win-loss record the previous year.

Lightning-rod: While telling Bart the story of how he procured his magical "Wonder Bat," he admits that during a thunderstorm he sheltered himself with a large piece of sheet metal while running for cover under a tall tree.

> **Movie Moment:**
> Homer makes his "WonderBat" from a tree that is struck by lighting, à la Roy Hobbs' bat in *The Natural*

What happens to knock each ringer recruited for the Springfield Nuclear Plant dream team out of commission: Wade Boggs (smacked by Barney during a bar argument), Jose Canseco (burned while rescuing items and pets from a burning house), Roger Clemens (inadvertently hypnotized into thinking he is a chicken), Ken Griffey, Jr. (gigantism brought on by an overdose of nerve tonic), Don Mattingly (booted from the team by Mr. Burns for wearing sideburns only Burns can see), Steve Sax (sentenced to six life terms for various murders in New York City), Mike Scioscia (radiation poisoning), and Ozzie Smith (vanishes into another dimension at the Springfield Mystery Spot).

The Rules of the Game:
Umpire: *Okay, let's go over the ground rules. You can't leave first until you chug a beer. Any man scoring has to chug a beer. You have to chug a beer at the top of all odd-numbered innings. Oh, and the fourth inning is the beer inning.*
Chief Wiggum: *(impatient) Hey, we know how to play softball.*

Carl: *Okay, Homer, bases loaded and you're up. Where's that secret weapon?*
Homer: *Check it out, boys. My magic bat.*
Carl: *That's it?*
Lenny: *(mocking) Yeah, I got a magic bat, too.*
Carl: *And I got an enchanted jock strap.*

(Smithers approaches Mike Scioscia, who is doing some hunting. Scioscia, not seeing him, fires a few bullets. One grazes Smithers.)
Mike Scioscia: *Hey, sorry! I thought you were a deer.*
Smithers: *Heh, heh, that's okay, happens all the time.*

Lyrics to "Talkin' Softball" (Sung by Terry Cashman to the Tune of "Talkin' Baseball"):
"Well, Mr. Burns had done it /The power plant had won it /With Roger Clemens clucking all the while /Mike Scioscia's tragic illness made us smile /While Wade Boggs lay unconscious on the barroom tile /We're talkin' softball /From Maine to San Diego /Talkin' softball /Mattingly and Canseco /Ken Griffey's grotesquely swollen jaw /Steve Sax and his run-in with the law /We're talkin' Homer.../Ozzie, and the Straw /We're talkin' softball /From Maine to San Diego /Talkin' softball /Mattingly and Canseco /Ken Griffey's grotesquely swollen jaw /Steve Sax and his run-in with the law /We're talkin' Homer.../Ozzie, and the Straw."

Homer: *Where do you think you're going?*
Lisa: *To the game.*
Homer: *No, no, no. I don't want you to see me sitting on my worthless butt.*
Bart: *We've seen it, Dad.*

Steve Sax: *Don't I at least get to call my lawyer?*
Chief Wiggum: *You watch too many movies, Sax.*

Burns: *I've decided to bring in a few ringers. Professional baseballers. We'll give them token jobs at the plant and have them play on our softball team! Honus Wagner, Cap Anson, Mordecai "Three Finger" Brown!*
Smithers: *Uh...sir...I'm afraid... all those players have retired and...uh...passed on. In fact, your right-fielder has been dead for a hundred and thirty years.*
Burns: *Damnation! All right, find me some good players. Living players! Scour the professional ranks! The American League! The National League! The Negro Leagues!*

THE STUFF YOU MAY HAVE MISSED

Marge wears a Smilin' Joe Fission-insignia cap atop her blue bouffant.

Smithers wears his plant ID badge even while at the baseball field, and elsewhere.

On the Springfield Nuclear Plant bulletin board, the safety poster of the Heimlich Maneuver shows a man choking on an entire lobster.

At the Springfield Heights Millionaire's Club, the sign in front reads, "You must have more than this to enter: $1,000,000." The "$1,000,000" is etched on a nameplate.

Bowling lothario Jacques is among those in the audience at the jazz club listening to The Steve Sax Trio.

It's the first game of the season, and the Springfield Nuclear Power Plant softball team trails by three runs in the ninth inning. Bases are loaded. Homer steps up to the plate with his homemade bat and hits a grand slam to win the game. The team remains undefeated, facing rival Shelbyville for the championship.

Mr. Burns bets Shelbyville's owner, Ari Amadopolis, a million dollars that his team will win. To hedge his bet, he hires Major Leaguers Jose Canseco, Don Mattingly, Ken Griffey, Jr., Ozzie Smith, Steve Sax, Darryl Strawberry, Roger Clemens, Wade Boggs, and Mike Scioscia to work at the plant and play on his team. The day before the game, all but Strawberry are involved in incidents that keep them from playing, forcing Burns to use real employees.

Only Homer is kept on the bench. With the score tied and bases loaded in the ninth inning, Burns sends in Homer to pinch-hit for Strawberry, preferring a right-hander to bat against the left-handed pitcher. The first pitch hits Homer and knocks him out, forcing in the winning run. Still unconscious, Homer is paraded around the field as a hero.

I WILL NOT AIM FOR THE HEAD.
I WILL NOT AIM FOR THE HEAD.
I WILL NOT AIM FOR THE HEAD.
I WILL NOT AIM FOR THE HEAD.
I WILL NOT AIM FOR THE HEAD.
I WILL NOT AIM FOR THE HEAD.

SEPARATE VOCATIONS

Episode 8F15 Original Airdate: 2/27/92 Writer: George Meyer Director: Jeffrey Lynch Guest Voice: Steve Allen as Himself

Lisa is heartbroken when her career test reveals her ideal future occupation — "homemaker." Bart's test shows that he should be a policeman. Lisa is determined to prove the test wrong. She goes to a music teacher to get his opinion. He informs her that, having inherited her father's stubby fingers, she can never be a very good saxophone player. Bart rides along with officers Lou and Eddie to see what it's like being a cop. During the ride, he assists in apprehending a suspect.

Her dreams shattered, Lisa loses interest in being a good student. When Principal Skinner discovers Bart's new interest in law enforcement, he enlists him as a hall monitor. Soon, Bart has order restored to the school.

After being punished for sassing Miss Hoover, Lisa steals the teachers' editions of the schoolbooks. Bart tracks down the thief, locker by locker. When he discovers that Lisa has stolen the books he takes the rap for her. He is stripped of his hall monitor sash and is given 600 days detention. Thankful to her

brother, Lisa plays her saxophone outside his classroom as he serves his time.

SHOW HIGHLIGHTS

Career Aptitude Normalizing Test or CANT: Test given to kids at Springfield Elementary, designed to pinpoint the children's individual careers.

EMMA: Computer in Iowa that evaluates CANT. Watched over by a rube in a wheelchair who pokes it with a broom when it breaks down.

"Well, I'm going to be a famous jazz musician. I've got it all figured out. I'll be unappreciated in my own country, but my gutsy blues stylings will electrify the French. I'll avoid the horrors of drug abuse, but I do plan to have several torrid love affairs. And I may or may not die young, I haven't decided."

"I'll be frank with you Lisa, and when I say frank, I mean, you know, devastating. You've inherited a finger condition known as 'stubbiness'. It usually comes from the father's side." Teacher at "Li'l Ludwig's Music Studio," telling Lisa why'll she'll never be a great blues musician.

Bart: *Hey, fellas, let's go shoot some bad guys.*
Lou: *(chuckles) Well, it doesn't quite work that way, son.*
Eddie: *People see movies like McBain and they think it's all bang bang, shoot-em-up, cops-n-robbers.*

Eddie: *(into CB) One ocean tango...We are in pursuit of a speeding individual, driving a red...car. License number...*
(Eddie squints at the license plate. It reads "EX CON")
Eddie: *Eggplant-Xerxes-Crybaby-Overbite-Narwhal.*

"I saw some awful things in 'Nam, but you really have to wonder at the mentality that would desecrate a helpless puma. I never thought I'd say this, but the no-goodniks rule this school!" Principal Skinner, after discovering the school mascot statue egged and teepeed.

"Shove it." Lisa, after Miss Hoover notes she is not putting sprinkles on her paste.

Bart: *...it's quite simple, really. I observed our friend Groundskeeper Willie burning leaves with a blatant disregard for our clean air laws.*
Skinner: *Bart Simpson on the side of law and order? Has the world gone topsy-turvy?*
Bart: *That's right, man. I got my first taste of authority and I liked it.*

Marge: *Bart's grades are up a little this term. But Lisa's are way down.*
Homer: *(moan) We always have one good kid and one lousy kid. Why can't both our kids be good?*
Marge: *We have three kids, Homer.*
Homer: *Maaaarge...The dog doesn't count as a kid.*
Marge: *No, Maggie!*
Homer: *Oh, yeah.*

"Sure, we have order—but at what price?"

Bart's punishment: 600 days detention, plus writing, "I will not expose the ignorance of the faculty" repeatedly on the blackboard.

Lisa: *Bart, why did you take the blame?*
Bart: *Cause I didn't want you to wreck your life. You got the brains and the talent to go as far as you want, no matter what anyone says. And when you do, I'll be right there to borrow money.*

Movie Moment:
When Principal Skinner asks Lisa what she is rebelling against, she answers, "Whattaya got?" as Marlon Brando did in *The Wild One*. She even has a toothpick in her mouth.

> I WILL NOT BARF UNLESS
> I'M SICK
> I WILL NOT BARF UNLESS
> I'M SICK
> I WILL NOT BARF UNLESS
> I'M SICK

THE STUFF YOU MAY HAVE MISSED

EMMA, the computer, is configured to look like she has a face.

A tiny skull hangs on a chain from Snake's rearview mirror.

One of the tough fifth grade girls Lisa befriends has skull earrings.

The tough fifth grade girls smoke Laramie Jr. cigarettes.

Bart searches the same locker twice. It is identifiable by the apple core and pencil on top.

THAT'S ENOUGH OUT OF YOU, SMART GUY.

IT'S TIMES LIKE THIS I'M GLAD I FLUNKED OUT OF DENTAL SCHOOL

DOG OF DEATH

Episode 8F17 Original Airdate: 3/12/92 Writer: John Swartzwelder Director: Jim Reardon

 o one in the Simpson family notices when Santa's Little Helper becomes seriously ill. While the family watches TV for the winning lottery numbers, the dog collapses. They rush him to the hospital, where they learn that he needs a $750 operation. The Simpsons do not have the money, but when Santa's Little Helper licks Homer, they resolve to find a way to help him.

In order to afford the operation, everyone in the family has to sacrifice something. Homer gives up beer, and Marge cooks no-frill meals. The operation is successful and Santa's Little Helper is completely healed. The Simpsons, however, are forced to live a life of austerity and take their frustrations out on the dog. One night, Homer inadvertently leaves the gate open and Santa's Little Helper wanders off. Guilt stricken, the family misses him and tries to find him.

Santa's Little Helper is picked up by the dog catcher and taken to the pound, where Burns sees him and adopts him as one of his attack dogs. When Bart enters Burns's mansion looking for his dog, Burns releases the hounds. Santa's Little Helper remembers Bart and saves him from the other dogs. Bart takes Santa's Little Helper home, where he receives a warm homecoming.

Movie Moment:
Burns brainwashes Santa's Little Helper by restraining him, prying his eyes open, and forcing him to watch images a dog would find horrifying, à la *A Clockwork Orange.*

SHOW HIGHLIGHTS

"Bart, I need some lucky numbers, fast! How old are you? Uh-huh, and what's your birthday? No kidding. And Lisa's birthday? What? You don't know your sister's birthday? What kind of brother are you?" Homer, calling home before buying his lottery ticket.

Lottery fever: A man goes to the Kwik-E-Mart and buys a wheelbarrow full of lottery tickets. They blow away as soon as he gets outside. Every copy of *The Lottery* by Shirley Jackson has been checked out of the library. The story is actually about a public stoning. With the education dividend, Skinner wants to buy books that explain how the Korean War came out and "math books that don't have that base six crap in them." He also has his sights on a detention hall where children are held in place with magnets. Homer buys fifty tickets. He imagines after winning he becomes a

I SAW NOTHING UNUSUAL IN THE TEACHER'S LOUNGE.
I SAW NOTHING UNUSUAL IN THE TEACHER'S LOUNGE.
I SAW NOTHING UNUSUAL IN THE TEACHER'S LOUNGE.

gilded giant, encrusted with gems. During the drawing, Chief Wiggum answers the emergency line and claims, "You have the wrong number. This is nine-one-two." Krusty puts his audience on hold while he waits for the drawing.

"I'm looking for something in an attack dog. One who likes the sweet gamey tang of human flesh. Mmm, why here's the fellow! Wiry, fast, firm, proud buttocks. Reminds me of me."

"I've figured out an alternative to giving up my beer. Basically, we become a family of traveling acrobats."

"The cat? What's the point?" Homer, after Marge suggests he pet the cat.

Doggie Heaven, Doggie Hell:
Homer: *I want to tell you about the most wonderful place in the world: Doggie Heaven. In Doggie Heaven, there are mountains of bones, and you can't turn around without sniffing another dog's butt!*
Bart: *Is there a Doggie Hell?*
Homer: *Well... of course! There couldn't be heaven if there weren't a hell.*
Bart: *Who's in there?*
Homer: *Oh, uh...Hitler's dog. And that dog Nixon had, whassisname, um, Chester...*
Lisa: *Checkers.*
Homer: *Yeah! One of the Lassies is in there, too. The mean one—the one that mauled Jimmy!*

Burns: *(to Smithers) Dogs are idiots. Think about it, Smithers. If I came into your house and started sniffing at your crotch and slobbering all over your face, what would you say?*
Smithers: *Uh...If YOU did it, sir...?*

(Homer dreams of what he will do if he wins the lottery. The scene shifts to the power plant cafeteria, where Lenny is eating a donut. Giant footsteps are heard and a large shadow falls over him.)
Lenny: *Hey, Homer, what'd you do, get a haircut or something?*
(Homer stands before him. He's huge and gold-plated.)
Homer: *(deep, echoed voice) Look closer, Lenny.*
Lenny: *Oh, I know what it is: you're the biggest man in the world now, and you're covered in gold.*
Homer: *Fourteen karat gold!*

THE STUFF YOU MAY HAVE MISSED

Photos of the missing dog are plastered over flyers of a missing Skinner. From 8F03, "Bart the Murderer."

A "Give a hoot! Read a book!" poster hangs in the library.

Secondary newspaper headline: "President, Rock Star to Swap Wives."

The ornamental lions outside the Springfield Veterinary Hospital are bandaged.

Ned Flanders wears his Assassins sneakers. He bought them in 7F14, "Bart's Dog Gets an F."

COLONEL HOMER

Episode 8F19 Original Airdate: 3/26/92 Writer: Matt Groening Director: Mark Kirkland

The family goes to the movies. Homer and Marge watch *The Stockholm Affair*, while Bart and Lisa see a monster movie. Homer gives the ending away and the audience boos him, embarrassing Marge. When Marge tells Homer to shut up, everyone applauds, embarrassing Homer. Dropping off Marge and the kids at home, he drives to a rowdy country western bar, where he listens to a beautiful waitress, Lurleen, sing a lonesome love song.

Several days later, still humming Lurleen's song, Homer drives back to the bar. He finds Lurleen and offers to take her to a recording booth at the mall. The booth attendant hears the song and offers to help air it on a local radio station. The song is a big success and Homer becomes Lurleen's manager. He spends more time with Lurleen than his wife, and Marge becomes jealous. Lurleen, attracted to Homer, asks him to spend the night with her but Homer feels guilty, and quickly leaves.

Realizing that Marge is the woman he loves, Homer sells Lurleen's contract to a music promoter for $50 and returns home to his wife and family. Marge and Homer watch Lurleen on television as she sings about how lucky Marge is.

> I WILL NOT CONDUCT MY
> OWN FIREDRILLS.
> I WILL NOT CONDUCT MY
> OWN FIREDRILLS.
> I WILL NOT CONDUCT MY
> OWN FIREDRILLS.

SHOW HIGHLIGHTS

Stinks: On his way to Spittle County, Homer passes a skunk, a fertilizer plant, a garbage dump a sulfur mine, and 40 miles of open sewers. He tries to hold his breath the whole way.

 "Marge, let's end this feudin' and a fussin' and get down to some lovin'."

 "As much as I hate that man right now, you gotta love that suit."

"Ya Hoo!": The Hee Haw-type show on which Lurleen makes a guest appearance.

 "Lurleen, I can't get your song outta my mind. I Haven't felt this way since "Funky Town."

Cast of "Ya Hoo!": Yodelin' Zeke, Butterball Jackson, Freddy-boy and Yuma, Cloris Mozelle, Big Shirtless Ron, Orville and Hurley, Cappy Maye, Hip Diddler, Rudy, and The Ya-Hoo Recovering Alcoholic Jug Band.

 "They don't call me Colonel Homer because I'm some dumb-ass army guy."

Lurleen's other songs include: "I'm Basting a Turkey with My Tears," "Don't Look Up My Dress Unless You Mean It," "I'm Sick of Your Lying Lips and False Teeth," and "Stand By Your Manager."

 "Marge, it takes two to lie. One to lie and one to listen."

Lurleen's Song:
You work all day for some old man/ You sweat and break your back/ Then you go home to your castle/ But your queen won't cut you slack/ That's why you're losin' all your hair/ That's why you're overweight.../ That's why you flipped your pick-up truck right off the interstate/ Now, you talk so tough and act so rough/ but darlin' you can't hide/ the heartache and the sadness/ that's buried deep inside/ There's a lot of bull they hand you/ There's nothin' you can do/ Your wife don't understand you/ But I do/ No, your wife don't understand you/ but I do/ I said your wife don't understand you/ but I do.

Homer's Comments during the Movie:
"Ah, this movie's too complicated... Hey, the floor's sticky..."
"Who's that guy?... What did that guy say when I said, 'who's that guy?'"
"Oh, that's so fake... Look, you can see the strings... ooh! An octopus!"
"I think that guy's a spy."
"Oh, wait, I heard how this ends. It turns out the secret code was the same nursery rhyme he told his daughter."

Marge's Annoyed Comments to Homer during the Movie:
"Well, of course he's a spy. You just saw him go through spy school!"
"Oh, shut up, Homer! No one wants to hear what you think!"

Movie Moment:
On entering Spittle County, Homer passes a kid playing a banjo on a porch à la *Deliverance*.

Now Playing at the Googoplex (in Theaters 22-28):
I'll Fry Your Face III
The Smell in Room 19
Space Mutants VI
Honey, I Hit a Schoolbus
Look Who's Oinking
The Stockholm Affair
Ernest vs. the Pope

THE STUFF YOU MAY HAVE MISSED

The sign at the Royal King Trailer Park reads "14 Days without a tornado"

The Capitol Building is directly in back of the Oval Office on *The Stockholm Affair* set.

Someone throws a candy bar at Homer in the movie theater. It bounces off his head and hits Marge.

A cow is on top of the garbage heap at the dump Homer passes by.

A horse is tethered outside the Beer 'N' Brawl.

The Beer 'N' Brawl sells Laramie High Tar cigarettes.

Yodelin' Zeke shows up on "Ya Hoo!" with a bandage around his head (he was beat up earlier in the episode at the Beer 'N' Brawl.

LURLEEN LUMPKIN

Occupation:
Cocktail waitress at the Beer 'N'Brawl; aspiring country singer.

Residence:
Trailer, at the Royal King Trailer Park.

Friends & family:
Mamma; Daddy; the triplets; Vonda Mae; Piney Jo.

Taste in men:
Slow-witted, bald family fellows.

Biggest talent:
Hiding love messages in the lyrics of her songs.

Schooling:
Didn't go.

WELL, C'MON BOYS. LET'S BREAK SOME HEARTS.

Guest Voice:
Beverly D'Angelo as Lurleen Lumpkin

BLACK WIDOWER

Episode 8F20 Original Airdate: 4/8/92 Writer: Jon Vitti Director: David Silverman Guest Voice: Kelsey Grammer as Sideshow Bob

Family tree spot:
Daughter of Jacqueline Bouvier; twin sister of Patty; both older sisters of Marge.

Pet iguana's name:
Jub-Jub.

Cigarette brand:
Laramie.

Employer:
Department of Motor Vehicles.

Hair:
Frizzy, grayish, with part in the middle distinguishing her from her twin sister.

Favorite TV show:
"MacGyver."

Favorite male:
Richard Dean Anderson.

Least favorite male:
Homer Simpson.

> NOW BRING US SOME EXTRA CHAIRS LIKE A GOOD BLUBBER-IN-LAW.

When Selma's prison pen pal is released, she invites him to the Simpsons' home to meet the family. To Bart's amazement, her pen pal and new beau is his mortal enemy, Sideshow Bob. Bob shares his new, positive outlook on life, but Bart does not trust him, even after he asks Selma to marry him.

Despite Bart's objections, Selma marries Sideshow Bob and sends back a videotape of their honeymoon. Watching the tape, Bart sees Sideshow Bob doting over his new bride. Although Selma is clearly in wedded bliss, Bart cannot help but feel something is not right. Realizing that Bob is up to no good, Bart and the police arrive at the hotel just in time to save Selma from Bob's deadly plot.

Bart explains to Sideshow Bob and Chief Wiggum how he figured out Bob's scheme. He explains that on the videotape, Bob vehemently demands a hotel room with a fireplace. Bart becomes suspicious because Selma lost her sense of smell in a freak bottle-rocket accident and would not notice a gas leak in the room. Bob could leave the gas on when Selma smokes her cigarettes—after meals and after her favorite TV show, "MacGyver." Selma would blow herself up, leaving Bob her life savings. As the police take Bob away, he vows that he'll be back.

SHOW HIGHLIGHTS

"Hey, you know the rules. Awards for excellence in entertainment are contraband. No Emmys, no Oscars, not even a Golden Globe." Prison guard, confiscating Bob's Emmy.

A first: The character formerly known as "Jailbird" is referred to as "Snake" for the first time.

 "Gee, if some snot-nosed little kid sent me to prison, the first thing out, I'd find out where he lives, and tear him a new bellybutton."

"Well, you can't go wrong with cocktail weenies. They taste as good as they look. And they come in this delicious red sauce. It looks like catsup – it tastes like catsup. But brother, it ain't catsup!"

"When I was a kid we were playing with bottle rockets and one shot straight up my nose. I permanently lost my sense of taste and smell." Selma, telling why all food tastes like Styrofoam to her.

FUNNY NOISES ARE NOT FUNNY
FUNNY NOISES ARE NOT FUNNY
FUNNY NOISES ARE NOT FUNNY
FUNNY NOISES ARE NOT FUNNY
FUNNY NOISES ARE NOT FUNNY
FUNNY NOISES ARE NOT FUNNY

 "We're a package. Love me, love MacGyver."

"It's been quite a week for you, Selma. First you were married and now you'll be buried." Bob, making plans for his new bride.

Final mystery: Sideshow Bob asks why the room blew up despite the fact that Bart came to the rescue. Chief Wiggum explains that his squad lit cigars to celebrate a job well done.

The Proposal:

Sideshow Bob: *Selma, would you mind if I did something bold and shocking in front of your family?*
Selma: *All right, but no tongues.*
Sideshow Bob: *Although kissing you would be like kissing some divine ashtray, that's not what I had in mind..Selma, will you marry me?*
Bart: *Don't be a fool, Aunt Selma. That man is scum.*
Selma: *Then call me Mrs. Scum!*

Guess Who's Coming to Dinner:

Patty: *You see, Aunt Selma has this crazy obsession about not dying alone, so in desperation, she joined this prison pen-pal program. Her new sweetie's a jailbird.*
Bart: *Cool, he can teach us how to kill a guy with a lunch tray.*

Springfield's Finest:

Bart: *Chief Wiggum, you've been around. You don't trust Sideshow Bob, do you?*
Wiggum: *Ahh, lighten up, son. If he was going to commit a crime, would he have invited the number one cop in town? (he pauses) Now, where did I put my gun? Oh, yeah. I set it down when I got a piece of cake...*

License Plates Bob Makes in Prison:

"DIE BART," "RIP BART," "I H8 BART," and "BART DOA."

The MacGyver Factor:

Selma: *That MacGyver's a genius.*
Sideshow Bob: *First of all he's not a genius, he's an actor. And second, he's not much of an actor.*
Selma: *You're lying! You're lying!*
Sideshow Bob: *No Selma, this is lying: that was a well-plotted piece of non-claptrap that never made me want to retch.*

Entertainment History Moment:

Bob's on-air reconciliation with Krusty at his "Telethon for Motion Sickness" parodies the reunion Jerry Lewis and Dean Martin had at one of Jerry's Labor Day telethons.

THE STUFF YOU MAY HAVE MISSED

Bob's chapstick is passed around the cell as he reads his first letter from Selma.

Selma works at window 6 at the Department of Motor Vehicles.

Wendell is one of the motion sickness sufferers at Krusty's telethon. (Wendell's uneasy stomach was last mentioned in 7F03, "Bart Gets an F.")

Before Patty announces the dinner guest, Lisa imagines it is going to be some type of elephant man.

THE OTTO SHOW

Episode 8F21 Original Airdate: 4/23/92 Writer: Jeff Martin Director: Wes Archer
Guest Voices: Spinal Tap members: Christopher Guest as Nigel Tufnel; Micheal McKean as David St. Hubbins; Harry Shearer as Derek Smalls

After attending a Spinal Tap concert, Bart announces that he wants to be a Heavy Metal rocker. Homer and Marge encourage Bart to follow his musical interests by buying him a guitar. However, no matter how hard Bart practices, he cannot master the instrument.

Bart brings his guitar on the school bus. Otto stops the bus to play some music. Realizing he is late, Otto races to school, crashing the bus in the process. When Principal Skinner discovers that Otto doesn't have a driver's license, he suspends him. At the DMV, Otto takes his test to get his job back, but fails when he asks Patty if she has always been female.

Out of a job and money, Otto is kicked out of his apartment. Bart tells him he can live in the Simpsons' garage. Otto is comfortable there, but Homer cannot put up with him and orders him to leave. Marge suggests Otto take the driver's license test over again, but it is only when Homer insults him that Otto decides to get his license so that he can staple it to Homer's head. Patty finds out that Otto dislikes Homer and makes sure he passes the exam.

> I WILL NOT SPIN THE TURTLE
> I WILL NOT SPIN THE TURTLE
> I WILL NOT SPIN THE TURTLE
> I WILL NOT SPIN THE TURTLE
> I WILL NOT SPIN THE TURTLE
> I WILL NOT SPIN THE TURTLE

SHOW HIGHLIGHTS

 "Tonight a city weeps as, for the first time ever, a hockey arena becomes a scene of violence following a concert by Spinal Tap."

Bart's T-shirt:
"Spinal Tap World Tour: London, Paris, Munich, Springfield."

"Check it out. Spinal tap kicking Mo-mar Kadaffy in the butt. The timeless classic, now two for a dollar." Comic Book Guy, selling bootleg T-shirts in the arena parking lot.

Bart's rock and roll fantasy: He is a burnt-out band front man who tells his manager and back up guitarist (Milhouse) to "slag off." He performs a chart topper called "Me Fans Are Stupid Pigs."

 "Although I'm sure I will receive a severe wedgie from my busmates, I must remind you we should have been at school ten minutes ago."

"If something's hard to do, then it's not worth doing. You just stick that guitar in the closet next to your short wave radio, your karate outfit, and your unicycle and we'll go inside and watch TV."

"Listen you drain clogging, last cookie-eating, collect-call getting sponge, I want you out of my house!" Homer's ultimatum to Otto.

Living with Otto:

He plays the guitar until all hours. His hair clogs the drain in the bathroom. He scares Lisa with interactive horror stories. He calls Homer "Pop'N' Fresh" and pokes him in the stomach.

Marge: *My little guy's first rock concert. I hope the Spinal Taps don't play too loud.*
Homer: *Oh Marge, I went to thousands of heavy metal concerts and it never hurt me.* (Marge says something to Homer, but he hears nothing but a ringing in his ears)
Homer: *I hear ya. Come on boy.*
Selma: *There goes Davy Crockett and his baldskin cap* (laughs).

Spinal Tap, on the Fall of the Iron Curtain:
Derek: *I can't think of anyone who's benefited more from the death of Communism than us.*
Nigel: *Oh, maybe the people who actually live in the Communist countries.*
Derek: *Oh yeah, hadn't thought of that.*

Officer Lou: *Let's see your license, pal.*
Otto: *No can do. Never got one. But if you need proof of my identity, I wrote my name on my underwear... (looking) Oh, wait, these aren't mine.*
Skinner: *Well, that tears it. Until you get a license and wear your own underwear, mister, you are suspended without pay.*
Otto: *...who's going to drive the bus?*
Skinner: *I drove an all terrain vehicle in Da Nang. I think I can handle it.*

Patty: *My name is Patty. I'll be testing you. When you do good, I use the green pen. When you do bad, I use the red pen. Any questions?*
Otto: *Yeah, one. Have you always been a chick? I mean, I, I y'know don't want to offend you, but you were born a man, weren't you? You can tell me, I'm open-minded.*
Patty: *(drops green pen) I won't be needing this.*

Bart: *Otto-man, you're living in a dumpster?*
Otto: *Oh, man, I wish. "Dumpster" brand trash bins are the top of the line. This is just a "Trash-Co" waste disposal unit.*
Bart: *Otto why don't you come home with me? You can stay in our garage.*
Otto: *A garage? Oh, somebody up there likes me.*

Marge: *I know we didn't ask for this, Homer, but doesn't the Bible say, "Whatsoever you do to the least of my brothers, that you do unto me...?"*
Homer: *Yes, but doesn't the Bible also say, "Thou shalt not take moochers into thy hut?"*

Bart: *Where's Otto?*
Skinner: *Otto. That's one palindrome you won't be hearing for a while.*

THE STUFF YOU MAY HAVE MISSED

The concert pyrotechnician is missing an arm.

Skinner gets a five o'clock shadow waiting for an opening in traffic while driving the bus.

There are bars of gold and jewels in the framework of the Simpsons' house.

OTTO

Main occupation:
Bus driver for Springfield Elementary School.

Side-gigs:
Driver for Springfield Nuclear Power Plant family events; Springfield Poolmobile; Springfield Seniors Gambling Junket Bus; Springfield Bloodmobile.

Favorite songs:
"Freebird"; "Purple Haze"; "Frankenstein"; "Iron Man."

Literary interests:
Stuff from the vampire's point of view.

Funky friend:
Snake.

Driving record:
Fifteen accidents and not a single fatality.

> THE ONLY THING I WAS EVER GOOD AT WAS DRIVING A BUS AND NOW "THE MAN" SAYS I NEED A PIECE OF PAPER TO DO THAT.

Position in Springfield society:
Bart's four-eyed sidekick and 4th-grade classmate.

Prime abuser:
Nelson Muntz.

Collects:
Bazooka Joe comics.

First girlfriend:
Samantha Stanky.

First human purchase:
Bart's soul, for $5.00.

MY DAD'S A PRETTY BIG WHEEL DOWN AT THE CRACKER FACTORY.

BART'S FRIEND FALLS IN LOVE

Episode 8F22 Original Airdate: 5/7/92 Writers: Jay Kogen & Wallace Wolodarsky Director: Jim Reardon Kimmy Robertson as Samantha Stanky

SHOW HIGHLIGHTS

Movie Moment:
The opening scene of Bart trying to steal Homer's penny jar parodies the opening scene of *Raiders of the Lost Ark*.

Bart: *You can read comics with us. Let's see, something for the lady. Ah, "Radioactive Man vs. the Swamp Hag."*
Samantha: *Got any girl comics? Like "Bonnie Craine, Girl Attorney;" "Punkin & Dunkin, the Twinkle Twins;" or "L'il Kneesocks?"*
Bart: *No, but my sister's got a wide selection of crappy comics.*

"She's faking it." Mrs. Krabappel, smoking a cigarette and commenting on Fuzzy Bunny and Fluffy Bunny's wedding night.

 "Hello, I'm actor Troy McClure. You kids might remember me from such educational films as *Lead Paint: Delicious but Deadly* and *Here Comes the Metric System!*".

"Homer Simpson. Born: 9 lbs. 6 oz. Died: 402 lbs., 1 oz." Homer's gravestone in Lisa's daydream, during which a sobbing Marge blurts, "I wish they had never invented fried cheese!"

"Did you know that 34 million American adults are obese? Taken together, that excess blubber could fill the Grand Canyon two-fifths of the way up. That may not sound impressive, but keep in mind it is a very big canyon."

 "This is the first time anyone has ever sat next to me since I successfully lobbied to have the school day extended by twenty minutes."

"Forbearance is the watchword. That triumvirate of Twinkies merely overwhelmed my resolve." Homer, after Marge comments that he ate three desserts that night.

"How could this happen? We started out like Romeo and Juliet but it ended up in tragedy."

"Marge, where's that...metal dealie...you use to...dig...food?" Homer, asking for a spoon after he stops listening to his vocabulary tapes.

"We just moved here from Phoenix. My dad owns a home security company. He came to Springfield because of its high crime rate and lackluster police force." Samantha, introducing herself to her new class.

Fuzzy Bunny's Guide to You Know What: The 1971 sex education film shown to Mrs. Krabappel's class.

Mazel Tov: We can see by Fuzzy Bunny and Fluffy Bunny's wedding day that Fuzzy is a Jewish bunny, wearing a yarmulke and stepping on a glass.

Fifty Rosaries a Kiss:
The punishment for boy-kissing at Samantha's new Catholic school.

THE STUFF YOU MAY HAVE MISSED

A reference to the Circus of Values store appears in 7G08, "Simpsons Roasting on an Open Fire."

There are only pennies in Homer's change jar, which says "Homer's Change: DON'T TOUCH!" on it.

Mrs. Krabappel's comment on Bart's test reads, "Very poor, even for you." Bart has written "Eat my shorts" in three of the answer areas.

When Milhouse and Samantha kiss for the first time, their joined upper bodies form a perfect heart shape—aping the comic book Bart is holding in front of him.

Films playing at the Springfield Googoplex: *Rip Roaring Reverend, Sing, Monkey, Sing, Space Mutants VII,* and *Hot Grits A-Flyin'.*"

I WILL NOT SNAP BRAS.
I WILL NOT SNAP BRAS.
I WILL NOT SNAP BRAS.
I WILL NOT SNAP BRAS.
I WILL NOT SNAP BRAS.
I WILL NOT SNAP BRAS.

A new girl, Samantha Stanky, moves into the neighborhood and joins Bart's and Milhouse's class. After school, a smitten Milhouse walks her home. Bart is stunned when Milhouse shows up at the treehouse with Samantha. Bart climbs down to get a few girl-type comic books from Lisa's room and when he returns, he is appalled to discover Milhouse and Samantha kissing.

Meanwhile, Lisa worries that Homer's overeating will shorten his life. She convinces Marge to order subliminal weight-loss tapes for him. Unaware that he has been sent vocabulary-building tapes instead, Homer puts on the headphones and falls asleep. When he wakes up, he is suddenly articulate.

To Bart's dismay, Milhouse and Samantha spend all of their free time together. Jealous and feeling excluded, Bart reveals Milhouse's and Samantha's relationship to her father. Mr. Stanky orders Samantha never to see Milhouse again and enrolls her in Catholic school. Meanwhile, after two weeks of listening to the vocabulary tapes, Homer gains thirteen pounds and throws the tapes away. He quickly loses his advanced verbal abilities and has trouble remembering the most basic words. Bart confides to Milhouse that he snitched, and they fight. Afterwards, they visit Samantha at St. Sebastian's. Bart apologizes to her and she and Milhouse share one last kiss.

BROTHER, CAN YOU SPARE TWO DIMES?

Episode 8F23 Original Airdate: 8/27/92 Writer: John Swartzwelder Director: Rich Moore
Guest Voices: Danny DeVito as Herb, Joe Frazier as Himself

 A routine physical at work reveals that Homer's sperm count has been damaged due to radiation exposure. Fearing a lawsuit, Mr. Burns's lawyers suggest that Homer receive a token sum of money in exchange for a legal waiver. To get Homer to accept the $2,000 and sign the waiver, Burns tells him that the money is for winning the fictitious First Annual Montgomery Burns Award for Outstanding Achievement in the Field of Excellence.

Meanwhile, Homer's half-brother, Herb, who has been a bum since staking his company on Homer's design for a car, needs an investor for a new invention. Reminding the family that Homer is responsible for his plummet from prosperity, Herb asks for the $2,000 to build a baby translator—a device capable of translating a baby's garbled gibberish into understandable speech. Homer gives him money instead of buying a massage chair and the invention becomes an instant money-maker.

Rich once again, Herb pays Homer back the $2,000 and buys the family various gifts, including an NRA membership for Bart, a washer/dryer for Marge, and a recliner for Homer. He also forgives Homer for ruining him in the first place.

Homer, considering the purchase of the vibrating Spine Melter 2000: "Marge, there's an empty spot I've always had inside me. I tried to fill it with family, religion, community service. But those were all dead ends. I think this chair is the answer."

Herb, explaining how his baby translator works: "It measures the pitch, the frequency, and the urgency of a baby's cry, and then tells whoever's around, in plain English, exactly what the baby's trying to say! Everything from 'Change me' to 'Turn off that damn Raffi record!'"

"That's the greatest invention in the world! You'll make a million dollars!" Homer, commenting on a drinking bird toy Herb has placed on the table.

SHOW HIGHLIGHTS

One of Herb's hobo friends, sharing his story with the group: "Yeah...I used to be rich. I owned Mickey Mouse massage parlors and those Disney sleazeballs shut me down. I said, 'Look, I'll change the logo, put Mickey's pants back on.' Some guys you just can't reason with."

"Why did this have to happen now, during primetime, when TV's brightest stars come out to shine?"

"Before you begin, let me make one thing clear for you. I want your legal advice. I even pay for it. But to me you're all vipers. You live on personal injury. You live on divorces. You live on pain and misery...but I'm rambling. Would anyone like some coffee?"

> **Classic Rock Moment:**
> Homer's line, "S'cuse me while I kiss the sky," is from the Jimi Hendrix tune "Purple Haze."

> **The Idea:**
> **Herb:** Lady, you just gave me the idea of a lifetime. How do I thank you?
> **Mother:** Please don't hurt me.
> **Herb:** Consider it done.

> **Singers:** It's the first annual Montgomery Burns / Award for —
> **Men Singers:** (singing) Outstanding Achievement In —
> **Female Singers:** (singing) The Field of
> **Singers:** (singing) Excellence!
> (Mr. Burns walks onstage in a tuxedo, clapping.)
> **Burns:** Yes, that was Bonita De Wolf & The Springfield Nuclear Power Plant Soft Shoe Society.

> **Homer:** All right, Herb. I'll lend you the 2,000 bucks. But you have to forgive me and treat me like a brother.
> **Herb:** Nope.
> **Homer:** All right, then just give me the drinking bird.

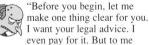
I WILL NOT FAKE SEIZURES.
I WILL NOT FAKE SEIZURES.
I WILL NOT FAKE SEIZURES.
I WILL NOT FAKE SEIZURES.
I WILL NOT FAKE SEIZURES.
I WILL NOT FAKE SEIZURES.

> **Movie Moment:**
> Homer's psychedelic, dreamy rush while in the Spine Melter 2000 chair is reminiscent of the penultimate scene in *2001: A Space Odyssey*.

> **Marge:** How was your day at work, dear?
> **Homer:** Oh, the usual. Stand in front of this, open that, pull down this, bend over, spread apart that, turn your head that way, cough...

THE STUFF YOU MAY HAVE MISSED

Teeth are seen flying when Joe Frazier beats up Barney outside the bar.

One of Homer's sperm has three eyes, like Blinky the fish.

One of the transients around the fire, dressed like Charlie Chaplin's Little Tramp character, eats a boot. Another transient is a hobo clown.

The train moving outside advertises "Krusty's Sulfuric Acid" and "Emily's Fluffy Pillows."

A sign at the Baby Expo reads: "No Triplets!"

Herb owns an "Oscilloscopes 4 Less" brand oscilloscope.

PROFESSOR FRINK

Profession:
Mad scientist.

Appearance:
Toussled hair; thick glasses; white smock.

Vocal lilt:
Annoying.

Shortcomings:
Creates inventions that never work properly.

Past flubs:
Constructed robots to protect Mr. Burns that turned violent toward the boss and exploded; blew up Moe's Tavern while attempting to strike a comet plunging toward Springfield; accidentally flew a radio-controlled, gas-powered plane carrying his own child through a window.

BRACE YOURSELVES, GENTLEMEN. ACCORDING TO THE GAS CHROMATOGRAPH, THE SECRET INGREDIENT IS... LOVE?! WHO'S BEEN SCREWING WITH THIS THING?

COUCH GAGS

whimper is heard, and Homer pulls Santa's Little Helper out from underneath. 8F04, 8F16–The family rushes in as a green octopus-type alien with four arms and one eye drinks a can of beer on the couch. It escapes via a trap door in the floor, just as the family members fling themselves onto the couch. 8F05, 8F15–The family rushes in. After Homer, Marge, Lisa, and Maggie sit down on the couch, Bart pounces

7G02, 7G07–The family rushes in and crams onto the couch. Bart pops out and comes crashing down seconds later in front of the TV as the opening credits end. 7G03, 7G10–The family rushes in and squeezes onto the couch, causing it collapse. 7G04, 7G13–The family rushes in and crowds onto the couch. Homer pops out and lands on the floor. 7G06, 7G12–The family rushes in and crams onto the couch. Maggie pops into the air, landing in Marge's arms. 7G09, 7G01–The family rushes in and sits on the sofa. No gag. 7F03, 7F12, 7F22, 9F06–The family rushes in. When they land on the couch, it crashes through the floor. 7F02, 7F13, 7F23–The family runs in and dances a cha-cha, first in one direction and then the other, with their arms extended. They leap in unison onto the couch, with their arms still extended. 7F01, 7F15–The family rushes in. When they sit down on the couch, it folds out into a bed. 7F05, 7F16–The family rushes in and sits on the couch, except Maggie, who is nowhere to be seen. A moment later, Maggie pokes her head out of Marge's hairdo. 7F08, 7F14–The family rushes in and everyone crowds on the couch, including Santa's Little Helper and Snowball II. 7F07, 7F17–The family rushes in. They wake up and startle Grampa, who is sleeping on the couch. 7F06, 7F18–The family rushes in and plops on the couch, which Homer tips sideways with his weight. Maggie flies through the air and lands on a cushion on the floor. 7F09, 7F19, 8F03, 8F14–The family rushes in and finds the couch missing. 7F10, 7F20–The family rushes in. When they sit on the couch, Homer squeezes them off one by one. 7F11, 7F21–The family rushes in. The couch falls backwards when they sit on it. Maggie pops up from behind. 7F24, 8F22–The family rushes in and jumps onto the couch, which tips over backwards, sending them crashing through the wall. 8F01, 8F12–The family rushes in and sits on the couch. A

across their laps. 8F06, 8F17–The family rushes in. Homer lies across the couch and they all sit upon him. 8F07, 8F19–The family rushes in. They sit on the couch, sinking deeply into the cushions. 8F08, 8F20–The family rushes in and find a pair of thieves carting away the couch. They leap onto it anyway, but the burglars dump them onto the floor before they carry out the couch. 8F09, 8F21, 3F31–Santa's Little Helper growls on the couch. The family slinks away. 8F10, 8F23–The family rushes in. They all cartwheel to the couch. Maggie falls. When they sit, they flourish with outstretched arms. 8F11–The family rushes in and leaps onto the couch, bouncing around and changing their positions with each bounce. 8F13–The family rushes in. Everyone except Maggie smacks heads and collapses in an unconscious heap. Maggie climbs aboard the couch alone. 8F24–The family rushes in. They can't sit down because the Flintstones are occupying the couch. 8F18, 9F15, 3F31–The family rushes in. When they sit, the couch turns into a monster and swallows them. 9F01, 9F12–The family rushes in. When they sit, the couch spins 180 degrees into a secret compartment, revealing an exact duplicate couch and wall. 9F02, 9F14, 3F31–The family rushes in, finds Maggie seated, sprints past the edge of the film, and scoots back into the frame and onto the couch. 9F04–The family's skeletons rush in and crowd onto the couch. Marge has a white streak in her hair, like the Bride of Frankenstein. 9F03–The family rushes in and the couch deflates. 9F05, 9F17–The family rushes in. When they sit, each has another's head. They swap until the heads are on the correct corresponding bodies. 9F07, 9F18–The family rushes in. Instead of the couch, there is a small chair which Homer and Marge share. The kids sit on their laps. 9F08, 9F13, 9F16, 9F22, 2F08, 3F31–The family rushes in. They dance in a chorus

line. Soon they are joined by high-kicking Rockettes, a variety of circus animals (including trained elephants), jugglers, trapeze artists, fire breathers, magicians, and Santa's Little Helper, who walks through a hoop as circus music plays. 9F09, 9F20, 3F31–A tiny version of the family rushes in and starts the long climb up to the couch. Bart helps Maggie up. 9F10, 3F31–The family rushes in and sits on the couch, as nearly all of Springfield joins them in front of the TV set. 9F11, 9F19–The family rushes in. Before they get to the couch, a large net snares them and sweeps them up off the ground. 9F21–The family rushes in. On the first take, they crash into each other and shatter like glass. Santa's Little Helper walks in and looks at the pieces. On the second take, they collide and blend into a five-headed blob on the couch. On the third take, they crash into each other and explode, leaving a burned patch on the living room floor. Maggie's pacifier drops to the ground. 1F02, 1F12, 2F33, 3F31–The family rushes in and sits on the couch. They are crushed by a giant Monty Pythonlike foot. 1F01–The family rushes in and finds doubles of themselves sitting on the couch. 1F04–The zombie family breaks through the living-room floor and sits on the couch. A painting over the couch depicts a sinking ship with sharks circling around it. 1F03–The family rushes in and crashes through the wall, which has been painted to resemble the living room. Their outlines remain. 1F05, 1F13–The family rushes in. A very large man is already on the couch. The Simpsons squeeze into what room is left. 1F06, 1F15, 2F04–Five pairs of eyes enter in the dark and take their positions. The lights go on. The family runs in. They sit down on the couch, cock their heads forward, and pop the eyes into their sockets. 1F07, 1F19–The family rushes in and sits down before noticing that the couch is in David Letterman's studio. David Letterman turns around in his chair to face them. 1F08, 1F21–The family rushes in. They crash into each other and shatter like glass. Santa's Little Helper walks in and looks at the pieces. 1F09, 1F20–The family rushes in. They crash into each other and explode, leaving a burned patch on the living room floor. Maggie's pacifier drops to the ground. 1F11–The family rushes in. They collide and blend into a five-headed blob on the couch. 1F10–Homer, Marge, Bart, and Lisa pop up one by one from behind the couch. Maggie pops up from behind the center cushion. 1F14–The family rushes run in. There are two couches. Each family member splits in two, taking a seat on each couch. 1F16–The family bounces into the living room as balls, resuming their usual shape once they land on the couch. 1F18–The family rushes in. Homer sees the Fox logo in the corner of the screen. He rips it off and stomps on it. The rest of the family joins in. 1F22, 2F12–The family sits in midair. There is no couch in sight. The couch runs in and puts itself together on top of them. They collapse under its weight. 1F17, 2F13, 3F31–The family swims in and climbs onto the couch. Bart wears a scuba mask and snorkel. 2F01, 2F14–The family materializes on the couch as if beamed down from the original Starship Enterprise. 2F03–A family of Simpson ghouls rushes into the living room sporting mismatched body parts. After sitting on the couch, they pass around one another's parts until they nearly match. 2F05, 2F15–The family rushes in. When they sit, the couch springs throw them off. Their heads stick through the ceiling. 2F06, 2F18, 3F31–The family rushes in and chases after the couch as it recedes down a long hallway. 2F07, 2F16–The family rushes in. Resembling Hanna-Barbera characters, they grin and run past the couch in a perpetually repeating background. 2F09, 2F19, 3F31–The house is distorted and surreal, like an Escher print. Each family member rushes into the living room from the ceiling and walls and sits on the couch. 2F10, 2F21–Homer is seen walking past the couch through the barrel of a gun, à la the opening of a James Bond film. He turns, draws his own gun, and shoots at the camera. The screen goes red. 2F11, 2F22, 3F31–The family rushes in. Everything is in black and white. The family, recalling cartoon characters from the twenties, wears white gloves and performs a bow-legged bounce in front of the television. 2F31, 2F32, 3F31–The family rushes in and sits down on the couch. Their sizes are reversed: Homer is the smallest and Maggie is the largest. 2F20–The family rushes in. The couch moves off to the side and a police lineup chart falls like a backdrop behind them. To "Dragnet"-like music they line up in front of the chart. 2F17, 3F12, 3F22–A life-size fax of the Simpsons comes up from the cushions, is ripped off, and floats to the ground. 3F02, 3F14–The Simpsons drive around the living room in tiny cars. Like Shriners, they wear fezzes on their heads. They park in a row in front of the television. 3F01, 3F13–Homer, Marge, Bart, Lisa, Maggie, Grampa, Santa's Little Helper, and Snowball II appear in their own square, à la "The Brady Bunch." The living room is featured in the center square. Each family member leaves his or her square and rushes onto the couch, except for Grampa, who is sleeping in his square. 3F03, 3F16–The family rushes in as gray shadows. Their features are airbrushed on

in color by machines that descend from the ceiling. 3F04–The family members drop down one at a time from the ceiling, hanging above the couch, their necks in nooses and their eyes wide open. 3F05, 3F15–The family rushes in as wind-up toys. They haphazardly meander to the couch by different methods of propulsion. Homer and Marge walk, but Homer falls. Lisa hops onto the couch, and Maggie flips onto it. Bart rolls towards the couch and spins in place. 3F06, 3F17–A bowling-lane cleaner removes Snowball II from the couch as an automatic pin-setter positions the family on the couch. 3F08, 3F18–The family rushes in, resembling Sea Monkeys. They swim to a couch made of clams and peer at a treasure chest instead of a television. 3F07, 3F19–The family rushes in and sits on the couch. Homer gets up to remove a plug cover from the floor. When he does, everyone and everything is sucked down. 3F10–The family rushes in and sits down on the couch. The camera moves to the right and zooms in on a mouse hole. Inside, a mouse family of five resembling the Simpsons rushes in to sit on a couch of their own. 3F09, 3F20–The family's heads are all mounted on the wall as trophies, except for Homer, who is a rug. A hunter walks in, sits on the couch, puts down his rifle, and lights his pipe. 3F11, 3F21–The family rushes in. Everything in the room has a neon tint to it, as though lit by a blacklight. Homer turns the light on, and the color returns to normal. 4F02–The Grim Reaper is sitting on the couch. As the family members rush in, each one keels over dead. The Reaper puts his feet up on Homer's corpse. 3F23, 3F24–The family parachutes down to the couch. Homer's chute does not open and he falls flat on the floor. 4F03, 4F15–The living room is a western plain. The family rushes in, dressed in western gear, and sits. The couch bucks off into the sunset like a horse. 4F05, 4F09–The family floats into the room as blue soap bubbles. They pop when they hit the couch. 4F06, 4F12–The family rushes in. They pose like the Beatles on the album cover of "Sgt. Pepper's Lonely Hearts Club Band." Homer is Paul. All of Springfield is in the living room. Among the characters in the background are older versions of the Simpsons, harkening back to their early days on "The Tracey Ullman Show." In the foreground are the head of the Jebediah Springfield statue, Blinky, a bottle of "Simpson & Son's Patented Revitalizing Tonic," a Happy Little Elf doll, a bowling ball, a Buddha statue that resembles Homer, several cans of Duff, various food products, and donuts that spell out "Simpsons." 4F04, 4F19–The family rushes in. Bart's image phases in and out like images on a broken

TV screen. Homer adjusts him by fiddling with the control knobs on the TV and smacking Bart on the back of the head until he "comes in." 4F01, 4F14, 4F21–The living room is upside down. The family rushes in, sits on the couch, and falls to the ceiling. 4F07, 4F18–The family rushes in. A "Vend-a-Couch" vending machine is in the wall. Homer deposits a coin, but nothing happens. He bangs the wall until a couch falls on him. 3G01–Homer, Marge, Lisa, and Bart fly into the room wearing rocket packs and land on the couch. Maggie zooms in, flying in loops, and plops down on Marge's lap. 4F08, 4F17–The living room is a Whack-a-Mole board. Carnival music plays as the Simpsons' heads pop out of different holes and are hit back in with a giant mallet. 4F10, 4F16–The family rushes in. The couch is folded out and Grampa is sleeping on it. They fold Grampa up in the couch and sit down. 3G03–The couch does not run in. The couch is empty. At the front door, Homer struggles with the lock and pounds on the door, his frustrated family behind him. 4F11–A computer screen is in view. One side of the screen shows a logo for "America Onlink." Two boxes are respectively labelled, "Load Family" and "Exit." On the other side of the screen is a graphic of the Simpsons' living room, covered by a message box and progress bar stating, "Adding artwork, please wait. . . . Receiving item 1 of 5." As the progress bar slowly advances, the "Exit" box is repeatedly clicked. 4F13–The TV and couch move back and forth on a rocky ship at sea. The family rushes in, wearing yellow ship gear and hats. They plop onto the swaying couch. A wave washes over them and deposits them in the sea. A TV bobs out of the water.

DOLPH AND KEARNEY

Positions:
Bullies; colleagues/lieutenants of Jimbo Jones.

Job:
Kamp Krusty counselors.

Where seen:
Shoplifting at the Leftorium, or more frequently, the Kwik-E-Mart.

Unexpected traits:
Hold a high regard for town founder, Jebediah Springfield.

Brazen acts:
They've beat up Bart on his own property.

Homer makes a deal with Bart. If Bart gets a "C" average on his report card, he can go to Kamp Krusty for the summer. If he does not, he stays home. When final grades are handed out, Bart receives straight D's. He forges them into A-pluses and shows Homer his report card. Homer knows Bart has doctored the grades but wants a Bart-free summer and lets him go to Kamp Krusty anyway.

Lisa, Bart, and friends arrive at the camp, which is run by a tyrant named Mr. Black and his squad of thugs, Dolph, Jimbo, and Kearney. Expecting fun, the kids instead are subjected to grueling exercises, squalid living conditions, and bad food. While their kids are suffering, Homer and Marge are living it up. Homer even grows hair and loses weight.

When Mr. Black tries unsuccessfully to pass off a look-alike Krusty to the kids, Bart leads a revolt. Krusty finds out how his camp is being run and immediately flies in from Wimbledon to apologize. Loading the kids onto a bus, he takes them to the happiest place on earth–Tijuana.

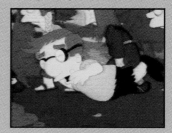

SHOW HIGHLIGHTS

"If you really want something in this life you have to work for it. Now quiet, they're about to announce the lottery numbers."

"Have a 'D'-lightful summer." Mrs. Krabappel, unmoved by Bart's appeal to have his grades changed so he can go to Kamp Krusty.

"Kamp Krusty is built on an actual Indian burial ground. We've got archery, wallet making, the whole megillah. And for you fat kids, my exclusive program of diet and ridicule will really get results!"

The Krusty brand seal of approval: It goes on clocks that get incredibly hot if left plugged in, short-circuiting electric toothbrushes and handguns.

Inside Bart and Lisa's Dingy Cabin:
Lisa: This is a little more rustic than I expected.
Bart: I'm not worried, Lis. You know why? Because of this...(Bart reveals a Krusty sticker) The Krusty brand seal of approval. You can only find it on products which meet the high personal standards of Krusty the Clown.

THIS PUNISHMENT IS NOT BORING AND POINTLESS
THIS PUNISHMENT IS NOT BORING AND POINTLESS
THIS PUNISHMENT IS NOT BORING AND POINTLESS
THIS PUNISHMENT IS NOT BORING AND POINTLESS

Lisa's letter home: "Dear Mom and Dad, I no longer fear Hell, because I've been to Kamp Krusty. Our nature hikes have become grim death marches. Our arts and crafts center is, in actuality, a Dickensian workhouse. Bart makes it through the days relying on his unwavering belief that Krusty the Clown will come through. But I am far more pessimistic. I am not sure if this letter will reach you as our lines of communication have been cut. Now, the effort of writing has made me lightheaded. So I close by saying, SAVE US! SAVE US NOW!"

"I've been scorched by Krusty before. I got a rapid heartbeat from his Krusty brand vitamins, my Krusty Kalculator didn't have a seven or an eight, and Krusty's autobiography was self-serving with many glaring omissions. But this time, he's gone too far!"

The Horrors of Kamp Krusty:
(Bart roasts something dark in front of a campfire.)
Bart: Don't we get to roast marshmallows?
Dolph: Shut up and eat your pine cone.

(Lisa stands at the edge of a dock, before a rickety canoe on a raging river.)
Lisa: Are you sure that's safe?
Kearney: Well, it ain't getting any safer!

(A hair-netted Dolph serves Lisa a bowl of gray slop.)
Lisa: You're serving us gruel?
Dolph: Not quite. This is "Krusty Brand Imitation Gruel." Nine out of ten orphans can't tell the difference.

Bart: If I don't get a C average, my dad won't let me go to Kamp Krusty.
Mrs. Krabappel: Well, it isn't fair to the other children, but, all right.
Bart: Much obliged, doll. (he pats her on the butt)
Mrs. Krabappel: Oh Bart Simpson, I'm gonna miss you.
Principal Skinner: (P.A.) Attention, everyone. This is Principal Skinner. I trust all you remembered to bring in your implements of destruction. Now let's trash this dump! (Alice Cooper's "School's Out" blares as the students and faculty of Springfield Elementary destroy the school. Bart mans a wrecking ball and bashes the school when he wakes up. It was a dream.)

Movie Moments:
Lisa bribes a stranger on horseback with a bottle of booze to smuggle out her letter home à la Meryl Streep in *The French Lieutenant's Woman*. The post-overthrow Kamp Krusty is similar to Kurtz's camp in *Apocalypse Now*.

THE STUFF YOU MAY HAVE MISSED

The bus pulls past a large totem pole of Indian faces. The sign reads: "Kamp Krusty – The Krustiest Place on Earth."

There is a "Give a hoot. Wash up." poster in Lisa's classroom.

Kids throw trash from their lockers on the floor, despite a sign that says, "Please use trash cans."

A kid streaks up the aisle of the bus (who looks strikingly similar to the kid who streaked through the "Ah Fudge" factory in 8F03, "Bart the Murderer.")

The horse in Krusty's TV ad is a show horse with a braided mane.

> HEY, SIMPSON. TELL YOUR MOTHER HER COOKIES SUCKED.

A STREETCAR NAMED MARGE

Episode 8F18 Original Airdate: 10/1/92 Writer: Jeff Martin Director: Rich Moore

arge tries out for a part in a musical version of "A Streetcar Named Desire" at the Springfield Community Center. At the audition, Ned Flanders is cast in the role of Stanley Kowalski, the slovenly and uncouth husband of Stella. The show's director, Llewellyn Sinclair, cannot find anyone fragile yet fiery enough for the role of Blanche DuBois, until he hears Marge talking to Homer on the phone. Sinclair gives her the role. When Maggie becomes a distraction during rehearsals, Marge places her in a daycare center, the Ayn Rand School for Tots, run by Sinclair's sister.

Marge rehearses her lines but cannot find the right fire for the role. She seeks support from Homer, but he is indifferent to her. Seething over Homer's insensitivity, Marge reads her lines with new determination at rehearsals. Her sudden anger gives her the rage she needs to play Blanche.

Meanwhile, at the daycare center, Maggie leads a revolt to recover the tots' pacifiers, which have been taken away from them. Homer, Bart, and Lisa pick up Maggie and go to see Marge's performance. Homer is very affected by the play. Afterwards, he goes backstage to tell Marge that she was terrific and admits that he sees himself in Stanley. He hugs his wife, showing his support.

SHOW HIGHLIGHTS

"Live, from beautiful Laughlin, Nevada: It's the Miss American Girl Pageant! Brought to you by Meryl Streep's 'Versatility.' Smell Like Streep...for Cheap!"

"There's the ol' face shredder." Ned, showing Marge how to break a bottle for the play.

"Do you know what a baby is saying when she reaches for a bottle? She's saying, 'I am a leech.' Our aim here is to develop the bottle within." Ms. Sinclair, telling Marge the Ayn Rand School for Tots philosophy.

"I just don't see why Blanche should shove a broken bottle in Stanley's face. Couldn't she just take his abuse with gentle good humor?"

Lyrics from "Oh! Streetcar!":

Introduction
Long before the Superdome
Where the Saints of football play...
Lived a city that the damned call home
Hear their hellish rondelet ...

New Orleans!
Home of pirates, drunks, and whores
New Orleans!
Tacky, overpriced souvenir stores

If you want to go to hell, you should take a trip
To the Sodom and Gomorrah of the Mississip'.

New Orleans!
Stinking, rotten, vomiting, vile
New Orleans!
Putrid, brackish, maggotty, foul

New Orleans!
Crummy, lousy, rancid and rank
New Orleans!

The Cast of "Oh! Streetcar!":

Blanche: Marge
Stanley: Ned
Stella: Helen Lovejoy
Steve, the Paperboy: Apu
Pablo: Otto*
Mitch: Lionel Hutz**
Chorus: Chief Wiggum, Jasper, Herman

*Later replaced by Llewellyn Sinclair.
**Also filing class action suit on behalf of those who did not get picked to be in play.

MY NAME IS NOT DR. DEATH
MY NAME IS NOT DR. DEATH
MY NAME IS NOT DR. DEATH
MY NAME IS NOT DR. DEATH
MY NAME IS NOT DR. DEATH
MY NAME IS NOT DR. DEATH

Marge: *I play an aging southern beauty who's driven to insanity by her brutish brother-in-law Stanley.*
Lisa: *Wow! My mother the actress. I feel like Lucie Arnaz-Luckinbill.*

Homer: *...I don't care, okay? I can't fake an interest in this and I'm an expert at faking an interest in your kooky projects.*
Marge (getting angry): *What kooky projects?*
Homer: *You know, the painting class, the First Aid course, that whole Lamaze thing.*
Marge: *Why didn't you tell me you felt this way?*
Homer: *You know I would never do anything to hurt your feelings.*

Movie Moment:
When the tab breaks off his pudding can, Homer stands outside in the yard and screams "Marge!" as Marlon Brando did in *A Streetcar Named Desire*.

Movie Moment II:
Maggie and the other children plot to get their pacifiers back in two scenes borrowed from *The Great Escape*.

Movie Moment III:
Homer picks up Maggie from childcare the night the show opens. The other toddlers are gathered around. The only sound is the echo of them sucking on their pacifiers. Homer moves through the children like Rod Taylor in *The Birds*.

Introducing the judges:
Troy McClure: *...and Mr. Bozwell, the man behind those infamous "Worst-Dressed Lists." Mr. Bozwell, can you give us a sneak peek at this year's list?*
Mr. Bozwell: *Memo to Goldie Hawn: Cheerleading tryouts were thirty years ago. Let's grow up, shall we?*
Bart (chuckling): *He's such a bitch.*

THE STUFF YOU MAY HAVE MISSED

Apu takes off his shirt to audition for Stanley, revealing his scars from his bullet wounds.

Ms. Sinclair reads *The Fountainhead Diet* when Maggie embarks on liberates the pacifiers.

Alfred Hitchcock walks by the childcare center when Homer picks up Maggie.

According to the marquee, "Oh! Streetcar! is a one-night-only performance."

Occupation:
Enfant terrible-type director of various Springfield theatrical productions.

Theatrical experience:
Three stage successes; three heart attacks (is planning on a fourth).

Greatest triumph:
"Hats off to Chanukah."

Favorite comforts:
Bed and bottle of Amaretto.

Temper:
Irritable to tempestuous.

Annoyed by:
Theatrical incompetence; Maggie; Homer.

Style:
Caftans for the portly man.

MRS. SIMPSON, IF YOU SET OUT TO PUSH THE BILE TO THE TIP OF MY THROAT; MISSION ACCOMPLISHED.

Guest Voice:
Jon Lovitz as Llewellyn Sinclair.

HOMER THE HERETIC

Episode 9F01 Original Airdate: 10/8/92 Writer: George Meyer Director: Jim Reardon

Favorite clothing:
A flowing robe and comfortable sandals.

Dislikes:
Reverend Lovejoy.

Quirks:
Uses roof instead of front door to enter a home.

Homer's description:
Perfect teeth; nice smell; a class act all the way.

Expertise:
Religion; the meaning of life.

> NOW, IF YOU'LL EXCUSE ME, I HAVE TO APPEAR ON A TORTILLA IN MEXICO.

Homer stays home while Marge and the kids go to church. He takes advantage of his freedom by running around in his underwear, making his favorite waffles, and watching television. Homer has such a wonderful time, he decides to stay home every Sunday morning.

Homer tells Marge he is giving up church and will instead practice his own religion. Marge is distressed, but that night, Homer dreams that God sanctions his new faith. The following Sunday, Homer stays home, pulls out his old *Playdude* magazines, and lights a cigar. He falls asleep, and the cigar sets the house ablaze.

Homer is trapped in the flames, but Flanders braves the intense heat and drags him to safety. Volunteer firemen Krusty, Apu, and Reverend Lovejoy pitch in to save what they can. Reverend Lovejoy assures Homer that God is not against him, but rather is in the hearts of those who saved his life and home. Homer denounces his new religion and the following Sunday attends church, where he falls fast asleep.

SHOW HIGHLIGHTS

Homer the chef: Having the house to himself, Homer raids the fridge, saying, "The perfect chance to make my patented, space age, out-of-this-world Moon Waffles! Let's see here: caramels...waffle batter...liquid smoke..." He pours the concoction onto the waffle iron, cleaning the side with his finger. "Oooh...waffle run-off," he says, tasting the raw waffle. He opens the waffle iron, peels off his creation, wraps it around a stick of butter, and takes a bite. "Mmm...fattening," he concludes.

(After dancing in his underwear. making waffles, winning a radio contest, and watching football, Homer finds a penny.)
Homer: Could this be the best day of my life?
(A thought balloon above Homer's head reveals memories of Homer marrying Marge and Homer gleefully running around a spraying, crashed beer truck in a swimsuit.)

Marge: I can't believe you're giving up church, Homer.
Homer: Hey, what's the big deal about going to some building every Sunday? I mean, isn't God everywhere?
Bart: Amen, brother.

Movie Moments:
While saving Homer, the floor burns out beneath Flanders's feet à la a rescue scene in *Backdraft*.
Homer dances in his underwear like Tom Cruise in *Risky Business*.

"The uh, Feast of...Maximum Occupancy." Homer, making up a holiday while looking at the sign behind the bar at Moe's.

 "No offense Apu, but when they were handing out religions, you musta been out taking a whizz."

"Sorry, this policy only covers actual losses, not made-up stuff." Insurance agent, to Homer, who claims he lost a Picasso and a collection of classic cars in the fire.

Marge: Don't make me choose between my man and my God, because you just can't win.
Homer: There you go again. Always taking someone else's side. Flanders...the water department... God...

Homer Talks to God:
Homer: I'm not a bad guy. I work hard and I love my kids. So why should I spend half my Sunday hearing about how I'm going to hell?
God: Hmm, you've got a point there. You know, sometimes even I'd rather be watching football. Does St. Louis still have a team?
Homer: No. They moved to Phoenix.

Homer: Apu, I see you're not in church.
Apu: Oh, but I am. I have a shrine to Ganesha, the god of worldly wisdom, located in the employee lounge.
Homer: Hey, Ganesha, want a peanut?
Apu: Please do not offer my god a peanut.

Bart: Hey, where's Homer?
Marge: Your father is...resting.
Bart: "Resting" hung over? "Resting" got fired? Help me out here.

THE STUFF YOU MAY HAVE MISSED

Despite the fact that it is freezing cold outside, none of the church-going Simpsons bundle up to go out.

In Homer's first dream sequence, God has four fingers and a thumb—in Homer's dream just before the end of the episode, God only has three.

Homer drools while dreaming about God.

The sermon title on the church marquee is: "When Homer Met Satan."

According to Homer's flashback, he was born feet first.

Milhouse's mom is with the Springfield Volunteer Fire Department.

Krusty: Hello, I'm collecting for the Brotherhood of Jewish Clowns. Last year, tornadoes claimed the lives of 75 Jewish clowns. The worst incident was during our convention at Lubbock, Texas. There were floppy shoes and rainbow wigs everywhere! (sobbing) It was terrible!
Homer: Wait a minute! Is this a religous thing?
Krusty: A religous clown thing, yes.
Homer: Sorry.
Krusty: Well, bless you anyw—
(Homer slams the door in his face.)

I WILL NOT DEFAME NEW ORLEANS
I WILL NOT DEFAME NEW ORLEANS
I WILL NOT DEFAME NEW ORLEANS*

*A number of people in New Orleans were upset by the song about their city in the episode "A Streetcar Named Marge."

LISA THE BEAUTY QUEEN

Episode 9F02 Original Airdate: 10/15/92 Writer: Jeff Martin Director: Mark Kirkland Guest Voice: Bob Hope as Himself

An artist at the school carnival draws a cartoon caricature of Lisa. When she sees it, Lisa is appalled with her appearance and develops an inferiority complex. Meanwhile, Homer wins a ride on the Duff Blimp. Noticing that Lisa is insecure about how she looks, he enters her in the Little Miss Springfield Pageant, selling his blimp ticket to come up with the $250 entry fee.

Lisa refuses to participate in the pageant. When Marge tells her that Homer sold his blimp ticket because he loves her, she finally agrees. Marge takes Lisa for a complete beauty makeover to help boost her confidence. The judges crown professional pageant participant Amber Dempsey as Little Miss Springfield, voting Lisa runner-up.

When Amber is struck by lightning, Lisa takes over the title and becomes spokesperson for Laramie Cigarettes. While riding the Laramie float in the Springfield parade, Lisa announces that smoking cigarettes is evil. Pageant officials strip Lisa of her crown. Relieved, Lisa thanks Homer for helping her to see her true beauty.

SHOW HIGHLIGHTS

Monte turns: Bart sets up an illegal three-card monte game at the carnival and, after Skinner busts him, disappears in a cloud of smoke.

 "Get yer haggis, right here! Chopped heart and lungs, boiled in a wee sheep's stomach! Tastes as good as it sounds. Good for what ails ya!"

"I heartily endorse this event or product." Krusty, giving his pre-filmed support to the Little Miss Springfield Pageant.

Pageant versatility: In the same week she was "Pork Princess," Amber Dempsey was crowned "Little Miss Kosher."

 "And later, I'll teach you the tricks of the trade: taping your swimsuit to your butt, putting petroleum jelly on your teeth for that frictionless smile, and the ancient art of padding."

"When it comes to compliments, women are ravenous, bloodsucking monsters, always wanting more, more, more! And if you give it to 'em, you'll get back plenty in return."

> (A lawyer and a pair of goons confront Principal Skinner at the school carnival, just below a banner for the event with the slogan, "The Happiest Place on Earth.")
> **Lawyer:** Principal Skinner, "The Happiest Place on Earth" is a registered Disneyland copyright.
> **Skinner:** Well, gentlemen, it's just a small school carnival.
> **Lawyer:** And it's heading for a great big lawsuit. You made a big mistake, Skinner.
> **Skinner:** Well, so did you. You got an ex-Green Beret mad.
> (Skinner sends a darting blow to the trachea of one of the goons and kicks the lawyer in the chest. One of the goons runs off, but Skinner takes the lawyer's briefcase and throws it at the escaping goon—knocking him out.)
> **Skinner** (à la James Bond): Copyright expired.

Krusty, singing at the end of the pageant: "'L' is for the losers in her wake/'I' is for the income she will make/'T' is for her tooth-filled mouth/'T' is for her tooth-filled mouth..."

Bob Hope, performing at Fort Springfield: "Hello, this is Bob 'What the hell am I doing in Springfield' Hope. Hey, how about that Mayor Quimby? He's some golfer! His golf balls spend more time under water than Greg Louganis."

"Oh, Lisa, this isn't real. It's just how you might look if you were a cartoon character." Homer, consoling Lisa about her ugly caricature.

> **Homer:** You're as cute as a bug's ear.
> **Lisa:** Fathers have to say that stuff.
> (Grampa walks by)
> **Homer:** Dad, am I cute as a bug's ear?
> **Grampa:** No! You're as homely as a mule's butt!
> **Homer:** (to Lisa) There, see?

> **Homer Tries the "Guess Your Age and Weight" Booth.**
> **Booth Man:** I'd say 53 years old and 420 pounds.
> **Homer:** Ha ha, you lose! 36 and 239!

> **The Commercial for the Little Miss Springfield Pageant:**
> **Jack Larson:** Your daughter could be crowned Little Miss Springfield by our host, the Maitre d' of Glee, Krusty the Clown!
> **TV daughter:** What a feeling! I'm as happy as a smoker taking that first puff in the morning.

THE STUFF YOU MAY HAVE MISSED

The carnival rocket car that broke off from the ride Otto was operating remains wedged into the side of the school everytime we see Springfield Elementary during the course of the episode.

At the Springfield Elementary School carnival, there are signs advertising "Haggis/50 Cents," "Jimbo's Spookhouse," "Caricatures $3," "The Paralyzer," and "The Happiest Place on Earth" (for the carnival itself).

In the ad for the Little Miss Springfield Pageant, the little girl the man is tossing up into the air gets lifted one time—and never comes down.

When Lisa is getting her makeover, her rejected hairstyles include a Princess Leia bun 'do, a Grace Jones-style 'do and a Bo Derek cornrow 'do, as well as a Marge Simpson beehive 'do.

> **Homer:** Moe, have you ever felt unattractive?
> **Moe:** Mmmm...no.

AMBER DEMPSEY

Vocation:
Professional Junior Miss beauty pageant participant; considered the Jack Nicklaus of the pageant circuit.

Appearance:
Curly blonde hair; fluttery eyelashes; glittery smile.

Threads of choice:
Sequined sailor suit; fur coat.

Estimated cost of dimples:
$5,000 apiece.

Secret shame:
Her eyelashes are implants.

HI, I'M AMBER DEMPSEY, AND WHEN I GROW UP, I WANT TO BE A SWEETIE PIE!

Guest Voice:
Lona Williams
as Amber Dempsey

"Good eeevening. I've been asked to tell you that the following show is very scary, with stuff that might give your kids nightmares. You see, there are some crybabies out there—religious types mostly—who might be offended. If you are one of them, I advise you to turn off your set now. C'mon, I dare you. Bock-bock-bock-bock-bock! Chicken!"

THE OPENING SEQUENCE

Headstones in Springfield Cemetery read, "Drexel's Class," "I'm with Stupid," "R. Buckminster Fuller," "Slapstick," and "American Workmanship." The "American Workmanship" headstone crumbles right after it is shown.

THE SET-UP

The Simpsons gather to tell scary stories during a Halloween party.

CLOWN WITHOUT PITY

Lisa's story begins as Homer buys Bart a Krusty the Clown doll for his birthday. When Bart pulls Krusty's string, the doll smiles and says, "I'm Krusty the Clown and I love you very much." But when Homer is alone with the doll, it speaks by itself and threatens to kill him. Terrified, Homer begs the family to keep the doll away from him. The family thinks that Homer is imagining things until Marge finds the doll clutching Homer's head and dunking him into the dog's water dish. A Krusty doll repairman finds a "Good/Evil" switch on the back and moves it to "Good." Relieved, Homer makes the doll his personal servant.

STORY HIGHLIGHTS

Krusty doll: *I'm Krusty the Clown and I'm going to kill you!*
Homer: *Hee, hee, hee! Didn't even pull the string that time.*
Krusty doll: *I said, I'm going to kill you! You, Homer Simpson!*

Kent Brockman: *And in environmental news, scientists have announced that Springfield's air is now only dangerous to children and the elderly.*
Homer: *Woo-hoo!*

(The shopkeeper hands Homer a Krusty doll.)
Shopkeeper: *Take this object, but beware, it carries a terrible curse!*
Homer: *Ooooh, that's bad.*
Shopkeeper: *But it comes with a free frogurt!*
Homer: *That's good.*
Shopkeeper: *The frogurt is also cursed.*
Homer: *That's bad.*
Shopkeeper: *But you get your choice of topping.*
Homer: *That's good*
Shopkeeper: *The toppings contain potassium benzoate.*
(Homer stares at the shopkeeper, not comprehending what this means.)
Shopkeeper: *That's bad.*

"The doll's trying to kill me and the toaster's been laughing at me." Homer, to Marge, as he fumbles into the kitchen, the Krusty doll grabbing at his head.

THE STUFF YOU MAY HAVE MISSED

The monkey's paw from 8F02, "Treehouse of Horror II" is on the counter at the House of Evil.

The phone number for the Krusty Doll Hotline is 1-900-DON'T-SUE.

A sign on the counter at the House of Evil reads "20% Rayon, 80% Shrunken Head."

Classic TV Moment:
A Krusty doll that is good to its child owner but evil to its father parodies the classic episode, "Living Doll," from "The Twilight Zone" ("My name is Talking Tina and I love you very much"), starring Telly Savalas.

House of Evil – "Your One-Stop Evil Shop": Where Homer shops for Bart's birthday present.

"We sell forbidden objects from places men fear to tread. We also sell frozen yogurt, which I call frogurt!" The House of Evil shopkeeper, to Homer.

"There goes the last lingering thread of my heterosexuality." Patty, when Homer runs by naked.

"Yep, here's your problem. Someone set this thing to 'Evil.'" The Krusty doll repairman, solving the Simpsons' homicidal doll problem.

HORROR III

Episode 9F04 Original Airdate: 10/29/92
Writers: Atrocious Al Jean, Morbid Mike Reiss, Johnny Katastrophe Kogen, Warped Wallace
Wolodarsky, Scarifying Sam Simon, Vicious Jack Vitti
Director: Bloodcurdling Carlos Baeza

KING HOMER

Grampa weaves a tale set in the 1930s that begins with Mr. Burns and Smithers setting off on an expedition to capture the monster ape, King Homer. They take Marge along as bait. Arriving at Ape Island, Smithers knocks out the giant ape with laughing gas and returns with him to Manhattan to star in a freak show on Broadway. King Homer breaks free from his chains and scales the Empire State Building. Out of breath at the second story, he falls from the building and crashes to the pavement below. Marge takes pity on him and marries him.

THE STUFF YOU MAY HAVE MISSED

The Nov. 19, 1938 edition of the *Springfield Shopper* reports that Marge has wed an ape. The headline reads, "Woman Weds Ape," with the subheadline, "Dick Cavett Born." The article includes a picture of the adult Dick Cavett—even though he was just born. As it spins into view, the article is titled "Woody Allen Born" and is accompanied by a picture of Woody Allen that is replaced by Cavett's photo for the final spin.

The island chief's shout—"Mosi Tatupu! Mosi Tatupu!"—is translated as, "The blue-haired woman will make a good sacrifice." In reality, Samoan native Mosi Tatupu was a runningback for USC in the 1970s and later went on to a career in the NFL with the New England Patriots.

STORY HIGHLIGHTS

"Smithers, this is a golden opportunity. If we get him alive, we can put him on Broadway. Dead, and we can sell monkey stew to the army!"

"You know, you look a little flushed. Maybe you should eat more vegetables and less people."

Before the Ship Sails:

(Marge asks to join the expedition.)
Burns: *What do you think, Smithers?*
Smithers: *I think women and seamen don't mix.*
Burns: *We know what you think.*

Captain Otto: *Hey, who's this Homer dude?*
Burns: *He's either a fifty-foot prehistoric ape or a tourist trap concocted by the Ape Island Jaycees. Either way, we're going ashore.*

C. Montgomery Burns, Showman:

Dave Shutton: *What kind of show you got for us, Mr. Burns?*
Burns: *Well the ape's going to stand around for three hours or so. Then we'll close with the ethnic comedy of Doogan and Dershowitz.*
Dave Shutton: *Sensational!*

Movie Moment:

This entire segment is a parody of the original *King Kong*.

DIAL "Z" FOR ZOMBIE

Bart tells a tale of the damned: Bart finds a book in the library that explains how to bring the dead back to life. He tries to bring Lisa's dead cat, Snowball I, back to life, but instead revives every person who has been dead for the past several hundred years. The zombies rise from their graves, seeking out living human brains. They rampage through Springfield, sucking out brains. Finally, they come looking for the Simpsons. Homer offers up himself to spare the family, but the zombies determine that he is brainless. Finally, Bart unearths a spell that sends the zombies back to their graves.

STORY HIGHLIGHTS

"Please, Lis, they prefer to be called the living-impaired." Bart, about the zombies.

"Take that, Washington! Eat lead, Einstein! Show's over, Shakespeare!" Homer, blasting and bashing historical zombies.

Movie Moment:

This story, about zombies who emerge from the grave to devour human flesh and organs, parodies George Romero's horror classic, *Night of the Living Dead*.

Bart: *From A-Apple to Z-Zebra, Baby's First Pop-Up Book is twenty-six pages of alphabetical adventure.*
Mrs. Krabappel: *Bart, you mean to tell me you read a book intended for preschoolers?*
Bart: *Well, most of it.*

Bart: *Dad, you killed the Zombie Flanders!*
Homer: *He was a zombie?*

THE STUFF YOU MAY HAVE MISSED

The gravestones at the pet cemetery include: a dog's grave with a headstone shaped like a bone, a hamster statue in a wire wheel, a picture of a lobster that says "Eaten by Mistake," and tombstones for the short-lived animal-oriented prime-time cartoon series "Fish Police," "Capitol Critters," and "Family Dog."

At the cemetery, Bart wears the album cover for Michael Jackson's "Thriller" on his head while he brings the zombies to life. The video for "Thriller" features zombies rising from their graves.

A zombie pops out of a grave with the headstone "Jay Kogan." Jay Kogen is a writer/producer for "The Simpsons."

To release the zombies, Bart chants "Cullen, Rayburn, Narz, Trebek!" representing four game-show hosts, and "Zabar, Kresge, Caldor, Walmart!" which are all stores.

Turning Lisa into a snail, Bart chants "Kolchak, Mannix, Banacek, Dano!" (all 1970s TV investigators), while his zombie spell-reversing chant, "Trojan, Ramses, Magnum, Sheik!" represents a quartet of condoms.

Born:
1928.

Died:
Endlessly.

Appearance:
Black & white.

First cartoon:
"That Happy Cat," featuring only Scratchy; performed poorly.

First teaming of Itchy with Scratchy:
"Steamboat Itchy."

First weapon of menace:
A tommy gun that Itchy uses to repeatedly shoot Scratchy in the knees.

Second weapon of menace:
A furnace into which Itchy leads Scratchy, closing the door before his body twitches and goes limp.

AHHHHHHHHHH!!!!!!

OH ME, OH MY.

During parent/teacher night at school, Marge is told that Bart needs serious discipline at home if he is ever become a respectable adult. Marge and Homer agree that they must be tougher on Bart. The next time Bart misbehaves, Marge sends him to his room without dinner. A starving Bart is just about to promise that he will change his ways when Homer sneaks in with a pizza, undermining Marge's disciplinary actions.

Marge and Homer leave Bart in charge of Maggie, who crawls out of the house into the family car and drives away, eventually crashing into Springfield's state penitentiary. This time, Homer issues a punishment: Bart can never see the new Itchy & Scratchy movie.

Bart is devastated that he is the only kid in Springfield who does not see the movie. Months later, he concedes victory to Homer, but Homer tells him that they have both won. Looking into the future, Homer finally takes his son—now Chief Justice of the Supreme Court—to see the Itchy & Scratchy movie.

SHOW HIGHLIGHTS

"Captain's Log Stardate 6051: had trouble sleeping last night...my hiatal hernia is acting up. The ship is drafty and damp; I complain but nobody listens." An aged Captain Kirk, in *Star Trek XII: So Very Tired.*

"Bart has been guilty of the following atrocities: synthesizing a laxative from peas and carrots, replacing my birth control pills with Tic-Tacs..."

"I will try to raise a better child." The sentence Mrs. Krabappel forces Marge to write over and over again on the blackboard.

Blood and more blood: A billboard advertising the I&S movie shows Itchy slamming a movie camera into the back of Scratchy's neck, causing his head to fall off and blood to spurt everywhere. The blood lands on a couple of newlyweds in a convertible. They look up, horrified, until they see the blood is from the billboard and laugh.

"But first, let's take a look back at the year 1928. A year when you might have seen Al Capone dancing the Charleston on top of a flagpole. It was also the year of the very first Scratchy cartoon, entitled, "That Happy Cat." The film did very poorly, but the following year, Scratchy was teamed up with a psychotic young mouse named Itchy and cartoon history was made."

How Itchy abuses Scratchy during the beginning of the trailer for *The Itchy & Scratchy Movie*: Poking his eyes, shaving his scalp in the center, scribbling on his face with a Magic Marker, firing a flame thrower into one ear and out the other, making two-finger bunny ears behind his head, blowing off the top of his skull with a cannon, and jumping into his skull and ripping out handfuls of brain.

"Chief Justice of the Supreme Court. What great men he would join: John Marshall, Charles Evans Hughes, Warren Berger... mmm...burger."

Bart: How was it?
Lisa: It wasn't that great.
Bart: Be honest.
Lisa: It was the greatest movie I've ever seen in my life! And you wouldn't believe the celebrities who did cameos. Dustin Hoffman, Michael Jackson... of course they didn't use their real names, but you could tell it was them.

THE STUFF YOU MAY HAVE MISSED

Among those waiting in line for *The Itchy & Scratchy Movie* are Milhouse, Martin, Ned and Rod Flanders, Otto in a sleeping bag, Abe and Jasper playing checkers, and Wendell.

The sign on an ice cream truck reads: "Native American Ice Cream (Formerly Big Chief Crazy Cone)."

Mr. T is on the cover of the issue of *TV Guide* that Homer reads to baby Lisa.

Forty years into the future, the "Do Not Sell to This Boy" picture of Bart in the Aztec Theater box office is still in place.

In the future, the Aztec Theater sells "Soylent Green."

Classic Cartoon Moment:
The first Itchy & Scratchy short, "Steamboat Itchy," parodies the first Mickey Mouse cartoon, "Steamboat Willie."

Marge: Do you want your son to become Chief Justice of the Supreme Court, or a sleazy male stripper?
Homer: Can't he be both, like the late Earl Warren?
Marge: Earl Warren wasn't a stripper!
Homer: Now, who's being naive?

Homer: If you don't start making more sense we're going to have to put you in a home.
Grampa: You already put me in a home.
Homer: Then we'll put you in the crooked home we saw on "60 Minutes."
Grampa: (small voice) I'll be good.

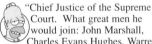

I WILL NOT BURY THE NEW KID

MARGE GETS A JOB

Episode 9F05   Original Airdate: 11/5/92   Writers: Bill Oakley & Josh Weinstein   Director: Jeff Lynch   Guest Voice: Tom Jones as Himself

SURLY JOE

Homer learns that his house, which has slid off its foundation, will cost $8,500 to repair. Marge applies for a job at the nuclear power plant so that the family will have enough money to fix it.

Marge embellishes her homemaker resume to include knowledge of Swahili. Impressed, Smithers hires her on the spot. Meanwhile, at school, Bart fakes being sick to get out of class. Grampa, who is watching the kids for Marge, reminds him of the story about the boy who cried wolf. Having never read the story, Bart is not too concerned.

At the plant, Mr. Burns is smitten by Marge and orders Smithers to arrange a romantic dinner for just the two of them. To help Mr. Burns ensure an unforgettable night, Smithers kidnaps Tom Jones for the evening's entertainment. When a wolf escapes from "The Krusty the Clown Show" and wanders into school, Bart cries "Wolf!" but Mrs. Krabappel ignores him. Meanwhile, Burns discovers that Marge is married and he fires her. Homer steps in to defend Marge. Impressed, Burns invites Homer and Marge to enjoy a romantic dinner at his mansion, where Tom Jones, still in shackles, performs.

> I WILL NOT TEACH OTHERS
> TO FLY.
> I WILL NOT TEACH OTHERS
> TO FLY.
> I WILL NOT TEACH OTHERS
> TO FLY.

SHOW HIGHLIGHTS

 "Hello, I'm Troy McClure. You might remember me from such instructional videos as "Mothballing Your Battleship" and "Dig Your Own Grave and Save!""

Musical Tribute to the Retiring Jack Marley:
There is a man/ A certain man/ A man whose grace/ And handsome face/ Are known across the land!/ You know his name/ It's Mister Burns/ He loves a smoke/ Enjoys a joke/ Why, he's worth ten times what he earns/ He's Mister Burns/ I'm Mister Burns/ He's Monty Burns!/ I'm MISTER Burns/ To friends he's known as Monty, but to you it's Mister Burns.

"Thou shalt not horn in on thy husband's... racket." Homer, making up a Bible passage to persuade Marge not to seek Jack Marley's old position at the plant.

Tibor: Non-anglophone on whom Homer pins his screw-ups at the plant.

"Oral thermometer, my eye! Think warm thoughts, boy, 'cause this is mighty cold."

Burns's synonyms for his employees: "Jackanapes... lolligaggers... noodle heads."

Burns's synonym for Marge: "Enchantress."

"I dreamed about her again last night, Smithers. You know that dream where you're in bed and they fly in through the window?" Burns, telling Smithers his fantasy about Marge. Smithers imagines Burns flying through his bedroom window, descending on his bed.

Willie to the rescue: Bart is saved when Willie cries, "Hey, Wolfie, put down that hors d'oeuvre—it's time for the main course!" Willie beats the wolf and soothes it with some Scotch whiskey, saying, "Don't feel bad for losin'. I was wrestling wolves back when you were at your mother's teat."

"I'm used to seeing people promoted ahead of me — friends, co-workers, Tibor. I never thought it'd be my own wife": Homer, to Marge.

Animal handler: Here we have an Alaskan timber wolf. He weighs 240 pounds and his jaws can bite through a parking meter. He does get spooked by loud noises.
Krusty: "Loud?" That's our secret word for the day!
(Sirens blare and a sign with the word "Loud" on it drops down from the ceiling, along with balloons and streamers. The children in the audience scream wildy. The wolf runs off in terror.)
Animal handler: Oh, my God!

Surly Joe: I'm afraid the whole west side of the house is sinking. I figure it's gonna cost you...oh, eighty-five hundred.
Homer: (shocked) Forget it. You're not the only foundation guy in town!
(Homer opens up the Yellow Pages to find one ad for foundation repair: "Surly Joe's Foundation Repair –The Only Foundation Repair Company in Town.")

(Sitting in the kitchen, Marge reads the resume Lisa has prepared for her.)
Marge: Chauffeur, seamstress, curator of large mammals?
(Homer enters, dressed in his underwear.)
Homer: Marge, have you seen my lunchbox?
(Homer grabs the lunchbox, scratches himself, and leaves.)
Marge: Oh, I see.
Lisa: They expect you to lie a little.
Marge: I worked for the Carter administration?
Lisa: Well you voted for him. Twice!
Marge: Shhh...someone might be listening.

(Ned Flanders passes by the window smoking a pipe. He is strangely tilted and his pipe smoke rises at a 45-degree angle.)
Flanders: Hey, howdy-do, neighbor! Good pipe weather; thought I'd fire up the briar.
Homer: Can't talk: busy.
Flanders: Okeley-dokeley-do.
Marge: Did you notice how slanted he looked?
Homer: All part of God's great plan.
Marge: (sliding down the floor) I think one side of our house is sliding.

THE STUFF YOU MAY HAVE MISSED

The famed photo of Burns and Elvis hangs in Smithers' office.

Tom Jones performs at the Copper Slipper in Las Vegas.

Occupation:
Founder and head of Surly Joe's Foundation Repair.

Attitude:
Actually, not that surly.

Smokes:
Cigars.

Surprising behavior:
Gives inexpensive plumbing supplies away for free.

How he can soak Springfielders:
He's the only foundation guy in town.

YOU KNOW, THE PROBLEM HERE WAS WATER LEAKAGE.

LAURA POWERS

Occupation:
Pubescent heartthrob babysitter.

Favorite game:
Messing with Dolph's and Kearney's minds.

Gifts:
Wet Willies; Hertz donuts; wedgies.

Rank (according to army jacket):
Corporal.

Taste in boys:
Rebellious quasi-thugs.

> MY UPBRINGING WAS PAINFULLY STRICT.

Guest Voice:
Sara Gilbert as Laura Powers

SHOW HIGHLIGHTS

"Hey, sometimes a guy just likes his skin to look it's yellowest." Bart, taking a bath before Laura comes over to babysit.

"She fell in with that *Guinness Book of Records* crowd. Suddenly, she didn't have any time for me. Oh, I wore a 15-pound beard of bees for that woman, but it just wasn't enough." Grampa, on his ill-fated romance with the oldest woman in the world.

"I wasn't really gonna kill ya; I was just gonna cut ya. Aah, forget it." Moe, showing mercy on Jimbo Jones.

"I wore my extra-loose pants for nothing. Nothing!" Homer, disappointed that he won't be able to go to the all-you-can-eat at the Frying Dutchman.

Movie Moment:
The courtroom scene in which bailiffs march in with bags and bags of letters addressed to Santa Claus is a parody of the film, *Miracle on 34th Street.*

Marge: *What about the bread? Does that have much fish in it?*
Waiter: *Yes.*
Marge: *Well, I have some Tic Tacs in my purse...*
Waiter: *Excellent choice. And for the gentleman?*
Homer: *All-you-can-eat! All-you-can-eat!*
Waiter: *All right, when you're ready, take this plate over—* (Homer is already at the buffet and carries away a steam tray of shrimp.)

(Homer consults with Lionel Hutz at "I Can't Believe It's a Law Firm!")
Homer: *All you can eat—hah!*
Hutz: *Mr. Simpson, this is the most blatant case of fraudulent advertising since my suit against the film, The Neverending Story.*
Homer: *Do you think I have a case?*
Hutz: *Now, Homer, I don't use the word "hero" very often. But you are the greatest hero in American history.*

"Hello, Moe's Tavern..."

(Moe answers the phone at the bar.)
Moe: *Hey, just a sec, I'll check.*
(to everyone) *Amanda Huggenkiss. Hey, I'm looking for Amanda Huggenkiss! Why can't I find Amanda Huggenkiss?*

Laura: *I'm so happy, I just had to tell someone. I have a boyfriend.*
(The scene blurs into Bart's fantasy. Laura casually reaches into Bart's chest and pulls out Bart's heart.)
Laura: *You won't be needing this!*
(Laura drop kicks Bart's heart into a wastebasket.)

Ruth Powers: *I actually had some doubts about moving to Springfield. Especially after reading Time magazine's cover story, "America's Worst City."*
Marge: *You could see our house in that photo!*

Lionel Hutz: *Mrs. Simpson, what did you and your husband do after you were ejected from the restaurant?*
Marge: *We pretty much went straight home.*
Lionel Hutz: *Mrs. Simpson, you're under oath.*
Marge: *We drove around until 3 a.m. looking for another "All You Can Eat" fish restaurant.*
Hutz: *And when you couldn't find one?*
Marge: *We went fishing.*
(Marge breaks down in tears.)
Hutz: (to jury) *Do these seem like the actions of a man who had, "all he could eat?"*

"Hello, Moe's Tavern..."

Laura: *Hello, I'd like to talk to Ms. Tinkle. First name... Ivana.*
(Moe has the phone to his ear at the bar.)
Moe: *Ivana Tinkle. Just a sec. Ivana Tinkle! Ivana Tinkle! Alright everybody, put down your glasses—Ivana Tinkle!*

THE STUFF YOU MAY HAVE MISSED

The Powers use the Clumsy Student Movers to haul their goods.

Items Marge gives Ruth Powers from the Springfield Welcome Mobile include a potholder from the Potholder Barn, a coupon for a "Free Tattoo with Every Tattoo Removal," and a copy of *Das Butt* (rated XXX).

Laura orders food from "Two Guys from Kabul."

Waiting to use the bathroom, Principal Skinner holds a copy of *Modern Principal.*

Bart tells Moe that the Simpsons' address is 1094 Evergreen Terrace.

I WILL NOT BRING SHEEP TO CLASS
I WILL NOT BRING SHEEP TO CLASS
I WILL NOT BRING SHEEP TO CLASS

Bart falls in love with his and beautiful new neighbor, Laura Powers, who babysits for the Simpsons while Homer and Marge enjoy the "all-you-can-eat" special at the Frying Dutchman. When Homer consumes almost all the food in the restaurant, Captain McCallister throws him out, before he is even finished eating.

Outraged, Homer decides to sue and hires Lionel Hutz to represent him. Meanwhile, Laura shows up at Bart's window wearing a pretty dress. Bart thinks that she has come to profess her love for him, but Laura has only come to tell Bart that she's now dating Jimbo Jones.

Homer's case goes to trial and Laura comes over to babysit. The Captain agrees to an out-of-court settlement, featuring Homer in the front window of his restaurant as "Bottomless Pete— Nature's Cruelest Mistake." Back at the Simpsons' home, Laura invites Jimbo over. To get rid of him permanently, Bart makes a prank phone call to Moe identifying himself as Jimbo and giving Moe the Simpsons' address. Moe charges over and corners Jimbo. Just as Moe is about to slice him up with butcher's knife, Jimbo starts to cry. Moe leaves and Laura sends Jimbo away, no longer seeing him as a tough rebel. Afterwards, Laura and Bart play one more prank on Moe for the evening.

MR. PLOW

Episode 9F07 Original Airdate: 11/19/92 Writer: Jon Vitti Director: Jim Reardon Guest Voices: Linda Rondstat as Herself, Adam West as Himself

D riving home from Moe's Tavern during a snow storm, Homer crashes into the family car parked in the driveway. Both cars are totaled. Homer attends the auto show to find a replacement. After encountering the Batmobile and Adam West, he buys a super deluxe snow plow and sets himself up in business as 'Mr. Plow.' He runs a late-night commercial and business booms. Thanks to Homer, Springfield remains operational during the snowy winter.

At Moe's, Barney mopes about his life. Homer advises him to take control and make something of himself, just like he did.

The next morning, Homer discovers that Barney has bought a snow plow. After airing his "Plow King" commercial featuring Linda Ronstadt, Barney takes away all of Homer's customers.

For revenge, Homer makes a phony call to the Plow King asking him to plow the driveway atop avalanche-prone Widow's Peak. Barney accepts the job and never returns. Homer's business booms again, but when he learns that Barney is stuck under an avalanche, Homer feels guilty. Using his snow plow, he saves Barney's life. Just as they agree to be partners instead of rivals, the snow thaws, putting them both out of business.

SHOW HIGHLIGHTS

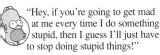

"Live from Hawaii's beautiful Molokai Island: we're not just for lepers anymore! It's 'Carnival of the Stars!' I'm your host, Troy McClure! You may remember me from such films as *The Erotic Adventures of Hercules* and *Dial M for Murderousness*. Tonight, we'll see Angela Lansbury walk on hot coals! Excitement, She Wrote!"

"Hey, if you're going to get mad at me every time I do something stupid, then I guess I'll just have to stop doing stupid things!"

"Eh, they shouldn't have been there in the first place." Moe, on why he didn't give free beer to the freed Iranian hostages.

The "Mr. Plow" Jingle: "Call Mr. Plow, that's my name, that name again is Mr. Plow!"

The adjuster: The man from the insurance company needs to know what kind of establishment Moe's is. Careful not to suggest he was drinking, Homer tells him, "It's a pornography store. I was buying pornography."

Movie Moment:
After Homer averts a possible snow day by plowing a path for the Springfield Elementary school bus, Bart is ambushed and riddled with snow balls à la Sonny Corleone in *The Godfather*.

(Barney drives away from the Flanders's house, having plowed their driveway.)
Flanders: *Thanks, Plow King-a-lee-ding.*
(Homer pulls up in his truck.)
Homer: *Flanders, I thought I was your plow man.*
Flanders: *(feeling guilty) Ah, you know, Homer, I think that other fella didn't do such a good job. Why don't you plow it again?*
(Ned holds up some cash.)
Homer: *Forget it pal. I don't need your phoney baloney job. I'll take your money but I'm not gonna plow your driveway.*

"Could this record-breaking heat wave be the result of the dreaded 'Greenhouse Effect?' Well, if 70-degree days in the middle of winter are the 'price' of car pollution, you'll forgive me if I keep my old Pontiac."

Reverend Lovejoy: *And now, to read from the Epistles of St. Paul, Homer Simpson.*
Homer: *Dear Lord, in your infinite wisdom, you know the number to call when you need a plow is KLONDIKE 5-3226.*
Reverend Lovejoy: *Homer, this is really low.*
Homer: *Not as low as my low, low prices!*

(On the steps of city hall, a ceremony to take the key to the city away from Homer and bestow it on Barney is being held.)
Quimby: *The torch has been passed to a new generation of, uh, snow plow people...* (to Homer) *Come, on give me the key!*
(Quimby wrestles the key to the city away from Homer. He sees small dents in it.)
Quimby: *These look like teeth marks.*
Homer: *I thought there was chocolate inside... Well, why was it wrapped in foil?*
Quimby: *It was never wrapped in foil!*

```
A  BURP  IS  NOT  AN  ANSWER
A  BURP  IS  NOT  AN  ANSWER
A  BURP  IS  NOT  AN  ANSWER
A  BURP  IS  NOT  AN  ANSWER
A  BURP  IS  NOT  AN  ANSWER
A  BURP  IS  NOT  AN  ANSWER
```

Moe: *Linda Ronstadt? How'd you get her?*
Barney: *Eh, we've been lookin' for a project to do together for a while.*

THE STUFF YOU MAY HAVE MISSED

"Crazy Vaclav's Place of Automobiles," the used car lot where Homer first looks to replace the cars.

Homer's head dents the steering wheel when he crashes.

The theme of the Springfield Auto Show: "We Salute the American Worker—Now 61% Drug Free."

Songs on Captain McAllister's album included: "Blow the Man Down," "Row, Row, Row, Your Boat," and "In the Navy."

When Homer needs a new ad for TV he goes to MacMahon and Tate, the ad firm of Darren Stevens on "Bewitched."

Linda Rondstat wears mariachi garb in her ad with Barney.

BARNEY

Occupation:
Barfly.

Best Friends:
Homer; Moe; Duff.

Favorite meal:
Peanuts from the garbage can; beer from ashtrays.

Expert on:
The sting of mace; cheese omelets; belching.

Regular source of income:
The Springfield Sperm Bank.

Past shames:
Dropped his cummerbund in the toilet at high school reunion; mistook a Girls Scout meeting for an AA meeting.

UH, OH. MY HEART JUST STOPPED... AH, THERE IT GOES.

LISA'S FIRST WORD

Episode 9F08 Original Airdate: 12/3/92 Writer: Jeff Martin Director: Mark Kirkland Guest Voice: Elizabeth Taylor as Maggie

BABY BART - 1983

Residence:
Lower East Side of Springfield.

Siblings:
None.

Level of guile:
Already growing.

Favorite activity:
Leaping on his sleeping father; smearing spaghetti all over himself; swinging naked around and around on a clothesline suspended 40 feet above the street for hours at a time.

Energy:
Boundless.

> I AM SO GREAT! I AM SO GREAT! EVERYBODY LOVES ME, I AM SO GREAT!

he Simpsons coax Maggie to say her first word. Homer tries in vain to get her to say "Daddy," but she only burps. Marge recalls Bart's first words, "aye carumba," and when Lisa asks what her first word was, Marge flashes back to 1983, when she first learned that she was pregnant with Lisa...

With a second baby on the way, Homer and Marge search for a bigger house. The year 1983 gives way to 1984, and the Summer Olympics begin. Krustyburger offers free burgers to customers who pick Olympic events won by the U.S. on their game cards. However, the games included in the promotion are ones that the Russians have traditionally won. When the Russians boycott the Olympics, the Americans win every event, and Homer gets a steady supply of free Krusty burgers.

When Lisa finally arrives, Bart has a difficult time adjusting. Jealous of all the attention she is getting, he decides to run away. However, when Lisa toddles into his bedroom and says her first word—"Bart"—he changes his mind. Homer tries to get Lisa to say "Daddy," but she can only say "Homer." Back in the present, Homer carries Maggie up to bed, turns out the light, and leaves. Alone in her room, Maggie utters her first word: "Daddy."

SHOW HIGHLIGHTS

"Ay carumba!" Bart's first spoken word, uttered at 10 months while seeing his parents cavorting on the bed.

"This story begins in that unforgettable spring of 1983: Ms. Pac-man struck a blow for women's rights, a young Joe Piscopo taught us how to laugh." Marge, setting the scene for the story of Lisa's first word.

Stickball™, Mumblety Peg™, Kick the Can™: The video games played on Springfield's Lower East Side in 1983.

"I'm a Little Teapot" and "The Itsy-Bitsy Spider": The two songs in Bart's "Spout Medley," which Patty pays him a dollar to sing.

"About three weeks." Homer, recalling how long it took him to ship Grampa off to the old folks home after asking Grampa to come and live with them.

"I'll tell you about the time I got locked in the bank vault with Mr. Mooney. It was another one of my harebrained schemes...Wait a minute. That was a 'Lucy Show.'"

"It's not easy to juggle a pregnant wife and a troubled child, but somehow I managed to squeeze in 8 hours of TV a day."

$44 million: The amount that Krusty stands to lose in his rigged Olympic Burger promotion now that the Russians have decided to boycott the games.

Homer's Cousin:
Marge: *I'm afraid we're going to need a bigger place.*
Homer: *No, we won't. I've got it all figured out. The baby can have Bart's crib and Bart'll sleep with us until he's 21.*
Marge: *Won't that warp him?*
Homer: *My cousin Frank did it.*
Marge: *You don't have a cousin Frank.*
Homer: *He became Francine back in '76. Then he joined that cult. I think his name is Mother Shabubu now.*

Realtor: *Once you get used to the smell of melted hog fat, you'll wonder how you ever did without it.*
Homer: *Mmmm...hog fat.*

Suppertime: In the Flanders home, Rod and Todd Flanders look forward to a meal.
Rod: *"Oh boy! Liver!"*
Todd: *"Iron helps us play!"*

Krusty, Filming His Olympic Krustyburger Ad:
Krusty: *(on TV) Heyyy, kids! Summer's just around the corner, and Krusty Burger is the official meat-flavored sandwich of the 1984 Olympics!*
(The scene switches to the studio where Krusty is filming the ad.)
Crew member: *And, cut!*
Krusty: *Bleh! (He spits out the burger.) Oh, I almost swallowed some of the juice. (He takes a drink from his flask.) Uhhhh, I'll be tasting that for weeks.*

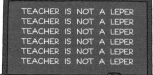

TEACHER IS NOT A LEPER
TEACHER IS NOT A LEPER
TEACHER IS NOT A LEPER
TEACHER IS NOT A LEPER
TEACHER IS NOT A LEPER
TEACHER IS NOT A LEPER

Movie Moment:
In the Itchy & Scratchy cartoon "100-Yard Gash," the music is taken from *Chariots of Fire* and the Vangelis soundtrack.

THE STUFF YOU MAY HAVE MISSED

The Krusty Burger is the "Official Meat-Flavored Sandwich" of the 1984 Olympics.

In the 1984 flashback, Homer is still driving his green car from high school, seen in 7F12, "The Way We Was."

Even though Abe seems younger during his talk with Homer in the 1984 flashback, a picture of his elderly self hangs on the wall of Homer and Marge's first apartment.

Homer and Marge use "Stinking Fish Realty" to help find their first home. Their motto is, "With a name this bad, we've got to be good."

Krusty the Clown is described as being illiterate in the 1990 episode 7G12, "Krusty Gets Busted," yet he is able to scan and decipher a wire report handed him (back in 1984) about the Soviets boycotting the Olympics.

HOMER'S TRIPLE BYPASS

Episode 9F09 Original Airdate: 12/17/92 Writers: Gary Apple & Michael Carrington Director: David Silverman

While driving his car, Homer hears strange thumping noises. He takes the car to a mechanic, who tells him that his car is fine, and that it is his heart that is making the noise. Mr. Burns catches Homer eating donuts instead of working, calls him into his office and taunts him with threats of dismissal. When Burns tells him that he is fired, Homer's heart stops.

After learning that he has suffered a mild heart attack, Homer is told that he needs a $40,000 coronary bypass operation. Lacking the money to pay for it, Homer tries to get health insurance. Just as he is about to sign the new policy, he suffers another heart attack and his application is rejected. Hearing a commercial featuring Dr. Nick Riviera, who will perform any operation for $129.95, Homer checks into the hospital, concluding that he has nothing to lose.

To brush up on the procedure, Dr. Riviera rents an instructional video. However, the most important part of the operation has been taped over. Homer says his final goodbyes to his family, just in case. An uncertain Dr. Riviera cuts into Homer and freezes, but Lisa, who has studied up on the operation, guides him through the surgery. Homer is soon back to his old self.

Identity:
Alcoholics who hang together at Moe's Tavern, because everybody knows their name.

Real names:
Sam (with hat) and Larry (without hair).

Favorite liquid:
Beer.

Favorite person:
Moe.

Favorite pastime:
Getting quietly toasted.

Favorite position:
Head down behind a beer, sitting on a stool, eyes nearly shut.

SHOW HIGHLIGHTS

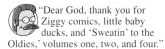

"This is Papa Bear. Put out an APB for a male suspect, driving a...car of some sort; heading in the direction of, uh, you know, that place that sells chili. Suspect is hatless. Repeat, hatless."

"Remember your hippopotamus oath." Homer, trying to get Dr. Hibbert to stop taunting and tickling him in the hospital.

"Dear God, thank you for Ziggy comics, little baby ducks, and 'Sweatin' to the Oldies,' volumes one, two, and four."

"Oh, no, what if they botch it? I won't have a dad...for a while." Bart, on Homer's surgery.

"They say the greatest tragedy is when a father outlives his son. I've never fully understood why that is. Frankly, I can see an up side to it."

Homer: *Kids, I have something to tell you.*
Marge: *Oh, Homie, I don't know. This might upset them.*
Bart: *Nothing you say can upset us. We're the MTV generation.*
Lisa: *We feel neither highs nor lows.*
Homer: *Really? What's it like?*
Lisa: *(shrugs) Eh...*

COFFEE IS NOT A DRINK
FOR KIDS
COFFEE IS NOT A DRINK
FOR KIDS
COFFEE IS NOT A DRINK
FOR KIDS

Barney, at Homer's hospital bed:
"When I first heard about the operation, I was against it. But then I thought, if Homer wants to be a woman, so be it."

Dr. Nick, entering the operation theater: "Now if something should go wrong, let's not get the law involved. One hand washes the other."

"What the hell is that?" The last thing Homer hears Dr. Riviera say before succumbing to the anesthesia.

The "COPS: In Springfield!" Theme:

Bad cops, bad cops / Bad cops, bad cops / Springfield cops are on the take / But what do you expect for the money we make? / Whether in a car or on a horse / We don't mind using excessive force / Bad cops, bad cops / Bad cops, bad cops.

(Mr. Burns watches Homer scarfing donuts on one of his security monitors.)
Mr. Burns: *Look at that pig, stuffing his face with donuts on my time. That's right, keep eating. Little do you know you're drawing ever closer to the poison donut.* (He chuckles evilly.) *There is a poison donut, isn't there, Smithers?*
Smithers: *Uh...no, sir. I discussed it with our lawyers and they consider it murder.*
Burns: *Damn their oily hides!*

(After Mr. Burns yells at Homer in his office, Homer collapses and his spirit rises out of his body.)
Smithers: *Mr. Burns, I think he's dead.*
Burns: *Oh, dear. Send a ham to his widow.*
Homer's spirit: *Mmm...ham...*
(Homer's spirit goes back into his body; his eyes open.)
Smithers: *No, wait. He's alive.*
Burns: *Oh, good. Cancel the ham.*
Homer: *D'oh!*

Homer: *I keep hearing this horrible irregular thumping noise.*
Gas station attendant: *It's your heart. And I think it's on its last thump.*
Homer: *Whew, I was afraid it was my transmission.*

THE STUFF YOU MAY HAVE MISSED

Snake's license plate reads "EX CON." There are also cows outside his house.

The Happy Widow Insurance Company features a neon sign with a stick-figure woman who goes from grieving over a grave to dancing over it and holding money.

The rabbi whom Homer hits up for money is Rabbi Krustofski, Krusty's father (introduced in 8F05, "Like Father, Like Clown").

Cops Eddie and Lou pull brass knuckles, a handgun, a grenade, and a knife out of Jasper's beard.

Space Mutants is playing at the drive-in in the "COPS: in Springfield" segment.

The puppets Homer uses to describe his coronary bypass operation look like "Life in Hell's" Akbar and Jeff, sans fez.

LYLE LANLEY

Occupation:
Fast-talking salesman/con man.

M.O.:
Selling damaged, possum-infested monorail systems to small towns including Ogdenville, North Haverbrook and Brockway — and then skipping out.

Preys on:
Small-town ignorance.

Attire:
A seersucker suit; straw boater; bow tie.

Expression:
Sly contempt.

Fears:
Investigative reporters, particularly those carrying hidden cameras.

YOU THERE, EATING THE PASTE.

Guest Voice:
Phil Hartman
as Lyle Lanley

MARGE VS

SHOW HIGHLIGHTS

Yabba-Dabba-Doo!: Homer slides down a pipe and crashes into the window of his car à la Fred Flintstone's exit, in which he slides off the tail of his construction dinosaur into his windowless stone vehicle.

"No. All of those bald children are arousing suspicion." Mr. Burns, after Smithers asks if they should dump a batch of nuclear waste in the playground.

Giant mechanical ants destroying Springfield Elementary: Bart's dream of how to spend Burns's $3 million.

Positive Role Model: Bart tells Homer he would like to follow in his monorail-conducting footsteps. Homer replies, "Do you want to change your name to Homer Jr.? The kids can call you Ho-Ju."

"I'd say this vessel could do at least Warp Five." Leonard Nimoy, grand marshal at the grand opening of the Springfield Central Monorail Station.

"Live long and prosper": Mayor Quimby says to Nimoy "May the force be with you." An annoyed Nimoy replies, "Do you even know who I am?" Quimby responds, "I

think I do. Weren't you one of the Little Rascals?"

"I call the big one 'Bitey.'" Homer, discussing the family of possums living in the monorail.

"Donuts. Is there anything they can't do?" Homer, after his makeshift anchor hooks on to a giant donut atop a donut shop.

**Homer's Opening Song
(to the tune of
"The Flintstones" Theme):**

Homer (driving off from work):
"Simpson! Homer Simpson/ He's the greatest guy in history/From the...town of Springfield/He's about to hit a chestnut tree." And he does.

Yet Another Lifelong Dream:

Homer: *Marge, I wanna be a monorail conductor.*
Marge: *Homer, no.*
Homer: *It's my lifelong dream!*
Marge: *Your lifelong dream was to run out on the field during a baseball game and you did it last year! Remember?* (Marge points to a framed sports page, with a picture of Homer running onto a baseball field in middle of a game, with the headline, "Idiot Ruins Game/Springfield Forfeits Pennant")

The Monorail Song:

Lyle Lanley: *Well, sir, there's nothing on Earth like a genuine, bona fide, electrified, six-car monorail! What'd I say?*
Ned Flanders: *Monorail!*
Lanley: *What's it called?*
Patty and Selma: *Monorail!*
Lanley: *That's right—Monorail!*
(Crowd softly chants "Monorail" in rhythm.)
Miss Hoover: *I hear those things are awfully loud.*
Lanley: *It glides as softly as a cloud.*
Apu: *Is there a chance the track could bend?*
Lanley: *Not on your life, my Hindu friend.*
Barney: *What about us brain-dead slobs?*
Lanley: *You'll all be given cushy jobs.*
Abe: *Were you sent here by the devil?*
Lanley: *No, good sir, I'm on the level.*
Chief Wiggum: *The ring came off my pudding can.*
Lanley: *Take my pen knife, my good man! I swear it's Springfield's only choice! Throw up your hands and raise your voice!*
Everyone: *Monorail!*
Lanley: *What's it called?*
Everyone: *Monorail!*
Lanley: *Once again!*
Everyone: *Monorail!*
Marge: *But Main Street's still all cracked and broken!*
Bart: *Sorry, Mom, the mob has spoken.*
Everyone: *Monorail!/Monorail!/ Monorail!/ Monorail!*
(finishing with a tuneful flourish)
Homer: *Mono...D'oh!*

THE MONORAIL

Episode 9F10 Original Airdate: 1/14/93
Writer: Conan O'Brien
Director: Rich Moore
Guest Voices: Leonard Nimoy as Himself,
Doris Grau as Lurleen Lumpkin and
Maggie Roswell as Maude Flanders

Mr. Burns is caught dumping highly toxic waste from the nuclear power plant in the park and is fined $3 million. He pays his debt to society in cash. The towspeople of Springfield hold a meeting to discuss how to spend the money. Lyle Lanley, a fast-talking stranger, convinces them that they need a monorail to put Springfield on the map. Caught up in his sales pitch, everyone votes for the monorail except Marge.

While Homer attends conductor school, Marge stops by Lanley's office to apologize for opposing the project. In his office, she discovers a notebook with drawings depicting Lanley making off with the money meant for the monorail. She drives to one of Lanley's past clients, nearby North Haverbrook, now a ghost town and a victim of Lanley's defective and ultimately worthless monorail. She heads back to Springfield to warn the others.

Marge is too late. Homer has already taken the monorail on its maiden voyage with Leonard Nimoy and a group of passengers. Lanley has left for the airport with the town's money. Running at full speed, the monorail zooms out of control. Homer fastens a crude anchor and throws it out the window. The monorail comes to a stop — but not before destroying a large portion of the city.

> **Number of Times Apu Has Been Shot This Year, Requiring Him to Nearly Miss Work:**
> Eight.

Movie Moments:

Lyle Lanley acts and sounds like traveling salesman Professor Harold Hill in *The Music Man*, except that Hill goes to River City, Iowa, rather than Springfield and is interested in starting a boys' band rather than stiffing the town on a monorail project. "The Monorail Song" also contains elements of *The Music Man* tune "Trouble."

The scene in which Mr. Burns and Smithers prepare to illegally dump nuclear waste is accompanied by an adaptation of "Axel F (Axel's Theme)" from *Beverly Hills Cop*. A similar adaption of the song was used in 8F15, "Separate Vocations.

Homer's Reasoning:

Marge: *I still think we ought to spend the money to fix Main Street.*
Homer: *Well, you should've written a song like that guy.*

A Country Song:

(Kent Brockman interviews a beaten-down Lurleen Lumpkin, fresh from her latest stay at the Betty Ford Clinic.)
Brockman: *"What ya been up to Lurleen?"*
Lumpkin: *"I spent last night in a ditch."*

Sittin' Next to Spock:

Leonard Nimoy: *A solar eclipse: the cosmic ballet goes on.*
Man sitting next to Nimoy: *Anybody want to switch seats?*

THE STUFF YOU MAY HAVE MISSED

Homer, Marge, Bart, Lisa and Maggie, Patty, Selma, Herman, Jasper, Grampa, Krusty, Apu, Mr. Burns, Smithers, Principal Skinner, Mrs. Krabappel, Miss Hoover, a woman in a bikini, Barney, Dr. Hibbert, Moe, Kent Brockman, Martin, Milhouse, Nelson and Otto appear in the couch gag.

Attendees at the Springfield Town Hall meeting include the receptionist from the Rubber Baby Buggy Bumper Babysitting Service (7G01, "Some Enchanted Evening"), the animated likeness of Simpsons producer Richard Sakai, and Ms. Mellon and school district psychologist Dr. J. Loren Pryor (both 7G02, "Bart the Genius").

Mr. Burns tries to disguise himself (poorly) at the Town Hall meeting as Mr. "Snrub," which is Burns spelled backwards.

A tree in the park has a heart carved on it that reads "M.B. + H.S."—which may or may not stand for Marge Bouvier + Homer Simpson.

A picture of a dinosaur is pinned to the Simpsons' bulletin board, à la the Flintstones.

Lyle Lanley's voice is a virtual dead-ringer for attorney Lionel Hutz and actor Troy McClure.

At sign at Swampy's Liquor on Main Street reads "Duff Spoken Here."

Another business on Main Street reads "Pizza on a Stick."

Homer drives down Main Street and says "Look at that pavement fly!", partially echoing his line, "Look at that blubber fly"in 9F09, "Homer's Triple Bypass."

I WILL NOT EAT THINGS
FOR MONEY
I WILL NOT EAT THINGS
FOR MONEY
I WILL NOT EAT THINGS
FOR MONEY
I WILL NOT EAT THINGS
FOR MONEY

PATTY

Occupation:
DMV clerk with her sister, Selma.

Voice:
Deep, graveled, scratchy.

Favorite vice:
Cigarettes, lots of cigarettes.

Quirks:
Bores others with detailed slide shows from trips abroad; considers a kiss "scoring."

Surrogate husband:
Twin sister, Selma.

Abilities:
Grows leg hair rapidly; insults brother-in-law with ease.

Loves:
Feet rubbed by nephews and nieces.

Hates:
Missing "MacGyver."

> RICHARD DEAN ANDERSON WILL BE IN MY DREAMS TONIGHT.

SELMA'S CHOICE

Episode 9F11 Original Airdate: 1/21/93 Writer: David M. Stern Director: Carlos Baeza

SHOW HIGHLIGHTS

Not thinking aloud: In the car, Patty mentions that Aunt Gladys's legend will live forever. Homer thinks to himself, "Yeah. The legend of the dog-faced woman." He thinks it's so funny he says it out loud, adding, "Legend of the dog-faced woman! Oh, that's good."

"Little Land of Duff" Song:
Duff beer for me/ Duff beer for you/ I'll have a Duff/ You have one too.
(repeated endlessly)

"That's a woman? Dear Lord!" Reverend, at the Lucky Stiff Funeral Home, after being corrected during his eulogy for what he believed to be a "a kind man."

"I want to have a baby before it's too late. You're looking at a free lunch, boys. Come and get it." Selma, filming her video for the "Low Expectations Dating Service."

"Ach! Back to the loch with ye, nessie!" Willie, after seeing Selma's video.

"A Nobel Prize winner! An NBA All-Star! Ooh, one of the 'Sweathogs!'" Marge, flipping through the "101 Frozen Pops" catalogue from the sperm bank.

"Oooh, this looks like fun… a bench! Kids, whaddya say you go get your Aunt Selma a beer smoothie?"

The Barrel Roll: Rollercoaster Bart hops on though he's too short. The protective bar locks behind his little body. Says Bart, "Whoa, that isn't good."

At the diner: Homer tries to complete a maze that is "Just for Kids." He ends up in the mouth of the alligator and angrily throws the kiddie activity sheet on the floor with his other failed attempts. The waitress comes by and asks, "Another placemat, sir?" Homer composes himself and answers, "Please."

(Walking into Duff Gardens, Lisa and Bart see several men in beer bottle costumes.)
Lisa: (gasps) *Look—the Seven Duffs!*
Bart: *There's "Tipsy!" and there's "Queasy!"*
Lisa: *There's "Surly" and "Remorseful!"*

The Postponement:
Homer: *But I wanna go to Duff Gardens. Right now!*
Marge: *Oh, Homer, quit pouting.*
Homer: *I'm not pouting. I'm… mourning. Stupid dead woman.*

Selma Visits Princess Opal's Potions, Hexes, and Fax Machine:
Princess Opal: *One drop of this love potion, and you will have any man you desire.*
(Princess Opal tastes a drop of the potion.)
Selma: *Really? What are the magical ingredients?*
Princess Opal: *Mostly corn syrup, a little rubbing alcohol. You'll be lucky if it doesn't make your hair fall out, actually.*
(Princess Opal looks at the bottle. It's labeled "Truth Serum.")

As Bart Hangs from the Safety Bar:
Selma: (to Surly) *Can't you do something?*
Surly: *'Ey, Surly only looks out for one guy — Surly.*
Selma: *Sorry, Surly.*
Surly: *Shut up.*

Homer: *Now, what do we say when we get to the ticket booth?*
Bart and Lisa: *We're under six.*
Homer: *And I'm a college student.*

Lisa: *Aunt Selma, this may be presumptuous, but have you ever considered artificial insemination?*
Homer: *Boy, I don't know. You gotta be pretty desperate to make it with a robot.*

Marge: *Kids, I have some bad news. Your Great Aunt Gladys has...passed on.*
Bart: (searching memory) *Gladys, Gladys… 'bout yay high, blue hair, big dent in her forehead?*
Marge: *No honey, Gladys looked more like your Aunt Patty.*
(Bart searches his memory. There's a noticeable shudder as he remembers.)
Bart: *Oh yeah, there she is.*

THE STUFF YOU MAY HAVE MISSED

Sign at The Lucky Stiff Funeral Home: "We Put the 'Fun' in Funerals."

This episode marks Lisa's first substance-induced hallucination. The second one, a *Yellow Submarine*-inspired delusion, occurrs in 9F15, "Last Exit to Springfield."

The Statue of Liberty drinks a Duff in the Duff Light Parade.

Marge learns that her Aunt Gladys has died and that the funeral will be held on the day the family plans to go to fun-filled Duff Gardens. The trip is postponed. Following the service, Lionel Hutz shows a videotape of Aunt Gladys's will. Included in the will are Patty and Selma, whom Aunt Gladys tells to have children so that they will not spend the rest of their lives alone.

Selma decides she wants to have a baby and searches for a half-way decent man to date, but the best she can do is Hans Moleman, whom she decides is too ugly to be the father of her children. As a last resort, she considers a sperm bank. When Homer wakes up sick on the day the family is scheduled to go to Duff Gardens Marge asks Selma to take the kids to Duff Gardens while she takes care of Homer at home, hoping to give Selma a taste of motherhood.

Bart and Lisa wear Selma out. Bart gets trapped on a roller coaster, while Lisa drinks the water in the "Little Land of Duff" boat ride and hallucinates. The day turns into Selma's worst nightmare. Happy to get Bart and Lisa home, she decides that kids are too much for her to handle. Instead, she happily adopts Jub-Jub, Aunt Gladys's pet iguana.

> I WILL NOT YELL "SHE'S DEAD" DURING ROLL CALL.
> I WILL NOT YELL "SHE'S DEAD" DURING ROLL CALL.
> I WILL NOT YELL "SHE'S DEAD" DURING ROLL CALL.

BROTHER FROM THE SAME PLANET

Episode 9F12   Original Airdate: 2/4/93   Writer: Jon Vitti   Director: Jeff Lynch   Guest Voice: Phil Hartman as Tom

himself off as an unwanted son and, without telling Homer, is assigned a Bigger Brother named Tom. The two hit it off, enjoying all the fun things Homer would never do.

Marge finds out that Lisa has been calling a 900 number to talk to Corey, Lisa's favorite teen heartthrob. Lisa promises to never call again, but can't stop. She decides to go cold-turkey and sets midnight as the goal. Counting the minutes and fighting temptation, Lisa finally loses the battle and grabs the phone. When Marge enters the kitchen, she finds Lisa asleep with the phone to her ear. Picking up the phone to listen, she hears the computer voice of the "time" operator and smiles.

When Homer finds out that Bart has a Bigger Brother, he decides to get even. Signing himself up, he becomes a Bigger Brother to a little boy named Pepi. Together, they do all the things Homer wants to do. At the aquarium, Bart and Tom run into Homer and Pepi. Believing Homer is a bad father, Tom beats him up. Bart tells Homer he never meant for him to get hurt and they renew their father-son bond. Tom becomes Pepi's Bigger Brother.

Homer forgets to pick up Bart after soccer practice. Wishing he had a better father, Bart responds to a television commercial for Bigger Brothers, an organization that offers companions to boys without positive role models. Bart passes

SHOW HIGHLIGHTS

"I know you're mad at me right now, and I'm kinda mad too… I mean, we could sit here and try to figure out 'who forgot to pick up who' till the cows come home. But let's just say we're both wrong and that'll be that."

Typical recorded messages on the Corey Hotline: "Here's a list of things that rhyme with Corey: Glory…Story… Allegory… Montessori," and "Let's see what's in the newspaper today...Canada Stalls on Trade Pact."

"This is even more painful than it looks." Homer, his back bent over a fire hydrant following his fight with Tom.

Agency worker: And what are your reasons for wanting a little brother?
Homer's brain: Don't say revenge. Don't say revenge.
Homer: Uh…Revenge.
Homer's brain: That's it, I'm getting outta here. (Footsteps are heard walking away, and then a door slams.) (The agency worker checks off "revenge" on a worksheet next to "spite," "malice," "boredom," and "profit.")
Agency worker: Welcome aboard, Mr. Simpson!

Homer: For your information, I'm his father!
Tom: The drunk and gambler?
Homer: (genial) That's right. And who might you be?

THE PRINCIPAL'S TOUPEE IS
NOT A FRISBEE.
THE PRINCIPAL'S TOUPEE IS
NOT A FRISBEE.
THE PRINCIPAL'S TOUPEE IS
NOT A FRISBEE.

Like Father and Son Again:

Bart: Dad, remember when Tom had you in that headlock and you screamed, "I'm a hemophiliac'"and when he let you go you kicked him in the back?
Homer: Yeah?
Bart: Will you teach me how to do that?
Homer: Sure, boy, First, you gotta shriek like a woman, and keep sobbing 'til he turns away in disgust. That's when it's time to kick some back.

Movie Moment:

Milhouse writes "Trab pu kcip! Trab pu kcip!" on the wall like the little kid in *The Shining*.

Homer: Hello, son. Where have you been?
Bart: Playing with Milhouse.
Homer: No you haven't! You've been out gallivanting around with that floozy of a Bigger Brother of yours! Haven't you? Haven't you? Look at me!
Bart: Dad, it just kinda happened. You're taking this too hard.
Homer: How would you like me to take it? "Go ahead, Bart, have your fun, I'll be waiting for you?" I'm sorry, I can't do it.
Bart: Well, what are you gonna do?
Homer: Ho, ho, you'll see.

Bart: I've been thinking. You've been really great to me...but there's probably some other kid who needs you even more.
Tom: Bart, I'd kiss you… if the Bigger Brother didn't make me sign a form promising I wouldn't.

Police Involvement:

Lou: There's a couple of guys fighting at the aquarium, Chief.
Wiggum: They still sell those frozen bananas?
Lou: I think so.
Wiggum: Let's roll.

THE STUFF YOU MAY HAVE MISSED

The driving woman Bart mistakes for Homer looks like Homer with a gray wig on.

One of the articles in *Non-Threatening Boys* magazine is "Meet Joey."

There is a billboard with Krusty's likeness and a very foreign caption in Pepi's neighborhood.

The items on the Springfield Elementary budget: fine arts, Doris, science, history, music & art, hot lunches, custodial, and playground.

Show and Tell:

Bart: Someday I want to be an F-14 pilot like my hero, Tom. He lent me this new weapon called a neural disruptor.
(Bart presses the trigger and a lazer shoots Martin who falls to the floor, twitching.)
Mrs. Krabappel: He's not dead, is he Bart?
Bart: Nah… but I wouldn't give him any homework for a while.
Mrs. Krabappel: Very good, Bart. Thank you.
Bart: Oh, don't thank me. Thank an unprecedented eight year military build-up.

PEPI

Economic status:
Disadvantaged.

Amazed by:
Electric garage doors;
Homer's wisdom.

Newest tidbit:
Whales aren't
really mammals.

Sex:
M.

Hair:
Black.

Eyes:
Huge.

OH, POPPA HOMER,
YOU ARE SO LEARNED.

RALPH WIGGUM

Age:
Eight.

Grade:
In his first year of fourth grade.

Accomplished at:
Sleeping; acting.

Connections:
Father is Chief of Police.

Happiest day:
When the doctor told him he didn't have worms anymore.

Favorite foods:
School supplies.

Shame:
His parents won't let him use scissors or the oven.

Misses most:
The point.

MY CAT'S BREATH SMELLS LIKE CATFOOD.

I LOVE LISA

Episode 9F13   Original Airdate: 2/11/93   Writer: Frank Mula   Director: Wes Archer

I t's Valentine's Day, and everyone in Lisa's class receives cards except Ralph. Feeling bad for Ralph, Lisa quickly signs a card and gives it to him. Ralph is instantly smitten with her. After school, he walks Lisa home, but Lisa has no feelings for Ralph except pity. She tries to avoid him at school, but they are chosen to perform in a play together.

Lisa is exasperated with Ralph, but when he asks her to go to Krusty's anniversary show with him, she is conflicted. She really wants to go but does not want to give Ralph the impression that she likes him. Homer advises her to go and enjoy the show. Arriving at the theater, Lisa is paranoid about being seen with Ralph. During the taping, Krusty interviews members of the audience. When Ralph is questioned, he introduces Lisa as his date. Horrified, Lisa blurts out that the only reason she gave Ralph a Valentine card was because she felt sorry for him. Ralph's heart breaks.

Lisa realizes that she embarrassed Ralph in front of everyone. She wants to apologize but does not get the chance before the night of the school play. Ralph transfers his grief into a good performance and mesmerizes the audience. After the play, young girls throw themselves at him. Later, Lisa gives Ralph another card, this time it is one that asks him to be her friend.

SHOW HIGHLIGHTS

"If you think I'm cuddly / And you want my company / Come on wifey let me know.../ Ugh, ugh, ugh..." Flanders, serenading his wife, dressed as a heart.

Miss Hoover: *Martha Washington will be played by Lisa Simpson. George Washington will be played by Ralph Wiggum.*
Rex: *What? This is a travesty! Everyone knows I'm the best actor in this ridiculous school!*
Hoover: *Sit down, Rex.*
Rex: *I will not sit down! Someone's gotten to you, you deceitful cow!*
Hoover: *That's absurd, Rex. Ralph won the part, fair and square.*
(Miss Hoover crosses to the window and shuts the venetian blinds repeatedly. Out in the parking lot, Wiggum, Lou, and Eddie see Miss Hoover at the window.)
Wiggum: *That's the signal. Take the boot off the car, boys.*

"Six simple words: I'm not gay, but I'll learn." Homer telling Lisa what to say to Ralph if he won't go away.

"Do you want to play John Wilkes Booth, or do you want to act like a maniac?" Miss Hoover, to Bart.

"Angry, angry young man." Krusty's description of former sidekick, Sideshow Raheem.

Lunch Room Conversation:
Truck Driver: *Where do you want these beef hearts?*
Lunchlady Doris: *On the floor.*
Truck Driver: *It doesn't look very clean.*
Lunchlady Doris: *Just do your job, heart-boy.*
(The driver pulls a lever and hundreds of beef hearts plop onto the floor.)

"Now you listen to me! I don't like you! I never liked you, and the only reason I gave you that stupid valentine is 'cause nobody else would!" Lisa, breaking Ralph's heart.

 "Good evening, everyone, and welcome to a wonderful evening of theater and picking up after yourselves."

"I dinna cry when me own father was hung for stealing a pig. But I'll cry now."

"We Are the Mediocre Presidents" Lyrics:

We are the mediocre presidents!/ You won't find our faces on dollars or on cents!/ There's Taylor, there's Tyler, there's Fillmore and there's Hayes!/ There's William Henry Harrison, "I died in thirty days!"/ We are the adequate, forgettable,/ occasionally regrettable caretaker presidents of the U.S.A.!

THE STUFF YOU MAY HAVE MISSED

Lisa erases someone else's name from the card before she re-signs it and gives it to Ralph.

The warning on Krusty's Home Pregnancy Test reads: "May Cause Birth Defects."

"I Choo-Choo-Choose You": Lisa's valentine to Ralph. It has a little train on it.

Lisa: *Ralph thinks I like him. But I only gave him a valentine 'cause I felt sorry for him.*
Homer: *Ah, sweet pity: where would my love life have been without it?*
Lisa: *What do you say to a boy to let him know you're not interested?*
Marge: *Well, honey—*
Homer: *Let me handle this, Marge. I've heard 'em all.* (counting them off on his fingers) *"I like you as a friend," "I think we should see other people," "I no speak English," "I'm married to the sea," "I don't want to kill you, but I will..."*

Bart: *We have to go to that show.*
Lisa: *To get tickets our parents would have to be part of Springfield's cultural elite.*
(Homer walks in trying out a toothbrush he got from Flanders's trash)
Homer: *Can you believe Flanders threw out a perfectly good toothbrush?*

I WILL NOT CALL THE PRINCIPAL 'SPUD HEAD'
I WILL NOT CALL THE PRINCIPAL 'SPUD HEAD'
I WILL NOT CALL THE PRINCIPAL 'SPUD HEAD'
I WILL NOT CALL THE PRINCIPAL 'SPUD HEAD'

H omer is arrested for drunk driving on his way home from a Duff Brewery tour with Barney. His license is revoked and he is required to attend Alc-Anon meetings. Meanwhile, Bart pelts Principal Skinner with a tomato that Lisa has grown for her science fair project. For revenge, Lisa secretly conducts an experiment to determine who is smarter, a hamster or her brother. The hamster passes the tests, while Bart fails miserably. Arriving home from an Alc-Anon meeting, Homer agrees to Marge's suggestion that he stop drinking for a month.

Bart discovers Lisa's plan to humiliate him at the science fair. He steals her hamster and dresses him in a mini-aviator suit for an experiment demonstrating that hamsters can fly airplanes. The judges award Bart's project first place.

Overcoming temptation, Homer makes it though the month without drinking and rushes to Moe's for a beer. However, realizing what drinking has done to the bar regulars, Homer puts down his beer and goes for a bicycle ride with Marge instead.

> GOLDFISH DON'T BOUNCE.
> GOLDFISH DON'T BOUNCE.
> GOLDFISH DON'T BOUNCE.
> GOLDFISH DON'T BOUNCE.
> GOLDFISH DON'T BOUNCE.
> GOLDFISH DON'T BOUNCE.

SHOW HIGHLIGHTS

"Well, Edna, for a school with no Asian kids I think we put on a pretty darn good science fair." Principal Skinner, to Edna Krabappel.

"I'm disrupting the learning process...and I love it!" Skinner, dancing "The Mashed Potato" in Bart's dream.

 "Hi! I'm actor Troy McClure. You might remember me from such Driver's Ed films as *Alice's Adventures Through the Windshield Glass* and *The Decapitation of Larry Leadfoot*."

"Wasting Squirrels with B.B. Guns": Nelson Muntz's project at the science fair.

 "Marge I'm goin' to Moe's. Send the kids to the neighbors. I'm comin' back loaded!"

Things found in bottles of Duff by Phil, the quality-control guy at the Duff Brewery: Mice, rat, syringe, and a nose.

Things he didn't find: Dentures, a fish, a broken bottle neck, and Adolf Hitler's head.

> (Homer stands up from the breakfast table.)
> **Homer:** *Well, time to go to work.*
> **Homer's brain:** *Little do they know, I'm ducking out early to take the Duff Brewery tour.*
> **Homer:** *Roll in at nine, punch out at five, that's the plan.*
> **Homer's brain:** *Heh, heh, heh. They don't suspect a thing. Well, off to the plant!*
> **Homer:** *Then to the Duff Brewery!*
> **Homer's brain:** *Uh, oh! Did I say that or just think it?*
> **Homer:** *I gotta think of a line, fast!*
> **Marge:** *Homer, are you going to the Duff Brewery?*
> **Homer:** *Aaaauuuggh!!!*

> **Types of Duff:**
> Duff, Duff Lite, Duff Dry, Raspberry Duff, Duff Dark, Tartar-Control Duff, Lady Duff, Duff Gummi Beers.

> **Movie Moment:**
> At the end of the episode, Homer rides Marge around on his bicycle handlebars to the song "Raindrops Keep Falling on My Head" in a takeoff of *Butch Cassidy and the Sundance Kid*.

> **The lyrics to "It Was a Very Good Beer"**
> (to the tune of "It Was a Very Good Year):
> *When I was 17 / I drank some very good beer / I drank some very good beer / I purchased with a fake I.D. / My name was Brian McGee / I stayed up listening to Queen / When I was 17.*

> **Lisa:** *I want the most intelligent hamster you've got.*
> **Owner:** *Okay, uh, this little guy writes mysteries under the name of J.D. MacGregor.*

> **The Sobriety Test :**
> (Homer stands on one foot touching his nose with his eyes closed.)
> **Homer:** *"W,X,Y & Z/ Now I know my ABC's / (hops to other foot) Won't you come and play with me?"*
> **Eddie:** *Flawless.*
> **Lou:** *We also would have accepted "Tell me what you think of me."*

> **Lisa:** *I've grown a futuristic tomato by fertilizing it with Anabolic steroids.*
> **Bart:** *The kind that help our Olympic athletes reach new peaks of excellence?*
> **Lisa:** *The very same. I think this tomato could wipe out world hunger.*

> **Homer Escapes the Plant:**
> **Homer:** *(reading the map) "To overcome the spider's curse, simply quote a Bible verse." Uh ...thou shalt not...oooh.*
> (Homer throws a rock at the spider, knocking it senseless, and jumps through an already broken window.)

THE STUFF YOU MAY HAVE MISSED

According to the Springfield Drivers License #C4043243 voided by the judge, Homer is 6', 240 pounds, has blue eyes and no hair. Date of Birth: 05-12-56. In 7F02, he was born in 1955.

A Prohibition-era sign at the Duff Brewery reads, "Prohibition Got You Down? Drink Doctor Duff's 'Health Tonic'."

A McCarthy-era sign reads "I Knew He Was a Commie 'Cause He Didn't Drink Duff Beer."

The state listed on Homer's license is NT.

Duff, Duff Lite, and Duff Dry are all fed from a common pipe at the Duff Brewery, indicating different names for the same product.

Lisa says, "I was just thinking of a joke I saw on "Herman's Head," a reference to Yeardley Smith, the voice of Lisa, as one of the stars of the former Fox comedy.

CHIEF WIGGUM

Full name:
Clancy Wiggum.

Father of:
Ralph Wiggum.

Position:
Chief of Police, Springfield.

Physique:
Rotund.

Personally handles:
All calls involving donut shops, ice cream parlors, and food processing plants.

Prime nemesis:
Mayor Quimby.

Morals and ethics:
Few.

Intellectual level:
Common sense-challenged; mixes up police terms, such as DOA and DWI.

> DO NOT BE ALARMED, CONTINUE SWIMMING NAKED. AWW, C'MON, CONTINUE! COME ON! AWWW...ALRIGHT, LOU, OPEN FIRE.

CARL

Position:
Homer's supervisor at the Springfield Nuclear Power Plant, Sector 7G; union organizer.

Best pal:
Worker drone Lenny.

Appearance:
Considered by Homer too handsome to fix up with Selma.

Enjoys:
The occasional donut, but not as occasional as Homer.

Turn-ons:
Union leadership; beating Homer in poker.

Turn-offs:
Inequitable treatment by management; when someone takes the last donut.

YOU KNOW, THOSE GERMANS AIN'T SO BAD.

The union leader who represents the workers at the nuclear power plant disappears, leaving the employees without a leader to renegotiate their contract. Taking advantage of the situation, Mr. Burns removes the dental plan from his employee benefits package, offering free beer in return. The workers agree to accept Burns's plan, including Homer, until he realizes that he'll have to pay for Lisa's new braces himself. At a union meeting, he stands up and urges the other members to reject the contract. Rallying them into a frenzy, he is elected the new plant union rep.

Without a dental plan, Marge gets Lisa the least expensive braces, which are crude and grotesque. Burns, unable to bribe or threaten Homer into giving in to his demands during negotiations, vows to crush him. The workers vote to strike.

Burns plays his trump card and turns off the city's power, but the workers' resolve remains firm. Realizing that he cannot compete against Homer's strong leadership, Burns proposes to reinstate the dental plan if Homer will resign his union leader post. Homer agrees, and Lisa gets brand-new, state-of-the-art braces.

SHOW HIGHLIGHTS

"You can't treat the working man this way. One day, we'll form a union and get the fair and equitable treatment we deserve! Then we'll go too far, and get corrupt and shiftless, and the Japanese will eat us alive!" A worker at Burns's grandfather's plant, after being dragged away for stealing six atoms.

Burns's trade: The nuclear power plant boss offers workers a free beer keg at their union meetings in exchange for giving up their dental plan.

Union man: Homer belongs to the International Brotherhood of Jazz Dancers, Pastry Chefs, and Nuclear Technicians union.

"Lisa and Marge, these braces are invisible, painless, and periodically release a delightful burst of Calvin Klein's 'Obsession—for Teeth.'" Dr. Wolfe, showing his top-of-the-line braces.

"Tonight, on 'Smartline': 'The Power Plant Strike: Argle Bargle or Fooforah?' With us tonight are plant owner, C.M. Burns; union kingpin, Homer Simpson; and talk show mainstay, Dr. Joyce Brothers."

Dr. Wolfe: *I'm afraid Lisa is going to need braces.*
Lisa: *Oh, no! I'll be socially unpopular—more so!*

Lisa's Protest Song:
Come gather 'round children/ It's high time ye learns/ 'Bout a hero named Homer/ And a devil named Burns/ We'll march 'til we drop the girls and the fellas/ we'll fight 'til the death/ or else fold like umbrellas/ So we'll march day and night/ By the big cooling tower/ They have the plant/ But we have the power.

Burns's Song of Lament:
Look at them all, through the darkness I'm bringing/They're not sad at all, they're actually singing!/They sing without juicers/They sing without blenders/They sing without flunjers, capdabblers and smendlers.

Dr. Wolfe: *How often do you brush, Ralph?*
Ralph: *Three times a day, sir.*
Dr. Wolfe: *Why must you turn my office into a house of lies?*
Ralph: *I don't brush! I don't bruuush!!*
Dr. Wolfe: *Let's look at a picture book, The Big Book of British Smiles.*
(Ralph is horrified as they flip through page after page of yellow rotting teeth. He thrusts the book away.)
Ralph: *That's enough! That's enoouuugh!*

Movie Moment:
Lisa smashes a mirror after looking at her braces in Wolfe's office à la the Joker in *Batman*.

Who's Homer Simpson?
Burns: *Who is that firebrand, Smithers?*
Smithers: *That's Homer Simpson, sir.*
Burns: *Simpson, eh? New man?*
Smithers: *Actually, sir, he thwarted your campaign for governor, you ran over his son, he saved the plant from meltdown, his wife painted you in the nude...*
Burns: *Eh, doesn't ring a bell.*

THE STUFF YOU MAY HAVE MISSED

Dr. Wolfe's business is called, "Painless Dentistry, Formerly Painful Dentistry."

X-rated clubs at the Springfield red-light district: "Nudes at Eleven," "Adam and Adam," and "The Horny Toad."

As Lisa floats along in her psychedelic-anesthetic daydream, we see the word "HATRED" rush by (it was "LOVE" in the original movie).

Burns: *We don't have to be adversaries, Homer. We both want a fair union contract.*
Homer's brains: *Why is Mr. Burns being so nice to me?*
Burns: *And if you scratch my back, I'll scratch yours.*
Homer's brain: *Wait a minute. Is he coming on to me?*
Burns: *I mean, if I should slip something into your pocket, what's the harm?*
Homer's brain: *Oh my god! He is coming on to me!*
Burns: *After all, negotiations make strange bedfellows.*
(Burns chuckles and winks at Homer.)
(Homer's brain screams.)
Homer: *Sorry, Mr. Burns, but I don't go in for these backdoor shenanigans. Sure I'm flattered, maybe even a little curious, but the answer is no!*

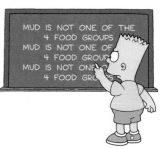

MUD IS NOT ONE OF THE 4 FOOD GROUPS
MUD IS NOT ONE OF THE 4 FOOD GROUP
MUD IS NOT ONE OF THE 4 FOOD GROUP

SO IT'S COME TO THIS: A SIMPSONS CLIP SHOW

Episode 9F17 Original Airdate: 4/1/93 Writer: Jon Vitti (with clip contributions from Al Jean & Mike Reiss, Jay Kogen & Wallace Wolodarsky, John Swartzwelder, Jeff Martin, George Meyer and Nell Scovell) Director: Carlos Baeza

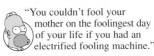

SHOW HIGHLIGHTS

"You couldn't fool your mother on the foolingest day of your life if you had an electrified fooling machine."

"You relive long lost summers, kiss girls from high school, it's like one of those TV shows where they show a bunch of clips from old episodes." Grampa, on what comas are like.

"And for an extra $20, I'll give Homer a tick bath, and then spay him." The veterinarian, to the Simpson family.

> **Movie Moment:**
> Barney's attempt to suffocate Homer (and his subsequent "escape" from the hospital) parodies the last scene in *One Flew Over the Cuckoo's Nest*.

A s an April Fools' Day prank, Homer exchanges good milk with sour milk in the refrigerator. Bart drinks the sour milk. Vowing revenge, he takes one of Homer's beers and brings it to the hardware store, where he puts it into a high-speed paint mixer before replacing it in the refrigerator. When Homer pops the can open, a violent explosion rocks the house and sends beer foam soaring into the sky.

The Episodes and the Scenes (In Order of Appearance):

7G11 *"Life on the Fast Lane,"* Bart throws a baseball and hits his father in the head.
8F13 *"Homer at the Bat,"* Homer gets hit by a pitch in the head.
8F06 *"Lisa's Pony,"* Homer is hit in the head with a circular saw that falls off of a shelf; he also falls asleep in the doors of the Kwik-E-Mart.
7F09 *"Itchy, Scratchy & Marge,"* Maggie whacks Homer on the head with a mallet.
7G04 *"There's No Disgrace Like Home,"* Homer and the rest of the Simpsons receive push-button shock therapy in Dr. Marvin Monroe's office.
7F06 *"Bart the Daredevil,"* Homer glides on a skateboard down Springfield Gorge and falls short, bumping around the rocky gorge and then getting jostled again after he is loaded into an ambulance.
8F17 *"Dog of Death,"* The veterinarian gives up on saving a hamster and flips him through a basketball hoop and into the trash can.
7G09 *"The Call of the Simpsons,"* Homer and Bart, lost in the forest.
7F04 *"The Simpsons Halloween Special"* (a.k.a. "Treehouse of Horror I"), The Simpsons are beamed onto a flying saucer.
7F09 *"Itchy, Scratchy & Marge,"* The "Itchy & Scratchy" short in which Itchy hits Scratchy on the back of the head with a sledgehammer, slamming out Scratchy's eyes. Itchy puts out two bombs that Scratchy picks up. Believing them to be his eyeballs, he screws them in and his head explodes.
7F11 *"Life on the Fast Lane,"* Marge pays Homer a surprise visit at the nuclear power plant.
8F09 *"Burns Verkaufen Der Kraftwerk,"* Homer cavorts in the Land of Chocolate.
8F06 *"Lisa's Pony,"* A drowsy Homer drives along in a Slumberland dream sequence complete with rolling beds.
8F17 *"Dog of Death,"* Homer asking Burns for money for his dog's operation before he is carried away by a pair of goons.
7F11 *"One Fish, Two Fish, Blowfish, Blue Fish,"* Lisa plays "When the Saints Go Marching In" for Homer on the sax.
8F22 *"Bart's Friend Falls in Love,"* A red-capped Bart tries to make off with Homer's penny jar, Indiana Jones-style.
7G05 *"Bart the General,"* Bart rolls downhill in the trash can after he is beaten up.
7F21 *"Three Men and a Comic Book,"* Homer checks on Bart and Milhouse in the treehouse.
7F11 *"One Fish, Two Fish, Blowfish, Blue Fish,"* Homer gives Bart a shaving lesson.

Homer is rushed to the hospital and given X-rays. When the doctor notices several abnormalities, Marge reflects on some of Homer's near run-ins with death. As Homer recovers, the Simpsons reminisce about their past fiascoes.

Homer tries to get a snack from the candy machine, but it crashes down on him, and puts him into a coma. Bart reminds Homer of all the good times they had and confesses that he tampered with the exploding beer can. Suddenly, Homer springs back to life, lunging at Bart and choking him.

"Mrs. Simpson, I'm afraid your husband is dead." Dr. Hibbert, pulling an April Fools' Day prank on Marge.

TV announcer: The following is a public service announcement. Excessive alcohol consumption can cause liver damage and cancer of the rectum.
Homer: *Mmm...beer.*

(Driving with Chief Wiggum, Lou sees an explosion in the distance.)
Lou: *That sounded like an explosion at the old Simpson place.*
Wiggum: *Forget it, that's two blocks away.*
Lou: *Looks like there's beer coming out of the chimney.*
Wiggum: *I am proceeding on foot; call in a code eight.*
Lou: *(into radio) We need pretzels; repeat, pretzels.*

NO ONE IS INTERESTED IN MY UNDERPANTS.
NO ONE IS INTERESTED IN MY UNDERPANTS.
NO ONE IS INTERESTED IN MY UNDERPANTS.

THE STUFF YOU MAY HAVE MISSED

During the sequence in which the Simpsons are depicted as pagans, the Lisa pagan does not participate in their ritual.

When Bart cranks up the temperature in the house to make Homer thirsty enough to go to the refrigerator for a Duff, among the things that melt is a Leo Sayer album from the late 1970s.

Number of candy bars that fall directly into Homer's mouth as he lay pinned and injured underneath the candy machine: 10.

Number of times Homer says "D'oh!" in succession from various episodes: 32.

Number of different episodes in which clips were utilized (aside from the "D'oh!s"): 14

PIMPLE-FACED KID

Places of employement:
Krustyburger; the Gulp 'N' Blow; Lard Lad; I.R.S. Burger; the Springfield Public Access station; Burns's casino.

Appearance:
Acne-encrusted.

Speaks:
Haltingly, and with an annoying lilt.

Reasoning ability:
Uncertain.

Strengths:
None evident.

I AM INTERESTED IN LONG-DISTANCE SAVINGS. *VERY* INTERESTED.

A fter watching a particularly bad "Itchy & Scratchy" episode, Bart and Lisa decide to write one of their own. However, the cartoon's producer rejects the script because they are too young. Undaunted, they put Grampa's name on the script and Grampa gets a job as a staff writer.

Meanwhile, Marge's and Homer's high school reunion approaches. When only Marge gets an invitation. Homer confesses that he didn't graduate because he flunked a class. Nevertheless, he goes to the reunion with Marge and racks up alumni awards, which are stripped when Principal Dondelinger reveals his secret. Homer decides to go back to school and get his diploma.

Grampa wins an award for his "Itchy & Scratchy" episode. After Brooke Shields presents him with the award, Grampa confesses that he had never seen the episode before that night and thinks that the show is too violent. At home, a beaming Homer shows Marge his diploma.

A short called "The Adventures of Ned Flanders" features Ned and his family.

"SCREAMS FROM A MALL"

ABRAHAM SIMPSON

THE STUFF YOU MAY HAVE MISSED

The "Dazed and Confused" Itchy & Scratchy short was written by Milt Fineburg and Hy Levine.

Lisa reads *How to Get Rich Writing Cartoons*, by Simpsons scribe John Swartzwelder.

An Itchy & Scratchy Duff ad hangs in Roger Meyers, Jr.'s office.

Twenty-seven nicotine patches are visible on Krusty when he introduces "Screams from a Mall."

The sign at the Springfield Civic Center reads, "Friday—Cartoon Awards Show," with the words "Saturday—Closed for Roach Spraying" underneath.

Attendees at the Cartoon Awards Show include many Simpsons writers as well as Matt Groening.

The band plays part of "The Simpsons" theme when Abe wins the award for his work on "Itchy & Scratchy."

SHOW HIGHLIGHTS

Pig Latin: Spoken twice during the episode, when Krusty says to the guest chef on his show, "Ix-nay on the Ew-jay!" and when Homer says to Marge, "Ix-Nay on the Uclear-Nay Echnician-Tay."

"When I read your magazine, I don't see one wrinkled face or a single toothless grin. For shame!" Grampa's letter to "the sickos at *Modern Bride* magazine."

"I can't believe I ate the whole thing." Homer's quote in the high school yearbook.

 "Well, whenever I'm confused, I just check my underwear. It holds the answer to all the important questions."

 "If I puked in a fountain pen and mailed it to the monkey house, I'd get better scripts!"

Homer's high school reunion awards: Most weight gained, most improved odor, most hair lost, oldest car, lowest-paying job, least distance traveled to get to the reunion.

"I discovered a meal between breakfast and brunch." Homer, explaining how he gained so much weight since high school.

> **Remedial Science 1A:**
> The class Homer failed.

Lisa: *Maybe he just doesn't take us seriously 'cause we're kids. Let's put a grown-up's name on it.*
Bart: *How about Grampa? He's pretty out of it; he let those guys use his checkbook for a whole year.*

Homer: *All right, brain, you don't like me and I don't like you. But let's just do this, and I can get back to killing you with beer.*
Homer's brain: *It's a deal!*

Lisa: *Look, there's only one way to settle this. Rock-Paper-Scissors.*
Lisa's brain: *Poor predictable Bart. Always takes rock.*
Bart's brain: *Good ol' rock. Nothin' beats that!*
Bart: *Rock!*
Lisa: *Paper!*
Bart: *D'oh!*

Homer's brain: *This is it, Homer. Time to tell the terrible secret from your past.*
Homer: *Marge, I ate those fancy soaps you bought for the bathroom.*
Marge: *Oh, my god!*
Homer's brain: *No, the other secret!*
Homer: *Marge, I never graduated from high school.*
Marge: *That still doesn't explain why you ate my soap. Wait. Maybe it does.*

I WILL NOT SELL MIRACLE CURES
I WILL NOT SELL MIRACLE CURES
I WILL NOT SELL MIRACLE CURES

"The Adventures of Ned Flanders" Theme Song:
Chorus: *Hens love roosters/ Geese love ganders/ Everyone else loves Ned Flanders.*
Homer: *Not me.*
Chorus: *Everyone who counts loves Ned Flanders.*

Episode 9F16
Original Airdate: 4/15/93
Writer: Adam I. Lapidus
Director: Rich Moore
Guest Voice: Brooke Shields as Herself, Alex Rocco as Roger Meyers, Jr.

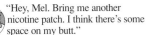 "Hey, Mel. Bring me another nicotine patch. I think there's some space on my butt."

"Thank you for this award. It is a tribute to this great country that a man who once took a shot at Teddy Roosevelt could win back your trust." Abe Simpson's planned acceptance speech.

The other nominees for Best Writing in a Cartoon Series: "Strondar, Master of Akom," the "Wedding" episode; "Action Figure Man," the "How to Buy Action Figure Man" episode; "Ren and Stimpy," season premiere.

Dondelinger: *Now, I'm, uh, going to burn this donut to show you how many calories it has.*
Homer: *Nooooo!*
Dondelinger: *The bright blue flame indicates this was a particularly sweet donut.*
Homer: *(sobbing) This is not happening! This is not happening!*

Lisa: *Then we put your name on the script and send it in.*
Bart: *Didn't you wonder why you were getting checks for absolutely nothing?*
Grampa: *I figured 'cause the Democrats were in power again.*

(Bart and Lisa see Homer walk into the living room, struggling to remove a plunger stuck on his head.)
Bart: *What are you going to change your name to when you grow up?*
Lisa: *Lois Sanborn.*
Bart: *(pointing to his chest) Steve Bennett.*

"Love That God":
Ned: *(seeing Rod and Todd praying) Knock that off, you two. It's time for church.*
Todd: *We're not going to church today.*
Ned: *(gasp) What? You give me one good reason.*
Todd: *It's Saturday.*
Ned: *Okelly-dokelly-do!*

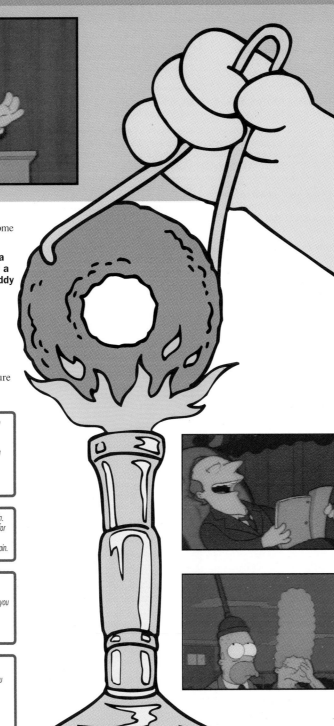

GRAMPA

Occupation:
Retired cranberry silo night watchman; patriarch of the Simpsons.

Residence:
Springfield Retirement Castle (where the elderly can hide from the inevitable).

Attire:
Bolo tie and bedroom slippers, except when attending funerals and award shows.

Prescriptions:
Two red pills for back spasms and a yellow one for arrhythmia.

Avoids:
Stairs; sticking to the point.

Favorite shop:
Herman's Military Antiques.

Favorite pastime:
Napping.

Least-favorite pastime:
Spending time with his family.

I CAN DRESS MYSELF.

RICHARD NIXON

WHACKING DAY

Episode 9F18 Original Airdate: 4/29/93 Writer: John Swartzwelder Director: Jeff Lynch Guest Voice: Barry White as Himself

Identity:
One-time president of the United States.

Nickname:
Tricky Dick.

Political affiliation:
Republican.

Relation to Springfield:
Participated in clubbing to death of snakes on Whacking Day; sold his soul to the Devil Flanders; Bart once did an imitation of him using his butt; tried to curry public favor by endorsing Duff.

I'D, UH, ALSO LIKE TO EXPRESS MY FONDNESS FOR THAT PARTICULAR BEER.

SHOW HIGHLIGHTS

Superintendent Chalmers's inspection includes: Counting the number of stars on the flags and tasting the sand in the sandbox for urine.

> **Nelson:** Imagine. A school out there with no bullies.
> **Jimbo:** Science geeks not gettin' beat up. Kids using their lunch money for food.
> **Nelson:** I can't take it!

Career opportunities for an elementary school dropout: 19th-century cockney bootblack or tester of dangerous food additives.

 "But first: A look at the local holiday that was called distasteful and puerile by a panel of hillbillies—Whacking Day! In a tradition that dates back to founding father Jebediah Springfield, every May tenth, residents gather to drive snakes to the center of town and whack them to snake heaven."

"Avert your eyes children, he may take on other forms!" Mr. Ogden, as he tosses Bart out of Springfield Christian School.

"Deformed? Why didn't you say so? They should call this book _Johnny Deformed_. Bart, accepting Marge's assignment to read _Johnny Tremain_.

> **Skinner:** Would the world judge me harshly if I threw away the key?
> **Groundskeeper Willie:** No. But the PTA would tear ya a new arse.
> **Skinner:** Wise counsel, William. But the potty talk adds nothing.
> **Groundskeeper Willie:** Aye, sir. You bath-taking, underpants-wearing lily-hugger.

"I'm an old man. I hate everything but 'Matlock.' Oooh! It's on now."

"Just squeeze your rage into a bitter little ball and release it at an appropriate time. Like that day I hit that referee with a whiskey bottle. 'Member that?" Homer, advising Lisa how to deal with her distaste for Whacking Day.

> **"Oh, Whacking Day" Lyrics**
> (Sung to the Tune of "O Christmas Tree"):
> Oh Whacking Day/ Oh Whacking Day/ Our hallowed snake skull-cracking day/ We'll break their backs/ Gouge out their eyes/ Their evil hearts we'll pulverize/ Oh Whacking Day/ Oh Whacking Day/ May God bestow His grace on thee.

Fort Sensible: So named after its inhabitants sacrificed the captain at the enemy's request so that they would be spared.

> **Lisa:** Dad, please, for the last time, I beg you: don't lower yourself to the level of the mob!
> **Homer:** Lisa, maybe if I'm part of that mob, I can help steer it in wise directions. Now, where's my giant foam cowboy hat and airhorn?

"Gentlemen, start your whacking!" Miss Springfield, starting Whacking Day.

> (Lisa sits in Lovejoy's office, looking for advice.)
> **Lovejoy:** (reading) And the Lord said "Whack ye all the serpents which crawl on their bellies and thy town shall be a beacon unto others." So you see, Lisa, even God himself endorses Whacking Day.
> **Lisa:** Let me see that.
> **Lovejoy:** No.

> **Mr. Ogden:** Now Bart, since you're new here, perhaps you'd favor us with a psalm.
> **Bart:** How about "Beans, Beans, the Musical Fruit?"
> **Mr. Ogden:** Well, beans were a staple of the Israelites... yes, proceed.

> **Skinner:** May I interest you in a Jello brick, sir? There's a grape in the center.
> **Chalmers:** Well, I'm not made of stone.

> (Bart questions Grampa about his days as a WWII cabaret singer in Dusseldorf.)
> **Bart:** Is that story true, Grampa?
> **Grampa:** Well, most of it. I did wear a dress for a period in the forties. Oh, they had designers then!

THE STUFF YOU MAY HAVE MISSED

Bob Woodward is the author of _The Truth about Whacking Day_.

The Springfield Christian School sign reads, "We Put the Fun in Fundamentalist Dogma."

Lisa plays back-up for Barry White on a pink electric bass guitar; she also plays guitar in 9F15, "Last Exit to Springfield."

Barry White also appears in 9F19, "Krusty Gets Kancelled."

The long car that pulls into Homer's $10 per-axle parking lot has 10 axles.

Principal Skinner prepares for Superintendent Chalmers's surprise inspection by locking Bart, Jimbo, Dolph, Kearney, and Nelson in the school's basement. Bart escapes and takes Groundskeeper Willie's tractor for a ride. Skinner expels Bart after he mows into Chalmers's backside.

Lisa is horrified by the approaching holiday, "Whacking Day," in which town residents beat snakes to death with clubs. Marge decides to teach Bart herself, turning the garage into a makeshift classroom. Bart reads _Johnny Tremain_ and willingly accompanies Marge to Olde Springfield Towne.

Whacking Day arrives and Lisa begs Homer not to participate, but he refuses to listen. With the help of the bass voice of Barry White, Bart and Lisa lure all the snakes in town into their house. An unruly mob arrives, so Bart reveals that his research has unearthed the holiday's original purpose: it was concocted as an excuse to beat up the Irish. To reward Bart for his studies, Skinner allows Bart to return to school.

I WILL RETURN THE SEEING EYE DOG
I WILL RETURN THE SEEING EYE DOG
I WILL RETURN THE SEEING EYE DOG

MARGE IN CHAINS

Episode 9F20   Original Airdate: 5/6/93   Writers: Bill Oakley and Josh Weinstein   Director: Jim Reardon   Guest Voice: David Crosby as Himself

The dreaded Osaka flu hits Springfield and Homer, Bart, Lisa, and Grampa all depend on Marge to nurse them back to health. While picking up supplies at the Kwik-E-Mart, Marge accidentally forgets to pay for Grampa's bottle of bourbon and is arrested for shoplifting.

Homer hires Lionel Hutz to defend Marge at her trial. The jury finds her guilty, and she is sentenced to thirty days in jail.

Now behind bars, Marge's absence is felt at home and at the annual bake sale. Without her famous marshmallow squares, the Springfield Park Commission fails to raise enough money to pay for a statue of Abraham Lincoln. Instead, they purchase one of Jimmy Carter. When the statue is unveiled, disappointed townspeople riot. Marge is released from jail, and the townspeople welcome her back, and apologizing for not trusting her.

SHOW HIGHLIGHTS

"Hello everybody. I'm Troy McClure, star of such films as *P is for Psycho* and *The President's Neck Is Missing*. But now I'm here to tell you about a remarkable new invention."

"Oh, the network slogan is true! Watch Fox and be damned for all eternity!" Ned Flanders, believing God is punishing him with the Osaka flu for watching "Married with Children."

"Can you get me some of those Flintstones' chewable morphine?" Bart, to Marge, sick at home with the flu.

"Mrs. Simpson! You did not pay for this bottle of Colonel Kwik-E-Mart's Kentucky Bourbon."

"All right. Come out with your hands up, two cups of coffee, an auto freshener that says Capricorn, and something with coconut on it. "

"From now on, I'll use my gossip for good, instead of evil." Helen Lovejoy, welcoming Marge back to Springfield.

"Now Apu, Mrs. Simpson claims she forgot she was carrying that bottle of delicious bourbon, brownest of the brown liquors... So tempting. What's that? You want me to drink you? But I'm in the middle of a trial!"

(Inside Bart's body, white blood cells are battling a virus.)
White blood cell #1: *Sarge, we keep getting orders to let the virus win!*
White blood cell #2: *Must be a school day. Lay down your arms.*
(The virus attacks and smothers the white blood cells.)
Virus: *All right! Let's make some pus.*

(Burns finds Homer eating a sandwich in his ultra-secure, microbe-free chamber.)
Burns: *Who the devil are you?*
Homer's brain: *Don't panic, just come up with a good story.*
Homer: *My name is Mr. Burns.*
Homer's brain: *D'oh!*

Revealed this Episode:
Marge has webbed toes.

Prosecutor: *Ladies and gentlemen of the jury, who do you find more attractive: Tom Cruise or Mel Gibson?*
Judge: *What is the point of all this?*
Prosecutor: *Your honor, I feel so confident of Marge Simpson's guilt, that I can waste the court's time by rating the Super-Hunks.*

THE STUFF YOU MAY HAVE MISSED

When the Japanese workers speak and laugh, their dialogue appears dubbed.

According to a sign Snake passes while leaving town with the Kwik-E-Mart, Mexico City is 678 miles away from Springfield.

The Mayor's seal says, "Corruptus in Extremis."

The Springfield Women's Prison's motto reads, "A Prison for Women."

A bumper sticker on one of the conjugal visit trailers reads, "Don't come a-knockin' if this van's a-rockin'."

After the hairdo is altered on the Jimmy Carter statue, its plaque is changed from "Malaise Forever" to "Marge Forever."

Hutz: *Now don't you worry, Mrs. Simpson, I— Uh-oh. We've drawn Judge Snyder.*
Marge: *Is that bad?*
Hutz: *Well, he's had it in for me since I kinda ran over his dog.*
Marge: *You did?*
Hutz: *Well, replace the word "kinda" with the word "repeatedly," and the word "dog" with "son."*

Hutz: *So, Mr. Nahasapeemapetilon—if that is your real name—have you ever forgotten anything?*
Apu: *No. In fact I can recite pi to 40,000 places. The last digit is one!*
Homer: *Mmm . . . pie.*

Homer: *Apu, I'd like you to drop the charges against my wife.*
Apu: *No offense, Mr. Homer, but we're putting that bitch on ice!*
Homer: *Now, c'mon! I'm your best customer!*
Apu: *I'm sorry, Mr. Homer, but it is the policy of the Kwik-E-Mart and its parent corporation Nordyne Defense Dynamics to prosecute shoplifters to the full extent of the law.*

Marge: *Knock, knock. I'm Marge Simpson. Your new cellmate.*
Phillips: *I'm Phillips. They call me that 'cause I killed my husband with a Phillips-head screwdriver.*

I DO NOT HAVE
DIPLOMATIC IMMUNITY
I DO NOT HAVE
DIPLOMATIC IMMUNITY
I DO NOT HAVE
DIPLOMATIC IMMUNITY

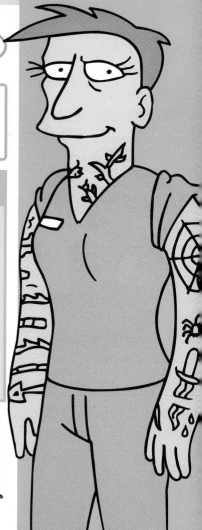

GABBO

What:
Dummy for ventriloquist Arthur Crandall; budding (if highly overhyped) TV star.

Appearance:
His hinges are visible.

Overall demeanor:
Mean-spirited and annoying.

Talents:
Can do both the "Hully Gully" and an imitation of Vin Scully.

I'M A BAD WIDDLE BOY.

The citizens of Springfield are bombarded with a media blitz hailing the arrival of Gabbo, a ventriloquist's dummy who resembles Howdy Doody and sounds like Jerry Lewis. Ventriloquist Arthur Crandall and Gabbo appear on TV every afternoon opposite Krusty the Clown, and Bart and Lisa fear that the competition will jeopardize Krusty's career. When Krusty's ratings plummet, his show is cancelled.

Krusty's efforts to find employment—and win at the racetrack—also fail. Determined to ruin Gabbo, Bart sneaks into the studio and activates a TV camera just as Gabbo is bad-mouthing his audience. Meanwhile, Bart and Lisa advise Krusty to relaunch his career with a TV special featuring major celebrities.

Bart and Lisa contact Bette Midler, Hugh Hefner, Elizabeth Taylor, and the Red Hot Chili Peppers. All but Taylor agree to appear on Krusty's show. With additional help from Johnny Carson and Luke Perry, the special is an enormous hit, and Krusty's show is reinstated.

SHOW HIGHLIGHTS

 "Everyone is saying 'Gabbo this' and 'Gabbo that.' But no one is saying 'Worship this' and 'Jericho that.'"

"Well, kids, this is where you would watch Itchy and Scratchy, except they're on the Gabbo show now. So, here's Eastern Europe's favorite cat-and-mouse team: Worker & Parasite!"

"I admit I used the city treasury to fund the murder of my enemies. But as Gabbo would say, 'I'm a bad widdle boy.'"

"Ah, Rex Morgan, M.D. You have the prescription for the daily blues."

"Thirty-five years in show business and already no one remembers me. Just like what's-his-name and whos-its and, you know, that guy, who always wore a shirt..."

Bart: Somebody ought to ruin Gabbo's career the way he ruined Krusty's.
Lisa: Two wrongs don't make a right, Bart.
Bart: Yes, they do.
Lisa: No, they don't.
Bart: Yes, they do.
Lisa: No, they don't.
Bart: Yes, they do.
Lisa: Dad!
Homer: Two wrongs make a right, Lisa.

(Krusty tries to get Mel to quit the "Gulp 'N' Blow.")
Krusty: But you gotta come back, Mel—we're a team!
Mel: No, Krusty. You always treated me rather shabbily. On our last show, you poured liquid nitrogen down my pants and cracked my buttocks with a hammer!

Ouch: Luke Perry is fired out of Krusty's cannon. He is catapulted through a studio window, into the Museum of Sandpaper, through a display of sulfuric acid bottles at the Kwik-E-Mart, and into a pillow factory, where he has a soft landing. The building is then demolished with him inside.

"Live, from Springfield Harbor, where the sewage meets the sand, it's the Springfield Squares!"
The opening line of the "Springfield Squares."

Krusty: I've had plenty of guys come after me, and I've buried 'em all. Hobos, sea captains, Joey Bishop...
Miss Pennycandy: Don't forget the Special Olympics.
Krusty: Oh, yeah; I slaughtered the Special Olympics!

Bart: I didn't know you knew Luke Perry.
Krusty: Know him? He's my worthless half-brother.
Lisa: He's a big TV star.
Krusty: Yeah. (dismissive) On Fox.

Lisa: Krusty! What have you done to yourself?
Krusty: I thought I'd get into shape, so I've been drinking nothing but milkshakes.
Lisa: You mean those diet milkshakes?
Krusty: Uh oh.

Bart: That cute little character could take America by storm. All he needs is a hook.
Gabbo: I'm a bad widdle boy.
Bart: Ay, carumba!

Gabbo: And now, it's time for another patented Gabbo Crank Call! Ooh, I love these!
Bart: I can't believe it. He stole this bit from Krusty!
Lisa: Yeah, well, Krusty stole it from Steve Allen.

I WILL NOT CHARGE ADMISSION TO THE BATHROOM.
I WILL NOT CHARGE ADMISSION TO THE BATHROOM.
I WILL NOT CHARGE ADMISSION TO THE BATHROOM.

THE STUFF YOU MAY HAVE MISSED

Gabbo's line, "That ought to hold the little S.O.B.'s," spoken after the camera has been turned off (a gaffe repeated by Kent Brockman), is taken from a 1950s kiddie show in which the host asked, "Are we off the air?" and then said, "That ought to hold the little S.O.B.s for another week." He did not know he was still on the air and was summarily dismissed.

A *Springfield Variety* headline reads, "Gabbo Fabbo Krusty Rusty."

After Quimby admits using the city treasury to fund the murder of his enemies, the *Springfield Shopper* features the headlines "Quimby Re-elected by Landslide," and, in smaller type, "Two More Bodies Surface in Springfield Harbor."

The sign, "Litter Removal Next Two Miles Courtesy of Bette Midler," is inspired by actual signs on the Los Angeles freeways.

The *Springfield Shopper* headline, "Krusty Special Airs Today" features a smaller headline that reads, "Gabbo to Have 'Real Boy' Operation Today."

Ratings on the Love-Tester at Moe's: "Hot Tamale," "Casanova," "Hubba Hubba," "Lukewarm Fish," "Coldfish."

KANCELLED

Episode 9F19 Original Airdate: 5/13/93
Writer: John Swartzwelder
Director: David Silverman
Guest Voices: Johnny Carson as Himself, Hugh Hefner as Himself, Bette Midler as Herself, Luke Perry as Himself, Elizabeth Taylor as Herself, Barry White as Himself, The Red Hot Chili Peppers as Themselves: Anthony Kiedis, Flea, Chad Smith, Arik Marshall

Gabbo Introduces Himself:

Gabbo: *You're gonna like me/you're gonna love me! 'Cause I can do most anything!*
(Gabbo leaps off Arthur Crandall's lap)
Gabbo: *I can do the hully gully!*
(he starts dancing wildly)
Gabbo: *I can imitate Vin Scully!* (à la Vin Scully) *Let's take time out from this triple-play to talk about Farmer Dan's pure pork sausages. Mmm, mmm!*
(back to normal) *I'll give out shiny dimes!*
(Gabbo tosses coins to the audience)
Gabbo: *I can travel back in time!*
(He disappears into thin air and suddenly reappears with a pilgrim)
(Toy soldiers march out, singing)
Toy soldiers: *You're gonna like him!*
(Toy bolsheviks dance out, singing)
Toy bolsheviks: *You're gonna love him!*
(The curtain opens, revealing giant juggling toy clowns and toy can-can girls kicking and singing, along with toy drummers and tromboners.)
All: *It's the greatest show in toooooowwn!! Gabbo!*
(Five jets roar over the stage, leaving colored rocket trails.)

Krusty and Johnny on the Special:

Krusty: *Now Johnny, whatcha got for us? Jokes? A little magic?*
Johnny Carson: *Actually, I thought I'd lift this 1987 Buick Skylark over my head.*
(Johnny walks over to the car, lifts it over his head, and nods to the audience.)
Krusty: *High-yo! Johnny, that's amazing!*
Johnny Carson: *Oh yeah? Get a load of this!*
(He spins the car over his head and sings opera.)

Krusty: *I'm a star again. I don't know how to thank you, kids.*
Bart: *That's alright, Krusty.*
Lisa: *We're getting fifty percent of the T-shirt sales.*
Krusty: *Whaat?!? That's the sweetest plum!! Ah, what the hell. You deserve it. Thanks, kids.*

(Krusty is backstage watching the Red Hot Chili Peppers perform in their briefs.)
Krusty: *Dancing around in your underwear. That is so degrading.*
(Krusty is dressed in an old-fashioned little kid's oufit, complete with curled wig, ruffled shirt, and tights.)
Stage director: *Thirty seconds to your "Li'l Stinker" sketch!*
Krusty: *Give me a bigger lolly!*

Krusty and the Red Hot Chili Peppers:

Krusty: *Now boys, ah, the network has a problem with some of your lyrics. Would you mind changing them for the show?*
Anthony: *Forget you, clown.*
Chad: *Yeah, our lyrics are like our children, man. No way.*
Krusty: *Well, okay, but here where you say, "What I got you gotta get and put it in ya," how about just, "What I'd like is I'd like to hug and kiss ya."*
Flea: *Wow. That's much better.*
Arik: *Everyone can enjoy that.*

SEEN AROUND SPRINGFIELD

Tonight Only, in Russian. Poster advertisement for the opera "Carmen," which the Simpson family attends. The conductor identified on the poster is Boris Csuposki, a play on the name of "The Simpsons" producer and supervising animation director, Gabor Csupo. (7G02)

50 Million Cigarette Smokers CAN'T BE WRONG!

Our Safety Record: [7] Days Since Last Accident. A sign at the Springfield Nuclear Power Plant. (7G03)

Poachers Will Be Shot. A sign on the gates of Burns's estate. (7G04)

We Give Credit to Everyone!; Bad Credit, Good!; Bankruptcy Schmankruptcy. Signs at Bob's RV Roundup. (7G09)

Half-Man, Half-Ape Burgers; Get Your Photo Taken with Bigfoot. Signs representing the arrival of the Bigfoot cottage industry. (7G09)

Florence of Arabia; Girlesque; Foxy Boxing; Mud City; The Sapphire Lounge. Girlie joints. (7G10)

Caution Radioactive. A sign on the floor of the Springfield Nuclear Power Plant. (7G11)

Honor System—Coffee Refills, 25 Cents. A sign beside the Springfield Nuclear Power Plant coffee urn. (7F02)

You Rip It, You Buy It. A sign inside the Royal Majesty—for the Obese or Gangly Gentleman haberdashery. (7F02)

Springfield Savings—Safe from 1890-1986, 1988-. A sign at the bank. (7F05)

Yes, We Have Rotgut! The sign on a liquor store "on the wrong side of the tracks." (7F07)

Everybody Gets a Trophy Day. One of the trophies Bart displays on his shelf. (7F08)

What If They Blew Up a Cat and Nobody Laughed? A sign at a protest against "The Itchy & Scratchy Show." (7F09)

If You Can Find a Cheaper Lion,

PUPPIES FOR FREE OR BEST OFFER

(9F08)

Painless Dentistry

You Must Be in Africa. A clause on a sign for Discount Lion Safari. (7F17)

You Don't Have to Be Crazy to Be Committed Here, But It Helps!; Your Mother Isn't Committed Here, So Clean Up after Yourself. Signs at the New Bedlam Rest Home for the Emotionally Interesting. (7F24)

Member of the Bonerland Medical Association. The sign on the front door of Dr. Marvin Monroe's office. (8F02)

The Straight and Narrow Storage Co. Advertisement on the jacket worn by the man who picks up cigarettes from Bart. (8F03)

For Your Thighs Only; Crocodile Done Me; Dr. Strangepants. Movie titles advertised on the Springfield X theater's marquee. (8F05)

All Creatures Great and Cheap. The sign on the pet store where Homer first looks for Lisa's pony. (8F06)

You Pet It, You Bought It. The sign inside the All Creatures Great and Cheap pet store. (8F06)

Non-Threatening Boys. The name of a magazine that Lisa reads. (8F11, 7F14)

We Cram Fun down Your Throat. The slogan at Wall E. Weasel's Pizzeria/Arcade. (8F11)

Where Logic Takes a Holiday; All Laws of Nature Are Meaningless. The slogan for the Springfield Mystery Spot. (8F13)

Ernest Needs a Kidney. The title of the film playing at the Aztec Theater. (8F16)

Science Made Very Very Simple. The title of the book Bart uses to explain how gas can be ignited by fire. (8F20)

We're Now Rat-Free! The sign at Ye Olde Off-Ramp Inn. (9F02)

Stinking Fish Realty. The name of the realty company that Homer and Marge use to find their first home. (9F08)

With a Name This Bad, We've Got to Be Good. Stinking Fish Realty's motto. (9F08)

(Formerly, Painful Dentistry). The sign on a dentist's office. (9F15)

Nudes at Eleven; Adam and Adam; The Horny Toad. The titles of X-rated flicks on the Springfield X theater's marquee. (9F15)

Entering Badlands—High-Speed

DON'T EAT BEEF.

EAT DEER.

Chases Use Diamond Lane. Sign on the highway. (1F03)

Models and Model Decals Store; Triple-G Rated; Sweet Tooth; Bootleg Records; All-Night Arcade; Booking; Batting; Bicycle Seat Covers. Glitzy kid-oriented nightspots and signs that Bart sees while in his sugar-high state during his night on the town. (1F06)

Sperms of Endearment; I'll Do Anyone. The titles of X-rated films advertised on a theater marquee. (1F08)

Seven Days without a Drink Makes Me Weak. A sign next to the bar in Flanders's basement. (1F09)

Petrochem Petrochemical Corporation. A sign in front of the Malibu Stacy factory. (1F12)

Proud Makers of Caustic Polypropylene and Malibu Stacy. A smaller sign in front of the Malibu Stacy Factory. (1F12)

No Mercury Dumping without a Permit. The sign at Lake Springfield. (1F14)

Springfield Tar Pits: The Best in Tar Entertainment—Time Magazine. The sign at the Springfield Tar Pits. (1F15)

Lionel Hutz (Also Expert Shoe Repair). The advertisement for attorney Lionel Hutz's services. (1F16)

Conformco Brain Deprogrammers—A Subsidiary of Mrs. Fields' Cookies. The sign outside the office that Homer and Marge visit. (1F16)

Li'l Bastard Clock-Tampering Kit. The name of the kit Bart uses to make the clocks at Springfield Elementary run fast. (1F19)

We Take the "Dolt" out of A-Dolt Education. The sign outside the Adult Education Annex. (1F20)

Hal Roach Apartments–Retirement Living in the Heart of the Cemetery District. The sign at the Hal Roach Apartments. (1F21)

Private Wedding–Please Worship Elsewhere. The sign at the First Church of Springfield. (1F21)

Today: Senior Citizens Swing Dance–Tomorrow: Cat Spay-a-Thon. The sign on the Springfield Community Center marquee. (1F21)

Not Affiliated with the Planet Venus. The message on the Venus Bridal Salon sign. (1F21)

Pool Sharks!–Where the Buyer Is Our Chum. The sign at Pool Sharks! pool shop. (1F22)

Li'l Bastard Traveling Kit. The label on Bart's fanny pack. (2F01)

Re-Neducation Center–Where the Elite Meet to Have Their Spirits Broken. The sign at the Re-Neducation Center. (2F03)

Welcome Candy Convention, Room I; Candy-Shaped Rat Poison Convention, Room II. Signs on the marquee in front of the convention hall. (2F06)

$1.99 Per Pound Special on Michener. An advertisement on the sign outside the Books! Books! And Additional Books bookstore. (2F07)

Kosher Erotic Sex; How to Seduce Your Lousy, Lazy Husband; Bordello Repair; Bork on Sex; Weight Loss through Laborious Sex. Sex titles on the shelves at the Books! Books! And Additional Books bookstore. (2F07)

I Told You Not to Flush That. The advertising slogan on the Stern Lecture Plumbing sign. (2F09)

Extra! Extra!–Bart Named World's Greatest Sex Machine. The headline in a novelty newspaper. (2F14)

Still Operating, Thanks to the Lengthy Appeals Process. The phrase on the Springfield Nuclear Power Plant sign. (2F15)

Building a Better Future . . . for Him. The slogan on the Burns Construction Company sign. (2F16)

Springfield Pet Shop: All Our Pets Are Flushable. The sign on the Springfield Pet Shop. (2F18)

Springfield Dog Track: Think of Them as Little Horses. The sign on the Springfield Dog Track. (2F18)

8:00–Medfly Spraying/8:15–Springfield Pops Concert/8:30–Spraying, 2nd Pass. The sign in Jebediah Springfield Park. (2F21)

Bear Baiter Magazine; Rock Jumper–The Magazine for People Who Like to Jump from Rock to Rock; Mosh Pitter; Danger Liker; Cliff Biker Magazine; Glass Eater Magazine. The titles of danger magazines. (2F21)

KJAZZ–152 Americans Can't Be Wrong. The sign for KJAZZ. (2F32)

Come for the Funerals, Stay for the Pie. The sign at the Springfield Cemetery. (2F32)

50 Million Cigarette Smokers Can't Be Wrong! The sign in the ad agency. (3F04)

When the H-Bomb Isn't Enough. The slogan on the sign at the Germ Warfare Laboratory. (3F06)

In Honor of the Birth of Our Savior, Try-N-Save Is Open All Day Christmas. The sign at the Try-N-Save. (3F07)

Proud Home of the Soap Bar Beating. The sign at Juvenile Hall. (3F07)

U.S. Air Force Base (Not Affiliated with U.S. Air). The sign at the U.S. Air Force Base. (3F08)

Duff and the Air Force–50 Years of Flying High. The sign at the Duff Beer stand. (3F08)

No Parcheesi Sets, Please. The mes-sage on the rummage sale flyers. (3F09)

Browse through Our Bra Barrel. An invitation at the Steppin' Out Fashion Mart. (3F11)

I Can't Believe It's a Law Firm. The name of Lionel Hutz's law firm. (3F16)

Ask about Our Sheet Rental. The sign on the marquee at a Worst Western Hotel, where Roger Myers stays after losing his fortune. (3F16)

Works on Contingency? No, Money Down! Lionel Hutz's remade business card. (3F16)

Red Light, Boris Yeltsin; Yellow Light, Stinkin ; Purple Light, Soused; Green Light, Tipsy. The results of Moe's Breathalyzer Test ("Yeltsin" is the drunkest). (3G01)

Human Blimp Sees Flying Saucer. The *Springfield Shopper* headline exposing Homer's UFO sighting. (3G01)

Invading Your Privacy for 60 Years. The sign at the FBI's Springfield Branch. (3G01)

Alien Dude: Need Two Tickets to Pearl Jam. Jimbo Jones's sign. (3G01)

Homer Was Right; No Fat Alien Chicks; Homer Is a Dope. Messages on T-shirts for sale. (3G01)

Now 40% Quainter. The sign at the Mt. Swartzwelder Historic Cider Mill. (4F05)

WILL DROP PANTS FOR FOOD

NIGEL

Occupation:
Star discoverer; fortune maker; hat blocker.

Modus operandi:
Lurking around small-town bars scouting flash-in-the-pan talent.

Country of origin:
Great Britain.

Description:
Long black hair pulled back into a ponytail; blue suit; red shirt; white tie; matching red and white hankie.

Unoriginal PR coups:
Press conferences at Kennedy Airport.

> GENTLEMEN, YOU'VE JUST RECORDED YOUR FIRST NUMBER ONE.

SHOW HIGHLIGHTS

 "Welcome, swappers, to the Springfield Swap Meet. Ich bin ein Springfield Swap Meet patron!"

"I wore this for two years in a Viet Cong Internment center. Never thought I'd see the old girl again. Still fits." Skinner, slipping on an iron mask labelled, "Prisoner 24601."

"Junk, junk, the airplane's upside down, Strad-i-who-vius?..." Homer rummaging through Mrs. Glick's box and pulling out the Declaration of Independence, a copy of "Action Comics" #1, a sheet of rare stamps, and a Stradivarius violin.

 "It all happened during that magical summer of 1985. A maturing Joe Piscopo left 'Saturday Night Live' to conquer Hollywood; People Express introduced a generation of hicks to plane travel; and I was in a barbershop quartet."

"Rock 'n' roll had become stagnant. 'Achy Breaky Heart' was seven years away. Something had to fill the void, and that something was barbershop." Homer, setting the stage for his story.

"Too Village-People." Nigel, giving his reason why Wiggum has to leave the quartet.

"Sure, why not? Now where's me toothpick?" Barney, on his hands and knees in the men's room, accepting the offer to sing with Homer's quartet.

"And the Grammy for Outstanding Soul, Spoken Word, or Barbershop Album of the Year goes to...The Be Sharps!" David Crosby, announcing the winner at the 29th Annual Grammy Awards.

Homer: *I'll never forget my five and a half weeks at the top.*
Bart: *Man, that's some story.*
Lisa: *But there's still a few things I don't get. Like, how come we never heard about this until today?*
Bart: *Yeah, and what happened to all the money you made?*
Lisa: *Why haven't you hung up your gold record?*
Bart: *Since when could you write a song?*
Homer: *Heh, heh, heh. There are perfectly good answers to those questions, but they'll have to wait for another night.*

The "Baby on Board" lyrics:
Baby on board/how I've adored/that sign on my car's windowpane/bounce in my step/loaded with pep/'cause I'm drivin' in the carpool lane/call me a square/friend, I don't care/that little yellow sign can't be ignored/I'm tellin' you it's mighty nice/each trip's a trip to paradise/with my baby on board.

Bart: *Dad, when did you record an album?*
Homer: *I'm surprised you don't remember, son. It was only eight years ago.*
Bart: *Dad, thanks to television, I can't remember what happened eight minutes ago.*

(Apu introduces himself to Nigel.)
Apu: *Apu Nahasapeemapetilon.*
Nigel: *Never fit on a marquee, luv. From now on, your name is Apu Du Beaumarchais.*
Apu: *It is a great dishonor to my ancestors and my God, but okay.*

The Name:
Skinner: *We need a name that's witty at first, but that seems less funny each time you hear it.*
Apu: *How about "The Be Sharps"?*
Skinner: *Perfect.*
Homer: *The Be Sharps.*

Lisa: *I can't believe you're not still popular.*
Bart: *What'd you do? Screw up like The Beatles and say you were bigger than Jesus?*
Homer: *All the time. It was the title of our second album!*

Homer: *...we were about to learn an iron law of show business: What goes up must come down.*
Lisa: *What about Bob Hope? He's been consistently popular for over 50 years.*
Bart: *So has Sinatra.*
Homer: *Well, anyway, we were all getting tired of —*
Lisa: *Dean Martin still packs 'em in.*
Bart: *Ditto Tom Jones.*
Homer: *Shut up!*

THE STUFF YOU MAY HAVE MISSED

At her swap meet table, Marge sells "Bald Adonis," a Ringo painting, and a Burns painting (from 7F18, "Brush with Greatness"). She also sells the sailboat painting that usually hangs above the couch.

David Crosby also appears in 9F20, "Marge in Chains."

Bart and Lisa browse at the flea market and discover a record album with Homer's picture on the cover. Homer recounts how in the summer of 1985, he, Chief Wiggum, Principal Skinner, and Apu formed a barbershop quartet...

At the behest of their manager, Nigel, the group replaces Wiggum with Barney, who has a beautiful tenor voice, and calls themselves "The Be Sharps." Inspired by Marge, Homer writes a song, "Baby on Board," which becomes a hit. The group's album receives a Grammy award for their first album and they become the focus of a mass merchandising campaign. Homer even meets George Harrison.

The band's meteoric success is short lived. Marge finds that with Homer constantly on the road, she cannot manage raising the kids by herself. There are disagreements over lyrics and personal friction among the band members. Barney dates a Japanese conceptual artist named Kako, whom the others regard with contempt. After five and a half weeks, the band finally splits up...

Homer finishes the story and, feeling nostalgic, gathers with his former band members for a reunion on the rooftop of Moe's Tavern.

```
I WILL NEVER WIN AN EMMY
I WILL NEVER WIN AN EMMY
I WILL NEVER WIN AN EMMY
I WILL NEVER WIN AN EMMY
I WILL NEVER WIN AN EMMY
I WILL NEVER WIN AN EMMY
```

CAPE FEARE

Episode #9F22   Original Airdate: 10/7/93   Writer: Jon Vitti   Director: Rich Moore
Guest Voice: Kelsey Grammer as Sideshow Bob

SIDESHOW BOB

Position:
Master thespian-turned-hardened convict; second banana on "The Krusty the Clown Show."

Real name:
Bob Terwilliger.

Description:
Red spiked hair; green hula skirt; oversized red shoes that house oversized feet.

Career pinnacle:
A prison production of "Evita."

Ultimate dream:
Until recently, to kill Bart Simpson.

Hobby:
Oozing refinement.

Bart receives an anonymous letter—written in blood—threatening kill him. He becomes paranoid, even suspecting members of his own family   In actuality, it is Sideshow Bob who has authored the letter from jail. Now released from prison and on parole, he plots his revenge against Bart for having sent him to jail.

Sideshow Bob launches a campaign to terrorize Bart. Homer and Marge seek help from the FBI, which recommends that the family join the Witness Relocation Program and moves them to Terror Lake, a community outside Springfield. Strapped underneath their car, Sideshow Bob accompanies the Simpsons to their new life.

Now renamed "The Thompsons," the Simpsons are given a houseboat as their new dwelling. The night they arrive, Sideshow Bob ties everyone up except Bart, sets the boat adrift, and enters Bart's room, planning to kill him. Bart escapes out the window, but is cornered by Sideshow Bob on the edge of the boat. As a last request, Bart asks Bob to sing the entire score from the "H.M.S. Pinafore," during which time the houseboat drifts back to

Springfield, where Chief Wiggum places Sideshow Bob under arrest.

SHOW HIGHLIGHTS

"Oh my god, someone's trying to kill me! Oh wait, it's for Bart." Homer, accidentally opening one of Bob's letters to Bart.

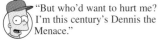 **"But who'd want to hurt me? I'm this century's Dennis the Menace."**

"No, that's German for 'The Bart, The.'" Sideshow Bob, when asked if the tattoo on his chest says "Die, Bart, Die."

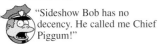 **"Sideshow Bob has no decency. He called me Chief Piggum!"**

Milhouse to Bart: "Um, I checked around. The girls are calling you 'Fatty Fat Fat Fat,' and Nelson's planning to pull down your pants, but...nobody's trying to kill you."

"Ooh–I wanna be John Elway": Homer's choice for a new identity.

The Arrest:
Chief Wiggum: *Hold it right there, Sideshow Bob. You're under arrest.*
Bob: *By Lucifer's beard!*
Chief Wiggum: *Uh, yeah. It's a good thing you drifted by this brothel.*
Bart: *I knew I had to buy some time, so I asked him to sing the score from the "H.M.S. Pinafore."*
Homer: *Ooh! A plan fiendishly clever in its in-trick-asies.*
Bart: *Take him away, boys.*
Chief Wiggum: *Hey, I'm the chief here! Bake him away, toys.*
Lou: *What'd you say, Chief?*
Chief Wiggum: *Do what the kid says.*

"I'll be Gus, the lovable chimney sweep. Clean as a whistle, sharp as a thistle, best in all Westminster." Bart, expressing his desire for a new identity.

Cape Feare, Terror Lake, New Horrorfield, Screamville: The options given the Simpsons for places where they can hide "in peace and security."

The Hearing:
Burns's lawyer: *Robert, if released, would you pose any threat to one Bart Simpson?*
Sideshow Bob: *Bart Simpson? Ha! The spirited little scamp who twice foiled my evil schemes and sent me to this dank, urine-soaked hellhole?*
Parole officer: *Uh, we object to the term "urine-soaked hellhole" when you could have said, "peepee-soaked heckhole."*
Sideshow Bob: *Cheerfully withdrawn.*

THE STUFF YOU MAY HAVE MISSED

Sideshow Bob writes a note to the "Life in These United States" section of *Reader's Digest*.

All of the notes are from Bob except for "I Kill You Scum," which Homer sent to Bart after Bart somehow tattooed the words, "WIDE LOAD" on Homer's butt.

Sideshow Bob's Tattoos: "Die, Bart, Die," "Ouch Man!" (with Bart's head on a skateboard), a skull and crossbones, "LUV" (on one hand), "HAT" (pronounced Hate, on the other hand—actually, the A is the phonetic, long "a" with the line above it.)

Sideshow Bob steps on nine rakes when he reaches the Thompson's houseboat.

Movie Moments:
The episode parodies the film *Cape Fear* and contains elements of *Psycho* (when Sideshow Bob stays at the Bates Motel in Terror Lake) .

Lisa: *Bart, I figured it out. Who's someone you've been making irritating phone calls to for years?*
Bart: *Linda Lavin?*
Lisa: *No, someone who didn't deserve it.*

Chief Wiggum: *I'd like to help you, ma'am, but, heh heh, I'm afraid there's no law against mailing threatening letters.*
Marge: *I'm pretty sure there is.*
Wiggum: *Ha! The day I take cop lessons from Ma Kettle–*
Lou: *Hey, she's right, chief.*
Wiggum: *Well, shut my mouth. It's ALSO illegal to put squirrels down your pants for the purpose of gambling.*

THE CAFETERIA DEEP FRYER IS NOT A TOY
CAFETERIA DEEP FRYER IS NOT A TOY
CAFETERIA DEEP FRYER IS NOT A TOY
CAFETERIA DEEP FRYER NOT A TOY

ATTEMPTED MURDER. NOW HONESTLY, WHAT IS THAT? DO THEY GIVE A NOBEL PRIZE FOR ATTEMPTED CHEMISTRY?

Guest Voice:
Kelsey Grammer as Sideshow Bob

BENJAMIN, DOUG, AND GARY

Position in community:
Nerd physics students and dorm roommates, Springfield University.

Identifying marks:
Benjamin wears a calculator on his hip; Doug is fat and wears a pocket protector; Gary wears black-rimmed glasses and has the most pronounced overbite.

Favorite game:
Computer solitaire.

Turns-ons:
Monty Python routines; *Star Trek* conventions; individually wrapped slices of American cheese.

Pet peeve:
Geeks on the Internet who insist that Captain Picard is better than Captain Kirk.

MR. SIMPSON? WE ALL HAVE NOSEBLEEDS.

HOMER GOES TO COLLEGE

Episode 1F02   Original Airdate: 10/14/93   Writer: Conan O'Brien   Director: Jim Reardon

The Nuclear Regulatory Commission makes a surprise inspection of the nuclear power plant. When Homer accidentally causes a meltdown during a test in a simulation van, the NRC officials tell Mr. Burns that Homer's job requires university training in nuclear physics. Homer applies to college, but when all his applications are rejected, Burns gets him accepted to Springfield University.

After Homer causes an accident in his nuclear physics class, his physics professor recommends that he be tutored by three young nerds, Gary, Doug, and Benjamin. Instead, Homer involves them in a prank to kidnap the pig mascot of nearby Springfield A&M. The nerds are caught and expelled from the university by Dean Peterson.

Homer schemes to get the nerds readmitted, but the caper goes awry and Homer runs the dean over in his car. At the hospital, Homer admits to Peterson that the pig prank was his idea and the nerds are allowed to return to school. When Homer flunks his final exam, the nerds change his grade on the computer to an A+. Marge finds out and tells Homer that he has to take the course over again.

SHOW HIGHLIGHTS

"There must be some mistake. We, uh, we make cookies here. Mr. Burns's old-fashioned, good time, extra chewy..." Mr. Burns, to the Nuclear Regulatory Commission agents.

 "The watchdog of public safety. Is there any lower form of life?"

"...It was the most I ever threw up, and it changed my life forever." Homer's closing statement for his college application essay.

Why Homer did not make it into college as a young man: Rather than signing the application which would have automatically granted admission to college, he rushed outside to fight a dog over a ham.

"Lighten up, Bitterman...that youngster will make a perfect addition to my cabinet: Secretary of Partying Down!" The President of the United States to the Dean, after Corey and Nerdlinger detonate their bra bomb, covering the campus in women's underwear. (Excerpted from the film, *School of Hard Knockers*).

 "Marge, try to understand. There are two kinds of college students: jocks and nerds. As a jock, it is my duty to give nerds a hard time."

"You've won this round dean, but the war isn't over."

"Wow! They'll never let us show that again, not in a million years!" Krusty, on the cartoon that Bart and Lisa just missed the ending of.

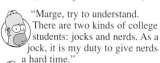 "Woo hoo! I'm a college man! I won't need my high school diploma anymore!"

Homer, Filling Out a College Application:
Lisa: *Dad, don't let these application essays throw you. Let's see...(reading) "List your three favorite books and how they've influenced your life."*
Homer: *Is "TV Guide" a book?*
Lisa: *No.*
Homer: *"Son of Sniglet"?*
Lisa: *No.*
Homer: *Katharine Hepburn's "Me"?*
Lisa: *No!*
Homer: *(moans) I suck.*

THE STUFF YOU MAY HAVE MISSED

Covering the walls of Homer and Marge's bedroom during his college attendance are posters of ballerina feet, W.C. Fields playing cards and Albert Einstein sticking out his tongue.

Sign in front of Springfield A&M University: "If You Were a Student Here, You'd Be Home by Now."

The dean's office features a Pink Floyd "Dark Side of the Moon" poster on one wall.

The closing credits include shots of Homer water-skiing in a toga, a naked Homer being spanked by frat boys, Nixon wearing a bra on his head, and Homer pushing the dean into the swimming pool.

Homer: *Look, I'm supposed to get a physics tutor.*
Doug: *Well, you've come to the right place then. If there's one thing we know, it is science...*
Benjamin: *And math...*
Gary: *And the words to every Monty Python routine.*
All Three in Unison: *We are the Knights who say, Nee! Nee!*
Homer: *Heh-Heh. "Nee."*

(Glowing intensely, the Nuclear Regulatory Committee simulator van melts into the earth. Homer climbs out of the crater. He is glowing bright green.)
Homer: *(ferociously) Must destroy mankind!*
(His watch alarm goes off and the green glow fades.)
Homer: *Ooh, lunch time.*

Professor: *Now, if anyone would like to stay, I'm going to hold a comprehensive review session after every class.*
Homer: *Do we have to?*
Professor: *No.*
Homer: *Then kiss my curvy butt goodbye.*
(Homer races out of the classroom. Moments later, he can be seen though a window, giggling and chasing squirrels with a stick.)

TV Moments:
The nerds work out of Room 222, the name of a popular TV show in the 1970s.
And Mr. Burns tries to get the nuclear inspectors to take the washer and dryer where Smithers is standing or trade it for a box, parodying the game show classic "Let's Make a Deal."

NRC agent: *I'm still not sure how he caused the meltdown. There wasn't any nuclear material in the truck.*
Mr. Burns: *Oh, very well, it's time for your bribe. Now, you can either have the washer and dryer where the lovely Smithers is standing, or you can trade it all for what's in this box.*
NRC agent: *The box! The box!*

ROSEBUD

Episode 1F01 Original Airdate: 3/18/93 Writer: John Swartzwelder Director: David Silverman Guest Voices: Maggie Roswell as Helen Lovejoy, The Ramones as Themselves: Joey Ramone, Johnny Ramone, C.J. Ramone, Marky Ramone

Mr. Burns's birthday celebration is coming up. Depressed, all he really wants is his lost childhood Teddy bear, Bobo. Nevertheless, Smithers organizes the best party he can, inviting dignitaries and arranging for the Ramones to play "Happy Birthday." When Homer gives his employer a tasteless birthday roast, Burns orders storm troopers to beat him up.

Bart goes to the Kwik-E-Mart to buy ice for Homer's injuries. In one of the bags of ice, he finds a stuffed bear and gives it to Maggie. When Homer learns that the bear is Bobo, he offers it to Burns for an exorbitant sum. Burns agrees on a settlement, but Homer realizes how attached Maggie is to the bear, and calls off the deal.

Burns and Smithers try in vain to steal Bobo. Their attempt to turn all of Springfield against the Simpsons also fails. Finally, Burns gives up, sadly telling Maggie to keep to the bear. Feeling sorry for Burns, Maggie gives Bobo back.

SHOW HIGHLIGHTS

Smithers's fantasy birthday present: Mr. Burns jumps out of a cake wearing nothing but a sash and singing, à la Marilyn Monroe, "Happy birthday, Mr. Smithers."

"Get away from me, loser." George Bush, to Jimmy Carter, after both men are removed from the line to Burns's party.

"Mmm...64 slices of American cheese." Homer, anticipating an all-night binge.

Mr. Burns's warnings – on TV: "As you can see, Simpson, I've taken over all seventy-eight channels. And you won't see any of your favorite shows again until you give in...what's that you say? You can live without television as long as you have beer?... Wrong. All beer trucks heading towards Springfield have been diverted. This town will be dry as a bone. And if the rest of you beer-swilling tube jockeys out there have a problem with this, talk to Homer Simpson."

> **TV Shows Interrupted by Burns:**
> "Barney, the Dinosaur."
> "Soul Mass Transit System,"
> "Bumblebee Man."

THE STUFF YOU MAY HAVE MISSED

Signs outside Burns Manor: "Warning, Keep Out," "Danger, Electrified Fence," "Tresspassers Will Be Shot," and "Free Kittens Inquire Within."

Hirschfeld's drawing of Burns at the party is complete with the name "Nina" spelled out in Burns's hair. (Hirschfeld works the name of his daughter into all his caricatures.)

Homer is brought out on stage to the Simpsons' theme.

A version of "Do You Know Where You're Going To?" plays during the slideshow at the party.

> (Burns sees Homer on a surveillance monitor.)
> **Burns:** That man who's getting all the laughs, Smithers. Who is he?
> **Smithers:** Homer Simpson, sir. One of the carbon blobs from Sector 7G. But I don't think that...
> **Burns:** I want this Simpson fellow to perform comedy at my party. I must harness his fractured take on modern life.

> **Mr. Burns:** (in his sleep) I want my ted-dy. Bobo! Bo-bo! (waking; to Smithers) Oh, it's you. The bed pan's under my pillow.
> **Smithers:** Who's Bobo, sir?
> **Burns:** Bobo? (lying) I meant Lobo. "Sheriff Lobo." They never should have cancelled that show.

> **The Journey of Bobo:**
> • The bear lays in the snow and is carried away in a stream when the snow thaws.
> • 1927–New York. The bear washes up on a riverbank. It is grabbed by Charles Lindbergh and flown to Paris in the *Spirit of St. Louis*. As Lindbergh throws it to the cheering crowd, Hitler jumps up and catches it.
> • 1945–Berlin. Hitler sits in his bunker with the bear; explosions are heard nearby.
> • 1957–The North Pole. The bear is enclosed in a block of ice on top of the *Nautilus* nuclear submarine.
> • 1993–The bear is uncovered by members of a polar expedition.
> • 1993–Springfield. The bear is sold in a bag of ice to the Kwik-E-Mart.
> • Bart discovers Bobo. "Hey, it's a Teddy bear!... Ew! Gross! It's probably diseased or something. Here, Maggie."

> **Bart:** Hey, Apu, this bag of ice has a head in it.
> **Apu:** Oooh! A head bag! Those are chock full of (pause) heady goodness.

> **Mr. Burns:** Ah, yes. Naturally, I can't pay you much of a reward because I'm strapped for cash. (The ceiling above gives way; money and jewels pour down on him) ...As you can see, this old place is falling apart. But I'm sure we can come to an understanding.

> **Movie Moments:**
> The opening shot of Burns Manor and the scene in which Mr. Burns breaks snow globes parody *Citizen Kane*. The guards outside Burns Manor march and chant à la the guards in *The Wizard of Oz*.

> **Burns Gets Bobo Back:**
> **Burns:** For me? Bobo? Smithers, I'm so happy. Something amazing has happened. I'm actually happy. Take a note. From now on, I'm only going to be good and kind to everyone.
> **Smithers:** I'm sorry, sir, I don't have a pencil.
> **Burns:** Don't worry, I'm sure I'll remember it.

> **The Ramones Insult Mr. Burns:**
> **Burns:** Have the Rolling Stones killed.
> **Smithers:** Sir, those aren't...
> **Burns:** Do as I say!

Seen in: The year 10,000 A.D., when apes rule the earth and all their slaves look like Homer.

Type of lifeform: Cyborg-robot body with human head.

Lifespan: Seemingly immortal.

Strengths: Super speed; super-extending arms.

Weaknesses: Misplaces his Teddy bear every century.

Allies: His loyal cyborg-dog assistant, Smithers.

THE OPENING SEQUENCE

The headstones at the Springfield Cemetery read, "Elvis—Accept It," "A Balanced Budget," and "Subtle Political Satire." A headstone reading "TV Violence" is riddled with bullets and bleeds.

THE SET-UP

Bart and other members of the Simpson family host three terrifying tales based on paintings on exhibit in a ghoulish gallery.

Marge's Warning for Parents:

(Bart, dressed in a suit, walks through a gallery of various paintings featuring the Simpsons.)
Bart: *Paintings. Lifeless images rendered in colorful goop. But at night, they take on lives of their own. They become portals to hell so scary and horrible and gruesome that—*
(Marge appears.)
Marge: *Bart! You should warn people this episode is very frightening and maybe they'd rather listen to that old "War of the Worlds" broadcast on NPR, hmm?*
Bart: *Yes, Mother.*

THE DEVIL AND HOMER SIMPSON

A t the power plant, Homer declares that he would sell his soul for a donut. He is visited by the Devil in the form of Ned Flanders, who grants Homer's request. That night, after Homer takes the last bite out of the donut, the Devil reappears to claim his prize. Marge and Lisa protest, demanding that Homer be given a fair trial. Satan agrees to hold court at midnight. At the trial, Marge convinces a jury of damned souls that Homer is her property, not the Devil's.

STORY HIGHLIGHTS

"Homer. I.O.U. one emergency donut. Signed, Homer." Homer, reading the note he finds inside his hollowed-out *Emergency Procedures* manual.

"Bastard! He's always one step ahead!" Homer, about himself.

"Hey, Bart." A nonchalant Devil Flanders, to Bart, after a fiery vortex to hell opens in the kitchen floor.

"Mr. Simpson, don't you worry. I watched 'Matlock' in a bar last night. The sound wasn't on, but I think I got the gist of it."

(Burns and Smithers see the Devil Flanders talking with Homer on the surveillance camera.)
Burns: *Hmm...who's that goat-legged fellow? I like the cut of his jib.*
Smithers: *Er, the Prince of Darkness, sir. He's your 11 o'clock.*

The Bargain:
Homer: *I'd sell my soul for a donut.*
Devil Flanders: *Heh, heh, that can be arranged.*
Homer: *What—Flanders! You're the Devil?*
Devil Flanders: *Ho-oh, it's always the one you least suspect.*

"Oh, you Americans with your due process and fair trials. This is always so much easier in Mexico." The Devil Flanders, after Lisa requests a trial to see if he can claim Homer's soul.

The Jury of the Damned:
Benedict Arnold, Lizzie Borden, Richard Nixon, John Wilkes Booth, Blackbeard the Pirate, John Dillinger, and the starting line of the 1976 Philadelphia Flyers.

Devil Flanders: *I simply ask for what is mine.*
Mr. Hutz: *That was a right-pretty speech, sir. But I ask you, what is a contract? Webster's defines it as "an agreement under the law which is unbreakable." Which is unbreakable! Excuse me, I must use the restroom.*

(Blackbeard looks at the back of Marge and Homer's wedding photo.)
Blackbeard: *'Tis some kind of treasure map!*
Benedict Arnold: *You idiot! You can't read!*
Blackbeard: *Aye, 'tis true. My debauchery was my way of compensatin'.*

THE STUFF YOU MAY HAVE MISSED

Bart's test, with an F-plus grade, is attached to the fridge.

Lionel Hutz combs his hair with a fork.

HORROR IV

Episode 3F04
Original Airdate: 10/30/95
Written by "Watch" Conan O'Brien, "The Late" Bill Oakley, "The Estate of" Josh Weinstein,
Greg "It's Alive!" Daniels, "The Disfigured" Dan McGrath and "Bilious" Bill Canterbury
Director: David "Dry Bones" Silverman

NIGHTMARE AT 5 1/2 FEET

Still jittery from a nightmare in which the school bus crashes in a thunderstorm, Bart boards the bus with Lisa during a storm. While riding on the bus, he sees a demonic gremlin ripping wires and metal from the side of the vehicle. When the other children look out the window, they see nothing. Bart watches as the monster loosens nuts from the bus's rear tire. In desperation, he pulls the emergency exit handle, hangs out the window, and shoots the monster with a flare.

STORY HIGHLIGHTS

"Hello, Simpson, I'm riding the bus today because Mother hid my car keys to punish me for talking to a woman on the phone. She was right to do it."

What Milhouse leaves himself open to if he leans out the window:
Wedgies, wet willies, and even "the dreaded rear admiral."

"Aw, isn't that cute. He's trying to claw my eyes out." Flanders, after picking up the injured gremlin in the street. He then hugs it.

Bart: Otto, you gotta do something! There's a gremlin on the side of the bus!
(Otto spots Hans Moleman driving an AMC Gremlin in the next lane.)
Otto: Eh, no problemo, Bart dude. I'll get rid of it.
(Otto rams Moleman off the road.)

Bart: There's a monster on the bus!
Skinner: The only monster on this bus is a lack of proper respect for the rules.

Bart: Look at the bus. I was right, I tell you, I was right!
Skinner: Right or wrong, your behavior was still disruptive, young man! Perhaps spending the reminder of your life in a madhouse will teach you some manners.
Nelson: Ha, ha!

THE STUFF YOU MAY HAVE MISSED

Uter is not mentioned by name; rather, he's referred to as "that foreign exchange student."

Uter's marzipan JoyJoys are "Mit Iodine!"

Movie Moment:
The story parodies "The Twilight Zone" episode, "Nightmare at 20,000 Feet," starring William Shatner, which takes place on a jet instead of a school bus.

BART SIMPSON'S DRACULA

After closing a deal to buy the Springfield Blood Bank, Mr. Burns invites the Simpsons to his castle in Pennsylvania. Lisa suspects that Burns is a vampire. At the castle, Burns bites Bart. Later that night, Lisa is awakened by Bart and his vampire friends, who float to her window. Homer and Marge are convinced that their son is one of the undead. They learn from Lisa that the only way to save Bart is to kill the head vampire, Mr. Burns. Although Homer drives a stake through his boss's heart, Bart remains a vampire. To her horror, Lisa discovers that her mother is really the head vampire.

STORY HIGHLIGHTS

"We think we're dealing with a supernatural being, most likely a mummy. As a precaution, I've ordered the Egyptian wing of the Springfield Museum destroyed." Wiggum, talking to the press about a Springfield local who is found drained of all blood and has teeth marks on his throat.

"Lisa, stop being so suspicious. Did everyone wash their necks like Mr. Burns asked?" Marge, to the family, on their way to Burns's midnight dinner.

Bashing the boss: Lisa tells Homer that the only way save Bart is to kill the head vampire, Mr. Burns. Homer replies, "Kill my boss? Do I dare to live out the American dream?"

"Uh, Dad? That's his crotch." Lisa, to Homer, who fails to drive a stake through vampire Burns's heart.

"I do have a life outside this house, you know." Marge, to her family, telling them that it is she who is the real head vampire.

Homer Simpson, Gracious Guest:
Homer: Ooh, punch!
Lisa: (sniffing it) Ew! Dad, this is blood!
Homer: Correction. Free blood.

Lisa: Mom, Dad! Mr. Burns is a vampire, and he has Bart!
Burns: Why, Bart is right here.
Bart: (monotone) Hello, Mother. Hello, Father. I missed you during my uneventful absence.
Homer: Oh, Lisa, you and your stories. "Bart is a vampire." "Beer kills brain cells." Now, let's go back to that...building...thingee...where our beds and TV...is.

THE STUFF YOU MAY HAVE MISSED

A painting of dogs playing poker appears above the Simpsons' couch.

Eddie the cop tosses a copy of the Mona Lisa into a fire after Chief Wiggum orders the Egyptian wing of the Springfield Museum destroyed.

Ghostlike neon sign at Burns's country estate: "To Secret Vampire Room—No Garlic."

The foreword of Mr. Burns's book, Yes, I Am a Vampire, is written by Steve Allen.

Lisa purposely spills a glass of blood all over herself and Bart, but moments after they sneak away from the dinner table, their clothes show no sign of stain.

Movie Moment:
The story's title and much of its plot parody Bram Stoker's Dracula and Francis Ford Coppola's film thereof.

MARGE ON THE LAM

Episode 1F03   Original Airdate: 11/4/93   Writer: Bill Canterbury   Director: Mark Kirkland   Guest Voice: George Fenneman as the Narrator

Status:
Divorcee; single mother.

Daughter:
Laura Powers, onetime love interest of Jimbo Jones.

Persona:
Daring, yet conventional.

Reason for divorce:
All her husband ever did was eat, sleep, and drink beer.

Transportation:
1966 Thunderbird Convertible stolen from her ex.

Packs:
Heat.

> I SHOULD GET HOME TO MY DAUGHTER BEFORE THAT NAKED TALK SHOW COMES ON.

Guest Voice:
Pamela Reed
as Ruth Powers

SHOW HIGHLIGHTS

Homer's ballet song: Imagining himself at the ballet, Homer envisions a circus bear wearing a fez who drives an electric cart around in circles to the strains of calliope music. Homer sings along to the scene in his head.

 "Hi, I'm Troy McClure. You might remember me for such telethons as 'Out with Gout '88' and 'Let's Save Tony Orlando's House.'"

"Always Do the Opposite of What Bart Says."
A message on a card that Homer keeps in his pocket.

Heard it twice: Both Homer and Marge say, "Your point being?" during the episode.

"Property of Ned Flanders": Sign on the side of the power sander Homer loans neighbor Ruth Powers. He adds "But remember, it's mine."

"Hey, can I throw up in your bathroom? I'll buy something." Barney, to a waiter at Jittery Joe's Coffee Shop.

"We're phasing out the games. People drink less when they're having fun." Moe, on why he is removing darts from the bar.

"Oh, uh, I'm, uh, I'm on a road. Uh, looks to be asphalt...um, oh, geez, trees, shrubs...uh, I'm directly under the Earth's sun...now!" Chief Wiggum, giving his precise location.

"Look, Marge, I'm sorry I haven't been a better husband, I'm sorry about the time I tried to make gravy in the bathtub, I'm sorry I used your wedding dress to wax the car, and I'm sorry—oh well, let's just say I'm sorry for the whole marriage up to this point."

Homer, the Brave:
Carl: *Careful, Homer. I heard someone lost an arm in there once.*
Homer: *Pfft, that's just an old wives' tale.*
(Homer's arm stretches up a windy path within the machine. We see a skeletal arm holding a can of Fresca.)

Ruth: *I envy you and Homer.*
Marge: *Thank you. Why?*
Ruth: *If you ever met my ex-husband, you'd understand. All he ever did was eat, sleep and drink beer.*
Marge: *Your point being?*

Lake Wobegon Moment:
The opening scene, featuring the humorist that the Simpsons find unfunny, parodies Garrison Keillor and his Minnesota-based public radio and TV show "A Prairie Home Companion."

Bearly Ballet:
Carl: *Hey, Homer, you wanna get a beer on the way home?*
Homer: *(bitter) I can't. I gotta take my wife to the ballet.*
Lenny: *Heh. You're gonna go see the bear in the little car, huh?*

THE STUFF YOU MAY HAVE MISSED

Volunteers at the pledge drive sleep, read, knit, and stare vacantly into space, waiting for the phone to ring.

The pledges received by the public television fund drive are a mere "0,000,023.58," or a little over 23 bucks.

A sign outside the Springfield High School gym reads, "Tonight: Professional Ballet. Tomorrow: Closed to Fix Gas Leak."

The neon sign at Jittery Joe's Coffee Shop shows a shaking hand grasping a coffee cup.

Highway Sign: "Entering Badlands. High Speed Chases Use Diamond Lane."

Marge's encounter with Mayor Quimby at the nightclub and his statement that he was there with his nephews is a reference to the Teddy Kennedy/William Kennedy Smith alleged rape incident.

Ruth flips the song, "Welcome to the Jungle," by Guns N' Roses into her cassette deck.

Wiggum and Homer, Giving Chase:
(Wiggum and Homer are making fried eggs on Wiggum's car's engine.)
Wiggum: *Mmm...engine-block eggs. If we can keep these down, we'll be sitting pretty.*
(Marge and Ruth whiz by in their car.)
Homer: *That's them!*
Wiggum: *Quiet! I can't hear the eggs.*

When Homer gets his arms stuck in two vending machines and cannot attend the ballet with Marge, she invites her neighbor, divorceé Ruth Powers, to take his place. The two women have a great time and agree to go out again. The following evening, Ruth pulls up in a 1966 T-Bird convertible wearing jeans and a leather jacket.

Homer wants his own night out and hires attorney Lionel Hutz to babysit. Meanwhile, Ruth and Marge hit several trendy nightspots before driving to the Springfield sign that overlooks the town. Homer arrives just as they are leaving, and runs into Chief Wiggum, who offers to drive him home. Homer hitches a ride with Chief Wiggum. When Wiggum tries to pull over Ruth's car for a minor infraction, Ruth speeds off, admitting to Marge that she stole the car from her ex-husband.

With Homer in the back seat, Wiggum gives chase. Soon he is joined by several other police cars. Ruth wants to give herself up, but Marge, loyal to her friend, turns the steering wheel towards the desert to help her escape. As their car approaches a chasm, Homer takes a bullhorn and apologizes to Marge for being a poor husband. Marge and Ruth stop the car just in time, but Wiggum and Homer, following closely behind, sail over the cliff, landing safely on a massive pile of garbage.

BART'S INNER CHILD

Episode 1F05 Original Airdate: 11/11/93 Writer: George Meyer Director: Bob Anderson

Homer buys a trampoline and, despite Marge's warnings about its danger, charges neighborhood kids a dollar each to use it. After numerous injuries, Homer tries to get rid of the trampoline. Eventually, it is stolen.

Marge orders a self-help videotape for herself and Homer that promises to change their relationship for the better. After watching it, they communicate better and their tensions ease. When the host of the tape, Brad Goodman, comes to Springfield, Marge and Homer decide that the whole family should attend his "Inner Child" seminar. Brad brings Bart on stage as an example of a child whose feelings are completely uninhibited. He recommends that everyone follow Bart's example.

Inspired, the people of Springfield let their repressed selves free. Realizing that his rebelliousness is no longer unique, Bart becomes depressed. At the "Do What You Feel Festival," events are out of control, and the townspeople blame Bart for the resulting disasters. Turning into an unruly mob, they chase Bart but soon lose interest in him and run off to the mill to drink cider.

BRAD GOODMAN

Occupation:
Soft-spoken self-help guru.

Description:
Tall; good-looking; slightly acromegalic.

A.K.A.:
"The man who put the 'you' in impr-you-vement."

Book:
Owning Your Okayness.

Video:
"Adjusting Your Self-O-Stat."

Education/ credentials:
Ph.D. in pain; (none)

Accessibility:
His infomercial plays 'round the clock on channel 77.

AND SOON YOU'RE NOT A HUMAN BE-ING YOU'RE A HUMAN DO-ING!

Guest Voice:
A. Brooks as Brad Goodman

SHOW HIGHLIGHTS

Personality disorders in the "Feel Bad Rainbow," according to Brad Goodman: Depression, insomnia, motor-mouth, darting eyes, indecisiveness, decisiveness, bossiness, uncontrollable falling down, Geriatric Profanity Disorder or GPD, and chronic nagging.

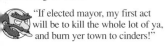 "Oh, hi. I'm Troy McClure. You might remember me from such self-help videos as *Smoke Yourself Thin* and *Get Confident, Stupid*. Well, now I'm here to tell you about the only real path to mental health. That's right, it's the...Brad Goodman... something or other."

"If elected mayor, my first act will be to kill the whole lot of ya, and burn yer town to cinders!"

"Lis, today I am a god." Bart, after the town is told to be like him.

Goodman Lingo:
Marge: *That video really opened my eyes. I can see that I'm just a passive-aggressive co-culprit. By nagging you when you do foolish things, I just enable your life script.*
Homer: *And that sends me into a shame spiral.*
Marge: *Exactly! So from now on, I'm going to quit nagging and have more fun.*

Everyone Yells Out Their Problems at the Seminar:
Quimby: *I, ah, can't commit to a relationship!*
Burns: *I'm too nice!*
Apu: *I have problems with—*
Lenny: *(interrupting) I'm always interrupting people!*

Movie Moment:
Kids injured in trampoline accidents are lined up in rows like the injured soldiers in *Gone with the Wind*.

Patty: *Your blood pressure is off the chart.*
Selma: *And I don't like this urine sample one bit.*
Patty: *You're headed for a nervous breakdown. You need Brad Goodman.*

Goodman: *What made you yell out that remark?*
Bart: *I 'unno.*
Goodman: *You just wanted to express yourself, yes?*
Bart: *(shrugs) I do what I feel like.*
Goodman: *That's marvelous! I couldn't have put it better myself. "I DO what I FEEL like." People, this young man here IS the inner child I've been talking about*

Bart: *Lis, everyone in town is acting like me, so why does it suck?*
Lisa: *It's simple, Bart. You've defined yourself as a rebel. And in the absence of a repressive milieu, your societal niche has been co-opted.*
Bart: *I see.*

More Goodman Lingo:
Marge: *Homer did you eat my whole pan of brownies?*
Bart: *Uh oh. You're in for it now, Dad.*
Homer: *Marge, I'm feeling a lot of shame right now.*
Marge: *I'm hearing that you feel a lot of shame.*
Homer: *And I feel you hear my shame.*
Marge: *I'm feeling annoyance and frustration, but also tolerance.*
Homer: *I feel validated by that.*
Marge: *Good. I'm glad we had this talk.*
Homer: *Me too.*

(Bart and Lisa play on the trampoline as the family looks on)
Lisa: *Dad, this one gesture almost makes up for years of shaky fathering.*
Bart: *I will never get tired of this.*
Lisa: *I'm going to have my wedding here.*
Marge: *I don't know if this is a good idea.*

THE STUFF YOU MAY HAVE MISSED

Krusty lives at 534 Center Street.

Nelson throws muck in Homer's imaginary "Homerland."

At the "Do What You Feel Festival," Marge wears a baseball cap backwards on top of her hairdo.

Divine-looking beams of sunlight stream through the clouds when Rod asks, "What have we done to make God angry?"

In the "For Free" section of the *Springfield Shopper*, one of the listings reads, "Fat Boy Bomb Free!!! Call Herman K19-4327." Herman also tried to sell nuclear devices in 9F21, "Homer's Barbershop Quartet" and 1F09, "Homer the Vigilante"

SEA CAPTAIN

Real name:
Captain McCallister.

Occupation:
Springfield entrepreneur.

Enterprises:
The Frying Dutchman restaurant (formerly The Rusty Barnacle); recordings of old sea shanties including "Blow the Man Down" and "In the Navy."

Secret shame:
Exposed by Lionel Hutz as not a real captain.

Dream:
To sail around the world on three vessels searching for riches.

> AAHRR! IS IT MORE ICE TEA YOU BE NEEDIN'?

Guest Voice:
Hank Azaria as the Sea Captain

BOY-SCOUTZ

SHOW HIGHLIGHTS

"Ah, finally, a little quiet time to read some of my old favorites. 'Honey Roasted Peanuts. Ingredients: salt, artificial honey roasting agents, pressed peanut sweepings!' Mmm." Homer, reading a jar on the couch.

"My Dinner with André." Martin's favorite video game. It has three controls: Trenchant Insight, "Tell Me More," and "Bon Mot."

"Okay, look, I made a terrible mistake. I wandered into a Junior Camper recruitment center. But what's done is done. I've made my bed and now I've got to weasel out of it."

The Ten Do's and Five Hundred Don't's of Knife Safety: Book Bart reads in order to handle a knife.

> *Marge:* Homer, I have to go out to pick up something for dinner.
> *Homer:* Steak?
> *Marge:* Money's too tight for steak.
> *Homer:* Steak?
> *Marge:* (lying) Sure, steak.

It Begins:

> *Apu:* Hello, gents, what will it be?
> *Milhouse:* Apu, give us a Super-Squishee.
> *Bart:* One that's made — entirely out of syrup.
> *Apu:* Entirely...(gulps) An all-syrup Super-Squishee? Oh, s-such a thing has never been done.
> (Bart slaps down the twenty.)
> *Bart:* Just make it happen.
> *Apu:* Ooof, oh dear.

> *Bart:* OK, we're young, rich, and full of sugar. What do we do?
> *Milhouse:* Let's go crazy, Broadway-style!

The Morning After:

> *Lisa:* Tsk, tsk. The remorse of the sugar junkie.
> *Bart:* I don't remember anything.
> *Lisa:* Really? Not even this?
> (Lisa yanks back the covers, revealing Bart dressed in the full khaki uniform of the Junior Campers)
> *Bart:* Oh, no. I joined the Junior Campers!
> *Lisa:* The few, the proud, the geeky.

> *Marge:* I know you think the Junior Campers are square and "uncool," but they also do a lot of neat things, like singalongs and flag ceremonies.
> *Homer:* Marge, don't discourage the boy. Weaseling out of things is important to learn. It's what separates us from the animals. (pause) Except the weasel.

> (Bart arrives at the Junior Campers meeting.)
> *Bart:* Hello, alternative to testing!
> (He walks in. Ned Flanders stands among the uniformed boys, also wearing a uniform.)
> *Ned:* Well, it's Bart Simpson! C'mon in! You're just in time for "Sponge-Bath the Old Folks Day."
> (Ned steps back to reveal Jasper sitting in a tub.)
> *Jasper:* Help yourself, but stay above the equator!

"Don't thank me–thank the knife!" Dr. Hibbert, responding to a man whose life he just saved by performing an emergency appendectomy with his pocket knife.

 "Ohhh. It seems like everywhere I look, people are enjoying knives!"

"'Don't do what Donny Don't does.' They could have made this clearer." Bart, reading his knife manual.

> (Bart walks into the living room, wearing his Junior Camper uniform.)
> *Homer:* How was jerk practice, boy? Did they teach you how to sing to trees? And make crappy furniture out of useless wooden logs? Huh?
> (The chair Homer is sitting in collapses.)
> *Homer:* D'oh! Stupid poetic justice!
> *Bart:* Actually, we were just planning the father-son river rafting trip.

N THE HOOD

Episode 1F06 Original Airdate: 11/18/93
Writer: Dan McGrath
Director: Jeffrey Lynch
Guest Voice: Ernest Borgnine as Himself

Bart and Milhouse find $20 and order an all-syrup Super-Squishee from Apu. Their senses reeling from the high-sugar content of the drink, they spend the rest of the money on a night out on the town. The next morning, Bart wakes up with a "hangover" and realizes that in the revelry of the night before he joined the Junior Campers, a Boy Scout-style organization.

Bart finds that belonging to the group has its advantages. He is excused from taking a test to attend a meeting and gets to carry a pocket knife. Homer joins Bart on a father-son river rafting trip, despite Bart's fears that his father will embarrass him. When Homer sends the raft hurling down the wrong rapids, the group finds itself drifting far out to sea.

As the days adrift take their toll Homer devours most of the food rations. When he drops a Swiss Army knife onto the bottom of the raft, its magnifying glass burns a hole through the rubber. As the raft sinks, Homer smells hamburgers and follows his nose to the safety of a Krusty-burger built on an oil rig. Bart hugs Homer and tells him he is proud.

"Well, if it isn't the leader of the weiner patrol, boning up on his nerd lessons!" Homer, finding Bart studying for his knife badge.

Pussy Willow: Rank Bart achieves when he receives his rubber training knife.

"Aahrr. I don't know what I'm doin'." Captain McCallister, after the boat he calls "the yarrest river goin' boat there be" suddenly sinks in the middle of his sales pitch.

"Want me to zinc your sniffer?" Flanders, offering Homer sunscreen for the nose.

> **Ned:** Howdilly hey, camper Bart! You ready for today's meeting?
> **Bart:** You knowdilly-know it, Neddy!
> **Ned:** Okilly-dokilly!

> **Simpsons' Psychology:**
> **Bart:** (thinking aloud) Look, Homer won't want to go, so just ask him, and he'll say no. Then it'll be his fault.
> **Homer:** (thinking aloud) I don't want to go, so if he asks me to go I'll just say yes.
> **Homer's brain:** Wait, are you sure that's how this sort of thing works?
> **Homer:** Shut up, or I'll stab you with a Q-tip.

"Godspeed, little doodle." Ned, to the cheese doodle that they use as bait to catch a fish.

"This ain't one of your church picnic flare-gun firings, Flanders! This is the real thing!" Homer, after yanking away the flare gun from Ned. Instead of getting the attention of a plane flying by, Homer accidentally shoots it down.

> (Bart and Ned sit at the front of the raft, rowing quickly to keep up with the river.)
> **Ned:** I guess now we know why they call 'em rapids and not slowpids, huh?
> (Bart laughs. Homer sees him.)
> **Homer:** You are not my son!

> **On the Lifeboat:**
> **Homer:** Flanders! My socks feel dirty! Gimme some water to wash 'em!
> **Ned:** Again? Homer, we have to ration the water carefully! It's our only hope!
> **Homer:** Oh, pardon me, mister let's-ration-everything, but what do you think we're floating on? Don't you know the poem, "Water, water everywhere, so let's all have a drink?"

THE STUFF YOU MAY HAVE MISSED

During the Squishee-soaked night-on-the-town sequence, glitzy kid-oriented nightspots and signs that blur by include, "Models and Model Decals Store," "Triple-G Rated," "Sweet Tooth," "Bootleg Records," "All Night Arcade," "Booking," "Batting," and "Bicycle Seat Covers."

Everyone is in line for the *Terminator* game at the arcade.

Bart has badges for archery, rent collecting, TV trivia, embalming, and patch forgery on his sash.

Fat Tony appears on a "Wanted" poster in Chief Wiggum's office.

The "Springfield" Song Lyrics:
Bart and Milhouse: *Springfield, Springfield!/ It's a hell of a town!/ The schoolyard's up and the shopping mall's down!/ The stray dogs go to the animal pound!/*
Springfield, Springfield !
Springfield, Springfield !
Sailor: *New York, New York!*
Bart: *New York is that-a-way, man.*
Sailor: *Thanks, kid!*
Bart and Milhouse: *It's a hell-of-a-towwwnnn!!*

THE LAST TEMPTATION OF HOMER

Episode 1F07   Original Airdate: 12/9/93   Writer: Frank Mula   Director: Carlos Baeza   Werner Klemperer as The Angel

Occupation:
Springfield Nuclear Power Plant engineer; temptress.

Transportation:
Motorcycle.

Faults:
Dominating Homer's thoughts, making him do even stupider things.

Quirks:
Runs into crushes in the strangest places.

Biggest mystery:
Keeps a svelte figure despite a passion for junk food.

Bart goes to the doctor for an eye exam and finds out that not only does he need glasses, he needs salve for his scalp and orthopedic shoes for his feet. He leaves the doctor's office looking like a nerd. Meanwhile, at the plant, Mr. Burns hires a female employee, Mindy. Homer is instantly smitten with her.

Homer and Mindy find they share many interests: eating donuts, drinking beer, watching television, and taking a nap before lunch. When the telephone booth he is using crashes to the sidewalk, Homer loses consciousness and meets his guardian angel, who shows Homer what life would be like had he married Mindy instead of Marge. Later, Burns

assigns Homer and Mindy to represent the power plant at the National Energy Convention in Capital City. In the meantime, after two weeks of wearing his new glasses, salve, and shoes, Bart finally tells the school bullies who have been beating him up that he is no longer a nerd. He gets beat up anyway.

Despite his best intentions, Homer enjoys his time with Mindy. They order room service together, trade insults with a passersby at the convention, then win a romantic dinner for two at a Chinese restaurant. After dinner, they return to Homer's room. However, instead of giving in to temptation, Homer invites Marge to stay with him at the hotel.

Guest Voice:
Michele Pfeiffer as Mindy Simmons

SHOW HIGHLIGHTS

"Why, that's a fabulous idea. Anything else you'd like? How about real lead in the radiation shields? Urinal cakes maybe? Smithers, throw this at him." Burns, responding to Charlie's request for a real emergency exit.

Unsexy Thoughts Homer Envisions to Keep His Mind off of Mindy:

Patty and Selma shaving their legs.
Barney in a jumbo thong bikini.

Homer's song (sung to tune of "Mandy"): "Oh Mindy, you came and you gave without flaking/But I sent you Ben-Gay/Oh Andy, you kissed me and stopped me from something/And I…"

(Bart finishes painting the lines for the parking spaces in the Springfield Elementary parking lot. Holding a can of paint and a brush, he and Milhouse stand at the edge and take a look at his handiwork.)
Bart: *The beauty of it is each parking space is a mere one foot narrower. Indistinguishable to the naked eye. But therein lies the game.*
Milhouse: *I fear to watch, yet I cannot turn away.*
(Simultaneously, all the teachers drive up and pull into their spaces. No one has the space to open their doors.)
Skinner: (to Mrs. Krabappel, banging his door into hers) *Blasted woman, you parked too close! Move your car.*
Krabappel: *I'm in the lines. You got a problem, go tell your mama.*
Skinner: *Oh don't worry, she'll hear about this.*

"Oy! Thanks nice lady! My voice is crazy with spraying already! Oy! I feel so much better, Mister Medical Science-Type Person!" Bart, à la Jerry Lewis, after getting his throat sprayed at the HMO.

"You will find happiness with a new love." Fortune Homer gets inside his cookie after eating the free meal he and Mindy won.

"Even the Chinese are against me." Homer, after reading his fortune.

The Talk with Mindy:
Homer: *Uh, so. Let's have a conversation. Uh, I think we'll find we have very little in common.*
Mindy: *Can't talk; eating.*
Homer: *Hey, my favorite, a raspberry swirl with a double glaze.*
Mindy: *Double glaze.* (Gurgling noise)
Homer: *D'oh! Ok, so we have one thing in common. But you know what I hate? Drinking beer and watching TV…*
Mindy: *Oh, not me. That's my idea of heaven.*
Homer: *D'oh! Me too.*
Mindy: *Really? I can see I'm gonna love working with you. Well, gotta go. I wanna sneak in a quick nap before lunch.*
Homer: *Foul temptress. I'll bet she thinks Ziggy's gotten too preachy too!*

ALL WORK AND NO PLAY
MAKES BART A DULL BOY
ALL WORK AND NO PLAY
MAKES BART A DULL BOY
ALL WORK AND NO PLAY
MAKES BART A DULL BOY

THE STUFF YOU MAY HAVE MISSED

When Homer tries to decipher the messy message he wrote on his hand to Mindy, he misreads it as a Buddhist chant.

"As Seen on '60 Minutes'": Sign at the Springfield Power Plant booth at the Energy Convention.

A few bars of the Capital City song (sung by Tony Bennett in 7F05, "Dancin' Homer") are played at the beginning of the Capital City scene.

"Legionnaires' Disease-Free Since 1990": Sign at the Capital City Plaza Hotel.

Mindy: *What's wrong?*
Homer: *…We're going to have sex.*
Mindy: *Oh… well, we don't have to.*
Homer: *Yes we do. The cookie told me so.*
Mindy: *Well, desserts aren't always right.*
Homer: *But they're so sweet.*

Renaissance Art Moment:

One of Homer's love hallucinations depicts Mindy as Venus in Botticelli's "Birth of Venus."

Homer's Dream:

Homer: *Col. Klink! Did you ever get my letters?*
Angel: *I'm not actually Col. Klink. I'm just assuming his form.*
Homer: *Hee, hee. Did you know Hogan had tunnels all over your camp?*

$PRINGFIELD (OR, HOW I LEARNED TO STOP WORRYING AND LOVE LEGALIZED GAMBLING)

Episode 1F08 Original Airdate: 12/16/93 Writers: Bill Oakley & Josh Weinstein Director: Wes Archer Guest Voice: Robert Goulet as Himself, Gerry Cooney as Himself

Springfield suffers an economic slowdown. The government closes Fort Springfield and Mr. Burns lays off employees. At a Town Hall meeting, Principal Skinner suggests that gambling be legalized to raise money for the town. The plan is adopted and things change overnight.

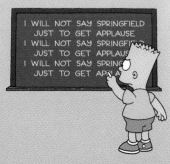

Mr. Burns builds his own casino in Springfield's boardwalk section, and employs Homer as a blackjack dealer. Bart converts his treehouse into a casino and encourages other kids to gamble. Marge slowly becomes addicted to slot machines and ignores her family. Mr. Burns grows even richer and, like Howard Hughes, becomes paranoid about germs.

Lisa senses that Marge has a gambling problem. She makes Marge promise to help her with a costume for the upcoming Geography Pageant, but Marge fails to return home in time from the casino. Enraged, Homer confronts Marge at the casino. She finally admits to Homer, and herself, that she has a serious gambling problem.

I WILL NOT SAY SPRINGFIELD
JUST TO GET APPLAUSE
I WILL NOT SAY SPRINGFI
JUST TO GET APPLAUS
I WILL NOT SAY SPRING
JUST TO GET APPLA

SHOW HIGHLIGHTS

"Hmm...better keep the egghead. He might come in handy." Mr. Burns, peering at a bespectacled Homer while deciding which employees to lay off.

"I propose that I use what's left of the town treasury to move to a more prosperous town and run for mayor. And, uh, once elected, I will send for the rest of you."

State of mind: Marge suggests that Lisa, for her school geography pageant, dress as the state of Nevada to honor Springfield's initiation of legalized gambling, but Lisa claims, "Nevada makes my butt look big."

Jaw of glass: Otto meets official casino greeter Gerry Cooney (the ex-heavyweight boxer) and feels that Cooney is harrassing him. He punches Cooney in the mouth. The champ falls instantly.

Homer's photographic memory: Recalling that Marge was opposed to legalized gambling, we see Homer's memory of the town meeting–Marge has green hair, Apu has three heads, and Homer's own body is buff and trim.

"Hey, how's it going? Hey, good to see you. Hey, friends, looking lucky. Hey, what's happening? Love the jacket." Bart, the casino boss.

Look who's talking: Barney sees Marge return immediately to the slot machine after an escaped albino tiger nearly eats Maggie, and says, "Man, that's classic compulsive behavior." He spots a waitress carrying cups and screams, "Wow, free beer!" He instantly downs all three cups, one of which contains quarters. As Barney begins burping up quarters, a woman rushes over with her coin bucket and screams, "This guy's paying off!"

Losing His Marbles:
(Burns ultimately grows shaggy hair, beard, and fingernails à la Howard Hughes and tells Smithers he has just designed a new plane called the Spruce Moose that "will carry 200 passengers from New York's Idyllwild Airport to the Belgian Congo in 17 minutes.")
Smithers: *That's quite a nice model, sir.*
Burns: *Model?*

(Homer finds a pair of black horn-rimmed glasses in a toilet stall. He puts them on and puts a finger to his temple, à la the Scarecrow at the end of *The Wizard of Oz*.)
Homer: *The sum of the square roots of any two sides of an isosceles triangle is equal to the square root of the remaining side.*
Man in stall: *That's a right triangle, you idiot!*
Homer: *D'oh!*

The Confession:
Homer: *Marge, I want you to admit you have a gambling problem.*
Marge: *You know, you're right, Homer. Maybe I should get some professional help.*
Homer: *No no, that's too expensive. Just don't do it anymore.*

Movie Moment:
The scene at the blackjack table between Homer and an autistic card-counter spoofs *Rain Man*.

Burns: *Aw, my beloved plant. How I miss her— bah! To hell with this. Get my razors! Draw a bath! Get these Kleenex boxes off my feet!*
Smithers: *Certainly, sir. And the jars of urine?*
Burns: *Oh, we'll hang on to those.*

Yet Another Lifelong Dream:
Homer: *I got a job at Burns's casino. As you know, it's been my lifelong dream to become a blackjack dealer.*
Marge: *Your lifelong dream was to be a contestant on "The Gong Show." And you did it in 1977, remember?*

THE STUFF YOU MAY HAVE MISSED

The porno movies *Sperms of Endearment* and *I'll Do Anyone* are spoofs on the James L. Brooks-produced films *Terms of Endearment* and *I'll Do Anything*. Brooks is an executive producer of "The Simpsons."

The germs dancing on Mr. Smithers's face squeal, "Freemasons run the country."

"Tonight: Milhouse. Next Week: An Evening with Jimbo." Sign on the marquee of Bart's treehouse casino.

Among the items tossed into the air to celebrate Springfield's decision to legalize gambling are a purse, a hair brush, dentures, and a whole bunch of hats.

Besides featuring Robert Goulet, Mr. Burns's Casino houses the Concrete and Asphalt Expo 1993.

A ROUND OF APPLAUSE FOR ANASTASIA. SO MUCH NICER THAN THE SAVAGERY OF THE JUNGLE, JA?

HOMER THE VIGILANTE

Episode 1F09 Original Airdate: 1/6/94 Writer: Jon Vitti Director: Rich Moore

Occupation:
Cat burglar.

Time of crime:
Steals the humble goods of Springfield while it lays sleeping.

Description:
Cool; suave; among the upper echelons of intelligence in Springfield.

Residences:
Springfield Retirement Castle; Springfield Jail.

Attire:
Hushed black tones that scream "low-keyed"; sneakers for sneaking.

Hobbies:
"Collecting" cubic zirconias from hither and yon.

I SINCERELY REGRET ANY INCONVENIENCE I MAY HAVE CAUSED. AND ALTHOUGH I'VE STOLEN YOUR MATERIAL GOODS, LET ME ASSURE YOU THAT YOUR DEAR TOWN HAS STOLEN MY HEART.

Guest Voice:
Sam Neill as Molloy

The Simpsons awaken one morning to discover that they have been robbed. The break-in is just one of a series of crimes attributed to the Springfield Cat Burglar. Residents arm themselves and install security devices. The Neighborhood Watch group elects Homer as its leader.

Homer's group patrols the streets, but its members break more laws than catch criminals. During an interview on Kent Brockman's "Smartline," Homer receives a call from the cat burglar threatening to steal the world's largest cubic zirconia from the Springfield Museum. He stakes out the museum, but is distracted by minors drinking beer. Joining them, he proceeds to get drunk, and the cat burglar steals the zirconia.

Grampa comes forward and identifies the cat burglar as Mr. Molloy, one of the residents from the retirement home. As citizens storm the home to find their stolen property, Chief Wiggum places Molloy under arrest. Molloy escapes from jail when he sends the townspeople on a wild goose chase to look for money hidden under a "big T."

SHOW HIGHLIGHTS

Entrance with ease: The cat burglar takes out precision instruments to break in to the Simpsons' home but notices a set of keys in the door. The keychain reads, "Homer."

The burglar's calling card: "You have just been robbed by the Springfield Cat Burglar. Est. 1957."

"Lisa, never ever stop in the middle of a hoedown!" Homer to Lisa, after Lisa shows him how pathetic playing the jug is.

"Thank you for coming. I'll see you in Hell." Apu, wielding a shotgun on the roof of the Kwik-E-Mart.

 "Aw, Dad, you've done a lot of great things, but you're a very old man, and old people are useless."

"Oh, my God! Underage kids drinking without a permit!" Homer, distracted from his watch at the museum.

 "So, Mr. Molloy, it seems that the cat has been caught by the very person who was trying to catch him."

Homer reads Molloy's note:
"'Frightfully sorry, but there is no hidden treasure. I have already used this time to escape from your jail. Fondest wishes...' Oh, I can't make out the signature!"

Jimbo Joins:
Jimbo: *Hey, you're that drunken posse. Wow! Can I join ya?*
Homer: *I don't know. Can you swing a sack of doorknobs?*
Jimbo: *Can I!*
Homer: *You're in. Here's the sack.*
Moe: *But you gotta supply your own doorknobs.*

Flanders Too:
Flanders: *Hidily ho, neighboreenos.*
Homer: *Can't talk. Robbed. Go hell.*
Flanders: *You folks get robbed too? The burglar took my Shroud of Turin beach towels.*

(Homer looks at the Springfield Shopper. Its headline reads, "Zirconia Ztolen," with the subheadline, "Simpson Asleep at the Switch.")
Homer: *Asleep at the switch! I wasn't asleep! I was drunk!*
Bart: (tenderly) *I believe you, Dad.*

I AM NOT AUTHORIZED TO FIRE SUBSTITUTE TEACHERS
I AM NOT AUTHORIZED TO FIRE SUBSTITUTE TEACHERS
I AM NOT AUTHORIZED TO FIRE SUBSTITUTE TEACHERS

Not Insured:
Lisa: *We are insured, aren't we, Mom?*
Marge: *Homer, tell your child what you bought when I sent you to town to get some insurance.*
Homer: *Curse you, Magic Beans!*
Marge: *Oh, stop blaming the beans.*

Movie Moment:
Molloy sends Springfield on a hunt for treasure that is buried underneath a giant letter as in *It's a Mad Mad Mad Mad World*. The end sequence of the show parodies the star-studded film—style of music, manic search for the money, recreation of the scene in which Phil Silvers drives his convertible into a river.

"Smartline," with Kent Brockman:
Kent: *Well, what do you say to the accusation that your group has been causing more crimes than it's been preventing?*
Homer: *Oh, Kent, I'd be lying if I said my men weren't committing crimes...*
(Brockman looks at Homer for a long pause)
Brockman: *Well, touché.*

THE STUFF YOU MAY HAVE MISSED

Pictures of Ms. Botz and Fat Tony still hang on the bulletin board at the police station.

A sign next to the bar in Flanders's basement reads, "Seven days without a drink makes me weak."

Words emblazoned across the front of the Springfield Museum are "truth," "knowledge," and "gift shop."

BART GETS FAMOUS

Episode 1F11 Original Airdate: 2/3/94 Writer: John Swartzwelder Director: Susie Dietter Guest Voice: Conan O'Brien as Himself

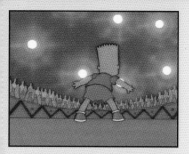

Bart's class takes a field trip to a local box factory. Bored, Bart sneaks away to the nearby television studio where "The Krusty the Clown Show" is taped. After Krusty fires his intern for not supplying him with a Danish, Bart steals a pastry from Kent Brockman and brings it back to Krusty. The grateful clown hires Bart as his new assistant.

Working for Krusty is not what Bart expected. Just as he is about to quit, Krusty offers him a one-line bit part in a comedy sketch. Bart accepts. While on stage he trips over a prop and causes a near disaster, uttering, "I didn't do it." The audience goes wild, and Bart becomes an instant celebrity.

With "I didn't do it" as his catch phrase, Bart's image soon appears on numerous products. He appears on "Late Night with Conan O'Brien" to prove that he is not just a fad. Bart tries to give his best performance on an upcoming episode of Krusty's show, but when his moment comes, no one laughs. Krusty explains that his stardom has ended, attributing it to the fickle nature of show business.

MY HOMEWORK WAS NOT
STOLEN BY A ONE-ARMED MAN
MY HOMEWORK WAS NOT
STOLEN BY A ONE-ARMED MAN
MY HOMEWORK WAS NOT
STOLEN BY A ONE-ARMED MAN

SHOW HIGHLIGHTS

"This is a dream factory, the birthplace of magic and enchantment. Now I need you to go clean out my toilet. Right in here, boy. I... Eww. I don't know what I was thinking last night." Krusty, showing Bart what it means to start at the bottom.

Tiny credits: Bart's name is so small in the credits for Krusty's show it looks like "Brad Storch," or "Betty Symington" to different people.

"I'm Kent Brockman, on the eleven o'clock news tonight...a certain kind of soft drink has been found to be lethal, we won't tell you which one until after sports and the weather with funny Sonny Storm."

The "I Didn't Do It" phenomenon: Bart's catch phrase becomes a skit series; a hip-hop dance quartet; a volume of rap singles; and an autobiography.

"Oh, don't worry about it. You're just finished, that's all... It happens all the time. That's show business for you. One day you're the most important guy who ever lived...the next day you're some schmo working in a box factory. "

Heard it twice: A passionless stagehand blurts in passing, "I wish I was dead." Bart says the same thing after Krusty needs Bart's fingerprints on a candlestick.

The Boring Box Factory:
Milhouse: *Do any of these boxes have candy in them?*
Box executive: *No.*
Milhouse: *Will they ever?*
Box executive: *No. We only make boxes to ship nails. Any other questions?*
Martin: *When will we be able to see a finished box, sir?*
Box executive: *Oh, we don't assemble them here. That's done in Flint, Michigan.*
Bart: *Have any of your workers ever had their hands cut off by the machinery?*
Box executive: *No...*
Bart: *...And then the hand started crawling around and tried to strangle everybody...?*
Box executive: *No, that has never happened.*
Bart: *Any popped eyeballs?*
Box executive: *I'm not sure what kind of factory you're thinking of; we just make boxes here.*

Bart's Promotion:
Krusty: *Bart! I need to use you in a sketch.*
Bart: *You want me to be on the show?*
Krusty: *It's just one line. Mel was supposed to say it, but he's dead.*
Bart: *Dead?*
Krusty: *Or sick. I dunno, I forget. Anyway, all you gotta do is say "I am waiting for a bus." Then I'll hit you with pies for five minutes. Got that?*
Bart: *(trying it) I am waiting for a bus.*
Krusty: *Makes me laugh. Let's go.*

The Conan O'Brien Show:
Bart: *You know, Conan, I have a lot to say. I'm not just a one-line wonder. Did you know that a section of rain forest the size of Kansas is burned every single...*
Conan: *Just do the line.*

Danish Delivery:
Bart: *Here's a Danish, Krusty.*
Krusty: *Gimme, gimme, gimme. (chewing) Now that's Danish. Where'd you get it?*
Bart: *I stole it from Kent Brockman.*
Krusty: *Great. (stops chewing) He didn't touch it, did he?*
Bart: *No.*
Krusty: *(resumes chewing) Good job, kid. What's your name?*
Bart: *I'm Bart Simpson. I saved you from jail... I reunited you with your estranged father... I saved your career, man! Remember your comeback special?*
Krusty: *Yeah, well what have you done for me lately?*
Bart: *I got you that Danish.*
Krusty: *And I'll never forget it.*

Lisa: *Forget it, Dad. If I ever become famous, I want it to be for something worthwhile, not because of some obnoxious fad.*
Bart: *Obnoxious fad?*
Homer: *Don't worry, son, they said the same thing about Urkle... that little snot. Boy I'd like to smack that kid.*

THE STUFF YOU MAY HAVE MISSED

The tune Bart whistles that Marge finds annoying is the Simpsons Theme Song.

Krusty's audience whoops like an "Arsenio" crowd.

There are gold albums by Bleeding Gums Murphy and the Larry Davis Experience hanging in the recording studio where Bart records his rap singles.

Mrs. Quimby resembles Jackie-O with her pink Chanel-ish dress and matching pillbox hat.

AY AY AY!
NO ME GUSTA!

Occupation:
International comedic sensation.
Country of origin:
Mexico.
Talent:
Getting hit, stuck, struck, pinched, caught, and shocked by various objects and making it look funny.
First network:
Channel Ocho.
Pets:
A little chihuahua with a head the size of a burnt-out comet.

APU

Full name:
Apu Nahasapeemapetilon.

Occupation:
Operator of the Kwik-E-Mart.

Economic policy:
Gouge, gouge, gouge.

Country of origin:
India.

Horrible memory:
Thought he was a hummingbird of some kind after working 96 hours straight.

Immigration status:
Semi-legal alien.

Diet:
Strict vegetarian: no meat, no milk, no eggs.

> I KNOW THE PROCEDURE FOR ARMED ROBBERY. I DO WORK IN A CONVENIENCE STORE, YOU KNOW.

SHOW HIGHLIGHTS

"Oh, stomach churning... bowels clenching... not much time... must finish." Homer, eating rancid ham on the couch.

Actor James Woods, explaining why he wants to work at the Kwik-E-Mart: "To be honest, in my upcoming movie I'm going to be playing this tightly-wound convenience store clerk and, you know, I kind of like to research my roles and really get into it. For instance, *True Believer*? I actually worked in a law firm for two months. And then, the film, *Chaplin*? I had a little cameo in that. I actually traveled back in time, back to the twenties, where...well, I've said too much."

The "Who Needs the Kwik-E-Mart" Lyrics:

Whether igloo, hut, or lean-to/ or a geodesic dome/ There's no structure I have been to/ which I'd rather call my home... When I first arrived you were all such jerks/ But now I've come to loooove your quirks/ Maggie with her eyes so bright/ Marge with hair by Frank Lloyd Wright/ Lisa can philosophize/ Bart's adept at spinning lies/ Homer's a delightful fella/ Sorry 'bout the salmonella/ Who needs the Kwik-E-Mart?/ Now here's the tricky part/ Oh won't you rhyme with me?/ Who needs the Kwik-E-Mart... (Marge) Their floors are sticky-mart/ (Lisa) They made Dad sicky-mart/ (Bart) Let's hurl a bricky-mart/ (Homer) That Kwik-E-Mart's is real-D'oh!/ (All) Who needs the Kwik-E-Mart? (Apu) Not me!

 "Come here, Apu. If it'll make you feel any better, I've learned that life is one crushing defeat after another until you just wish Flanders was dead."

"Ah! The searing kiss of hot lead; how I missed you! I mean, I think I'm dying." Apu, after saving James Woods's life.

Customer #1: *I need one twenty-nine cent stamp.*
Apu: *That's a dollar eighty-five.* (rings it up)
Customer #2: *Hi, I want two dollars worth of gas, please.*
Apu: *Four-twenty.* (rings it up)
Martin: *How much is your penny candy?*
Apu: *Surprisingly expensive.*

Dissatisfied Customer:
Homer: *Your old meat made me sick!*
Apu: *I'm so sorry. Please accept five pounds of frozen shrimp.*
Homer: *This shrimp isn't frozen and it smells funny.*
Apu: *Okay, ten pounds.*
Homer: (accepting) *Woo hoo!*

(Homer watches a Def Jam-type comedy show on TV)
Comedian: *See, black guys drive a car like this here.* (He mimes driving while leaning back in the seat, one hand on the wheel.) *But white guys, white guys drive like this.* (He mimes driving while leaning up to the windsheild, both hands on wheel.)
Homer: (laughing) *It's true, it's true. We're so lame.*

Spiritual Discourse:
Kwik-E CEO: *You may ask me three questions.*
Apu: *That's great, because all I need is one.*
Homer: (interrupting) *Are you really the head of the Kwik-E-Mart?*
Kwik-E CEO: *Yes.*
Homer: *Really?*
Kwik-E CEO: *Yes.*
Homer: *You?*
Kwik-E CEO: *Yes. I hope this has been enlightening for you.*
Apu: *But I must...*
Kwik-E CEO: *Thank you, come again.*

Homer Goes Undercover:
Brockman: *Alright, are you willing to go undercover to nail this creep?*
Homer: (pacing) *No way. No way, man. Get yourself another patsy, man. No way I'm wearing a freakin' wire.*
Brockman: *Would you be willing to wear a hidden camera and microphone?*
Homer: *Oh, that I'll wear.*

(Homer and Apu near a majestic Kwik-E-Mart, deep within a mountain range.)
Apu: *There she is, the world's first convenience store.*
Homer: *This isn't very convenient.*
Apu: *Must you dump on everything we do?*

THE STUFF YOU MAY HAVE MISSED

The Kwik-E-Mart does not accept checks from the following people: Chief Wiggum, Reverend Lovejoy, Homer J. Simpson, Homer S. Simpson, H. J. Simpson, Homor Simpson, Homer J. Fong.

A sign in the world's first Kwik-E-Mart: "The Master Knows Everything Except Combination to Safe."

The can of chicken soup on the Kwik-E-Mart bargain table is affected by botulism.

A t the Kwik-E-Mart, Apu lowers the price on meat that has expired instead of throwing it out. Homer buys the meat, eats it, and is rushed to the hospital. Lisa urges Homer to expose Apu, and Homer takes his story to "Bite Back with Kent Brockman." Apu is fired by the Kwik-E-Mart company after a sting in which Homer helps to reveal Apu's violations.

Apu tells Homer that he wishes to make amends by becoming Homer's personal valet. While Apu works for the Simpsons, actor James Woods takes his job at the Kwik-E-Mart. Apu enjoys his work with the Simpsons but longs to return to the Kwik-E-Mart.

Homer agrees to accompany Apu to Kwik-E-Mart's corporate headquarters in India to help him win back his job. The company's benevolent enlightened president and CEO grants three questions, but Homer intervenes, costing Apu his chance to be rehired. Apu finally returns to the Kwik-E-Mart, where he saves James Woods's life during a robbery attempt. Eternally grateful, Woods offers Apu his job back.

I WILL NOT GO NEAR THE KINDERGARTEN TURTLE.

LISA VS. MALIBU STACY

Episode 1F12   Original Airdate: 2/17/94   Writer: Bill Oakley & Josh Weinstein   Director: Jeff Lynch   Pamela Hayden as Malibu Stacy

Confronted by his own mortality, Grampa decides to give his relatives their inheritance before he passes away. Homer takes Grampa and the family shopping at the mall to buy gifts for themselves. Lisa purchases a talking Malibu Stacy doll, but discovers that the doll can only utter vacuous phrases that reinforce sexist stereotypes.

Marge takes Lisa to the factory where Malibu Stacy is manufactured, but Lisa's complaints receive the standard corporate response. With Smithers's help, Lisa tracks down Stacy Lovell, Malibu Stacy's reclusive inventor. Meanwhile, Grampa, feeling useless and tired of complaining about life, takes a job at a local Krustyburger.

Lisa convinces Lovell to challenge the big toy companies and create an entirely new doll that embodies qualities she respects. The doll is named "Lisa Lionheart." The company that produces Malibu Stacy responds by introducing "Malibu Stacy Plus," the same old doll with a new hat. At the Krustyburger, Grampa realizes that he really belongs on the other side of the counter, with all the grumpy, complaining old men.

On the day of Lisa Lionheart's debut, children flock to the new Stacy doll, ignoring Lisa Lionheart. Lisa concludes that even if her doll makes an impression on just one little girl, her efforts will have been worthwhile.

STACY LOVELL

Occupation:
Inventor, Malibu Stacy doll.

Social status:
A total recluse; has not appeared in public in more than 20 years.

Appearance:
Resembles the Malibu Stacy doll.

House:
Resembles the Malibu Stacy Dream House in the catalog.

Marital status:
Has had five husbands (Ken, Johnny, Joe, Dr. Colossus, Steve Austin).

Vices:
Smokes and drinks to excess.

> I WAS FORCED OUT OF MY COMPANY IN 1974; THEY SAID MY WAY OF THINKING WASN'T COST-EFFECTIVE. WELL, THAT, AND I WAS FUNNELING PROFITS TO THE VIET CONG.

Kathleen Turner as Stacy Lovell

SHOW HIGHLIGHTS

"What's eatin' you, Abe? For three weeks, all you been talkin' 'bout was meeting Matlock. Now you met him, swiped his pills..."

"Hey, horse-face! Get your ugly pie hooks off that Summer Fun Set!" Lisa, getting tough with other girls while competing for dolls in the "Valley of the Dolls" section of Kidstown USA.

Grampa's rant: "Hey, why didn't you get something useful, like storm windows, or a nice pipe organ? I'm thirsty! Ooh, what smells like mustard? There sure are a lot of ugly people in your neighborhood. Oh, look at that one! Ow, my glaucoma just got worse. The President is a Demmy-crat..."

"Eh. This ain't so bad." Grampa, after flying off a bicycle into a freshly dug grave.

Fact: Waylon Smithers is the owner of the world's largest Malibu Stacy collection.

"We need some more secret sauce. Put this mayonnaise in the sun." Mr. Peterson, teenage manager of Krustyburger, to his worker drones.

"I'm a white male, aged 18 to 49. Everyone listens to me! No matter how dumb my suggestions are."

"I've got a solution — you and I are going to make our own talking doll. She'll have the wisdom of Gertrude Stein and the wit of Cathy Guisewite, the tenacity of Nina Totenberg and the common sense of Elizabeth Katy Stanton. And to top it off, the down-to-earth good looks of Eleanor Roosevelt!"

Bart's suggested names for Lisa and Stacy's new doll:
"Blabbermouth—The Jerky Doll for Jerks," "Wendy Windbag," "Ugly Doris," "Hortense: The Mule-Faced Doll," "Loudmouth Lisa," "Stupid Lisa Garbage Face."

Lisa Plays with Her New Malibu Stacy:
Lisa: Come on, Stacy. I've waited my whole life to hear you speak. Don't you have anything relevant to say? (Lisa pulls the string.)
Malibu Stacy: Don't ask me — I'm just a girl. (Stacy giggles.)
Bart: Right on! Say it, sister!
Lisa: It's not funny, Bart! Millions of girls will grow up thinking that this is the right way to act—that they can never be more than vacuous ninnies whose only goal is to look pretty, land a rich husband, and spend all day on the phone with their equally vacuous friends talking about how damn terrific it is to look pretty and have a rich husband!!
Bart: Just what I was gonna say.

Movie Moments:
The "We Love You, Matlock" song parodies the "We Love You, Conrad" tune from *Bye Bye Birdie*. Homer plays obsessively on the giant keyboard in the toystore à la *Big*.

THE STUFF YOU MAY HAVE MISSED

Stores at the Springfield Mall: "House of No Refunds," "Simply Shoes," "One Size Fits All Lingerie," "The Leftorium," "Origami Designs," "Just Videos," "Yogurt Nook," "Kidstown USA (Not Affiliated with Kidstown Juvenile Correction Farm)."

We can see Bart in a *Springfield Gazette* photo accompanying a story on a gay rights march.

Sign in front of Malibu Stacy factory: "Petrochem Petrochemical Corporation." Smaller sign: "Proud Makers of Caustic Polypropylene and Malibu Stacy."

Claire Harper: Well, that's the tour. If you have any questions, I'd be happy to—
Lisa: I have one.
Claire Harper: Yes?
Lisa: Is the remarkably sexist drivel spouted by Malibu Stacy intentional, or is it just a horrible mistake?
Harper: Believe me, we're very mindful of such concerns. (A man opens an adjacent boardroom door filled with male executives.)
Executive: (wolf whistles) Hey, Jiggles! Grab a pad and back that gorgeous butt in here!
Harper: (coy) Oh, you, get away... (girlish giggles).
Executive: Aw, don't act like you don't like it.

N ASA scientists believe that their agency has lost the American public's interest. Realizing that most popular sitcoms on television feature blue-collar workers, the scientists embark on a search to find just the right "blue-collar slob." Their prayers are answered when Homer calls the Space Administration to complain about TV's boring space coverage.

NASA offers both Homer and Barney a chance to join the next space mission. When the men realize that only one of them will be chosen, a competition develops. Barney gives up drinking and is suddenly smarter, thinner, and motivated. He ultimately beats Homer out for the spot. But when Barney celebrates with nonalcoholic champagne, he reverts to his old self and Homer is chosen by default.

Once in space with astronauts Buzz Aldrin and Race Banyon, Homer spills potato chips and smashes an experimental ant farm. Chips and ants dangerously clog the instrument panel. Musician James Taylor sings a song for the crew, then suggests that the men blow the debris into the vacuum of space. The plan works until Homer nearly gets sucked out of the airlock, in the process breaking a critical door handle. He pins the door shut using an inanimate carbon rod, allowing the ship to return safely to Earth.

SHOW HIGHLIGHTS

Why Homer feels he's finally going to win the Worker of the Week Award: "Union Rule 26: 'Every employee must win 'Worker of the Week' at least once, regardless of gross incompetence, obesity or rank odor.' Heh heh heh."

"Compadres, it is imperative that we crush the freedom fighters before the start of the rainy season. And remember, a shiny new donkey for whoever brings me the head of Colonel Montoya." Mr. Burns, a little confused in his remarks to employees gathered for the Worker of the Week announcement.

"Stupid carbon rod. It's all just a popularity contest."

Homer's admission: He claims to have a file with the FBI regarding harassing phone calls.

"Gentlemen, you've both worked very hard, and in a way, you're both winners. But in another more accurate way, Barney's the winner." Stillwater, breaking the news to Homer and Barney.

Ironic landing: Barney goes berserk after drinking nonalcoholic champagne. He steals a jet pack and flies away. The jet pack runs out of fuel and Barney falls from the sky towards a pillow factory. He bounces off of the factory's hard metal roof and plummets to the street below. A marshmallow truck then runs over him.

"Ladies and gentlemen, uh, we've just lost the picture, but what we've seen speaks for itself. The Corvair spacecraft has apparently been taken over—'conquered,' if you will—by a master race of giant space ants. It's difficult to tell from this vantage point whether they will consume the captive Earthmen or merely enslave them. One thing is for certain: there is no stopping them; the ants will soon be here. And I, for one, welcome our new insect overlords. I'd like to remind them that as a trusted TV personality, I can be helpful in rounding up others to toil in their underground sugar caves."

"Well, this reporter was...possibly a little hasty earlier and would like to...reaffirm his allegiance to this country and its human president. It may not be perfect, but it's still the best government we have. For now." Kent Brockman, apologizing for welcoming alien invaders.

(Grampa and Lisa watch Homer's reentry on television.)
Lisa: C'mon, dad, you can make it.
Grampa: Oh, of course he'll make it! It's TV!

Movie Moment:
Several scenes in the episode spoof *The Right Stuff*, including Homer and Barney's training regimen and when the crew sings while sweating out reentry.

Scientist Dr. Babcock: Sir, we've run into a serious problem with the mission. These Nielsen ratings are the lowest ever.
NASA Executive Jack Stillwater: (reading) Oh, my God! We've been beaten by "A Connie Chung Christmas."

HOMER

Episode 1F13
Original Airdate: 2/24/94
Writer: David Mirkin
Director: Carlos Baeza
Guest Voices: Buzz Aldrin as Himself and James Taylor as Himself

INANIMATE CARBON ROD

Identity:
Heroic material object.

Color:
Green.

Efforts:
Tireless and long-overlooked at the Springfield Nuclear Power Plant.

Greatest feat:
Holding the door hatch on the space shuttle after Homer breaks the handle, allowing Homer and his fellow astronauts to make it back to Earth.

Greatest honor:
Making the cover of *Time* magazine ("In Rod We Trust") and receiving its own parade.

Greatest disparager:
Homer.

Awards:
Worker of the Week at Springfield Nuclear Power Plant.

"When I found out about this, I went through a wide range of emotions. First I was nervous, then anxious, then wary, then apprehensive, then... kind of sleepy, then worried, and then concerned. But now I realize that being a spaceman is something you have to do."

"You're right, Marge. Just like the time I could have met Mr. T at the mall. The entire day, I kept saying, 'I'll go a little later, I'll go a little later...' And when I got there, they told me he just left. And when I asked the mall guy if he'll ever come back again, he said he didn't know. Well, I'm never going to let something like that happen again! I'm going into space right now!"
Homer, responding to Marge urging him not to miss his once-in-a-lifetime opportunity.

James Taylor's advice: "Ants, huh? We had quite a severe ant problem at the Vineyard this year. I had Art Garfunkel come by with his compressor and we created a total vacuum outside the house and we blew the ants out the front door. But I'm sure you high-tech NASA people could care less about our resort town ways."

"Yeah. Maybe I do have the right... What's that stuff?"

Homer: *Nobody respects me at work.*
Marge: *Well, we respect you.*
(Bart secretly writes "INSERT BRAIN HERE" on the back of Homer's head.)

Stillwater: *People, we're in danger of losing our funding. America isn't interested in space exploration anymore.*
Babcock: *Maybe we should finally tell them the big secret, that all the chimps we sent into space came back super intelligent.*
(A chair swivels around, revealing a chimp in a suit, wearing glasses, and smoking a pipe.)
Chimp: *(arrogant; English accent) No, I don't think we'll be telling them that.*

Reporter: *Uh, question for the barbecue chef: Don't you think there is an inherent danger in sending underqualified civilians into space?*
Homer: *I'll field this one. The only danger is if they send us to that terrible Planet of the Apes.*
(Homer thinks for a moment and realizes something.)
Homer: *Wait a minute, Statue of Liberty—that was our planet! You maniacs! You blew it up! Damn you! Damn you all to hell!*

Buzz Aldrin: *So Barney, we hear you're kickin' ass.*
Homer: *I, uh, don't think this contest is over yet, Buzz. If that is your real name. I believe there is still a little something called the swimsuit competition.*
Aldrin: *There's no swimsuit competition, Homer.*
Homer: *You mean I shaved my bikini zone for nothing?*

Stillwater: *(sighs) Well, Homer. I guess you're the winner by default.*
Homer: *(jubilant) De-fault! The two sweetest words in the English language.*

THE STUFF YOU MAY HAVE MISSED

Sign at launch site: "Cape Canaveral—Formerly Cape Kennedy—Formerly Cape Arbuckle."

Homer knows the telephone numbers for both NASA and President Clinton.

Homer wears his "Hail to the Chef" apron to the NASA press conference.

The space shuttle is named "Corvair." The Chevrolet Corvair of the 1960s was judged to be one of the road's most unsafe cars.

Homer calls up President Clinton, and says, "I figured if anyone knew where to get some Tang, it'd be you." This may or may not be meant as a double entendre.

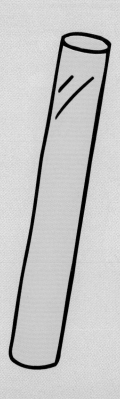

ROD FLANDERS

Family tree branch:
Youngest child of the Springfield Flanders.

Idea of blasphemy:
The talking dog on "Davey and Golitath."

Most positive influences:
His family; The Bible.

Worst influences:
Homer and Bart Simpson.

Biggest miracle:
Hasn't been beaten up by Jimbo, Dolph, Kearney, or Nelson.

> DAD, CAN I ANOINT THE SORES ON HIS FEET?

HOMER LOVES FLANDERS

Episode 1F14   Original Airdate: 2/24/94   Writer: David Richardson   Director: Wes Archer

Homer tries to obtain tickets to a football game but fails. Flanders wins two tickets during a radio contest and invites Homer as his guest. Desperate, Homer accepts. Flanders pays for all the food and even gets the winning quarterback to give the game ball to Homer. Overwhelmed by Flanders's generosity and no longer ashamed to be associated with him, Homer becomes friends with Ned and his family.

Marge complains that Homer is now ignoring his own family. Homer arranges a camping trip with both families, but the families do not get along. When the Simpsons initiate a food fight, Ned tells Maude he now hates his neighbor.

Back home, Homer is oblivious to Ned's animosity. He arrives at the Flanders's home expecting to play golf, but Ned and his family get in their car and race off. Pulled over by police for speeding, Ned takes a sobriety test as the disapproving townspeople watch. At church, Ned yells at Homer, alarming the congregation. However, Homer sticks up for Ned and convinces the townspeople to give him another chance. The next week, everything returns to normal, as Homer once again is annoyed by Flanders.

SHOW HIGHLIGHTS

"Oh, golly, if that doesn't put the shaz in shazam. Oh listen, what's the cash value of those tickets so I can report it on my income taxes?" Flanders, winning the football tickets over the radio.

"What's so special about this game anyway? It's just another chapter in the pointless rivalry between Springfield and Shelbyville. They built a mini mall so we built a bigger mini mall. They made the world's largest pizza so we burnt down their City Hall."

Nacho hat: The snack Ned buys Homer at the game. It consists of a giant, wearable tortilla-chip sombrero with nacho cheese in the top.

"Losers! Losers! Kiss my big Springfield behind, Shelbyville!" Homer, taunting the crowd before getting hit with a flying beer keg.

"Bless the grocer for this wonderful meat, the middleman who jacked up the price, and let's not forget the humane but determined boys at the slaughterhouse."

> I AM NOT
> DELIGHTFULLY SAUCY
> I AM NOT
> DELIGHTFULLY SAUCY
> I AM NOT
> DELIGHTFULLY SAUCY

"We're heading back. Todd's got Zesty Italian in his eye." Flanders, to Homer, after the Simpson-initiated food fight.

"Hey Flanders! Over here. I got us some kick-ass seats!" Homer, at church, calling to Ned.

"Oh can't you see this man isn't a hero! He's annoying. He's very, very annoying!" Flanders, erupting over Homer in church.

"Stop it! How dare you talk about Ned Flanders like that! He's a wonderful, kind caring man. Maybe even more so than me. There have even been times when I've lost patience with him, even lashed out at him. But this man has turned every cheek on his body. If everyone here were like Ned Flanders, there'd be no need for heaven: we'd already be there."

Homer Loves Flanders:
Homer: *I want everyone to know that* (sticking head out the window) *this is Ned Flanders... my friend!* (Lenny and Carl walk by.)
Lenny: *What'd he say?*
Carl: *I dunno. Somethin' about being gay.*

Comments on Ned:
Helen Lovejoy: *Well Ned Flanders is just jealous!*
Moe: *Aw, the guy's hepped up on goofballs.*
Grampa: *Let's sacrifice him to our god! We did it all the time in the 30s.*

Movie Moments:
"Where's your messiah now, Flanders?" parodies a line from *The Ten Commandments*. Homer sprints after Flanders's car with the golf irons à la *Terminator 2*.

Flanders Pulled Over for Speeding:
Flanders: *I told you, officer. I'm not "hepped up" on "goofballs."*
Wiggum: *Yeah right.*
(Moments later, Flanders loses balance in his dexterity test, embarrassed that a church bus is passing by.)
Wiggum: *High as a kite, everybody! Goofballs!* (à la Edward G. Robinson) *Where's your messiah now, Flanders?*

THE STUFF YOU MAY HAVE MISSED

Headline in *Springfield Shopper* under "Big Fat Man Has Big Fat Heart" is "Little Thin Man Accused in Armed Robbery."

Springfield Community Church boasts "The Loosest Bingo Cards in Town."

The sign on the soup kitchen where Ned Flanders volunteers says, "Helter Shelter, Father James Helter, Founder."

Flanders's boat is named: *Thanks for the Boat, Lord II.*

The sign for Lake Springfield: "No mercury dumping without a permit."

Flanders's license plate reads JHN 143. This could refer to John 14:3 of the New Testament.

Da Vinci's "Last Supper" hangs in Flanders's den.

BART GETS AN ELEPHANT

Episode 1F15 Original Airdate: 3/31/94 Writer: John Swartzwelder Director: Jim Reardon

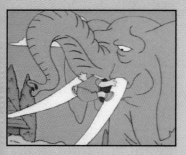

Identity:
Full-grown African elephant won by Bart on the "Bill & Marty Show" on KBBL radio.

Smells:
Like an elephant.

Thinks:
He's people.

Hates:
Being chained up in the backyard.

Craves:
Other elephant company.

Eats:
Lots.

Daily food bill:
$300.

W hen Bart wins a KBBL radio contest, deejays Bill and Marty give him the choice of two prizes: $10,000 in cash or a full-grown African elephant. Bart chooses the elephant. Never thinking that anyone would choose the gag gift, Bill and Marty are caught off guard. They offer Bart a variety of other prizes, all of which he refuses. Their jobs at stake, they arrange delivery of a full-grown elephant to the Simpsons' house.

Bart names the elephant Stampy and ties him to a post in the backyard. Lisa thinks that keeping the animal away from the jungle is cruel, while Homer is concerned that the pachyderm is eating him out of house and home. To help offset food costs, Bart offers rides on Stampy for $2.00 apiece, but Homer decides that Stampy's upkeep is too high and sells the elephant to an ivory dealer. Before the dealer can claim him, Bart sets Stampy free.

Stampy blazes a trail of destruction through the town. Bart insists that Homer give him to an animal refuge, but Homer does not want to lose thousands of dollars from the ivory dealer. Homer gets stuck in the tar pits, and is in danger of sinking, when Stampy pulls him out. Grateful to Stampy for saving his life, Homer gives the elephant to an animal refuge.

SHOW HIGHLIGHTS

 "Son, when you participate in sporting events, it's not whether you win or lose: it's how drunk you get."

"Bart! With $10,000, we'd be millionaires! We could buy all kinds of useful things, like...love." Homer, trying to convince Bart to take the $10,000 cash.

"I'm tired. I'm hungry. Can't we just get a new house?"

"Lisa, go to your room." Homer, after Lisa tells them it is "wrong to imprison an animal."

"So isn't that what we're all asking in our own lives? 'Where's my elephant?' I know that's what I've been asking."

"Oh, everything's cruel according to you. Keeping him chained up in the backyard is cruel. Pulling on his tail is cruel. Yelling in his ears is cruel. Everything is cruel. So excuse me if I'm cruel."

"We Love You": Santa's Little Helper and Snowball II walk across the room balancing on balls to try to get the family's attention away from Stampy.

Bart's sign: "See the Elephant—$1. Ride the Elephant—$2."

First appearance of Cletus, the slack-jawed yokel: Lisa's defense of Stampy's ill-temperedness is, "You'd be grumpy too if you were taken out of your natural habitat and gawked at by a bunch of slack-jawed yokels." Cletus approaches and says, "Hey, Maw. Look at that pointy-haireded little girl. Hu-yuck!"

"See the Elephant—$100. Ride the Elephant—$500." Homer's new pricing structure.

Mr. Blackheart, not denying that he's an ivory dealer: "Little girl, I've had lots of jobs in my day. Whale hunter, seal clubber, president of the Fox Network. And like most people, yeah I've dealt a little ivory."

> **Movie Moment:**
> A curious Stampy looks directly into the window outside the Simpsons' living room à la the T-Rex peering into the jeep in *Jurassic Park*.

> **Lisa:** *Dad, I think he's an ivory dealer. His boots are ivory, his hat is ivory, and I'm pretty sure that check is ivory.*
> **Homer:** *Lisa, a guy who's got lots of ivory is less likely to hurt Stampy than a guy whose ivory supplies are low.*

> **Mr. Blackheart:** *All right, I'll be back in the morning to pick up Stampy.*
> **Homer:** *Here's the keys.*
> **Mr. Blackheart:** *Elephants don't have keys.*
> **Homer:** *Well, I'll just keep these then.*

> **Homer:** *Well, these bills will have to be paid out of your allowance.*
> **Bart:** *You'll have to raise my allowance to about a thousand dollars a week.*
> **Homer:** *Then that's what I'll do, smart guy!*

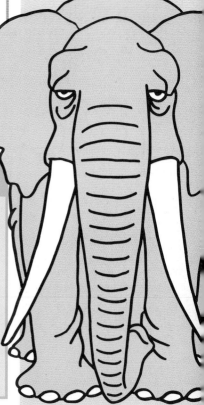

THE STUFF YOU MAY HAVE MISSED

Simpson house clutter and filth include: pizza and footprints on the cieling, splattered eggs on the walls, a sandwich on the staircase, Homer's bowling ball in the refrigerator, and underpants on the banister and in the refrigerator.

Signs seen inside the Republican Convention as Stampy walks through to cheers:
"We want what's worst for everyone" and "We're just plain evil."

Signs seen inside the Democratic Convention as Stampy walks through to boos: "We hate life, and ourselves" and "We can't govern."

Sign at the tar pits: "Springfield Tar Pits. 'The Best in Tar Entertainment' —*Time Magazine*."

ORGAN TRANSPLANTS ARE BEST LEFT TO THE PROFESSIONALS
ORGAN TRANSPLANTS ARE BEST LEFT TO THE PROFESSIONALS

BURNS' HEIR

Episode 1F16 Original Airdate: 4/14/94 Writer: Jack Richdale Director: Mark Kirkland

SIMPSON ACTORS

Occupations:
Actors; frauds for hire.

Latest job:
Retained by Mr. Burns to portray members of the Simpson family.

Technique:
Using dialogue designed to convince Bart his mother, father and sisters no longer love him.

Judgemental error:
Treating this as a real job.

Skill level:
Poor.

Commitment to roles:
Questionable.

SORRY, M.B., BUT I'M HAVING TROUBLE WITH THIS CHARACTER. IS HE SUPPOSED TO HAVE SOME SORT OF NEUROLOGICAL IMPAIRMENT LIKE RAIN MAN OR AWAKENINGS?

A fter nearly drowning in a bathtub, Mr. Burns realizes that he is without an heir and launches a search for a suitable young man to inherit his vast fortune. Homer coaches Bart for his "audition." Reading Homer's words from cue cards, Bart sounds like a moron. Humiliated, he vandalizes Burns's mansion. Impressed by the boy's sheer malevolence, Burns chooses Bart as his heir.

Bart spends time at Burns's mansion, where Burns caters to his every whim and demand. When Bart returns home, spoiled and unbearable, Homer attempts to punish him. Refusing to obey, Bart moves in with Mr. Burns. Homer and Marge hire Lionel Hutz to regain custody of their son, but Hutz loses the case.

Burns tries to convince Bart that his family does not miss him. He even hires actors to portray uncaring versions of Homer, Marge, Lisa, and Maggie. Bart falls for the ploy, embracing Burns and calling him "Dad." As a sign of complete loyalty, Burns asks Bart to fire Homer from his job. Instead, Bart, deciding to return to his family, triggers a trap door that sends the evil millionaire plummeting down a dark shaft.

SHOW HIGHLIGHTS

Near-death experience: When Mr. Burns sinks in his bathtub under the weight of a sponge placed atop his head, his life flashes before his eyes. A baby Burns drinks from a bottle handed to him by his nanny and suddenly spits it out. He fires her on the spot. Next, a teenage Monty fires a pistol at the feet of a street beggar, imploring him to dance. The man does a jig and then stops while Burns reloads. Finally, Burns wears a bad hippie wig on a Greenpeace boat, sinking it and declaring, "It was I, you fools! The man you trusted isn't Wavy Gravy at all!" He tosses away his guitar and says, "And all this time, I've been smoking harmless tobacco."

(When Bart tells Mr. Burns that he wants to go home, Burns shows Bart a monitor that is supposedly connected to a camera in the Simpson household; it shows the Simpsons on the couch.)
Homer: (blank delivery, wrong voice) *I do not miss Bart at all.*
Marge: *I am glad he's gone.*
Lisa: *As am I.*
Homer: (dropping his sandwich) *B'oh!*
Bart: (to Mr. Burns) *It's probably my imagination, but something about them didn't seem right.*

 "Smithers, do you realize, if I had died there would be no one to carry on my legacy? Due to my hectic schedule and lethargic sperm, I never fathered an heir."

"Hello Mr...Kurns? I bad want...money now. Me sick." Bart, reading Homer's cue cards at the audition.

"He's the perfect one to suckle at my proverbial teat." Burns, after seeing a sample of Bart's malevolence.

Pizza man: Bart demands that Krusty the Clown deliver a pizza to him at the mansion. He wonders how Krusty can be on both live TV and standing there with a pizza at the same time. Krusty explains he's just playing a rerun, but this one is the show he taped the day the Falkland Islands were invaded.

"I've argued in front of every judge in this state. Often as a lawyer."

The things Bart runs through while driving his new red sports car: A fire hydrant, a loaded mailbox, several bales of hay, a "Santa's Christmas Village" sign, several candy canes, reindeer cutouts, an elf, and a menorah.

> **Movie Moment:**
> A cockney boy says to Burns, "Why, today is Christmas Day, sir," parodying a scene with Ebeneezer Scrooge in *A Christmas Carol*.

The Audition:
Milhouse: *I have nothing to offer you but my love.*
Burns: *I specifically said, "No geeks!"*
Milhouse: *But my mom says I'm cool.*
Burns: *Next.*
Nelson: *Gimme your fortune or I'll pound your withered old face in!*
Burns: *Oh, I like his energy. Put him on the call back list.*
Martin: (singing) *Clang, clang, clang went the trolley / Ring, ring, ring went the bell / Zing, zing, zing went my heartstrings... / (Oooh! (Nelson cold-cocks him.)*
Burns: *Thank you. Give the bully an extra point.*

THE STUFF YOU MAY HAVE MISSED

Some stores at Springfield Mall: "Shoes for Tots," "The Creamatorium," "Gum for Less," and "Lionel Hutz (Also Expert Shoe Repair)."

The Happy Earwig Hotel marquee message: "Our crawlspace now body-free."

Sign: "Conformco Brain Deprogrammers—A Subsidiary of Mrs. Fields's Cookies."

Mr. Burns's "Let's All Go to the Lobby" song is taken from an actual intermission snack-bar tune once played at movie theaters and drive-ins, in the 1960s and '70s.

Krusty reads a TelePrompTer in a 1982 edition of his show, even though he is supposedly illiterate.

THE PLEDGE OF ALLEGIANCE DOES NOT END WITH 'HAIL SATAN'!
THE PLEDGE OF ALLEGIANCE DOES NOT END WITH 'HAIL SATAN'!

SWEET SEYMOUR SKINNER'S BAADASSSSS SONG

Episode 1F18 Original Airdate: 4/27/94 Writers: Bill Oakley & Josh Weinstein Director: Bob Anderson

Bart brings Santa's Little Helper to school for "Show & Tell." When the dog disappears into the school's vents, Grounds-keeper Willie is sent in to catch him. Soon Willie is stuck inside the vents and both he and Santa's Little Helper must be rescued by the fire department. Superintendent Chalmers witnesses the debacle, fires Principal Skinner, and replaces him with Ned Flanders.

Bart feels responsible for Skinner's dismissal. When Skinner invites him to his home, the two become friends. Bart tells Skinner how the school is falling apart under Flanders's disciplineless regime.

Skinner re-enlists in the army. Missing his new friend, Bart plots to have Flanders fired and Skinner rehired by exposing Flanders's poor leadership. Chalmers is unfazed by the chaos. When he hears Flanders say "Lord" over the loudspeaker, Chalmers fires him for introducing prayer in the school. Skinner resigns from the army and is reinstated.

I WILL NOT CELEBRATE MEANINGLESS MILESTONES

SHOW HIGHLIGHTS

 "I know Weinstein's parents were upset, Superintendent, but, but, ah, I was sure it was a phony excuse. I mean, it sounds so made up: 'Yom Kip-pur.'"

"I said 'Make way for Willie,' ye bloated gas-bag!" Willie, landing on Superintendent Chalmers.

"Bart, look. It's Principal Skinner, and I think he's gone crazy. He's not wearing a suit or tie or anything!"

"All right you little punks, pick up your freakin' ears, because I'm only going to be saying this once. From now on things are going to be very, very different around here...with your new principal, Ned Flanders!" Leopold, to the students of Springfield Elementary.

"That photo was taken shortly before I was shot in the back, which is very strange, because it was during a Bob Hope show. I was trying to get Joey Heatherton to put on some pants for God's sake." Skinner, reminiscing to Bart about Vietnam.

"I think you need Skinner, Bart. Everybody needs a nemesis. Sherlock Holmes had his Dr. Moriarty, Mountain Dew has its Mello Yello, even Maggie has that baby with the one eyebrow."

"God has no place within these walls, just like facts have no place within organized religion! Simpson, you get your wish. Flanders is history." Chalmers, after catching Ned say, "Let's Thank the Lord" over the intercom.

(Bart lifts the box revealing Santa's Little Helper.)
Mrs. Krabappel: Oh, he is a gem! Here boy. Would you like these cookies Martin made for me? (She puts the box of cookies on the floor, and the dog wolfs them down.)
Martin: My raisin roundees!

Skinner: Willie, go into the vent and get him.
Groundskeeper Willie: What!? Have ye gone waxy in yer beester?! I canna fit in the wee vent, ye croquet-playin' mint-muncher!
Skinner: Grease yourself up and go in, you— guff-speaking work-slacker.
Groundskeeper Willie: Ooh. Good comeback.

Bart: Here's the plan: Once Chalmers comes for his next inspection and sees how crappy the school has gotten, he'll fire Ned on the spot.
Skinner: Uh, one question remains. How do I get out of the army?
Bart: No problemo. Just make a pass at your commanding officer.
Skinner: Done and done. And I mean done.

Movie Moment:
The scene in which Willie looks for Santa's Little Helper in the air ducts as Skinner watches on a radar monitor parodies a scene from *Alien.*

Superintendent Chalmers: You're fired.
Skinner: I'm sorry, did you just call me a liar?
Superintendent Chalmers: No, I said you were fired.
Skinner: Oh. That's much worse.

Skinner's New Recruits:
Hayseed #1: Hi. Where do I get my grenades at?
Hayseed #2: Uh, they don't have them group terlets here no more, do they?

Nelson, at Show 'N' Tell:
Nelson: The ingredients were (reading) "Fresh pureed tomatoes, water, salt, and Sodium Benzoate used to retard spoilage." Once again, if I'm not mistaken, this can contained tomato paste.
Mrs. Krabappel: Thank you, Nelson. I look forward to seeing it again next week. Bart, you're up.

THE STUFF YOU MAY HAVE MISSED

The line "It thinks it's people," spoken by Mrs. Krabappel after Santa's Little Helper sneezes is the same line Bart says after Stampy scratches himself on the Simpsons' house in 1F18, "Bart Gets an Elephant."

Lunchlady Doris scoops meat out of a drum labeled, "Assorted Horse Parts," with the additional line "Now with More Testicles."

Principal Skinner barbecues with a "Principals Do It Nine Months a Year" apron.

The sign outside Fort Springfield reads, "Proud Home of the Secret Civilian Mail-Opening Project."

Skinner has sweat stains under his arms while talking on the phone with Chalmers.

SUPERINTENDENT CHALMERS

Occupation:
Superintendent of Springfield schools.

Demeanor:
As threatening as a school official can possibly be.

Least favorite place:
Springfield Elementary School.

Least favorite principal:
Principal Skinner.

Often shouts:
"Skinner!"

Surprising behavior:
He sometimes believes Skinner's lame excuses.

Dates:
Skinner's mom.

I HAVE HAD IT WITH THIS SCHOOL! THE LOW TEST SCORES, CLASS AFTER CLASS OF UGLY, UGLY CHILDREN!

FREDDY QUIMBY

Occupation:
Recreational golf and tennis; recreation in general.

Place in society:
So high up he is only seen by Springfield rank-and-file on his court dates.

Proud distinctions:
Didn't graduate from high school; pays for his dates; didn't work for his money.

Benefactor:
Daisy, the never-seen Quimby matriarch.

Quirks:
Has a bizarre link to New England apparent in his nasal tone, accent, and his zest for chowdah.

Unpaid debt:
To Bart Simpson for clearing his name.

AND TO THINK I GOT ALL THIS AFTER DROPPING OUT OF THE FOURTH GRADE.

Bart forges a note from Marge that excuses him early from school for a dental appointment. Principal Skinner reads the note and is suspicious. He tracks Bart through town. Bart escapes by jumping inside the passing car of Freddy Quimby, the Mayor's 18-year-old nephew. Arriving at Freddy Quimby's birthday party, he hides beneath a table and witnesses an altercation between Freddy and a waiter.

Freddy Quimby is charged with beating the waiter and Homer is selected to serve on the jury at his trial. Bart confesses to Lisa that he saw what happened and can prove that Freddy Quimby is innocent, but that if he comes forward, Skinner will expel him for skipping school.

All the members of the jury conclude that Freddy is guilty—except Homer, who enjoys being

SHOW HIGHLIGHTS

"If I were a truant boy out for a good time, I'd be right here. The Springfield Natural History Museum. You're mine, Simpson."

"His brand of gum—Doublemint. Trying to double your fun, eh, Bart? Well, I'll double your detention. I wish someone was around to hear that." Skinner, after finding a clue on Bart's trail.

"Wow! This is the biggest Rice Krispies square I've ever seen. Boy, the rich sure know how to live." Bart, hiding out in Quimby's kitchen.

"I know you can read my thoughts, Bart. Just a little reminder: if I find out you cut class, your ass is mine. Yes, you heard me. I think words I would never say." Principal Skinner, telepathically communicating with Bart from the jury box.

"Well, only one in two million people has what we call the evil gene. Hitler had it. Walt Disney had it. And Freddy Quimby has it."

"I just want to say how great it is to finally see some chicks on the bench. Keep up the good work, toots."

Mrs. Krabappel: *Well, children, our new ultra-hard Posturific chairs have arrived. They've been designed by eminent posturologists to eliminate slouching by the year 3000.*
Martin: *Mrs. Krabappel, I'm having back spasms.*
Mrs. Krabappel: *I know they seem a little uncomfortable right now, but eventually your bones will change shape.*
Milhouse: *I've lost all feeling in the left side of my body.*

Quimby's lawyer: *Mr. Quimby, did you assault Mr. Lacoste?*
Freddy: *Of course not. I love each and every living thing on God's green earth.*
Lawyer: *Therefore, you certainly would never lose you temper over something as trivial as the pronunciation of "chowder."*
Freddy: *That's chowdah. Chowdah! I'll kill you! I'll kill all of you—especially those of you in the jury!*

KNEW TOO MUCH

Episode 1F19
Original Airdate: 5/5/94
Writer: John Swartzwelder
Director: Jeffrey Lynch

sequestered in a hotel with free room service and cable TV. Lisa convinces Bart to testify. Bart states that Freddy never touched the waiter and that the waiter slipped in the kitchen and injured himself. The charges against Quimby are dropped. Skinner praises Bart for his bravery and only sentences him to four months detention.

THERE ARE PLENTY OF
BUSINESSES LIKE SHOW BUSINESS
THERE ARE PLENTY OF
BUSINESSES LIKE SHOW BUSINESS
THERE ARE PLENTY OF
BUSINESSES LIKE SHOW BUSINESS

What Really Happens to the Waiter:

He slips on a piece of Rice Krispies square, sliding face-first into a row of hanging skillets. This sends him backwards across the kitchen and headfirst into the microwave oven. One hand gets stuck in a mixing bowl and the other in a toaster. Shrieking, he falls forward into the oven, then knocks over a pot of steaming water on to his back. He screams, falling backwards into a closet marked "Rat Traps." The waiter emerges covered head-to-toe with the traps and knocks into a row of hanging wine glasses, teetering across the room and falling to the floor.

Homer, the Juror:

Homer: *What does "sequestered" mean?*
Skinner: *If the jury is deadlocked, they're put up in a hotel together so they can't communicate with the outside world.*
Homer: *What does "deadlocked" mean?*
Skinner: *It's when the jury can't agree on a verdict.*
Homer: *Uh-huh. And "if"?*
Skinner: *A conjunction meaning "in the event that" or "on condition that."*
Homer: *So "if" we don't all vote the same way, we'll be "deadlocked" and have to be "sequestered" in the Springfield Palace Hotel…*
Patty: *That's not going to happen, Homer.*
Jasper: *Let's vote, my liver is failing.*
Homer: *Where we'll get… a free room, free food, free swimming pool, free HBO—oooh, Free Willy!*
Skinner: *Justice is not a frivolous thing, Simpson. It has little, if anything to do with a disobedient whale. Now let's vote.*

At the Aztec:

Bart: *Look, if I was under 17 I'd be in school, right?*
Ticket seller: *Yeah, I guess you're right. Enjoy Boob-A-Rama, sir.*

The Chowder Affair:

Freddy: *Hey, what the hell is this?*
Waiter: *It's a bowl of show-dair, sir.*
Freddy: *Wait a minute. Come here. What did you call it? Say it loud enough for everyone to hear. Come on! Say it.*
Waiter: *Show-dair.*
Freddy: *(mocking) "Show-dair?" "Show-dair?" It's "chowdah." Say it right.*
Waiter: *Show-der.*
Freddy: *Come back here! I'm not through demeaning you.*

THE STUFF YOU MAY HAVE MISSED

This episode marks the second time Apu quashes Skinner's excitement: the first such incident occurs in 1F18, "Sweet Seymour Skinner's Baadasssss Song," when Apu informs Skinner that his novel is a rip-off of *Jurassic Park.*

Bart uses the "Li'l Bastard Clock-Tampering Kit."

Sign posted in front of the Quimby compound: "Thursday Is Ladies' Night."

Matt Groening is the courtroom artist.

Springfield Shopper headline: "Quimby Nephew Charged in Beating." Subheadline: "Chowder Said Wrong."

MRS. JACQUELINE BOUVIER

Identity:
Mother of Marge, Patty, and Selma.

Residence:
The Hal Roach Apartments, "Retirement Living in the Heart of the Cemetery District."

Wears:
Dentures; sports a grey bouffant resembling daughter Marge's blue number.

Claim to fame:
Originator of the Bouvier family grumble, and a onetime flapper.

Most embarrassing moment:
Arrested for indecent exposure in 1923.

Friends at one time with:
Zelda Fitzgerald; Frances Farmer; and little Sylvia Plath.

Favorite song:
Glenn Miller's "Moonlight Serenade."

Biggest regret:
Having Homer as a son-in-law.

AT THE RISK OF LOSING MY VOICE, LET ME SAY JUST ONE MORE THING: I'M SORRY I CAME.

SHOW HIGHLIGHTS

The Baby with One Eyebrow returns: During Maggie's birthday party, the Baby with One Eyebrow is pushed in its stroller. Maggie and the baby exchange mean looks. (A previous confrontation occurs in 1F18, "Sweet Seymour Skinner's Badasssss Song.")

 "Y'know, you remind me of a poem I can't remember, and a song that may never have existed, and a place I'm not sure I've ever been to."

"If he marries your mother, Marge, we'll be brother and sister! And then our kids, they'll be horrible freaks with pink skin, no overbites, and five fingers on each hand." Homer, expressing concern about Grampa falling in love with Mrs. Bouvier.

"Hello, I'm Troy McClure. You might remember me from such films as *The Boatjacking of Super-Ship 79* and *Hydro: The Man with the Hydraulic Arms*."

"My darling, since my kneecaps are filling with fluid as we speak, I'll be brief. Will you marry me?" Mr. Burns's marriage proposal to Mrs. Bouvier.

Over the Closing Credits, to the Tune of "The Sounds of Silence":
Hello Grampa, my old friend/Your busy day is at an end/Your exploits have been sad and boring/They tell a tale that's worth ignoring/When you're alone, the word of your story/Will echo down the rest home hall/'Cause no one at all can stand /The sound of Grampa.

Troy: *Coming up this hour on the Impulse Buying Network, your chance to own a piece of Itchy & Scratchy, the toontown twosome beloved by everyone, even cynical members of Generation X!*
Gen X guy: *Yeah, (using his hand to make air quotes) "groovy."*
Roger Meyers, Jr.: *Troy, I'm proud to offer your viewers these hand-drawn Itchy & Scratchy animation cels. Each one is absolutely, positively 100% guaranteed to increase in value!*
Voiceover announcer: *(quickly & quietly) Not a guarantee.*

(Grampa, having been ditched by Mrs. Bouvier, walks home along a row of streetlights. He holds up his hat.)
Grampa: *Goodnight, Mrs. Bouvier...Wherever you are.*
(The lawyer and thugs suddenly arrive.)
Lawyer: *Mr. Simpson, I represent the estate of Jimmy Durante. I have a court order demanding an immediate halt to this unauthorized imitation. Boys?*
(The thugs grab Grampa's hat and stomp on it.)
Grampa: *Well, would it be all right with you if I just laid down in the street and died?*
Lawyer: *Yes, that would be acceptable.*

Movie Moment:
Mr. Burns and Mrs. Bouvier get married in the First Church of Springfield (as Grampa screams from the glassed-in organist's booth) and Grampa and Mrs. Bouvier run out to the minibus to the strains of "Sounds of Silence"-esque music in a direct parody of *The Graduate*.

Homer: *Marge, please, old people don't need companionship. They need to be isolated and studied, so it can be determined what nutrients they have that might be extracted for our personal use.*
Marge: *Homer, would you please stop reading that Ross Perot pamphlet?*

The Play-It-Cool Song:
Homer: *Now, what you gotta do/If you want to get a kiss/Is act real smooth/And make your move like this.* (He does the yawn-and-stretch routine, putting his arm over Grampa's shoulder.)
Grampa: *Oh, I see. So if I take your advice/And make your patented move/Then my chances for love/Will slightly improve?*
(Grampa practices the move on Homer.)
Homer: *Hee, hee, hee! Now what's that rule?*
Grampa: *Play it cool.*

THE STUFF YOU MAY HAVE MISSED

Sign: "Hal Roach Apartments—Retirement Living In the Heart of the Cemetery District."

Sign at the First Church of Springfield: "Private Wedding. Please Worship Elsewhere."

Restaurant where Marge, Homer, Grampa, and Mrs. Bouvier dine: P. Piggly Hogswine's Super-Smorg.

On the Springfield Community Center marquee: "Today: Senior Citizens Swing Dance, Tomorrow: Cat Spay-a-Thon."

Red Breem and His Band of Some Esteem play Glenn Miller's "Moonlight Serenade" and Benny Goodman's "Sing! Sing! Sing!" at the Springfield Community Center.

Patty, Selma, Mrs. Bouvier, and Grampa help celebrate Maggie's first birthday. After the party, Marge tells Homer that her mother and his father seem lonely. They take the elderly pair to dinner, hoping to spark a relationship. At Mrs. Bouvier's apartment after dinner, Grampa sees photos of Mrs. Bouvier from her flapper days and falls in love with her.

Meanwhile, Bart orders a genuine Itchy & Scratchy animation cel, advertised on TV, with Homer's credit card. However, when the cel arrives, it vaguely resembles part of Scratchy's arm. Grampa takes Mrs. Bouvier to a senior citizens' swing dance, but Mr. Burns cuts in and dances with Mrs. Bouvier the entire night. Grampa is heartbroken.

The following day, Burns arrives at the Simpsons' house to pick up Mrs. Bouvier for another date. Bart extorts money from him to pay for the worthless cel and gives the money to Homer. Mr. Burns proposes to Mrs. Bouvier, and despite Marge's warnings, she accepts. During the wedding ceremony, however, Mr. Burns kicks Bart when he drops the wedding ring. Repulsed by Burns's behavior, Mrs. Bouvier leaves with Grampa, deciding not to marry either man.

I WILL NOT RE-TRANSMIT WITHOUT THE EXPRESS WRITTEN PERMISSION OF MAJOR LEAGUE BASEBALL

SECRETS OF A SUCCESSFUL MARRIAGE

Episode 1F20 Original Airdate: 5/19/94 Writer: Greg Daniels Director: Carlos Baeza

Homer requests an instructing position himself. He is hired to teach a course on marriage. Enthusiastic at first, Homer soon realizes that he does not know how to run a class. As the students begin to leave the classroom, he reveals personal secrets about his marriage. Soon, the class is paying close attention.

Marge finds out that Homer is disclosing private information about her. She tells him that she does not want the public knowing details of their lovelife, but Homer cannot stop himself. When Moe teases Homer about one of the personal secrets right in front of Marge, she kicks Homer out of the house.

Marge refuses to forgive Homer, telling him that he betrayed her trust. Homer takes up temporary residence in Bart's treehouse, hoping Marge will change her mind. Reverend Lovejoy encourages Marge to seek a divorce, but Homer pours his heart out to her and promises that he will never lose her trust again. Moved by Homer's sincerity, Marge forgives him.

When Homer's poker-playing friends call him "slow," Marge suggests he enroll in an adult education course to sharpen his intellect. However, Homer's friends are teachers, so

Occupation:
Button-down educator.

Demeanor:
No-nonsense.

Quirks:
A slight speech impediment that makes it difficult for him to say "Simpson."

Believes:
It's impossible for anyone to tell the difference between butter and I Can't Believe It's Not Butter.

Also believes:
Homer has all the tools to make a decent instructor.

SHOW HIGHLIGHTS

"Look Marge, you don't know what it's like—I'm the one out there every day putting his ass on the line. And I'm not out of order! You're out of order! The whole freaking system is out of order! You want the truth? You want the truth? You can't handle the truth! 'Cause when you reach over and put your hand into a pile of goo that used to be your best friend's face, you'll know what to do! Forget it, Marge, it's Chinatown!"

"Oh, uh, hi, Marge. I heard you and Homer broke up so I'm declaring my intentions to move in on his territory. Here, I brung you some posies."

"Marge, you'll never guess what. My whole class is here. They're going to observe the human peep show that is our lives."

Homer's New Approach:
Homer: I do have a story about two other young marrieds. Now, the wife of this couple has an interesting quirk in the bedroom. It seems she goes wild with desire if her husband nibbles on her elbow.
Mrs. Krabappel: We need names!
Homer: Well let's just call them, uh, "Mr. X" and "Mrs. Y." So anyway, Mr. X would say, "Marge, if this doesn't get your motor running, my name isn't Homer J. Simpson!"

Homer Figures It Out:
Homer: Wait a minute! Wait, that's it! I know now what I can offer you that no one else can. Complete and utter dependence!
Marge: Homer, that's not a good thing.
Homer: Are you kidding? It's a wonderous, marvelous thing. Marge, I need you more than anyone else on this entire planet could possibly ever need you. I need you to take care of me, to put up with me, and most of all, I need you to love me, because I love you.
Marge: But how do I know I can trust you?
Homer: Marge, look at me! We've been separated for a day, and I'm as dirty as a Frenchman. In another few hours, I'll be dead. I can't afford to lose your trust again.
Marge: I must admit, you really do make a gal feel needed.
Homer: Wait until my class hears about this. Kidding!

What They Teach at the Adult Education Annex:
Patty & Selma: "Turn a Man Into Putty In Your Hands."
Moe: "Funk Dancing for Self-Defense."
Lenny: "How to Chew Tobacco."
Hans Moleman: "How to Eat an Orange."

Marge's Warning #1:
Marge: Homer, I really don't like you telling personal secrets in your class.
Homer: Marge, I didn't tell 'em personal stuff.
Marge: Today at the Kwik-E-Mart everybody knew I dyed my hair!
Homer: Oh, you mean about you.

> FIVE DAYS IS NOT TOO LONG TO WAIT FOR A GUN.
> FIVE DAYS IS NOT TOO LONG TO WAIT FOR A GUN.
> FIVE DAYS IS NOT TOO LONG TO WAIT FOR A GUN.

Lovejoy's Advice:
Lovejoy: Get a divorce.
Marge: But, isn't that a sin?
Lovejoy: Marge, just about everything is a sin. (holds up the Bible) Y'ever sat down and read this thing? Technically, we're not allowed to go to the bathroom.

Putting on a Show:
Homer: And how's my little major leaguer? Catch any Junebugs today?
Bart: Well, me and Milhouse took some mail from a mail truck and threw it down the sewer.
Homer: Son, I know you meant well, but that wasn't the right thing to do.
Bart: What the hell are you talking about? You're the one who double-dared us.
Homer: Why you little... (choking Bart)

THE STUFF YOU MAY HAVE MISSED

Adult Education Annex's motto: "We Take the 'Dolt' out of A-Dolt Education."

In the treehouse, Homer sleeps in a burlap sack labelled, "U.S. Mail."

The stores that remind Marge of her problems with Homer are, "Broken Home Chimney Repair," "Splitsville Ice Cream Sundaes," and "Painful Memories Party Supplies."

Lenny's "How to chew tobacco" seminar is attended by Otto, Groundskeeper Willy, Abe Simpson, Captain McCallister, Hans Moleman, Jasper, and the Crazy Old Man.

WHAT IS YOUR AREA OF EXPERTISE?

Burning Love. Scratchy lies in a hammock. When he turns over, Itchy fires a flaming arrow at his rear. It connects, and Scratchy leaps up, on fire and screaming. (7G12, "Krusty Gets Busted") **Let Them Eat Scratchy.** Brandishing a rapier, Scratchy chases after Itchy. Itchy traps Scratchy in a guillotine and chops off his head. He

inserts a stick of dynamite into the mouth of Scratchy's severed head. The dynamite explodes, leaving only Scratchy's skull. (7F03, "Bart Gets an F") **Hold That Feline.** Itchy lights the fuse of an exploding football and kicks it towards Scratchy. Scratchy catches the football, which explodes on contact. As the hapless cat lays in a crater, several hefty football players dogpile on top of him. (7F09, "Itchy & Scratchy & Marge") **Kitchen Kut-Ups.** Itchy and Scratchy smash each other with meat tenderizers. Itchy pins Scratchy down with butcher knives and attempts to stab him as Scratchy wriggles around. Finally, Itchy pins him through the heart. Afterwards, Itchy chases after Scratchy with an electric hand-blender. (7F09, "Itchy & Scratchy & Marge") **Messenger of Death.** Scratchy answers a knock at his door and finds Itchy dressed as a messenger. Itchy fires a bazooka at Scratchy. When the smoke clears, all the flesh is blown off of Scratchy's skull, which topples off. Later, Itchy hits Scratchy in the back of the head, knocking out his eyeballs. As Scratchy gropes around for his eyeballs, Itchy hands him two lit cherry bombs, which Scratchy pops into his eye sockets. Combing his hair in front of a mirror, Scratchy notices the bombs and screams in terror. Finally, his head explodes. (7F09, "Itchy & Scratchy & Marge") **Porch Pals.** Sitting in rocking chairs, Itchy and Scratchy share a pitcher of lemonade. (7F09, "Itchy & Scratchy & Marge") **Sundae Bloody Sundae.** Itchy works as a soda jerk. Scratchy sits at the counter and tries to order, but Itchy grabs him and shoves him into a milkshake cup. Itchy puts Scratchy through the blender and pours his bloody, liquefied body into a tall, old-fashioned soda glass. (7F16, "Oh Brother, Where Art Thou?") **Bang the Cat Slowly.** Itchy gives Scratchy a bomb inside a box and ties the box with Scratchy's tongue. When Scratchy swallows the box, the bomb blows his head off. As Scratchy's head falls to the ground, it is impaled on a pointy birthday hat. (7F24, "Stark Raving Dad") **O Solo Meow.** Scratchy eats a plate of Itchy's spaghetti, with a bomb substituting for a meatball. Scratchy realizes what he has eaten and, in a panic, races out the door so quickly that he knocks off his head. As his body explodes, a dog waiter walking by with a tray trips over Scratchy's head and crashes to the ground. (7F23, "When Flanders Failed") **The Sounds of Silencers.** With his Thompson submachine gun, Itchy pumps hundreds of bullets into seven tough-looking cats lined up against a wall. He fires his gun, spelling out "The End." (8F03, "Bart the Murderer") **My Dinner with Itchy.** At "Itchy's" restaurant, Itchy pours drinks for himself and Scratchy. Scratchy drinks his down and realizes that he drank acid. As Scratchy's body burns away, Itchy throws his glass of acid into Scratchy's face. Blinded, Scratchy runs out of the restaurant. A streetcar runs him over. (8F04, "Homer Defined") **Field of Screams.** A combine comes bearing down on Scratchy and his son as they play catch in a wheatfield.

Itchy and his son look out from inside the combine as blood splashes up against the windshield. Afterwards, Itchy and his son play catch with Scratchy's head. (8F05, "Like Father, Like Clown") **House of Pain, Or This Old Mouse.** Itchy ties Scratchy to a post in a house that he is building. He drives a nail through Scratchy's head and into the post and hangs up a picture of both of Itchy and Scratchy smiling. (8F09, "Burns Verkaufen der Kraftwerk") **Cat Splat Fever.** Dedicated to Timmy O'Toole, the short features Scratchy, who finds a note in his bedroom that reads, "Good-bye, cruel world." Looking out the window, he sees Itchy jump down a well in his backyard. As Scratchy descends into the well to save Itchy, he sees Itchy sitting on a brick. Scratchy desperately tries to stop his fall but fails, landing in an alligator's jaws. Now a harp-playing cat angel, Scratchy rises from the well, but Itchy shoots him in the head. (8F11, "Radio Bart") **I'm Getting Buried in the Morning.** Itchy officiates at Scratchy's wedding. As Scratchy kisses his bride, Itchy pulls off his broad-brimmed black priest's hat and throws it at Mrs. Scratchy. The hat slices through her neck and her body falls to the floor. Scratchy opens his eyes and is horrified to see what has happened to his bride. The hat flies back towards him, slicing his head off as well. Itchy drives the wedding car, with Scratchy and Mrs. Scratchy's heads tied to the bumper like tin cans. (8F22, "Bart's Friend Falls in Love") **Flay Me to the Moon.** While Scratchy reads in his rocking chair, Itchy ties his tongue to a rocket that is launched to the moon. Scratchy's tongue gets tangled on the moon, stopping the rocket's flight. By the time Scratchy realizes what is happening, the moon is being pulled towards his house. As

Scratchy hides in the closet, the house is crushed. Mouse Mission Control celebrates its success. (9F01, "Homer the Heretic") **Steamboat Itchy.** On a steamboat, Itchy shoots off Scratchy's kneecaps with a machine gun. Scratchy crawls around, leaving a trail of blood. Itchy stuffs his head in the steamboat's furnace and pulls out a charred skull. (9F03, "Itchy & Scratchy: The Movie) **100-Yard Gash.** Representing the U.S.A. Olympic team, Scratchy lines up for the 100-yard race. Itchy nails Scratchy's tail to the track as the starter's pistol fires. Scratchy tries to run but is held back. Finally, his skeleton bursts out of his skin and his flesh and muscles sag in a heap. Scratchy's skeleton wins a gold medal and appears on a Wheaties box. The episode ends with the message, "Good luck to all our athletes, from Itchy and Scratchy, the official animated cat-and-mouse team of the 1984 Olympics." (9F08, "Lisa's First Word") **Kitty Kitty Bang Bang.** At a bowling alley, Itchy catches Scratchy's tongue in the automatic ball return. He lights the fuse of a bomb and rolls it down the lane. Scratchy tries to free himself from the automatic ball return by cutting off his tongue with a hacksaw, but the bomb hits him before he can escape and blows him to smithereens. Itchy sells Scratchy's ligaments and intestines to several hungry dogs. (9F12, "Brother from the Same Planet) **My Bloody Valentine.** Scratchy presents Itchy with a valentine. Itchy doesn't have one to give Scratchy, so he rips out Scratchy's own heart and presents it to him. Scratchy takes his heart home, puts it on his mantel, and sits down

to read the paper. He reads a headline that informs him that he needs a heart to live. He runs to the mantel to get the heart, but dies before he can reach it. (9F13, "I Love Lisa") **Dazed and Confused.** Itchy taps Scratchy on the head four times with a mallet. Both characters turn to the camera and deliver the message, "Kids: Say No to Drugs" (9F16, "The Front") **Little Barbershop of Horrors.** Bart and Lisa's cartoon features Itchy and Scratchy in a barbershop, where Itchy covers Scratchy's head with barbecue sauce and pours a box of flesh-eating ants on top of it. Scratchy screams as Itchy hurls the barber's chair through the ceiling. His skull crashes into a TV that Elvis is watching. Elvis says, "Aw, this show ain't no good," and shoots the TV. (9F16, "The Front") **Screams from a Mall.** Itchy nails Scratchy's feet to the stairs of an escalator. When Scratchy reaches the top, he is pulled into the machine, which tears his fur off. Itchy grabs the fur and sells it to a fur shop. A snooty woman wears Scratchy's fur out of the shop. A skinned Scratchy confronts her and takes back his fur, swinging it over his shoulder like a stole. As he walks out of the mall, anti-fur protesters beat him with their signs. (9F16, "The Front") **Untitled, with Guest Director Oliver Stone.** Black-and-white footage features Scratchy, who is led through a crowd à la Lee Harvey Oswald. Itchy leaps out and shoots him. (9F18, "Whacking Day") **Germs of Endearment.** Scratchy enters Itchy's doctor's office and points to a blackboard that reads, "Today's Special: Tonsillectomies." Itchy grabs some tissue from the back of Scratchy's throat, ties it to a brick, and throws it out the window. The weight of the brick yanks out all of Scratchy's internal organs. Scratchy dives out the window after his organs and manages to replace them. In the process, he impales himself on a cactus. (9F20, "Marge in Chains") **Spay Anything.** Itchy stands in front of a sign that reads, "We Pay Your Pet, $75." He steps away, revealing the "S" that precedes the word "Pay." The sign now reads, "We Spay Your Pet, $75." Scratchy enters the storefront and a pair of huge dogs strap him to a table. Dr. Itchy enters and turns on the spay ray, which moves closer towards Scratchy's crotch. Screaming, Scratchy desperately tries to unplug the machine with his tongue. He pulls it out, stopping the laser just in time. However, Dr. Itchy plugs it back in and the laser zooms over Scratchy's body, slicing him to bits. (9F22,

FILMOGRAPHY

"Cape Feare") **Burning Down the Mouse.** Scratchy ties Itchy to a post and shoves dynamite in his ears and under his eyelids. He molds a beard and stovepipe hat for him out of plastic explosives and hangs a pair of grenades from his ears like earrings. He aims two nuclear missiles at his eyeballs, lights the fuse, hails a cab, and drives away. As Itchy struggles frantically to escape, Lisa remarks, "My purpose in life is to witness this moment." Bart holds Lisa's hand. Just as the fuse is about to ignite the dynamite, the picture goes black. Gary has pulled the plug, explaining, "We need the outlet for our rock tumbler." Bart and Lisa scream at Gary to reconnect the TV,

but by the time he does, the cartoon is over. (1F02, "Homer Goes to College") **Ahhh! Wilderness!** Scratchy sits at a campfire, strumming a guitar, while Itchy roasts a marshmallow. It starts to rain, and the rain quenches the fire. Itchy grabs some tent spikes and pounds them into each of Scratchy's paws. He jams a tall stick under Scratchy's stomach and creates a shelter out of Scratchy's body. Hammering spikes through Scratchy's tongue and tail, he completes his tent. As Itchy lies down in his makeshift tent, lightning strikes Scratchy repeatedly. (1F06, "Boy-Scoutz N the Hood") **Scar Trek: The Next Laceration.** Scratchy eats a sandwich while piloting a spaceship. His stomach bulges and Itchy pops out à la Alien. Itchy eats the last bite of sandwich and throws Scratchy into the airlock, pressing a button that will blow him into space. Scratchy zips up his spacesuit and dons a helmet just as he is sucked out of the airlock. Itchy chases Scratchy in a space pod with robotic claws and pulls Scratchy towards Saturn, sawing the cat in half on the planet's spinning rings. Scratchy watches his pelvis and legs float away and chases them, but they burn up after they enter the planet's atmosphere. A robotic claw then rips off Scratchy's helmet, exposing his head to the vacuum of space. Scratchy's head and eyeballs puff up and the robotic claw pops them. The splatter of head tissue on the windshield of the pod spells out "The End." (1F13, "Deep Space Homer") **The Buck Chops Here.** Itchy and Scratchy stand under a tour sign outside the U.S. Mint in Washington, D.C. They shake hands and walk in. Itchy grabs a sack of coins and smashes Scratchy on the head with it. He throws Scratchy on a conveyor belt, which flattens the cat into a large sheet and prints him into dollar bills. Sliced up by huge whirring blades, the Scratchy money is stacked into two bundles. Itchy loads them into an armored car and drives into a tycoon convention. Dogs in suits stand around smoking cigars. Itchy hands one a Scratchy bill. The dog uses it to light his cigar. An eye above the pyramid on the dollar bill begins to panic as the flame spreads. Scratchy lets out a blood-curdling scream. (1F16, "Burns' Heir") **Planet of the Aches.** Itchy barricades Scratchy behind the brick wall of a dungeon. Three thousand years later, futuristic tools rip out the bricks. An emaciated, elderly Scratchy is led away. His liberators are a race of futuristic Itchys with big pulsating brains, wafer-thin bodies, and telekinetic powers. They groom Scratchy, bathe him, put him into a white robe, and lead him into a Roman-style coliseum. Futuristic Itchys fill the stands.

Suddenly, all the Itchys' brains pulse, and destructive tools (knives, axes, and others) fly at Scratchy and slice him to pieces. Scratchy falls into a pile of bloody goo as the big-brain Itchys applaud and smile. (1F22, "Bart of Darkness") **The Last Traction Hero.** Scratchy works out with a barbell and gets stronger. Buffed-up, he flexes for Itchy, who tries to pop Scratchy's muscles like balloons. When the pinprick has no effect on Scratchy, Itchy pokes his entire chest. Scratchy bleeds heavily and sits down. With a chainsaw, Itchy slices off his biceps and pectoral muscles. (2F01, "Itchy & Scratchy Land") **Four Funerals and a Wedding.** Scratchy is getting married. At the altar, Itchy replaces his betrothed with a bride made out of bombs and dynamite. Scratchy has children with his bomb-wife and grows old with her. On the porch of the old folks' home, she finally explodes, killing Scratchy. An aged, bearded Itchy runs out of the home, laughing hysterically. He has a heart attack and dies. (2F31, "A Star Is Burns") **Skinless in Seattle.** Scratchy walks with a bouquet of flowers reading a note that says, "Meet me at the Space Needle." When he arrives, he unknowingly stops on a big "X." Itchy is waiting for him at the very top. Ignoring the sign, "Do not throw pennies from the tower," Itchy drops one at Scratchy and misses. He buys up all of the souvenir Space Needles and aims them at Scratchy, but the needles simply make an outline of a heart around him. Frustrated, Itchy saws off the top half of the tower. It falls over and impales one of Scratchy's eyes. Scratchy runs around, screaming. (3F02, "Bart Sells His Soul") **Foster Pussycat! Kill! Kill!** Scratchy sits in a rocking chair, reading Nice magazine, when the doorbell rings. He looks through the peephole, unlocks the door, and opens it a crack. A basket sits on his doorstep. Scratchy pokes a shotgun at it, then looks inside. He discovers a baby Itchy sucking on a bottle. He holds the toddler, and, smiling, hearts rise up from his body. Itchy breaks his bottle with an evil laugh and jabs the jagged end into Scratchy's chest, leaving two bloody wounds. Scratchy falls over, and Itchy runs into his house. Laughing, he walks away with Scratchy's TV, trailing bloody footprints behind him.

Scratchy calls out weakly, "Why? Why? My only son." (3F01, "Home Sweet Homediddly-Dum-Doodily") **Esophagus Now.** Scratchy eats in a restaurant. Itchy is his waiter. After Scratchy orders his food, Itchy sneaks under Scratchy's table, shaves Scratchy's belly, stretches it, and puts it on a plate with an olive in the bellybutton, placing on a sign that reads, "rare." Itchy serves the belly to Scratchy, who cuts off a piece and swallows it. The piece comes out of the hole Scratchy cut in his belly, and he takes the piece and repeats the process, swallowing and re-swallowing. Finally, Itchy puts the piece in a take-out box, and gives Scratchy a bill for $100. Scratchy is so shocked, his head explodes. (3F03, "Lisa the Vegetarian") **Remembrance of Things Slashed.** Itchy reads a headline in the newspaper: "Scratchy Dead! Peace after Long Illness." Scratchy's ghost appears before Itchy and Itchy tries to stab it with a knife. When that fails, he sucks up Scratchy's ghost in a vacuum cleaner and blows it into the freezer. A second later, Itchy opens the freezer and

finds Scratchy frozen in a block. He stabs him with an ice pick and crumbles him into cubes for his drink. Inside Itchy's glass, Scratchy's frozen eyeballs blink. (3F16, "The Day Violence Died") **Good Cats, Bad Choices.** Scratchy appears on a talk show and dabs his eyes. A caption on the bottom of the screen explains, "Says mouse friend mistreats him." Itchy is backstage with a bottle. His caption reads, "Feels he is the victim." Itchy breaks the bottle and walks onstage. The camera cuts back to Scratchy. The caption at the bottom of the screen now reads, "Doesn't know slashing is imminent." When Scratchy sees the caption, his eyes bug out. As Itchy advances, the audience applauds. Just as he is about to drive the bottle into Scratchy, the cartoon is interrupted by a special report.

(4F06, "Bart after Dark") **Reservoir Cats, with Special Guest Director Quentin Tarantino.** Wearing a black suit and thin tie, Scratchy is tied to a chair in a garage à la *Reservoir Dogs*. He sadistically dances around the chair to the Stealers Wheel song "Stuck in the Middle with You" and splashes gasoline on Scratchy. When he finally slices off Scratchy's ear, Tarantino enters and says, "What I'm trying to say in this cartoon is that violence is everywhere in our society, you know, it's like even in breakfast cereals, man..." Itchy chops off Tarantino's head and he and Scratchy dance to a *Pulp Fiction* guitar riff. (3G03, "Simpsoncalifragilisticexpiala[ANNOYED GRUNT]cious") **Why Do Fools Fall in Lava?** Scratchy pays Itchy the five-dollar fee to "Volcano Bungee Jump." Itchy slashes open Scratchy's stomach, yanks out one end of his intestine, and pushes into the volcano, using the intestine as a bungee cord. Screaming, Scratchy plummets towards the heart of the volcano but, thanks to his intestinal bungee chord, stops just short of the fiery lava. Meanwhile, Itchy pours gasoline into the other end of Scratchy's intestine. Scratchy's cheeks balloon with gasoline until they burst, and he is consumed with flames. (4F12, "The Itchy & Scratchy & Poochie Show") **The Beagle Has Landed.** Itchy and Scratchy drive a car. They pass signs that indicate that they are approaching a fireworks factory. Seeing Poochie at the side of the road, they stop. Poochie introduces himself in a rap song and slam-dunks a basketball while he rides a bike. Finally, he takes off in Itchy and Scratchy's car, driving past the fireworks factory. (4F12, "The Itchy & Scratchy & Poochie Show") **Deaf Comedy Blam!** Dressed as a doctor, Itchy enters the Ear Trauma Ward, where Scratchy lays on a bed with cotton in his ears. Itchy puts the hearing piece of a stethoscope in Scratchy's ears and pulls the stethoscope's drum with him out the door. Holding the drum, he boards a taxi and takes a plane to an island, where an atomic bomb is being tested. He passes a sign that reads, "Aujourd'hui: Le Bombe Atomique," and holds up the stethoscope drum as a countdown in French is broadcast over a PA system. As a nuclear weapon detonates in the distance, the thunderous explosion gathers in the drum and travels in a bulge down the length of the stethoscope hose, through the ocean, past Hollywood, across the land, and finally into Scratchy's ears. Scratchy's head explodes, causing the patient in the next bed to lean over and say, "Shhhh!" (4F18, "In Marge We Trust").

MAUDE FLANDERS

Identity:
God-fearing, attractive wife of God-fearing Ned Flanders; mother of religious-zealots sons Rod and Todd.

Life code:
No profanity; no unkind thoughts; no lustful thoughts; no non-puritanical thoughts; no alcohol or drugs of any kind; no questioning of her husband; no Sundays off of church; no taking of the Lord's name in vain.

Hobbies:
Reading the Bible; quoting the Bible; studying from the Bible; highlighting passages in the Bible; following the Bible; holding the Bible; cherishing the Bible; raising ficus plants.

Favorite book:
The Bible.

Secret admirer:
Homer.

Silent shame:
Has a more masculine scream than Ned.

NEDDY DOESN'T BELIEVE IN INSURANCE. HE CONSIDERS IT A FORM OF GAMBLING.

When a heat wave hits Springfield, Bart and Lisa lobby Homer for a swimming pool of their own. Homer gives in, but the moment the pool is installed, children from around Springfield invade the Simpsons' backyard. Bart attempts an ambitious dive from the roof of his treehouse. He loses his balance and breaks his leg.

The cast on his leg prevents Bart from enjoying the new pool and he takes refuge inside his bedroom, where he remains isolated and in darkness. Lisa realizes that Bart is lonely and bitter and gives him her telescope to help him pass the time. Using the telescope to spy on his neighbors, Bart sees Ned Flanders digging a grave in his backyard and hears him muttering about killing Maude. Bart concludes that Flanders has killed his wife.

Lisa promises to help Bart gather evidence that will prove that Flanders murdered Maude. While Flanders is away, she sneaks inside the house. Bart watches from his bedroom as Ned returns carrying an ax, and he hobbles across the lawn to warn Lisa. Confronting Flanders, he accuses him of killing his wife. Flanders explains that the only thing he buried was Maude's favorite plant.

SHOW HIGHLIGHTS

Homer's idea: To keep cool, Homer sets up a tent in front of the open refrigerator door and rubs boxes of frozen food on his body.

"We gotta fill this thing with Epsom salts and jam it on over to the old folks' home." Otto, telling the kids that their Poolmobile time is up.

"Uh, hello, uh, Mrs. uh, Bart. Is your pool ready yet?" Jimbo Jones, to Marge, as he stands with dozens of bathing suit-clad neighborhood kids at the Simpsons' front door.

In perfect harmony: Just as Bart rationalizes that a pool is no more fun than being "in a bathtub with a garbage bag taped around your cast," he sees the neighborhood kids performing a synchronized Busby Berkeley-style number with Lisa in the center, à la Esther Williams.

Bart: *Look, Lis! I snatched five bathing suits–all Martin's!*
(Martin stands nearby with his arms folded, wearing layers and layers of bathing suits.)
Martin: *Take your best shot! I'm wearing seventeen layers!*
(All the kids in the pool rush to Martin, grabbing his various swimming trunks. Within moments, he has none left.)
Martin: *I brought this on myself.*

Young Krusty: During the summer hiatus, Krusty's show runs "Klassic Krusty" episodes. The first, from Feb. 6, 1961, features a discussion on collective bargaining agreements with AFL-CIO chairman George Meany.

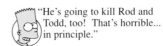
"He's going to kill Rod and Todd, too! That's horrible... in principle."

Lisa and Bart Bargain:
Lisa: *Dad, as you know, we've been swimming, and we've developed a taste for it. We both agree that getting our own pool is the only way to go. Now before you respond, you must understand that your refusal would result in months and months of...*
Bart/Lisa: *CanwehaveapoolDad? CanwehaveapoolDad? CanwehaveapoolDad?*

(Bart stands on top of the treehouse. Nelson calls up to him from the pool.)
Nelson: *Hey, Bart, your epidermis is showing!*
Bart: *It is?*
(Bart, embarrassed, shifts around, looking to see what's exposed. He falls off the treehouse. Nelson turns to Kearney as Bart screams on his way to the ground.)
Nelson: *See epidermis means your hair...*
(Bart slams into the ground.)
Nelson: *...so technically, it's true. That's what makes it so funny. Pardon me a moment.* (turning to Bart's unconcious body) *Ha ha!*
Milhouse: *Hey Nelson, he's really hurt! I think he broke his leg!*
Nelson: *I said, "Ha ha."*

Dr. Hibbert: *I'm sorry, that leg's going to have to come off.*
(Bart and Homer gasp.)
Dr. Hibbert: (chuckling) *Did I say "leg"? I meant that wet bathing suit. I'm afraid you'll need a cast on that broken bone.*
Bart: *Aww, I'm going to miss the whole summer.*
Homer: *Don't worry, boy. When you get a job like me, you'll miss every summer.*

Bart's brain: *Well, it looks like it's just you and me, Barty Boy.*
Bart: *Oh, great. I get to spend the summer with my brain.*

THE STUFF YOU MAY HAVE MISSED

The wall of Dr. Hibbert's workout room (seen through Bart's telescope lens) features white family portraits.

The pictures on the wall of Jimmy Stewart's room, featuring a race car wreck and a plane, are the same ones used in Hitchcock's *Rear Window*.

Number of kids at the Pool Mobile: 19.

Sign at the pool shop: "Pool Sharks—Where the Buyer Is Our Chum."

Bart wears his underwear instead of a swimsuit in the Pool Mobile.

Milhouse swims in the overchlorinated pool and instantly develops bleached skin and hair.

DARKNESS

Episode #1F22
Original Airdate: 9/4/94
Writer: Dan McGrath
Director: Jim Reardon
Executive Producer: David Mirkin

"Hello and welcome to the Springfield Police Department Resc-U-Fone. If you know the name of the felony being committed, press one. To choose from a list of felonies, press two. If you are being murdered or are calling from a rotary phone, please stay on the line." The recording Bart gets when he calls the cops.

Movie Moment:
Numerous elements of the murder plot, including the music, parody Hitchcock's *Rear Window*.

(Kids crowd around Lisa in the Simpsons' pool.)
English Boy: *Lisa, please join my family for a weekend in the country. They'll be hunting, charades, and ever so many delightful romantic misunderstandings.*
Lisa's Brain: *They're only using you for your pool, you know.*
Lisa: *Shut up, brain! I got friends now, I don't need you anymore!*

The Simpsons Go Pool Shopping:
Marge: *Is it true that we should wait at least an hour after eating before we go in?*
Pool salesman: *Look, question lady, this job is not what I really do. I play keyboards.*

(Homer and Marge skinny dip in the pool.)
Marge: *This was a lovely idea, Homey. Come here and kiss me.*
(A helicopter whirs and a searchlight shines down on their bodies. They scream and try to cover themselves. It's the Springfield Police helicopter.)
Chief Wiggum: *(through a megaphone) Do not be alarmed. Continue swimming naked. Aw, come on. Continue. Come on, aw. All right, Lou, open fire.*

Bart the Witness:
(Through his telescope, Bart spies Flanders digging a grave in his backyard.)
Bart: *Uh, uh, no. This can't be what it looks like. There's got to be some other explanation.*
Flanders: *I wish there was some other explanation for this. But there isn't. I'm a murderer! I'm a murderer!*
Bart: *Then that's not the real Ned Flanders.*
Flanders: *I'm a mur-diddley-urdler!*
Bart: *If that's not Flanders, he's done his homework.*

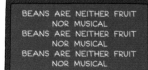

BEANS ARE NEITHER FRUIT NOR MUSICAL
BEANS ARE NEITHER FRUIT NOR MUSICAL
BEANS ARE NEITHER FRUIT NOR MUSICAL

Episode 1F17   Original Airdate: 9/11/94   Writer: Mike Scully   Director: Mark Kirkland

ALLISON TAYLOR

Description:
Seven-year-old gifted new student at Springfield Elementary School.

Temperament:
Cool, collected, even after people replace her diorama with a beef heart.

Favorite game:
Anagrams.

Talent:
Besting Lisa at most things she's good at.

Lung capacity:
Better than Lisa's.

> I'M ACTUALLY KINDA GLAD I LOST. NOW I KNOW LOSING ISN'T THE END OF THE WORLD.

Guest Voice:
Winona Ryder as Allison

A new student, Allison Taylor, joins Lisa's class. She's as intelligent and as talented a saxophone player as Lisa. Vying for first chair in the band, each girl blows complicated riffs in an attempt to outplay the other. Lisa faints from the effort, and Allison is awarded first chair.

Meanwhile, Homer steals 100 pounds of sugar from an overturned truck and tries to sell his booty door-to-door. His efforts, however, are futile, and Marge insists that he dispose of the sugar. Homer refuses, but nature intercedes: a sudden rainstorm soaks the mound of sugar, causing it to dissolve.

Lisa feels increasingly average around Allison. Her spirits rise when Bart offers to sabotage Allison's entry to the school's diorama contest, replacing her elaborate scene of Poe's "The Telltale Heart" with a box containing a cow's heart. However, Lisa feels guilty and uncovers Allison's original project. Surprisingly both girls lose to Ralph Wiggum, who receives the prize for his display of action figures. Lisa and Allison patch up their differences and become friends.

SHOW HIGHLIGHTS

"I can't live the button-down life like you. I want it all! The terrifying lows, the dizzying highs, the creamy middles! Sure, I might offend a few of the blue-noses with my cocky stride and musky odors—oh, I'll never be the darling of the so-called 'City Fathers' who cluck their tongues, stroke their beards, and talk about 'What's to be done with this Homer Simpson?'"

"It's okay, Marge. I've learned my lesson. A mountain of sugar is too much for one man. It's clear now why God portions it out in those tiny packets, and why he lives on a plantation in Hawaii."

"Ah, Diorama-Rama, my favorite school event next to 'Hearing-Test Thursday.'"

Bart: *Hey, I know... How about if I dig up some dirt on Allison? Remember how I got Milhouse's picture on America's Most Wanted?*
(The scene switches to two F.B.I. agents driving up. One peers through binoculars.)
FBI #1: *There he is on the monkey bars.*
FBI #2: *Try to take him alive.*
(The car crashes through the fence, sending children running away, screaming.)
Milhouse: *Oh no, not again!*

Marge: *Believe me, honey. She's more scared of you than you are of her.*
Lisa: *You're thinking of bears, Mom.*

Miss Hoover: *Now, here's an oral extra credit question: What was Christopher Columbus actually looking for when he discovered America?*
Lisa: *(raises hand) Ooh! Ooh!*
Miss Hoover: *Anyone besides Lisa for a change?*
Ralph: *Oh! Eh! Eh!*
Miss Hoover: *Ralph, this better not be about your cat.*
(Ralph sadly puts down his hand.)
Miss Hoover: *Oh, all right, Li—*
Allison: *Columbus was looking for a passage to India.*
Miss Hoover: *Correct Allison! And on your very first day in our class!*

Lisa: *Hi, Allison? I'm Lisa Simpson. It's great to finally meet someone who converses above the normal eight-year-old level.*
Allison: *Actually, I'm seven. I was just skipped ahead because I was getting bored with first grade.*

(Homer and Bart stand before the jack-knifed sugar truck.)
Homer: *We hit the jackpot, here! White gold! Texas tea... sweetener.*
(Homer starts shoveling the sugar into his trunk.)
Bart: *Dad, isn't that stealing?*
Homer: *Read your town charter, boy. "If food stuffs should touch the ground, said food stuffs shall be turned over to the village idiot." Since I don't see him around, start shoveling!*

Lisa: *Why am I still rotting away in the second grade instead of being skipped ahead?*
Marge: *I don't know, honey. I guess that's the school's decision to make.*
Lisa: *Well, did you ever talk to anyone at the school? Make a few calls on my behalf? Maybe you could have been "nicer" to Principal Skinner, if you know what I mean.*
Marge: *Lisa! I am nice.*

(Allison and Lisa, each trying to outplay the other, hold a prolonged note on the sax. After turning red, Lisa passes out. She wakes up.)
Lisa: *What's happening? Oh...it was just a dream.*
Mr. Largo: *That was a close one, Lisa, but you made it.*
Lisa: *I won first chair?*
Mr. Largo: *No, you regained consciousness... Allison got first chair. And believe me, this is not a dream.*

Lisa: *Hey Ralph. Want to come with me and Allison to play anagrams?*
Allison: *We take proper names and rearrange the letters to form a description of that person.*
Ralph: *My cat's breath smells like cat food.*

THE STUFF YOU MAY HAVE MISSED

Bart reads *Bad Boys Life* magazine, which advertises Laramie Jrs. on the back cover.

Marge reads, *Love In the Time of Scurvy.*

Bart is using a cellular phone at the beginning of the episode.

Allison has a picture of Bleeding Gums Murphy in her room.

After Milhouse jumps into the raging waterfall, and shouts, "My glasses!", his glasses are taped together and cracked.

NO ONE IS INTERESTED IN
MY UNDERPANTS
NO ONE IS INTERESTED IN
MY UNDERPANTS
NO ONE IS INTERESTED IN
MY UNDERPANTS

Episode 2F33 Original Airdate: 9/25/94 Writer: Penny Wise (with clip contributions from John Swartzwelder, John Vitti, Frank Mula, David Richardson, Jeff Martin, Bill Oakley & Josh Weinstein, Matt Groening, Sam Simon, Al Jean & Mike Reiss, Jay Kogen & Wallace Wolodarsky, Nell Scovell, David Stern, George Meyer, Conan O'Brien, Robert Cohen, Bill Canterbury, and Dan McGrath) Director: David Silverman

SHOW HIGHLIGHTS

 "Mom, romance is dead. It was acquired in a hostile takeover by Hallmark and Disney, homogenized, then sold off piece by piece."

 "Okay, Marge, as long as we're traumatizing the kids, I have a scandalous story of my own."

Number of Episodes from Which Clips Were Taken:
28.

"Well, as Jerry Lee Lewis would say, 'There's a whole lot of frowning going on.'" Marge, trying to cheer up the family as their discussion about romance leads to depression.

"Love isn't hopeless. Look, maybe I'm no expert on the subject, but there was one time I got it right." Homer, on falling in love with Marge.

(Marge sits in bed, reading *The Bridges of Madison County*, as Homer sleeps. A tear wells in her eye.)
Marge: (sniffling) *This romance is so full of heartfelt passion. I can really identify with this corn-fed heroine. Homer, are you awake? This is important. Give me some sign you're awake.*
(Homer belches.)
Marge: *Wake up!*
Homer: (sleepy) *Wha? Wuzz wrong? House run away? Dog's on fire?*
Marge: *Homie, do you think the romance has gone out of our lives?*
(Homer belches again.)
Marge: *Wake up!*
Homer: *Marge, it's 3 a.m. and I worked all day!*
Marge: *It's 9:30 p.m. and you spent your whole Saturday drinking beer in Maggie's kiddie pool.*

(Bart and Lisa watch the Itchy & Scratchy short, "Flay Me to the Moon" and laugh. Marge walks in.)
Marge: *How many times can you laugh at that cat getting hit by the moon?*
Bart: *It's a new episode.*
Lisa: *Not exactly. They pieced it together from old shows, but it seems new to the trusting eyes of impressionable youth.*
Bart: *Really?*
Lisa: *Ren and Stimpy do it all the time.*
Marge: *Yes, they do, and when was the last time you heard anyone talk about Ren and Stimpy?*

Marge: *I made the right decision to stay with my Homey, and there was no harm done.*
(Homer moans in distress.)
Marge: *So if you kind of mentally snip out the part where I already had a husband, that's my idea of romance.*
Homer: *Marge, I want you to stop seeing this Jacques! You can let him down gently, but over the next couple of months, I want you to break it off.*
Marge: *Um, okay Homer.*
Homer: *Whoof! That was a close one, kids.*

Bart: *What happened to Mindy?*
Marge: *Yes, what did happen to her?*
Homer: *Well, she hit the bottle pretty hard and lost her job.*
Marge: *Hmm. Good.*

Marge: *Lisa, not all romances turn out that way. Bart, do you have a love story that doesn't end in heartbreak?*
Bart: *Yes, I do. The only girl I ever loved invited me up to the treehouse. She had something very important to tell me . . .*
(Bart relates the story of Laura Powers from 9F06, "New Kid on the Block.")
Bart: *Wait, that did end in heartbreak. Thanks for opening up old wounds, Mom.*

Marge: *Does anyone else have a love story?*
Lisa: *Yes, I do. And just like your love stories, it's tragic and filled with hurt feelings and scars that will never heal.*

Lisa: *That didn't seem like a happy ending. That seems more like a detached tale of modern alienation.*
Marge: *I give up. Did anybody learn anything about love tonight?*
Bart: *I learned it screws everybody up.*

The Selected Kisses of Homer and Marge:
After twirling Marge around on the stage after his speech in front of the Sapphire Lounge patrons, 7G10, "Homer's Night Out"; after making up in Moe's Tavern, 7F10, "Bart Gets Hit by a Car"; after singing "You Are So Beautiful to Me" to Homer, 7F02, "Simpson and Delilah"; after telling Marge she's as pretty as Princess Leia and as smart as Yoda, 8F10, "I Married Marge"; after singing "You Light Up My Life," 8F10, "I Married Marge"; after the performance of the play, 8F18, "A Streetcar Named Marge"; making up after Marge admits her gambling problem, 1F03, "Springfield."

The Selected "Hello, Moe's Tavern...":
"Al Coholic," (7G01); "Jacques Strap," (7G06); "I.P. Freely," (7G03); "Seymour Butz," (7F11); "Homer Sexual," (7F15); "Mike Rotch," (7F22); "Amanda Hugenkiss," (9F06); "Hugh Jass," (8F08); "Ivana Tinkle," (9F06); "I'm a stupid moron with an ugly face and a big butt and my butt smells and I like to kiss my own butt," (8F02).

The Selected Homer's "Mmmm..." Lines:
"Mmmm...chocolate," (9F17); "Mmmm...invisible cola," (1F03); "Mmmm...forbidden donut," (1F04); "Mmmm...sacrilicious," (1F14); "Mmmm...snouts," (8F17); "Mmmm...free goo," (1F06); "Mmmm...something," (2F33).

After tearfully reading *The Bridges of Madison County* one night in bed, Marge awakens Homer to tell him that they should teach the kids about romance. The next day, the Simpsons reflect on cherished memories—Bart, on his numerous prank calls to Moe and Homer on eating donuts and goo. Realizing she is not getting her point across, Marge tells them about her near-affair with bowling instructor Jacques.

Emboldened by Marge's honesty, Homer relates a scandalous story of his own: his mutual attraction with ex-nuclear plant employee Mindy. Lisa shares her painful memories of Ralph Wiggum's Valentine-inspired crush on her, while Bart remembers how Laura Powers once broke his heart.

Recalling so much anguish leads Marge to nearly give up on teaching the children about love. Homer reminds her that at least the two of them got it right, and the kids leave to watch "The Itchy & Scratchy Show."

I WILL NOT USE ABBREV.
I WILL NOT USE ABBREV.
I WILL NOT USE ABBREV.
I WILL NOT USE ABBREV.
I WILL NOT USE ABBREV.
I WILL NOT USE ABBREV.

ITCHY & SCRATCHY

Identity:
Popular, extraordinarily violent, animated TV cat-and-mouse adversaries.

Home:
"The Krusty the Clown Show."

Homicidal sadist:
Itchy.

Perpetual victim:
Scratchy.

Number of times Itchy has killed Scratchy:
Infinite.

Number of times Scratchy has killed Itchy:
Zero (almost once).

Amazing fact:
In spite of it all, they remain the best of friends.

ROGER MEYERS, SR.

Identity:
Founder of Itchy & Scratchy International; disputed creator of Itchy & Scratchy cartoon characters.

Stars in:
The Roger Meyers Story, which calls him a "gentle genius" and "beloved by the world."

Chief successes:
The Itchy & Scratchy Show; full-length musical Scratchtasia; the wildly successful Pinitchyo.

Criticized for:
The controversial 1938 cartoon, Nazi Supermen Are Our Superiors.

ITCHY & SCRATCHY LAND

Episode 2F01 Original Airdate: 10/2/94 Writer: John Swartzwelder Director: Wes Archer

SHOW HIGHLIGHTS

The many lands of Itchy & Scratchy Land: Torture Land, Explosion Land, Searing Gas Pain Land, and Unnecessary Surgery Land.

"Attention, Marge Simpson. Your son has been arrested... Attention, Marge Simpson, we've also arrested your older, balder, fatter son." Announcements at Itchy & Scratchy Land.

"You've got to listen to me! Elementary chaos theory tells us that all robots will eventually turn against their masters and run amok in an orgy of blood and kicking and the biting with the metal teeth and the hurting and shoving!"

"My hair! You chopped off my hair! Oh God, I'm ugly!" Homer, as the robots start to lose control.

"Hey, you're the guys that didn't like our capering. When you get to hell, tell 'em Itchy sent you." Itchy actor, kicking Bart and Homer away from the helicopter.

"Heh, heh, heh! Hey, look Marge, they're still not fighting back! Hee, hee! I can be a jerk and no one can stop me!" Homer, taunting an Amish man on the Simpsons' last vacation.

THE STUFF YOU MAY HAVE MISSED

After the "shortcut" the Simpson family car has no roof; a missile labeled "US Army" is sticking in it; a banner with the word "Homecoming" hangs off the back; one of the tires has been replaced with a wagon wheel; and a traffic sign is connected to that side.

Itchy's 70's Disco has a smaller sign reads, "Est. 1980."

The full name of the bar "where it's constantly New Year's Eve" is "T.G.I. McScratchy's Goodtime Fooddrinkery."

A sign in the background of the parade reads, "Penny Arcade–All Games, 75¢."

Bart's fanny pack is labeled "Li'l Bastard Traveling Kit."

The rides that aren't in operation: Head Basher, Blood Bath, Mangler, Nurses Station.

Itchy ties up Scratchy and feeds him chili in the illustration for "Searing Gas Pain Land."

(Lisa pulls a wagon holding a seemingly-dead Bart into Marge and Homer's bedroom)
Lisa: Mom! Dad! Bart's dead!
(Homer and Marge gasp. Bart quickly sits up.)
Bart: That's right! Dead serious about going to Itchy & Scratchy Land!
Lisa: You know, Itchy & Scratchy Land isn't just for kids. They have a place called "Parents' Island." Yeah, (reading pamphlet) "Dancing, bowling, fashionable shops, over one hundred bars and saloons, and a world-class chemical dependency center." (Homer takes the pamphlet.)
Homer: (gasps) TV Town! Hammock Land!
Marge: Oooh. Recipe-related bumper cars.

Lisa: Who are all these characters?
Bart: Well, you're probably too young to remember the short-lived "Itchy & Scratchy and Friends Hour." They had to come up with some friends. There's Disgruntled Goat, Uncle Ant, Klu Klux Clam...
Lisa: Oh yeah. They weren't very funny.

"Tavern on the Scream" Fine Dining:
Bart: I'll have a brain burger with extra pus, please.
Marge: Bart!
Homer: Eyeball stew.
Marge: Homer! We just got here and already I'm mortified beyond belief by your embarrassing behavior. You're placing our happy vacation in serious jeopardy.
Bart: I was just ordering a cheeseburger, Mom. They have violent names for everything here.
Marge: Oh, I see. All right. I'll have the baby guts.
Waiter: Lady, you disgust me.
Lisa: Mom, that's veal.

Park spokesman: There's no need to murmur, ma'am. Here at Itchy & Scratchy Land, we're just as concerned about violence as you are. That's why we're always careful to show the consequences of deadly mayhem so that we may educate as well as horrify.
Marge: When do you show the consequences? On TV, that mouse pulled out that cat's lungs and played them like a bagpipe. But in the next scene he was breathing comfortably.
Park spokesman: Just like in real life.

Homer's Amnesty:
Marge: I have nothing to say to you.
Homer: But, Marge, I was a political prisoner.
Marge: How were you a political prisoner?
Homer: I kicked a giant mouse in the butt. Do I have to draw ya a diagram?

Movie Moments:

The family is surrounded by robots running amok in a theme park à la *Westworld*. Frink's comment about chaos theory and the insignia on the park choppers parody *Jurassic Park*. Moleman's phone booth bird attack is reminiscent of *The Birds*.

Bart and Lisa beg their parents to take them to Itchy & Scratchy Land, advertised as "the violentest place on earth." Marge is reluctant, but agrees to go when the family promises that they will not turn the trip into a miserable, embarrassing experience.

After an arduous journey by car, the Simpsons arrive at the theme park. Marge is shocked by the gratuitously violent rides but finds a pleasant escape with Homer at Parents' Island. However, her respite from the violence is short-lived when Bart and Homer are arrested for abusing costumed park employees.

Marge bails Homer and Bart out of the theme park's jail. Soon afterwards, defective Itchy & Scratchy robots brandishing weapons attack the Simpsons. When Lisa figures out that the bright lights from their camera's flashes scramble the robots' circuitry, the Simpsons turn their cameras into weapons and take the robots' pictures. A battle ensues and the robots are defeated. Marge admits that the family's visit to Itchy & Scratchy Land was their best vacation ever, but curtly requests that no one ever speak of it again.

> I AM NOT THE REINCARNATION OF SAMMY DAVIS, JR.
> I AM NOT THE REINCARNATION OF SAMMY DAVIS, JR.
> I AM NOT THE REINCARNATION OF SAMMY DAVIS, JR.

SIDESHOW BOB ROBERTS

Episode 2F02 Original Airdate: 10/9/94 Writers: Bill Oakley & Josh Weinstein Director: Mark Kirkland Guest Voices: Larry King as Himself, Dr. Demento as Himself, Kelsey Grammer as Sideshow Bob

Lisa studies Mayor Quimby's reelection campaign for a school project. While listening to a call-in talk show hosted by ultra-conservative Birch Barlow, she recognizes the voice of one of the callers: Sideshow Bob. Bob has an instant rapport with Barlow, who makes Bob's release from prison his top priority. Bart is horrified that his arch-nemesis is manipulating the media in hopes of winning his freedom. As support for Bob's release grows, Mayor Quimby grants him a pardon.

Backed by members of Springfield's Republican elite, Bob announces his candidacy for Mayor. A game of one-upmanship ensues between Bob and Mayor Quimby. When Quimby ingests too many flu caplets just before a televised debate with Bob, his poor performance leads to Bob's landslide victory.

The moment he assumes power, Bob condemns the Simpson home to permit construction of a new expressway. Convinced that the election is fraudulent, Lisa and Bart discover that many voters who cast their ballots for Bob are dead.

Lisa tricks Bob into admitting that he rigged the election. He is arrested and sentenced to serve time at a minimum security prison.

SHOW HIGHLIGHTS

"Good morning, fellow freedom-likers. Birch Barlow, the fourth branch of government, the 51st state..." Radio talk show host Birch Barlow's signature sign-on.

"Hey, I am no longer illiterate." Mayor Quimby, after Birch Barlow calls him an "illiterate, tax-cheating, wife-swapping, pot-smoking Spend-o-crat."

"My friends, i-i-isn't this just typical? Another intelligent conservative here, railroaded by our liberal justice system—just like Colonel Oliver North, Officer Stacey Koon, and cartoon 'smokesperson' Joe Camel. Well, I've had it!!" Birch Barlow, announcing his new crusade to set Sideshow Bob free.

Revealed this episode: Sideshow Bob's middle name is "Underdunk."

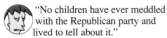 **"No children have ever meddled with the Republican party and lived to tell about it."**

"Quimby. If you were running for mayor, he'd vote for you." The Quimby campaign slogan.

(Bart is reading comic books in his room when Lisa runs in.)
Lisa: *Bart, your mortal enemy is on the radio!*
(Lisa turns on a boom box next to Bart's bed.)
Dr. Demento: *(on the radio) It's time for more deeementia with Dr. Demento! And now, the funny five!*
(Bart screams and throws the boom box through the window.)
Lisa: *I meant your other mortal enemy. Sideshow Bob.*
Bart: *Sideshow Bob? Oh, I'm only ten and I already got two mortal enemies.*

The inner circle of the Republican Party of Springfield: Burns, Birch Barlow, a green vampire-like humanoid, the Lawyer (introduced in 7F10, "Bart Gets Hit by a Car"), Dr. Hibbert, Ranier Wolfcastle, and a man in a cowboy hat and a bolo.

"Duh, stay out of Riverdale." Moose, to Homer, after he, Archie, Jughead, and Reggie toss Homer out of their car and onto the Simpson lawn.

"And the results are in. For Sideshow Bob—100%. For Joe Quimby—1%. And we remind you there is a 1% margin of error."

Barlow: *(on the radio) My friends, Bob is a political prisoner. I want every loyal listener to do everything they can to get him out of jail.*
Moe: *All right, you heard the man. (pulling out a box) One grenade each.*
Barney: *Moe, I think he meant through nonviolent, grassroots political action.*
Moe: *Aw geez... really, ya think so? All right, give 'em back. Come on, everybody give 'em back. (mad) Hey, hey, who pulled the pin on this one?*

Birch Barlow: *Mayor Quimby, you're well-known, sir, for your lenient stance on crime. But let's suppose for a second that your house was ransacked by thugs, your family tied up in the basement with socks in their mouths. You try to open the door, but there's too much blood on the knob—*
Quimby: *What is your question?*
Barlow: *My question is about the budget, sir.*

Lisa: *You don't have the intelligence to rig an election by yourself, do you?*
Bart: *You were just Barlow's lackey!*
Lisa: *You were Ronnie to his Nancy!*
Bart: *Sonny to his Cher!*
Lisa: *Ringo to the rest of the Beatles!*

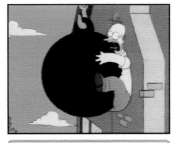

The Mayor Quimby Campaign Jingle: "Without a Mayor Quimby / Our town would really stink! / We wouldn't have a tire yard / Or a mid-size roller rink! / We wouldn't have our gallows / Or our shiny Bigfoot traps! / It's not the Mayor's fault / That the stadium collapsed."

THE STUFF YOU MAY HAVE MISSED

The first *Springfield Shopper* we see in this episode features the headline, "Bob Pardon: #1 Local Issue." The subheadline reads, "Edges Out 'No Fat Chicks' Ordinance."

The sign at the Springfield Community Center reads, "Tonight: Mayoral Debates. Tomorrow: Mass Wedding of Cult Members."

Smithers meets with Bart and Lisa at the Pay & Park & Pay.

Larry King was last featured in 7F11, "One Fish, Two Fish, Blowfish, Blue Fish."

Another headline in the *Spingfield Shopper* reads, "Call for Probe in Bob Flap," with the subheadline, "Editorial: Why Not Let Dead Pets Vote?"

BIRCH BARLOW

Occupation:
Springfield's favorite conservative radio talk show host.

Wrote:
The bestselling book Only Turkeys Have Left Wings.

Appeal:
Really speaks to Homer and people like Homer.

Deepest regret:
Supporting the prison pardoning and mayoral candidacy of Sideshow Bob Terwilliger.

Turn-ons:
Republicans; conservatism in all its forms; the moneyed class; donuts.

Turn-offs:
Democrats; liberalism in all its forms; Mrs. McFearly's compost heap; the bats in the public library.

...SO MY FRIENDS, LET'S JUST JUNK THOSE DUMB-O-CRATS AND THEIR BLEEDING-HEART SMELLFARE PROGRAM.

Marge's warning: "Hello, once again. As usual, I must warn you all that this year's Halloween show is very, very scary and those of you with young children may want to send them off to bed and—oh, my. It seems the show is so scary that Congress won't even let us show it. Instead, they suggested the 1947 classic Glen Ford movie *200 Miles to Oregon*."

THE OPENING SEQUENCE

A tombstone at the Springfield Cemetery reads, "Amusing Tombstones: R.I.P." Moe's body falls from a tree, hanging from a noose, and he opens his eyes. Rev. Lovejoy burns Patty and Selma at the stake. They use the fire to light cigarettes. ·Principal Skinner watches as Bart chops the heads off of Mrs. Krabappel, Chief Wiggum, and Groundskeeper Willie on a guillotine. Skinner gives the thumbs-up sign before he himself is beheaded.

Homer: *So, what do you think, Marge? All I need is a title. I was thinking along the lines of "No TV and No Beer Make Homer...something something."*
Marge: (worried) *Go crazy?*
Homer: *Don't mind if I do!*

Movie Moment:

The story parodies the Stephen King novel and Stanley Kubrick film, *The Shining*–from blood that pours out the elevator to a maniacal Homer, who screams, "Heeeeeeeeeeere's Johnny!"

THE SHINNING

The Simpsons are employed as caretakers at Mr. Burns's remote estate. Before leaving, Burns and Smithers kill the cable TV signal and remove all beer from the premises. Deprived of his two favorite things, Homer slowly goes insane. He threatens Marge, who locks him inside a pantry. Homer chops his way out with an ax. Using a telepathic power called "the shinning," Bart contacts Groundskeeper Willie. Willie arrives at the estate to help but is instantly killed by Homer. Chasing his family through the snow with the ax, Homer discovers Willie's mini-TV set. His urge to kill subsides.

STORY HIGHLIGHTS

 "This house has quite a long and colorful history. It was built on an ancient Indian burial ground and was the setting for satanic rituals, witch burnings, and five John Denver Christmas specials."

 "Tell you what. We come back and everyone's slaughtered, I owe you a Coke."

"I'm Mike Wallace. I'm Morley Safer. And I'm Ed Bradley. All this and Andy Rooney tonight on '60 Minutes.'" Homer, chopping through the dining room door, holding a stopwatch.

"Television—teacher, mother, secret lover!"

Mr. Burns: *Oh, goody, the sea monkeys I ordered have arrived. Look at them cavort and caper.*
Smithers: *Sir, they're the new winter caretakers for the lodge.*
Mr. Burns: *Yes, they work hard and they play hard.*

Groundskeeper Willie: *Boy, you read my thoughts! You've got the "shining"!*
Bart: *You mean "shining."*
Willie: *Shhh! You wanna get sued? Now look, boy. If your Da goes ga-ga, you just use that..."shin" of yours to call me and I'll come a-runnin'. But don't be readin' my mind between four and five. That's Willie's time.*

"No TV and No Beer Make Homer Go Crazy."

The message scrawled all over the walls of a darkened room discovered by Marge.

THE STUFF YOU MAY HAVE MISSED

There are "Wanted" posters of Sideshow Bob, Fat Tony, and Snake at the police station.

A bagpipe and a painting of a Scottish woman adorn Willie's room.

HORROR V

Episode 2F03 Original Airdate: 10/30/94
Writers: Count Greg Danula, Dearly Departed Dan McGrath, David Cohen's Severed Hand, Blob Kushell
Director: Jaundiced Jim Reardon

TIME AND PUNISHMENT

While fixing a toaster, Homer gets sucked into a vortex and is whisked backwards in time to a prehistoric jungle. He accidentally kills a mosquito and, in doing so, alters the course of time. When Homer returns to the present-day, he is horrified to learn that Ned Flanders rules the world. He travels back and again changes history. Returning to the present, he finds that Patty and Selma have just died but that no one has heard of a donut. Homer travels from past to present continuously in search of normalcy. He settles on a universe where his family eats with froglike tongues.

THE STUFF YOU MAY HAVE MISSED

The sign at the Re-Neducation Center: "Where the Elite Meet to Have Their Spirits Broken."

Homer's reference to himself as the "first non-Brazilian person to travel backwards through time" alludes to hallucinogen-inspired author Carlos Castaneda.

STORY HIGHLIGHTS

Good Advice:
Homer: *Aaah! OK. Don't panic. Remember the advice your father gave you on your wedding day.*
A tuxedoed Abe in Homer's thought bubble: *"If you ever travel back in time, don't step on anything, because even the tiniest change can alter the future in ways you can't imagine."*
Homer: *Fine. As long as I stand perfectly still and don't touch anything, I won't destroy the future.*
(A prehistoric mosquito buzzes by.)
Homer: *Stupid bug. You go squish now!*
(He swats it and kills it.)

Fellow Travellers:
(Homer floats through a time vortex accompanied by backwards-running clocks.)
Homer: *Look at that. I'm the first non-Brazilian person to travel backwards through time.*
(Mr. Peabody and Sherman appear.)
Mr. Peabody: *Correction, Homer, you're the second.*
Sherman: *That's right, Mr. Peabody!*
Mr. Peabody: *Quiet, you.*

Homer: *You know, Marge, I've had my share of troubles, but sitting here now with you and the kids in our cozy home in this beautiful free country, it just makes me feel that I'm really a lucky guy.*
Lisa: *Dad! Your hand is jammed in the toaster!*

(Homer arrives back in the present. The house has been transformed into a luxurious estate.)
Lisa: *Are we taking the new Lexus to Aunt Patty and Selma's funeral today?*
Homer: *Hmm. Fabulous house, well-behaved kids, sisters-in-law dead, luxury sedan. Woo hoo! I hit the jackpot! Marge, dear. Would you kindly pass me a donut?*
Marge: *Donut? What's a donut?*
(Homer runs back to the time toaster, screaming.)
(Marge looks out the window and sees donuts falling from the sky.)
Marge: *Hmph. It's raining again.*

NIGHTMARE CAFETERIA

Principal Skinner sentences Bart to detention in the school cafeteria. When Bart's fellow students begin disappearing one by one, he and Lisa suspect that Skinner and Lunchlady Doris are cooking kids and serving them as cafeteria food. As the student population dwindles, Bart and Lisa try to escape, but they are cornered by Skinner and Doris, who slowly back them into a giant food processor. Bart awakens from his nightmare only to find that he and his family are turned inside-out by a mysterious fog.

STORY HIGHLIGHTS

 "Oh, relax, kids. I've got a gut feeling Uter's around here somewhere. After all, isn't there a little Uter in all of us? In fact, you might even say we just ate Uter and he's in our stomachs right now! Wait. Scratch that one."

"Easy there, young man. You'll only make yourself tired and stringy. Now, to check on the free-range children." Principal Skinner, to Martin, as he struggles against the bars of his cage.

Hat trick: Willie gets an axe in the back in all three Treehouse of Horror V stories.

Principal Skinner: *This overcrowding in detention is becoming critical; it's a powderkeg waiting to go off in an explosion of unacceptable behavior.*
Lunchlady Doris: *Don't bitch to me, boss-man. Thanks to the latest budget cuts, I'm down to using Grade-F meat.*
Principal Skinner: *Wouldn't it be wonderful if there was some sort of common solution to both our problems?*

Mrs. Krabappel: *Are you saying you killed Jimbo, processed his carcass, and served him for lunch?*
(Skinner taps his nose and nods.)
Mrs. Krabappel: *Hah!*

THE STUFF YOU MAY HAVE MISSED

Lunchlady Doris's Grade-F meat is made up of "mostly circus animals, some filler."

The word "OKTOBERFEST" has umlauts over the K, the second O, the last T and both E's.

One of the settings on the Hamilton Beach Student Chopper is "Gooify."

JESSICA LOVEJOY

Description:
Discreetly incorrigible only daughter of Helen and Reverend Lovejoy.

Educational status:
Currently suspended from boarding school.

Turn-ons:
Causing trouble; finding trouble; guys that like causing and finding trouble.

Turn-offs:
Lack of parental attention; following the rules.

Nemesis:
Sarah, Plain and Tall.

Evil powers:
She can make boys do whatever she wants.

REMEMBER, I'M THE SWEET, PERFECT MINISTER'S DAUGHTER AND YOU'RE JUST YELLOW TRASH.

Guest Voice:
Meryl Streep as Jessica Lovejoy

BART'S GIRLFRIEND

Episode 2F04   Original Airdate: 11/6/94   Writer: Jonathan Collier   Director: Susan Deitter

Bart falls in love with Reverend Lovejoy's daughter, Jessica. When she fails to notice him, he re-enrolls in Sunday School and sits next to her, hoping to impress her with good behavior. However, his efforts prove fruitless. When Skinner catches Bart in a detention sting operation, Jessica takes pity on him and invites him over for dinner.

During dinner with the Lovejoys, Bart uses the word "butt" and is promptly kicked out of the house. Jessica, however, likes Bart's bad behavior and joins him in committing acts of vandalism throughout town. Bart discovers that he is no match for Jessica and gets into trouble for things she talked him into doing. As the Reverend's daughter, she is never suspected, even when she steals money from the church collection plate.

Bart is blamed for the theft and becomes a pariah. Determined not to allow her brother to take the blame for something he did not do, Lisa addresses the congregation and urges them to search Jessica's

room, where they find the the money. Jessica admits her guilt, explaining that all she wanted was attention.

SHOW HIGHLIGHTS

Dances In Underwear, Thinks Too Much: Bart's and Lisa's names, respectively, when playing Cowboys and Native Americans.

"Hi, I'm Bart Simpson. I was incredibly moved by your reading. I don't think God's words have ever sounded so plausible." Bart, introducing himself to Jessica Lovejoy.

"I just think you and Jessica are too different from each other to get along. She's a sweet, kind reverend's daughter and you're the devil's cabana boy."

"Now the kilt was only for day-to-day wear. In battle we donned a full-length ball gown covered in sequins. The idea was to blind your opponent with luxury."

Bart Dines with the Lovejoys:

Mrs. Lovejoy: Hmm. I didn't know the rocket sled was an Olympic event.
Bart: Well, no offense, lady, but what you don't know could fill a warehouse.
(Reverend and Mrs. Lovejoy gasp, horrified.)
Reverend Lovejoy: Young man, explain yourself!
Bart: Sorry. I have kind of a short fuse...which some find charming! Speaking of charming, watching Fox last night, I heard a rather amusing story. This character named Martin was feeling rather...randy, and he was heard to remark—
(We cut to Reverend Lovejoy kicking Bart out of the house.)
Reverend Lovejoy: Don't you ever come near my daughter again! Never have I heard such gratuitous use of the word "butt!"
Bart: (struggling to explain) But—but—but—but—but—but—but—but—but—
Mrs. Lovejoy: (covering her ears) Make him stop! Make him stop!

Groundskeeper Willie, explaining Scotch warrior garb at "Scotchtoberfest."

Bart and Jessica's fun: Bart and Jessica loiter together under a "No Loitering" sign, they eat ice cream in front of obese people exercising at a weight-loss center, and they tee-pee the statue of Jebediah Springfield.

"Well, Jessica. I don't think we should hang out together anymore. You're turning me into a criminal when all I want to be is a petty thug."

"She's like a Milk Dud, Lis. Sweet on the outside, poison on the inside." Bart, on Jessica.

Lisa: Doesn't the Bible teach us "Judge not lest ye be judged," Reverend?
Reverend Lovejoy: I think it may be somewhere towards the back.
Lisa: There is someone among us with a guilty conscience. After much soul searching I decided it would be wrong of me to name names, but I urge that guilty person here, under the eyes of God, to come forward and confess and save yourself from the torment of your own personal hell.
Skinner: I smelled some marijuana smoke in Vietnam!
Grampa: I was the one that canceled Star Trek!
Dr. Hibbert: I left my Porsche keys inside Mrs. Glick!
Lisa: I'm talking to the collection money thief: only you can come forward and end this injustice!
(Lisa pauses, waiting for Jessica to confess.)
Lisa: Oh, what the heck, it was Jessica Lovejoy.

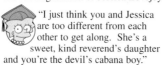

I WILL NOT SEND LARD
THROUGH THE MAIL
I WILL NOT SEND LARD
THROUGH THE MAIL
I WILL NOT SEND LARD
THROUGH THE MAIL

Jessica: You're bad, Bart Simpson.
Bart: No, I'm not! I'm really—
Jessica: Yes you are. You're bad...and I like it.
Bart: I'm bad to the bone, honey.
Jessica: Let's go find some fun.
Bart: But you're father said—
Jessica: (scoffing) I told the "Rev" I was going to my room to say my prayers.
Bart: (in love) Smart, beautiful, and a liar!

Bart: Give it up, Lis. She's a criminal mastermind. She's got a 108 IQ, she reads at a fifth-grade level, and (sigh) her hair smells like red Froot Loops.
Lisa: Yeah, well I eat Froot Loops for breakfast.

THE STUFF YOU MAY HAVE MISSED

This episode marks the second time a Hannibal Lecter-type restraint device is used on a Springfielder. (The first time occurred in 9F10, "Marge vs. the Monorail.")

Sign on the marquee of the Springfield Community Church: "Evil Women in History: From Jezebel to Janet Reno."

A woman in the "Scotchtoberfest" audience faints upon seeing what's under Willie's kilt.

The Lovejoys have a replica of Leonardo Da Vinci's "The Last Supper" hanging in their dining room.

LISA ON ICE

Episode 2F05 Original Airdate: 11/13/94 Writer: Mike Scully Director: Bob Anderson

Lisa leads Apu's team, the Gougers, to their best season ever. Homer lavishes attention on Lisa, making Bart feel jealous. The conflict heightens between brother and sister when Homer announces that Lisa's team and Bart's team will face off in a game.

News spreads about the match and blood-thirsty Springfield gets caught up in the Simpson rivalry. The game comes down to a penalty shot that pits Bart against Lisa. As they stare each other down, they each realize how many memories they share together. Taking off their equipment, Bart and Lisa embrace, ending the game in a tie.

SHOW HIGHLIGHTS

"This way your parents won't have to wait for report card time to punish you." Principal Skinner, introducing the "Academic Alert" program to the students.

"Me fail English? That's unpossible." Ralph Wiggum, being handed his first Academic Alert.

"Oh, yes, we won! We won! We won! Um, unfortunately, since I bet on the other team, a-heh heh, we won't be going out for pizza." Chief Wiggum, coach of the Mighty Pigs, on his team's victory.

 "Lisa, if the Bible has taught us nothing else—and it hasn't—it's that girls should stick to girls' sports, such as hot oil wrestling and foxy boxing and such and such."

Principal Skinner initiates a new system that alerts parents when their children do poorly in school. Lisa receives notice that she is failing gym class and unsuccessfully tries out for various teams to make up for her grades. After one of his hockey games, Bart flings garbage at Lisa with his stick. Apu notices how well Lisa deflects the projectiles and signs her up as his team's goalie.

> **Kearney:** *Hey Dolph–take a memo on your Newton.*
> (Dolph writes "Beat Up Martin"; the mini-computer translates it into "Eat Up Martha.")
> **Kearney:** *Bah!*
> (Kearney throws it at Martin.)

> **Lisa the Jock:**
> **Lisa:** *Hey, Milhouse! Knock him down if he's in your way. Jimbo! Jimbo, go for the face! Look! Ralph Wiggum lost his shin guard. Hack the bone! Hack the bone!*
> **Homer:** *Wow. Eye of the tiger. Mouth of a Teamster!*

> **Friendly Visit:**
> **Moe:** *Hello.*
> **Homer:** *Moe, what are you doing here?*
> **Moe:** *What? What? A bartender can't come by and say "hi" to his best customer? Hey, hey there, Midge! Oh gee, I like what you done to your hair.*
> **Marge:** *You caught me at a real bad time, Moe. I hope you understand I'm too tense to pretend I like you.*
> **Moe:** *And how are the little kids doin'? I mean really how are they doin'? Any disabling injuries? Something, say, the gambling community might not yet know about? (to Bart) C'mere, lemme see those knees.*
> **Marge:** *Moe, I think you should leave.*
> **Moe:** *But, Blanche! You gotta help me out here. Please! I'm sixty-four grand in the hole. They're gonna take my thumbs!*

> **Bart:** *Hello, Queen Lisa.*
> **Lisa:** *Bart! What are you doing in my room?*
> **Bart:** *Lisa, certain differences, rivalries, if you will, have come up between us. At first I thought we could talk it over like civilized people. But instead, I just ripped the head off Mr. Honeybunny.*
> **Lisa:** *Bart, that was your cherished childhood toy.*
> **Bart:** *Aah! Mr. Honeybunny!*

 "Sorry, Bart, I'm gonna hang out with Lisa, for protection. And to be seen!"

 "Oh, my God, Marge. A penalty shot, with only four seconds left. It's your child versus mine! The winner will be showered with praise, the loser will be taunted and booed until my throat is sore."

> **Mixed Messages:**
> **Marge:** *We love you both! You're not in competition with each other! Repeat: You are not in competition with each other!*
> **Homer:** *Hey! Apu just called. This Friday Lisa's team is playing Bart's team. You're in direct competition. And don't go easy on each other just because you're brother and sister. I want to see you both fighting for your parents' love!*

> **Bart:** *Come watch TV with me, Dad. We missed the first two episodes of "Cops," but if we hurry we can catch the last three.*
> **Homer:** *Ah, sorry Bart, Lisa and I are going out for gelato. We'd ask you to come, but, you know?*

THE STUFF YOU MAY HAVE MISSED

Homer teases Maggie with his beer can at the beginning of the episode.

The logo on Dolph's Newton is of a worm coming out of an apple.

The slogan of the Springfield Youth Center reads, "Building Unrealistic Hopes Since 1966."

Apu has a picture of the original Kwik-E-Mart hanging in his home. The first Kwik-E was last seen in 1F10, "Homer and Apu."

When Homer's head hits the top of the stove, it makes a large dent.

A sign for Moe's bar at the skating rink reads, "The 70s Are Back So Let's Drink Like It." Another sign reads, "Hey Kids, Menthol Moose Says, Smoke Laramies."

I WILL NOT DISSECT THINGS
UNLESS INSTRUCTED.
I WILL NOT DISSECT THINGS
UNLESS INSTRUCTED.
I WILL NOT DISSECT THINGS
UNLESS INSTRUCTED.

UTER

Description:
Exchange student at Springfield Elementary.

Country of origin:
Germany.

Talent:
Can keep a seat on the schoolbus to himself even if the bus is full.

Style:
Alpine casual: lederhosen, etc.

Passion:
Candy, particularly Flavor Wax and Marzipan Joy Joys mit iodine.

Shame:
Once created a chocolate diorama of Charlie and the Chocolate Factory as a school project, but ate it before it could be judged.

WOULD YOU LIKE A BITE OF MY FLAVOR WAX?

ASHLEY GRANT

Identity:
Grad student and feminist crusader.

Believes:
Boys are susceptible to video-game lures.

Sensitive to:
Sexual harassment, particularly from balding, paunchy, drooling sugar freaks.

Turn-offs:
Having her butt grabbed; having her space invaded; having sexist interaction.

> SEE, LISA? MALES AREN'T HARD TO TAME. THEY ALL FOLLOW THEIR VIDEO CARTRIDGES.

Homer takes Marge to the Candy Industry Trade Show, leaving feminist grad student Ashley Grant to watch the children. At the show, Homer steals a rare gummy Venus de Milo. When he drops Ashley off at home, he notices that the Venus is stuck to her backside and he snatches it off—a move that Ashley mistakes for a sexual advance.

Soon afterwards, outraged protesters calling Homer a sexist pig surround the Simpsons' home. They follow Homer everywhere, making his life unbearable. Homer agrees to sit for an interview with tabloid reporter Godfrey Jones, who twists the story into a sensationalized, highly inaccurate piece for his TV show "Rock Bottom." After the story airs, the media descend on the Simpson home and monitor Homer's every move.

At Lisa's and Marge's urging, Homer appears on public access TV and declares his innocence. However, no one watches him. Groundskeeper Willie informs Homer that he secretly videotapes couples in their cars and shows Homer a tape of the Ashley Grant incident. The tape exonerates Homer and his life returns to normal.

SHOW HIGHLIGHTS

A university grad student and a scary-looking hobo: Marge's only choices for a babysitter for Bart and Lisa. She picks the grad student.

"Oh, I feel like a kid in some kind of a store." Homer, at the candy convention.

Busted: A security guard approaches Marge as she pulls a celery stalk out of her purse. He warns, "All right, you're going to have to put some sugar on that celery or get out, ma'am."

Gummy Bears, Gummy Calves' Heads, Gummy Jaw breakers: Some of the gummy products admired by Homer at the candy convention.

"See you in hell—candy boys!!" Homer, escaping the candy convention by hurling a Buzz Cola/Pop Rox grenade at his pursuers.

"Okay, don't panic. She can't have gotten far. She has no arms." Homer, searching for his gummy Venus de Milo.

"Two-four-six-eight/Homer's crime was very great! (Pause) 'Great' meaning large or immense/We used it in the pejorative sense." The protesters' chant against Homer.

Bear time: The talk show "Ben" features the bear Gentle Ben with a microphone jutting from a helmet strapped to his head. During the taping, he rushes to a table of food, savagely knocks away a trainer, and is tranquilized by a "Ben Control" team.

> **Homer S.: Portrait of an Ass-Grabber:**
> New Fox TV-movie, starring Dennis Franz as Homer.

"You mean, I'm on my own? I've never been on my own. Oh no! On own! On own! I need help. Oh, God help me! Help me, God!" Homer, after Marge tells him she cannot make everything all better.

BADMAN

Episode 2F06   Original Airdate: 11/27/94
Writer: Greg Daniels
Director: Jeff Lynch
Guest Voice: Dennis Franz as Himself

I WILL NOT WHITTLE HALL
PASSES OUT OF SOAP.
I WILL NOT WHITTLE HALL
PASSES OUT OF SOAP.
I WILL NOT WHITTLE HALL
PASSES OUT OF SOAP.

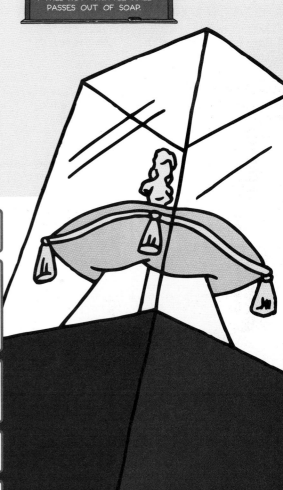

Gummy salesman: *That is the rarest gummy of them all: the gummy Venus de Milo. Carved by gummy artisans who work exclusively in the medium of gummy.*
Marge: *Will you stop saying "gummy" so much?*

"Somebody had to take the babysitter home. Then I noticed she was sitting on the gummy Venus, so I grabbed it off her. Just thinking about that sweet, sweet candy....I just wish I had another one right now!" Homer, in his statement to Godfrey Jones.

"Somebody had to take the babysitter home. Then I noticed she was sitting on *(edit)* **her** *(edit)* **sweet** *(edit)* **can.** *(edit)* **so I grabbed** *(edit)* **her** *(edit)* **sweet can.** *(edit)* **(drooling) Oh, just thinking about** *(edit)* **her** *(edit)* **can** *(edit)* **I just wish I had** *(edit)* **her** *(edit)* **sweet** *(edit)* **sweet** *(edit)* **s-s-sweet** *(edit)* **can."** Homer, in his statement on the "Rock Bottom" broadcast.

"This is hour 57 of our live, 'round-the-clock coverage outside the Simpson estate. Remember, by the way, to tune in at 8:00 for highlights of today's vigil, including when the garbage man came and when Marge Simpson put the cat out. Possibly because it was harassed, we don't know."

"That's your solution to everything: move under the sea—it's not gonna happen!" Marge, to Homer.

"You know, the courts might not work anymore, but as long as everyone is videotaping everyone else, justice will be done." Marge, after Groundskeeper Willie's amateur videotape clears Homer of butt-grabbing.

Homer: *Oh, that! No, I was grabbing a gummy Venus de Milo that got stuck to your pants.*
Protester: *Yeah, right! That's the oldest excuse in the book.*

Lisa: *Dad, I don't understand. What is she saying you did?*
Homer: *Well, Lisa, remember that postcard that Grampa sent us from Florida of that alligator biting that woman's bottom?*
Bart: *Oh, yeah. That was brilliant.*
Homer: *That's right, we all thought it was hilarious. But it turns out we were wrong. That alligator was sexually harassing that woman.*
Bart: *And the dog in the Coppertone ad? Same deal, Dad?*
Homer: *Well, that's kind of a gray area.*

Godfrey Jones: *Tonight on "Rock Bottom," we go undercover at a sex farm for sex hookers.*
Farmer: *I keep telling you, I just grow sorghum here.*
Voice: *Uh huh, and where are the hookers?*
Farmer: *'Round back...oops.*

Ashley: *Hmm. Homer, I thought you were an animal, but your daughter said you were a decent man. I guess she was right.*
Homer: *You're both right.*

Godfrey Jones: *(on TV) Tomorrow, on "Rock Bottom," he's a foreigner who takes videos of you when you least suspect it. He's "Rowdy Roddy Peeper."*
Homer: *Oooh, that man is sick!*
Marge: *Groundskeeper Willie saved you, Homer.*
Homer: *But listen to the music, he's evil!*
Marge: *Hasn't this experience taught you you can't believe everything you hear?*
Homer: *Marge, my friend, I haven't learned a thing.*

Homer's "Under the Sea" Song Lyrics:
Under the sea/Under the sea/There'll be no accusations/Just friendly crustaceans/Under the sea!

MAYOR QUIMBY

Occupation:
Chief Executive of the town of Springfield.

A.K.A:
Diamond Joe Quimby.

Duties:
Includes polling the electorate; declaring meaningless holidays; fact-finding missions on tropical islands.

Pains in rear:
Getting caught with his pants down; Chief Clancy Wiggum; Sideshow Bob.

Secret shames:
He is a tax-cheat; wife-swapper; pot smoker; former illiterate.

Best pick-up line:
"How would you like a street named after you?"

BY THE WAY, THIS YOUNG WOMAN IS NOT MY WIFE, BUT I AM SLEEPING WITH HER. I'M TELLING YOU THIS BECAUSE I'M COMFORTABLE WITH MY WOMANIZING.

GRAMPA VS. SEXUAL INADEQUACY

Episode 2F07 Original Airdate: 12/4/94 Writers: Bill Oakley & Josh Weinstein Directed by: Wes Archer

SHOW HIGHLIGHTS

"Marge, there's just too much pressure, what with my job, the kids, traffic snarls, political strife at home and abroad. But I promise you, the second all those things go away, we'll have sex." Homer, reassuring Marge about their lovelife.

 "I got a home remedy that'll put the zowzers back in your trousers."

Mr. and Mrs. Erotic American:
Paul Harvey's book on tape. Homer and Marge buy it to help improve their relationship.

Homer Sulks:

Marge: Homie, are you really going to ignore Grampa for the rest of your life?
Homer: Of course not, Marge, just for the rest of his life. He said I was an accident. He didn't want to have me.

"Legend has it, my Great-grandpappy stumbled upon this recipe when he was tryin' to invent a cheap substitute for Holy Water." Grampa, explaining the origin of his love tonic.

"No offense, Homer, but your half-assed underparenting was a lot more fun then your half-assed overparenting."

"Kids-here's-fifty-dollars-Why-not-go-to-the-movies-then-take-a-cab-to-your-Aunts'-house-Stay-there-Phone-call-you-later-Now-now-now." Homer, to the kids, after drinking Grampa's love potion.

 "Step right up, folks, and witness the magnificent medicinal miracle of Simpson & Son's Patented Revitalizing Tonic! Put some ardor in your larder with our energizing, moisturizing, tantalizing, romanticizing, surprising, her-prizing, revitalizing tonic!"

Frigid Falls, Mount Seldom, and Lake Flaccid: The towns Grampa and Homer plan to visit to sell their tonic.

(Bart and other kids from the neighborhood try to figure out what's going on with the grown-ups.)
Bart: Okay, it's now painfully clear, the adults are definitely paving the way for an invasion by the saucer people.
Milhouse: You fool! Can't you see it's a massive government conspiracy? Or have they gotten to you, too?
(Milhouse dives on Bart and they start to struggle.)
Lisa: Hey, hey, hey! Stop it! Why are you guys jumping to such ridiculous conclusions? Haven't you ever heard of Occam's Razor? "The simplest explanation is probably the correct one."
Bart: So, what's the simplest explanation?
Lisa: (sarcastic) I don't know; maybe they're all reverse vampires and they have to get home before dark.
Everyone: Aaaah! Reverse vampires! Reverse vampires!

Homer: I'm a screw-up. I burned down our house.
Grampa: No, I'm a screw-up. I burned down our house.
Homer: You know what?
Grampa: What?
Homer: We're both screw-ups.

Homer Sits in Bed, Watching TV:

Announcer: We now return to the 1971 film Good Time Slim, Uncle Doobie, and the Great Frisco Freak-Out! starring Troy McClure.
(An amorous Marge snuggles up and kisses Homer as he watches.)
Homer: Please, Marge. How often can I see a movie of this caliber on late-night TV?
Marge: Is there anything wrong, Homie?
Homer: No. It's just that I've only seen this movie twice before, and I've seen you every night for the last eleven ye—aha. What I mean to say is… We'll snuggle tomorrow, sweetie. I promise.

THE STUFF YOU MAY HAVE MISSED

The sign outside of BOOKS! BOOKS! AND ADDITIONAL BOOKS! boasts "Today's Special: Michener, $1.99/Lb."

Sex books on the shelf: *Kosher Erotic Cakes, How to Seduce Your Lousy, Lazy Husband, Bordello Repair, Vol. I, Bork on Sex, Weight Loss through Laborious Sex.*

Marge and Homer grab books to read in front of Bart and Lisa, entitled *Tanks of the Third Reich* and *Mapplethorpe.*

Homer ushers Bart, Lisa, and Maggie out of the house to go to the movies, but they end up at the "Stock Footage Festival."

Marge and Homer's sex life becomes nonexistent, and sensing that the couple's marriage is in deep trouble, Grampa concocts a home remedy that he guarantees will put sparks back into the relationship. Homer is skeptical but takes a swig. He immediately runs home to make love to Marge.

At Marge's suggestion, Homer and Grampa go into business together and sell the tonic from town to town. During one outing, they visit the farmhouse where Homer grew up and have a disagreement. Homer accuses his father of never encouraging him, while Grampa tells Homer that his conception was an accident. Incredibly hurt, Homer kicks Grampa out of the car.

Homer vows to show his children the attention they deserve, but he overcompensates. Bart and Lisa tell him that they were better off without so much attention. Homer and Grampa each return separately to the farmhouse. Homer discovers an old photo of his father dressed as Santa. He realizes that his father did care about him after all. Accidentally setting fire to the farmhouse, Homer and Grampa both admit that they are "screw-ups."

MY HOMEWORK WAS NOT STOLEN BY A ONE-ARMED MAN MY HOMEWORK WAS NOT STOLEN BY A ONE-ARMED MAN

FEAR OF FLYING

Episode 2F08 Original Airdate: 12/18/94 Writer: David Sacks Director: Mark Kirkland
Guest Voices: Ted Danson as Sam, Woody Harrelson as Woody, Rhea Pearlman as Carla, John Ratzenberger as Cliff, and George Wendt as Norm

DR. ZWEIG

After pulling a prank on Moe, Homer is banned from the bar and looks for another place to drink. He settles for "The Little Black Box" at the airport, but is mistaken for a pilot and whisked into the cockpit of an airplane, which he promptly damages. Fearing public humiliation, the airline gives Homer free tickets for the family. However, the idea of plane travel fills Marge with anxiety, and after a panic attack on the plane, the trip is postponed.

Marge begins to act strangely and Lisa convinces Homer that she needs professional help. Homer takes Marge to see a psychiatrist named Dr. Zweig, despite his fear that he will be blamed for his wife's condition.

Dr. Zweig gradually helps Marge remember back to the time she found out that her father was an airline steward and not a pilot, as she was told. Marge's shame is erased when Dr. Zweig tells her that her father helped clear the way for all of today's male stewards. Marge is cured of her anxiety.

Occupation:
Soothing Springfield psychoanalyst; exposes the roots of peoples' fears; relieves cases of high anxiety.

Proud of:
Her wall full of qualifications.

Quirks:
Believes The Monkees were about rebellion as well as social and political upheaval; knows Murray the window washer's work schedule.

School of thought:
The husband is to blame.

Pet peeve:
When her patients' checks bounce.

> YES, YES. IT'S ALL A RICH TAPESTRY.

SHOW HIGHLIGHTS

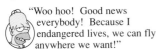 "I've been wasting my life away in that dump for years. That's it! I'm going to find a new bar to drink in and I'm going to get drunker than I've ever been in my entire life!"

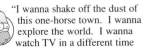 "Woo hoo! Good news everybody! Because I endangered lives, we can fly anywhere we want!"

"I wanna shake off the dust of this one-horse town. I wanna explore the world. I wanna watch TV in a different time zone. I wanna visit strange, exotic malls. I'm sick of eating hoagies! I want a grinder, a sub, a foot-long hero! I want to live, Marge! Won't you let me live? Won't you, please?

"My father was a stewardess."
Marge, confronting one of her demons.

Moe: *I'm taking your caricature down from Mt. Lushmore. And I'm pulling your favorite song out of the jukebox.*
Homer: *"It's Raining Men"?*
Moe: *Yeah, not no more it ain't.*

"Marge, what's wrong? Are you hungry? Sleepy? Gassy? Gassy? Is it gas? It's gas, isn't it?"
Homer, trying to get to the root of Marge's anxiety on the plane.

"Let me off! Let me off! Let me off! Let me off! Let me off! Let me off! Let me off! Let me off! Let me off! Let me off! Let me off! Let me off! Let me off! Let me off!"
Marge, running up and down the aisle of the plane before takeoff.

At the Little Black Box:
Bartender: *Uh, sorry, you gotta be a pilot to drink in here.*
Homer: *Uh, but I am a pilot.*
Bartender: *Where's your uniform?*
Homer: *Um, I stowed it safely in the overhead compartment.*
Bartender: *Well, you talk the talk. Here's a loaner.*

At the She-She Lounge:
Homer: *Wait a minute, there's something bothering me about this place. I know! This lesbian bar doesn't have a fire exit! Enjoy your death trap, ladies!*
Woman: *What was her problem?*

In the "Cheers"-like Bar:
Norm-type: *Woody, gimme a beer.*
Woody-type: *I think you had enough, Mr. Peterson. My chiropractor says I can't carry you home anymore.*
Norm-type: *Just give me another beer, you brain dead hick! I'll kill ya! I'll kill all of ya!*

RALPH WON'T "MORPH" IF YOU
SQUEEZE HIM HARD ENOUGH
RALPH WON'T "MORPH" IF YOU
SQUEEZE HIM HARD ENOUGH
RALPH WON'T "MORPH" IF YOU
SQUEEZE HIM HARD ENOUGH

(A man who looks like Homer enters Moe's bar. He has a mustache and wears a suit and tophat.)
Guy: *Greetings, good man. Might I trouble you for a drink?*
Moe: *Oh, get out of here, Homer.*
Guy: *Homer? Who is Homer? My name is Guy Incognito.* (Moe roughs up Guy and throws him out, just as Homer walks by.)
Homer: *(gasp) Oh my god! This man is my exact double! (gasp) That dog has a puffy tail! Hee hee hee hee hee hee hee hee! (chasing the dog) Here puff! Here puff! Hee hee hee hee hee!*

Dr. Zweig: *Now, let's talk about your father.*
Marge: *Sure, okay. I'll talk about father. Father Christmas. That's what they call Santa Claus in England. They drive on the wrong side of the road there. Now that's crazy. People are always saying how small England is. But you couldn't fit it all in here. Not by a long shot. You know what? I'm cured.*
Dr Zweig: *Marge, get back here! Tell me about your father! What did he do for a living?*

THE STUFF YOU MAY HAVE MISSED

Homer's caricature on Mt. Lushmore is reminiscent of a classic cover of *The New Yorker* magazine.

Although Kelsey Grammer has guest-starred numerous times as the voice of Sideshow Bob, during the "Cheers" scene, Grammer's character does not speak.

Marge last flew—without incident—in 8F01, "Mr. Lisa Goes to Washington."

The She-She Lounge is located across the street from a church.

The Crazy Clown Airline executive wears a toupee.

Skinner reads *Principal's World* magazine at Dr. Zweig's office.

Guest Voice:
Anne Bancroft as Dr. Zweig.

Homer notices that Lenny and Carl are acting strangely. He follows them after work to an ominous-looking temple, where they participate in a strange ceremony with Moe, Chief Wiggum, and others. Homer learns that they are all members of The Stonecutters, an exclusive, secret organization. He discovers that Grampa is also a member, which guarantees Homer membership. He survives the initiation ceremony and is inducted by the club's leader, Number One.

After Homer joins The Stonecutters, his popularity soars. However, he uses a sacred parchment as a table napkin and is stripped of his membership. As Number One kicks Homer out, he notices a distinct birthmark on Homer's back that identifies him as The Stonecutters' true leader. The Stonecutters rejoice that The Chosen One has arrived.

Homer's initial enthusiasm with his new role soon fades as his disciples pander to his every whim. When Homer takes Lisa's suggestion that he use his power to help others in the community, The Stonecutters reject him. They vote to form a new club called the Ancient Mystic Society of No Homers and resort to their old ways.

SHOW HIGHLIGHTS

"Yeah, I probably won't be able to get the parts I need for two, three weeks. And that's if I order 'em today. Which I won't." The Simpsons' plumber, giving them the news about their flooded basement.

"This is is Arnie Pie. Looks like we got a little accident that's backing traffic up as far as this reporter can see." Arnie Pie, sitting in his crashed helicopter, in front of three lanes of traffic.

"I saw weird stuff in that place last night. Weird, strange, sick, twisted, eerie, godless, evil stuff. And I want in."

"Why don't those stupid idiots let me in their crappy club for jerks?" Homer, talking to Marge about feeling left out.

"Homer, a man who called himself 'You Know Who' just invited you to a secret 'wink wink' at the 'you know what.' You certainly are popular now that you're a Stonecutter." Marge, to Homer, in the living room.

"I'm an Elk, a Mason, a Communist...I'm president of the Gay and Lesbian Alliance for some reason...Ah, here it is. The Stonecutters."

Homer's initiation rituals into The Stonecutters: "The Leap of Faith," "Crossing the Desert," "The Unblinking Eye," "The Wreck of the Hesperus," and "The Paddling of the Swollen Ass...with Paddles."

"You have joined the sacred order of The Stonecutters, who, since ancient times, have split the rocks of ignorance that obscure the light of knowledge of light and truth. Now let's all get drunk and play Ping-Pong!" Number One, welcoming Homer.

> **Homer:** So anyway, Lenny and Carl are never around on Wednesdays and they don't tell me where they go. It's like a conspiracy.
> **Bart:** A conspiracy, eh? You think they might be involved in the Kennedy assassination in some way?
> **Homer:** (thoughtfully) I do...now. Anyway, I'm going to follow them tonight and see where they go.
> **Marge:** Oh, Homer. Don't start stalking people again. It's so illegal. Remember when you were stalking Charles Kuralt because you thought he dug up your garden?
> **Homer:** Well, something did.

> **Homer:** I'd give anything to get into the Stonecutters.
> **Lisa:** What do they do there, Dad?
> **Grampa:** I'm a member!
> **Homer:** What do they do? What don't they do!? (laughs) Oh, they do so many things...they never stop...oh, the things they do there! My stars.
> **Lisa:** You don't know what they do there, do you?
> **Homer:** Not as such, no.

> **Taking the Oath:**
> **Homer:** And by the Sacred Parchment, I swear that if I reveal the secrets of The Stonecutters, may my stomach become bloated and my head be plucked of all but three hairs.
> **Moe:** Um...I think he should have to take a different oath.

> **Lisa:** Dad, I know you think you're happy now, but it's not going to last forever.
> **Homer:** Everything lasts forever.

> **Burns, the Underling:**
> **Lenny:** We call each other by number, not by name. Carl is number 14, I'm number 12. Burnsie is number 29.
> **Homer:** You outrank Mr. Burns here?
> **Lenny:** Sure. Watch. Hey 29! Get over here!
> (Lenny squeezes Burns's nose hard and makes a honking noise.)
> **Mr. Burns:** Thank you, sir, may I have another?
> (to himself) Patience, Monty...climb the ladder.

THE STUFF YOU MAY HAVE MISSED

"Econo-Save Budget Stool, Factory Second": The label of Homer's work stool, which collapses.

A car in a parking lot has the license plate "3MI ISL" (Three-Mile Island).

The Simpsons use "Stern Lecture Plumbing." Their motto is, "I told you not to flush that."

Homer's revenge list: Bill of Rights, Grandpa, Fat-Free Lard, Gravity, Emmys, Darwin, H2WHOA! (the waterslide Homer got stuck in at Mt. Splashmore, featured in 7F18, "Brush with Greatness"), Billy Crystal, God, Soloflex, The Boy, Stern Lecture Plumbing, Econo Save.

The Stonecutters members: Lenny, Carl, Homer, Jasper, Barney, Adolf Hitler, Sideshow Mel, Chief Wiggum, Mr. Burns, Smithers, Grampa, Principal Skinner, Moe, Herman, Dr. Hibbert, Mayor Quimby, Groundskeeper Willie, Steve Guttenberg, Krusty, Mr. Van Houten, Kent Brockman, Dewey Largo, Scott Christian, Asst. Superintendent Leopold, "Number One," Apu, Homer Glumplich, a small green alien, and the Egg Council guy.

Stonecutter World Council members: George Bush, Jack Nicholson, Orville Reddenbacher, and Mr. T.

When Homer goes bowling with The Stonecutters, he bowls on aisle number 13.

At the site of The Stonecutter's first charitable gesture, the sign reads: "Stonecutter's Day Care Center (License Pending) Grand Opening."

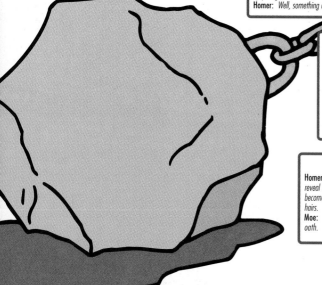

GREAT

Episode 2F09
Original Airdate: 1/8/95
Writer: John Swartzwelder
Director: Jim Reardon

Number 908:

Homer's number in The Stonecutters.

(Homer pulls a sticker with a hammer on it out of the membership pack Lenny gives him.)
Homer: *What's this?*
Lenny: *You put that sticker on your car so you won't get any tickets. And this other one keeps paramedics from stealing your wallet while they're working on you.*
Carl: *Oh, and don't bother calling 911 anymore. Here's the real number.*
(Carl hands Homer a card that reads "912.")

What Really Happened at the Signing of the Declaration of Independence, According to The Stonecutters:

Founding Father #1: *And a nation is born. Now let us party, like 'twas 1799!*
(The gathered Founding Fathers start chugging from casks and breaking windows with chairs. The owner of the hall approaches one of the men.)
Hall owner: *Please sir, you're destroying my establishment.*
Founding Father #2: *We just created the greatest democracy on earth, you lowlife commoner!*
(The man kicks away the hall owner.)

Lisa: *Well, maybe you could reach out to the community and help other people.*
Homer: *Hmmmm. I could help others. I'll get a bunch of monkeys, dress 'em up, and make 'em reenact the Civil War! Heh, heh, heh!*
Lisa: *Dad, that doesn't help people!*
Homer: *Couldn't hurt. Unless the monkeys started hurting people. Which they almost certainly would.*

ADDING "JUST KIDDING"
DOESN'T MAKE IT OKAY TO
INSULT THE PRINCIPAL
ADDING "JUST KIDDING"
DOESN'T MAKE IT OKAY TO
INSULT THE PRINCIPAL

The Stonecutters' Song:

Who controls the British crown? /
Who keeps the metric system down? /We do! We do! /
Who leaves Atlantis off the maps?/
Who keeps the Martians under wraps? /We do! We do! /
Who holds back the electric car? /
Who makes Steve Guttenberg a star? /We do! We do! /
Who robs the cave fish of their sight? /Who rigs every Oscar night? /We do! We do!

Homer's Idea:

Homer: *Brothers, I've learned a wonderful lesson. Helping others makes our own lives better, and makes us better people. So instead of just shooting pool and drinking beer, let us Stonecutters use what we have to help the less fortunate.*
Moe: *He's gone mad with power. Like that Albert Schweitzer guy.*

(Marge and the kids find Homer presiding over a group of monkeys dressed in Civil War uniforms at The Stonecutters' headquarters.)
Marge: *Homer, you can't just keep hanging out with these Globus monkeys. Somebody's gonna get parasites.*
Homer: *Aw, Marge, kids, I miss my club.*
Marge: *Oh, Homey. You know, you are a member of a very exclusive club.*
Homer: *The Black Panthers?*
Marge: *No. The family Simpson. Which has just five members. And only two of those members have special rings.*

NUMBER ONE

Position:
Head of The Stonecutters.

Obsession:
Butt-paddling.

Vocal style:
Commanding, dramatic, and Shakespearean.

Favorite celebration:
Getting drunk and playing ping-pong.

Takes his position:
Very seriously.

Constantly in search of:
The Chosen One.

TONIGHT WE ARE HERE TO COMMEMORATE OUR GLORIOUS SOCIETY'S 1500TH ANNIVERSARY. AND IN HONOR OF THIS MOMENTOUS OCCASION, WE'RE HAVIN' RIBS.

Guest Voice:
Patrick Stewart
as **Number One**

KNIGHT BOAT

Identity:
Talking boat on television.

Alias:
The Crime-Solving Boat.

Specialty:
Chasing sea poachers and various other sea scum.

Skipper:
Michael.

Attitude:
Touchy.

YOU DON'T HAVE TO YELL, MICHAEL. I'M ALL AROUND YOU.

AND MAGGIE MAKES THREE

Episode 2F10 Original Airdate: 1/22/95 Writer: Jennifer Crittenden Director: Swinton O. Scott III

While browsing through the family photo album, Lisa notices that there are no pictures of Maggie and asks for an explanation. Homer explains by recounting the story of Maggie's birth. Homer had received a paycheck that finally cleared him of all his debts. Overjoyed, he quit his job and insulted Mr. Burns. To make ends meet, he took a job at a local bowling alley, satisfying a lifelong dream. To celebrate his new life, Homer took Marge out for a night of romance.

Not long afterwards, Marge discovered that she was pregnant. She knew the news would end Homer's new lifestyle and affect his happiness, because it meant he could no longer support his family on his bowling alley salary. Marge kept her pregnancy a secret as long as she could, but Patty and Selma, eager to ruin Homer's life, spread the news throughout the town. When Homer found out, he was devastated.

Knowing he now needed more money for his family, Homer quit his job at the bowling alley and returned to the power plant to ask for forgiveness. Mr. Burns gave him his job back, but soon Homer was once again unhappy at his work. The only thing that cheered him up was Maggie's birth. Homer explains to Lisa that all of Maggie's baby pictures are on the wall of his work station.

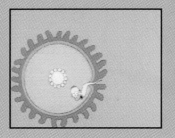

SHOW HIGHLIGHTS

"I should be resisting this, but I'm paralyzed with rage... and island rhythms." Mr. Burns, reacting to Homer playing his head like a bongo.

"If horseracing is the sport of kings, then surely bowling is a...very good sport as well."

"Mmm...bowling fresh"/"Mmm... urinal fresh." Homer, after spraying shoes and putting cakes in the urinals at the bowling alley.

"Mom, make Dad tell the story right!" Lisa, after hearing that Homer stood outside the bowling alley firing a shotgun into the air to increase business. Marge sadly tells her, "That's what really happened."

"Wow, Dad, you really threw a tantrum like a little sissy girl?"

Revealed this episode: Homer lost his hair by tearing it out each time he learned Marge was pregnant.

(Homer, Bart, and Lisa watch TV as Marge walks in holding Maggie.)
Marge: *Okay, TV off. It's family time.*
Homer: *Oh, but Marge, Knight–boat - the crime solving boat.*
Marge: *Homer, you promised. One night of family time a week. Besides, that back-talking boat sets a bad example.*
Bart: *Says you, woman.*

"Sorry you had to 'Split'": The message stitched on the back of the satin jacket the crew at the bowling alley gives to Homer as a going away present.

"You're a pin monkey? Wow! Finally, I don't have to be ashamed of my father's job!"

Crawling back: When Homer returns to the plant, he is sent past the door labelled, "Applicants" to a small doggy door labelled, "Supplicants." Homer gets on his hands and knees and makes his way through a small tunnel to Burns's office. When Mr. Burns sees Homer, he says, "So, come crawling back, eh?"

TV Moment:

Reminiscent of the opening to "The Mary Tyler Moore Show," Homer dances around, singing, "I'm gonna make it after all!" He finishes off with a flourish, throwing his bowling ball into the air à la Mary's hat. It crashes to the ground, making a crater in the bowling lane.

"BAGMAN" IS NOT A LEGITIMATE CAREER CHOICE "BAGMAN" IS NOT A LEGITIMATE CAREER CHOICE "BAGMAN" IS NOT A LEGITIMATE CAREER CHOICE

"It's wonderful, it's magical. Oh boy, here it comes. Another mouth." Homer's poorly feigned excitement at Maggie's delivery.

"Don't forget: you're here forever." The plaque Burns and Smithers install in front of Homer's station at work.

Pictures in the Simpson Family Album:

Baby Bart wearing nothing but a cowboy hat and boots riding Snowball I.

Lisa next to a block fort she built. The fort after Bart knocks it down. Lisa crying.

Various other pictures of Bart sleeping, Bart dozing, Bart "after a visit from the sandman," Bart during nappy time, and Bart all tuckered out.

THE STUFF YOU MAY HAVE MISSED

Homer sports sweat stains as he exercises in his office on his last day of work.

In all the flashback scenes, Homer has three hairs on top of his head—until he tears one out after learning Marge is pregnant.

Homer's sperm have three hairs on top of their heads as well.

Jacques (introduced in 7G11, "Life on the Fastlane") is seen bowling at the Bowl-A-Rama.

Dr. Hibbert's flashback haircut is modelled after Arsenio Hall's.

BART'S COMET

Episode 2F11 Original Airdate: 2/5/95 Writer: John Swartzwelder Director: Bob Anderson

 As punishment for a prank, Bart is sentenced to assist Principal Skinner with his astronomy project, which begins at 4:30 a.m. each morning. While on detail with Skinner, Bart spots a comet and reports it to an observatory. The astonomers at the observatory congratulate Bart for the discovery and name the comet after him. Skinner is crestfallen.

It becomes apparent that "The Bart Simpson Comet" is on a collision course with Springfield. Scientists launch a rocket to intercept the mass and blow it to pieces, but the rocket misses its target and destroys the bridge that is the only way out of town.

The residents of Springfield take refuge in Flanders's bomb shelter. However, not everyone can fit in the tiny space. Homer forces Flanders out of the shelter, but, feeling horribly guilty, he opens the shelter door. Homer and the others step outside. As the comet enters the atmosphere, it encounters a thick layer of pollution and begins to break up until it seems harmlessly small. The comet lands on Flanders's empty shelter, causing it to collapse instantly.

> CURSIVE WRITING DOES NOT
> MEAN WHAT I THINK IT DOES
> CURSIVE WRITING DOES NOT
> MEAN WHAT I THINK IT DOES
> CURSIVE WRITING DOES NOT
> MEAN WHAT I THINK IT DOES
> CURSIVE WRITING DOES NOT
> MEAN WHAT I THINK IT DOES

SHOW HIGHLIGHTS

"I'm going to punish you for this, Bart. And it won't just be a simple caning this time."

"Oh, it won't come down for months. Curse the man who invented helium. Curse Pierre Jules Cesar Janssen!" Skinner, after giving up on catching the balloon.

"Sounds like the Doomsday Whistle. Ain't been blown for nigh onto three years." Grampa, at the sounding of the town's alarm.

Bart impedes science: As Skinner's weather balloon is launched, Bart pulls a string revealing his handiwork. He has transformed the balloon into a likeness of Skinner bending forward with his pants down and holding a sign that says, "Hi! I'm Big Butt Skinner."

"With the bridge gone and the airport unfortunately on the other side of the bridge, a number of citizens are attempting to jump the gorge with their cars. It's a silent testament to the 'never give up' and 'never think things out' spirit of our citizens." Arnie Pie in the Sky, reporting on the bombed out bridge.

"I've said it before and I'll say it again. Democracy simply doesn't work. Now, over the years, a newsman learns a number of things that, for one reason or another, he just cannot report. It doesn't seem to matter now, so... the following people are gay..."

Homer's prediction: "What's everyone so worked up about? So there's a comet. Big deal. It'll burn up in our atmosphere, and whatever's left will be no bigger than a chihuahua's head."

"Okay, let's start again. We'll need laughter, religious enlightenment, gossip—that's Mrs. Lovejoy..." Rev. Lovejoy, going over the list of people who should stay in the shelter and who should leave.

 "Let's go burn down the observatory so this will never happen again."

Irony: When the tiny remnant of the comet falls to earth, it pops the "Skinner Big Butt" weather balloon on the way down.

> ### Homer the Sage:
> **Bart:** *But what's really amazing is that this is exactly what Dad said would happen.*
> **Lisa:** *Yeah, Dad was right.*
> **Homer:** *I know, kids. I'm scared, too.*

> (A group of nerdy-looking kids calls Bart over in the cafeteria.)
> **Database:** *As the first student at Springfield Elementary to discover a comet, we're very proud to make you a member of our very select group. Welcome to SuperFriends!*
> **Ham:** *I am called "Ham," since I enjoy ham radio. This is "E-Mail," "Report Card," "Database," and "Lisa."*
> (Lisa smirks at Bart.)
> **Ham:** *Your nickname will be "Cosmos."*

> (The Simpsons watch the rocket launch from the roof. They see the rocket fall out of the sky and blow up the only bridge out of town.)
> **Lisa:** *It blew up the bridge! We're doomed!*
> **Homer:** *It's times like this I wish I were a religious man.*
> **Rev Lovejoy:** (running down the street, crazed) *It's all over, people! We don't have a prayer!*

> ### Congressional Assistance:
> **Congressman #1:** *Then it is unanimous. We are going to approve the bill to evacuate the town of Springfield in the great state of...*
> **Congressman #2:** *Wait a second, I want to tack on a rider to that bill. Thirty million dollars of taxpayer money to support the perverted arts.*
> **Congressman #1:** *All in favor of the amended Springfield-slash-Pervert bill?*
> (Members of Congress boo.)
> **Congressman #1:** *Bill defeated.*

THE STUFF YOU MAY HAVE MISSED

Springfield Shopper headlines during this episode: "Boy Discovers Comet" and "Rocket to Kick Comet's Tail."

A sign on the side of the rocket sent to blow up the comet reads, "Caution! Aim Away from Face."

Two slingshots are thrown at Skinner's car in attempts to get the weather balloon down.

When people who had been in the bomb shelter go to join Flanders on the hill, Apu appears yellow.

DATABASE:

Founding member of:
SuperFriends, Springfield Elementary's "very select group" of academically-gifted students.

Favorite activities:
Playing "Pop goes the Weasel" in the school band; dancing around lemon trees; inducting new members of SuperFriends.

Finest moment:
Participating in the raid on Shelbyville to return Springfield's lemon tree.

> I MAKE IT A POINT NEVER TO TURN MY HEAD UNLESS I EXPECT TO SEE SOMETHING.

HOMIE THE CLOWN

Episode 2F12 Original Airdate: 2/12/95 Writer: John Swartzwelder Director: David Silverman Guest Voices: Dick Cavett as Himself, Johnny Unitas as Himself, Joe Mantegna as Fat Tony

Occupation:
Greater Springfield Mafia head.

Country of origin:
Italy.

Voice:
As raspy as Moe's, only deeper.

Favorite garment:
Fancy black cape.

Favorite entertainment:
Clown capering.

Pet peeve:
Unpaid debts.

GRAZIE, GRAZIE. YOU HAVE BROUGHT GREAT JOY TO THIS OLD ITALIAN STEREOTYPE.

SHOW HIGHLIGHTS

"Ahh, there's nothing better than a cigarette... unless it's a cigarette lit with a $100 bill!"

"If there has to be a bastardized version of Krusty, I'm glad it's you." Lisa, to Homer on his new job.

"Welcome to the noble family of skilled Krustaceans. You will now go back to your home towns and do kids' parties, swap meets, and all the other piddling crap I wouldn't touch with a ten-foot clown pole. Now, come and get your catskins... uh, I mean, sheepskins."

Homer's first "regional" Krusty gigs: Parachuting out of a plane to introduce the new Krusty Burger, entertaining at Milhouse's birthday party, dedicating a new Jiffy Lube, and co-hosting the Regional Ace Awards.

"Hey Krusty, Krusty, remember the time we got loaded and set those beavers loose in that pine furniture store?"

"How could I charge full price to the man whose lust for filthy magazines kept me in business during that first shaky year? Oh, by the way, here's your new issue of *Gigantic Asses*." Apu, to Homer (posing as Krusty).

"Aw, being a clown sucks. You get kicked by kids, bit by dogs, and admired by the elderly. Who am I clowning? I have no business being a clown! I'm leaving the clowning business to all the other clowns in the clowning business."

"I'm seeing double here: four Krustys!" Legs, looking at Homer and Krusty side by side.

The Spin Cycle Fantastique Stunt:

With Homer on his shoulders, Krusty rides the tiny bike towards the loop. Homer causes them to ride up a pool cue onto the pool table where they knock in all the balls. They sail onto the bar where Homer's head plays the theme from The Godfather on the hanging wine glasses. Seeing that the pass-way door to the bar is up, Krusty grabs a seltzer bottle and shoots a stream of water, knocking the leaf down and clearing the way. They land on a barstool which spins them around until they are thrown off. Shot towards the loop with so much speed, they go around three times and fly into the air. They land on their feet. Homer steps in front of Krusty, swallows the bike, and rings the bell.

Identity Crisis:

Homer: But wait. You can't kill me for being Krusty. I'm not him. I'm Homer Simpson.
Fat Tony: The same Homer Simpson who crashed his car through the wall of our club?
Homer: Uh... actually my name is Barney. Yeah. Barney Gumble.
Legs: The same Barney Gumble who keeps taking pictures of his sister?
Homer: Uh, actually my real name is uh, think Krusty, think, Joe Valachi.
Louie: The same Joe Valachi who squealed to the Senate Committee about organized crime?
Homer: Benedict Arnold!
Legs: The same Benedict Arnold who plotted to surrender West Point to the hated British?
Homer: D'oh!

Movie Moment:

Homer sculpts a circus tent out of mashed potatoes at the dinner table à la Richard Dreyfuss in *Close Encounters of the Third Kind*.

Louie: Hey! It's Krusty all right. Should I shoot him gangland-style or execution-style?
Fat Tony: Listen to your heart.

THE STUFF YOU MAY HAVE MISSED

Sign beneath the front gate to Krusty's Clown College: "Formerly Willie Nelson's House."

Krusty merchandise featured in the episode includes a Weeble-Wobble Sideshow Mel and a Krusty big-haired troll doll.

Krusty has a "Kroon along with Krusty" gold record in his office.

Homer and Krusty can be told apart by the tops of their head. Krusty has a tuft of green hair where Homer only has his regular two.

Accountant: Let me get this straight. You took all the money you made franchising your name and bet it against the Harlem Globetrotters?
Krusty: (miserable) Oh, I thought the Generals were due! (to TV) He's spinning the ball on his finger! Just take it! Take the ball! That game was fixed. They were using a freakin' ladder for God's sakes!

In order to generate more income to pay for his extravagant lifestyle, Krusty opens a clown college. Homer sees a billboard advertising the college and, obsessed by it, enrolls to learn the secrets of the trade from the master himself. Upon successfully graduating, Homer appears as Krusty at events throughout Springfield.

The grueling schedule of his second job as "Krusty the Clown" runs Homer ragged. Just as he is about to quit, Chief Wiggum tears up a speeding ticket because he thinks that Homer is the real Krusty. People all over Springfield also believe that Homer is Krusty, and Homer takes advantage of all the perks, until mobster Fat Tony and his gang try to collect on Krusty's gambling debt.

Homer tries to tell the gangsters who he really is, but they ignore him. Their leader, Don Vittorio, tells Homer that his life will be spared if he performs the "Spin Cycle Fantastique" bicycle trick. Homer fails the stunt. When the real Krusty arrives to settle his debt, Vittorio orders them to do the trick together. They succeed with extra flair and Vittorio spares their lives.

NEXT TIME IT COULD BE ME ON THE SCAFFOLDING
NEXT TIME IT COULD BE ME ON THE SCAFFOLDING
NEXT TIME IT COULD BE ME ON THE SCAFFOLDING

BART VS. AUSTRALIA

Episode 2F13 Original Airdate: 2/19/95 Writers: Bill Oakley & Josh Weinstein Director: Wes Archer

Lisa tells Bart that water in the Northern Hemisphere always drains counter-clockwise. In an effort to prove her wrong, Bart places a collect call to a boy in Australia and discovers that the water in the Southern Hemisphere drains in a clockwise direction, proving Lisa right. However, the phone line remains open for six hours and the boy's father receives a bill for $900. Sometime later, Bart receives an official notice from the Australian government informing him that he is being indicted for fraud in Australia.

The Simpsons are visited by Evan Conover, U.S. Undersecretary for International Protocol, Brat and Punk Division, who explains that he has arranged for Bart to fly with his family to Australia to issue a personal apology to the Australian government. In Australia, Bart is brought before Parliament and apologizes. However, the Prime Minister also decrees that Bart must receive a "booting" to atone for his act of fraud.

Homer is outraged. He and Bart escape and a chase ensues. They run back to the American Embassy, meeting up with Marge and Lisa on the way. The United States ambassador negotiates one more method of making amends: Bart is to be kicked once by the Prime Minister himself. However, just as Bart is about to receive his punishment, he drops his pants and moons the Prime Minister. Angry Australians storm the embassy, and the Simpsons are airlifted to safety by helicopter.

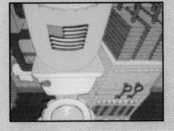

SHOW HIGHLIGHTS

"No way! Water doesn't obey your 'rules.' It goes where it wants. Like me, babe." Bart, refuting the Coriolis effect.

"Nine hundred dollaridoos?! Tobias! Did you accept a six-hour collect call from the States?" Hopping mad Aussie, Bruno Drundridge, finding out why his phone bill is so expensive.

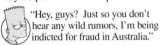 "Hey, guys? Just so you don't hear any wild rumors, I'm being indicted for fraud in Australia."

"Unfortunately, Bart, your little escapade could not have come at a worse time. Americo-Australianian relations are at an all-time low. As I'm sure you remember, in the late 1980s the U.S. experienced a short-lived infatuation with Australian culture. For some bizarre reason, the Aussies thought this would be a permanent thing. Of course, it wasn't." Evan Conover, explaining the seriousness of Bart's situation.

"Booting": A form of Australian corporal punishment administered by an angry-looking man wearing a huge boot. According to Andy, Australia's Prime Minister, "it's just a little kick in the bum."

"You sold us out, Conover!" Homer, reacting the news that Parliament plans to boot Bart.

 "When will you Australians learn? In America, we stopped using corporal punishment, and things have never been better. The streets are safe. Old people strut confidently through the darkest alleys. And the weak and nerdy are admired for their computer-programming abilities. So, like us, let your children run wild and free, because as the old saying goes, let your children run wild and free."

"Don't Tread on Me": The words Bart writes on his butt before mooning the Australian Prime Minister.

"I'm impressed you were able to write so legibly on your own butt."

Final Settlement:
Ambassador: We did it! We've worked out a compromise that will allow both nations to save face.
Conover: We've argued them down to a booting.
Simpsons: What?!
Ambassador: The Prime Minister just wants to kick you once. Through the gate. With a regular shoe.
Conover: I believe it's a wing-tip.

I WILL NOT HANG DONUTS ON MY PERSON.
I WILL NOT HANG DONUTS ON MY PERSON.
I WILL NOT HANG DONUTS ON MY PERSON.

The Great Escape:
Homer: Hey, do we get to land on an aircraft carrier?
Helicopter pilot: No, sir. The closest vessel is the U.S.S. Walter Mondale. It's a laundry ship. They'll take you the rest of the way.

Bruno: You're just some punk kid, aren't you? Ooh, you picked the wrong guy to tangle with here, mate.
Bart: (laughs) I don't think so. You're all the way in Australia. Hey, I think I hear a dingo eatin' your baby.

THE STUFF YOU MAY HAVE MISSED

The places in the Southern Hemisphere that Bart calls: Chile, Antarctica, New Ouagadougou, Burkina Faso, Unnamed Settlement, and Disputed Zone.

Bart's collect call costs Bruno Drundridge $900—the exact same amount the Springfield Gas Company bills the Simpsons after one of Bart's stunts detaches the family dryer and ignites the gas main in 4F11, "Homer's Phobia."

Motto on commemorative Australian stamp: "30 Years of Electricity."

A sign at the American embassy in Australia reads, "U.S. Embassy. Restroom for Citizens Only."

Bart receives a notice from the Hopping Mad Collection Agency of Sydney, Australia.

The statue hailing Australia's founding inmates is a likeness of Snake.

The Simpsons fly Transhemispheric Airlines.

EVAN CONOVER

Occupation:
Undersecretary of State for International Protocol, Brat and Punk Division.

Expertise:
Australian correctional history; footwear.

Strengths:
Introductions; selling out fellow Americans to angered foreign interests.

Incompetent at:
Editing slide shows; diplomacy.

Secret shame:
Cuba Plan-B.

Favorite munchy:
Candied apples.

DISPARAGING THE BOOT IS A BOOTABLE OFFENSE.

Guest Voice:
Phil Hartman as Evan Conover

HOMER VS. PATTY AND SELMA

Episode 2F14 Original Airdate: 2/26/95 Writer: Brent Forrester Director: Mark Kirkland Mel Brooks as Himself

BALLET TEACHER

Occupation:
Ballet teacher, Springfield Elementary.

Accent:
Russian.

Teaching style:
Firm, yet loving.

Theory:
It takes more than "fire in the belly" to be the next Baryshnikov.

BALLET IS FOR THE STRONG, THE FIERCE, THE DETERMINED. BUT FOR THE SISSIES? NEVER. NOW PUT ON THIS FUCHSIATARD. YOU ARE A FAIRY.

Guest Voice:
Susan Sarandon as the Ballet Teacher

Homer invests heavily in pumpkins futures, but fails to sell them before Halloween, losing his life savings. His credit ruined, he is refused loans. In desperation, Homer turns to Patty and Selma, who write him a check and save him from financial ruin. In return, he makes them promise not to tell Marge and agrees to wait on them hand and foot.

Meanwhile, Bart fails to show up at school in time to sign up for P.E. The only available class is ballet. Despite insisting that ballet is for sissies, Bart discovers a natural ability and falls in love with dancing. Fearing ridicule from his classmates, he dons a ski mask before his first performance. His dancing prowess is highly praised, but the praise soon turns to derisive comments and threats from the school bullies when Bart removes his mask.

Homer kicks Patty and Selma out of the house after they disclose his secret to Marge. To free himself of his debt to Patty and Selma, he takes on a second job as a limousine driver, but is pulled over for not having the proper license. At the DMV, Homer takes the exam for a limousine license, but Patty and Selma take revenge and fail him. When a supervisor catches the two sisters smoking inside the DMV building, Homer takes the blame. In exchange for saving their jobs, Patty and Selma reluctantly forgive Homer's debt.

SHOW HIGHLIGHTS

"All right, let's not panic. I'll make the money back by selling one of my livers. I can get by with one."

"Marge, we had a deal. Your sisters don't come here after six, and I stop eating your lipstick." Homer, shortly before wiping lipstick from his teeth.

"What a day, eh Milhouse? The sun is out, birds are singing, bees are trying to have sex with them—as is my understanding..."

"Time to fertilize the lawn. A couple of 500-pound bags should do it!" Homer, grabbing Patty and Selma by the neck and escorting them to the front door.

"Hmm...Am I wrong, or did it just get fatter in here?" Patty, after Homer walks into the house.

"See that? I started to do like a little arabesque, but then I just fully went for it and pulled off the demi-entrechant. *(suddenly gruff)* Not that I'm into that kind of thing."

I WILL REMEMBER TO TAKE MY MEDICATION.
I WILL REMEMBER TO TAKE MY MEDICATION.
I WILL REMEMBER TO TAKE MY MEDICATION.

(Homer, Barney, Moe, and the barflies smoke cigars at the bar.)
Homer: *This year I invested in pumpkins. They've been going up the whole month of October, and I got a feeling they're gonna peak right around January. Then, bang! That's when I'll cash in.*
Barney: *(toasting) To Homer! And to Sergeant Pepper, who is growing out of the middle of your back.*
Moe: *Ah Barn, you got to unwrap the plastic before you smoke these.*

"Listen, why don't you play Carl Reiner, and let me play Police Chief Wiggum? I hate Carl Reiner!" Mel Brooks, to Chief Wiggum.

"We know something you don't want Marge to know. Now, we own you like Siegfried owns Roy."

Marge: *I'm sorry. Homer doesn't mean to be rude, he's just a very complicated man.*
Homer: *(leaning out the window and breaking a plate over his head) Wrong!*
Selma: *When are you going to wake up and smell your husband, Marge?*
Patty: *Granted, you got some kids out of him. But when the seeds have been planted, you throw away the envelope.*

Homer: *Oh, wow. I can't believe my very first passenger is comedy legend Mel Brooks. I love that movie Young Frankenstein. Scared the hell out of me.*
Mel Brooks: *Uh, thanks.*
Homer: *Hey! Let's do that 2,000-pound man thing. I'll be that Carl Reiner guy, and you be what's-his-face.*

Jimbo and Nelson, on Bart's Ballet:
Jimbo: *He's graceful yet masculine. So it's okay for me to enjoy this.*
Nelson: *This reminds me of the movie Fame and to a lesser extent the TV series, which was also called "Fame."*

THE STUFF YOU MAY HAVE MISSED

A-1 Discount Broker's motto: "Our Commissions Offset Your Losses."

A sign for Bart's recital reads, "Ballet Performance. The 'T' is Silent."

Patty and Selma still have their souvenir pyramid lamp from Egypt, first seen in 7F15, "Principal Charming."

Logo abbreviation for the First Bank of Springfield: "BS."

Headline in novelty newspaper: "EXTRA EXTRA — BART NAMED WORLD'S GREATEST SEX MACHINE."

Homer never tells the man that he telephones at the casino in Las Vegas his name when he bets (and loses) $100 on roulette, yet he feels compelled to say he will still send a check.

Homer: *That's it! I'll make money with a chauffeur job. Good thing you turned on that TV, Lisa.*
Lisa: *I didn't turn it on, I thought you turned it on.*
Homer: *No. Well anyway, turn it off.*
Lisa: *It is off.*

A STAR IS BURNS

Episode 2F31 Original Airdate: 3/5/95 Writer: Ken Keeler Director: Susie Dietter

At a Town Hall meeting, Marge suggests that Springfield boost its image by holding a film festival. With the townspeople's consent, she assembles a distinguished jury, including Jay Sherman, a critic from New York.

The Simpsons invite Sherman to stay at their home. Homer becomes jealous of Sherman and asks Marge if he can be on the jury as well. Marge reluctantly assigns Homer to the jury in place of Martin Scorsese. Meanwhile, Mr. Burns uses the film festival as a public relations vehicle to improve his own image. He hires a director to glorify his achievements in a high-budget epic. However, when the film is shown at the festival, Burns is booed.

Burns bribes two members of the jury to vote for his film, forcing the panel into a deadlock. Sherman selects Barney's artistic black-and-white film, while Homer picks a short called *Man Getting Hit by Football*, by Hans Moleman. Homer reconsiders and votes for Barney's quality entry, which wins first prize. Disgraced, Burns leaves the festival and brings his film to the Oscars. He loses the Oscar to George C. Scott's remake of *Football in the Groin*.

SHOW HIGHLIGHTS

 "Listen, Spielbergo. Schindler and I are like peas in a pod! We're both factory owners. We both made shells for the Nazis, but mine worked, damn it! Now, go out there and win me that festival."

A Burns for All Seasons: Burns's propaganda film about himself.

Bright Lights, Beef Jerky: Apu's entry in the Springfield Film Festival.

Man Getting Hit by Football: Hans Moleman's film, featuring him getting hit in the groin by a football and instantly collapsing.

"But the ball! His groin! It works on so many levels." Homer, raving about Moleman's film.

Pukahontas: Barney Gumble's sensitive documentary about his alcoholism.

Bart Sells a Stars' Home Map to a Japanese Tourist Family:

(Father knocks on door of run-down house. Moe answers, wearing only his underwear.)
Father: *Excuse me, are you Drew Barrymore?*
Moe: *What? Get outta here, I'm hung-over.*
Mother: *Sorry, Miss Barrymore.*
Moe: *What?*

Lisa: *I like him; he's smart, he's sensitive, he's clearly not obsessed with his physical appearance.*
Homer: *My ears are burning.*
Lisa: *Uh, I wasn't talking about you, Dad.*
Homer: *No, my ears are really burning. I wanted to see inside so I lit a Q-Tip.*

Marge: *I think we should hold a film festival and give out prizes...*
Wiggum: *Could we make our own movies and enter them?*
Marge: *Yes!*
Wiggum: *At last—an excuse to wear make-up!*

Smithers: *A film biography might help them get to know the real you—virtuous, heroic, nubile...*
Burns: *You left out pleasant!* (he hits Smithers with his scepter) *But I like that film biography idea. A slick Hollywood picture to gloss over my evil rise to power, like Bugsy, or Working Girl. Get me Steven Spielberg!*
Smithers: *He's unavailable.*
Burns: *Then get me his non-union Mexican equivalent.*

Marge: *Hello, I'm Marge Simpson, and this is my husband, Homer.*
Jay Sherman: *Oh, nice to meet you, Marge. I saw your hair from the plane. And you must be the man who didn't know if he had a pimple or a boil.*
Homer: *It was a Gummi Bear.*

Jay Sherman: *How can you vote for Burns's movie?*
Krusty: *(quietly) Let's just say, it moved me. (loudly) To a bigger house! (to self) Oops. I said the quiet part loud and the loud part quiet.*

Jay: *And if you ever want to visit my show...*
Bart: *Nah, we're not going to be doing that.*

Rainier Wolfcastle's "McBain: Let's Get Silly" Plug:
McBain: *The film is just me in front of a brick wall for an hour and a half. It cost 80 million dollars.*
Jay: *How do you sleep at night?*
McBain: *On top of a pile of money, with many beautiful ladies.*

Moe's Musical Number for His Film, Moe Better Booze.

Money gets you one more round/ Drink it down/ Ya stupid clown/ Money gets you one more round/ Then you're out on your ass!

(Bart sits in the living room, watching TV.)
TV announcer: *Coming up next, "The Flintstones Meet the Jetsons!"*
Bart: *Uh, oh. I smell another cheap cartoon crossover.*
(Homer and Jay enter.)
Homer: *Bart Simpson, meet Jay Sherman, the critic.*
Jay: *Hello.*
Bart: *Hey, man. I really love your show. I think all kids should watch it. (shudders) Ew. I suddenly feel so dirty.*

THE STUFF YOU MAY HAVE MISSED

Krusty acts in the play "Sunrise at Campobello."

In this episode, a *Springfield Shopper* headline referring to Mr. Burns reads, "Incontinent Old Man Wins Miss Teen America Pageant." Mr. Burns's incontinence is mentioned in 8F23, "Brother, Can You Spare Two Dimes."

The airplane from New York is defaced like a New York subway train.

Jay Sherman's belch knocks food off of everyone's plate.

Two of the writers on Burns's film are named Lowell Burns and Babaloo Smithers.

CRAZY OLD MAN

Identity:
Anonymous nut case; entertainer.

Age:
Old.

State of mind:
Crazy.

Favorite activity:
Dropping his pants and dancing without provocation.

Past achievement:
Hosted his own TV show on which he dropped his pants and danced a lot.

THE OLD GRAY MARE SHE AIN'T WHAT SHE USED TO BE, AIN'T WHAT SHE USED TO BE, AIN'T WHAT SHE USED TO BE...

HUGH PARKFIELD

Identity:
Brilliant student; suave individual; and humorless vegetarian.

Nation of Origin:
Great Britain.

Area of Study:
The enviroment.

Favorite Band:
The Rolling Stones (due to their effort to preserve buildings).

Parentage:
The finest.

Suffers Fools:
Poorly.

First Great Love:
Lisa Simpson.

> I'VE NEVER MET ANYONE WHO SO UNDERSTOOD THE MAGIC OF JIM CARREY.

Guest Voice:
Mandy Patinkin
as Hugh Parkfield

LISA'S WEDDING

Episode 2F15 Original Airdate: 3/26/95 Writer: Greg Daniels Director: Jim Reardon

he Simpsons go to a Renaissance Faire, where Lisa has her fortune read. The fortune teller describes how—in the year 2010—Lisa will meet her first love, the British-bred Hugh Parkfield..

Initially, Lisa hates Hugh but grows to love him. Hugh brings her home to England to meet his well-heeled family and asks for her hand in marriage. Lisa accepts. She phones home to share the good news and to prepare the family for a visit, reminding Marge to make sure that Homer does not ruin anything. Sure enough, Homer's and Bart's plan to raise the British Union Jack over the house turns disastrous when the flag brushes their bug zapper and catches fire.

Although life with the Simpsons is anything but genteel, Hugh never complains. However, on their wedding day, he tells Lisa that after they are married they will never again deal with her family. Hurt by Hugh's insensitivity, Lisa hands him back the ring and calls off the wedding... The fortune teller ends her tale, explaining to Lisa that although she specializes in foretelling unsuccessful relationships, Lisa will have a true love one day.

SHOW HIGHLIGHTS

Future shock: In the future, Lisa approaches a vending machine that sells only Soy Pops. The wrappers reads, "Now with Gag Suppressant."

"Lisa, will you do me the honor of giving me your hand in the holy tradition of matrimo—" Hugh's flaming, firework-marriage proposal, which burns out before the final "ny."

"Lisa, hello! How are you doing in England? Remember, an elevator is called a 'lift,' a mile is called a 'kilometer,' and botulism is called 'steak and kidney pie.'"

Hugh's full name: Hugh St. John Alastair Parkfield.

Future Nukes: In 2010, the Springfield Nuclear Power Plant is operated primarily by robots. Carl and Lenny are in charge, and Homer works in the same spot at the same job, but Milhouse is now his supervisor.

"Homer, don't take this personally, but I've obtained a court order to prevent you from planning this wedding."

Hugh: I can't believe how much we have in common. We're both studying the environment, we're both utterly humorless about our vegetarianism, and we both love the Rolling Stones.
Lisa: Yes, not for their music, but for their tireless efforts to preserve historic buildings.

Lisa: That's the book I need. You'll probably take forever with it, too.
Hugh: I can read faster than you.
Lisa: I read at a 78th grade level.
(Hugh opens the book and throws it on the table.)
Hugh: Right here!
(They both start speed reading, their pupils darting back and forth in a blur.)
(It's much later. They're still stilling together, reading.)
Lisa: Finished this page!
Hugh: Ages ago.
(Lisa grumbles.)
Hugh: I'll get a dictionary.
Lisa: Why?
Hugh: You'll see when you get there. The word "stochastic."
Lisa: "Pertaining to a process involving a randomly-determined sequence of observations."
(They look at each other and kiss passionately. It's love.)

"You can be the first to try out the new guest bedroom I built. Remember, if the building inspector comes by, it's not a room, it's a windowbox."

Oink, oink: Homer gives Hugh the same pig bride-and-groom cufflinks to wear that his father gave him on his wedding day. Hugh is momentarily stunned.

"You know, Fox turned into a hard-core sex channel so gradually, I didn't even notice."

I WILL NOT STRUT AROUND
LIKE I OWN THE PLACE.
I WILL NOT STRUT AROUND
LIKE I OWN THE PLACE.
I WILL NOT STRUT AROUND
LIKE I OWN THE PLACE.
I WILL NOT STRUT AROUND
LIKE I OWN THE PLACE.

Hugh: Lisa, darling, don't worry. I'm sure I'll get along with your family. You've so thoroughly prepared me for the worst, as long as they're not squatting in a ditch poking berries up their noses...
Lisa: And if they are?

THE STUFF YOU MAY HAVE MISSED

There is a "Steel Wheelchair Tour 2010" Rolling Stones poster in Lisa's college dorm room.

Quimby drives his cab for the Otto Cab Co., established 2003.

In the year 2010, Kent Brockman works for CNNBCBS, a division of ABC. It's transmitted into Moe's with an huge, ultrathick "1500 (Channel) Cable."

The skeleton of a miner, a treasure chest, and an abandoned mine can be seen on the way to Martin's underground chamber beneath Springfield Elementary.

As a teen, Maggie has a motorcycle trophy as part of her messy room's decor.

Sound effects reminiscent of "The Jetsons" and "Star Trek" can be heard throughout this episode. Also, Homer's white shirt of the future resembles George Jetson's.

Movie Moment:
Lisa and Hugh meet in a library and argue over getting a book, parodying Ryan O'Neal and Ali McGraw in *Love Story*.

TWO DOZEN AND ONE GREYHOUNDS

Episode 2F18 Original Airdate: 4/9/95 Writer: Mike Scully Director: Bob Anderson

The Simpsons are concerned with Santa's Little Helper's behavior. He digs holes in the backyard, has seemingly endless energy, and disobeys commands. A pet store clerk suggests they buy new toys for the dog. On the drive home from the pet store, Santa's Little Helper jumps out of the car. The Simpsons eventually find him at the dog track mating with a female greyhound. Marge takes the new dog into their home, and not long afterwards, they have a litter of 25 puppies.

Small and playful at first, the puppies soon drive the family crazy. Despite Bart and Lisa's protests, Homer and Marge decide to give them away and put a sign in front of the house, advertising free puppies. Mr. Burns shows up wanting them all, but Marge is suspicious and refuses to give the puppies to him. With Smithers's help, Burns steals the dogs.

Bart and Lisa sneak into Burns's estate and overhear his plans to make a tuxedo out of the puppies. As they are escaping with the puppies down the laundry chute, Burns intercepts them. Aware that Burns has a particular fondness for one of the puppies, Bart and Lisa foil his attempt to separate it from the group. Burns realizes how special all the puppies are. He raises them as racing dogs and earns millions of dollars in winnings.

SHOW HIGHLIGHTS

 "Hmmm. I guess Bart's not to blame. He's lucky, too, because it's spanking season, and I got a hankering for some spankering!"

"Don't worry. As soon as they find out he doesn't have any money, they'll throw him out. Believe me. I know." Homer, as Santa's Little Helper runs off to the dog track.

 "Ah, so that's what's been wrong with the little fella. He misses casual sex."

"We sure could use a pooch to guard the flock at the Flanderosa."

"I'm sorry, kids. I don't think we're ever gonna find your greyhounds. Maybe Mr. Burns will sell you one of the 25 he got last night." Chief Wiggum, to Bart and Lisa.

A Dog's Dream:
Burns: *I know the little fellas would love romping around my many acres, chasing my many cars, drinking from my many toilets...*
Homer: *Who wouldn't?*

Lyrics to "See My Vest"
(Sung to the Tune "Be Our Guest" from *Beauty and the Beast*):
You see, some men hunt for sport,
Others hunt for food.
The only thing I'm hunting for
is an outfit that looks good.
See my vest, see my vest,
Made from real gorilla chest.
Feel this sweater, there's no better
Than authentic Irish Setter!
See this hat, 'twas my cat.
My evening wear, a vampire bat.
These white slippers are albino
African endangered rhino!
Grizzly bear underwear,
Turtles' necks, I've got my share.
Beret of poodle on my noodle it shall rest!
Try my red robin suit,
It comes one breast or two...
See my vest, see my vest, see my vest.
Like my loafers,
Former gophers,
It was that or skin my chauffeurs,
But a greyhound fur tuxedo would be best...
So let's prepare these dogs,
Kill two for matching clogs!
See my vest!
See my vest!
Oh, please, won't you see my veessssst!

Movie Moment:
The scene with all of the puppies watching TV and the episode's basic plot parody *101 Dalmatians.*

TV announcer: *Your cable TV is experiencing difficulties. Please, do not panic. Resist the temptation to read or talk to loved ones. Do not attempt sexual relations, as years of TV radiation have left your genitals withered and useless.*

THE STUFF YOU MAY HAVE MISSED

Sign: SPRINGFIELD PET SHOP "All Our Pets Are Flushable."

Sign: SPRINGFIELD DOG TRACK "Think of Them as Little Horses"

Homer puts two of the newborn puppies in a barbecue apron that reads, "Cook Those Dogs."

Mr. Burns's bathroom has a telephone, magazine rack, and a bidet, but apparently, no toilet paper.

Homer puts a sign in the front yard that reads, "Puppies for Free—Or Best Offer."

There are 26 puppies eating from doggie dishes in the kitchen rather than 25.

Marge: *All right, who broke my vase?*
Lisa: *Who took all my test papers off the refrigerator and tore them up?*
Homer: *Who spread garbage all over Flanders's yard before I got a chance to?*
Bart: *Oh, please! This is senseless destruction, with none of my usual social commentary.*

Homer: *Your mother and I have been thinking about giving the puppies away.*
Bart and Lisa: *Nooooo!*
Homer: (quickly) *...Mainly your mother.*
Lisa: *Is that what we do in this family? When someone becomes an inconvenience, we just get rid of them?* (The scene switches to Grampa sitting alone in his room, staring at the phone.)
Grampa: (picking up the phone) *Hello? Is anybody there? Oh...*

THE GOOD HUMOR MAN CAN ONLY BE PUSHED SO FAR
THE GOOD HUMOR MAN CAN ONLY BE PUSHED SO FAR
THE GOOD HUMOR MAN CAN ONLY BE PUSHED SO FAR

PET STORE MAN

Job:
Clerk at Springfield Pet Shop

Special talent:
Claims to be able to accomplish a canine/human mind meld, an incredibly rare psychic power possessed only by him and three other clerks in his store.

Ethical shortcoming:
Tends to abuse his ability to connect with dogs, using it solely to peddle such retail products as imported leather leashes, doggie contact lenses, and 200-volt shock training collars.

No advancement:
His talent has not advanced him beyond pet shop clerk because the technique only works with gullible families.

LADY, I'LL TELL YOU WHAT I'M TELLING EVERYONE ELSE. I'M SORRY IF YOUR DOG WENT BLIND, BUT YOUR GRIPE IS WITH HARTZ MOUNTAIN, NOT WITH ME.

LEOPOLD

Position:
Henchman for Superintendent Chalmers.

Height:
Hulking.

Known for:
Introducing other people.

Attitude:
Mean.

Vocal style:
Intimidating.

The kids don't know:
He's all bark and no bite.

> ALL RIGHT, YOU, LISTEN UP, YOU LITTLE FREAKS. THE FUN STOPS HERE. YOU'RE GONNA HAVE TO SHUT YOUR STINKING TRAPS AND BEHAVE, DAMMIT. THIS IS ONE SUBSTITUTE YOU'RE NOT GONNA SCREW WITH... MARGE SIMPSON.

SHOW HIGHLIGHTS

Revealed This Episode:
Jimbo lives in an elegantly decorated home and enjoys soap operas.

Moe Takes Attendance:
Moe: *All right, settle down. Anita Bath here?* (All the kids laugh even more.)
Moe: *All right, fine, fine. Ah, Maya Buttreeks?* (The kids continue to roar.)
Moe: *Hey, hey, what are you laughing at, what? Oh, oh, I get it, I get it. It's my big ears, isn't kids? Isn't it?* (breaking down) *Well, children, I can't help that.*

"All right, the battlefield is just a half-mile ahead. Begin braking procedure!" Principal Skinner, to a school bus full of kids on a field trip. Students stick their coats out the window, à la racing parachutes.

"I'm worried about the kids, Homey. Lisa's becoming very obsessive. This morning I caught her trying to dissect her own raincoat."

"Lisa, if you don't like your job you don't strike. You just go in every day and do it really half-assed. That's the American way."

"Replace teachers with super-intelligent cyborgs. Or if cyborgs aren't invented yet, use people from the neighborhood." Ned Flanders, reading from the official Springfield school district emergency plan in the event of a prolonged strike.

(Mrs. Krabappel and Principal Skinner sit across from each other in the cafeteria.)
Mrs. Krabappel: *Seymour, the teachers are fed up. You have to start putting money back into the school. You've cut back on everything: salaries, supplies, the food—I don't care what you say, I can taste the newspaper.*
Principal Skinner: *Posh. Shredded newspapers add much-needed roughage and essential inks. Besides, you didn't notice the old gym mats.*
(Lunchlady Doris pushes a gym mat into a grinder.)
Lunchlady Doris: *There's very little meat in these gym mats.*

Principal Skinner: *Five dollars a child?! Last year it was free.*
Ticket lady: *Hmm. New ownership.*
(She points to a sign that reads, "DIZ-NEE HISTORICAL PARK. Sorry, But There's Profit to Be Had.")
Skinner: *But we don't have that kind of money. In fact, no school could afford to...*
(A brand new Shelbyville Elementary double-decker bus pulls up. Students, followed by a well-dressed principal, get out of the bus and approach the ticket booth.)
Shelbyville Principal Valiant: *Here's the admission, plus, uh, something for you. See that they get a little extra education, would you?*
Ticket lady: *Yes, sir, Principal Valiant!*
Skinner: *He thinks he's so hot ever since he swept the "Princi" awards. Those things are rigged.*

Bart: *Ah, I think I got your lunch.*
(He shows Lisa a hand-written note from inside his lunch bag: "I am very proud of you. Love, Mom.")
Lisa: *Oh, yeah. I didn't think this was for me.* (She hands Bart a note: "Be good. For the love of God, please be good.")

Lisa: *There's no way I'll get into an Ivy League school now. At this rate, I probably won't even get into Vassar.*
Homer: *I've had just about enough of your Vassar-bashing, young lady!*

"Relax? I can't relax. Nor can I yield, relent, or... Only two synonyms? Oh my god! I'm losing my perspicacity!"

Hey, they're trying to learn for free!" Soldier at the Civil War battle reenactment, noting the Springfield Elementary class peering over the wall after Principal Skinner refuses to pay the admission charge.

THE STUFF YOU MAY HAVE MISSED

Video games at the Springfield Arcade: Larry the Looter, Time Waster, Razor Fight II: The Slashening, Escape from Death Row.

Signs held by striking teachers: "2+2, A Raise Is Due!" "A, is for Apple, B, is for Raise," and "Gimme! Gimme! Gimme!"

"Honk If You Love Cookies." Sign held up by Mrs. Krabappel to elicit what sounds like strike support from passing motorists.

According to his list, the substitute teachers Bart previously eliminated before Moe were Chief Wiggum, Barney, Lionel Hutz, and Gabe Kaplan.

Lisa's strike kit includes a math book, a picture of Springfield Elementary, a tape recording of Miss Hoover, and fish sticks from the cafeteria.

Principal Skinner cuts back funding for school supplies, cafeteria food, and instructor salaries. Enraged at his penny pinching, Mrs. Krabappel rallies support from her fellow teachers and warns Skinner that a strike is imminent. Taking advantage of their discord, Bart manipulates both parties, hoping to close down the school.

Bart succeeds, and the teachers go on strike. Suddenly, the students have too much free time. Lisa experiences education withdrawal symptoms. Even Bart shows signs of strange behavior. Marge sets out to reopen the school and organizes a PTA meeting. However, both sides refuse to resolve their differences. Left with little choice, the PTA replaces the striking teachers with ordinary citizens.

Marge is called on to teach Bart's class. When Jimbo and Kearney single Bart out for retaliation, Bart devises a strategy to reunite Skinner and Krabappel, trapping them in a room together and locking the door. The school reopens after Skinner and Krabappel reconcile, deciding to lease classroom closet space to overcrowded prisons in order to raise enough capital to increase teachers' salaries.

I DO NOT HAVE POWER OF ATTORNEY OVER FIRST GRADERS
I DO NOT HAVE POWER OF ATTORNEY OVER FIRST GRADERS
I DO NOT HAVE POWER OF ATTORNEY OVER FIRST GRADERS

'ROUND SPRINGFIELD

**Episode 2F32 Original Airdate: 4/30/95 Writers: Joshua Sternin & Jeffrey Ventimilia (teleplay) and Mike Reiss & Al Jean (story)
Director: Steven Dean Moore Guest Voices: Ron Taylor as Bleeding Gums Murphy, Steve Allen as Himself**

LUNCHLADY DORIS

Bart ingests a free jagged metal Krusty-O and is rushed to the hospital, where his appendix is removed. While visiting Bart, Lisa runs into Bleeding Gums Murphy, who is a patient at the hospital. Bleeding Gums recounts his career in show business and offers Lisa his prized sax to use at her upcoming jazz recital.

After the recital, Lisa learns that Bleeding Gums has passed away. Depressed, she attends the jazzman's funeral services and is angered at her discovery that no one in town really knew Bleeding Gums or his music.

Meanwhile, Lionel Hutz offers to represent Bart in a suit against Krusty-O Cereal Corporation. Bart settles for $100,000, but receives only $500 after attorney's fees. When Lisa asks a local DJ to honor Bleeding Gums with a tribute, she finds out that his lone album is very rare and costs $500. Bart buys the album for his downcast sister with his settlement. As the record plays at the low-power radio station, a bolt of lightning strikes the station's antenna, broadcasting the music throughout Springfield.

LUNCHLADY DORIS

Occupation:
Heavily lipsticked, ponytailed chief food server in the Springfield Elementary School cafeteria.

Chief preoccupation:
Getting the schoolkids the protein and iron they need in their diet on her meager budget.

Ways she adds nutrition to meals:
Stretches meat dishes with horse testicles.

Always:
Stirring something.

Major vice:
Mokes cigarettes and does not always watch where the ashes go.

Dirty secret:
Once served Jimbo Jones and Uter as entrees.

SHOW HIGHLIGHTS

Um, the guy who chopped up "George Washington?" Bart, answering the question, "Who is George Washington Carver?"

"No teacher shall be held accountable if Bart Simpson dies. We're also absolved if Milhouse gets eaten by the school snake."

"Bonjour, you cheese-eatin' surrender monkeys." Groundskeeper Willie, teaching French class due to school budget cuts.

"Whoopsie. Heh. Maybe if I fiddle with these knobs. Hey, I smell gas. Pleasant gas. Night-night gas." Dr. Nick Riviera, preparing to anesthetize Bart for surgery.

"Hello, I'm Dr. Cheeks. I'm doing my rounds and, uh, I'm a little behind." Bart, mooning Lisa and Bleeding Gums Murphy.

"This just in. Krusty the Clown staged a press conference today to defend himself against charges that his products are unsafe, his theme park is a death trap, and that he's marketing videos of Tonya Harding's wedding night."

```
NERVE GAS IS NOT A TOY
NERVE GAS IS NOT A TOY
NERVE GAS IS NOT A TOY
NERVE GAS IS NOT A TOY
NERVE GAS IS NOT A TOY
NERVE GAS IS NOT A TOY
```

"What I'm saying is, all we have to do is go down to the pound and get a new Jazzman." Homer, to Lisa after Bleeding Gums Murphy's death.

"Lady, he's putting my kids through college." A hot dog vendor, to Marge, on why he shows up wherever Homer goes.

THE STUFF YOU MAY HAVE MISSED

Attorneys Robert Chaporo and Albert Dershman (who can hold three billiard balls in his mouth at once) are parodies of trial attorneys Robert Shapiro and Alan Dershowitz.

Krusty's Percodan addiction was last mentioned in 9F07, "Mr. Plow." The addiction is yet another similarity between Krusty and Jerry Lewis.

A sign outside Springfield Elementary reads, "Tonight: School Recital, Sold Out; Tomorrow: Barbra Streisand, Tickets Still Available."

The sign underneath the KJAZZ logo reads, "152 Americans Can't Be Wrong."

Homer sports a "Starland Vocal Band" tattoo on his arm.

Bleeding Gums Murphy: *I cut my first and only album, "Sax on the Beach." But then I spent all my money on my $1500 a day habit.*
(The scene shifts to Bleeding Gums standing at the counter of a fancy department store.)
Bleeding Gums: *I'd like another Faberge egg please.*
Store clerk: *Sir, don't you think you've had enough?*
Bleeding Gums: *I'll tell you when I've had enough!*

Bleeding Gums: *I don't really have a family. All I had was a little brother who grew up to become a doctor. He used to laugh at the most inappropriate times.*
Dr. Hibbert: *Hey, I've got an older brother that I'll never see. He's a jazz musician or some such.*

Bleeding Gums Murphy on "The Cosby Show":
Cliff: *Hey, kids! Meet Grandpa Murphy!*
Rudy: *But we have three grandpas already.*
Cliff: *This one's a great jazz musician.*
Rudy: *They all are.*
Cliff: *Oh, you see, the kids, they listen to the rap music, which gives them the brain damage. With their hippin' and the hoppin' and the bippin' and the boppin', so they don't know what the jazz is all about. You see, jazz is like the Jell-O Pudding Pop. No, actually, it's more like Kodak film. No, actually jazz is like the New Coke—it'll be around forever. Heh heh heh.*

Lisa: *That was for you, Bleeding Gums.*
(The clouds in the sky gather and form the head of Bleeding Gums Murphy.)
Bleeding Gums: *You've made an old jazzman happy, Lisa.*
(Mufasa from The Lion King forms in the cloud, behind Bleeding Gums.)
Mufasa: *You must avenge my death, Kimba...dah, I mean, Simba!*
(Darth Vader appears in the cloud, behind Mufasa and Bleeding Gums.)
Darth Vader: *Luke, I am your father.*
(James Earl Jones forms beside the other three.)
James Earl Jones: *This is CNN.*
Bleeding Gums: *Will you guys pipe down? I'm saying goodbye to Lisa.*
Mufasa/Vader/Jones: *We're sorry.*

(Over the closing credits, Lisa and Bleeding Gums end their duet.)
Lisa: *One more time!*
Bleeding Gums Murphy: *Oh, come on, Lisa. I got a date with Billie Holliday.*

HOW COME YOU KIDS NEVER WANT SECONDS?

THE SPRINGFIELD CONNECTION

Episode 2F21 Original Airdate: 5/7/95 Writer: Jonathan Collier Director: Mark Kirkland

JERICHO

Identity:
Sinister criminal with an eye for counterfeit fashion.

Operates:
A bogus designer jeans ring.

Likes to:
Sample the merchandise before buying.

Weakness:
Lack of patience.

Also wears:
A medallion and a fishing hat.

THESE ARE FABULOUS!

While walking the streets of Springfield with Marge, Homer encounters a con artist playing a game of three card monte. He makes a $20 bet and loses. Marge confronts the con artist, who attempts a hasty getaway. However, Marge gives chase and knocks him out cold. Enjoying the great adrenaline rush of police work, she enlists in the Springfield Police Academy.

Soon, Marge realizes that her day-to-day job is less fulfilling than she expected. Her new career also affects her social life: people consider her a cop even when she is off duty. One day on her beat, she sees Homer parked across three handicapped spaces. She warns him to move the car, but Homer only taunts and makes fun of her. When he takes her hat, Marge slaps handcuffs on him and places him under arrest.

Homer is released from jail. Later, while playing poker with his friends at home, he discovers that Herman is running a counterfeit jeans ring out of the Simpsons' garage and threatens to expose him. Just as Herman's henchmen advance on Homer, Marge arrives and rescues him. She learns that Wiggum and his men have stolen the counterfeit jeans for themselves. Outraged at the corruption within the force, Marge resigns.

SHOW HIGHLIGHTS

"Laser effects, mirrored balls—John Williams must be rolling around in his grave." Homer, reviewing the Springfield Pops' performance of the theme to *Star Wars*.

"How dare you prey on the greedy and stupid like this?" Marge, to Snake, after he cheats Homer out of $20.

"Strange, regular ham doesn't thrill me anymore. Hmph. I'm crossing over to deviled ham."

"Marge, you being a cop makes you the man! Which makes me the woman—and I have no interest in that, besides occasionally wearing the underwear, which, as we discussed, is strictly a comfort thing."

"Wow, Mom, I never pictured you as any kind of authority figure before."

"Well, these days my roots don't stay so chestnut on their own, Officer Simpson." Moe, explaining his presence in the beauty parlor to an off-duty Marge.

"Boy, when Marge first told me she was going to the Police Academy, I thought it'd be fun and exciting, you know, like the movie *Spaceballs*. But instead, it's been painful and disturbing, like the movie *Police Academy*."

"It's too late for me, Marge! Sell the jeans and live like a queen." Homer, taken hostage.

"Years of buying pants for two active children and a full-seated husband has given me a sixth sense for shoddy stitching, which these jeans have in spades."

Homer: *Whoa, careful now. These are dangerous streets for us upper-lower-middle-class types. So avoid eye contact, watch your pocketbook, and suspect everyone.*
Snake: *Three card monte!*
Homer: *Woo hoo! Easy money!*

Chief Wiggum: *Cuff him boys, we're putting this dirtbag away.*
Snake: *Ha! I'll be back on the street in twenty-four hours.*
Wiggum: *We'll try to make it twelve.*

(Homer is spraying his eggs with something.)
Marge: *Homer, give me my pepper spray.*
Homer: *Oh, Marge, one squirt and you're south of the border.*
(Homer takes a bite of his eggs).
Homer: *Mmm...incapacitating.*

Officer Marge: *I got a report on a domestic disturbance at this address.*
Skinner: *Yes, indeed there is. There's an inflatable bath pillow that mother and I both enjoy. She claimed it was her day to use it. I maintained she was mistaken. We quarreled. Later, as I prepared to bathe, I noticed to my horror that "someone" had slashed the pillow.*

Homer: *Hey, Herman, I had to come out here to see what's so funny... (gasps) A counterfeit jeans ring operating out of my car hole! I'm going to tell everyone! Wait here.*
(Homer walks to the door.)
Herman: *(pulling a gun) Not so fast.*
Homer: *(slowing down) Okay.*
Herman: *Maybe you should just stop entirely.*
Homer: *Herman, how could you? We've all thought about counterfeiting jeans at one time or another, but what about the victims? Hard-working designers, like Calvin Klein, Gloria Vanderbilt, or Antoine Bugle Boy. These are the people who saw an overcrowded marketplace and said, "Me, too!"*

THE STUFF YOU MAY HAVE MISSED

Sign in Jebediah Springfield Park:
8:00 Medfly Spraying
8:15 Springfield Pops
8:30 Spraying: 2nd Pass

Magazines Marge peruses at the newsstand: *Sponge and Vacuum, Bear Baiter Magazine, Rock Jumper: The Magazine for People Who Like to Jump from Rock to Rock, Mosh Pitter, Danger Liker, Cliff Biker Magazine,* and *Glass Eater Magazine.*

I WILL NOT MOCK
MRS. DUMBFACE.
I WILL NOT MOCK
MRS. DUMBFACE.
I WILL NOT MOCK
MRS. DUMBFACE.

LEMON OF TROY

Episode 2F22 Original Airdate: 5/14/95 Writer: Brent Forrester Director: Jim Reardon

SHELBY

After defacing a wet segment of cement on the sidewalk, Bart receives a talk from Marge about respecting his town. Bart takes the talk to heart, and when Springfield's lemon tree is stolen by Shelbyville kids, he vows to get it back.

Bart leads an expedition of friends into Shelbyville. With a black wig and fake scar, he infiltrates the Shelbyville gang, but gets no information. Finally, the Springfield posse follows a trail of lemons to an impound lot.

Homer commandeers Flanders's RV and enlists the other fathers to find the children. When the parents and children meet up, Homer leads them to the impound lot where he demands the return of the tree. However, the lot's owner refuses and Homer's group retreats. Following Bart's Trojan Horse plan, they park the RV illegally in a hospital loading zone and are towed to impound lot. After the sun goes down, the Springfielders get out of the RV and grab the tree. Taunting the Shelbyvillians, they narrowly escape and make their way home with the lemon tree.

SHOW HIGHLIGHTS

 "Bart, you have roots in this town and you ought to show respect for it. This town is a part of us all, a part of us all, a part of us all. Sorry to repeat myself, but it'll help you remember."

"That lemon tree's a part of our town, and as kids, the backbone of our economy. We'll get it back, or choke their rivers with our dead!"

"Okay, folks. Look, I called the police captain in Shelbyville and he says he hasn't seen our kids, but if they show up in the morgue he's gonna fax us."

"Okay, here's how it goes. I'm the leader. Milhouse is my loyal sidekick. Nelson's the tough guy, Martin's the smart guy and Todd's the quiet religious guy who ends up going crazy."

"This is the darkest day in the history of Springfield. If anybody wants me, I'll be in the shower." Homer, in Flanders's RV, as they leave without having recaptured the lemon tree.

The Birth of Springfield:

Jebediah Springfield: *People, our search is over! On this site we shall build a new town where we can worship freely, govern justly, and grow vast fields of hemp for making rope and blankets.*
Shelbyville Manhattan: *Yes! And marry our cousins.*
Springfield: *I was…Who—what are you talking about, Shelbyville? Why would we want to marry our cousins?*
Shelbyville: *Because they're so attractive. H, I thought that was the whole point of this journey.*
Springfield: *Absolutely not!*
Shelbyville: *I tell you I won't live in a town that robs men of the right to marry their cousins.*
Springfield: *Well then, we'll form our own town. Who will come and live a life devoted to chastity, abstinence, and a flavorless mush I call root marm?*

Marge: *This town is a part of who you are. This is a Springfield Isotopes cap; when you wear it, you're wearing Springfield. When you eat a fish from our river, you're eating Springfield. When you make lemonade from our trees, you're drinking Springfield.*
Bart: *Mom, when you give that lecture, you're boring Springfield.*

THE STUFF YOU MAY HAVE MISSED

When we first see the lemon tree, Martin, Todd, and Database are dancing around it.

Database (of the "SuperFriends") was last seen in 2F19, "The PTA Disbands." During all the chases in this episode, he is seen consistently bringing up the rear.

A machine dispensing the *Shelbyville Daily* reads, "Once a week, every week."

The grasses in Shelbyville and Springfield are different shades of green.

Milhouse wears red shoes with his camouflage outfit.

The Shelbyvillians drink Fudd beer (introduced in 8F19, "Colonel Homer"), shop at the the Speed-E-Mart, and drink at Joe's (a tavern that looks exactly like Moe's). Their elementary school is tended by a Scottish, female groundskeeper who looks very similar to Willie.

(Marge vacuums in the living room as Bart walks out the front door, wearing a backpack.)
Marge: *Where're you going, Bart?*
Bart: *Mom, you won't believe this, but something you said the other day really got through to me. And now, I'm going to teach some kids a lesson.*
Marge: *I choose to take that literally.*
(Bart runs out.)
Bart: *(from outside) Death to Shelbyville!*
Homer: *Yes, Bart's a tutor, now. Tute on, son! Tute on!*

(Milhouse is ambushed by a blue-haired Shelbyville kid.)
Milhouse: *Is this the untimely end of Milhouse?*
Blue-haired kid: *But Milhouse is my name!*
Milhouse: *And I thought I was the only one.*
Blue-haired kid: *A pain I know all too well.*
(The two embrace.)
Milhouse: *So this is what it feels like when doves cry.*

Homer's Stand:

Homer: *That tree's been in Springfield since the time of our forefathers. Give it back, or we'll bust in there and take it!*
Tow truck man: *Bust in here and take it? You must be stupider than you look.*
Homer: *Stupider like a fox!*

(As the fathers and sons of Springfield make off with the lemon tree, Bart and Homer call back to the Tow Truck Man.)
Bart: *Eat my shorts, Shelbyville!*
Homer and Bart: *Eat my shorts!!*
Ned: *Yes, eat all of our shirts!*

THE FIRST AMENDMENT DOES NOT COVER BURPING. THE FIRST AMENDMENT IS NOT COVER BURPING. E FIRST AMENDMENT NOT COVER BURPING.

Likes:
Taunting; threatening; ordering around lackeys; acting like his father.

Residence:
Shelbyville.

Hobbies:
Skateboarding; citric horticulture.

Best friends:
Six kids and a viciously mean mongrel.

Sense of style:
Wears his baseball cap backwards.

LOOK AT THE WEAK LITTLE BABY. YOU'RE STUPID, YOU STUPID WEAK BABY.

 175

WHO SHOT MR. BURNS?

While digging a grave for a dead gerbil in the school basement, Groundskeeper Willie accidentally strikes oil. The ensuing geyser leads the townspeople to believe that the school is now rich. Mr. Burns decides that he wants to buy the oil well to protect his interests, but Principal Skinner rejects his offer.

Burns takes matters into his own hands. He erects his own derrick, which drills into the school's oil source. When Burns's well strikes the school's oil, a burst of crude destroys Bart's treehouse, injures his dog, and cheats the school out of the millions of dollars it could have made. The townspeople vow revenge against Burns.

Burns retaliates with his own diabolical scheme: to block out all the energy from the sun. The entire town is outraged, even Smithers, whom Burns fires for insubordination. Surprising the townspeople, Burns appears at a Town Hall meeting and enacts his plan, pushing a button on a remote-control device that effectively blocks out the sun's rays. As he walks happily away, he is shot in the chest by a mystery assailant.

SHOW HIGHLIGHTS

"Why is it when I heard the word 'school' and the word 'exploded,' I immediately thought of the word 'Skinner?'" Chalmers, yelling at Skinner.

"A nonprofit organization with oil? I won't allow it! An oil well doesn't belong in the hands of Betsy Bleeding Heart and Maynard G. Muskievote!"

"Hello, Lenny, Carl, Guillermo, hello, um, oh, oooh...um." Burns, in the elevator, trying to remember Homer's name, even though he wears a nametag.

"I'll get even with whoever did this to you, boy. I swear it!" Bart, to Santa's Little Helper, after he's injured by Burns's slanted oil well.

"Argh, I'll kill that Mr. Burns!! And wound that Mr. Smithers!" Groundskeeper Willie, after losing his job.

"Yeah, I'd like to settle his hash, too." Lisa, talking to Tito Puente about Mr. Burns.

"But sir, every plant and tree will die; owls will deafen us with incessant hooting; the town sundial will be useless. I don't want any part of this project. It's unconscionably fiendish." Smithers, refusing to participate in Burns's plan to block out the sun.

"Oh, you all talk big, but who here has the guts to stop me?" Burns, taunting the surly crowd at the Town Hall meeting.

"After all these years, things are finally starting to go my way. I feel like celebrating. I...oh, it's you. What are you so happy about? _(gasp)_ I see. I think you'd better drop it. I said drop it! Get your hands off!" Burns's last words, before he is shot.

> **Skinner:** _Mr. Burns, it was naive of you to think I would mistake this town's most prominent 104-year-old man for one of my elementary-school students._
> **Burns:** _I want that oil well! I've got a monopoly to maintain. I own the electric company and the waterworks, plus the hotel on Baltic Avenue!_
> **Skinner:** _That hotel's a dump and your monopoly is pathetic! The school's oil well is not for sale, particularly to a blackhearted scoundrel like yourself!_

> **Barney:** _These fumes aren't as fun as beer. Sure, I'm all dizzy and nauseous, but where's the inflated sense of self-esteem?_
> _(One of the barflies passes out.)_
> **Moe:** _Hey! If you guys are getting loaded off them fumes, I'm gonna have to charge ya._

THIS IS NOT A CLUE
...OR IS IT?
THIS IS NOT A CLUE
...OR IS IT?
THIS IS NOT A CLUE
...OR IS IT?

> _(Burns watches construction of the oil well through binoculars.)_
> **Mr. Burns:** _That's it. Frimble about with your widgets and doobobs. It'll all be a monument to futility when my plan comes to fruition._
> **Smithers:** _Sir, uh, what I'm about to say violates every sycophantic urge in my body, but: I wish you would reconsider. This isn't a rival company you're battling with, it's a school—people won't stand for it._
> **Mr. Burns:** _Pish-posh. It will be like taking candy from a baby._
> _(Through the binoculars, Burns sees a baby sitting in a sandbox, licking a lollypop.)_
> **Burns:** _Say, that sounds like a larf—let's try it right now!_

> **EPA Man:** _All right, everybody out! As long as Burns is pumping oil, this bar is closed!_
> **Moe:** _Damn Burns! Let me just get one thing!_
> _(Moe grabs his shotgun.)_
> **Barney:** _Me too!_
> _(Barney pulls out a small handgun.)_

> Mr. Burns at the Town Hall Meeting:
> **Captain McCallister:** _Aahrr! Burns, your scurvy schemes will earn ye a one-way passage to the boneyard!_
> **Ned:** _I'd like to hear from Sideshow Mel._
> **Sideshow Mel:** _I'll see to it that Mr. Burns suffers the infernal machinations of hell's grim tyrant!_
> **Otto:** _Yeah!_

THE STUFF YOU MAY HAVE MISSED

Burns reads the _Springfield Shopper_ headline, "Awful School Is Awful Rich."

A sign in town reads, "BURNS CONSTRUCTION CO.—Building a Better Future...for Him."

There are numerous references to 3:00: When Bart writes his punishment, the clock on the wall reads 3:00; the TV set in Moe's Tavern advertises "Pardon My Zinger," airing weekdays at 3:00; Burns refers to the 3:00 sunset; when Burns falls onto the sundial, the clock tower rings three times.

Another _Springfield Shopper_ headline reads: "BURNS PLANS SUNSHINE HALT— Special Section: Your Guide to Perpetual Darkness."

A picture of the Springfield Nuclear Power Plant hangs in the Simpsons' living room.

The TV at Moe's is tuned to "Mystery Science Theater 3000."

Mr. Burns's arms reach toward the compass points "S" and "W" when he falls onto the town square sundial.

(PART ONE)

Episode 2F16
Original Airdate: 5/21/95
Writers: Bill Oakley & Josh Weinstein
Director: Jeffrey Lynch
Guest Voice: Tito Puente as Himself

MAIN SUSPECTS

Groundskeeper Willie:
Burns cost him his job at Springfield Elementary.

Moe:
Burns made him lose his bar.

Grampa:
Burns destroyed his room at the Springfield Retirement Castle.

Barney:
Burns caused him to lose Moe's bar.

Lisa:
Burns robbed her school of music.

Principal Skinner:
Burns robbed the school of financial security.

Tito Puente:
Burns robbed the school of him.

Homer:
Burns can't remember his name.

Bart:
Burns disabled Santa's Little Helper.

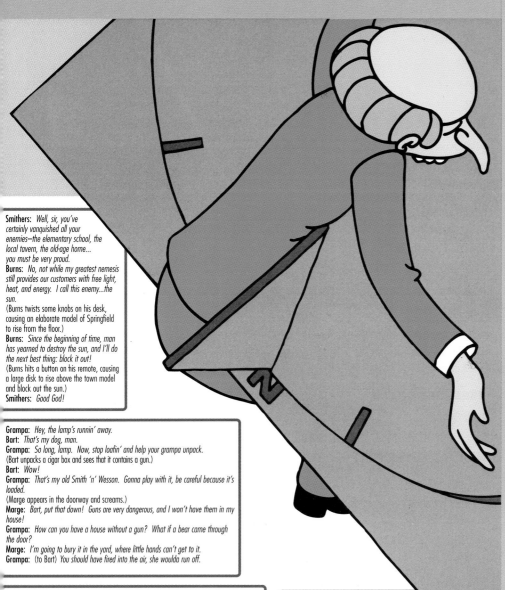

Smithers: *Well, sir, you've certainly vanquished all your enemies—the elementary school, the local tavern, the old-age home... you must be very proud.*
Burns: *No, not while my greatest nemesis still provides our customers with free light, heat, and energy. I call this enemy...the sun.*
(Burns twists some knobs on his desk, causing an elaborate model of Springfield to rise from the floor.)
Burns: *Since the beginning of time, man has yearned to destroy the sun, and I'll do the next best thing: block it out!*
(Burns hits a button on his remote, causing a large disk to rise above the town model and block out the sun.)
Smithers: *Good God!*

Grampa: *Hey, the lamp's runnin' away.*
Bart: *That's my dog, man.*
Grampa: *So long, lamp. Now, stop loafin' and help your grampa unpack.*
(Bart unpacks a cigar box and sees that it contains a gun.)
Bart: *Wow!*
Grampa: *That's my old Smith 'n' Wesson. Gonna play with it, be careful because it's loaded.*
(Marge appears in the doorway and screams.)
Marge: *Bart, put that down! Guns are very dangerous, and I won't have them in my house!*
Grampa: *How can you have a house without a gun? What if a bear came through the door?*
Marge: *I'm going to bury it in the yard, where little hands can't get to it.*
Grampa: *(to Bart) You should have fired into the air, she woulda run off.*

I Am Homer Simpson:

Burns: *Who the devil are you?*
Homer: *(charging at Burns) Homer Simpson!*
Burns: *What?*
Homer: *(fast) Homer Simpson!*
Burns: *What are you talking about?*
Homer: *Homer Simpson.*
Burns: *Talk clearly, make sense, man!*
Homer: *Shut up! Homer Simpson!*
Burns: *I can't understand a word you're saying.*
Homer: *My name is Homer Simpson!*
Burns: *You're just babbling incoherently...*
Homer: *(guards drag him off) Oh, you're a dead man, Burns. Oh, you're dead! You're dead, Burns!*

Patty: *Mr. Burns has been shot.*
Wiggum: *Just a minute! This isn't Mr. Burns at all! It's a mask!*
(Wiggum pulls at Burns's face.)
Wiggum: *Wait, it is Burns. Heh, his wrinkly skin luh-looks like a mask.*
Marge: *I don't think we'll ever know who did this. Everyone in town is a suspect.*
(The townspeople eye each other suspiciously. Hibbert laughs.)
Hibbert: *Well, I couldn't possibly solve this mystery. Can you?*
(Hibbert points directly at the camera; it turns out that he is actually pointing at Wiggum.)
Wiggum: *Yeah, I'll give it a shot. I mean, you know, it's my job, right?*

WANTED
FOR QUESTIONING IN CONNECTION WITH THE SHOOTING OF MONTGOMERY BURNS

HOMER J. SIMPSON

WANTED
FOR QUESTIONING IN CONNECTION WITH THE SHOOTING OF MONTGOMERY BURNS

HERSCHEL SHMOIKEL KRUSTOFSKY

WANTED
FOR QUESTIONING IN CONNECTION WITH THE SHOOTING OF MONTGOMERY BURNS

SEYMOUR SKINNER

WHO DOES WHAT VOICE

DAN CASTELLANETA

Homer J. Simpson

Grampa Simpson

Santa's Little Helper

Barney Gumble

Krusty the Clown

Groundskeeper Willie

Mayor Quimby

Hans Moleman

Sideshow Mel

Itchy

Arnie Pie

Kodos

Scott Christian

Louie

Bill

Ugolin (7G13)

Cpt. Lance Murdock (7F06)

Thomas Jefferson (8F01)

Aristotle Amandopolis (8F13)

Zombie Shakespeare (9F04)

Human Fly (9F21)

Gary (1F02)

Gremlin (1F04)

Actor Homer (1F16)

Actor Lisa (1F16)

Freddy Quimby (1F19)

Leopold (2F19)

Luigi (3F10)

George Washington (3F13)

Etch (3F19)

Kearney's Father (4F03)

Poochie (4F12)

Laddie (4F16)

JULIE KAVNER

Marge Simpson

Patty

Selma

Jacqueline Bouvier

Aunt Gladys

YEARDLEY SMITH

Lisa Simpson

NANCY CARTWRIGHT

Bart Simpson

Nelson

Todd Flanders

Ralph Wiggum

Kearney

Database (2F11)

Jimmy (3F03)

HANK AZARIA

Apu

Moe

Chief Wiggum

Comic Book Guy

Lou

Carl

Dr. Nick Riviera

Snake

Kirk Van Houten

Captain McCallister

Bumblebee Man

Superintendent Chalmers

Professor Frink

Cletus

Legs

Akira

Drederick Tatum

Bob Arnold (8F01)

Fritz (8F09)

Vet (8F17)

House of Evil Shopkeeper (9F04)

Gabbo (9F19)

Doug (1F02)

Dean Bobby Peterson (1F02)

Brad Goodman (1F05)

G.I. Joe (1F12)

Knightboat (2F10)

Don Vittorio (2F12)

Bruno Drundridge (2F13)

Pet Store Man (2F18)

Jericho (2F21)

Shelbyville Milhouse (2F22)

Iggy Wiggum (3F19)

Ox (3F19)

Rick (3F22)

Jimbo's Father (4F03)

Dr. Foster (4F07)

Ranger (4F10)

Hippie (4F17)

Frank Grimes (4F19)

HARRY SHEARER

C. Montgomery Burns
Smithers
Ned Flanders
Principal Skinner
Otto
Reverend Lovejoy
Dr. Julius Hibbert
Kent Brockman
Jasper
Lenny
Eddie
Ranier Wolfcastle/McBain
Scratchy
Mr. Bouvier
Kang
Dr. Marvin Monroe
Herman
Mr. Largo
Marty
Dave Shutton
Jebediah Springfield
Dr. J. Loren Pryor (7G02)
Cesar (7G13)

Bad Dream House (7F04)
Smilin' Joe Fission (7G03)
Hans (8F09)
Woodrow (8F16)
Nixon (9F18)
Nigel (9F21)
Ben (1F02)
Kwik-E-Mart CEO (1F10)
Birch Barlow (2F02)
Godfrey Jones (2F06)
George Bush (3F09)
Sheldon Skinner (3F19)
Dolph's Father (4F03)

MARCIA WALLACE

Edna Krabappel

RUSSI TAYLOR

Martin Prince
Uter
Sherri
Terri
Lewis
Wendell

PAMELA HAYDEN

Milhouse
Rod Flanders
Janey Powell
Dolph
Maria Dominguez (8F01)
Ms. Pennycandy (8F05)
Tattoo Annie (9F20)
Malibu Stacy (1F12)
Actor Marge (1F16)
Ashley Grant (2F06)
Ham (2F11)
Tobias Drundridge (2F13)
Susan (3F11)
Cypress Creek Milhouse (3F23)
"Lisa" (4F20)

TRESS MACNEILLE

Jimbo
Dolph
Sunday School Teacher
Brandine
Agnes Skinner
Adil Hoxha (7G13)
Millicent (8F06)

Shelby (2F22)
Pepi (9F12)
Phillips (9F20)
Nana Van Houten (3F02)
Gavin (3F07)
Barbara Bush (3F09)
Evelyne Peters (3F11)
Lester (3F16)
Dean (3F22)
Belle (4F06)

MAGGIE ROSWELL

Maude Flanders
Helen Lovejoy
Miss Hoover
Mrs. Van Houten
Princess Kashmir
Mary Bailey
Barbara Bush (8F01)
Shary Bobbins (3G03)

DORIS GRAU

Lunchlady Doris
Lurleen Lumpkin (9F10)

179

DOCTOR COLOSSUS

Role:
Master of cartoon supervillainy.

Accent:
Germanic.

Demeanor:
Arrogant, but easily humbled.

His greatest advantage and disadvantage:
His amazing Colosso-boots.

BAH! HE WAS A RANK AMATEUR COMPARED TO DOCTOR COLOSSUS! OH-HAH-HAH-HAH!

WHO SHOT MR.

Smithers awakens one morning with a severe hangover. He recalls the events leading up to Mr. Burns's shooting outside Town Hall and concludes that while he was drunk, he pulled the trigger. Wracked with guilt, Smithers confesses to a priest. The confession booth turns out to be a police trap, and Smithers is taken into custody.

Shortly thereafter, Smithers remembers that he was home watching TV when the shooting occurred and therefore is innocent. The police release him. Meanwhile, Lisa approaches Chief Wiggum with a list of possible suspects. The police search Homer's car and discover a gun covered with his fingerprints. Homer becomes a chief suspect. When Burns regains consciousness, he utters Homer's name, prompting his arrest.

The paddy wagon transporting Homer to jail overturns and Homer escapes. He sneaks into the hospital and, in a demented rage, advances on Burns. Just then, Lisa races in to announce that she has solved the mystery. However, Mr. Burns, now coherent, reveals the truth: after a struggle over candy in the Town Hall parking lot, his gun fell into Maggie's hands and discharged.

SHOW HIGHLIGHTS

"Speedway Squad!": Smithers's imagined 1965 TV show, in which he and Mr. Burns play detectives on the hot-rod circuit.

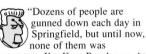 "Dozens of people are gunned down each day in Springfield, but until now, none of them was important. I'm Kent Brockman. At 3 p.m. Friday, local autocrat C. Montgomery Burns was shot following a tense confrontation at Town Hall. Burns was rushed to a nearby hospital where he was pronounced dead. He was then transferred to a better hospital where doctors upgraded his condition to 'alive.'"

"Kids, kids, kids. As far as Daddy's concerned, you're both potential murderers."

Innocent: Sideshow Mel points out that Smithers could not possibly have shot Mr. Burns because he was home at 3 o'clock watching his favorite TV show, "Pardon My Zinger." What Smithers is guilty of is shooting Jasper in his wooden leg (the left one).

Agatha Christie's *Ten Trite Tales*: Chief Wiggum's crime-solving reference guide.

 "When I took your father's name, I took everything that came with it, including DNA."

"If you've ever handled a penny, the government's got your DNA."

BURNS? (PART TWO)

Episode 2F20 Original Airdate: 5/17/95
Writers: Bill Oakley & Josh Weinstein
Director: Wes Archer
Executive Producers: Bill Oakley and Josh Weinstein
Guest Voices: Tito Puente as Himself, Tito Puente
and his Latin Jazz Ensemble as Itself

I WILL NOT COMPLAIN ABOUT
THE SOLUTION WHEN I HEAR IT
I WILL NOT COMPLAIN ABOUT
THE SOLUTION WHEN I HEAR IT
I WILL NOT COMPLAIN ABOUT
THE SOLUTION WHEN I HEAR IT

Why do you think they keep them in circulation?" DNA expert, to Chief Wiggum.

Police-file photo: A beaten-up Homer wears a "Haig in '88" T-shirt.

 "We all got to stick together if we're going to have any hope of bringing that awful Homer to justice."

 "Be careful when we capture him! We cannot claim the reward unless we have 51% of the carcass."

"Gee, I hope all the suspects are this much fun." Chief Wiggum, after interviewing Tito Puente.

"The one who shot me was... Maggie Simpson!" Burns, revealing the mystery assailant.

Smithers: *Father, I'm not a Catholic, but...well, I tried to march in the St. Patrick's Day Parade. But, anyway, I've got a...rather large sin to confess. (sniffles) I'm the one who, who... shot Mr. Burns!*
Chief Wiggum: *(opening confessional window) That's all I needed to hear. Boy, this thing works great.*

Chief Wiggum: *Hey, what about that jazz teacher that got laid off? You know, uh, Mr. Samba? Señor Mambo, what was it?*
Lisa: *Tito Puente?*
Chief Wiggum: *Yeah.*
Lisa: *Well, he did vow revenge, heh-heh. But I can't see him doing something illegal. He's in show business. He's a celebri–*
Chief Wiggum: *Let's roll, boys.*

Doctor Colossus Is Freed:

Wiggum: *All right, Colossus, you're free to go, but stay away from Death Mountain.*
Doctor Colossus: *But all my stuff is there.*

THE STUFF YOU MAY HAVE MISSED

Smithers's Scotch: "Vagrant's Choice Fortified Scotch—May Cause Ejection of Stomach Contents."

Church Sign: "Cathedral of the Downtown—Archbishop Carries Less Than $20."

Tito Puente is questioned at Chez Guevara, named after the Argentinean revolutionary.

"El Barto" graffiti appears on the front steps of the police station.

When Lisa says, "I don't think anyone in this family is capable of attempted murder," Maggie wakes up and eyes Snowball II.

Lisa's Suspects Poster:
"Moe—Lost His Bar"
"Barney—Lost Moe's Bar"
"Principal Skinner—Lost His Oil Well"
"Groundskeeper Willie—No Crystal Slop Bucket."

Mr. Burns's room number at the hospital is 2F20, the same as the episode's production code.

Some names in the DNA Computer: Burns, Smithers, Flanders, Szyslak, Oakley, Nahasapeemapetilan, Hutz, Wolfcastle, Kompowski, Nixon, Puente, Prince, Moleman, Brokaw, McCartney, Starr, Harrison, Weinstein, Frink, Lovejoy, Reiss, Quimby, Krustofski, Terwilliger, Simpson, Hapablap, Borgnine, Murphy.

Movie Moments:

Groundskeeper Willie's interrogation while he wears a kilt recalls Sharon Stone's in *Basic Instinct*.

Homer's escape at the Krustyburger drive-thru parodies *The Fugitive*.

(Lou and Eddie interrogate Moe while he's hooked up to the lie detector.)
Eddie: *Did you hold a grudge against Montgomery Burns?*
Moe: *No! (piercing buzz) All right, maybe I did. But I didn't shoot him. (pleasant ding)*
Eddie: *Checks out. Okay, sir, you're free to go.*
Moe: *Good, 'cause I got a hot date tonight. (buzz) A date. (buzz) Dinner with friends. (buzz) Dinner alone. (buzz) Watching TV alone. (buzz) All right! I'm going to sit at home and ogle the ladies in the Victoria's Secret catalog. (buzz) (ashamed) Sears catalog. (ding) Now would you unhook this already please?! I don't deserve this kind of shabby treatment! (buzz)*

Chief Wiggum: *This bullet matches the one we took out of Burns. Homer Simpson, you're under arrest for attempted murder.*
Homer: *D'oh!*
Chief Wiggum: *Yeah, that's what they all say. They all say "D'oh."*

Kent Brockman: *How does it feel to be accused of the attempted murder of your boss and mentor?*
Smithers: *Kent, I... I feel about as low as Madonna when she found out she missed Tailhook.*

Classic TV Moments:

Chief Wiggum's cream-induced, backward-talking dream is inspired by "Twin Peaks." "Dallas" is honored twice with the 1979 "Who Shot J.R.?" cliffhanger and the season-erasing "shower scene" during the 1986 premiere.

Marge: *Well, I'm just relieved that Homer's safe and that you've recovered and that we can all get back to normal. If Maggie could talk, I'm sure she'd apologize for shooting you.*
Mr. Burns: *I'm afraid that's insufficient. Officer, arrest the baby!*
Chief Wiggum: *Ha. Yeah right, pops. No jury in the world's going to convict a baby. Uhm, maybe Texas.*

Tito Puente's "Slanderous Mambo":

Wounds won't last long/But an insulting song/Burns will always carry with him./So I'll settle my score/on the salsa floor/with this vengeful Latin rhythm!/Burns!/Con el corazon de perro/Señor Burns!/El diablo con dinero!/ It may not surprise you/but all of us despise you./Please die and fry/in hell/you rotten/rich/old wretch!/Adios viejo!

RADIOACTIVE MAN

Episode 2F17 Original Airdate: 9/24/95 Writer: John Swartzwelder Director: Susie Dietter Guest Voice: Mickey Rooney as Himself

Occupation:
Overpaid portrayer of action hero, McBain.

Country of origin:
Someplace where they speak German.

Biggest theatrical stretch:
Playing Radioactive Man.

Turn-offs:
Nerds; being washed away in a tide of sulfuric acid.

Biggest mystery:
How an obvious teutonophone can get away with playing an Irishman.

Drives:
A Humvee.

UP AND AT THEM.

SHOW HIGHLIGHTS

On the Set:
Milhouse: *Uh, these aren't real X-rays, are they?*
Director: *Good question. We'll check into that. Okay, X-ray machine to full power and … Action!*

Bart: *George Burns was right. Show business is a hideous bitch goddess.*
Lisa: *Cheer up, Bart. Milhouse is still going to need a true friend, someone to tell him he's great. Someone to rub lotion on him. Someone he can hurl whiskey bottles at when he's feeling low.*
Bart: *You're right, Lis. I can suck up to him, like the religious suck up to God.*

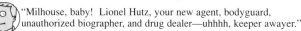
"Milhouse, baby! Lionel Hutz, your new agent, bodyguard, unauthorized biographer, and drug dealer—uhhhh, keeper awayer."

"OK, listen up, everybody: this is the hardest, most expensive scene in the movie, and we only get one shot at it, so we have to do it right. Fallout Boy will untie Radioactive Man and pull him to safety, moments before he's hit with a forty-foot wall of sulfuric acid that will horribly burn everything in its path. Now that's real acid, so I want to see goggles, people." The director, explaining the million-dollar scene.

"But Milhouse, they haven't cured anything! Heart disease and world hunger are still rampant. Those do-gooders are all a bunch of pitiful losers. Every last one of them. Want results? You have to go to the Schwarzeneggers, the Stallones, and, to a lesser extent, the Van Dammes."

Older executive: *I don't see why Rainier Wolfcastle should be the star. I think we should bring back Dirk Richter. Kids will wanna see the original Radioactive Man.*
Producer: *I keep telling you. He's 73 years old and he's DEAD.*

(Visiting the set, Homer encounters three burly guys leaning against a truck.)
Homer: *You guys work on the movie?*
Teamster: *You saying we're not working?*
Homer: *Oh, I always wanted to be a teamster. So lazy and surly. Mind if I relax with you?*

"All right. This place must be hot. They don't need a big ad or even correct spelling." One of the producers, after seeing a tiny "FLIM SPRINGFIELD" ad in *Variety.*

Revealed this episode: Moe tells Barney how he was one of the original Little Rascals until he killed the original Alfalfa for stealing his car-exhaust-in-the-face bit.

"'Congratulations, Bart Simpson, you're our new Fallout Boy.' That's what I'd be saying to you if you weren't an inch too short. Next." *Radioactive Man* director, breaking Bart's heart.

Director: *We've got to do the "jiminy jillikers" scene again, Milhouse.*
Milhouse: *But we already did it. It took seven hours, but we did it. It's done.*
Director: *Yes! But we got to do it from different angles. Again and again and again and again and again.*

Platforms, Chihuahua, Vertical-Striped Suit:
What Bart uses in an attempt to appear taller to get the role of Fallout Boy.

THE STUFF YOU MAY HAVE MISSED

Doug, one of the nerds from 1F02, "Homer Goes to College," is part of the chain of internet geeks that relay the Radioactive Man casting information.

"BORT!", "POO!", "MINT!", "NEWT!", "ZAK!", "SNUH!", "PAN!", "ZUFF!" Various sound effects of the campy 70s Radioactive Man series. "Bort" was a name on a novelty license plate in 2F01, "Itchy & Scratchy Land" and "Snuh" was an acronym for an organization Marge founded, "Springfieldians for Niceness, Understanding, and Helping" in 7F09, "Itchy & Scratchy & Marge."

The comics in the rack at the Android's Dungeon include "Cat Girl," "Batboy," "Birdguy," "Mr. Smarty Pants," "Dog Kid," "Snake Kid," "Batchick," "Tree Man," "Mr. Hop," "Nick," "Radiation Dude," The Human Bee," "Iguana Girl," "Mister Amazing," "Power Person," and "Star Dog."

Hollywood producers choose Springfield as the location for their big-budget feature film, *Radioactive Man*, based on the popular comic book series, with Rainier Wolfcastle, star of the popular McBain films, in the title role. They hold local auditions for Radioactive Man's trusted sidekick, Fallout Boy. Bart gives a brilliant reading, but loses the part to Milhouse because he is too short.

Springfield Shopper
MILHOUSE DISAPPEARS!
Movie On Hold

As film production begins, city officials and local retailers greet the production crew with outrageously expensive permit fees and overpriced merchandise. Milhouse runs away when the pressure of publicity and demands on him escalate. A manhunt is organized.

Bart finds Milhouse hiding in his treehouse. Milhouse insists that stardom is hollow and meaningless. Despite Mickey Rooney's attempts to convince him to return to the film, Milhouse refuses to go back to work. Without their co-star, and already over-budget, the production company shuts down.

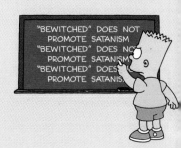

"BEWITCHED" DOES NOT PROMOTE SATANISM

BART SELLS HIS SOUL

Episode 3F02 Original Airdate: 10/8/95 Writer: Greg Daniels Director: Wesley Archer

To prove that there is no such thing as a soul, Bart sells his to Milhouse for 5.00. Shortly afterwards, Bart's pets act hostile to him and he thinks that Itchy & Scratchy are no longer funny. After witnessing the changes in Bart, Lisa suspects that he really did lose his soul.

Bart tries to buy back his soul from Milhouse, but Milhouse wants $50 for it. At the grand opening of Moe's new family style restaurant, Lisa taunts Bart with a prayer before dinner. Bart jumps up and leaves the restaurant to make one last attempt to reclaim his soul.

Bart tracks down Milhouse at his grandmother's house, where he learns that Milhouse traded his soul for Alf pogs at the Android's Dungeon. Bart camps outside the comic book store only to find out that the dealer sold his soul to someone else. As Bart prays for his soul, Lisa hands it back to him, having bought it from the comic book dealer the night before.

NANA VAN HOUTEN

Residence:
A one bedroom apartment on 257th Street.

Family:
Son, Kirk; daughter-in-law, Luanne; grandson, Milhouse.

Talent:
Can rouse herself at the blink of an eye to answer the door in the middle of the night.

Moved By:
The fact her family comes to visit her since she is too old to eat at Uncle Moe's.

SHOW HIGHLIGHTS

"In the Garden of Eden": The disguised rock anthem, "In-A-Gadda-Da-Vida," which Bart distributes as a hymn at church.

"Soul? Come on, Milhouse, there's no such thing as a soul! It's just something they made up to scare kids, like the Boogie Man or Michael Jackson!"

"Way to breathe, no-breath." Jimbo, commenting on Bart's inability to fog up the glass on the ice cream freezer at the Kwik-E-Mart.

"Well, whether or not the soul is real, Bart, it's the symbol of everything that is fine inside us."

"An alligator with sunglasses? Now I've seen everything!" Marge, seeing all the knick-knacks covering the walls of "Uncle Moe's Family Feedbag."

Milhouse: It's kinda in here. (pointing to his chest) And when you sneeze, that's your soul trying to escape. Saying "God bless you" crams it back in. And when you die, it squirms out and flies away.
Bart: Uh-huh, what if you die in a submarine at the bottom of the ocean?
Milhouse: Oh, it can swim. It's even got wheels in case you die in the desert and it has to drive to the cemetery.
Bart: How can someone with glasses so thick be so stupid? Listen. You don't have a soul, I don't have a soul, there's no such thing as a soul!
Milhouse: Fine. If you're so sure about that, why don't you sell your soul to me?
Bart: How much you got?
Milhouse: Five bucks.
Bart: Deal.

"If you like good food, good fun, and a whole lotta crazy crap on the walls, then come on down to 'Uncle Moe's Family Feedbag.' Now that's "Moe" like it. So bring the whole family—mom, dad, kids. Uh, no old people. They're not covered by our insurance. It's fun! And remember our guarantee: If I'm not smiling when your check comes, your meal's on me, Uncle Moe."

"Oh, dude, you did not smile. We eat for free. Come on Shoshana, let's roll." Snake, holding Moe to his promise.

Little Girl: My sodie is too cold—my teef hurt.
Moe: Aw, your "teef" hurt, huh? Your "teef" hurt? Well, that's too freakin' bad! Ya hear me? I'll tell you where you can put your freakin' "sodie," too!

Reverend Lovejoy: I know one of you is responsible for this. So repeat after me: If I withhold the truth, may I go straight to hell, where I will eat naught but burning hot coals and drink naught but burning hot cola...
Ralph: (scared) ...where fiery demons will punch me in the back...
Bart: (nonchalant) ...where my soul will be chopped into confetti and strewn upon a parade of murderers and single mothers...
Milhouse: (nervous) ... where my tongue will be torn out by ravenous birds...
(A crow outside the window stares at Milhouse.)
Milhouse: Bart did it! That Bart right there!

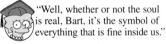

I AM NOT A LEAN MEAN
SPITTING MACHINE.
I AM NOT A LEAN MEAN
SPITTING MACHINE.
I AM NOT A LEAN MEAN
SPITTING MACHINE.

Homer's Name Suggestions for Moe's New Restaurant:
"Chairman Moe's Magic Wok" and "Madman Moe's Pressure Cooker."

Bart: Lisa! You bought this?
Lisa: With the change in my piggy bank.
Bart: There's no change in your piggy bank.
Lisa: Not in any of the ones you know about.
Bart: Oh, Lisa, thank you.

Moe: Everybody is going to family restaurants these days, seems nobody wants to hang out in a dank pit no more.
Carl: You ain't think of gettin' rid of the dank, are you Moe?
Moe: Ah, maybe I am.
Carl: Oh, but Moe, the dank! The dank!
Moe: Yeah, family restaurants—that's where the big bucks are. I could turn this joint into a place where you wouldn't be ashamed to bring your family!

THE STUFF YOU MAY HAVE MISSED

The sign outside the Springfield Church reads, "No Shirt No Shoes No Salvation."

The deep fryer Moe buys is labeled, "USS Missouri" with the designation, "C Deck Mess."

Some of the family restaurants of the greater Springfield area: The Spaghetti Laboratory, FaceStuffers, Professor V.J. Cornucopia's Fantastic Foodmagorium and Great American Steakery, and The Texas Cheescake Depository.

One of the specials on Moe's board is "Ranchy Wingy Things."

When Chief Wiggum shines his flashlight at Bart, Bart's pupils become catlike.

A CALLER AT THIS HOUR? YOU DIAL 9–1, THEN WHEN I SAY SO, DIAL 1 AGAIN.

HOME SWEET HOMEDIDDLY-DUM-DOODILY

Episode 3F01 Original Airdate: 10/1/95 Writer: Jon Vitti Director: Susie Dietter Guest Voice: Joan Kenley as Phone Voice

SEYMOUR, DO YOU WANT ME TO TELL YOU WHEN IT'S SEVEN O'CLOCK?

Homer surprises Marge with tickets for a three-hour visit to a health spa, arranging for Grampa to watch the kids. While they are gone, Bart is found to have head lice at school, and after bullies steal her shoes and she's hit on the head with a soccer ball, it appears that Lisa is a victim of neglect. Principal Skinner calls the county welfare office and the kids are put in foster care at the Flanders's home.

Horrified at the thought of letting the Flanders raise their children, Marge and Homer plead their case in court. The judge orders them to complete a class in child rearing in order to get the children back.

When Ned finds out that none of the Simpson children have been baptized, he rushes them to the Springfield River, intending to baptize them himself. Homer learns of Flanders's plans just as he and Marge complete their class. Rushing to the river, they stop Bart, Lisa, and Maggie from being baptized. The family is reunited.

SHOW HIGHLIGHTS

Bully Girls: *You have cooties! You have cooties!*
Lisa: *No I don't!*
Skinner: (over P.A.) *Lisa Simpson, report to the principal's office for head lice inspection.*

Welfare Board assessment of the Simpson house: Sink full of dirty dishes. Trash not taken out. Living room a mess, stacks of old newspapers from twenty years ago. A disheveled and malnourished man found sleeping in his own filth, seems confused and dehydrated. Baby drinking from dog dish, wearing a sign indicating she is a "stupid baby."

Toilet paper hung in improper overhand fashion. Dogs mating on dining room table.

 "The only thing I'm high on is love. Love for my son and daughters. Yes, a little LSD is all I need."

 "Come on, honey. You work yourself stupid for this family. If anyone deserves to be wrapped up in seaweed and buried in mud, it's you."

Welfare agent to Lisa, after a baby tooth falls from her mouth: "Don't you worry, little girl. We'll get you some nice county dentures."

Bart: *Wow, Dad, you took a baptismal for me. How do you feel?*
Homer: *Oh, Bartholomew, I feel like St. Augustine of Hippo after his conversion by Ambrose of Milan.*
Flanders: *Wait, Homer. What did you just say?*
Homer: *I said shut your ugly face, Flanders!*

"Sweet Georgia Brown! Something is rotten at the Simpson house."

"Gone Baptizin'": Sign Homer and Marge read on the Flanders's front door.

"Heydilly-ho! Welcome to your new home, neglect-areenos!"

Krabappel: *Ahh! Lice?! How on earth does a boy get head lice in this day and age?*
(We flashback to Bart with a screeching monkey crawling around his head, sitting on the couch with Milhouse next to a wicker basket.)
Milhouse: *We bought a wicker basket from Pier One, and he was passed out inside!*
(The flashback ends.)
Bart: *Hey, how come I get lice and nothing happens to Milhouse.*
(Milhouse has a pallid complexion, his eyes are half-open, and he shivers as he holds himself.)
Milhouse: *So c-cold, so very, very cold...*

Homer: *Okay, okay, don't panic. To find Flanders, I just have to think like Flanders!*
Homer's Brain: *I'm a big four-eyed lame-o and I wear the same stupid sweater everyday, and—*
Homer: *The Springfield River!*

The Flanders House:
Bart: *Oh, I hate this place.*
Lisa: *Yeah. It seems like our house, but everything's got a creepy Pat Boone-ish quality to it.*
(Flanders enters holding a tray.)
Ned: *Hey, kids! Nachos, Flanders style. That's cucumbers with cottage cheese.*

Job Poorly Done:
Homer: *We leave you the kids for three hours and the county takes them away?!*
Grampa: *Oh, bitch, bitch, bitch.*

THE STUFF YOU MAY HAVE MISSED

A statue of writer/producer John Swartzwelder stands outside the courthouse.

Headlines on the old newspapers Marge gives Lisa include: "America Loves Ted Kennedy" and "40 Trampled at Poco Concert."

The state seal of the state that Springfield is in, last featured in 8F01, "Mr. Lisa Goes to Washington," is shown.

The child welfare "ambulance" runs over a tricycle on its way to the Simpsons' house.

Homer becomes shiny in the sauna.

Playing the Game "Bombardment" with Bible Questions:

Flanders: *No, son, we've got to let Bart and Lisa get one. C'mon, this one's easy.*
Lisa: *We give up.*
Flanders: *Well, guess! Book of Revelations... Fire-breathing lion's head... tail made out of snakes... Who else is it gonna be?*
Bart: (unsure) *Jesus?*
Flanders: *Jes— Jes— Don't you kids know anything? The serpent of Rehaboam? The Well of Zohossadar? The bridal feast of Beth Chadruharazzeb?*
Maude: *Why, that's the kind of thing you should start learning at baptism.*
Lisa: *Uh, actually, you see... We were never baptized.*

NO ONE WANTS TO HEAR FROM MY ARMPITS
NO ONE WANTS TO HEAR FROM MY ARMPITS
NO ONE WANTS TO HEAR FROM MY ARMPITS

LISA THE VEGETARIAN

Episode 3F03   Original Airdate: 10/15/95   Writer: David S. Cohen   Director: Mark Kirkland   Guest Voices: Paul and Linda McCartney as Themselves

After meeting a cute baby lamb at a petting zoo, Lisa becomes a vegetarian. However, her new lifestyle is under constant attack. At school, Principal Skinner learns of Lisa's new philosophy and shows the students an outdated film that encourages them to eat meat. Meanwhile, Homer is insulted when he is not invited to Flanders's family barbecue and instead plans a big barbecue of his own.

Lisa brings gazpacho to the barbecue as an alternative to meat but is laughed at by everyone. As Homer proudly presents a roast suckling pig to his happy guests, Lisa gets her revenge. Driving Homer's sit-down lawn mower, she hijacks the rolling grill, sending it and the pig down a steep incline.

A rift between Homer and Lisa ensues. The tension mounts until Lisa can no longer stay in the house. Believing that she cannot fight the forces of meat consumption, she goes to the Kwik-E-Mart and eats a hot dog. Apu informs her that the hot dog is actually made of tofu. He brings her to the roof of the Kwik-E-Mart, where he introduces her to Paul and Linda McCartney, who teach Lisa how to be a good vegetarian—vigilant yet respectful of others' choices. Lisa apologizes to Homer for ruining his barbecue, and the two make up.

SHOW HIGHLIGHTS

"Yum. It's rich in bunly goodness." Lunchlady Doris, after serving Lisa the cafeteria's vegetarian alternative—a hot dog bun.

 "I never realized before, but some Itchy & Scratchy cartoons send the message that violence against animals is funny."

"You don't win friends with salad." Homer, explaining to Lisa why he must serve meat at his barbecue. It turns into a chant and conga line formed by Bart, Homer, and Marge.

"Don't Have a Cow, Man": Vegetarian slogan on the T-shirt Apu shows Lisa.

 "Hi, I'm Troy McClure. You may remember me from such educational films as *Two Minus Three Equals Negative Fun!* and *Firecrackers: The Silent Killer.*"

"Don't kid yourself, Jimmy. If a cow ever got the chance, he'd eat you and everyone you care about." Troy McClure, hosting the film, *The Meat Council Presents: Meat and You–Partners in Freedom.*

 "Wait, Dad! Good news, everyone! You don't have to eat meat. I made enough gazpacho for all! It's tomato soup served ice cold!"

"Marge, tell Bart I just want to drink a nice glass of syrup like I do every morning." Homer, at breakfast.

"…I learned long ago, Lisa, to tolerate others rather than forcing my beliefs on them. You know, you can influence people without badgering them always. It's like Paul's song, 'Live and Let Live.'"

Ned Introduces Homer to His Cousins:
Ned: *Here's Jose Flanders!*
Jose Flanders: *Buenas ding-dong-diddly-dias, señor.*
Ned: *And this is Lord Thistlewick Flanders!*
Lord Thistlewick Flanders: *Charmed.*
(Ned nudge him with his elbow. Lord Thistlewick looks reluctant, but relents.)
Lord Thistlewick Flanders: *Eh, a-googily-doogily.*

(At the dinner table, Lisa looks down to her lamb chop. A thought balloon of the lamb from the petting zoo appears above her head.)
Lamb: *Please, Lisa. I thought you lo-o-o-ved me. Lo-o-o-ved me!*
Marge: *What's wrong, Lisa? Didn't you get enough lamb chops?*
Lisa: *I can't eat this. I can't eat a poor little lamb!*
Homer: *Lisa, get a hold of yourself. This is lamb—not a lamb.*
Lisa: *What's the difference between this lamb and the one that killed me?*
Bart: *This one spent two hours in the broiler.*

(Lisa pushes the grill Homer is barbecuing the pig on down a steep hill. Homer and Bart run after it as it rolls through some shrubs.)
Homer: *It's just a little dirty—it's still good! It's still good!*
(The pig flies off its spit, into a river.)
Homer: *It's just a little slimy—it's still good! It's still good!*
(The pig blocks off the intake of a dam. The water builds up behind it, until the pressure sends the pig rocketing off towards the horizon.)
Homer: *It's just a little airborne—it's still good! It's still good!*
Bart: *It's gone.*
Homer: *I know.*

THE BOYS ROOM IS NOT
A WATERPARK
THE BOYS ROOM IS NOT
A WATERPARK
THE BOYS ROOM IS NOT
A WATERPARK

THE STUFF YOU MAY HAVE MISSED

The Meat Council Presents–Meat and You: Partners in Freedom is Number 3F03 in the *Resistance Is Useless Series.* (3F03 is also the production number of this episode.)

Reverend Lovejoy drinks a bottle of beer at Homer's barbecue.

The only person who eats the gazpacho at the barbecue is Santa's Little Helper.

A sign in a Krustyburger Lisa passes reads: "Try Our New Beef-flavored Chicken."

A billboard featuring a stern female doctor reads: "Don't Eat Beef." It then changes to the smiling doctor at a dinner table cutting a steak, and reads: "Eat Deer."

JIMMY

Identity:
Child co-star of the carnivore-friendly educational film "The Meat Council Presents: Meat and You--Partners in Freedom" with Troy McClure.

Persona:
Alternately curious and naive.

Reaction to visiting meat-packing plant:
Nauseous.

Ability to reason independently:
Minimal.

WOW, MR. McCLURE, I WAS A GRADE-A MORON TO EVER QUESTION EATING MEAT!

THE OPENING SEQUENCE

Krusty, as a headless horseman, gallops through the woods at night. He holds up his laughing head and flings it at the camera. It splatters with bloody impact and forms the words "The Simpsons Halloween Special VI."

ATTACK OF THE 50-FOOT EYESORES

A strange ionic disturbance brings to life gargantuan statues of popular advertising mascots. The icons, including Lard Lad, Professor Peanut, and the Duff Cowboy, begin to destroy Springfield. Lisa discovers a copyright notice in a footprint left behind by one of the mascots and tracks down the ad agency that created many of the characters. The head of the agency theorizes that if the townspeople stop paying attention to the monsters, they will lose their powers and die. Assisted by singer Paul Anka, Lisa spreads the word not to look at the mascots. The monsters soon fall over and die.

STORY HIGHLIGHTS

"Ah, the Miracle Mile—where value wears a neon sombrero and there's not a single church or library to offend the eye." Homer, driving on Springfield's business strip.

"Well, I acquired it legally, you can be sure of that." Homer to Marge, about the giant donut in the living room.

 "Good morning everybody, panic is gripping Springfield as giant advertising mascots rampage through the city. Perhaps it's part of some daring new ad campaign, but what new product could justify such carnage?"

"Whoa! Another acid flashback!" Otto, after the Red Devil Realty mascot picks up the schoolbus.

"Hello? Yes? Oh! Heh, heh, uh...if you're looking for that big donut of yours... um, Flanders has it. Just smash open his house." Homer, when Lard Lad comes to his front door. After closing the door, Homer says, "He came to life. Good for him."

THE STUFF YOU MAY HAVE MISSED

In the opening credits, Matt Groening is identified as Matt "Funk Lord of USA" Groening.

Professor Peanut is a parody of the Planters mascot, Mr. Peanut.

A poster in the advertising agency reads, "50 Million Cigarette Smokers Can't Be Wrong!"

A mascot on a flying carpet destroys the birthplace of Norman Vincent Peale, author of *The Power of Positive Thinking.*

Homer's "Mmm...sprinkles" also occurs in 8F02, "Treehouse of Horror II."

The mascot with the tuxedo and top hat is inspired by Western Exterminator Co. of Los Angeles.

"Just Don't Look" Song Lyrics:
Paul Anka: *To stop those monsters 1-2-3/Here's a fresh new way that's trouble-free/It's got Paul Anka's guarantee...*
Lisa: *Guarantee void in Tennessee!*
Paul Anka and Lisa and Townspeople: *Just don't look!/Just don't look!/Just don't look!/Just don't look!*

(Wiggum spots an incredibly tall young man in a basketball uniform and shoots him. The young man falls over dead.)
Chief Wiggum: *Aw, they're not so tough.*
Lou: *Ah, Chief, that wasn't a monster. That was the captain of the high school basketball team.*
Chief Wiggum: *Uh, yeah...well, he was turning into a monster, though.*

HORROR VI

Episode 3F04
Original Airdate: 10/30/95
Writers: John Swartzwelder, Steve Tompkins, David S. Cohen
Director: Bob Anderson
Guest Voice: Paul Anka as Himself

NIGHTMARE ON EVERGREEN TERRACE

Bart suffers a nightmare in which he is terrorized by Groundskeeper Willie. Shortly thereafter, Martin falls asleep during class and dies. Marge reveals how Willie was burned alive in an accident during a PTA meeting. Although he screamed for help, the parents continued to discuss lunch menus and allowed him to die. Willie vowed to make the parents pay for his death with the blood of their sleeping children. Bart and Lisa fear that if they fall asleep, Willie will get them. After desperately trying to stay awake, Bart deliberately dozes off to slay Willie in his dreams. Lisa, too, falls asleep. Willie, as a bagpipe-spider creature, captures both of them and is about to kill them. Just then Maggie appears and uses her pacifier to seal the bagpipe's vent. Willie explodes. Bart and Lisa wake up, hoping they are free of Willie forever.

THE STUFF YOU MAY HAVE MISSED

Many of the elements of Bart's first dream—the backgrounds, the music, the behavior of the characters—parody Tex Avery's cartoons.

The Secret Revealed:

Lisa: *Mom, Dad, Martin died at school today!*
Marge: *Mmm...I don't see what this has to do with Groundskeeper Willie.*
Bart: *Um...we didn't mention Groundskeeper Willie, Mom.*
Marge: *Kids, it's time we told you the true story and put your fears to rest. It's a story of murder and revenge from beyond the grave.*

Grampa's Two Cents:

Lisa: *Bart, do you realize what this means? The next time we fall asleep we could die!*
Grampa: *Ehh, welcome to my world.*

STORY HIGHLIGHTS

"Glad to rake your acquaintance." Groundskeeper Willie, pursuing Bart with a rake in Bart's nightmare.

"Children, I couldn't help monitoring your conversation. There's no mystery about Willie. Why, he simply disappeared. Now, let's have no more curiosity about this bizarre cover-up."

"Willie, please, Mr. Van Houten has the floor." Principal Skinner, as Willie, screaming for help, burns to a crisp during a PTA meeting.

"Good-bye Lis. I hope you get reincarnated as someone who can stay awake for 15 minutes." Bart, to his sister in their Spider-Willie nightmare.

HOMER³

Desperately trying to avoid Patty and Selma during a visit, Homer accidentally steps into a third dimension, becoming three dimensional. He calls for help. Soon the Simpson's house is filled with concerned friends. However, no one can help him. Homer accidentally creates a vortex that threatens to envelop him and everything around him. Just as he is about to be freed, the dimension collapses, catapulting Homer into our world—the most frightening dimension of all.

STORY HIGHLIGHTS

"That's weird. It's like something out of that twilighty show about that zone." Homer, when his hand goes into the wall as he leans on it.

"Mmm...unprocessed fish sticks." Homer, looking into a reflecting pool and seeing beautiful golden fish swimming by.

"Take that, you lousy dimension!" Chief Wiggum, firing his gun into the dimensional gateway.

"Well, we hit a little snag when the universe sorta collapsed on itself, but Dad seemed cautiously optimistic."

"Ooh, erotic cakes!" Homer, finding a store he likes in the odd new universe.

Classic TV Moment:

The entire segment is based on the "Little Girl Lost" episode of "The Twilight Zone."

Marge: *Homer? Where are you?*
Homer: *(from beyond) Uh, I'm somewhere where I don't know where I am.*
Marge: *Do you see towels? If you see towels, you're probably in the linen closet again.*
Homer: *(from beyond) Just a second. (pause) No, it's a place I've never seen before.*
Selma: *Ah, the shower!*

Homer: *Um, it's, like, uh...did anyone see the movie Tron?*
Dr. Hibbert: *No.*
Lisa: *No.*
Chief Wiggum: *No.*
Marge: *No.*
Bart: *No.*
Patty: *No.*
Chief Wiggum: *No.*
Flanders: *No.*
Selma: *No.*
Prof. Frink: *No.*
Rev. Lovejoy: *No.*
Chief Wiggum: *Yes. I mean, uh, I mean, no. No.*

Selma: *Have we got a family activity for you!*
Patty: *A pillowcase full of seashells from our trip to Sulfur Bay.*
Selma: *You can help us clean and organize them.*
Patty: *And pry out all the dead hermit crabs. Get a screwdriver.*

THE STUFF YOU MAY HAVE MISSED

Patty's greeting to Marge—"How's it hangin'?"—is an allusion to her mannishness. Another such reference occurs in 1F03, "Marge on the Lam," in which Patty refuses to join Marge at the ballet, referring to it as "girl stuff."

Homer's reference to "that wheelchair guy" alludes to Dr. Stephen Hawking, the wheelchair-bound scientist and author of *A Brief History of Time*.

DR. NICK RIVIERA

Occupation:
Springfield's professional medical alternative to Julius Hibbert.

Alma maters:
Hollywood Upstairs Medical College; Club Med School; Mayo Clinic Correspondence School.

Office location:
The Springfield Mall, next to Gum for Less and two doors down from I Can't Believe It's a Law Firm.

Patented treatments:
Slow, steady gorging process combined with assal horizontology for weight gain; transdermal electomicide to soothe edginess in older people.

Ethics problems:
Uses cadavers so he can drive in the carpool lane; uses plastic restaurant cutlery to perform operations.

THE CORONER. I'M SO SICK OF THAT GUY. WELL, SEE YOU IN THE OPERATING PLACE.

KING-SIZE HOMER

Episode 3F05 Original Airdate: 11/5/95 Writer: Dan Greaney Director: Jim Reardon

Homer decides that he wants to work at home and discovers how to attain his goal: he gorges himself until he reaches a target weight of 300 pounds and is officially declared disabled. The power plant installs a computerized workstation for Homer in his home.

Looking for shortcuts in his job performance, Homer uses a novelty bobbing-head bird as a substitute for his fingers at the keyboard and goes to the movies. Refused admittance because of his size, he returns home only to find that the bird has failed and the reactor core is about to explode.

Homer hijacks an ice cream truck and races to the plant. He climbs a ladder to get to the manual shut-down lever, but the catwalk buckles under his enormous weight. When the tank's sealing cap ruptures, Homer falls and his body seals the leak. To reward Homer for saving the plant, Mr. Burns agrees to pay for liposuction so that Homer can return to his normal size.

SHOW HIGHLIGHTS

Burns, leading the plant exercises: "Raise your right hock. Aerate! Raise your left hock. Aerate! I want to see more Teddy Roosevelts and less Franklin Roosevelts!"

Homer, reading about possible disabilities: "Carpal Tunnel Syndrome? No. Lumber Lung? No. Jugglers despair? No. Achy-Breaky Pelvis? No. Oh, I'm never going to be disabled. I'm sick of being so healthy! Hey, wait--'Hyper-Obesity. If you weigh more than 300 pounds, you qualify as disabled."

 "Arnie Pie in the Sky with the morning commute. Traffic this morning is as bad as it gets. Due to a fire at the army testing lab a bunch of escaped, infected monkeys are roaming the expressway. Despite the sweltering heat, don't unroll your windows 'cause those monkeys seem confused and irritable!"

"I wash myself with a rag on a stick." Bart, in his fantasy about being a "lardo on workman's comp, just like Dad."

 "But let me tell you, the slim lazy Homer you knew is dead. Now I'm a big fat dynamo."

Jimbo, referring to Homer: "I heard that guy's ass has its own congressman."

Homer: *Hey, where's Charlie? How'd he get out of this?*
Carl: *Aw, he's at home on disability.*
Lenny: *Yeah, he got injured on the job and they sent him home with pay. Pfft. It's like a lottery that rewards stupidity.*
Homer: *Stupidity, eh?*

Recording Homer hears on the phone when he tries to call the plant: "The fingers you have used to dial are too fat. To obtain a special dialing wand, please mash the key pad with your palm, now."

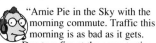 "Homer, your bravery and quick thinking have turned a potential Chernobyl into a mere Three-Mile Island. Bravo!"

Dr. Nick: *You'll want to focus on the neglected food groups, such as the whipped group, the congealed group, and the choc-o-tastic.*
Homer: *What can I do to speed the whole thing up, doctor?*
Dr. Nick: *Well, be creative. Instead of making sandwiches with bread, use Pop-Tarts. Instead of chewing gum, chew bacon.*
Bart: *You could brush your teeth with milkshakes!*
Dr. Nick: *Hey, did you go to Hollywood Upstairs Medical College, too? And remember, if you're not sure about something, rub it against a piece of paper. If the paper turns clear, it's your window to weight gain.*

Marge: *Have you lost your mind?! Have you thought about your health or your appearance?*
Homer: *Oh, so that's it, isn't it, Marge? Looks. I didn't know you were so shallow.*
Marge: *Oh, please. I would love you if you weighed 1,000 pounds but . . .*
Homer: *Beautiful. G'night.*

Salesman: *Well, sir, many of our clients find pants confining. So we offer a range of alternatives for the ample gentleman: ponchos, muu-muus, capes, jumpsuits, uni-sheets, muslin body rolls, academic and judicial robes.*
Homer: *I don't want to look like a weirdo. I'll just go with a muu-muu.*

Homer: *Shame on all of you. Give me my dignity! I just came here to see Honk If You're Horny in peace.*
Manager: *Sir, if you'd just quiet down, I'd be happy to treat you to a garbage bag full of popcorn.*

Mr. Burns: *I am pleased to dedicate this remote work terminal. It will allow our safety inspector here to perform his duties from home. And so, excelsior to you, Mr., Er . . . What's the name of this gastropod?*
Smithers: *Simpson, Sir. One of your chair moisteners from Sector 7G.*
Burns: *Yes, Simpson.*

THE STUFF YOU MAY HAVE MISSED

The marquee at the Aztec reads, "Pauly Shore and Faye Dunaway in *Honk If You're Horny!*"

Ham Ahoy!, Much Ado About Stuffing, Tubbb!, Cheezus-N-Rice, Uncle Jim's Country Fillin' are products Homer buy at the grocery store.

There are prehistoric Itchy and Scratchy skeletons near the underground gas-venting pipe.

After Homer okays the sounding of the horn from his workstation, it can be heard in the background.

There are two food groups shown on the Nutrition Pyramid diagram which Dr. Nick doesn't mention: Fats & Sweets and Empty Calorie Group.

INDIAN BURNS ARE NOT OUR CULTURAL HERITAGE
INDIAN BURNS ARE NOT OUR CULTURAL HERITAGE
INDIAN BURNS ARE NOT OUR CULTURAL HERITAGE

MOTHER SIMPSON

Episode 3F06 Original Airdate: 11/19/95 Writer: Richard Appel Director: David Silverman Guest Voice: Harry Morgan as Bill Gannon

H omer fakes his own death so that he can enjoy his Saturday at home rather than help his co-workers collect litter. After friends stop by to offer their condolences, Marge realizes what Homer has done and tells him to set things straight. At the Hall of Records, he reads a clerk's computer screen and discovers that his mother is still alive. He visits the family plot and meets his long-thought-dead mom, who has snuck in to town to pay her final respects to her son.

Mother Simpson recounts how, 25 years earlier, she tired of her dull husband Abe and joined germ warfare protesters at Springfield State College. Caught while staging a raid on a germ lab operated by Mr. Burns, she was forced to flee the family and hide underground. Now, 25 years later, she has risked her freedom by coming back to Springfield. Soon after, Mr. Burns sees her at the post office and identifies her.

While FBI agents begin an extensive manhunt for the fugitive mom, while Grampa explains to his wife why he told Homer she had died rather than admit the truth. The FBI determines Mother Simpson's whereabouts and storms the Simpson home. But Mother has already fled, tipped off by Chief Wiggum, who was repaying an old debt.

SHOW HIGHLIGHTS

"I can't believe I'm spending my Saturday picking up garbage. I mean, half these bottles ain't even mine." Lenny, picking up trash beside the highway for Mr. Burns.

"When I asked you if that dummy was to fake your death, you told me 'no!'" Marge

"Homer J. Simpson. We Are Richer for Having Lost Him": Tombstone brought to the Simpson front door by Patty and Selma.

The power line man, to Marge: "Oh, no. No mistake. Your electricity is in the name of Homer J. Simpson, deceased. The juice stays off till you get a job or a generator. Oh, and, uh, my deepest sympathies."

"Damn you, Walt Whitman! I-hate-you-Walt-freakin'-Whitman! _Leaves of Grass_ my ass!" Homer, upon discovering that the grave he thought was his mother's is actually Walt Whitman's.

"This is so weird. It's like something out of Dickens or 'Melrose Place.'" Lisa

The '60s protesters chant against Mr. Burns's germ warfare lab: "Anthrax, gangrene, swimmer's ear, get your germ lab outta here!"

"Only one member of the Springfield Seven was identified. She's been described as a woman in her early thirty's, yellow complexion, and may be extremely helpful. For channel six news, I'm Kenny Brockelstein."

"I had help from my friends in the underground. Jerry Rubin gave me a job marketing his line of health shakes. I proofread Bobby Seale's cookbook. And I ran credit checks at Tom Hayden's Porsche dealership."

Bill Gannon voice: _How does it happen, Joe?_
Joe Friday voice: _How does what happen?_
Bill Gannon voice: _How does a sweet young lady mortgage her future for a bunch of scraggly ideals and greasy-haired promises?_
Joe Friday voice: _Maybe she just thought the war in Southeast Asia was so immoral, her end justified the means._
Bill Gannon voice: _Gee, Joe. You haven't been the same since your son went crazy in Vietnam._
Joe Friday voice: _It's a pain that never ends._

Homer Stages His Own Violent Death:

Carl: _Oh, no! He's going over the falls!_
Lenny: _Oh, good! He snagged that tree branch!_
Carl: _Oh, no! The branch broke off!_
Lenny: _Oh, good. He can grab onto them pointy rocks._
Carl: _Oh, no! The rocks broke his arms and legs!_
Lenny: _Oh, good! Those helpful beavers are swimming out to save him!_
Carl: _Oh, no! They're biting him! And stealing his pants!_
Smithers: _Good lord! He'll be sucked into the turbine!_
Mr. Burns: _Smithers, who was that corpse?_
Smithers: _Homer Simpson, sir._ (sniffs) _One of the finest, bravest men ever to grace Sector 7G._ (he stops crying and returns to normal) _I'll cross him off the list._

Homer: _Listen here. My name is Homer J. Simpson. You guys think I'm dead, but I'm not. Now I want you to straighten this out without a lot of your bureaucratic red tape and mumbo-jumbo._
County clerk: _Okay, Mr. Simpson, I'll just make the change here_ (taps computer keyboard) _and you're all set._
Homer: _I don't like your attitude, you water-cooler dictator. What do you have in that secret government file, anyway? I have a right to read it._
County clerk: _You sure do._

Homer: _I thought you were dead._
Mother Simpson: _I thought you were dead._
Gravedigger: _Dang blasted! Isn't anybody in this dad-gummed cemetery dead?_
Hans Moleman: (popping out of a nearby coffin) _I didn't want to make a fuss, but now that you mention it . . ._

Among the trash littering the highway are a toilet seat lid, a dead frog, and part of a New Bedlam Asylum for the Emotionally Interesting straitjacket. (New Bedlam was last seen in 7F24, "Stark Raving Dad.")

While cleaning up trash, Lenny lifts a bird's nest off of a tree limb and throws it away, eggs and all.

Protest signs at rally: "Anthrax Isn't Groovy," "Germs Off Campus," "Make Love, Not Germs," "Take the U.S. Out of Pus," "Pax Not Pox."

"Rocking Pneumonia" and "Boogie-Woogie Influenza" are two of the germs in Burns's lab.

As a child, Homer slept with a Pillsbury doughboy doll.

Sign: "Germ Warfare Laboratory–When the H-Bomb Isn't Enough."

Sign: "Springfield Hall of Records– Not the Good Kind of Records, Historical Ones."

MOTHER SIMPSON

Identity:
Long-lost mother of Homer; presumed dead.

Reason for hiding:
Was seen by Mr. Burns on the day she participated in the protest destruction of his germ warfare lab in the late 1960s.

Aliases:
Mona Simpson; Mona Stevens; Martha Stewart; Penelope Olsen; Muddie Mae Suggins.

Plays:
The guitar, specializing in 1960's folk tunes.

WE'D MET THE ENEMY AND IT WAS MONTGOMERY BURNS. DRASTIC ACTION HAD TO BE TAKEN TO STOP HIS WAR MACHINE.

Guest Voices:
Glenn Close as Mother Simpson

IF YOU DON'T OPEN THAT DOOR, I'LL TEAR YOU UP LIKE A KLEENEX AT A SNOT PARTY!

Guest Voice:
R. Lee Ermey as Colonel Hapablap.

SIDESHOW BOB'S LAST GLEAMING

Episode 3F08   Original Airdate: 11/26/95   Writer: Spike Ferensten   Director: Dominic Polcino

While serving his time in a minimum security prison, Sideshow Bob becomes obsessed by TV's detrimental effect on society. During work detail at an Air Force base, he sneaks away and gains access to a restricted hangar that stores nuclear materials. Meanwhile, the Simpsons travel to the base to watch an air show.

During the show, Bob appears on a gigantic monitor and threatens to detonate a nuclear bomb unless all television is abolished in Springfield. In the ensuing panic, Bart and Lisa are separated from their parents. In response to Bob's threat, Mayor Quimby shuts down Springfield's TV stations, but Krusty, sensing a ratings windfall, broadcasts his show from a civil defense shack. Outraged, Bob sets off the bomb, but the antiquated weapon fails to explode.

As military forces close in on him, Bob kidnaps Bart and commandeers the original Wright Brothers' plane, on loan from the Smithsonian, towards Krusty's makeshift studio on a kamikaze mission. The slow-moving craft bounces harmlessly off the shack's roof and Bob is taken into custody.

COL. HAPABLAP

SHOW HIGHLIGHTS

"The common box-kite was originally used as a means of drying wet string!"

"Fly Me To the Moon": What Sideshow Bob whistles as he opens a hatch leading to the bomb.

"By the way, I'm aware of the irony of appearing on TV in order to decry it, so don't bother pointing that out."

"Would it really be worth living in a world without television? I think the survivors would envy the dead."

"And as my final newscast draws to a close, I'm reminded of a few of the events that brought me closer to you: the collapse of the Soviet Union, premium ice cream price wars, dogs that were mistakenly issued major credit cards and others who weren't so lucky. And so, farewell. Eh, and uh, don't forget to look for my new column in *PC World* magazine."

Bob Appears on the Giant Television Screen at the Air Show.

Sideshow Bob: *Hello, Springfield. Sorry to divert your attention from all the big noises and shiny things, but something's been troubling me lately: television. Wouldn't our lives be so much richer if television were done away with?*
Moe: *What!?*
Dr. Hibbert: *Surely he's not talking about VH-1!*

The Alkali Flats of the Springfield Badlands: The location of the civil defense shack where Krusty is broadcasting.

"Kids, Itchy and Scratchy can't be here today, but instead we've got the next best thing—it's the Sting-y and Battery Show! They bite, and light, and bite and light and dite, ligh, ligh, ligh—yadda yadda, you know what I'm talking about." Krusty, holding up a scorpion and corroded lantern battery while broadcasting from the civil defense shed.

"How ironic. My crusade against television has come to an end so formulaic it could've spewed from the Powerbook of the laziest Hollywood hack..."

Grampa and Bart Looking at the Wright Brothers' Plane:

Bart: *Look at that hunk o' junk.*
Grampa: *Oh, ja, wha...You're ignorant! That's the Wright Brothers' plane! At Kitty Hawk in 1903, Charles Lindbergh flew it 15 miles on a thimbleful of corn oil. Single-handedly won us the Civil War, it did.*
Bart: *So how do you know so much about American history?*
Grampa: *I pieced it together, mostly from sugar packets.*

Chief Wiggum: *Hey, where is Sideshow Bob and that guy who eats people and takes their faces?*
Normal-looking prisoner: *I'm right here, Chief!*
Wiggum: *Oh. Then where's Sideshow Bob?*
Another prisoner: *Uh, he ran off.*
Wiggum: *Oh, great. Well...if anyone asks, I beat him to death, okay?*

THE STUFF YOU MAY HAVE MISSED

Frink appears in the underground "war room," with a different hairstyle, wearing dark glasses, and sitting in what appears to be a wheelchair.

The "representatives of television" are Kent Brockman, Krusty the Clown, Bumblebee Man, a Dr. Who lookalike, and an Urkel lookalike.

The ad for the air show depicts an F-14 with giant truck wheels.

Sign: "U.S. AIR FORCE BASE (Not affiliated with U.S. Air)."

Magazines in the Air Force base war room: *Granny Fanny*, *Cheek Week*, and *American Breast Enthusiast*.

The giant television screen at the air show is called "Tyranno-Vision."

Movie Moments:

Colonel Hapablap asks Sideshow Bob "What's your major malfunction?" à la the Drill Sergeant (also played by R. Lee Ermey) in *Full Metal Jacket*.

The underground "war room" where Quimby decides what to do parodies *Dr. Strangelove*.

WEDGIES ARE UNHEALTHY FOR CHILDREN AND OTHER LIVING THINGS.
WEDGIES ARE UNHEALTHY FOR CHILDREN AND OTHER LIVING THINGS.

THE SIMPSONS 138TH EPISODE SPECTACULAR

Episode 3F31 Original Airdate: 12/3/95 Writer: Penny Wise Director: Pound Foolish
Guest Voices: Glenn Close as Mother Simpson, Buzz Aldrin as Himself.

Job:
Gun-toting creator of
"The Simpsons"; creator of such
comics as "Damnation,"
"Johnny Reb,"
and "True Murder Stories."

Appearance:
Bald, with scar and eye-patch.

Demeanor:
Angry.

Accent:
Southern.

Drinks:
Tequila (at his desk.)

SHOW HIGHLIGHTS

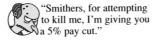 "Hello, I'm Troy McClure. You may remember me from such Fox network specials as 'Alien Nose Job' and 'Five Fabulous Weeks of 'The Chevy Chase Show.''" Tonight we're here to honor America's favorite nonprehistoric cartoon family."

Scene Cut from 3F06, "Mother Simpson":

Homer: *Mmmm...*
Mother Simpson: *Homer, please, you don't have to wolf down that 25-year-old candy just to make me happy.*
Homer: *(eating) But it won't make you unhappy, right? Hey, space food sticks! Oh, I wish I had these on my space adventure. Did you know I blasted into space two years ago, Mom?*
Mother Simpson: *Oh, sure, I read all about it. It was national news. Do you still work for NASA?*
Homer: *No, I work for the nuclear power plant.*
Mother Simpson: *Oh, Homer...*
Homer: *Well, you'll be happy to know I don't work very hard. Actually, I'm bringing the plant down from the inside.*

"NRA4EVER": The message on the cash register when Maggie is scanned in the opening credits. Or so says Troy. Adds McClure: "...Just one of the hundreds of radical right-wing messages inserted into every show by creator Matt Groening."

April 19, 1987: The date the Simpsons first appeared, as a short on "The Tracey Ullman Show."

 "Smithers, for attempting to kill me, I'm giving you a 5% pay cut."

Captain Wacky: Homer's original name in "The Simpsons," according to Troy.

"Which popular 'Simpsons' characters have died in the past year? If you said Bleeding Gums Murphy and Dr. Marvin Monroe, you are wrong. They were never popular." The announcer, giving the answer to the episode's second Simpsons trivia question.

The solutions to "Who Shot Mr. Burns?" that we never intended to air: Barney shoots him, Tito Puente shoots him, Moe shoots him, Apu shoots him, Santa's Little Helper shoots him.

Tracey Ullman Shorts
(or Parts of Shorts) Shown:

MG01, "Goodnight"; MG16, "The Perfect Crime"; MG13,"Space Patrol"; MG20, "World War III"; MG44, "Bathtime."

Never-Seen Scene from 1F04, "Treehouse of Horror IV":

Bart: *I'd sell my soul for a formula one racing car.* (The Devil Flanders appears.)
Devil Flanders: *Heh, heh, heh, that can be arranged.*
Bart: *Changed my mind. Sorry.* (The Devil Flanders vanishes.)
Bart: *Cool.*
Marge: *Bart! Stop pestering Satan!*

A Portion of the Phony Ending to "Who Shot Mr. Burns?":

Burns: *The one who shot me was... Aah! Aah! Waylon Smithers!*
Smithers: *Nooooo! Wait a minute. Yes.*

A Scene We Didn't See from "Krusty Gets Kancelled":

Network executive #1: *Krusty, we're from the network. Uh, we have some bad news: I'm afraid your show's been canceled.*
Krusty: *Oh, I thought this would happen. I just hope you replace me with something as educational and uplifting as I tried to be.*
Network executive #2: *Actually, it's a hemorrhoid infomercial starring Claude Akins.*
Krusty: *Can I play hemorrhoid sufferer number one? Ooh! Oh, that hurts! Ah! Oh, is there no relief?*
Network executive #1: *I don't think so.*
Krusty: *How about one of the "after" guys? Aah. Ooh, that's better! I can ride a bike again.*
Network executive #1: *Sorry.*

T elevision, movie, and infomercial personality Troy McClure hosts this retrospective from the Springfield Civic Auditorium. The show begins with a brief history of "The Simpsons." Series creator Matt Groening is portrayed as an elderly, alcoholic Southern patriot and onetime pulp comic book creator. Clips from "The Simpsons" shorts, originally aired on "The Tracey Ullman Show," are featured.

Troy answers viewer mail, fielding questions regarding Homer's stupidity, how many people it takes to produce the show, and the "real deal" about Smithers.

The Simpsons "cutout classics" are screened, featuring scenes never before aired from 9F19, "Krusty Gets Kancelled"; 1F08, "$pringfield"; 3F06, "Mother Simpson"; 1F04, "Treehouse of Horrors IV"; 1F10, "Homer and Apu"; and 1F16, "Burns' Heir."

Several alternate solutions to the "Who Shot Mr. Burns?" mystery follow, featuring a montage of Barney, Tito Puente, Moe, Apu, and Santa's Little Helper shooting Burns. The phony ending, which reveals Smithers as the triggerman, is also screened.

Troy closes the show with, "Yes, the Simpsons have come a long way since an old drunk made humans out of his rabbit characters to pay off old gambling debts. Who knows what adventures they'll have between now and when the show becomes unprofitable?"

THE STUFF YOU MAY HAVE MISSED

Matt Groening is depicted as an old bald man with an eye patch. A "Life in Hell" poster hangs on his office wall.

James L. Brooks resembles Mr. Moneybags from Monopoly.

Sam Simon, with his grotesque fingernails and gaunt profile, resembles Howard Hughes at his most eccentric.

The note that spills out of Homer's bowling-ball brain reads, "IOU one brain, signed, God."

The sign at the Springfield Civic Auditorium reads, "Tonight—Gala Spectacular" and "Tomorrow—Alternate Lifestyle Senior Prom."

GET OUTTA MY OFFICE!

DETECTIVE DON BRODKA

Job:
Head of security, Try-N-Save store.

Demeanor:
Tough.

Modus operandi:
Scaring the living tar out of young boys who steal through intimidation and ratting to their parents.

Chief vice:
Smoking.

Chief area of confusion:
Tends to get his commandments mixed up.

Food of choice:
Little packs of Cheez 'n' Crackers.

> IF I WANTED SMOKE BLOWN UP MY ASS I'D BE AT HOME WITH A PACK OF CIGARETTES AND A SHORT LENGTH OF HOSE.

Guest Voice:
Lawrence Tierney as Detective Don Brodka

MARGE BE NOT PROUD

Episode 3F07 Original Airdate: 12/17/95 Writer: Mike Scully Director: Steven Dean Moore

Bart sees a TV commercial for the new ultraviolent video game, "Bonestorm," and must have it. However, all of his attempts to purchase, rent, or borrow "Bonestorm" fail. Stealing the game from a local discount store, Bart is caught by store security man Don Brodka.

Brodka escorts Bart to a darkened back room and tells him never to enter the store again. When Marge takes the family to the same store for their annual Christmas picture, Bart struggles to escape detection. However, Brodka spots him and shows a disbelieving Marge and Homer the security tape of Bart shoplifting the game.

Bart notices that Marge acts differently towards him, and fears he has lost her love. He goes to the discount store and returns home with a bulge under his jacket. When Marge confronts him, he produces a framed photograph of himself, smiling, along with a receipt that states "Paid in Full."

SHOW HIGHLIGHTS

"It's 'A Krusty Kinda Kristmas!' brought to you by: I.L.G.— selling your body's chemicals after you die,' and by Li'l Sweetheart Cupcakes, a subsidiary of I.L.G."
TV announcer, introducing Krusty's latest special.

"Tuck in time! All aboard the sleepy train to visit Mother Goose. Barty's stop is snoozy lane to rest his sweet caboose!"

Thrillhouse: Milhouse's video game "handle." It registers as "Thrillho."

"Hi, I'm Troy McClure. You might remember me from such public-service videos as 'Designated Drivers: The Life-Saving Nerds' and 'Phony Tornado Alarms Reduce Readiness.' I'm here today to give you the skinny on shoplifting, thereby completing my plea bargain with the good people at 'Foot Locker of Beverly Hills.'"

Detective Brodka: *You think you're pretty smart, don't you?*
Bart: *No.*
Detective Brodka: *Don't smart off to me, smart guy.*

(Bart looks at the video game case, and sees the video game characters come to life.)
Luigi: *Go ahead-a, Bart. Take-a the Bonestorm.*
Mario: *The store is-a so rich, she'll-a never notice.*
Donkey Kong: *Duh, it's the company's fault for making you want it so much.*
Lee Carvallo: *Don't do it, son. How's that game gonna help your putting?*
Sonic the Hedgehog: *Just take it! TakeItTakeItTakeIt TakeItTakeIt! Take IT!*

"Stealing?! How could you?! Haven't you learned anything from that guy who gives those sermons at church? Captain What's-his-name? We live in a society of laws. Why do you think I took you to all those *Police Academy* movies? For fun? Well, I didn't hear anybody laughin', did you?"

"I've figured out the boy's punishment. First: he's grounded. No leaving the house, not even for school. Second: no eggnog. In fact, no nog, period. And third, absolutely no stealing for three months."

"I love you so much, my little Bitty Barty." Marge, after Bart gives her a framed picture of himself, along with a receipt that says, "Paid in Full."

Wild Santa Claus: (on TV) *So tell your folks: Buy me "Bonestorm" or go to hell!*
(Bart gets up from the living room and runs into the kitchen.)
Bart: *Buy me Bonestorm or go to hell!*
Marge: *Bart!*
Homer: *Young man, in this house, we use a little word called "please."*
Bart: *But it's the coolest video game ever!*
Marge: *I'm sorry, honey, but those games cost up to and including seventy dollars. And they're violent and they distract you from your schoolwork.*
Bart: *Those are all good points, but the problem is they don't result in me getting the game.*
Homer: *I know how you feel, Bart. When I was your age, I wanted an electric football game more than anything in the world, and my parents bought it for me, and it was the happiest day of my life. Well, goodnight.*

THE STUFF YOU MAY HAVE MISSED

The stockings lined up for the boys in Juvenile Hall have numbers on them instead of names.

Detective Don Brodka has a USMC (United States Marine Corps) tattoo on his left arm.

Detective Brodka says that Bart violated "The 11th Commandment—Thou Shalt Not Steal.'" It's actually the 8th Commandment. (As revealed in 7F13, "Lisa vs. Homer and 8th Commandment.")

Brodka has a "Try-N-Save Security School" certificate on his wall.

The sign in front of the Try-N-Save reads, "In Honor of the Birth of Our Savior, Try-N-Save Is Open All Day Christmas."

A sign in Juvenile Hall reads, "Proud Home of the Soap Bar Beating."

Signs in Try-N-Save read, "Eterna-Logs, $2.99/each" and "Folding Chair Riot, $9.99."

Rich suburban mom: *Gavin, don't you already have this game?*
Spoiled boy: *No, Mom, you idiot. I have Bloodstorm and Bonesquad and Bloodstorm II, stupid.*
Rich suburban mom: *Oh, I'm sorry, honey. We'll take a Bonestorm.*
Spoiled boy: *Get two. I'm not sharing with Caitlin.*

> I WILL STOP TALKING ABOUT THE TWELVE INCH PIANIST
> I WILL STOP TALKING ABOUT THE TWELVE INCH PIANIST
> I WILL STOP TALKING ABOUT THE TWELVE INCH PIANIST

TEAM HOMER

Episode 3F10 Original Airdate: 1/6/96 Writer: Mike Scully Director: Mark Kirkland

U nable to afford the $500 registration fee to join a bowling league, Homer asks an anesthetized Mr. Burns for the money and receives a check. Meanwhile, at Springfield Elementary, Bart's "Down with Homework" T-shirt incites a student riot that leads to the implementation of a uniform dress code.

Homer's bowling team, the Pin Pals, begins to win after Homer initiates team-supporting cheers. Mr. Burns recovers from his stupor and discovers the canceled check he gave Homer. He decides to replace Otto as the team's fourth member, but the team suffers, since he can barely roll the ball down the lane.

The Pin Pals make it to the league championship match against the Holy Rollers. Two pins away from victory, Mr. Burns takes his turn. Otto tips over a novelty machine and the vibrations help the Pin Pals win by knocking down the pins. Back at the school, Principal Skinner's dress code demoralizes the students until a rainstorm soaks through the uniforms, revealing psychedelic colors. The children go wild.

SHOW HIGHLIGHTS

"Down with Homework": The *Mad* magazine iron-on that causes the riot and leads to the institution of uniforms at Springfield Elementary.

 "Man, you go through life, you try to be nice to people, you struggle to resist the urge to punch 'em in the face, and for what?! For some pimply little puke to treat you like dirt unless you're on a team. Well, I'm better than dirt— well, most kinds of dirt. I mean, not that fancy, store-bought dirt. That stuff's loaded with nutrients. I—I can't compete with that stuff."

"Call this an unfair generalization if you must, but old people are no good at everything." Moe, on the prospect of Mr. Burns joining the bowling team.

> I AM NOT CERTIFIED TO
> REMOVE ASBESTOS
> I AM NOT CERTIFIED TO
> REMOVE ASBESTOS
> I AM NOT CERTIFIED TO
> REMOVE ASBESTOS

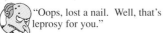 "Oops, lost a nail. Well, that's leprosy for you."

"Haw...Ho?" Nelson, forgetting his trademark taunt.

 "I'm tired of being a wanna-be league bowler, I wanna be a league bowler!"

"Go, Moe! Go, Moe! Don't make Homer shout out 'D'oh!'" Homer, Apu, and Otto, cheering on Moe.

"I spent the next three years in a POW camp, forced to subsist on a thin stew made of fish, vegetables, prawns, coconut milk, and four kinds of rice. I came close to madness trying to find it here in the States, but they just can't get the spices right."

"This just in, a new addition to our 'worst dressed list'— those guys!"

Bart: *Omigod! The Mad Magazine Special Edition! They only put out 17 of these a year!*
Milhouse: *Boy, they're really socking it to that Spiro Agnew guy! He must work there or something.*

(As Burns is "doped-up" on ether, Homer enters his office. Mr. Burns sees Homer as The Pillsbury Doughboy.)
Homer: *Mr. Burns, I, uh, was wondering if you'd like to sponsor my bowling team...for five hundred dollars.*
Burns: *Oh, why, certainly, Pop 'n Fresh. I—I owe my robust physique to your tubes of triple-bleached goo!*

Homer: *You can do it Otto / You can do it Otto / Help each other out, that'll be our motto!*
Homer/Apu/Moe: *You can do it Otto/You can do it Otto!*
Apu: *Make this spare, I'll give you free gelato!*
Moe: *Then back to my place where I will get you blotto!*
Homer: *Domo arigato, Mister Roboto!*

Marge: *No, I will not pay you five hundred dollars for sex!!*
Homer: *Aw, come on, Marge! You're getting something in return! And I'm getting a bowling team. It's win-win!*
Marge: *It's sick! And I don't have that kind of money to spend on sex! Maybe you could get someone with money to sponsor your team. Like Mr. Burns.*
Homer: *Pfft. Burns never gives money to anybody. Just last week, I asked him for fifteen hundred dollars.*
Marge: *For what?*
Homer: *Oh, I've got to get the third degree from you, too?*

Bart: *Mo-o-om! My slingshot doesn't fit in these pockets. And these shorts leave nothing to the imagination. These uniforms suck!*
Marge: *Bart, where do you pick up words like that.*
Homer: *Yeah, Moe, that team sure did suck last night! That just plain sucked! I've seen teams suck before, but they were the suckiest bunch of sucks that ever sucked!*

Burns: *I don't remember writing a check for bowling!*
Smithers: *Uh, sir. That's a check for your boweling.*
Burns: *Oh, yes. That's very important.*
Smithers: *Yes, sir. Remember that monkey didn't do it?*

In Loving Memory of Doris Grau:

This episode was dedicated to Grau, the voice of Lunchlady Doris, who died in December 1995.

THE STUFF YOU MAY HAVE MISSED

Barney's uncle Al, last seen in 2F10, "And Maggie Makes Three," appears during this episode.

Homer stole the Oscar belonging to Dr. Haing S. Ngor, who won Best Supporting Actor for *The Killing Fields* in 1984. He crossed out Dr. Ngor's name and put in his own.

LUIGI

Occupation:
Italian chef/waiter.

Attire:
White, with a huge white chef's hat.

Nationality:
Italian.

Accent:
Pronounced.

Attitude:
Gracious to your face; sarcastic; condescending behind your back.

Bowls for:
"The Stereotypes" in the bowling league.

HEY, SALVATORE, GIVE-AH THE UGLY KID A PLATE OF THE RED-AH CRAP-AH!

DISCO STU

Identity:
1970s retro nerd.

Hair:
Afro.

Attitude:
Arnold Horshack meets
Arthur Fonzarelli.

Dress:
Tacky.

Refers to himself:
In the third person.

HEY, DISCO STU
DOESN'T ADVERTISE.

TWO BAD NEIGHBORS

Episode 3F09   Original Airdate: 1/14/96   Writer: Ken Keeler   Director: Wes Archer

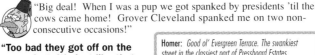

SHOW HIGHLIGHTS

Marge: *Can we get rid of this "Ayatollah" T-shirt? Khomeini died years ago.*
Homer: *But, Marge, it works on any Ayatollah! Ayatollah Nakhbadeh, Ayatollah Zahedi...Even as we speak, Ayatollah Razmara and his cadre of fanatics are consolidating their power!*

(Rummaging through the attic, Homer holds up a denim jacket with "Disco Stu" shakily lettered in rhinestones on the back.)
Marge: *Who's "Disco Stu?"*
Homer: *Oh, I wanted to write "Disco Stud" but I ran out of space. Not that "Disco Stu" didn't get his share of the action!*

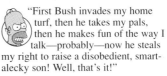

"Big deal! When I was a pup we got spanked by presidents 'til the cows came home! Grover Cleveland spanked me on two non-consecutive occasions!"

"Too bad they got off on the wrong foot. It's just like that Noriega thing. Now he and George are the best of friends." Barbara Bush, on Homer and George's bad blood.

"All right. His story checks out." Homer, checking in the encyclopedia under "Bush, George."

Homer: *(singing to the tune of "Big Spender") Hey, big spender! / Dig this blender! / Rainbow suspenders! Hey, big spender!*
Crowd: *We surrender!*
Homer: *(big finish) Speeeeend some dough at Table Three!*
(The crowd cheers and applauds.)
Homer: *Thank you, neighbors, thank you! Now let's give it up for Table Five. (to the tune of "Stayin' Alive") Ah-ah-ah-ah / Table Five, Table Five /Ah-ah-ah-ah/Table Fi-i-i-i-i-ve...*

Lisa: *Actually, this is one of the nine states where Mr. Bush claims residency, Dad. I wouldn't have voted for him, but it's nice to have a celebrity in the neighborhood.*
Homer: *Wait a minute. If Lisa didn't vote for him, and I didn't vote for him—*
Marge: *You didn't vote for anybody.*
Homer: *I voted for Prell to go back to the old glass bottle. After that, I became deeply cynical.*

Flanders: *Howdily-doodily there, President Bush—or should I say, President Neighbor! I'm Ned Flanders, and this is Maude, Rod, and Todd.*
George Bush: *And howdily-doodily yourself there, Ned. This is my wife, Barbara. I call her Bar. 'Dja like some lemonade?*
Flanders: *Tip-top-notch!*
George Bush: *Okily-dokily!*
Flanders: *Thankily-dankily!*
George Bush: *Scrumpdiddlerific!*
George Bush and Flanders: *Fine and dandy! Like sour candy!*

"First Bush invades my home turf, then he takes my pals, then he makes fun of the way I talk—probably—now he steals my right to raise a disobedient, smart-alecky son! Well, that's it!"

"Ahem. Disco Stu likes disco music." Disco Stu, upset after Homer's music stops.

"Hmm. A 'Krusty' burger. That doesn't sound too appetizing. What kind of stew do you have today?" George Bush, ordering at the Krustyburger drive-thru.

Homer: *Good ol' Evergreen Terrace. The swankiest street in the classiest part of Pressboard Estates.*
Bart: *Well, If you love it so much, why are you always littering?*
Homer: *It's easier. Duh.*

Gerald Ford: *Say, Homer, do you like football?*
Homer: *Do I ever!*
Gerald Ford: *Do you like nachos?*
Homer: *Yes, Mr. Ford.*
Gerald Ford: *Well, why don't you come over and watch the game and we'll have nachos, and then some beer.*
Homer: *Ooooh!*
(Homer and Gerald Ford cross the street together.)
Homer: *Jerry, I think you and I are going to get along just—*
(Both Homer and Ford trip at Ford's driveway.)
Homer and Ford: *D'oh!*

THE STUFF YOU MAY HAVE MISSED

Homer eats "Chippos" brand snack chips; its bag features an anthropomorphic hippo.

At the rummage sale, the Simpsons sell old "I Didn't Do It" T-shirts last seen in 1F11, "Bart Gets Famous"; the Mary Worth telephone from 1F21, "Lady Bouvier's Lover"; a copy of the album "Bigger Than Jesus," by The Be Sharps from 9F21, "Homer's Barbershop Quartet"; Simpson and Son's Revitalizing Tonic from 2F07, "Grampa vs. Sexual Inadequacy"; the Olmec Indian head from 7F22, "Blood Feud"; and a painting of Ringo Starr from 7F18, "Brush with Greatness."

Gorbachev is mentioned in 1F08, "Springfield," when Krusty theorizes that the spot on his head is a symptom of herpes.

Gorbachev brings the Bushes a coffee maker as a housewarming present.

A t a rummage sale held by the Simpsons and their neighbors on Evergreen Terrace, Homer discovers a talent for hawking items. He draws a huge crowd. However, his sudden popularity is upstaged by former President George Bush and his wife, Barbara, who purchase a home across the street from the Simpsons.

Bart makes regular trips to the Bush home and becomes a total nuisance to George, who takes an immediate dislike to him. One day, Bart accidentally engages an outboard motor in the Bush's garage, shredding George's typed memoirs. George puts Bart over his knee and spanks him, prompting Homer to confront his new neighbor. Each man vows to make trouble for the other.

Homer launches bottle rockets at the Bush's home and glues a rainbow wig onto George's head. George retaliates by flying crudely rendered drawings of the Simpsons on a banner and by chewing up their lawn with his car. The war comes to a head in a sewer beneath the street, where Homer and Bart unleash a locust swarm. Realizing that the neighborhood is bringing out the worst in George, Barbara tells Marge that they are selling the house.

SCENES FROM THE CLASS STRUGGLE IN SPRINGFIELD

Episode 3F11 Original Airdate: 2/4/96 Writer: Jennifer Crittenden Director: Susie Dietter Guest Voice: Tom Kite as Himself

Marge purchases a Chanel suit for $90 dollars at a discount fashion store. Without any place special to wear it, she runs errands around town in it. She meets a wealthy ex-classmate, Evelyn, who invites Marge to her country club.

Marge's visit to the club is a success and she is invited back. Even Homer is invited to play a round of golf with Mr. Burns. Homer discovers that Smithers, Burns's caddy, cheats for his boss. Burns gives Homer his word that he will support Marge's membership if Homer keeps the secret.

Marge accidentally ruins her suit and buys another one for the upcoming membership initiation. On the evening of her initiation into the club, she realizes that her desire to fit in has changed her personality and that she was happier being her old self. She decides she'd rather go back to the way things were than continue to pursue lofty social ambitions.

EVELYN PETERS

Occupation:
Socialite.

Purpose:
To pass time chit-chatting with other friends/club members; to act as arbiter of Springfield society.

Drives:
A Mercedes wagon.

Incompetent at:
Doing menial jobs herself.

Secret shame:
Graduated from Springfield High School instead of an expensive prep school.

Biggest mysteries:
Why she doesn't know the Kwik-E-Mart pumps are self-serve; where her money came from.

I WON'T EAT ANYTHING UNLESS IT'S SHIPPED OVERNIGHT FROM VERMONT OR WASHINGTON STATE.

SHOW HIGHLIGHTS

"Well, you've come a long way from the girl I knew nothing about in high school."

"That's the trouble with first impressions: you only get to make one." Club socialite Sue-Sue, meeting Marge.

"Uh, c'mon, kids let's go sit in the car till your Mom's done fitting in."

"Love your outfit, Marge. The vest says 'Let's have lunch,' but the culottes say, 'your paying!'" Roberta, on Marge's revamped suit.

Who's Homer Simpson?

Burns: Hmmm. Who is that lavatory linksman, Smithers?
Smithers: Homer Simpson, sir. One of the fork-and-spoon operators from sector 7G.
Burns: Well, he's certainly got a loose waggle. Perhaps I've finally found a golfer worthy of a match with Monty Burns, eh?
Smithers: Oh, his waggle is no match for yours, sir. I've never seen you lose a game... except for that one in '74 when you let Richard Nixon win. That was very kind of you, sir.
Burns: Oh, he just looked so forlorn, Smithers, with his "Oh, I can't go to prison, Monty! They'll eat me alive!" Say, I wonder if this Homer Nixon is any relation?
Smithers: Unlikely, sir. They—they spell and pronounce their names differently.

Lisa: C'mon, Mom, you never treat yourself to anything.
Marge: Oh, sure I do. I treated myself to a Sanka not three days ago. But this is a real find.
Lisa: Just buy it. You don't have to rationalize everything.
Marge: All right, I will buy it. It'll be good for the economy.

"Maybe for once, someone will call me 'sir' without adding, 'You're making a scene.'"

"Yes, you're in deep 'D'oh' now." Burns, after Homer's shot lands in a sand trap.

Oh, Homie, I like your in-your-face humanity. I like the way Lisa speaks her mind. I like Bart's... I like Bart." Marge, accepting her family for who they are.

Evelyn: Marge, your family is fitting in perfectly here. If all goes well at Saturday's ball, I'd love to sponsor you for membership.
Marge: Oh, that would be a dream come true! I'll be there with bells on!
Sue-Sue: Bells? Where exactly will you be attaching them to that mangled Chanel suit?
Evelyn: Oh, don't worry, Marge. Her idea of wit is nothing more than an incisive observation humorously phrased and delivered with impeccable timing. I'm sure you'll be a smash at the ball and I just know you'll have a lovely new outfit.

Bart/Lisa/Homer: Yay!! We're getting a new TV!!
Bart: Let's go to the Sharper Image. They've got a TV shaped like a fifties diner!
Lisa: No, let's go to the Nature Company. They've got a TV assembled by Hopi Indians!
Marge: Mmmm...we can't afford to shop at any store that has a philosophy. We just need a TV. We're going to the outlet mall in Ogdenville.

Salesman: Listen, I'm not going to lie to you: those are all superior machines. But if you like to watch your TV—and I mean really watch it—you want: the Carnivale. It features: two-pronged wall plug, pre-molded hand-grip well, durable outer casing to prevent fall-apart...
Homer: Sold! You wrap it up, I'll start bringing in the pennies.

(Marge and Lisa dig through piles of clothes at the outlet store as Cletus does the same.)
Marge: I don't think these clothes are us.
Lisa: Who are they?
Cletus: Hey, Brandine! You can wear this shirt to work!
(Cletus holds up a tasseled, rhinestoned half-shirt with the words "Classy Lassy" emblazoned across the front.)
Brandine: Oh, Cletus, you know I got to wear the shirt what Dairy Queen give me.

Burns: Oh, quit cogitating, Steinmetz, and use an open-faced club! The sand wedge!
Homer: Mmm...open-faced club sandwich.

Evelyn: Well, I wonder where Marge could be?
Socialite: I hope she didn't take my attempts to destroy her too seriously.

THE STUFF YOU MAY HAVE MISSED

Ogdenville, the site of the outlet mall, is mentioned in 9F10, "Marge vs. the Monorail."

The Simpsons buy their TV at the Appliance Zone. Their slogan is, "Your grey-market superstore."

Apu sells mini-Space Mutants at his cash register.

Marge and Lisa go shopping at the Steppin' Out Fashion Mart. A sign out front reads, "Browse through Our Bra Barrel."

The motto under the gate to the Springfield Glen Country Club reads, "Proud Home of the Tippling Gadabout." It also features a duck with a golf club wrapped around its neck.

Homer reads, Our Caddies, Ourselves: A Book by and for Golfers.

BART THE FINK

Episode 3F12 Original Airdate: 2/11/96 Writer: John Swartwelder Director: Jim Reardon Guest Voice: Bob Newhart as Himself.

Occupation:
Dances for nickels down at the docks.

Special deal:
Will dance for hours on a quarter.

Agent:
Captain McCallister.

Favorite accompaniment:
That song from "Popeye" played on the concertina.

Irony:
He ain't all that handsome.

Bart opens a checking account for his share of an inheritance from a long-lost aunt. He plans to get Krusty the Clown's autograph by slipping a 25-cent check into the clown's back pocket and waits for the bank to return the endorsed check. However, when Bart receives the check, it is endorsed with a stamp instead of the signature. Dismayed, he brings the check to the bank, where officials trace the endorsement and expose Krusty as one of the biggest tax cheats in history.

The IRS takes control of Krusty's assets and his show, reducing his lifestyle to that of an average citizen. One evening, as the town watches, a depressed Krusty pilots his airplane into a mountainside. He is later pronounced dead.

A memorial service is held for Krusty at which Bob Newhart offers condolences. Shortly thereafter, Bart sees a man whom he recognizes as Krusty. With Lisa's help, he finds and identifies Krusty, who lives under the name of Rory B. Bellows. Bart convinces Krusty that he deserves the life of respect he once knew and urges him to drop his phony identity and return to public life.

Krusty kills off his pseudonym in order to collect the life insurance premium—ending his tax woes.

SHOW HIGHLIGHTS

"Yes, this should supply adequate sustenance for the 'Dr. Who' marathon." Comic Book Guy, rolling out a wheelbarrow full of tacos from the TacoMat.

"If he wants these 25 cents, he'll have to endorse the check by signing it on the back. Then when my monthly bank statement comes, I'll get the check back complete with autograph. No fuss, no muss."

"Cayman Island Offshore Holding Corporation": The stamp on the back of Bart's cancelled check to Krusty.

"The IRS Presents Herschel Krustofski's Clown-Related Entertainment Show": The name of Krusty's new show.

"Don't let Krusty's death get you down, boy. People die all the time. Just like that. Why, you could wake up dead tomorrow. Well, good night."

"I'm sorry. I can't divulge information about that customer's secret illegal account. Oh, crap, I shouldn't have said he was a customer. Oh, crap, I shouldn't have said it was a secret. Oh, crap, I certainly shouldn't have said it was illegal! Ahhh, It's too hot today." Krusty's Cayman Islands Holding Corporation representative.

"Okay, folks, show's over. Nothing to see here, show's… Oh, my God! A horrible plane crash! Hey, everybody, get a load of this flaming wreckage! Come on, crowd around, crowd around! Don't be shy, crowd around!"

"Hello, I'm Troy McClure. You might remember me from such show business funerals as 'Andre the Giant, We Hardly Knew Ye,' and 'Shemp Howard: Today We Mourn a Stooge.'"

Marge: *What are you gonna spend your money on, kids?*
Bart: *There's a special on tacos down at the TacoMat. A hundred tacos for a hundred dollars. I'm gonna get that.*
Lisa: *I'm going to contribute my money to the Corporation for Public Broadcasting.*
Marge: *Tacos! Public Broadcasting! I won't have you kids throwing your money away like that. You're both coming downtown with me and you're putting that money in the bank.*

(Bart stands at the teller window at closing time.)
Teller: *Sorry, the bank is— Oh, kid! Gosh, I meant to tell ya. Turns out that Krusty is one of the biggest tax cheats in history and they nailed him, all thanks to you.* (Bart gasps.)
Teller: *Some might say you're a hero, kid. Not me, however. I love Krusty.*

Revealed This Episode:

Jimbo Jones's real first name is "Corky." Principal Skinner's mother's first name is Agnes.

Krusty: *Oh, I can't go to jail! I got a swanky lifestyle! I'm used to the best!*
I.R.S. official: *Krusty, this is America; we don't send our celebrities to jail. We're just going to garnish your salary.*
Krusty: *Garnish my celery??*
I.R.S. official: *Please, Krusty, no jokes.*
Krusty: *Who's joking?? Ahhh, I don't know what you're saying, it all sounds so crazy to me.*
I.R.S. official #2: *It simply means we will be taking part of your salary until your debt is repaid. Say 75% for forty years.*
Krusty: *But I don't plan to live that long!*
I.R.S. official: *Better make it 95%.*

THE STUFF YOU MAY HAVE MISSED

Bart remarks to Jimbo that the payment is for on his check "Services Rendered."

Bart chooses the Hindenburg flip book series of checks. Officially, they are known as "Check Style No. 9 'Oh, the Humanity…'"

A sign on a bus dropping off Krusty reads, "Are You Missing 'Mad About You' Right Now? NBC—Must See TV Sundays at 8."

At the IRS Plaza, one sign points to Probate Court; another points to the Food Court.

Mourners at Krusty's funeral include: Don King (or possibly Lucius Sweet), David Crosby, Kermit the Frog, and Rainier Wolfcastle.

A message on a wreath at Krusty's funeral reads, "Krusty—You can never be replaced. Laffs, 369-3084."

LISA THE ICONOCLAST

Episode 3F13 Original Airdate: 2/18/96 Writer: Jonathan Collier Director: Mike B. Anderson

SHOW HIGHLIGHTS

"1796. A fiercely determined band of pioneers leaves Maryland after misinterpreting a passage in the Bible. Their destination: New Sodom. This is their story." The narrator of *Young Jebediah Springfield*, a "Rental Films" presentation.

"I hope they show the time where they traded guns to the Indians for corn, and then the Indians shot them and took the corn."

"A noble spirit embiggens the smallest man." Jebediah Springfield, on how to achieve greatness.

"Homer, y' know I support most any prejudice you can name, but your hero-phobia sickens me. You and your daughter ain't welcome here no more."

"No, no, no, no, no, no, no! Take that down! As a semilegal immigrant, your poster could land me in a predicament as red-hot as the candies which bear that name."

> **The Lyrics to the Closing "Jebediah Springfield Theme":**
> *It's that team of Jebediah Springfield/Whip those horses, let that wagon roll/That a people might embiggen America/That a man might embiggen his soul, his soul, his souuuul!*

> **Lisa:** *Jebediah was really a vicious pirate named Hans Sprungfeld. His tongue was bitten off by a Turk in a grog house fight!*
> **Homer:** *No tongue, eh? How did he talk and eat and laugh and love?*
> **Lisa:** *He had a prosthetic tongue made out of silver.*
> **Homer:** *Yes, that'd do.*

> **Quimby:** *Congratulations, Ned, you are our new town crier. May your shrill, nasal voice ring throughout our streets and brains.*
> **Flanders:** *Thankily-dank, Mayor, I shan't disappoint. Har ye, har ye! I declare myself pickled tink about Springfield's Bicen-ciddily- ti-ten-toodily-rin-tin-tennial Day.*
> **Homer:** *You suck-diddily-uck, Flanders! Gimme that! Hear ye! Hear ye! Ye olde town crier proclaimed crappy by all! Chooseth Homer Simpson and he shalt rock thy world!*
> **Wiggum:** *Good god, he is fabulous!*
> **Skinner:** *He's embiggened that role with that cromulent performance!*

"That's preposterous! Now get out—you're banned from this Historical Society! You and your children and your children's children! (pause) For three months." Hollis Hurlbut, President of the Springfield Historical Society, responding to Lisa's claim.

"Well, that settles that. There is no silver tongue. Is there, Bonesy?" Wiggum, before picking up Springfield's skull and operating it like a ventriloquist's dummy.

"We had quitters in the Revolution, too. We called them 'Kentuckians.'" George Washington, convincing Lisa to continue her fight for the truth.

> **Homer:** *Dig him up!!! Dig up that corpse! If you really love Jebediah Springfield, you'll haul his bones out of the ground to prove my daughter wrong! Dig up his grave! Pull out his tongue!*
> **Quimby:** *Can't we have one meeting that doesn't end with us digging up a corpse?*

> **Miss Hoover:** *Lisa, for you essay, "Jebediah Springfield: Superfraud," F.*
> **Lisa:** *But it's all true!*
> **Miss Hoover:** *This is nothing but dead white male-bashing from a P.C. thug. It's women like you who keep the rest of us from landing a good husband.*

THE STUFF YOU MAY HAVE MISSED

One of the settlers in *Young Jebediah Springfield* pushes the fake buffalo forward that "Jebediah Springfield" tamed.

This episode features the first reference to Kearney's adulthood when he talks about his memories of the '76 bicentennial. In later episodes, it's revealed that he has a son (4F04, "A Milhouse Divided"), owns a car (4F01, "Lisa's Date with Density"), and is of drinking age (3F24, "The Mysterious Voyage of Homer").

Homer reads a copy of the Springfield Shopper with the headline, "Parade to Distract Joyless Citizenry."

The handwritten letters that scroll quickly offscreen at the end of the film reads "Young Jebediah Springfield' - —- Rental Films——."

WANTED FOR TREASON

As Springfield's bicentennial celebration approaches, Homer wins the role of town crier in the city's parade. At school, Lisa writes an essay on town founder, Jebediah Springfield, who, her research reveals, was a murderous, silver-tongued pirate.

For her accusations, Lisa is banned from the Springfield Historical Society by its president, Hollis Hurlbut, and ostracized by the townspeople. She and Homer convince the city officials to exhume Jebediah's body to prove that he had a silver tongue. However, when the body is exhumed, no tongue is found.

Lisa deduces that Hurlbut stole the tongue and confronts him. Hurlbut confesses but explains that he only wanted to protect the image of the local hero. Lisa realizes that the myth of Jebediah is more important than historical fact and decides to keep the information from the public. She leads the parade as Homer rings his crier's bell.

Occupation:
President of the Springfield Historical Society "where the dead come alive. (metaphorically)."

Ideal snack:
Fresh brewed chicory and microwave johnnycakes.

Illnesses:
Jebeditis; denial.

Secret talent:
The old swipe-the-silver-tongue-from-the-mouth-of-a-corpse trick.

Secret shame:
Sweeps dirt under the hoop skirts of his mannequins.

HERE'S HIS FIFE, UPON WHICH HE SOUNDED THE SWEET NOTE OF FREEDOM; HIS HATCHET, WITH WHICH HE HACKED AT THE CHAINS OF OPPRESSION; AND HIS CHAMBER POT.

Guest Voice:
Donald Sutherland as Hollis Hurlbut

HOMER THE SMITHERS

Episode 3F14 Original Airdate: 2/25/96 Writer: John Swartzwelder Director: Steve Moore

SMITHERS

Occupation:
Professional lickspittle to Mr. Burns.

Duties:
Squeezing juice for Burns in the morning; tucking him in at night; moistening his eyeballs; removing his dead skin; lying to Congress; 2,795 other odd jobs.

Calling:
To be the sobering yin to Mr. Burns's raging yang.

Secret shame:
Home computer screen-saver featuring a naked Mr. Burns.

Proudest accomplishment:
Owns the largest Malibu Stacy collection in the world.

Smithers puts undue pressure on himself at work and Mr. Burns insists that he take a vacation. To ensure that his replacement won't outshine him, Smithers chooses Homer to look after Burns. However, Homer is barely able to do any of Smithers's jobs. When Burns criticizes him once too often, Homer hits his boss in the face.

Homer attempts to apologize, but Burns sends him away, fearing that Homer will hit him again. Without anyone to assist him, Burns learns to do many things for himself. When Smithers returns from his vacation, Burns no longer needs him and fires him.

Homer offers to help Smithers get his job back. They devise a plan in which Smithers rescues Burns from a phone call with his mother. However, Homer bungles the scheme, and a fight ensues between Homer and Smithers. During the scuffle, Burns is accidentally pushed out of the window. Confined to his bed, he once again becomes dependent on Smithers to meet his every need.

I'VE NEVER GONE BEHIND MR. BURNS'S BACK BEFORE, BUT SIDESHOW BOB'S ULTRA-CONSERVATIVE VIEWS, ER, CONFLICT WITH MY...CHOICE OF LIFESTYLE.

SHOW HIGHLIGHTS

 "You should have seen the murderous glint in his eye, Smithers. And his breath reeked of beer and pretzeled bread."

 "I think Smithers picked me because of my motivational skills. Everyone always says they have to work a lot harder when I'm around."

"Your new duties will include answering Mr. Burns's phone, preparing his tax return, moistening his eyeballs, assisting with his chewing and swallowing, lying to Congress, and some light typing."

 "Here are your messages: 'You have thirty minutes to move your car.' 'You have 10 minutes to move your car,' 'Your car has been impounded,' 'Your car has been crushed into a cube,' 'You have 30 minutes to move your cube.'"

 "Dough-nuts? I told you I don't like ethnic foods!"

"Everything's fine, Smithers. This Simpson fellow seems to be getting dumber by the minute. I've never seen anything quite like it… Anyhoo, you just enjoy your vacation." Burns, on the phone to Smithers.

"I've got Bobo, hot from the dryer! Careful not to burn yourself on his eye." Smithers, back with Mr. Burns.

Burns: *Pull yourself together, man! I dare say you're in need of a long vacation.*
Smithers: *No! Don't make me take a vacation! Without you, I'll wither and die!*
Burns: *That's a risk I'm willing to take.*

Smithers: *Mr. Burns can't stand talking to his mother. He never forgave her for having that affair with President Taft.*
Homer: *Heh, heh, heh! Taft, you old dog!*

Burns: *Really, Smithers, I'll be fine! I'm sure your replacement will be able to handle everything. Who is he anyway?*
Smithers: *Uh, Homer Simpson. One of your organ banks from sector 7G. All the recent events of you life have revolved around him in some way.*

Burns: *Good lord, Smithers! You look atrocious. I thought I told you to take a vacation.*
Homer: *Uh, Smithers already left, sir. I'm his replacement, Homer Simpson.*
Burns: *Ah, yes, Simpson. I'll have my lunch now. A single pillow of shredded wheat, some steamed toast, and a dodo egg.*
Homer: *But I think the dodo went extinct—*
Burns: *Get going! And answer those phones, install a computer system, and rotate my office so the window faces the hills.*

(Smithers calls Burns from a nightclub where men are dancing with each other.)
Smithers: *Mr. Burns, 48 rings! Are you all right? What did Simpson do to you?*
Burns: *Nothing other than drive me to distraction with his incompetent boobery. Terrible at everything. A complete moron. But I'm not really free to talk right now.*

Homer: *Mr. Burns, is there anything at all I can do for ya?*
Burns: *No, Homer. You've already done more for me than any man. Your brutal attack forced me to fend for myself. I realize now that being waited on hand and foot is okay for your average Joe, but it's not for me. I want to thank you.*

Mr. Burns's Criticisms of Homer:
"60 watts! What do you think this is, a tanning salon?"
"I asked for light starch on my nightcap!"
"You call this Postem?!"
"You call this a tax return?!"
"You call this a super computer?!"
"You're a travesty of a joke of an assistant."

Smithers's New Resume:
Piano Mover,
Neat and Tidy Piano Movers.
Announcer, Springfield Dragway.
Barney Guarder, Moe's Tavern.

THE STUFF YOU MAY HAVE MISSED

Smithers uses a Macintosh OS computer.

One of the drag racers at the Springfield Dragway is sponsored by Amalgamated Pornography.

Burns throws shredded environmental reports out the window.

Smithers brings pineapples back from his vacation.

While imitating Burns's mother, Homer calls Burns "Montel."

A FISH CALLED SELMA

Episode 3F15 Original Airdate: 3/24/96 Writer: Jack Barth Director: Mark Kirkland Guest Voice: Jeff Goldblum as MacArthur Parker

Troy McClure talks Selma into illegally letting him pass his driver's license vision test in exchange for a dinner date. At the end of the evening, the two run into a group of paparazzi, who snap their picture. When the photo is published in the next day's *Springfield Shopper*, it instantly erases McClure's image as a fish fetishist. His estranged agent, MacArthur Parker, renews contact and tells him if he keeps dating, he can get work again.

As McClure continues to see Selma, his popularity soars. To maintain his image, he proposes. Before the wedding, McClure admits to Homer that he is only marrying Selma for the good publicity. Homer waits until after the wedding to tell Marge the truth about Selma's marriage.

Marge and Patty confront Selma, but she doesn't want to believe the news. Upon returning home, however, Selma asks Troy if their marriage is a sham. He immediately confesses, but convinces her that the marriage will be fun. Selma goes along with his plan until Troy tells her that they must have a child if his success is to continue. Selma decides not to bring a child into a loveless marriage and leaves with her iguana, Jub-Jub.

SHOW HIGHLIGHTS

 "Hi, I'm Troy McClure. You may remember me from *The Greatest Story Ever Hula-ed* and *They Came to Burgle Carnegie Hall*.

"Tell ya what—just go down to the DMV tomorrow and try to pass that eye test. I'll tear up this ticket, but I'm still going to have to ask you for a bribe." Chief Wiggum, letting Troy McClure off easy.

"You're Troy McClure! I remember you from such films as *Meet Joe Blow* and *Give My Remains to Broadway*. Stars like you don't need glasses."

"Hello, Selma Bouvier? It's Troy McClure. You may remember me from such dates as last night's dinner!"

The Contrabulous Fabtraption of Professor Horatio Hufnagel: Troy McClure turns down the supporting lead in *McBain 4: Fatal Discharge* for this film. He plans to direct and star in the film for Twentieth Century Fox.

"Oh, Princess Fair, willst thou grant me thine dainty hoof in marriage?" Onscreen Troy, to Miss Piggy, and the real Troy, to Selma.

"Tonight, 70's leading man Troy McClure has finally met the woman of his dreams. We may remem—woman? Huh. Okay. We may remember Troy from such films as *The Verdict Was Mail Fraud* and *Leper in the Backfield*." Entertainment show co-host, announcing the news of Troy and Selma's romance.

"Hi. I remember you from such filmstrips as *Locker Room Towel Fight: The Blinding of Larry Driscoll*."

> **The Truth:**
> *Selma:* Is this a sham marriage?
> *Troy:* Sure, baby. Is that a problemo?

> *Marge:* It was a beautiful wedding. I've never seen Selma happier.
> *Homer:* That reminds me—Troy said something interesting last night at the bar. Apparently he doesn't really love Selma and the marriage is just a sham to help his career. Well, enough talk. Let's snuggle.

> **The "Thank You" Dinner:**
> *Selma:* What are you working on now?
> *Troy:* I've been reading a lot of scripts lately. You know, it's a lot cheaper than going to the movies.

> *Parker:* Ever hear of "Planet of the Apes?"
> *Troy:* The movie or the planet?
> *Parker:* The brand-new, multi-million dollar musical. And you are starring as the human!
> *Troy:* It's the part I was born to play, baby!

> *Parker:* I think they want you to play McBain's sidekick in—brace yourself— the new McBain movie!
> *Troy:* McBain's sidekick?! Hot damn! I'm going to Sea World!

> **"Dr. Zaius Dr. Zaius" Lyrics:**
> *Dr. Zaius, Dr. Zaius!/ Dr. Zaius, Dr. Zaius!/ Dr. Zaius!/ Oh, Dr. Zaius/Dr. Zaius, Dr. Zaius!*
> *Troy:* What's wrong with me?
> *Dr. Zaius:* I think you're crazy.
> *Troy:* I want a second opinion.
> *Dr. Zaius:* You're also lazy.
> *Chorus*
> *Troy:* Can I play the piano anymore?
> *Dr. Zaius:* Of course you can.
> *Troy:* Well, I couldn't before.
> *Chorus*

THE STUFF YOU MAY HAVE MISSED

A picture of Rainier Wolfcastle with the caption, "Look Who's Drunk," appears on the society page of the *Springfield Shopper*.

Among the pictures of stars on the wall of the Pimento Grove are Conan O'Brien and Birch Barlow (both seen in 2F17, "Radioactive Man.")

Troy reads a book called *Bean Bag Furniture Repair* when he gets the call from MacArthur Parker.

The following movie posters hang on Troy McClure's walls: *Astro-Heist Gemini 3, Incident at Noon,* and *My Darling Beefeater.*

The marquee at the Aphrodite Inn welcomes "Mr. and Mrs. McClure" and "Cher and Contest Winner."

TROY MCCLURE

Occupation:
Past B-Movie idol, and present host of all informercials, funerals, award shows, telethons, Do-It-Yourself videos, TV specials, and educational films relating to Springfield.

Car:
Delorean.

House:
Early seventies decrepit aquatic; For sale by owner.

Favorite dinner spots:
The Pimento Grove; Ugli.

Secret shame:
His prescription glasses make him look like a geek; And the fish thing.

HAVE IT YOUR WAY, BABY.

Guest Voice:
Phil Hartman as Troy McClure

CHESTER J. LAMPWICK

Identity:
Bum in Bumtown,
the bad part of Springfield.

Demeanor:
Bitter.

Claims:
To have invented Itchy the cartoon mouse as well as the whole concept of cartoon violence.

Goals:
To live in a solid-gold house; to have millions of dollars; to own a rocket car; to have his health.

Tends to:
Take food as payment for work he never performs.

Favorite meal:
Liver and onions.

Favorite food to toss:
Tomatoes.

BEFORE I CAME ALONG, ALL CARTOON ANIMALS DID WAS PLAY THE UKULELE. I CHANGED ALL THAT.

Guest Voice:
Kirk Douglas as Chester.

While watching the Itchy & Scratchy parade, Bart encounters Chester J. Lampwick, who claims that Roger Meyers, Sr., stole the Itchy character from him. As proof, Chester produces an old cartoon reel of his original Itchy from 1919, but after he shows it to Bart and Milhouse, the projector melts the print.

Bart and Chester pay a visit to Roger Meyers, Jr., at Itchy & Scratchy Studios, where Chester asks Meyers for $800 million in damages. When Meyers kicks them out of the studio, they hire Lionel Hutz to handle the case in court. Just as Chester is about to lose his case, Bart produces a rare pen-and-ink Itchy drawing and proves that it predates the first Meyers cartoon. The court rules in Chester's favor, and Itchy & Scratchy Studios is shut down.

Now forced to watch boring cartoons, Bart and Lisa work unsuccessfully to strike a deal between Meyers and Chester. Meanwhile, Lester and Eliza, two children who bear an uncanny physical resemblance to Bart and Lisa, bring an end to the stalemate by exposing the U.S. Postal Service's plagiarism of another Roger Meyers, Sr., character. After receiving a sizable settlement from the government, Itchy & Scratchy Studios reopens and is soon back in business.

DEDICATED TO:

LESTER and ELIZA
FOR MAKING ALL THIS POSSIBLE

SHOW HIGHLIGHTS

"He stole the character from me in 1928. When I complained, his thugs kicked me out of his office and dropped an anvil on me. Luckily, I was carrying an umbrella at the time." Chester, on inventing Itchy.

Early Itchy: Lampwick's cartoon short, "Itchy, the Lucky Mouse in: Manhattan Madness," finds Itchy smashing an Irishman over the head with a light bulb, pulling him by his beard through a clothes wringer. Then he hacks off Teddy Roosevelt's head with an axe. Splattered with blood, he winks at the camera.

"He's a good man. Every Christmas, he goes down to the pound and rescues one cat and one mouse and gives them to a hungry family."
Bart, on Roger Meyers, Jr.

"Look out Itchy! He's Irish!"

The other members of the Itchy & Scratchy family: Brown-Nose Bear, Disgruntled Goat, Flatulent Fox, Rich Uncle Skeleton, Dinner Dog.

Bart: *You invented Itchy? The "Itchy & Scratchy" Itchy?*
Chester: *Sure. In fact, I invented the whole concept of cartoon violence. Before I came along, all cartoon animals did was play the ukulele. I changed all that.*
Bart: *Well, I'm not calling you a liar, but...(pause) but I can't think of a way to finish that sentence.*

The "Amendment to Be" Short:

(On TV, a little boy encounters a sad, cartoon bill sitting in front of Congress.)
Little boy: *Hey, who left all this garbage on the steps of Congress?*
Amendment: *I'm not garbage...(Breaking into song) I'm an amendment to be/Yes, an amendment to be/And I'm hoping that they'll ratify me/There's a lot of flag-burners who have got too much freedom/I want to make it legal for policemen to beat 'em/'Cause there'd limits to our liberties/'Least I hope and pray that there are/'Cause those liberal freaks go too far.*
Little boy: *But why can't we just make a law against flag-burning?*
Amendment: *Because that law would be unconstitutional. But if we change the Constitution—*
Little boy: *—then we could make all sorts of crazy laws!*
Amendment: *Now you're catchin' on!*

(Bart and Lisa sit on the couch, watching and frowning.)
Bart: *What the hell is this?*
Lisa: *It's one of those crappy seventies throwbacks that appeals to Generation Xers.*
Bart: *We need another Vietnam to thin out their ranks a little.*

(Back on the TV, the little boy and the bill keep talking.)
Little boy: *But what if they say you're not good enough to be in the Constitution?*
Amendment: *Then I'll crush all opposition to me!/And I'll make Ted Kennedy pay/If he fights back I'll say/That he's gay.*
Congressman: *Good news, amendment! They ratified ya! You're in the U.S. Constitution!*
Amendment: *Oh yeah! Door's open, boys!*

(Wild, gun-wielding bills race up the steps to the Capitol, firing their weapons.)

"Animation is built on plagiarism. If it weren't for someone plagiarizing 'The Honeymooners,' we wouldn't have 'The Flintstones.' If someone hadn't ripped off 'Sergeant Bilko,' there'd be no 'Top Cat.' 'Huckleberry Hound,' 'Chief Wiggum,' 'Yogi Bear'? Ha! 'Andy Griffith,' 'Edward G. Robinson,' 'Art Carney.'"

Marge: *Bart, Lisa it's eleven o'clock at night! Where do you think you're going?*
Bart: *Downtown.*
Lisa: *We've got to get seats for the Itchy & Scratchy parade.*
Marge: *I won't have my children sitting alone on a cold, dangerous street all night. Homer, you go, too.*
Homer: *Ooohh, why can't they just take the gun?*

THE STUFF YOU MAY HAVE MISSED

Charlie Chaplin is one of the people hanging out in Bumtown.

Bumtown has a "4-H Club" with the name "Moe" painted on the side of a building.

The Olmec Indian head Mr. Burns gave the Simpsons in 7F22, "Blood Feud," is still in the basement.

Roger Meyers stays at a Worst Western Hotel. Its marquee recommends, "Ask about Our Sheet Rental."

Lester and Eliza look like Bart and Lisa as seen on the Simpson shorts appearing on the "Tracey Ullman Show" from 1987-1989.

Principal Skinner closes school the day before spring vacation and invents Go to Work with Your Parents Day to keep the students occupied. Bart spends his time with Patty and Selma at the DMV. When the sisters are distracted, he creates his own driver's license and uses the ID to get into an R-rated movie. Bart, Milhouse, and Nelson later run into Martin, who has earned $600 trading commodities at his father's job. Armed with money and the fake ID, the boys rent a car. Meanwhile, Lisa accompanies Homer to the power plant and spends the day at his work station.

Bart, Milhouse, Nelson, and Martin tell their parents that they are attending the National Grammar Rodeo in Canada and sneak off for a trip in Bart's rental car. Scanning an outdated AAA guidebook, they choose Knoxville, Tennessee, as their Spring Break destination, planning to see the World's Fair, which was held there 14 years earlier. In Knoxville, their car is destroyed, and they are stranded without money or transportation.

Bart places a collect call to Lisa, who has spent the entire spring vacation with Homer at work, to ask her for advice. Lisa obtains Homer's promise that he won't get upset and reveals Bart's predicament. Homer orders equipment for the power plant and ships it via courier from Knoxville, with the boys stowed away inside the crate.

SHOW HIGHLIGHTS

"Hot damn! No more sittin' in the dirt in the drive-in!" Cletus, upon taking the picture for his driver's license.

> **Lisa:** *Bart rented a car with a phony driver's license and drove Milhouse, Nelson and Martin to a wig outlet in Knoxville and the car got crushed and they're out of money and they can't get home and Bart's working as a courier and just came back from Hong Kong.*
> **Homer:** *(eerily calm) Yes, that's a real pickle. Would you excuse me for a moment?*
> *(Homer puts on a radiation suit hood and yells out indistinguishable profanities.)*
> **Homer:** *All right, I have thought this through. I will send Bart the money to fly home, then I will murder him.*

"I can think of at least two things wrong with that title." Nelson, after seeing the film, *Naked Lunch.*

 "Yes, Go to Work with Your Parents Day. Tomorrow, you will learn by doing and apply your knowledge of fractions and gym to real-world situations."

"The way I figure it, if the candy stays in the machine for more than a year, it's up for grabs." Homer, showing Lisa how to take candy from the vending machine.

"Simpson, how'd you like to escort 500 Big Macs to Marlon Brando's island?" Knoxville Bonded Courier Service Owner, to Bart.

 "Dad, you tell everybody everything! Even Moe knew when I threw up on the dentist!"

> **Nelson:** *What is this place?*
> **Bart:** *Branson, Missouri. My dad says it's like Vegas if it were run by Ned Flanders.*

"He's very quiet and he enjoys puzzles." Lisa, describing Langdon Alger, the boy she currently likes.

> **Patty:** *Some days, we don't let the line move at all.*
> **Selma:** *We call those "weekdays."*

 "Well, I realize it's trite, but we could tour the bridges of Madison County."

> **"Hello, Moe's Tavern..."**
> **Homer:** *Hello, I'd like to speak with a Mr. Snotball, first name Ura.*
> **Moe:** *Ura Snotball?*
> **Homer:** *What? How dare you? If I find out who this is, I'll staple a flag to your butt and mail you to Iran!*

> *(In the car, Bart hands Milhouse, Martin, and Nelson envelopes.)*
> **Bart:** *Gentlemen, for our road trip, I have taken the liberty of preparing an airtight and utterly plausible alibi for use on our parents.*
> *(In the Van Houtten household, Milhouse talks to his parents.)*
> **Milhouse:** *I've been selected to represent the school at the National Grammar Rodeo at the Sheraton Hotel in Canada.*
> *(In the Prince household, Martin talks to his parents.)*
> **Martin:** *I've been selected to represent the school at the National Grammar Rodeo at the Sheraton Hotel in Canada.*
> *(Nelson walks out of his house, calling behind him.)*
> **Nelson:** *I'm goin' away for a week. See ya.*

> *(Bart and the guys alongside a family in a stationwagon.)*
> **Father:** *If you kids can't keep your hands to yourself, I'm going to turn this car around and there'll be no Cape Canaveral for anybody!*
> *(Nelson leans out of the car and furtively slaps the father on the back of the neck.)*
> **Father:** *That's it! Back to Winnipeg!*
> *(The stationwagon peels off the road and turns around, roaring off.)*

THE STUFF YOU MAY HAVE MISSED

Principal Skinner refers to himself as "Principal" even when speaking with a worker with an airline.

Bart's driver's license lists his birthday as Feb. 11, 1970 and identifies him as being 4'0" tall, 85 pounds, with BL eyes (probably blue).

The song Bart and the boys listen to in the car is 1975's "Radar Love" by Golden Earring.

Some of the shows playing in Branson, Mo.: "Waylon Jennings and Madam," "Phantom of the Opry," "Up with White People," "Fent Dixon and the Second Helping Band," "Lurleen Lumpkin and Pip Diddler," "Alabamania," "Show Show Show."

The review on the marquee advertising Andy Williams reads, "Wow! He's still got it! — *Look* magazine." (*Look* magazine went out of business more than two decades ago.)

CLETUS

Identity:
Slack-jawed yokel.

Speaks with:
Pronounced Southern drawl.

His woman:
Brandine.

Father of:
26 children.

Dog:
Geech (a "smellhound").

Bowls for:
The Stereotypes.

HEY MA, LOOK AT THAT POINTY-HAIREDED LITTLE GIRL!

VERY TALL MAN

Identity:
Perhaps Springfield's tallest resident.

Auto of choice:
Volkswagen Beetle.

Pet peeve:
Being made fun of, particularly by young bullies.

Chief adversary of the moment:
Nelson Muntz.

DO YOU FIND SOMETHING COMICAL ABOUT MY APPEARANCE WHEN I AM DRIVING AN AUTOMOBILE?

A s Bart and Milhouse wonder aloud if anything truly interesting ever happens to anyone in Springfield, a series of interconnected vignettes focus on the events in the lives of parents, lovers, friends, relatives, businessmen, and children.

At the Kwik-E-Mart, Sanjay convinces Apu to close the store for five minutes of wild merriment. Marge tries to remove a wad of bubble gum from Lisa's hair. A bee sting sends Smithers to the hospital. Moe is elated when Barney pays $2,000 on his bar tab—until Snake comes in and steals the money.

Meanwhile, Principal Skinner invites Superintendent Chalmers to his home for dinner, substituting Krusty Burgers when his roast burns, and sets the kitchen on fire.

Homer accidentally locks Maggie in a newspaper box. Chief Wiggum and Lou discuss the differences between Krustyburger and McDonald's. Bumblebee Man's real-life dilemmas rival his sitcom skits. Reverend Lovejoy's dog soils Flanders's lawn as Marge experiments on gum-removal techniques for Lisa's hair.

The stories continue. Milhouse traps his father inside a *Pulp Fiction*-like nightmare in Herman's military antiques store. Slack-jawed yokel Cletus rescues a pair of boots from a power line to give to his woman, Brandine. Wiggum, Snake, and Mr. Van Houten are taken hostage by antiques store owner Herman. A barber gives Lisa a trendy hairdo. A tall man takes revenge on Nelson, forcing the bully to march down the street with his pants around his ankles.

SHOW HIGHLIGHTS

"Ho! Goodbye student loan payments!" Snake, upon emptying Moe's cash register.

"Smithers, you infernal ninny! Stick your left hoof on that flange now! Now if you can get it through your bug-addled brain, jam the second mephitic clodhopper of yours on the right doo-dad! Now pump those scrawny chicken legs, you stuporous funker!"

"C'mon, it's eleven o'clock. I need some sugar."

"Come on, boy. This is the spot—right here. That's a good boy. Good boy. Do your dirty, sinful business." Reverend Lovejoy, with his dog on Ned Flanders's lawn.

What Marge uses to try to get the gum out of Lisa's hair: Olive oil, lemon juice, tartar sauce, chocolate syrup, gravy, bacon fat, hummus, baba ghanouj, peanut butter, and mayonnaise.

"Hey everybody, look at this, it's that boy who laughs at everyone! Let's laugh at him!" The Tall Man, while forcing Nelson to march down the street with his pants around his ankles.

(Cletus presents Brandine with a pair of old boots.)
Cletus: *Hey, Brandine, you might could wear these to your job interview.*
Brandine: *And scuff up the topless dancin' runway? Naw, you best brang 'em back from where you got 'em.*

ABOUT SPRINGFIELD

Episode 3F18   Original Airdate: 4/14/96
Writers: Richard Appel, David S. Cohen, John Collier, Jennifer Crittenden, Greg Daniels, Brent Forrester, Rachel Pulido, Steve Tompkins, Josh Weinstein and Matt Groening.
Writing Supervisor: Greg Daniels
Director: Jim Reardon

Movie Moments:
The episode title is a play on the film *Thirty-Two Short Films about Glenn Gould*. The McDonald's discussion and Herman segments parody *Pulp Fiction*.

"Skinner & the Superintendent" Theme Song Lyrics:
Skinner with his crazy explanations/The superintendent's gonna need his medication/When he hears Skinner's lame exaggerations/ There'll be trouble in town, tonight!

"The Tomfoolery of Professor John Frink" Theme Song Lyrics:
Professor Frink, Professor Frink/He'll make you laugh/He'll make you think/He likes to run and then the thing with the...person...

"Cletus, the Slack-Jawed Yokel" Theme Song Lyrics:
Some folks'll never eat a skunk/but then again some folks'll/like Cletus, the Slack-Jawed Yokel.

THE STUFF YOU MAY HAVE MISSED

In order to ring up a $14 billion tab at Moe's, Barney would need to drink 10 beers a day, at $2 apiece, for roughly 1.95 million years.

Homer's pasteurized process imitation cheese product in the can is called Cheesy Does It.

This episode features the third appearance of the Capital City Goofball, last seen in 9F19, "Krusty Gets Kancelled."

The name of the barbershop Lisa goes to is called Snippy Longstocking's.

There are more than 2,000 McDonald's restaurants in the state where Springfield is located, but none in Springfield itself.

When Homer gets Maggie stuck in the newspaper machine, she holds up a newspaper article headlined "Deadbeat Dad Beat Dead."

The chihuahua in this episode was previously seen in 2F11, "Bart's Comet" and 2F17, "Radioactive Man."

This is one of only four "Simpsons" episodes to be broadcast with its title on screen, the others being 7G07, "The Telltale Head," 7F10, "Bart Gets Hit by a Car," and 3F31, "The Simpsons 138th Episode Spectacular."

Skinner: *Oh, well, that was wonderful. A good time was had by all; I'm pooped.*
Chalmers: *Yes, I should be—Good Lord! What is happening in there?*
Skinner: *Aurora Borealis?*
Chalmers: *Aurora Borealis? At this time of year, at this time of the day, in this part of the country, localized entirely within your kitchen?*
Skinner: *Yes.*
Chalmers: *May I see it?*
Skinner: *No.*
Agnes Skinner: *(from upstairs) Seymour, the house is on fire!*
Skinner: *No, Mother, it's just the Northern Lights.*

(Smithers and Burns ride on a bicycle built for two; Burns reads a magazine with his feet on Smithers's back as Smithers stops pedaling.)
Mr. Burns: *Smithers, what is the meaning of this slacking off?*
Smithers: *Uh, there's a bee in my eye, sir.*
Burns: *And?*
Smithers: *I'm allergic to bee stings. They cause me to, uh, die.*
Burns: *But we're running out of forward momentum!*
Smithers: *Uh, perhaps you could pedal for just a little while, sir.*
Burns: *Quite impossible. I can try to bat him off if you like.*
Smithers: *Uh, really, that's o—aaaaah!*
(He slumps over the handlebars).

Dr. Nick Faces the Medical Review Board:
Dr. Nick: *Hi, everybody!*
The Board: *Hi, Dr. Nick.*
Board chairman: *Dr. Nick, this malpractice committee has received a few complaints against you. Of the 160 gravest charges, the most troubling are performing major operations with a knife and fork from a seafood restaurant...*
Dr. Nick: *But I cleaned them with my napkin!*
Board chairman: *...misuse of cadavers—*
Dr. Nick: *I get here earlier when I drive in the carpool lane!*

Sanjay: *I wish you'd come to my party, Apu. You could use some merriment!*
Apu: *Listen, serving the customer is merriment enough for me. (to exiting Bart and Milhouse) Thank you, come again. (to Sanjay) You see? Most enjoyable.*
Sanjay: *Oh, I guarantee a wing-ding of titanic proportions. You will be there or kindly be square.*
Apu: *Well, I don't like to leave the store, but...*
(Apu reaches under the counter, dusts off "Back in 5 Minutes" sign.)
Apu: *...for the next five minutes, I'm going to party like it's on sale for $19.99!*

Description:
The fightingest squad in the fightingest company in the third fightingest battalion in the army.

Commander:
Sgt. Abraham Simpson.

Roster:
Iggy Wiggum, Sheldon Skinner, and Arnie Gumble; there was also Griff, Asa, Ox, Etch, and a troublemaker named Montgomery Burns.

War of service:
World War Two.

Biggest success:
Liberating priceless works of art from defeated Germans.

Biggest misfortune:
The Veterans' Day float disaster of '79, resulting in five fatalities.

Proof of membership:
A tattoo of a fish making a muscle with "Flying Hellfish" written around it.

RAGING ABE SIMPSON AND HIS GRUMBLING GRANDSON IN "THE CURSE OF THE FLYING HELLFISH"

Episode 3F19   Original Airdate: 4/28/96   Writer: John Collier   Director: Jeff Lynch

 fter attending Grandparents' Day at school and embarrassing Bart in front of his class, Grampa learns that a member of his old army unit has died. Now, either he or Mr. Burns, who also served in the unit, will inherit a fortune from the past—depending on which one survives the other. After the funeral, Burns plans to have Grampa killed.

Following three attempts on his life, Grampa seeks refuge at the Simpsons' home. He tells Bart the story of his old platoon, the Flying Hellfish: during the war, the members of the platoon made a pact to determine which one of them would eventually own the priceless art that the unit stole from the Nazis. Each one received a key to a special safe. As each member died, his key was added to the safe's giant lock. The last surviving member would own the treasure. Bart refuses to believe Grampa until Burns tries to steal Grampa's key by forcing his way into the house on a mechanical platform. Bart manages to get both keys in his possession.

Together, Bart and Grampa set out to capture the booty at the bottom of Lake Springfield. However, as soon as they recover the case of masterpieces, Burns steals it. Grampa and Bart give chase and a fight ensues between Grampa and Burns, which is broken up by representatives of the State Department, who have arrived to return the paintings to their proper heir. Although Grampa has lost his chance of inheriting a fortune, Bart is proud of him.

SHOW HIGHLIGHTS

"Second class? What about Social Security, bus discounts, Medic-Alert jewelry, Gold Bond powder, pants all the way up to your armpits, and all those other senior perks? Oh, if you ask me, old folks have it pretty sweet."

"Look, if you're going to stay in my room, could you at least stop making up gibberish?" Bart, incredulous at Grampa's claim to fortune.

"I tried to meet you halfway on this, Simpson, but you had to be Little Johnny Live-a-lot. Now give me your key to the Hellfish Bonanza."

Priorities:
Bart: I'm sorry I cost you your fortune, Grampa.
Grampa: Ah, the fortune doesn't matter, boy. The important thing is you're safe. Now, let's get that fortune!

The Rightful Owner:
Von Wortzenburger: Ja, ja, ja. Mach schnell mit der art things, huh? I must get back to the Dance Centrum in Stuttgart in time to see Kraftwerk. Hey, and dumbkopf! Watch out for the CD changer in my trunk, huh?! Idiot!
Grampa: I guess he deserves it more than I do... Well at least I got to show you I wasn't always a pathetic old kook.
Bart: You never were, Grampa.
Grampa: Aw, I'd hug ya, but I know you'd just get embarrassed.
Bart: I won't get embarrassed. I don't care who knows I love my Grampa.
Von Wortzenburger: Hey, funboys! Get a room!

"I'll thank you to stop pinching my Botticelli." Burns, showing up to claim the art.

"Now Burnsie, there's one thing we don't stand for in the Hellfish, and that's trying to kill your commanding officer. So consider this your dishonorable discharge. You're outta my unit. You're outta the frontline. And that means the paintings are mine. Private, you are dismissed."

Bart: Hey, Grampa, do you think I could've been a Flying Hellfish?
Grampa: You're a gutsy daredevil with a give-'em-hell attitude and a fourth-grade education. You coulda made sergeant.

Grampa: Let me in! Someone's trying to kill me! Sweet Merciful McGillicuddy, ya gotta open the door!
Homer: Who is it?

Grampa Speaks before Bart's Class:
Grampa: Now, my story begins in 19-dickety-two. We had to say "dickety" 'cause the Kaiser had stolen our word "twenty." I chased that rascal to get it back, but gave up after dickety-six miles.
(The children laugh.)
Martin: Dickety? Highly dubious.
Grampa: What're you cackling at, Fatty? Too much pie, that's your problem!
(Martin is shocked. The children laugh at him.)
Now, I'd like to digress from my prepared remarks to discuss how I invented the terlet.
Mrs. Krabappel: "Terlet." Hah!
Grampa: Stop your snickering! I spent three years on that terlet!

Nuts to That:
Homer: Where are you two going at this hour?
Bart: On a treasure hunt.
Homer: Oh, can I come?
Grampa: Only if you're ready to stare danger in the face, put your manhood to the ultimate test, and take—
Homer: Pass.

THE STUFF YOU MAY HAVE MISSED

The banner for Grandparents' Day reads, "A Low-Cost Outing for Seniors."

Homer plays with a Chinese finger trap as Grampa arrives at his door.

A school of three-eyed fish swims in Lake Springfield.

Bart says, "consarn it" in this episode. He uses this expression in 9F21, "Homer's Barbershop Quartet."

Although Grampa's squad was named "The Flying Hellfish," the Hellfish stationery and the memorial at the cemetery both read, "Fighting Hellfish."

MUCH APU ABOUT NOTHING

Episode 3F20   Original Airdate: 5/5/96   Writer: David S. Cohen   Director: Susie Dietter

 After a bear wanders into Springfield, Mayor Quimby raises taxes to establish a Bear Patrol, angering the townspeople. To distract them, he blames the high taxes on illegal immigrants and initiates Proposition 24, calling for the deportation of illegal immigrants from Springfield.

Apu worries that he, too, will be deported, since his visa expired after his graduation from an American college. To avoid scrutiny, he buys a new American identity from Fat Tony, but realizes that he is betraying his Indian heritage.

Lisa tells Apu that he qualifies for amnesty and can therefore apply for American citizenship. Apu passes the citizenship test, but Proposition 24 still passes.

SHOW HIGHLIGHTS

"This is Kent Brockman with a special report from the Channel 6 Newscopter. A large bearlike animal, most likely a bear, has wandered down from the hills, in search of food or perhaps employment. Please remain calm. Stay in your homes."

> **Homer:** *I'm sick of these constant bear attacks! It's like a freakin' country bear jamboroo around here.*
> **Ned:** *Well, now realistically, Homer, I've lived here some thirty-odd years; this is the first and only bear I've ever seen.*
> **Homer:** *Hey, if you want wild bears eatin' your children and scarin' away your salmon, that's your business. But I'm not gonna take it! Who's with me?*

"We're here! We're queer! We don't want any more bears! We're here! We're queer! We don't want any more bears!"

> **Quimby:** *Are these morons getting dumber or just louder?*
> **Aide:** *Dumber, sir. They won't give up the Bear Patrol, but they won't pay taxes for it either.*

"In one week, the town will vote on a special referendum: whether or not to deport all illegal immigrants from Springfield. It shall be known as Proposition 24!" Quimby, giving birth to an illegitimate law.

"Oh, my God. I got so swept up in the scapegoating and fun of Proposition 24, I never stopped to think it might affect someone I cared about. You know what, Apu. I am really, really gonna miss you."

"Whoa, whoa, whoa, whoa, whoa, whoa, whoa. Can the courtesy, you're an American now. Remember: you were born in Green Bay, Wisconsin. Your parents were Herb and Judy Nahasapeemapetilon. And if you do not wish to arouse suspicion, I strongly urge you to act American."

"I cannot deny my roots and I cannot keep up this charade. I only did it because I love this land, where I have the freedom to say, and to think, and to charge whatever I want!"

"Wow. You must love this country more than I love a cold beer on a hot Christmas morning. Darn it, Apu, I'm not gonna let them kick you out!" Homer, changing his mind about Proposition 24.

"I'd rather eat poison. My name's already Selma Bouvier Terwilliger Hutz McClure. God knows it's long enough without Nahasapeetapet—whatever. From now on, I'm only marrying for love. And possibly once more for money."

"All right men, here's the order of deportations. First we'll be rounding up your tired, then your poor, then your huddled masses yearning to breathe free." Wiggum, readying his force.

> **Marge:** *But, Apu, the vote on Proposition 24 is on Tuesday. You'll have to pass the test before then.*
> **Apu:** *Oh, no. That is not nearly enough time to learn over 200 years of American history.*
> **Homer:** *Oh. It can't be that many! C'mon, Apu. I'll be your tutor.*

> **Nelson:** *Hey, German boy, go back to Germania!*
> **Uter:** *Aaaha...I do not deserve this. I have come here legally as an exchange student!*
> **Skinner:** *Young man, the only thing we exchanged for you is our national dignity.*

THE STUFF YOU MAY HAVE MISSED

Signs that Barney, Moe, and Homer paint at the Yes on 24 Headquarters (at Moe's): "Yes on 24!" "United States for United Statesians," and "Homer say 'Get Out.'"

Signs held by protesters outside the Kwik-E-Mart: "The Only Good Foreigner Is Rod Stewart," "Buy American," and "Get Eurass Back to Eurasia."

Apu falls asleep at the kitchen table, on top of Homer's open notebook; when he wakes up, it's shut.

Sign outside the Immigration and Naturalization Service Building: "The United States: 131 Years Without a Civil War."

Dr. Nick has crib notes on his arm to help him cheat on his naturalization exam.

Lisa reads the book, *Backdoors to Citizenship.*

Characters taking the test for citizenship include: Akira, Apu, Luigi, Bumblebee Man, Dr. Nick, and Moe.

THE BEAR

Identity:
The bear that started the immigration controversy in Springfield.

Color:
Brown.

Eyes:
Curious.

Claws:
Significant.

Diet:
Garbage; mailboxes.

Tends to:
Wander into residential neighborhoods.

HOMERPALOOZA

Episode 3F21 Original Airdate: 5/19/96 Writer: Brent Forrester Director: Wes Archer Guest Voices: Sonic Youth as Themselves, Cypress Hill as Themselves, Smashing Pumpkins as Themselves, Peter Frampton as Himself

W hile driving Bart and Lisa to school, Homer discovers how "uncool" his children think he is. To prove them wrong, he buys tickets to the Hullabalooza music festival for himself, Bart, and Lisa.

As the rock bands perform, Homer tries unsuccessfully to blend in. Forcibly escorted to the fringe of the crowd, a projectile prop pig flies into his gut at point-blank range. Homer's rugged abdominal constitution helps him withstand the force of the pig. When this talent is recognized, he joins the Hullabalooza freak show, during which a cannonball is shot at his stomach.

When Homer's stomach starts making strange noises, a veterinarian warns him not to perform anymore. However, Homer is determined to pursue his new career in rock and roll. Hullabalooza's next stop is Springfield, where Homer's family attends the show. Homer strides out on stage, but when the cannon is fired he steps aside, explaining to his family that they mean more to him than having a "cool" job.

> I'VE BEEN LOOKING FOR A BIG FATSO TO SHOOT WITH A CANNON. I'D LIKE VERY MUCH FOR YOU TO BE THAT FATSO.

SHOW HIGHLIGHTS

 "Nobody knows the band Grand Funk? The wild, shirtless lyrics of Mark Farner? The bong-rattling bass of Mel Shocker? The competent drum-work of Don Brewer? Oh, man!"

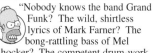 "Dad! No one cares about any of your stupid dinosaur bands! You have the worst, lamest taste in music ever!"

"That's fine for you, Marge. But I used to rock and roll all night and party every day. Then it was every other day. Now I'm lucky if I can find half an hour a week in which to get funky. I've got to get out of this rut and back into the groove!"

"It smells like Otto's jacket."
Lisa, commenting on a strange scent she and Bart smell coming from the crowd during Cypress Hill's set.

Pageant of the Transmundane: The name of Hullabalooza's freak show.

"You know, my kids think you're the greatest. And thanks to your gloomy music, they've finally stopped dreaming of a future I can't possibly provide." Homer, to

Billy Corgan of Smashing Pumpkins.

"Homer, nothing's more important to me than the health and well-being of my freaks. I'm sending you to a vet." The manager of the freak show, to Homer.

 "Wow, it's like Woodstock, only with advertisements everywhere and tons of security guards."

The veterinarian, examining Homer: "My God. Those cannonballs have practically demolished your stomach. From now on, no cannonballs, no spicy food, and when you lie in a hammock, please—rest your beer on your head or your genitals."

> **Homer:** *Where can I find the latest releases by Bread?*
> **Sales kid:** *Oldies.*
> **Homer:** *Oldies?* (he flips through the oldies bin) *But you've got all the top bands in here. Styx? I just heard them on "The King Biscuit Flour Hour." Now, here are some of your no-name bands: Sonic Youth, Nine Inch Nails, Hullabalooza...*
> **Sales kid:** *Hullabalooza is a music festival—the greatest music festival of all time.*

> **Homer's Flashback:**
> **Abe:** *What the hell are you two doing?*
> **Barney:** *It's called rockin' out.*
> **Homer:** *You wouldn't understand, Dad. You're not "with it."*
> **Abe:** *I used to be "with it." But then they changed what "it" was. Now what I'm "with" isn't "it" and what's "it" seems weird and scary to me. It'll happen to you.*
> **Homer:** *No way, man. We're gonna keep on rockin' forever!*

> **Marge:** *You don't have to join a freak show just because the opportunity came along.*
> **Homer:** *You know, Marge, in some ways you and I are very different people.*

> **Homer:** *Cool concert, am I right?*
> **Sour kid:** *Yeah, nice try, narc!*
> **Kid:** *Where's the narc?*
> **Girl #2:** *Who?*
> **Other kid:** *That fat Jamaican guy.*
> **Homer:** *What did I say? What's going on?*
> **Kid #2:** *Hey, we're just trying to have a good time, narc! Why do you want to destroy us?*
> **Sour girl:** *Don't commit your hate crimes here. Hate crime!*

> **Bart:** *Dad, do you wear boxers or briefs?*
> **Homer:** *Nope.*
> **Bart:** *What religion are you?*
> **Homer:** *You know, the one with all the well-meaning rules that don't work out in real life, uh, Christianity.*

THE STUFF YOU MAY HAVE MISSED

The sign on the record store Homer visits reads, "Suicide Notes" with the message underneath, "Formerly Good Vibrations."

The rack of the oldies section of "Suicide Notes" is made of plywood.

One teenager wears a T-shirt version of Münch's "The Scream"; another wears a "Great Gazoo" T-shirt.

Hullabalooza advertises a "Free Nose Piercing with Every Admission."

Two booths at Hullabalooza advertise, "Register Not to Vote" and "Bungee Jump against Racism."

The teen salesclerk at Suicide Notes music store reads *Mondo Frowno* magazine.

Homer's strut parodies famous cartoonist R. Crumb's "Keep on Truckin'" illustration.

SUMMER OF 4 FT. 2

Episode 3F22   Original Airdate: 5/19/96   Writer: Dan Greaney   Director: Mark Kirkland

ERIN

Lisa finds out how unpopular she is at the end of the school year when no one signs her yearbook. While the family packs for their summer vacation at Flanders's beach house, she prepares to change her life.

Arriving in Little Pwagmattasquarmsettport, Lisa buys clothes befitting a generation X wannabee. Avoiding the pitfalls of her superior vocabulary and intellect, she succeeds in making friends with a group of "cool" beach kids.

Jealous of Lisa's new-found popularity, Bart plots revenge. He shows the beach kids Lisa's yearbook and points out all the nerdy, unhip things she did at school. Lisa is furious at Bart, thinking that his disclosure has turned her friends away. Arriving home from a carnival, however, she finds them in the act of decorating the Simpsons' car with hundreds of seashells in her honor. They explain that they like Lisa for who she is. To make up with Lisa, Bart has them all sign her yearbook.

Description:
Somewhat inarticulate youth who summers at Little Pwagmattasquarmsettport with her family.

Favorite activity:
Idleness.

Pet peeve:
When her mother butts in on her and her friends with a pitcher of Tang and Rice Krispies Squares.

Strongest suspicion:
The cops are confiscating the skateboards of Little Pwagmattasquarmsettport to use down at the station.

Treasures most:
Necklaces made with cinnamon dental floss.

Favorite TV show:
"Baywatch."

SHOW HIGHLIGHTS

"Retrospecticus": The name of Springfield Elementary's yearbook, Lisa Simpson, editor.

"I don't get it. Straight A's, perfect attendance, Bathroom Timer... I should be the most popular girl in school." Lisa, wondering why no one signed her yearbook.

"Hello, Mr. Brown Ground, whatcha got for me?" Flanders, rolling up his sleeves to inspect the Simpson septic tank.

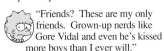
"Friends? These are my only friends. Grown-up nerds like Gore Vidal and even he's kissed more boys than I ever will."

"Like, you know, whatever. Like, you know, whatever." Lisa, rehearsing to introduce herself to some potential friends.

"Ooh, captain of the football team! He's a dreamboat! Don't wait up, Marge." Homer, playing Dream Date, the board game, with Marge, Bart, and Milhouse.

"Um... let me have one of those porno magazines... a large box of condoms... a bottle of Old Harper... a couple of those panty shields... andsomeillegalfireworks... and one of those disposable enemas. Ah, make it two." Homer, slyly trying to buy some fireworks for the 4th of July.

Homer's celebration: After chiding Bart for not having any matches or a lighter, Homer lights his M-320 on the stove. Most of the fuse burns off, leaving Homer with little time to dispose of it. Out of desperation, he throws it into the dishwasher, causing the sink to overflow with black ooze. He walks away, hands behind his back, whistling. Marge is later seen drying the badly damaged dishes.

"Oh, this is the worst Fourth of July ever. I hate America!"

(Bart sits on the porch with Milhouse as Marge mops the kitchen with the door open. Further down the beach, Lisa sits with her friends.)
Marge: Let Lisa be alone with her new friends.
Bart: They're my friends rightfully! She only got them by copying me.
Lisa: Don't have a cow, man!
(Lisa's new friends laugh.)
Bart: See? That's my expression!
Marge: Oh, you haven't said that in four years. Let Lisa have it.
Bart: It's the principle! She's gotta learn!
Marge: No! Now park your keister, meester!
Lisa: Ay carumba!
(Lisa's new friends laugh again.)

"You taught us about cool things like nature and why we shouldn't drink sea water." Dean to Lisa, on why the group still likes her despite discovering her "nerd leanings."

"Hey, he looks just like you, Poindexter!" Homer, pointing out that "the Dud" in Dream Date resembles Milhouse.

On Vacation:
Homer: Bye-bye, job.
Bart: Bye-bye toothbrush.
Lisa: Bye-bye, Lisa Simpson.

Bart: Where the hell are we going?
Marge: Little Pwagmattasquarmsettport. It's known as America's scrod basket.
Bart: I thought Springfield was America's scrod basket.
Marge: No, Springfield is America's crud bucket. At least, according to Newsweek.

THE STUFF YOU MAY HAVE MISSED

Achievements listed under Lisa's yearbook picture include Junior Overachiever; Record for Most Handraises in a Single Semester (763); Most Popular Student's Sister; Spelling Bee Queen; Camera Club; and Tidiest Locker.

In Little Pwagmattasquarmsettport, there is a deli called "Tern for the Wurst" and a newsstand called "Gull Things Considered."

The episode features the second time someone has been squirted in the face with a water gun intended for a "squirt the clown-head, blow up the balloon" carnival booth. Lisa soaks Bart as Nelson soaked Martin in 9F02, "Lisa the Beauty Queen."

In the back room of the convenience store there is a an explosive labeled, "Bangtime fun bomb."

Lisa, Irate at Breakfast:
Bart: I guess my little yearbook stunt was pretty rough, but it did teach you a lesson: It's important to be yourself.
Lisa: I know exactly who I am. I'm the sister of a rotten, jealous, mean little sneak. You cost me my only friends! You ruined my life!

Lisa: My goony brother's always going to libraries. I usually hang out in front.
Erin: Oh, you like hangin' out, too?
Lisa: Well, it beats doin' stuff.
Erin: Yeah. Stuff sucks.

I CAN TOTALLY HEAR HIM GOING THAT.

Guest Voice:
Christina Ricci as Erin

MERCHANDISING, THY NAME IS KRUSTY...

Krusty Mug. A mug that features a smiling Krusty on its side and the saying, "Who Do You ♥ ?" (7G12)

Krusty Dolls. The classic Krusty doll, in both talking and nontalking versions. (7G12, 7F04, 7F05, 9F04, 2F12)

Krusty Alarm Clock. An alarm clock that features Krusty's face. (7G12)

Krusty Pencil-Tops. Mini-Krusty heads, placed on top of pencil erasers for decoration. (7G12)

Krusty Pacifier. A pacifier, with a Krusty head on its front. (7G12)

Krusty Balloons. Krusty's head, including his hair, on a balloon. (7G12)

Krusty Costume. In a box that features a smiling Krusty face. (7G12)

Krusty Lunchboxes. A lunchbox, with a Krusty the Clown graphic on the front. (7G01, 7G12, 2F12, 4F09)

Krusty T-Shirt. A shirt that features "I ♥ Krusty." (7G12)

Krusty Tote Bag. An image of Krusty is on the front of the bag. (7G12)

Krusty Baby Bottle. Baby bottle, with a smiling Krusty on the front. (7G12)

Krusty Banner. A sports-style banner, with the phrase, "I ♥ Krusty." (7G12)

Krusty Towel. A beachtowel, featuring Krusty. (7G12)

Krusty Bedspread. A bedspread, with a giant Krusty face on it. (7G12)

Krusty Punch Doll. An inflatable Krusty doll that rolls back when you punch it. (7G12)

THE KRUSTY HOME PREGNANCY TEST
WARNING: MAY CAUSE BIRTH DEFECTS!

Krusty Lamp. A lamp, with Krusty's body as the base and the lampshade as his head. (7G12)

Krusty Phone. A telephone sculpture of Krusty holding the receiver. (7G12)

Krusty Wall Clock. A wall clock, featuring Krusty. His arms act as the clock's hands. (7G12)

Krusty Slippers. Slippers that resemble Krusty's face. (7G12)

Krusty Beanbag Chair. A beanbag chair, with Krusty's head on the top. (7G12)

Krusty Giant Toy Drum. A big toy drum, with Krusty's face on the sides. (7G12)

Krusty Trash Basket. A trash basket, featuring the words, "The Krusty the Clown Show." (8F22)

Krusty Bumper Sticker. A bumper sticker that says, "I ♥ Krusty." (8F22)

Krusty Walkie-Talkies. Walkie-Talkies, in the shape of Krusty's face. (8F04, 8F22, 3F12)

Krusty Poster. A poster in the nurse's office, featuring the slogan "Give a hoot...Brush," and depicting Krusty the Clown holding a toothbrush. (7F03)

Krusty Poster. A poster from Krusty's Literacy Campaign that reads, "Give a hoot! Read a book!" (7G12, 7F19, 8F12, 8F17)

Frosty Krusty Flakes. Bart's favorite breakfast cereal. (7G02, 7F24)

Chocolate Frosted Frosty Krusty Flakes. Bart's other cereal of choice, which boasts that "Only Sugar Has More Sugar!" (8F02, 8F03)

Krusty Brand Ham. The ham Homer is awarded for saving Springfield from a nuclear meltdown. (8F04)

Krusty Non-Toxic Kologne. Advertised on the label as "The Smell of the Bigtop," warning, "Use in well-ventilated area. May stain furniture. Prolonged use can cause chemical burns." (8F05)

Krusty's Sulfuric Acid. Advertised on train cars that contain the industrial product. (8F23)

Krusty Poster. A "Give a hoot . . . Wash up" poster, adorning the wall in Lisa's classroom. (8F24)

Krusty Brand Seal of Approval. The seal identifying products

that meet the high personal standards of Krusty the Clown. (8F24)

Krusty Handguns. Seen among the products approved quickly by Krusty before he leaves for Wimledon. (8F24)

Krusty Non-Narkotik Kough Syrup. Krusty's own brand of expectorant, also used as the secret ingredient in the Flaming Homer/ Flaming Moe. (8F08)

Krusty Flip-Flop Sandals. Sandals that feature Krusty's face. (3F12)

Krusty Pajamas. Pajamas that feature a repeating pattern of Krusty's face. (3F12)

Krusty Klump Bar. The Krusty chocolate bar, with or without almonds. (2F06)

"Kroon Along with Krusty." Krusty's album that went gold. (2F12)

Lady Krusty Mustache Removal System. A feminine hygienie product. (2F12)

Krusty's Monopoly. An unauthorized knock-off of the board game. (2F12)

Sideshow Mel Weeble-Wobbles. Another unauthorized knock-off, featuring Sideshow Mel. (2F12)

Krusty Mini-Basketball Hoops. A mini-basketball hoop, featuring Krusty's face on the back board. (2F12)

Krusty Flying Disk. A flying disk that features Krusty's face. (2F12)

Krusty Troll Doll. A version of the big-haired doll, with Krusty's features and clown-white complexion. (2F12)

Krusty Dart Game. A suction-cup dart game, with Krusty's face as the target. (2F12)

Krusty Lamppost Statue. A small keepsake statue, featuring Krusty leaning on a lamp-post. (2F12)

Krusty Jack-in-the-Box. The tradional children's toy, with Krusty as the jack-in-the-box. (2F12)

Krusty Cannon Toy. Cannon that shoots out a tiny Sideshow Mel. (8F24, 3F12)

Krusty-Head Knife Doll. A doll with a removable head that hides a stiletto. (8F24)

Krusty Electric Toothbrush. A sparking electric toothbrush. (8F24)

Krusty Bomb Doll. A doll that features Krusty with a lit bomb. (8F24)

Krusty Pez Dispenser. A Krusty-head dispenser, probably unauthorized. (8F24)

Krusty Wagging-Tongue Wall Clock. A wall clock that features Krusty's face, with his tongue as the clock's pendulum. (8F24)

Kamp Krusty. Krusty's summer camp, advertised as "The Krustiest Place on Earth." The sign appears on a large totem pole. (8F24)

FLESH-EATING BACTERIA IN EVERY BOX!

Krusty Brand Imitation Gruel. The chief foodstuff served at Kamp Krusty. (8F24)

Krustyburger. Krusty's fast-food chain, whose product, the Krusty Burger, is designated the "Official Meat-Flavored Sandwich" of the 1984 Olympics. (7F21, 9F08, 1F06, 1F12, 2F12, 2F20, 3F03, 3F09, 3F12, 3F18)

Krusty Trading Cards. Now in their eighth series. They feature Krusty visiting relatives and posing for trading card photos. (1F04)

Krusty's Home Pregnancy Test. Accompanied by a warning on the label admonishing that the test "May Cause Birth Defects." (9F13)

Krusty-O's. Krusty's cereal, touting "Flesh-Eating Bacteria in Every Box!" (2F32)

Krusty Hot Line. Advertised on a Krusty Flakes cereal box. Callers get a daily message from Krusty the Clown by dialing 1-909-O-U-KLOWN. (7F24)

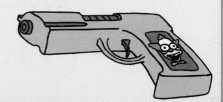

THE OPENING SEQUENCE

Homer lights a jack-o'-lantern. It erupts in flame, and the fire spreads to his hand. As his entire body catches on fire, he runs back and forth, screaming like a maniac.

THE THING AND I

Bart and Lisa investigate strange noises emanating from the attic. They discover an empty cage with steel bars. In explanation, Homer and Marge admit that Bart has an evil Siamese twin brother named Hugo, who was separated from Bart at birth and kept in the Simpsons' attic. Everyone races out to search for the missing twin except Bart, who is unaware that Hugo is still inside. Armed with a steak knife, Hugo finds Bart and discloses his plan to surgically reconnect Bart to his side. Dr. Hibbert appears just in time to save Bart and knocks Hugo out. He notices that Hugo's surgical scar is not on the left side of his body, that he is not the evil twin, and that Bart is the true incarnation of evil.

STORY HIGHLIGHTS

"Yeah, yeah. I'll go feed it." Homer, walking upstairs with a bucket of fishheads, after he tells his children that nothing is up there.

"You went into the attic? I'm very disappointed and terrified." Marge, to the kids.

"Normally, the birth of Siamese twins is a joyous occasion, but unfortunately, one of them was pure evil." Dr. Hibbert, on delivering Bart and Hugo into the world.

"I think I'll bottle feed that one." Marge, after seeing one of her newborn Siamese twins start to gnaw on the other.

Homer Lets It Slip:

Lisa: *What's up there?*
Bart: *Is it a monster?*
Lisa: *We have to know.*
Bart: *Yeah, what's the secret?*
Homer: *No more questions. I work my butt off to feed you four kids and all you do is...*
(Marge stares at him)
Homer: *What?*
Marge: *Three. We have three kids, Homer.*

Dr. Julius Hibbert, Sensitive Physician:

Dr. Hibbert: *Yes, I remember Bart's birth well. You don't forget a thing like...Siamese twins!*
Lisa: *I believe they prefer to be called "conjoined twins."*
Dr. Hibbert: *And Hillbillies prefer to be called "sons of the soil," but it ain't gonna happen.*

Dr. Hibbert: *But what to do with poor Hugo? Too crazy for Boy's Town, too much of a boy for Crazy Town. The child was an outcast. So, we did the only humane thing.*
Homer: *We chained Hugo up in the attic like an animal and fed him a bucket of fish heads once a week.*
Marge: *It saved our marriage!*

Homer: *We'll search out every place a sick, twisted, solitary misfit might run to.*
Lisa: *I'll start with Radio Shack.*

Bart: *You're crazy!*
Hugo: *Am I? Well, perhaps we're all a little crazy. I know I am. I went mad after they tore us apart. But I'll be sane once I sew us back together.*

Dr. Hibbert: *You know, isn't it interesting how the left, or sinister, twin is invariably the evil one. I had this theory tho—wait a minute, Hugo's scar is on the wrong side; he couldn't have been the evil left twin. That means the evil twin is—and always has been—Bart!*
(Everyone turns to Bart.)
Bart: *Oh, don't look so shocked.*

(The family has gathered for dinner with Dr. Hibbert. Hugo is sitting in Bart's place.)
Dr. Hibbert: *Care for a drumstick, Hugo?*
(Hugo grabs the drumstick and devours it. He starts to chew his napkin.)
Lisa: *Mom, Hugo's eating his napkin.*
(Bart looks out of the grate of the air vent.)
Bart: *Hey, can I have some turkey?*
Marge: *You finish your fish heads, then we'll talk.*

THE STUFF YOU MAY HAVE MISSED

In the attic: the Mary Worth telephone that Bart traded his bad "Itchy & Scratchy" cel for (1F21, "Lady Bouvier's Lover"), an "I Didn't Do It" T-shirt (1F11, "Bart Gets Famous"), one of Marge's Ringo Starr paintings (7F18, "Brush with Greatness"), several boxes of the Lisa Lionheart doll (1F12, "Lisa vs. Malibu Stacy"), a box of The Be Sharps merchandise (9F21, "Homer's Barbershop Quartet"), the Spine Melter 2000 (8F23, "Brother, Can You Spare Two Dimes?"), and Bart's electric guitar (8F21, "The Otto Show").

Homer's autobiography is called *Homer, I Hardly Knew Me*.

HORROR VII

Episode 4F02
Original Airdate: 10/27/96
Writers: Ken Keeler, Dan Greaney and David S. Cohen
Additional Material by: Jacqueline Atkins
Director: Mike Anderson
Executive Producers: Bill Oakley and Josh Weinstein

THE GENESIS TUB

Lisa conducts a science fair project with a baby tooth that falls out of her mouth. She places the tooth inside a margarine tub and pours soda over it. Bart zaps her with static electricity, and she, in turn, accidentally zaps the tooth. The next morning, Lisa examines the tooth with a microscope and discovers evidence of a tiny society. Bart mistakes the miniature city for a model and crushes it with his finger. That night, the tiny society retaliates, deploying spaceships that attack Bart in his bed. Meanwhile, a series of energy rings shrinks Lisa to microscopic size and beams her down into the minute town. The tiny townspeople mistake her for God. Lisa explains that "the Dark One" is her brother. Afterwards, Bart enters the margarine tub experiment in the science fair and wins first prize.

THE STUFF YOU MAY HAVE MISSED

The story was inspired by a "Twilight Zone" episode, in which spacemen land on an asteroid to repair their ship and one of the men stumbles upon a tiny civilization, making him drunk with power.

Lisa is barefoot at the end of the segment, despite the fact that she was wearing slippers when she was beamed down to the Tub World.

"Unshrink you?? Well, that would require some sort of a re-bigulator, which is a concept so ridiculous it makes me want to laugh out loud and chortle, mmm, hey, ahhhh, but not at you, oh holiest of gods, with the wrathfulness and the vengeance and the blood reign and the hey, hey, hey, it hurts me." The Frinkian scientist of the Tub World, responding to Lisa.

STORY HIGHLIGHTS

"Wait, one of them is nailing something to the door of the cathedral. Oh, I've created Lutherans!" Lisa, staring at the tiny society in the margarine tub that she brought into being.

 "Principal Skinner—wait! I created the universe! Give me the gift certificate!"

Lisa: Tiny little people! My God, I've created life!
Marge: (from downstairs) Lisa, breakfast! We're having waffles!
Lisa: Ooh, waffles!
(She runs off.)

Bart: Your microjerks attacked me!
Lisa: Well, you practically destroyed their whole world.
Bart: You can't protect them every second. Sooner or later, you'll let your guard down and then flush, it's toilet time for Tinytown.

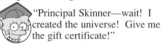

CITIZEN KANG

Aliens Kang and Kodos interrogate Homer about the identity of Earth's leaders. Homer names Bill Clinton as president but cautions that Bob Dole could replace him if he wins the election. The aliens kidnap both men, place them in suspended animation, and then morph into their exact duplicates. Hoping to expose their sinister plan, Homer interrupts a political debate between the alien candidates, but he is quickly whisked away by the Secret Service. In desperation, he rushes the candidates and tears off their fake skin, exposing Kang and Kodos. However, the aliens point out that, in a two-party system, the citizens have to vote for one of the candidates, and, therefore, one of them will still win the election.

STORY HIGHLIGHTS

 "Oh, my God! Space aliens! Don't eat me, I have a wife and kids! Eat them!"

Mumbly Joe: What Homer calls Bob Dole.

"Uhh, Bob Dole doesn't need this." Dole, upon being abducted by Kang and Kodos.

"Oh no! Aliens, bioduplication, nude conspiracies. Oh, my God! Lyndon LaRouche was right!" Homer, witnessing Kang and Kodos bioduplicate Clinton and Dole.

"We are merely exchanging long protein strings. If you can think of a simpler way, I'd like to hear it." Dole-Kang, when told that people are becoming confused by seeing him and Clinton constantly hold hands.

"These candidates make me want to vomit in terror! I've got to stop them."

Homer Simpson, Gracious Abductee:
Homer: I suppose you want to probe me. Well, you might as well get it over with.
(He pulls down his pants and starts bending over.)
Kang: Stop! We have reached the limits of what rectal probing can teach us.

Kent Brockman: Senator Dole, why should people vote for you instead of President Clinton?
Dole-Kang: It makes no difference which one of us you vote for. Either way, your planet is doomed! Doomed!
Brockman: Well, a refreshingly frank response there from Senator Bob Dole.

(The family watches Kent Brockman on TV.)
Kent Brockman: Kent Brockman here, with "Campaign '96: America Flips a Coin." At an appearance this morning, Bill Clinton made some rather cryptic remarks, which aides attributed to an overly tight necktie.
(The scene cuts to the news conference.)
Clinton-Kodos: I am Clin-Ton. As overlord, all will kneel trembling before me and obey my brutal commands. End communication.
Marge: Hmm, that's Slick Willie for you, always with the smooth talk.

Dole-Kang: Fooling these Earth voters is easier than expected.
Clinton-Kodos: Yes, all they want to hear are bland pleasantries embellished by an occasional saxophone solo or infant kiss.

(Before a huge crowd at the Capital Building, Homer reveals the candidates as space aliens.)
Kodos: It's true, we are aliens. But what are you going to do about it? It's a two-party system! You have to vote for one of us.
(The crowd murmurs.)
Man in crowd: Well, I believe I'll vote for a third-party candidate.
Kang: Go ahead, throw your vote away! Ah-hah-hah-hah-haaaah!

THE STUFF YOU MAY HAVE MISSED

The Kang and Kodos presidential debate charges $5.00 admission.

Bob Dole is holding a pencil in his "bad" hand as he is lifted into the Rigellian spaceship.

The only one who does not cheer and clap at the debates is Lisa.

HANK SCORPIO

Occupation:
President of Globex Corporation.

Interests:
World domination; fun runs.

Dislikes:
Being called "boss"; walls.

Nemesis:
James Bont.

Invented:
Wearing jeans with sports coats.

Prized possession:
The doomsday device.

The Simpsons move to Cypress Creek, where Homer has accepted a job at Globex Corporation. While Homer enjoys his work and is impressed by his boss's friendly, down-to-earth style, the rest of the family has trouble adjusting. Marge is bored living in the self-maintaining house, Bart is moved to a remedial program at school, and Lisa is allergic to all of the area's plant life.

Homer fails to notice that his boss, Hank Scorpio, is a terrorist and Globex, his vehicle for international extortion. Instead, he basks in the attention of his boss and becomes a relatively competent manager. When he finds out his family is unhappy, however, he must make a choice between Cypress Creek and Springfield.

In the midst of a siege on the Globex compound, Homer resigns. The Simpsons return to Springfield and Hank Scorpio takes over the East Coast. In appreciation for Homer's services, Scorpio gives him the Denver Broncos.

> DON'T DO THAT. MY BUTT IS FOR SITTING, NOT FOR KISSING.

Guest Voice:
A. Brooks
as Hank Scorpio

SHOW HIGHLIGHTS

Homer, announcing his new job to the family: "Marge! I got a new job! It's with Globex Corporation. I get more money plus health benefits, for me and my life partner. And they'll move us and give us a nice house and…"

"We have roots here, Homer. We have friends and family and library cards… Bart's lawyer is here." Marge, protesting the move.

Yet another lifelong dream: Homer always wanted to own the Dallas Cowboys.

"Homer, I don't want to leave Springfield. I've dug myself into a happy little rut here and I'm not about to hoist myself out of it."

The Simpsons' new address: 15201 Maple Systems Road.

"Don't call me that word. I don't like things that elevate me above the other people. I'm just like you. Oh sure, I come later in the day, I get paid a lot more, and I take longer vacations, but I don't like the word 'boss.'"

The household conveniences: Self-cleaning oven, autovac, Swing-a-majig baby swinger, automatic sprinklers.

Hank Scorpio, introducing Homer to his team: "Now Homer, these gentlemen here will be your eyes and your ears and, should the need arise, they'll fill in for any other part of your body. Your job will be to manage and motivate them. Give them the benefit of your years of experience."

"You got a fresh sound. It'll play well at this school." One of Bart's new classmates, critiquing Bart's armpit playing.

"Mr. Scorpio says productivity is up 2%, and it's all because of my motivational techniques, like donuts and the possibility of more donuts to come."

"When you go home tonight, there's gonna be another story on your house." Hank, thanking Homer for foiling James Bont's escape.

"Homer, on your way out, if you want to kill somebody, it would help me a lot."

Diagnosis:
Mr. Doyle: *So, you never learned cursive?*
Bart: *Um, well, I know hell, damn, bit…*
Mr. Doyle: *Cursive handwriting. Script. Do you know the multiplication tables? Long division?*
Bart: *I know of them.*
Mr. Doyle: *You know, Bart, I think you'd profit from a more remedial environment. I'm sure you'll feel right at home in… The "Leg-Up" Program.*

Bart's Disorder:
Bart: *Look, lady, I'm s'posed to be in the fourth grade.*
Teacher: *Sounds to me like someone's got a case of the "spose'das."*

Scorpio's Video Conference with the UN:
Hank: *Good afternoon, gentleman. This is Scorpio. I have the doomsday device. You have 72 hours to deliver the gold. Or you face the consequences. And to prove I'm not bluffing, watch this…*
UN member #1: *Oh, my God! The 59th Street Bridge!*
UN member #2: *Maybe it just collapsed on its own.*
UN member #1: *We can't take that chance.*
UN member #2: *You always say that. I want to take a chance!*

THE STUFF YOU MAY HAVE MISSED

Many of the students at Cypress Creek Elementary resemble the students at Springfield Elementary.

The power sander and TV tray that Homer takes from Flanders originally appeared in 1F03, "Marge on the Lam" and 9F08, "Lisa's First Word," respectively.

Cypress Creek Elementary's internet address is http://www.studynet.edu.

Homer buys his autographed Tom Landry hat at a store called "The Spend Zone."

Homer is disappointed with Scorpio's gift of the Denver Broncos, despite the fact that he requests to be John Elway when the family is given new identities as a part of the Witness Relocation Program in 9F22, "Cape Feare."

> I DID NOT LEARN EVERYTHING I NEED TO KNOW IN KINDERGARTEN I DID NOT LEARN EVERYTHING I NEED KNOW IN KINDERGART

THE HOMER THEY FALL

Episode 4F03 Original Airdate: 11/10/96 Writer: John Collier Director: Mark Kirkland
Guest Voices: Paul Winfield as Lucius Sweet, Michael Buffer as Himself

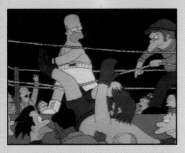

Bart is beaten up at school by Jimbo, Dolph, and Kearney, who steal his high-tech belt. Homer takes matters into his own hands, confronting the assailants' fathers at Moe's. But he himself becomes a victim of their pummelings when he tries to recount the events at school. Although Homer is unable to make his point, he withstands the beating. Impressed with Homer's stamina, Moe talks him into becoming a boxer with Moe as his manager.

Homer's ability to take punches becomes his sole strategy. As his opponents knock themselves out while pounding on him, Homer fights his way up the ranks of hungry hobos. His rise catches the attention of promoter Lucius Sweet, who wants Homer to fight heavyweight champ Drederick Tatum. Moe accepts the challenge.

Before the fight, Moe promises Sweet that Homer will stay up for three rounds. He also promises Marge that he will throw in the towel as soon as Homer is in danger. When the fight begins, it is clear Homer will not last the three rounds. Just as he is about to be knocked out in the first round, Moe airlifts Homer to safety.

SHOW HIGHLIGHTS

"Son, there's only one thing punks like that understand: squealing. You've got to squeal to every teacher and every grown-up you can find. Coming to me was a good start."

"Compass, matches, whistle, saw, panic button, squirrel snare, radon-slash lie detector, sphygmomanometer... and it's even got turn signals!" Bart, showing Milhouse the features of his Tactical Pants-Retaining System.

"They called me 'Kid Gorgeous.' Later on, it was 'Kid Presentable.' Then 'Kid Gruesome.' And finally, 'Kid Moe.'" Moe, summarizing his boxing career for Homer.

"You're 38 years old, you don't know how to box, and you haven't gotten any exercise since grade school. Before you even consider this, I insist you consult a doctor." Marge, protesting Homer's choice to box.

"Well, the fans are weary of fights that are over before they even have an opportunity to get drunk. I just need a body who can sustain verticality for three rounds." Lucius, wanting Homer for a bout with Tatum.

"Who's Drederick Tatum, anyway? Is he another hobo?" Homer, researching his new opponent.

"Society put Drederick Tatum away for his brutal crime. But he's paid his debt, and, and now he's going to get revenge... on Homer Simpson." Ominous announcer, in the TV ad for "Tatum vs. Simpson: PAYBACK."

"I think he's a good man, I like him, I got nothing against him, but I'm definitely gonna make orphans of his children." Drederick Tatum, on Homer Simpson.

"This just in: go to hell!" Kent Brockman, reacting to the crowd booing his name.

Tatum enters the ring to gangsta rap in a robe that says, **"Mr. Armageddon."**

Homer enters the ring to War's "Why Can't We Be Friends?" in a robe that says, **"Opponent."**

Hibbert: You have an absolutely unique genetic condition known as "Homer Simpson's Syndrome."
Homer: Oh, why me?
Hibbert: Don't worry, it's quite beneficial. Your brain is cushioned by a layer of fluid one eighth of an inch thicker than normal. It's almost as if you're wearing a football helmet inside your own head. Why I could wallop you all day with this surgical two by four, without even knocking you down.

Saint Moe:
Homer: Are you an angel?
Moe: Yes, Homer, I'm an angel. All us angels wear Farah slacks.

Comic book guy: Yes, finally. I would like to return your quote-unquote ultimate belt.
Salesman: I see, do you have receipt, quote-unquote sir?
Comic book guy: No, I do not have a receipt. I won it as a door prize at the Star Trek convention, although I find their choice of prize highly illogical, as the average trekker has no use for a medium size belt.
Salesman: Whoa, whoa, a fat, sarcastic Star Trek fan! You must be a devil with the ladies.
Comic book guy: Hey, I, uh, de—oh...
Salesman: Gee, I hate to let you down, Casanova, but no receipt, no return.
Bart: I'll give you four bucks for it.
Comic book guy: Huuuuh. Very well. I must hurry back to my Comic Book Store where I dispense the insults rather than absorb them.

THE STUFF YOU MAY HAVE MISSED

The dads of Jimbo, Dolph, and Kearney all hang out together.

A sign outside the Springfield Coliseum: "Championship Boxing Tasteful Attire Prohibited."

Homer boxes under the auspices of the ASSBOX (Association of Springfield Semi-Pro Boxers).

ASSBOX boxers include: Switchyard Sullivan, Boxcar Fritz, Snuffy, Manny the Mooch, Soupcan Sam, and Boxcar Ira.

As Homer advances in his boxing career, his taste in car washes becomes more refined: he goes from Premium Wash to Ultra Deluxe Wash to Super Premium Wash to Mega Tycoon Wash.

Drederick Tatum was introduced in 7F13, "Homer vs. Lisa and the Eighth Commandment."

Occupation:
Boxing manager/promoter.

Biggest client:
Drederick Tatum, who was temporarily imprisoned for pushing his mother down a flight of stairs.

Hair:
Electrified and frizzed-up.

Reputation:
Shady.

Soul:
None evident.

YOUR BOY LOOKS A LITTLE SOFT, MOE. YOU DO REMEMBER OUR ARRANGEMENT?

BURNS, BABY BURNS

Episode 4F05 Original Airdate: 11/17/96 Writer: Ian Maxtone-Graham Director: Jim Reardon

Resume:
Orphanage until the age of 18; job selling souvenirs at a stand; once saw a blimp.

Residence:
Waynesport, somewhere between New Haven, CT, and Springfield.

Sometimes mistaken for:
A corpse.

Favorite advice:
"Hey, relax"; "Hey, don't worry about it."

Coping mechanism:
Making up similes.

WHOA, THIS GUY'S GOT MORE BREAD THAN A PRISON MEATLOAF.

Guest Voice:
Rodney Dangerfield as Larry Burns

SHOW HIGHLIGHTS

"Twenty of the suckiest minutes of my life." Homer, describing to Flanders his trip to the historic cider mill.

Flanders's device for identifying apple products: "If it's clear and yella', you've got juice there, fella! If it's tangy and brown, you're in cider town. Now, there's two exceptions and it gets kinda tricky here..."

 "Hey, how ya doin'? Welcome to scenic Waynesport. And remember your visit with a googly-eyed walnut. How 'bout a googly-eyed rock?"

How Larry was conceived:
Burns met Lily, the 21-year-old daughter of his college sweetheart, at his 25th college reunion. He took her to the movies and to the Peabody Museum, where they expressed their love physically, "as was the style at the time." Larry was given up for adoption, and Lily's parents shipped her off to a convent in the South Seas.

"Well, he is a bit rough around the edges, sir. One might blame his truly heroic intake of cocktails." Smithers, assessing Larry.

"It's the principle, Smithers! Nobody steals from Montgomery Burns, whether it be my Sunday newspaper or my loutish oaf of a son."

> **Bart:** That's a hitchhiker, Homer.
> **Homer:** Ooh, let's pick him up!
> **Marge:** No! What if he's crazy?
> **Homer:** And what if he's not? Then we'd look like idiots.

> **Burns:** You're what? Selling light bulbs? Worried about the whales? Keen on Jesus? Out with it!
> **Larry:** Oh, Mr. Burns—I'm your son. Oh, and I stepped on one of your peacocks. You got a paper towel?

> (Larry shows the Simpsons an old picture of Monty Burns.)
> **Larry:** Hey, I'm looking for this guy. Anybody know who he is?
> **Bart:** Yeah, sure, we know him. That's Mr. Burns.
> **Lisa:** He tried to kill our puppies.
> **Marge:** He sexually harassed me.
> **Grampa:** He stole my fiancee.
> **Homer:** He made fun of my weight.
> **Larry:** Okay, so there's been a little friction. Know his address?

> **Dowager:** Oh, Monty, this must be the son I've heard so much about! Larry, you must meet our daughter, the debutante. She came out last spring.
> **Larry:** Whoa! Put her back in, she's not done yet!

> **Larry:** Geez, come on, Dad, we got company. Make with the yakkety-yak-yak.
> **Burns:** Yakketty-yak-ya... You, Foodbag—do you have a son?
> **Homer:** Yes, sir. I do.
> **Burns:** And is he a constant disappointment? Does he bring home nitwits and make you talk to them?
> **Homer:** Oh, all the time! Have you ever heard of this kid Milhouse? He's a little weiner who—
> **Burns:** Fascinating. Goodnight.

> **Conductor:** Attention, passengers. The train has been temporarily delayed because of a discarded couch on the tracks.
> **Burns:** This may take a while, Smithers. Why don't you get drunk and stumble around comically for my amusement?
> **Smithers:** I'll be a one-man conga line.

> **Wiggum:** Don't be a fool, Simpson! Let the kid go!
> **Burns:** The negotiations have failed! Shoot him!
> **Larry:** Wait! I mean, Homer's no kidnapper. He's the best friend I ever had! We faked the whole thing.
> **Burns:** I should've known. You're the only one stupid enough to kidnap you. Now get down here so I can spank you in front of this gawking rabble. Smithers, take off my belt.
> **Smithers:** With pleasure, sir.

THE STUFF YOU MAY HAVE MISSED

The Simpsons visit Mt. Swartzwelder Historic Cider Mill, "Now 40% Quainter," named after Simpsons writer John Swartzwelder.

The grounds of the Burns estate feature statues of Mr. Burns dressed like an ancient Roman.

The Olmec Indian Head from 7F22, "Blood Feud," is still in the Simpsons' basement.

Mr. Burns was a member of Yale's class of 1914.

Disco Stu and a Hassidic Jew can be seen dancing at the party in front of the Aztec.

This episode marks the second time Homer has spoken badly of Milhouse behind his back. The first time occurred in 8F04, "Homer Defined," when Homer referred to him as, "that four eyes with the big nose."

Mr. Burns's train ride back to Springfield from Yale is interrupted by an obstacle on the tracks. While the train sits, a man named Larry hawks souvenirs to the passengers. When he sees Mr. Burns, his jaw drops in surprise, and he packs up his gear to follow the train to Springfield.

The Simpsons see Larry hitchhiking to town and stop to pick him up. In Springfield, Larry heads to Burns's estate and identifies himself as Burns's long-lost son. Burns, acknowledging the resemblance, admits that Larry is the result of a one-night fling during a college reunion.

At first, Burns accepts his son but tires of him when Larry proves to be an incurable oaf. However, Homer befriends Larry, realizing that they share many of the same interests. They fake Larry's kidnapping to help Larry win back his father's love. Marge convinces Homer and Larry to abandon their plan, but as they leave to confess their scheme to Mr. Burns, they are chased by reporters and police. Burns forgives Larry for the hoax, but explains that he cannot continue as his father. Announcing that he is returning home, Larry stages an impromptu street party.

BART AFTER DARK

Episode 4F06 Original Airdate: 11/24/96 Writer: Richard Appel Director: Dominic Polcino

L isa and Marge go to help clean up an oil spill, leaving Bart and Homer at home. While they are gone, Bart damages property in the yard of a spooky house. A woman, Belle, comes out and leads Bart home by the ear. She tells Homer that Bart should be punished. Homer makes Bart do chores for Belle to pay for his misdeed.

Belle's house turns out to be the Maison Derriere, a burlesque salon. Upon Marge's and Lisa's return, a group of concerned citizens confront Homer on Bart's work. Marge joins the group in its attempt to oust the Maison Derriere from Springfield.

At a Town Hall meeting, Marge convinces the townspeople that it is in their best interest to demolish the old house. When the townspeople gather with implements of destruction at the Maison Derriere and begin to destroy the house, Homer sings a song that changes everyone's mind. The demolition is stopped. However, Marge's bulldozer slips out of gear and damages to the house. To pay her debt, she must perform a ventriloquist act.

SHOW HIGHLIGHTS

Marge, to Homer, before she leaves with Lisa to Baby Seal Beach:
"And if anything happens, just use your best judg—just do what I would do."

 "Where is Bart, anyway? His dinner's getting all cold and eaten."

Smithers, explaining his visit to the Maison Derierre: "My… my parents insisted I give it a try, sir."

Homer, Missing the Point:

Kent Brockman: *Kent Brockman at the Action News desk. A massive tanker has run aground on the central coastline, spilling millions of gallons of oil on Baby Seal Beach.*
Lisa: *Oh, no!*
Homer: *It'll be okay, honey. There's lots more oil where that came from.*

Milhouse: *Thanks a lot! Now it's stuck on that haunted house!*
Nelson: *I heard a witch lives there.*
Ralph: *I heard a Frankenstein lives there.*
Milhouse: *You guys are way off. It's a secret lab where they take the brains out of zombies and put them in the heads of other zombies to create a race of Super-Zombies!*
Nelson: *That's the house?!*

Homer, the Disciplinarian:

Woman: *Your son was trespassing on my property and destroyed a very valuable stone gargoyle, and—Are you wearing a grocery bag?*
Homer: *I have misplaced my pants.*
Woman: *I'm not going to press charges, but I assume you'll want to punish him.*
Homer: *(chuckles) 'Preciate the suggestion, lady, but he hates that. And I gotta live with him.*
Bart: *You're the man, Homer.*

Belle: *When you work the door, the main things are to greet the visitors and toss out the troublemakers.*
Bart: *Oh, the ol' greet 'n' toss. No problemo.*

Bart: *Wow, man! What is this place?*
Woman: *I prefer not to be called "man." My name is Belle, and this is the Maison Derriere. That means the, uh, "back house."*

Skinner: *Ah, there's no justice like angry mob justice.*
Lenny: *I'm gonna burn all the the historic memorabilias!*
Moe: *I'm going to take me home a toilet!*
Groundskeeper Willie: *There'd a-better be two!*
Ned: *Uh, it's an angry mob, ma'am. Could you step outside for a twinkle while we knock down your house?*

THE STUFF YOU MAY HAVE MISSED

The mess on the living room floor includes a box of donuts, a carton of eggs, an orange juice jug, paper bags, a book, an envelope, a half-eaten candy bar, a pizza box, and Homer's bowling ball.

Marge's slide show of men leaving the Maison Derriere features Dr. Hibbert, Chief Wiggum (twice), Skinner, Patty, Cletus, Barney, Smithers, Mayor Quimby.

Mayor Quimby's wife makes her second appearance in the episode. Her first was in 1F11, "Bart Gets Famous."

Princess Kashmir, introduced in 7G10, "Homer's Night Out," fan dances at the Maison Derriere.

"The Spring in Springfield" Song Lyrics:

Homer: *You could close down Moe's, Or the Kwik-E-Mart, And nobody would care/ But the heart and soul of Springfield's in our Maison Derriere…*
Belle: *We're the sauce on your steak, we're cheese in your cake/ We put the spring in Springfield.*
Dancer #1: *We're the lace on the nightgown,*
Dancer # 2: *The point after touchdown,*
Belle and dancing girls: *Yes, we put the spring in Springfield.*
Belle: *We're that little extra spice that makes existence extra-nice/ A giddy little thrill/At a reasonable price!*
Lovejoy: *Our only major quarrel's with your total lack of morals.*
Dancer #1: *Our skimpy costumes ain't so bad!*
Dancer # 2: *They seem to entertain your dad!*
Belle and dancing girls: *The gin in your martini, the clams on your linguine/Yes we keep the ("boing" sound effect) in Springfield!*
Wiggum, Krusty, and Skinner: *We remember our first visit,*
Mayor Quimby: *The service was exquisite!*
Mrs. Quimby: *Why, Joseph, I had no idea!*
Mayor Quimby: *Come on now, you were working here!*
Grampa and Jasper: *Without it we'd have had no fun since the March of 1961!*
Bart: *To shut it down now would be twisted,*
Jimbo, Dolph, and Kearney: *We just heard this place existed!*
Dancers: *We're the highlights in your hairdo,*
Apu: *The extra arms on Vishnu!*
Dancers: *So don't take the (Barney opens a jack-in-the-box)*
Men: *We won't take the (Sideshow Mel blows on his slide-whistle)*
Everyone: *Yes, let's keep the (Moe crashes two garbage can lids together) in Springfield!*
Marge: *Well I also have a song to sing! Don't make up your mind until you hear both songs! "Morals, and ethics and carnal forbearance…"* (Marge, pleading her case as her bulldozer slips into gear and crashes into the Maison Derriere.)

I THINK I KNOW WHAT SPRINGFIELD WANTS, SUGAR.

T he Simpsons invite the Flanders, the Hibberts, the Lovejoys, and the Van Houtens to a dinner party. During the course of the evening, it becomes clear that Kirk and Luann Van Houten's marriage is in trouble. In front of the dinner guests, Luann announces that she wants a divorce.

Homer is confident that he and Marge will never get a divorce until Kirk tells him how quickly things can change: one day he was eating his favorite meal with his wife and the next, thawing hot dogs in a gas station sink.

When Homer arrives home, he finds frozen hot dogs thawing in the sink and realizes that he has taken his marriage for granted.

Homer overcompensates by smothering Marge. When she gets fed up, he goes to the courthouse to file for divorce. That evening, he arrives home and calls Marge into the living room. He surprises her by asking for her hand in marriage again. Reverend Lovejoy performs the ceremony as well-wishers witness their new vows. Inspired by Homer and Marge, Kirk asks Luann if she will marry him again. She flatly refuses.

SHOW HIGHLIGHTS

"Hey, this ain't the Ritz." Bart, to Marge, explaining why he is eating dinner in his underwear.

"Man, that is flagrant false advertising!" Otto, outside Stoner's Pot Palace, Springfield's upscale kitchen store.

 "Marge, if this was my last meal, I'd tell the warden, 'Bring on the lethal injection!'"

"Can I Borrow a Feeling?" The title of Kirk's demo tape.

 "I didn't want a hokey second wedding like those ones on TV! This one's for real!"

 "I will now read the special vows which Homer has prepared for this occasion. Do you, Marge, take Homer, in richness and in poorness?—Poorness is underlined—In impotence and potence? In quiet solitude or blasting across the alkali flats in a jet-powered monkey-navigated... and it goes on like this."

> **Marge:** *I feel terrible. The Van Houtens split up at our party.*
> **Homer:** *Marge, please, that was twenty minutes ago.*

> **Marge:** *Homer, is this the way you pictured married life?*
> **Homer:** *Yup, pretty much. Except we drove around in a van solving mysteries.*

DIVIDED

Episode 4F04
Original Airdate: 12/1/96
Writer: Steve Tompkins
Director: Steve Moore

KIRK VAN HOUTEN

Occupation:
(Former) Factory manager at Southern Cracker.

Alma mater:
Gudger College.

Secret shame:
His (ex) wife was born in Shelbyville.

Connections:
Jerry, the major player down at the sewing store.

Pet peeve:
Drowned possums in the Casa Nova pool.

> YOU KNOW ME. AND I'M A SUPERSTAR AT THE CRACKER FACTORY.

Kirk's Latest:
Name: Starla.
Occupation: Temp at K-ZUG Radio 530.
Drives: Kirk's car.
Says: "Can I have the keys to the car, lover? I feel like changing wigs."

Luann's Latest:
Name: Chase aka Pyro.
Occupation: American Gladiator.
Drives: American Gladiator cage ball.
Says: "Go ahead, break a chair on me."

Casa Nova:
The apartment complex into which Kirk moves. The sign indicates "A Transitional Place for Singles."

Marge's Preparations for the Party:
Putting doilies under the coasters.
Nibbling down a candle to make it match its mate.
Cleaning toilet seats in the dishwasher.

Kirk: How about it, Luann? Will you marry me—again?
Luann: Ewwww! No!

Luann: If you want to talk nervous, you should have seen Kirk deal with the high school boys who egged our Bonneville.
Kirk: Heh. I should have asked them to hurl some bacon, then maybe I could've had a decent breakfast for once.

Kirk: You're letting me go?
Cracker executive: Kirk, crackers are a family food, happy families. Maybe single people eat crackers, we don't know. Frankly, we don't want to know. It's a market we can do without.
Kirk: So that's it after twenty years? "So long. Good luck."
Cracker executive: I don't recall saying "good luck."

"Can I Borrow a Feeling?" Song Lyrics:
Can I borrow a feeling? / Could you lend me a jar of love? / Hurtin' hearts need some healin' / Take my hand with your glove of love.

Kirk: You wanna talk? Go ahead, Luann, talk! Why don't you tell 'em one of your little bedtime stories, huh? Like how rotten it is to be married to a loser; or how about the one about how I carry a change-purse? Yeah, a purse!
Homer: Shut up and let the woman talk!
Luann: Okay, Kirk, I'll tell a story. It's about a man whose father-in-law gave him a sweet job as manager of a cracker factory—
Homer: Boooring.
Luann: A man whose complete lack of business sense and managerial impotence—
Homer: Ooh, here we go!
Luann: Sent the number one cracker factory in town into a tie for sixth with Table Time and Allied Biscuit.

Kirk: That's how it is, though. One day your wife is making you your favorite meal, the next day you're thawin' a hot dog in a gas station sink.
Homer: Oh, that's tough, pal. But it's never gonna happen to me.
Kirk: Well, how do you know? What makes you guys so special?
Homer: Because Marge and I have one thing that can never be broken—a strong marriage built on a solid foundation of routine.

THE STUFF YOU MAY HAVE MISSED
Homer reads *Hot Lottery Picks* in bed.
According to the sign in front, the Southern Cracker Company makes "the dryyyyyy cracker."
A cracker fountain, cracker paintings, and cracker sculptures decorate the Southern Cracker executive offices.
Marge gets her hair cut at "The Perm Bank."
Plato's Republic Casino is within eyeshot of Shotgun Pete's Wedding Chapel.
The wedding scene appears in 8F10, "I Married Marge." Plato's Republic Casino appears in 7F17, "Old Money."

JIMMY THE SCUMBAG

Occupation:
Criminal.

Appearance:
Unshaven and tired.

Latest scam:
Involved autodialer telemarketing.

Fate:
Will rot in the slammer for the next 20 years, subsisting on bread and water, taking icy showers, having guards "whompin' his ass" round-the-clock.

Says:
Nothing without his attorney present.

LISA'S DATE WITH DENSITY

Episode 4F01 Original Airdate: 12/15/96 Writer: Mike Scully Director: Susie Dietter

Homer finds a phone autodialer in the trash and takes it home to use for electronic panhandling. Meanwhile, Principal Skinner finds proof that Nelson has vandalized Superintendent Chalmers's car. Nelson's punishment is to help Willie around the schoolyard. As Lisa watches Nelson torment Willie, she develops a crush on him.

Lisa decides to change Nelson into a good person. They go on a date to the observatory, where they kiss. Soon after, however, Nelson is convinced by Jimbo, Dolph, and Kearney to join them in throwing expired cole slaw at Skinner's house. Following the attack, which he is accused of, Nelson seeks refuge with Lisa. Nelson tells Lisa that he is being framed but, later, he unintentionally reveals the truth. Lisa realizes that he is still a liar, and loses her crush on him.

Homer is caught harassing neighbors with his phone scam, and is ordered by the court to apologize. He uses the auto-dialer to fulfill his sentence . . . and asks them for more money.

SHOW HIGHLIGHTS

"Oh, you think this stolen 'H' is a laugh riot, don't you? Well, I'll tell you something that's not so funny: right now, Superintendent Chalmers is at home crying like a little girl! Well, I guess it is a little funny": Skinner, before searching the lockers to find the missing "H" from Chalmers's '79 Honda.

"Frankly, I would have expected better from Jimmy 'the Scumbag.'"

"Bite me. Cram it. You're dead. Get bent, ma'am." Nelson, apologizing to the rightful owners of the items he stole.

"Greetings, friend. Do you wish to look as happy as me? Well, you've got the power inside you right now. So use it. And send one dollar to Happy Dude, 742 Evergreen Terrace, Springfield. Don't delay! Eternal happiness is just a dollar away." The message Homer records for the AT-5000 autodialer.

"I will not be a snickerpuss." The message Mr. Largo makes Lisa write on the board over and over again after music class.

"How does Bart do this every week?" Lisa, as her hand cramps while doing her punishment.

 "He's not like anybody I've ever met. He's like a riddle wrapped in an enigma wrapped in a vest. He sure is ugly, though. So why can't I stop staring at him? Oh, no! I think I'm getting a crush on Nelson Muntz!"

"I like you too, Milhouse, but not in that way. You're more like a big sister": Lisa, to Milhouse, making her relationship clear to him.

"Okay. But if anybody sees us, I'm just there to steal your bike." Nelson, accepting an invitation to Lisa's house.

"Well, most women will tell you that you're a fool to think you can change a man—but those women are quitters!"

"I missed you guys. Let's never fight again." Nelson, showing up to slaw Skinner's house.

"See ya in court, Simpson. Oh, and bring that evidence with ya, otherwise, I got no case and you'll go scot-free."

(Nelson gets busted.)
Skinner: *Well, who's "haw-hawing" now, hmmm?*
Nelson: *I 'unno, but he's got lethal tuna breath.*

Dolph: *You asked for it, man. You're broadcasting geek rays all over the entire valley.*
Nelson: *'Fraid not! I'm still wicked bad.*
Jimbo: *Oh, yeah? Then prove it, assbutt. Come raid Skinner's house with us.*

Lisa: *"Nuke the whales?" You don't really believe that, do you?*
Nelson: *I don't know. Gotta nuke somethin'.*

THE STUFF YOU MAY HAVE MISSED

There is a medieval mace and a green knit cap in Jimbo's locker.

The "Wee Monsieur" clothing store that Lisa takes Nelson to is seen in 8F12, "Lisa the Greek."

Among the stolen items in Nelson's locker: a crystal ball, a box of Two-Star brand cigars, a globe, a football, a bat, a mitt, a shoe, a baseball, a book, and a toy plane.

One of the items Nelson must return is a lobster in a trap. The Old Sea Captain can be seen in the line of rightful owners, claiming their stolen goods.

Nelson: *Wait'll he finds what I left in his birdbath!*
Lisa: *I thought you weren't there.*
Nelson: *Huh? Oh, yeah, I guess I was.*
Lisa: *You lied to me.*
Nelson: *Nuh-uh!*
Lisa: *There, you did it again!*
Nelson: *All right, all right, I lied! I'm sorry. Let's kiss.*
Lisa: *No. You don't understand, Nelson. A kiss doesn't mean anything if it's dishonest.*

The Lyrics to Nelson's Song:

Joy to the world/ The teacher's dead!/ We bar-b-qued her head!/ What happened to her body?/ We flushed it down the potty!/ And round and round it goes/ And round and round it goes.

Movie Moment:
Parts of this episode occur at an observatory that looks a great deal like the one in *Rebel without a Cause.*

The Flanders's house is demolished by a hurricane and, without homeowners' insurance, Ned and his family move into the church basement. There, he learns that the Leftorium was looted in the storm's aftermath.

The people of Springfield gather to rebuild Ned's house. When it is finished, Ned inspects their work and, finding poor workmanship, angrily berates everyone who helped rebuild the house. Feeling that he is having a total breakdown, Ned commits himself to a mental institution.

Dr. Foster, Ned's childhood psychiatrist, treats Ned and discovers that Ned's past therapy has taught him to suppress his anger rather than use it constructively. Using Homer as a role model, Dr. Foster teaches Ned to express his angry feelings. Cured once again, Ned returns home.

SHOW HIGHLIGHTS

"... and the Weather Service has warned us to brace ourselves for the onslaught of Hurricane Barbara. And if you think naming a destructive storm after a woman is sexist, you obviously have never seen the gals grabbing for items at a clearance sale."

"There's so little left: Creamed Eels? Corn Nog? Wadded Beef?" Marge, shopping for hurricane supplies at the Kwik-E-Mart.

"Ooh, I better take down the manger scene! If baby Jesus got loose, he could really do some damage!"

"The University of Minnesota Spankological Protocol": The experimental therapy that helps Young Ned contain his anger. It consists of eight months of constant spanking.

"Dear God, this is Marge Simpson. If you stop this hurricane and save our family, we will be forever grateful and recommend you to all our friends."

"We don't believe in rules. Like we gave them up when we started living like freaky beatniks." Young Ned's dad, explaining to young Dr. Foster why Ned is such a terror.

"Down here at Springfield mall, a storm-addled crowd appears to have turned its rage on the Leftorium. Surprisingly, people are grabbing things with both hands, suggesting it's not just southpaws in this rampaging mob."

"Why me, Lord? Where have I gone wrong? I've always been nice to people! I don't drink or dance or swear! I've even kept kosher just to be on the safe side! I've done everything the Bible says; even the stuff that contradicts the other stuff! What more could I do?"

"Ned, you so crazy." Homer, to Flanders upon release from Calmwood.

Ned: Reverend Lovejoy, with all that's happened to us today, I kinda feel like Job.
Lovejoy: Well, aren't you being a tad melodramatic, Ned? Also, I believe Job was right-handed.
Ned: But, Reverend, I need to know. Is God punishing me?
Lovejoy: Ooh, short answer, "yes" with an "if." Long answer, "no" with a "but."

Ill Winds:

Homer: Oh, Lisa, there's no record of a hurricane ever hitting Springfield.
Lisa: Yes, but the records only go back to 1978, when the Hall of Records was mysteriously blown away!

Ned: I attacked all my friends and neighbors just for trying to help me. I'd like to commit myself.
Nurse: Very well, shall I show you to your room, or would you prefer to be dragged off kicking and screaming?
Ned: Ooh. Kicking and screaming, please.

Ned: Calm down, Neddily-diddily-diddily-diddily-diddily... They did their best... Shoddily-iddly-iddly-diddly... Gotta be nice... hostility-ilitity-bility-dility—Aw, hell, diddily-ding-dong-crap! Can't you morons do anything right?
(The crowd gasps.)
Marge: Ned, we meant well and everyone here tried their best!
Ned: Well my family and I can't live in good intentions, Marge! Oh, your family is out of control but we can't blame you because you've got gooood intentions.
Bart: Hey, back off, man!
Ned: Oh, okay, duuude! I wouldn't want you to have a cow, maaan! Here's a catch-phrase you better learn for your adult years: "Hey buddy, got a quarter?"
(The crowd gasps again.)
Bart: I am shocked and appalled.

THE STUFF YOU MAY HAVE MISSED

Apu stands on top of the Kwik-E-Mart wielding a shotgun in 1F09, "Homer the Vigilante."

Todd wears a Butthole Surfers T-shirt he found in the church's donation bin.

It appears that Dean Peterson (from 1F02, "Homer Goes to College") is present at the execution in Springfield State Prison.

Ned commits himself to Calmwood Mental Hospital.

The Juvenile Aggression Study that Foster shows Ned is sponsored by "Swanson's Angry Man Dinners."

The marquee at the Springfield Community Church reads, "God Welcomes His Victims."

Claim to fame:
Single-handedly remedied the troubled young Ned Flanders's behavior problems.

Secret shames:
His remedies work so well they come back to haunt him; he leaves his shoes in the den.

Favorite expression:
"May God have mercy on us all!"

Professional aids:
Books that have yet to be discredited.

JUST REMEMBER, ONE OF OUR PATIENTS IS A CANNIBAL. TRY TO GUESS WHICH ONE I THINK YOU'LL BE PLEASANTLY SURPRISED.

Marge fears that Homer will embarrass her at the annual Springfield Chili Cook-Off. She reminds him about his behavior the previous year, when he consumed too much beer and frolicked nude inside a cotton candy machine. Homer promises to behave. Sampling this year's various chilis, he dismisses them as bland and timid. However, when he eats a dish laced with potent Guatemalan peppers, he begins to hallucinate.

In his altered mind-state, Homer experiences a fantasy involving a pyramid and a mystical coyote. The coyote tells him that in order to become a complete person, Homer must find his soul mate.

When Homer arrives home from the cook-off, disoriented, Marge accuses him of breaking his promise.

Concerned that Marge is not really his soul mate, Homer leaves the house and roams the city. He notices a lighthouse in the distance and convinces himself that only the lighthouse keeper, "the loneliest man in the world," will understand him. Once inside the structure, however, Homer finds that the lighthouse is directed by an automated computer system. Marge arrives at the lighthouse and apologizes to Homer for accusing him of getting drunk. Homer realizes that Marge is his soul mate after all.

SHOW HIGHLIGHTS

"Not me. I'm more of a mail-tamperer." Bart, responding to Homer's question about whether he cut a story out of the newspaper.

"Well, I just felt like filling the house with the rich, satisfying smell of tobacco." Marge, on why she is smoking a cigarette.

"Look at me! I'm a puffy pink cloud!" Homer, drunk and naked inside a cotton candy machine at the Springfield Chili Cook-Off.

"Oh, well, of course, everything looks bad if you remember it."

"That Homer Simpson! He thinks he's the Pope of Chilitown!" Chief Wiggum, watching Homer's inspection of the cook-off.

"I've added an extra ingredient, just for you. The merciless peppers of Quetzlzacatenango. Grown deep in the jungle primeval by the inmates of a Guatemalan insane asylum."

"Look, just gimme some inner peace, or I'll mop the floor with ya!"

Marge: Ooh, look at that adorable spice rack! Eight spices! Oh, some must be doubles. Or-uh-gahn-o? What the hell?
Homer: Marge, we're missing the chili! Less artsy, more fartsy!
Marge: Homer, I happen to like handicrafts much more than stuffing my face.
Homer: Fine. I'll come find you when I'm ready to stop having fun.

Helen Lovejoy: Howdy, howdy, Marge and Hom— oh, my mistake, Homer's not even with you! Probably just knocking back a few "refreshments."
Marge: Thank you for your concern, Helen. Homer isn't drinking today.
Helen: Oh. I think it's lovely that he said that—and that you believed him!
Rev. Lovejoy: Now, Helen, let us not glory in Homer's binge-drinking. There but for the grace of God goes Marge herself.

"Look at these records! Jim Nabors, Glen Campbell, the Doodletown Pipers! Now look at her records—they stink!" Homer, comparing his albums to Marge's.

"Alone! I'm alone! I'm a lonely, insignificant speck on a has-been planet orbited by a cold, indifferent sun!"

"Ma'am, I wouldn't honk the honk if I couldn't tonk the tonk." Smithers, asking Marge to dance.

"Oh, honey, I didn't get drunk, I just went to a strange fantasy world." Homer, defending his behavior at the cook-off.

E.A.R.L.: The Electronic Automatic Robotic Lighthouse that Homer initially believes is a human being.

Sylvania 40,000-watt Energy-miser: The type of lightbulb used at the lighthouse.

NUESTRO JOMER

Episode 3F24
Original Airdate: 1/5/97
Writer: Ken Keeler
Director: Jim Reardon

COYOTE

Identity:
Coyote.

Mindset:
Wise and mystical.

Hangs out in:
Hallucinogenic dreamscapes.

Role:
Homer's spiritual guide.

Homer: *Five-alarm chili, eh? (He tastes it.) One...two...hey, what's the big idea?*
Flanders: *Oh, I admit it! It's only two-alarm, two-and-a-half, tops! I just wanted to be a big man in front of the kids.*
Todd: *Daddy, are you going to jail?*
Flanders: *We'll see, son. We'll see.*

(Homer swallows some of Wiggum's peppers.)
Quimby: *This can't be happening!*
Dr. Hibbert: *By all medical logic, steam should be coming out of his ears!*
Krusty: *His ears, if we're lucky!*

(Bart points to a souvenir cap from the cook-off; it reads "Time for Chili" and has a clock on the front.)
Bart: *Lis, check it out, "Time for Chili."*
Lisa: *I saw it, Bart.*
Bart: *You're just mad 'cause there's no clock in your hat.*
Lisa: *What hat?*
Bart: *Aw, this baby's wasted on an idiot like you.*

Coyote: *Fear not, Homer. I am your spirit guide.*
Homer: *Hiya.*
Coyote: *There is a lesson you must learn.*
Homer: *If it's about laying off the insanity peppers, I'm way ahead of ya.*

Homer: *Hey, Barney! Soul mate! Let me buy you a beer.*
Barney: *Okay, but I'm not your soul mate. I'm really more of a chum.*
Homer: *Well, what about you, Lenny?*
Lenny: *I'm a crony.*
Homer: *Carl?*
Carl: *I'd say acquaintance.*
Larry: *Colleague.*
Sam: *Sympathizer.*
Bumblebee man: *Compadre.*
Kearney: *Associate.*
Dr. Hibbert: *Contemporary.*
Moe: *I'm a well-wisher, in that I don't wish you any specific harm.*

(Homer's silhouette can be seen in the lighthouse's spotlight, à la the bat-signal.)
Bart: *Hey, look! Is that Dad?*
Lisa: *Either that, or Batman's really let himself go.*

Marge: *I woke up and you weren't there and I was so worried!*
Homer: *Really? You were? But how did you find me?*
Marge: *Well, I was sure you would be on foot, because you always say public transportation is for losers. And, I was sure you'd head west, because Springfield slopes down that way. And then I saw the lighthouse, and I remembered how you love blinking lights, like the one on the waffle iron.*
Homer: *Or the little guy on the "Don't Walk" sign.*
Marge: *Yeah...*

Homer: *Maybe we do have a...*
Marge: *Profound, mystical understanding?*
Homer: *We do! Oh, Marge! We're number one! We're number one! In your face, space coyote!*
Marge: *Space coyote?*

Movie Moment:

The music from *The Good, the Bad, and the Ugly* accompanies the scenes when Homer walks through the chili festival and when he meets Chief Wiggum at the chili stand.

Classic TV Moment:

Substituting the man in the lighthouse with a computer spoofs an old episode from "The Twilight Zone," in which a man in a cave turns out to be a machine.

THE STUFF YOU MAY HAVE MISSED

Marge cuts the curtains in the kitchen and later sews them back together.

The purple entertainment center owned by the Simpsons is a DisCabinetron 2000 model.

A vagrant sells water for $3 a bottle at the Chili Cook-Off.

The sign for the chili festival reads, "Springfield Chili Cook-Off—Please lick spoons clean after each use."

Janis Ian's song, "At Seventeen," plays as Homer wanders around.

Signs at Chili Cook-Off: "Apu's Vegetarian Chili," "Professor Frink's Virtual Chili," "A Little Bit of Lenny," "Firehouse Ned's Five-Alarm Chili," "Moe's Chili Bar," "Old Elihu's Yale-Style Saltpeter Chili," "Muntz Family Chili—It Takes Weeks to Make Muntz," "Beer Garden—Proof of age or exact change required."

An evil-looking gargoyle carrying a spoon adorns Wiggum's booth.

Telephone wires labelled "NSA," "FBI," "ATF," "CIA," "KGB," and "MCI" can be seen in the floorboards between the first and second floor of the Simpson home.

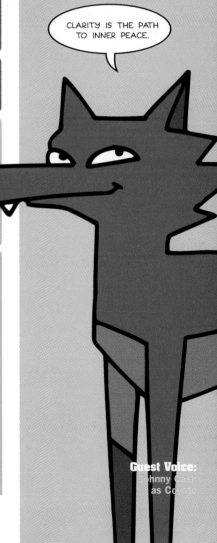

> CLARITY IS THE PATH TO INNER PEACE.

Guest Voice:
Johnny Cash
as Coyote

THE SPRINGFIELD FILES

Episode 3G01   Original Airdate: 1/12/97   Writer: Reid Harrison   Director: Steven Dean Moore   Guest Voice: Leonard Nimoy as Himself

SCULLY AND MULDER

Occupation:
Agents with the FBI, Division of Paranormal Activities.

First names:
Dana (Scully) and Fox (Mulder).

Relationship:
Platonic (or so they say).

Favorite letter of the alphabet:
X.

Demeanor:
Truth-seeking (Mulder); Skeptical (Scully).

How they view Homer:
As a bumpkin who could stand to lose a few pounds.

AGENTS MULDER AND SCULLY. FBI.

Guest Voices:
Gillian Anderson as Scully,
David Duchovny as Mulder

In a tale hosted by Leonard Nimoy, Homer drinks too much at Moe's Tavern and opts to walk home late one night. He hears something strange and encounters an eerie glowing creature with bulbous eyes and a contorted body emerging from the woods. At home, disheveled and shaken, he wakes up Marge, but the entire family passes off Homer's sighting as a product of his drinking.

The next day, the *Springfield Shopper* prints a story about Homer's UFO encounter. The story finds its way to the Washington bureau of the FBI, where it is read by "X-Files" agents Scully and Mulder. Mulder convinces his skeptical partner to investigate the sighting further. They travel to Springfield to interview Homer and visit the site. Finding Homer's credibility shaky and the people of Springfield annoying, they quickly leave.

Bart and Homer set up camp at the site and videotape the alien during a return visit. The following Friday, hundreds of Springfielders gather to glimpse the alien. When the creature finally appears, Lisa shines her flashlight on it, revealing its true identity. The being is actually Mr. Burns, who has been receiving appearance-altering longevity treatments from Dr. Riviera.

SHOW HIGHLIGHTS

"I saw this in a movie about a bus that had to speed around a city, keeping its speed over fifty, and if its speed dropped, it would explode! I think it was called 'The Bus That Couldn't Slow Down.'"

The horror: After Homer leaves Moe's, he passes through a creepy part of town. He screams in terror when he sees a billboard that reads, "DIE." A gust of wind moves a tree branch, revealing the billboard's complete message: "DIET." Even more terrified, Homer screams again!

"His jiggling is almost hypnotic." Mulder, watching Homer jogging on a treadmill in his underwear.

"All right, they're on to us. Get him back to Sea World!" Moe, spooked by the FBI's visit into unloading the killer whale in the back of his tavern.

"Now, son, you don't want to drink beer. That's for Daddys, and kids with fake I.D.'s."

Mulder: There's been another unsubstantiated UFO sighting in the heartland of America. We've got to get there right away.
Scully: Well, gee, Mulder, there's also this report of a shipment of drugs and illegal weapons coming into New Jersey tonight.
Mulder: I hardly think the FBI's concerned with matters like that.

"Take a look at this, Lisa. You don't see any "Homer Is a Dope" T-shirts, do ya?" Homer, holding up a "Homer Was Right" T-shirt. He later learns that the "Dope" T-shirt sold out in five minutes.

"A lifetime of working in a nuclear power plant has given me a healthy green glow. And left me as impotent as a Nevada boxing commissioner."

Movie Moments:
Milhouse puts 40 quarters into "Kevin Costner's *Waterworld*" videogame, satirizing the overbudgeting fiasco of *Waterworld*. The episode also features references to *The Shining*, *E.T.*, and *Close Encounters of the Third Kind*.

Mulder: All right, Homer. We want you to recreate your every move the night you saw this alien.
Homer: Well, the evening began at the Gentleman's Club, where we were discussing Wittgenstein over a game of backgammon.
Scully: Mr. Simpson, it's a felony to lie to the FBI
Homer: We were sitting in Barney's car eating packets of mustard. Ya happy?

THE TRUTH IS NOT OUT THERE
THE TRUTH IS NOT OUT THERE
THE TRUTH IS NOT OUT THERE
THE TRUTH IS NOT OUT THERE
THE TRUTH IS NOT OUT THERE
THE TRUTH IS NOT OUT THERE

Homer: (sipping a Red Tick beer) Hmm, bold, refreshing, and something I can't quite put my finger on. (The scene shifts to the Red Tick Brewery, where dogs are swimming in vats of beer.)
Brewery worker: Needs more dog.

Lisa: All right! It's time for ABC's TGIF lineup!
Bart: Lis, when you get a little older, you'll learn that Friday is just another day between NBC's Must-See Thursday and CBS's Saturday Night Crap-o-rama.

Lisa: Dad, according to Junior Skeptic Magazine, the chances are 175 million to 1 of another life actually coming in contact with ours.
Homer: So?
Lisa: It's just that the people who claim they've seen aliens are always pathetic low-lifes with boring jobs. Oh, and you, Dad. Heh, heh.

THE STUFF YOU MAY HAVE MISSED

The Simpsons have a *Better Homes Than Yours* magazine on their coffee table.

Leonard Nimoy was last seen in 9F10, "Marge vs. the Monorail."

Moe's Breathalyzer Test's ratings go from "Tipsy" to "Soused" to "Stinkin'" to "Boris Yeltsin."

The official F.B.I. portrait on the wall of F.B.I. headquarters is of J. Edgar Hoover in a sundress.

Springfield Shopper headline regarding Homer's UFO sighting: "Human Blimp Sees Flying Saucer."

The sign at the FBI's Springfield branch: "Invading Your Privacy for 60 Years."

THE TWISTED WORLD OF MARGE SIMPSON

Episode 4F08   Original Airdate: 1/19/97   Writer: Jennifer Crittenden   Director: Chuck Sheets   Guest Voice: Joe Mantegna as Fat Tony

Marge is voted out of the Springfield Investorettes for being too conservative. To beat her former colleagues at their own game, Marge attends a franchise fair and buys a pretzel franchise.

The Investorettes, however, strike back. When Marge tries to sell her pretzels, she is overshadowed by their new falafel van. Marge tries to hand out free samples at a baseball game, but they are hurled at Mr. Burns instead of being eaten. In an attempt to help his wife, Homer asks Fat Tony for assistance.

Soon, orders for Marge's pretzels pour in while the Investorettes' falafel business mysteriously fails. Marge's sales skyrocket, and Fat Tony attempts to collect all the profits. Marge, however, refuses to comply. Fat Tony and his goons arrive at the Simpsons' home for a showdown but are headed off by the Japanese mafia, who are sent by the Investorettes to rub out Fat Tony and his boys.

> I AM NOT LICENSED TO DO ANYTHING.
> I AM NOT LICENSED TO DO ANYTHING.
> I AM NOT LICENSED TO DO ANYTHING.

SHOW HIGHLIGHTS

Municipal House of Pancakes: Where Marge meets the Investorettes: Helen Lovejoy, Maude Flanders, Agnes Skinner, Edna Krabappel, and Luann Van Houten.

"I'm not wild about these high-risk ventures. They sound a little risky."

"Well, Marge, you're about as popular as rug burn. All in favor of expelling Marge from 'The Investorettes?'"

> **The Investorettes Plan Their Next Move:**
> **Edna:** Oh, oh! How about OklaSoft? It's Oklahoma's fastest-growing software company.
> **Maude:** Um—cushions! Everybody likes to sit on cushions.
> **Agnes:** Children are so fat today. Isn't there some way we could make money off that?

"Wow, check out that van. It looks like it doesn't even need our business." Lenny, as the Fleet-A-Pita parks in Marge's territory.

> **Bart:** Oh, cheer up, Mom. You can't buy publicity like that. Thousands and thousands of people saw your pretzels injuring Whitey Ford.
> **Homer:** You can call them Whitey-whackers!

Cletus's kids: Tiffany, Heather, Cody, Dylan, Dermott, Jordan, Taylor, Brittany, Wesley, Rumer, Scout, Cassidy, Zoe, Chloe, Max, Hunter, Kendall, Katlin, Noah, Sasha, Morgan, Kira, Ian, Lauren, Q-Bert, Phil.

"Copyright 1968? Hmm. Determined or not, that cat must be long dead. That's kind of a downer." Marge, reading the fine print "Hang in there, Baby," on her achievement poster, which features a cat dangling from its front paws on a clothesline.

"Ladies and gentlemen, a winner has been chosen for today's giveaway. And the 1997 Pontiac AstroWagon goes to the fan sitting in seat number zero, zero, zero, one—C. Montgomery Burns": The announcement that makes the fans hurl their pretzels.

"This is a pretzel town, pretty boy." Fat Tony, as he and Louie knock over Hans Moleman's hot dog cart.

> (A line forms in front of Marge's table advertising "Pretzels $1.00.")
> **Lenny:** Uh, let's see…I'll have one…Uh…
> **Carl:** Hey, hurry up. I wanna get my pretzel.
> **Lenny:** One pretzel.
> **Marge:** Thank you.
> **Carl:** Let's see…Um, I will have one of your uh…
> **Burns:** Come on, come on…while we're young.

> **Marge:** That'll be three hundred dollars.
> **Cletus:** Hey, I don't think so. I got me three hundred coupons.
> **Marge:** I should've said "Limit—one per customer."
> **Cletus:** Shoulda, but didna. So hands 'em over.

> **Marge:** Well, I guess Macy's and Gimbels learned to live side by side.
> **Agnes:** Gimbel's is gone, Marge. Long gone. You're Gimbels.

> **Fleet-A-Pita-Speak:**
> Falafel = crunch patties.
> Tahini = flavor sauce.
> Pita = pocket bread.

> **Literary/Movie Moment:**
> Frank Ormand's speech, "Wherever a young mother is ignorant of what to feed her baby, you'll be there. Wherever nacho penetration is less than total, you'll be there. Wherever a Bavarian is not quite full, you will be there," parodies Tom Joad's speech in *The Grapes of Wrath*.

THE STUFF YOU MAY HAVE MISSED

In the Whack-A-Mole Couch Gag, Homer's head is the only one to actually get whacked.

The Municipal House of Pancakes has four kinds of syrup on each table.

The Mexican wrestler that the Investorettes invested in is "El Bombastico."

The sign hanging at the Springfield Convention Center reads, "Franchise Expo, Where You Can Make Your Nonsexual Dreams Come True."

At the Picture Perfect franchise booth, the crooked picture is of a sad clown, the level picture is of a happy clown.

Disco Stu's business is called "Disco Stu's Can't Stop the Learnin' Disco Academies."

FRANK ORMAND, THE PRETZEL MAN

Occupation:
Founder of the "Pretzel Wagon" franchise.

Weakness for:
Statuettes and bric-à-brac for the front lawn.

Demise:
A car accident, that also killed the executor of his will.

Pet peeve:
Millipedes in the pretzel flour.

Synonyms for pretzels:
Knot bread; tasty golden-brown life preservers.

> CONGRATULATIONS! AND WELCOME TO THE DYNAMIC WORLD OF MOBILE PRETZEL RETAILING.

Guest Voice:
Jack Lemmon as The Pretzel Man

MOUNTAIN OF MADNESS

Episode 4F10   Original Airdate: 2/2/97   Writer: John Swartzwelder   Director: Mark Kirkland

Duties:
Maintaining Mt. Useful as a public-friendly national park; tacking leaf samples to bulletin boards; humoring children; digging corpses out of avalanches.

Challenges:
Budget cuts; lack of fun atop Mt. Useful; decrepit chair-lifts; avalanches.

Entertainment:
The Mountain Music Festival (March 14-18).

RIDING THE CHAIR-LIFT GIVES US AN EAGLE-EYE VIEW OF THE AREA DIRECTLY BENEATH THE CHAIR-LIFT.

In order to create teamwork among his workers, Mr. Burns holds a survival retreat for employees and their families. All the employees team up in pairs. Homer becomes Burns's partner, while Smithers must go off solo. The challenge is to find a cabin hidden on the snowy mountainside. The last team to reach the cabin will be fired.

Burns and Homer make it to the cabin with the benefit of a snowmobile previously hidden by Burns. Bart and Lisa meet up with Smithers and volunteer to help him. While the rest of the employees toil through the wilderness, Homer and Burns make themselves comfortable at the cabin and start their celebration early.

Their tranquillity is shattered by the onset of avalanches, and the cabin is buried. The rest of the employees mistake the ranger station for the cabin and congregate there. Made insane from the cold, Homer and Burns get into a fight. In the scuffle, they rupture a propane tank, which ignites and sends the cabin rocketing to safety.

SHOW HIGHLIGHTS

Burns, deciding how to bring excitement to the plant: "No, no, something fun. Something the men will enjoy, like a safety drill, but what kind? Ah, meltdown alert? Mad dog drill? Blimp attack? Ah, I think a good old-fashioned fire drill today."

 "So Burns is going to make us all go on a stupid corporate retreat up in the mountains to learn about teamwork. Which means we'll have to cancel our plans to hang around here."

 "Mm, hmm. If you can take advantage of a situation in some way, it's your duty as an American to do it. Why should the race always be to the swift or the jumble to the quick-witted? Should they be allowed to win merely because of the gifts God gave them? Well, I say, cheating is the gift Man gives himself."

"We have several hours before the others arrive. What say we get comfy?" Burns, arriving with Homer at the cabin.

 "Oh, yes, sitting—the great leveler. From the mightiest pharaoh to the lowliest peasant, who doesn't enjoy a good sit?"

"Hmm. No books, no radio, no board games. Ah! A Bazooka Joe comic. Ech! I heard that one 75 years ago." Mr. Burns, trying to keep occupied while trapped in the cabin.

Burns marvels at his snowman: "Ah. 206 bones, fifty miles of small intestine, full, pouting lips. Why, this fellow is less a snowman than a god."

The Ranger, setting out to look for Homer and Burns: "Okay, search party. Before we set out, let's take a moment to humor the children. Kids, your father's gonna be just fine. Okay, everybody, put on your corpse handling gloves. We've got two frozen bodies buried somewhere in this mountain."

Homer, praying as the propane-powered cabin shoots down the mountain. "Oh Lord, protect this rocket house and all who dwell within the rocket house."

Smithers: *Sir, this can't be right. You assured me this drawing was rigged so we'd be teammates.*
Burns: *Yes, well, frankly, you've been a bit of a pill lately.*
Smithers: *Why do we always fight on vacation?*

THE STUFF YOU MAY HAVE MISSED

Location of Burns's wilderness teamwork seminar is "Mt. Useful, Strategic Granite Reserve."

The "rocket house" knocks an innocent squirrel out of its way as it roars down the mountain.

Mr. Burns fires Lenny in this episode; the last time he did so was in 1F16, "Burns's Heir."

Burns: *Well, Simpson, I must say, once you've been through something like that with a person, you never want to see that person again.*
Homer: *You said it, you weirdo.*

Burns: *Now as an added incentive, the second to last team to arrive at the cabin will receive an [sic] hilarious "World's Worst Employee" trophy.*
Homer: *Hey, this sounds like fun.*
Burns: *And the last team to arrive will be fired.*
Homer: *Heh-heh...uh, oh.*
Burns: *And to show that I'm not playing favorites, both Smithers and I will be participating. Who knows? I might be the unlucky one who gets fired.* (muttering) *Not bloody likely.*

After the Avalanche:
Carl: *According to the map, the cabin should be right here.*
Lenny: *Hey, maybe there is no cabin. Maybe it's one of them, um, metaphorical things.*
Carl: *Oh, yeah, yeah. Like maybe the "cabin" is the place inside each of us created by our goodwill and teamwork.*
Lenny: *Ohhh. Nah, they said there'd be sandwiches.*

Burns's brain: *I'm trapped with a madman. Look at him, staring into me, filling my mind with paranoid thoughts.*
Homer's brain: *Hmmm, look at his eyes. He's trying to hypnotize me, but not in the good Las Vegas way.*
Burns's brain: *(gasp) I know what he's up to. He's thinking of killing me and riding my carcass down the mountain to safety. He's truly gone mad if he's thinking that. Well, he can't kill me if I kill him first!*
Burns: *I'll kill you, you bloated museum of treachery.*
Homer: *You and what army?*
(Homer envisions Burns's army: it's a regiment of snowmen in German spiked helmets and hair comb mustaches on either side of Burns.)
Homer: *Stay back! I have powers! Political powers!*
(Burns imagines Homer's army: a regiment comprised of Abe Lincoln, Teddy Roosevelt, Mao Tse Tung, Mahatma Gandhi, and Ramses.)

SHARY BOBBINS

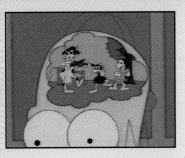

Marge is overwhelmed by the demands of motherhood. When her hair begins to fall out in huge clumps, she consults Dr. Hibbert, who suggests that she hire a nanny to reduce her stress level. After rejecting several nanny applicants, the Simpsons receive a visit from a magical British stranger, who floats down from the sky holding an umbrella.

Assuring the family that she will do everything for them—from telling stories to changing diapers—the new nanny, Shary Bobbins, uses her gifts of song and imagination to teach Bart and Lisa how to clean. A miracle worker, she charms the entire town with her charisma and wisdom, even warming the heart of Mr. Burns. Marge's hair grows back, and the Simpsons are the happiest they've been in years.

However, one miracle that Shary cannot perform is helping the Simpson family to amend their listless, messy ways. Her spirit crushed, Shary leaves, realizing that she has taught the family nothing. As she floats away on her umbrella, she is sucked into a jet plane's engine.

> I WILL NOT HIDE THE
> TEACHER'S PROZAC
> I WILL NOT HIDE THE
> TEACHER'S PROZAC
> I WILL NOT HIDE THE
> TEACHER'S PROZAC

SHOW HIGHLIGHTS

"Your mother seems really upset. I better go have a talk with her—during the commercial."

"Wait a minute, Marge. I saw *Mrs. Doubtfire*. This is a man in drag!" Homer, yanking on the hair of one of the nanny applicants.

Bart: *Pop quiz, hotshot. I'm s'posed to be doing my homework, but you find me upstairs readin' a Playdude. What do you do? What do you do?*
Shary Bobbins: *I make you read every article in that magazine, including Norman Mailer's latest claptrap about his waning libido.*
Homer: *Oh, she is tough.*

The Family Sing to Shary Bobbins:

Homer: *Around the house, I never lift a finger/As a husband and father I'm sub-par/I'd rather drink a beer /than win Father of the Year/I'm happy with things the way they are.*
Lisa: *I'm getting used to never getting noticed.*
Bart: *I'm stuck here till I can steal a car.*
Marge: *The house is still a mess, and I'm going bald from stress—*
Bart/Lisa/Marge: *But we're happy just the way we are!*
Flanders: *They're not perfect, but the Lord says love thy neighbor—*
Homer: *Shut up, Flanders*
Flanders: *Okely-dokely-do.*
Shary: *Don't think it's sour grapes but you're all a bunch of apes/And so I must be leaving you!*

Shary: *Oh, Mr. Burns, I think you'll find all life's problems just float away when you're flying a kite.*
Mr. Burns: *Balderdash. This is the silliest load of—ooh, look at it fly. Whee! Look at me, Smithers, I feel practically superduperfragicaliexpiala-dohhhhh!*
(Lighting strikes the kite, electrocuting Burns.)
Mr. Burns: *I have this strange sensation in my chest.*
Smithers: *I think your heart's beating again.*
Mr. Burns: *Aw, that takes me back. God bless you, Shary Bobbins!*

Krusty: *Now I'd like to introduce a new feature never before seen on TV; "Dumb Pet Tricks!" Oh boy. Here's a dog that's been trained to catch this red rubber ball.*
(The dog leaps up and bites onto Krusty's red rubber nose.)
Krusty: *Auggh! Oww! Somebody shoot it! Somebody shoot it!*

Krusty: *Hey! Hey Hey! It's great to be back at the Apollo Theater!*
(He looks behind him at the KKK sign for "Krusty Komedy Klassic.")
Krusty: *KKK?! That's not good.*
(nervous laugh)

Music Plays and the Family Sings:

Lisa: *If you wish to be our sitter/Please be sweet and never bitter/Help us with math and book reports/*
Bart: *Might I add, eat my shorts.*
Lisa: *Bart!*
Bart: *Just cuttin' through the treacle.*
Lisa: *If Maggie's fussy, don't avoid her.*
Bart: *Let me get away with moider.*
Lisa: *Teach us songs and magic tricks.*
Homer: *Might I add—no fat chicks.*
Marge: *Homer!*
Lisa: *The nanny we want is kindly and sage.*
Homer: *And one who will work for minimum wage!*
Lisa: *Hurry nanny, things are grim—*
Grampa: *I'll do it!*
Bart and Lisa: *Any-one but him.*

Bart: *A nanny?*
Homer: *But how am I supposed to pay for a that?*
Lisa: *We'll find a way. Mom has made so many sacrifices for us, it's time we gave up something for her. I'll stop buying Malibu Stacy clothing.*
Bart: *And I'll take up smoking and give that up.*
Homer: *Good for you, son. Giving up smoking is one of the hardest things you'll ever have to do. Have a dollar.*
Lisa: *But he didn't do anything!*
Homer: *Didn't he, Lisa? Didn't he? (pause) Hey, wait a minute, he didn't!*

Shary Sings a Song to Lisa, Bart, and Maggie:

Shary Bobbins: *In front of a tavern, flat on his face/A boozehound named Barney is pleading his case...*
(The scene changes to a snowy day in front of Moe's.)
Barney: *Buy me beer, two bucks a glass/Come on, help me—I'm freezing my ass/ Buy me brandy/A snifter of wine/Who am I kidding?/I'll drink turpentine.*
Moe: *Move it ya drunk or I'll blast your rear end!*
Barney: *I found two bucks.*
Moe: *Then come in, my friend.*
(Bart, Lisa, and Maggie are nearly asleep.)
Shary: *And so let us leave on this heartwarming scene.*
Bart: *Can I be a boozehound?*
Homer: *Not till you're 15.*

THE STUFF YOU MAY HAVE MISSED

During the "Mad about Shoe" sketch on the Krusty special, a shoe, a brick, two tomatoes, a wine bottle, and a crumpled-up piece of paper are hurled at Krusty.

This episode marks the second appearance of President Gerald Ford, last seen in 3F09, "Two Bad Neighbors."

During the "Half-Assed Job" song, Apu cleans a hot dog that has dirt, hair, and a Band-Aid on it, much like the hot dog that gets him fired in 1F10, "Homer and Apu."

In scripts for The Simpsons, "D'oh!" is written as "(ANNOYED GRUNT)."

Identity:
Magical nanny of British ancestry.

Last employer:
Lord and Lady Huffington of Sussex.

Chief mode of transportation:
Floating by umbrella.

Personality:
Magnetic.

Nanny philosophy:
Sing a lot; cut corners when cleaning to have more time for play; life's problems float away when flying a kite.

Dirty little secret:
Dumped former fiancée Groundskeeper Willie after getting her eyesight back.

> I'VE BEEN SINGING YOU SONGS ALL DAY. I'M NOT A BLOODY JUKEBOX.

POOCHIE

Purpose:
To increase "The Itchy & Scratchy Show" ratings.

Paradigm:
The original dog from hell—part-rasta, part-surfer.

Attributes:
Gets "biz-zay;" a dog with attitude; in-your-face.

Downfalls:
Too "biz-zay;" too much attitude; too in-your-face; doesn't make much sense.

Poochie's end:
He dies on the way back to his home planet.

> CATCH YOU ON THE FLIP SIDE, DUDEMEISTERS! NOT!

The ratings of "The Itchy & Scratchy Show" plummet, sending producer Roger Meyers, Jr., on a market-research mission to discover the reason. When Lisa tells him that the characters in the show have lost their impact, Meyers creates a new character, Poochie.

Bart and Lisa convince Homer to audition for Poochie's voice. He gets the part and is teamed with June Bellamy, who does the voices of Itchy and Scratchy. Together, they make publicity appearances, fielding questions from nerdy fans.

Poochie's debut is not well received by the show's viewers. When Homer finds out that his character will be killed off, he refuses to cooperate and creates his own lines instead of reading from the script. Homer thinks he has succeeded in convincing Meyers to keep Poochie alive, but in the next episode, the character is edited out.

SHOW HIGHLIGHTS

Roy: Mysterious teenager in baggy jeans and sunglasses who lives with the Simpsons. He bears a striking resemblance to Poochie and calls Homer, "Mr. S."

Auditioning for the voice of Poochie: Lionel Hutz, Jimbo, Kearney, Miss Hoover, Hans Moleman, Troy McClure, Otto, and Homer.

"Ruff, ruff! I'm Poochie the rockin' dog!" The line of dialogue used to audition potential Poochies.

"Hi, I'm Troy McClure. You may remember me from such cartoons as 'Christmas Ape' and 'Christmas Ape Goes to Summer Camp.'"

"Far be it from me to gloat in another's downfall, but I have a feeling no children are going to be crying when this puppy is put to sleep."

"I have to go now. My planet needs me." Words edited into Poochie's script to speed up his departure.

"Now, kids, we all know that sometimes when cartoon characters die, they're back again the very next week. That's why I'm presenting this sworn affidavit that Poochie will never, ever, ever return."

Research Group:

Moderator: *Okay. How many of you kids would like "Itchy & Scratchy" to deal with real-life problems, like the ones you face every day?*
All kids: *Me! / I would.*
Moderator: *And who would like to see them do just the opposite, getting into far-out situations involving robots and magic powers?*
All kids: *Me! / I would.*
Moderator: *So, you want a realistic, down-to-earth show that's completely off the wall and swarming with magic robots?*

Poochie's Rap:

The name's Poochie D. / And I rock the telly. / I'm half Joe Camel and a third Fonzarelli. / I'm the Kung-Fu hippie / from gangsta city. / I'm a rappin' surfer. / You the fool I pity.

& POOCHIE SHOW

Episode 4F12
Original Airdate: 2/9/97
Writer: David S. Cohen
Director: Steve Moore
Guest Voice: Alex Rocco as Roger Meyers, Jr.

Lisa's Suggestion:

Lisa: *Um, excuse me, sir. The thing is, there's not really anything wrong with "The Itchy & Scratchy Show." It's as good as ever. But after so many years, the characters just can't have the same impact they once had.*
Roger Meyers, Jr.: *That's it. That's it, little girl!! You've saved "Itchy & Scratchy"!*
Lawyer: *Please sign these papers indicating that you did not save "Itchy & Scratchy."*

Brainstorm:

Network executive: *We at the network want a dog with attitude. He's edgy. He's in your face. You've heard the expression "Let's get busy?" Well, this is a dog who gets biz-zay. Consistently and thoroughly.*
Krusty: *So he's proactive, huh?*
Network executive: *Oh, God, yes. We're talking about a totally outrageous paradigm.*
Writer #3: *Excuse me, but "proactive" and "paradigm?" Aren't those just buzzwords that dumb people use to sound important? Not that I'm accusing you of anything like that. (pause) I'm fired, aren't I?*
Roger Meyers, Jr: *Oh, yes. The rest of you writers start thinking up a name for this funky dog. I don't know, something along the lines of, say, Poochie. Only more proactive.*

Homer Tries Out for Poochie:

Roger Meyers, Jr.: *Now that's just bad; you got no attitude, you're barely outrageous, and I don't know what you're in but it's not my face. Next.*
Homer: *(harsh) Oh, "no attitude," eh? Not "in your face," huh? Well, you can cram it with walnuts, ugly!*
Roger Meyers, Jr.: *That's it! That's the Poochie attitude! Do that again!*
Homer: *Huh? I can't. I don't remember what I did.*
Roger Meyers, Jr.: *Then you don't get the job. Next.*
Homer: *(harsh) I don't get the job, do I? Well, boo-hoo! I don't get to be a cartoon dog!*
Roger Meyers, Jr.: *That's it! You've got the job!*
Homer: *Oh, now I got the job, huh? (instantly softening) Oh, thank you.*

Homer's First Recording Session:

Roger Meyers, Jr.: *You folks ready to begin?*
Homer: *Uh, I guess. Is this episode going on the air live?*
June Bellamy: *No, Homer. Very few cartoons are broadcast live—it's a terrible strain on the animators' wrists.*

At the "Meet the Voices of Itchy & Scratchy & Poochie" Signing:

Doug: *Hi, question for Ms. Bellamy. In episode 2F09, when Itchy plays Scratchy's skeleton like a xylophone, he strikes the same rib twice in succession yet he produces two clearly different tones. I mean, what are we, to believe that this is some sort of a, a magic xylophone or something? Boy, I really hope somebody got fired for that blunder.*
June Bellamy: *Uh, well, uh...*
Homer: *I'll field this one. Let me ask you a question. Why would a man whose shirt says "Genius at Work" spend all of his time watching a children's cartoon show?*
Doug: *I withdraw my question.*
Database: *Excuse me, Mr. Simpson, on the Itchy & Scratchy CD-ROM, is there a way to get out of the dungeon without using the wizard's key?*
Homer: *What the hell are you talking about?*

Springfield Responds to Poochie:

(Various Springfield residents gather in the Simpsons' home to watch the debut episode of "The Itchy & Scratchy & Poochie Show." The show ends and the audience reacts.)
Nelson: *Aagh. That stunk.*
Homer: *Well, what did everybody think?*
(People grumble and walk out. Ned Flanders and Lenny stay for a moment.)
Ned: *Homer, I can honestly say that was the best episode of "Impy and Chimpy" I've ever seen.*
Carl: *Yeah, you should be very proud, Homer. You, uh…got a beautiful home here.*

Homer: *I'm the worst Poochie, ever.*
Lisa: *No, it's not your fault, Dad. You did fine. It's just that Poochie was a soulless by-product of committee thinking. You can't be cool just by spouting a bunch of worn-out buzzwords.*
Bart: *Hey, don't have a cow, Lis.*

Comic Book Guy: *Last night's "Itchy & Scratchy" was, without a doubt, the worst episode ever. Rest assured, I was on the Internet within minutes, registering my disgust throughout the world.*
Bart: *Hey, I know it wasn't great, but what right do you have to complain?*
Comic Book Guy: *As a loyal viewer, I feel they owe me.*
Bart: *What? They've given you thousands of hours of entertainment for free! What could they possibly owe you? If anything, you owe them!*
Comic Book Guy: *Worst episode ever.*

JOHN

Occupation:
Owner/operator of Cockamamie's collectible shop.

Taste:
Things that are tragically ludicrous or ludicrously tragic.

Favorite article of clothing:
Second-hand bowling shirt from Goodwill, formerly belonging to a guy named Homer.

Knows:
Where Kent Brockman was caught cheating in the Springfield Marathon; where Lupe Velez bought the toilet she drowned in; all the deer in Springfield migrated north when they converted the park into AstroTurf.

Belief:
Ultrasuede is a miracle.

> THIS IS A SORDID LITTLE BURG, ISN'T IT? MAKES ME SICK, IN A WONDERFUL WAY.

Guest Voice:
John Waters as John

SHOW HIGHLIGHTS

Bouvier Heritage:
Lisa: *Aw, Mom, are you sure you want to sell a family heirloom to pay the gas bill? I mean, what would your grandma say?*
Marge: *I'm sure she'd be proud that her descendants had piping-hot tap water and plenty of warm, dry underwear.*

At the Shop:
Marge: *Oh, Homer, look! Look! A TV Guide owned by Jackie O.!*
John: *Oh, you should see the crossword puzzle! She thought that "Mindy" lived with "Mark."*
Homer: *Give her a break! Her husband was killed!*

"**OhmyGod! OhmyGod! OhmyGod! OhmyGod! I danced with a gay! Marge, Lisa, promise me you won't tell anyone. Promise me!**" Homer, after Marge informs him that John is a homosexual.

"**Ohh, my son doesn't stand a chance! The whole world has gone gay!**" Homer, at the factory where he takes Bart to see real men. It turns out to be a gay steel mill.

"**Something about a bunch of guys alone together in the woods... seems kinda gay.**" Bart's take on hunting.

"**Well, the sound is just brutal. And I figured reindeer would naturally be afraid of their cruel master, Santa Claus. I mean, wouldn't you be?**" John, on his plan to save the day with his remote-controlled Japanese Santa.

"**Is it okay to come out now, Mr. Gay Man, sir?**" Barney, from underneath a trough.

Discovery:
John: *Hmmm. Well, see... here's—here's the thing on this. It's a Johnny Reb bottle, early 70's. One of the J&R Whiskey "Liquor Lads." Two books of Green Stamps, if I'm not mistaken.*
Marge: *Oh, no. Oh, no, no, no, no. No. It's a very, very old figurine.*
John: *No, it's—it's a liquor bottle. See?*

(Marge is awakened by Homer's strange noises. She turns on the light.)
Marge: *Homie, I can hear you chewing on your pillow. What's wrong?*
Homer: *Marge, the boy was wearing a Hawaiian shirt!*
Marge: *So?*
Homer: *There's only two kinds of guys who wear those shirts—gay guys and big fat party-animals. And Bart doesn't look like a big fat party-animal to me.*

"**All right, everybody got their ticket? Then get ready for today's Super-Barto jackpot drawing!**" Bart, to his friends, as he puts numbered balls in the dryer and turns it on.

"**He didn't give you gay, did he? Did he?**"

"**Homer, you are the living end!**" John, to Homer, as the two do the Bump in the living room.

"**No refunds! Force majeure! Read the back of your ticket!**" Bart, to his fleeing friends after the gas line on the dryer ruptures.

Albums John Eyes in the Simpson Collection:
"The New Christy Minstrels," "Ballads of the Green Berets," "Loony Luau," "The Wedding of Linda Bird Johnson."

Marge Spells It Out for Homer:
Marge: *Homer, didn't John seem a little festive to you?*
Homer: *Couldn't agree more, happy as a clam.*
Marge: *He prefers the company of men!*
Homer: *Who doesn't?*
Marge: *Homer, listen carefully: John is a ho-mo-*
Homer: *Right.*
Marge: *-sexual! (Homer screams.)*

THE STUFF YOU MAY HAVE MISSED

The name of John's store is "Cockamamie's."

Buttons in John's shop include "Quayle Can't Fail," "Click with Dick," "I Fell for Dole."

One of the stores in the mall is called "One-Size-Fits-All Lingerie Store."

The caption on Jackie O's *TV Guide* cover reads: "Laverne and Shirley: Too Daring for TV?"

When John is introduced in this episode, a plastic pink flamingo is lying against the wall behind him. *Pink Flamingos* is the title of one of John Waters's films.

A sign for Fudd beer (introduced in 8F19, "Colonel Homer") hangs in John's store.

After one of Bart's stunts detaches the family dryer and ignites the gas main, the Simpsons are left with a $900 bill from the Springfield Gas Company. They try to sell an old family heirloom at a collectibles store to pay for it, but they find out that the heirloom is actually a liquor bottle. Nonetheless, the family strikes up a relationship with John, the store owner.

The Simpsons invite John over to assess their other belongings and Homer takes a liking to him. However, when Marge informs him that John is gay, Homer refuses to see John again. Soon afterwards, Homer notices changes in Bart's behavior and fears that John is influencing his son.

Homer embarks on a campaign to make Bart more "manly." Following a trip to a gay steel mill, Homer, Moe, Barney, and Bart leave on a hunting trip, and find themselves at a reindeer pen at a Christmas theme park. The men urge Bart to kill a reindeer, but he refuses. Suddenly, the herd gets aggressive and surrounds the group. Just as the reindeer attack Homer, John arrives with a remote-controlled Santa, which neutralizes the herd. Homer thanks John for saving his life.

BROTHER FROM ANOTHER SERIES

Episode 4F14   Original Airdate: 2/23/97   Writer: Ken Keeler   Director: Pete Michels   Guest Voice: Kelsey Grammer as Sideshow Bob

With the help of Reverend Lovejoy, Sideshow Bob is released from prison. His brother, Cecil, puts him up and hires him to supervise the construction of the Springfield Hydroelectric Dam. Bart suspects that Bob is masterminding another diabolical scheme.

Bart and Lisa trail Bob to see what he is up to. They sneak into his office and discover a suitcase filled with money. A moment later, Bob catches them. He tries to explain his innocence, but Bart and Lisa refuse to believe him until

Cecil enters and holds them all at gunpoint.

Cecil's plan is to blow up the dam, along with Bob, Bart, and Lisa, while he gets away with the $15 million he embezzled from the project. He assumes that Bob will be blamed, allowing him to get revenge on Bob for stealing his role as Krusty's sidekick. Cecil locks Bart, Lisa, and Bob in a chamber, but they escape and foil Cecil's plan. Although he is innocent, Bob is sent to prison along with his brother.

CECIL

SHOW HIGHLIGHTS

"Oh, great. Whenever a woman passes by, I suppose it will be my job to lead the hooting. 'Oh, yeah. Shake it, madam. Capital knockers.'" Sideshow Bob, finding out he will supervise the construction crew.

"Well, Krusty, as you remember, after I tried to frame you for armed robbery, I tried to murder Selma Bouvier. Let's see, I rigged the mayoral elections, I tried to blow up Springfield with a nuclear device, and I tried to kill you, and whenever I could find spare time, I've tried to murder Bart Simpson."

"Free comedy tip, slick: the pie gag's only funny when the sap's got dignity—like that guy! Hey Hal, pie job for Lord Autumnbottom, there!"

Lisa: It's hopeless. Utterly, utterly hopeless.
Sideshow Bob: Oh, I see. When it's one of my schemes, you can't foil it fast enough. But when Cecil tries to kill you, it's "Hopeless, utterly hopeless."

Cecil: I'm aware of your felonious past, but you are still my brother. And blood is thicker than bread and water.
Sideshow Bob: You don't have to worry about me, brother. I'm all murdered out.

Bart: Man, those cons love Krusty! Inside that hardened criminal beats the heart of a ten-year-old boy.
Lisa: And vice-versa.

"I'm telling you, Cecil, I can't take much more of this! Rustic workmen who've turned the saniJohn into a smokehouse! Coveralls that don't quite cover all! And a psychotic little boy who won't stop hounding me!"

"And now to kill you. There may be a slight ringing in your ears. Fortunately, you'll be nowhere near them." Cecil, poised to blow up Bob and Bart.

"Oh, poppycock! I called it at the arraignment!" Cecil, fighting Bob for the top bunk in their cell.

Krusty the Clown Prison Special Song Lyrics:

I slugged some jerk in Tahoe / They gave me one to three / My high-priced lawyer sprung me on a tech-ni-cal-i-ty / I'm just visiting Springfield Prison / I get to sleep at home tonight.

(Cecil and Bob follow Cletus down to the cement mixer, where a dog stands rigid, covered in cement.)
Cecil: See, Cousin Merle and me was playin' fetch with Geech—that's our old smellhound, and—
Cousin Merle: Geech gone to heaven, Mr. Terwilliger.
Bob: Oh, Cousin Merle—really!
Cecil: Temper, temper. You know Cousin Merle "ain't been quite right" lately.

Cecil: At last, I'm going to do what Bob never could—kill Bart Simpson!
Bart: By throwing me off a dam? Isn't that a little crude for a genius like you?
Cecil: Ooh, I suppose it is. Heh. If anyone asks, I'll lie.

Homer: Sure, you're the one who ruined all of Sideshow Bob's criminal schemes—
Marge: We're very proud of you, by the way.
Homer: And sure, he's probably so insane with rage that he'd butcher you horribly if he could—
Marge: But he's safely locked away!
Homer: In a medium security prison.
Marge: For life.
Homer: Unless he gets out somehow.
Marge: Which is impossible!
Homer: Or so you'd think, except he's done it so many times before.

Sideshow Bob: You—saved my life, Bart.
Bart: Yeah—I guess that means you can't ever try to kill me again, huh?
Sideshow Bob: Oh, I don't know about that. Joking! Joking!

THE STUFF YOU MAY HAVE MISSED

A sign in the Springfield Prison visiting room reads, "Please Visit Only YOUR Convict."

All of the stained-glass windows in the prison chapel have bars on them.

A *Springfield Shopper* headline reads, "Maniac to Live at Brother's Apartment."

Pictures of Tom Brokaw and Birch Barlow hang behind Bob's table at the Pimento Grove.

Bart and Lisa rummage for clues in a "Trash-Co waste disposal unit"; Otto sleeps in a Trash-Co in 8F21, "The Otto Show."

Signs held by the crowd upon Bob's release: "Keep Bob Locked Up," "You're Making a Mistakes," "Ban the Bob," and "Crime Yes, Criminals No."

HEY, CHILDREN, MEET ME... SIDESHOW CECIL.

SANDWICH DELIVERY GUY

Occupation:
Oversized submarine sandwich maker/deliverer.

Nationality:
Italian, by way of the Bronx.

Identifying characteristics:
Wears short-sleeve shirt sporting colors of the Italian flag.

Tends to:
Skimp on the vinegar unless you tell him differently.

> GOOD EVENING THERE, MISS. HERE'S YOUR GIANT PARTY SUB, SWIMMING IN VINEGAR, JUST HOW YOU LIKE IT. IT'S GONNA BE $2.25, PLUS TIP.

MY SISTER, MY SITTER

Episode 4F13   Original Airdate: 3/2/97   Writer: Dan Greaney   Director: Jim Reardon

SHOW HIGHLIGHTS

"I'm walking on the waterfront, once the center of a thriving squid-gutting industry, now abandoned by all but a few longshoremen and allied tradespeople. But, the decades of rot will end with the opening of the South Street Squidport, an upscale shopping promenade with authentic maritime theming."

"Simpson?! Look, we've already been out there tonight for a sisterectomy, a case of severe butt-rot, and a leprechaun bite. How dumb do you think we are?"   The 911 operator, to Lisa.

"This is an outrage! I'm two years and thirty-eight days older than she is! This is the greatest injustice in the history of the world!"

Lisa: Where are the dice?
Todd: Daddy says dice are wicked.
Rod: We just move one space at a time. It's less fun that way.

"Well, I'm not leaving 'til I get paid. I get five hundred just for 'Hey hey!'"

Air Force Officer: We got a report that a Lisa Simpson spotted a UFO.
Lisa: I didn't see any UFO!
Air Force Officer: That's right, miss. You didn't.

"Ew, your arm! It's got extra corners!"   Lisa, to Bart, after he dislocates his arm.

"Joe, um, I must've, like, fallen on a bullet and it, like, drove itself into my gut."   Snake, dripping blood from his stomach in Dr. Nick Riviera's office.

(When Bart refuses to go to bed, Lisa begins pulling him across the carpet; Bart goes limp.)
Lisa: Why do you have to make this so hard?
Bart: I'm using nonviolent resistance.
Lisa: Uch! The idea that you would compare yourself to Mahatma Gandhi...
Bart: Who?

Marge: Oh, that sounds fabulous, Homer. Stores throw the best parties.
Homer: You like parties, huh? Well, I just remembered they're having a big one down at the waterfront this weekend.
Marge: You didn't remember that. You just saw it on TV.
Homer: The important thing is I didn't imagine it.

(The crowd at the Squidport looks at Lisa hunched over Bart's body at the bottom of the hill.)
Maude Flanders: She's murdered her brother!
Lenny: And she's tryin' to dump the body in the harbor!
Otto: Well, duh...
Sideshow Mel: And as a grim finale, she plans to drown that poor caged baby!
Lisa: (squinting into the glare) Oh, what's happening? Where am I?
Helen Lovejoy: And she is on drugs!!!

Flanders: Homer, I've got a fozzie of a bear of a problem. Y'know, Maude and her mother were visiting Tyre and Sidon, the twin cities of the Holy Land. They must've kneeled in the wrong place and prayed to the wrong God, because, well, they're being held prisoner by militants of some sort.
Homer: Militants, huh? Well, if I were you, I'd kick their asses.
Flanders: Well, any hoodily-doodle, the embassy says it's just a routine hostage-taking—but I have to drive to Capital City, fill out some forms to get 'em out. Could you possibly watch the kids tonight?
Homer: Uh, gee, I'd really love to want to help you, Flanders, but...uh, Marge was taken prisoner in the...Holy Land and uh...
Lisa: I'll do it! I'll babysit!
Flanders: Well, I don't know, Lisa. You're awfully young, and the boys can be a handful. Todd's been pinching everyone lately.
Lisa: But I'm smart and responsible, and my parents will be right next door!
Flanders: Well, what do you say, Homer? Can Lisa babysit for my kids?
Lisa: Please, please, please!
Homer: Eh, I'll have to ask her.

THE STUFF YOU MAY HAVE MISSED

When Kent Brockman talks about the "allied tradespeople" who remain at Springfield's waterfront district, the camera flashes on a hooker in shorts and halter top and smoking a cigarette.

The marquee of the Springfield Community Church reads, "No Synagogue Parking."

The Babysitter Twins books that Lisa and Janey read are *The Formula Formula* and *The President's Baby Is Missing.*

Flanders wears a yellow ribbon on his sweater as he tells Homer that Maude and her mother have been taken hostage.

The ad for "Dr. Nick's Walk-In Clinic" boasts "Complete Confidentiality" and that it's "As Good as Dr. Hibbert."

Lisa expresses an interest in babysitting, but Marge worries that she is too young. One night, Flanders urgently needs a sitter and offers Lisa the job. He gives her a glowing review, and Lisa gets steady work. Homer and Marge are so impressed that they ask her to babysit for Bart one evening while they attend the Squidport gala.

Bart is outraged that his younger sister is permitted to babysit him. After Homer and Marge leave, he feeds Maggie caffeine-rich coffee ice cream and embarks on a series of pranks that unnerve Lisa. When Bart refuses to go to bed, Lisa lunges at him, knocking him down the stairs and dislocating his arm.

To make his injuries appear more severe and get Lisa in further trouble, Bart bangs his head against a door until he is unconscious. Lisa panics and places Bart's limp body in a wheelbarrow in order to transport him to Dr. Nick's clinic. However, Bart falls out and rolls down a hill, stopping only yards from the location of the gala. The townspeople are mortified, but the next day, Lisa receives even more offers for babysitting jobs.

HOMER VS. THE EIGHTEENTH AMENDMENT

Episode 4F15 Original Airdate: 3/16/97 Writer: John Swartzwelder Director: Bob Anderson Guest Voice: Joe Mantegna as Fat Tony

During Springfield's St. Patrick's Day Parade, a Duff Beer float sprays beer into the crowd. Bart, holding a novelty horn to his mouth, catches most of the liquid and becomes very drunk. After images of Bart in his inebriated state are broadcast on TV, a group of women bursts into City Hall and demands an all-out ban on the sale of alcohol. Responding to their concerns, a clerk discovers a prohibition law that has been on the books for 200 years but has never been enforced. On the basis of this law, Mayor Quimby declares an end to liquor sales.

Unable to stop gangster Fat Tony from smuggling alcohol into Moe's speakeasy, Chief Wiggum is replaced by Rex Banner, an Elliott Ness-type from Washington, who puts Fat Tony out of business. When Moe's liquor supply dries up, Homer steals Duff barrels from the city dump and masterminds a complex plan to bring the beer into the speakeasy.

"Beer Baron" Homer's beer supply is soon depleted, and Homer concocts his own "bathtub hooch" in the basement. Eventually, he ends his bootlegging career and approaches Chief Wiggum with a plan: the Chief will restore his good name by "exposing" Homer. As Homer is about to receive his punishment under the ancient prohibition law by being catapulted out of town, he is saved by an impassioned speech by Marge. As Banner rebuts, he steps into the catapult and is cast away by Wiggum. Belatedly, the City Hall clerk announces that the statute had, in fact, been repealed. The townspeople celebrate by getting drunk.

BEER BARON BEATS BANNER — Family Sedan Outruns Cops

LISTEN, RUMMY, I'M GOING TO SAY IT PLAIN AND SIMPLE. WHERE'D YOU PINCH THE HOOCH? IS SOME BLIND TIGER JERKING SUDS ON THE SIDE?

SHOW HIGHLIGHTS

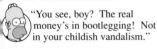
"Top o' the mornin' to ye on this gray, drizzly afternoon. Kent O'Brockman live on Main Street, where today, everyone is a little bit Irish! Eh-heh, except, of course, for the gays and the Italians."

"Parades just bring out so many emotions in me: joy, excitement, looking..."

"Duff Zero": The new alcohol-free Duff marketed to counter the new prohibition. It puts Duff out of business within 30 minutes.

"You see, boy? The real money's in bootlegging! Not in your childish vandalism."

"Well, I'll tell you what we're looking at, young man—a town gone mad. A town whose very conscience was washed away in a tide of beer and green vomit."

Mayor Quimby: *You can't seriously want to ban alcohol. It tastes great, makes women appear more attractive, and makes a person virtually invulnerable to criticism.*
Helen Lovejoy: *Oh, won't somebody please think of the children?!??*
Maude Flanders: *What kind of an example are we setting?*
Mayor Quimby: *Ladies, please. All our founding fathers, astronauts, and World Series heroes have been either drunk or on cocaine.*

"To alcohol! The cause of— and solution to—all of life's problems!"

"Tuck in that shirt! Get those shoes shined! Take that badge out of your mouth! You're police officers!" Rex Banner, taking control of the Springfield Police Department.

Moe: *Yeah, all right, listen up. This is the busiest drinkin' day of the year. Where are the designated drivers?*
(A few men raise their hands.)
Moe: *Beat it! I got no room for cheapskates.*

Marge: *What happened to you, Homer? And what happened to the car?*
Homer: *Nothin'.*
Marge: *I don't think it had broken axles before.*
Homer: *Before, before! You're livin' in the past, Marge. Quit livin' the past!*

Rex Banner: *Are you the Beer Baron?*
Comic Book Guy: *Yes, but only by night. By day, I'm a mild-mannered reporter for a major metropolitan newspaper.*
Rex Banner: *Don't crack wise with me, Tubby!*
Comic Book Guy: *Tubby?* (he looks at his stomach) *Oh, yes, Tubby.*

Narrator: *Dateline: Springfield. With prohibition back in force, sobriety's peaceful slumber was shattered by its noisy neighbor: the speakeasy!*
Homer: *Glad you're finally back in business, Moe.*
Moe: *Yeah, that was a scary coupla hours.*
Narrator: *The suppliers of the illegal booze? Gangsters, running truckloads of smuggled hooch all the way from Shelbyville. And John Law was helpless!*

> **Moe's Pet Shop:**
> The marquee fronting Moe's new speakeasy.

THE STUFF YOU MAY HAVE MISSED

Moe carries a jug that reads "Green Dye— Poison" into his tavern on St. Patrick's Day.

Businesses along the parade route include: "Twelve-Day Dry Cleaners," "Pawn Shop," and "Heinrich's Monocle Shop."

Signs held by the angry group of temperance women at City Hall: "Draft Men, Not Beer," "Prohibition Now!" and "Say No to Drunks."

A banner in Springfield reads, "Springfield— Clean and Sober for .75 Days!"

A parade float carries the banner, "2000 Years of Irish Cops." Another says, "The Drunken Irish Novelists of Springfield."

Flashed on the TV screen as Bart stumbles around in a drunken stupor is the label, "Drunken Boy–Live."

Quimby: *I run this town. You're just a bunch of low-income nobodies.*
Quimby's aide: (low) *Uh, election in November. Election in November.*
Mayor Quimby: *What, again? This stupid country.*

Guest Voice:
Dave Thomas as Rex Banner.

MATHEMAGICIAN

Identity:
Party mathematics entertainer.

Wears:
Wizard's blue robe; pointy hat; and horn-rimmed glasses.

Tools of trade:
Chalkboard; chalk.

Secret shame:
Can't divide well.

> NOW, PREPARE TO MARVEL AT THE MYSTERIES OF THE UNIVERSE AS I MAKE THIS REMAINDER DISSAPEAR.

Mrs. Krabappel and Principal Skinner strike up a conversation at Martin's birthday party and suddenly take a romantic interest in one another. When a batch of bacteria-laden oysters sends most of the children, except Bart, to the hospital, they sneak away to Martin's playhouse, where a shocked Bart sees them kiss.

The following Monday, Skinner and Krabappel overhear Bart preparing to tell his classmates about their romance. In exchange for his silence, they arrange for Milhouse to inherit Bart's permanent record. Bart becomes their go-between and exchanges their love notes. Tired of being used, he assembles his classmates and opens the janitor's closet, exposing Skinner and Krabappel locked in a passionate embrace.

As word about the children's discovery spreads, the story is exaggerated, suggesting more illicit behavior between Skinner and Krabappel than simply kissing. Superintendent Chalmers gives Skinner an ultimatum: end the relationship or face dismissal. Skinner refuses, and Chalmers fires them both. Following Bart, Skinner and Krabappel lock themselves on the roof of the school with him and alert the news media. When the police arrive, they announce their one demand: that the town respect and celebrate their love. After a tense standoff, the townspeople confront the couple for having sex in the closet. Skinner maintains that they never had sex, revealing that he, in fact, is still a virgin. The matter is cleared up, and Skinner and Krabappel are reinstated.

SHOW HIGHLIGHTS

 "As you know, Bart, your permanent record will one day disqualify you from all but the hottest and noisiest jobs."

"Good morning, students. Way to go there, Wendell. There's Ralph—he knows the score. Jimbo, how's that hat today? Janey, Janey, bo-faney!"

"The only way to survive a deadly blaze is...ah heck, life's too short for fire safety. Let's go outside and pick wildflowers!"

"Dear Edna, I want to 'Seymour' ('see more') of you! How about another secret rendezvous? Forever yours, Principal Skinner."
The note Skinner asks Bart to deliver to Krabappel.

"Wait a minute. Bart's teacher is named 'Krabappel'? Oh, I've been calling her 'Crandall.' Why didn't someone tell me? Ohhh, I've been making an idiot out of myself!"

> **Ralph:** *Mrs. Krabappel and Principal Skinner were in the closet making babies and I saw one of the babies and the baby looked at me.*
> **Chief Wiggum:** *Baby looked at you? Sarah—get me Superintendent Chalmers.*

 "That's why I love elementary school, Edna. The children will believe anything you tell them."

"Obviously, you two have no experience causing a scene."
Bart, to Skinner and Krabappel.

> **Skinner:** *Mrs. Krabappel, Bart has something he wants to say to you.*
> **Bart:** *I won't say it!*
> **Skinner:** *Bart!*
> **Bart:** *Oh, I love you, Edna Krabappel.* (The class erupts in laughter.)
> **Sherri and Terri:** *Bart's going to marry the teacher!*
> **Nelson:** *Where are you registered, Simpson?*

> **Skinner:** *Mmmm. This dessert is quite exquisite. What do you call it?*
> **Krabappel:** *Applesauce.*
> **Skinner:** *(chuckling) Oh, of course. I'm sorry, I-I don't get out to restaurants much.*
> **Krabappel:** *That's okay. I don't entertain much. Usually it's just soup for one, salad for one, wine for three...*

> **Skinner:** *Well, this party is certainly a break in my routine. You know, normally I spend my Saturdays carefully laying out my clothes for the following week, then I stroll down to the car wash to see if Gus is there...*
> **Krabappel:** *Oh, yeah, you gotta keep busy. I collect matchbooks from glamorous nightclubs. It's amazing. If you just write to them and ask them nicely...*
> **Skinner:** *Is this how you imagined your life, Edna?*
> **Krabappel:** *Well, yes, but then I was a very depressed child.*
> **Skinner:** *(raising a glass) To poor decisions.*

Saturday, at Martin's:

> **Bart:** *Uh—Mrs. K! Hey, it's Saturday! Your powers are useless against me.*
> **Mrs. Krabappel:** *Relax. I'm just here to have fun like everybody else. Don't think of me as a teacher.*
> **Bart:** *Okay. So...*
> **Mrs. Krabappel:** *Mmmm-hmmm?* (Bart and Mrs. Krabappel look at each other and laugh nervously. A few moments of awkward silence pass.)
> **Bart:** *Excuse me.*

> **Krabappel:** *Well, it's going to be hard to say goodbye to all of you. We've had a lot of fun together...Nelson, Nelson, Nelson. Oh, how many kids have you beaten up this year?*
> **Nelson:** *I 'unno. Fifty.*
> **Krabappel:** *Ah, fifty. Where does the time go?*

Episode 4F16 Original Airdate: 4/13/97 Writer: Ron Hauge Director: Dom Polcino

 Bart fills out an application for a credit card in Santa's Little Helper's name. The card is approved. Bart uses it to shop for catalogue items and buys a collie named Laddie from Vermont. The dog is well trained and the family falls in love with him.

Bart fails to pay the balance on his credit card and the bank repossesses Laddie. When the repo men arrive, Bart gives them Santa's Little Helper instead. He immediately feels guilty. Tiring of Laddie, Bart wants Santa's Little Helper back.

Bart gives Laddie to the police and sets off to find Santa's Little Helper. His search ends at the house of a blind man named Mr. Mitchell. Bart tries to kidnap his dog, but Mitchell traps him in a closet and calls the police, who arrive shortly afterwards. Laddie seems to take an immediate liking to Mitchell, but is, in fact, sniffing out a bag of marijuana in his pocket. Bart leaves with Santa's Little Helper as other police arrive at Mitchell's house with beer and party to reggae music.

> A FIRE DRILL DOES NOT
> DEMAND A FIRE
> A FIRE DRILL DOES NOT
> DEMAND A FIRE
> A FIRE DRILL DOES NOT
> DEMAND A FIRE

SHOW HIGHLIGHTS

"You gave both dogs away?? You know how I feel about giving!"

Revealed This Episode:
The Baby with One Eyebrow's name is Gerald.

Bart gets the family: 15 pounds of Vancouver smoked salmon; radio cookware for Marge; a golf shirt for Homer with his own corporate logo; "Truckers Choice Stay-Alert Tablets" for Lisa.

"This limited edition Collie comes fully trained by Major Jonas Fong, A.L.B.D.A. Only 800 will be bred; quite possibly the World's Best Dog." The ad that catches Bart's eye.

Santos L. Halper: Name on Bart's fraudulent credit card.

"Sprinkles": Santa's Little Helper's new name, given to him by Mitchell.

"You sound like a mature responsible person who wouldn't want an unpaid credit card bill to spoil all his hopes and dreams for the future, dreams such as home ownership, boat ownership, and event attendance." The representative from Moneybank Credit Services, calling Bart for payment.

"He unholied the holy water!" Agnes Skinner, complaining about Santa's Little Helper.

"I can't promise I'll try. But I'll try to try." Bart, to Lisa, after she tells him to "try not to freak out the blind man."

> **Lisa:** *Where's Santa's Little Helper?*
> **Bart:** *I took him to a kennel, two towns over. Just 'til the new dog gets settled.*

> **Bart:** *Put it all on my credit card, my good man.*
> **Comic Book Guy:** *Ooh, pardon me, "Santos"—if that is your real name, Bart Simpson—but your phony credit card is not good here. Now make like my pants and split.*

> **Lisa:** *Ooh, I knew you were up to no good.*
> **Bart:** *Okay, so I committed a little mail fraud. Haven't I been punished enough?*

> **Marge:** *Bart says he won him at a church carnival, two towns over.*
> **Lisa:** *In a truth-telling contest. Right, Bart?*
> **Bart:** *Uh, to the best of my recollection, yes.*

> **Bart:** *Santa's Little Helper? Guess I was the only one who loved him.*
> **Milhouse:** *You got that right. Remember the time he ate my goldfish? And you lied and said I never had any goldfish? Then why did I have the bowl Bart? Why did I have the bowl?*

> **Homer:** *Well, crying isn't gonna bring him back unless your tears smell like dog food. So you could either sit their crying and eating can after can of dog food until your tears smell enough like dog food to make your dog come back, or you can go out there and find your dog.*
> **Bart:** *You're right. I'll do it!*
> **Homer:** *Rats. I almost had him eatin' dog food.*

THE STUFF YOU MAY HAVE MISSED

Bart orders items from "The Covet House Catalog."

Repo Depot: Company that reclaims all of the merchandise purchased on Bart's card.

Bart's account number according to the card is 4123 0412 3456 7890. It expires on 12/03/99. It has a dovelike graphic on it.

The Simpsons take Laddie to the Springfield Dog Park, "Where Dogs Meet to Sniff Each Other and Bark."

The Springfield Community Church's gift shop's slogan is, "Nobody Beats the Rev."

Bart is wearing a monogrammed robe when he opens Laddie's crate.

Santa's Little Helper is chewing on a picture of Bart when Bart gives him away.

> **Bart:** *I'm gonna break into the blind man's yard and swipe the dog.*
> **Lisa:** *Bart, that is a new low.*
> **Bart:** *Hey, I'm not saying it's gonna be a dance around the maypole.*

> **Mitchell:** *So, what this comes down to is you want a blind man to give up his only companion.*
> **Bart:** *Yes, please.*
> **Mitchell:** *Tell you what. Why don't we let the dog decide?*

Description:
Well trained collie bred in Vermont.

Package:
Unlocked crate with greeting card and literature on maintenance.

Talents:
Rescuing babies; catching and tossing Frisbees; back-flips; sniffing out narcotics.

Secret shame:
Allows other dogs to be repossessed in his place.

Loved:
By all.

Episode 4F17 Original Airdate: 4/20/97 Writer: John Swartzwelder Director: Mark Kirkland

HIPPIE

Occupation:
Operator of the Uriah's Heap recycling center.

Badly kept secret:
Smokes hemp.

Wears:
Tie-dyes and sandals.

Hair accessory:
Red rubber band.

> IT SOUNDS LIKE YOU'RE WORKING FOR YOUR CAR. SIMPLIFY, MAN!

SHOW HIGHLIGHTS

 "Aw, recycling is useless, Lis. Once the sun burns out, this planet is doomed. You're just making sure we spend our last days using inferior products."

 "I'll keep it short and sweet. Family, religion, friendship: these are the three demons you must slay if you wish to succeed in business. When opportunity knocks, you don't want to be driving to the maternity hospital or sitting in some phony baloney church. Or synagogue. Questions?"

"Oh, so Mother Nature needs a favor? Well, maybe she should have thought of that when she was besetting us with droughts and floods and poison monkeys. Nature started the fight for survival and now she wants to quit because she's losing? Well, I say 'Hard cheese!'" Mr. Burns, reacting to Lisa's question about recycling.

"We're not allowed to read newspapers; they angry up the blood."

"Uh, well, if I did agree to help you, you could only earn money by doing good, socially responsible things. Nothing evil."

"Um, Dad... ten percent of 120 million dollars isn't twelve thousand. It's—" Lisa gives Homer another heart attack.

(A realtor shows a professional wrestler Burns's former house as Burns and Smithers leave.)
Bret "the Hitman" Hart: Eww. This place's got old man stink.
Mr. Burns: Ooooh...
Smithers: Don't listen to him, sir. You've got an enchanting musk.

(Burns leads Lisa out of the factory to a balcony over the sea. Below them, a giant net of sewn-together six-pack holders hangs over the water.)
Burns: I figured if one six-pack holder will catch one fish, a million sewn together will catch a million fish. Watch—
(Burns flips a lever and the net pulls in fish, squid, seaweed, dolphins, and a whale.)
Lisa: What's going on?
Burns: I call it the Burns Omni-net. It sweeps the sea clean!
(Saws and mashers transform the sea life into a reddish goo that travels down a trough into industrial drums.)
Lisa: (gasp) Oh, dear God.
Burns: I call our product: Li'l Lisa's Patented Animal Slurry! It's a high-protein feed for farm animals. Insulation for low-income housing, a powerful explosive, and a top-notch engine coolant. And best of all, it's made from 100% recycled animals!

Confederated Slave Holdings:
One of the many outdated stocks in Burns's stock portfolio.

Burns: It doesn't matter what your name is, you idiot! What I want to know is: will you help me get my money back?
Lisa: Ha! I'd never help you. You're the worst man in the world.
Burns: Yes, that's the kind of moxie I'm looking for—you're hired!

TV Moment:
Mr. Burns chases Lisa down for her assistance in a scene reminiscent of the opening to "That Girl."

Burns: Smithers, why didn't you tell me about this market crash?!
Smithers: Um, well, sir, it happened 25 years before I was born.
Burns: Oh, that's your excuse for everything!

Movie Moment:
Lisa runs around Springfield revealing the truth about Burns's recycling center à la Charlton Heston in Soylent Green.

THE STUFF YOU MAY HAVE MISSED

Homer gives Lisa a book by Leon Uris to recycle. Uris's books include Exodus and QB VII.

Posters on clubroom wall: "Up... ...with Business."; "I'm High... On Capitalism."

An entry in Burns's mental dictionary reads, "running dog, n: one who does someone else's bidding: LACKEY, ie. (SMITHERS)."

Burns wrote his autobiography, Will There Ever Be a Rainbow?, during the events that occur in episode 7F22, "Blood Feud."

Smithers's grocery list includes ointment, greens, and luncheon meat.

Smithers's Malibu Stacy collection is displayed on shelves in his apartment.

A Springfield Shopper headline reads, "Burns to Open Recycling Plant," with the subheadline, "Makes Other Bums Look Bad."

While addressing a Junior Achievers club at Springfield Elementary, Mr. Burns learns from Lisa that according to his autobiography, he is not worth as much money as he thinks he is. Smithers, his lawyers, and his accountants confirm that his holdings have depreciated in value considerably. Unwisely, he invests the rest of his money in archaic companies and loses everything. Penniless, Burns moves in with Smithers.

One day, while Burns is shopping, two grocery clerks catch him muttering to himself and commit him to the Springfield Retirement Castle. Disgusted by his surroundings, he vows to regain his fortune. When Lisa goes to the home to collect recyclables, Mr. Burns recalls her contrary nature towards him. He realizes that he lost his fortune by surrounding himself with "yes men." He asks Lisa to help him get his fortune back.

Lisa introduces Burns to recycling. Soon Burns has enough money to build his own recycling plant. He names it after Lisa and gives her the first tour. With pride, he shows her how he captures aquatic life and "recycles" it into an all-purpose "goo." Lisa is horrified. When Burns regains his fortune, he buys back the power plant. He pays Lisa her share of his profits, but she rips up the check, giving Homer a multiple heart attack.

Episode 4F18   Original Airdate: 4/27/97   Writer: Donick Cary   Director: Steve Moore

Concerned that Reverend Lovejoy is not meeting all the needs of his parishioners, Marge volunteers to help him. She begins to give advice to the members of the congregation who call in crisis. As Marge gains a loyal following in Springfield, Lovejoy laments that he is a "shepherd without a flock." Meanwhile, Homer is troubled by his discovery of a box of Japanese dish soap bearing his likeness. He calls the company that manufactures the soap to learn why his face is on the box.

Homer receives a videotape from the soap manufacturer that shows a bizarre commercial for the product featuring a character named "Mr. Sparkle." The video also illustrates how two company logos were combined to create "Mr. Sparkle," who happens to look just like Homer.

Unable to help Ned with a crisis, Marge calls Lovejoy, who finds Ned and rescues him from a den of baboons at the zoo. Telling the story in his next sermon, Lovejoy miraculously captures his congregants' interest.

SHOW HIGHLIGHTS

"Wh... what's going on? Wh... wha... why am I on a Japanese box?"

The Mr. Sparkle commercial:
(A housewife in her kitchen blows a whistle, bringing the Mr. Sparkle to life off of his box. He calls to her.)
Mr. Sparkle: I'm disrespectful to dirt! Can you see I am serious!
(Mr. Sparkle hovers over her dirty dishes, releasing sparkles over them. The dishes' grime disappears. Mr. Sparkle floats to the living room, where he bounces over a baby's xylophone. He then appears underwater, where three women are dancing.)
Mr., Sparkle: Get out of my way, all of you! This is no place for loafers. Join me or die. Can you do any less?
(The women stop dancing.)
Two of the women: What a brave corporate logo! I accept the challenge of "Mr. Sparkle."
Woman: Awsoma power!
(Mr. Sparkle blows magic dust over the girls as a graphic of a drumming monkey toy hovers in the upper left of the screen. The dust turns the girls into blue Sumos.)
(The scene changes to a reporter interviewing a two-headed cow.)
Reporter: Any plans for the summer?
(Mr. Sparkle appears and shatters the cow. Its disembodied eyes blink at him. The scene changes to Mr. Sparkle coming at us from an orange background.)
Mr. Sparkle: For lucky best wash, use Mr. Sparkle.

Lovejoy Meets Flanders:
(In a flashback to the seventies, Reverend Lovejoy is setting up his office when a forlorn Ned Flanders walks in.)
Flanders: Reverend, I'm, uh, I'm afraid something has happened.
Lovejoy: Well sit down and rap with me brother, that's what I'm here for.
Flanders: Well, I was talked into doing a dance called "the Bump," but my hip slipped and my buttocks came into contact with the buttocks of another young man!

"Mother's gone too far. She's put cardboard over her half of the television. We rented *Man without a Face*--I didn't even know he had a problem!"

The greeting of the English speaking Mr. Sparkle factory employee: "Hello chief, let's talk why not?"

"Don't thank me—thank Marge Simpson. She taught me that there's more to being a minister than not caring about people" Lovejoy, to Ned after the rescue.

(Marge answers Lovejoy's phone and talks to Moe.)
Moe: Uh, yeah, hi, I'm callin' for Reverend Lovejoy. Who is this?
Marge: Oh, well, this is… um… the, uh… the Listen Lady!
Moe: Yeah? Well, listen lady, I got so many problems I—I don't know where to begin here.
Marge: Okay. Why don't you start from the top?
Moe: Allrighty. Number one, I've lost the will to live.
Marge: Oh, that's ridiculous, Moe. You've got lots to live for.
Moe: Really? That's not what Reverend Lovejoy's been tellin' me. Wow, you're good, thanks.

Reverend Lovejoy's sermon, "Conquest of the County of the Apes."
"Baboons to the left of me, baboons to the right, the speeding locomotive tore through a sea of inhuman fangs. A pair of the great apes rose up at me, but BIFF! BAM! I sent them flying like two hairy footballs. A third came screaming at me—and that's when I got mad…"

Marge: But you can't let a few bad experiences sour you on helping people!
Lovejoy: Oh, sure I can.

Marge: The Lord only asks for an hour a week.
Homer: In that case, he should have made the week an hour longer. Lousy god.

Marge: Sermons about "constancy" and "prudissitude" are all very well and good, but the church could be doing so much more to reach out to people.
Lovejoy: Oh, I don't see you volunteering to make things better.
Marge: Well, okay. I will volunteer!
Lovejoy: I wasn't prepared for that.

THE STUFF YOU MAY HAVE MISSED

Ambulance, Bird, Disco Whistle: Alarm options on Lovejoy's pulpit, to awaken the congregation during or after a dull sermon.

Waiting in line to see Marge after Lenny are: Kirk Van Houten, Ruth Powers, The Skinners, Dr. Nick, Miss Hoover, and Larry the barfly.

Other messages on the Springfield Community Church's marquee read, "Sunday, The Miracle of Shame" and "The Listen Lady Is In."

Homer, Bart, and Lisa go to "The Happy Sumo" (introduced in 7F11, "One Fish, Two Fish, Blowfish, Blue Fish") to ask Akira about the box they found.

MR. SPARKLE

Occupation:
Magnet for foodstuffs. Banishes dirt to the land of wind and ghosts.

Residence:
Hokkaido, Japan.

Model:
The melding of a fish face and a light bulb.

Guest Voice:
Sab Shimono as Mr. Sparkle

FRANK GRIMES

Occupation:
New (late) Springfield Nuclear Power Plant worker.

Prized possessions:
His briefcase; his haircut; his personalized pencils.

Education:
Correspondence school diploma in nuclear physics—with a minor in determination.

Worst birthday:
His 18th, when he was blown up in a silo explosion.

Biggest success:
Teaching himself to hear and feel pain after his accident.

I CAN'T STAND IT ANYMORE! THIS WHOLE PLANT IS INSANE! INSANE, I TELL YOU!

A hard-working employee, Frank Grimes, is hired at the plant and takes an instant dislike to Homer. Disapproving of Homer's poor job performance and lackadaisical attitude, Grimes eventually declares that he and Homer are enemies. Meanwhile, at City Hall, Bart steps into a tax auction and buys an abandoned factory for a dollar. He hires Milhouse, and the two spend their days wreaking havoc at the factory until it collapes during Milhouse's graveyard shift.

Hoping to win Grimes's favor with a nice family dinner, Homer invites him over to discuss an important work issue. However, when Grimes sees Homer's beautiful home and family, he becomes even more bitter. To expose Homer's stupidity, he enters Homer in a children's contest to design a nuclear power plant. Homer wins the childrens' contest and when he is lauded by his peers, Grimes goes berserk. Imitating Homer's behavior, he runs amok through the plant and electrocutes himself. As he is laid to rest, the mourners laugh good-naturedly at Homer, who drools and mumbles in his sleep.

SHOW HIGHLIGHTS

"Looks like all my years of hard work have finally paid off." Bart, seeing his run-down factory for the first time.

"Stop laughing, you imbecile! Don't you realize how close you just came to killing yourself?!" Frank, saving Homer from taking a sip of sulfuric acid.

 "How dare you destroy my valuable wall and spill my priceless acid?! Did you really think you were going to get away with it?"

 "I'm not your buddy, Simpson. I don't like you. In fact, I hate you. Stay the hell away from me! Because from now on... we're enemies."

Moe: *As hard as it is to believe, some people don't care for me, neither.*
Homer: *(shaking head) No, I won't accept that.*
Moe: *No, it's true. I got their names written down right here, in what I call my, uh, "enemies list."*
Barney: *(taking the list and reading it) Jane Fonda, Daniel Schorr, Jack Anderson... Hey, this is Richard Nixon's enemies list! You just crossed out his name and put yours.*

Lisa: *Can I go downstairs and see what Dad's doing?*
Marge: *I wouldn't bother him, honey. He's making some kind of model for a contest. He says it's really high-tech stuff that we wouldn't understand.*
(Homer sticks his head in the kitchen.)
Homer: *Marge, do we have any elbow macaroni and glue-on sparkles?*

"Good morning, fellow employee. You'll notice that I am now a model worker. We should continue this conversation later, during the designated break periods. Sincerely, Homer Simpson."

"Well, basically I just copied the plant we have now. Then I added some fins to lower wind resistance. And this racing stripe here I feel is pretty sharp." Homer, describing his prize-winning power plant model.

"I'm peeing on the seat. Give me a raise?! Now I'm returning to work without washing my hands. But it doesn't matter, because I'm Homer Simpson! I don't need to do my work, 'cause someone else will do it for me. D'oh! D'oh! D'oh!" Frank Grimes, angrily impersonating Homer Simpson.

(Homer sits in the lunchroom, eating a sandwich.)
Homer: *Hiya Stretch, what's the good word?*
Frank: *My name is Grimes, uh, Simpson. Frank Grimes. I took the trouble to learn your name, the least you can do is learn mine.*
Homer: *Okay, Grimey.*
Frank: *Uh, you're eating my special dietetic lunch.*
Homer: *Who?*
(Annoyed, Frank clears his throat and points to the bag labeled "Property of Frank Grimes.")
Homer: *A ho-ho-ho, gee, oh, I'm sorry.*
Frank: *The bag was clearly marked; please be more careful in the future.*
Homer: *Check.*
(Homer takes another two bites out of the sandwich and puts it back in the bag.)

Grimes: *God, he eats like a pig!*
Lenny: *I dunno. Pigs tend to chew. I'd say he eats more like a duck.*
Grimes: *Well some kind of farm animal, anyway. And earlier today, I saw him asleep inside a radiation suit! Can you imagine that? He was hanging from a coat hook!*
Lenny: *He had three beers at lunch. That would make anybody sleepy.*

THE STUFF YOU MAY HAVE MISSED

A shoe falls to the ground following the silo explosion.

The framed picture of Lenny that Homer keeps on his console reads, "Homer—Have a good summer!—Lenny."

The pictures featuring Homer with Gerald Ford, Homer with Smashing Pumpkins, Homer and The Be Sharps with David Crosby, and Homer in outer space are from 3F09, "Two Bad Neighbors"; 3F21, "Homerpalooza"; 9F21, "Homer's Barbershop Quartet"; and 1F13, "Deep Space Homer," respectively.

Mr. Largo is at the tax seizures auction.

There is a softball sign-up sheet on the bulletin board at the power plant.

THE SIMPSONS SPIN-OFF SHOWCASE

Episode 4F20 Original Airdate: 5/11/97 Writers: David S. Cohen, Dan Greaney, Steve Tompkins Story: Ken Keeler Director: Neil Affleck
Guest Voices: Tim Conway as Himself, Gailard Sartain as Big Daddy

In a show hosted by Troy McClure, a trio of spin-offs features "The Simpsons" characters.

"Chief Wiggum, P.I." Chief Wiggum is a New Orleans detective and Principal Skinner is "Skinny Boy," his associate. A mysterious crime figure named Big Daddy kidnaps Wiggum's son, Ralph. Chasing Big Daddy through the streets of New Orleans, Wiggum recovers Ralph, but lets Big Daddy slip away, certain he'll meet the villain again.

"The Love-matic Grampa." The show's opening theme song explains how Grampa's soul gets lost on the way to heaven and ends up inhabiting the Love Tester machine at Moe's Tavern. Thanks to coaching from Grampa, Moe lands a date with a brassy brunette named Betty. Wanting Grampa's advice on his date, he brings the Love Tester on to the restaurant, hiding it in the men's room. Betty discovers Moe's scheme, but is flattered by his efforts to impress her.

"The Simpson Family Smile-Time Variety Hour." The entire Simpson clan, except Lisa, participates in this series of musical comedy skits, joined by special guest Tim Conway, playing a clan of beavers and 1950s teenyboppers.

SHOW HIGHLIGHTS

"'Spin-off:' is there any word more thrilling to the human soul? Hi! I'm Troy McClure! You may remember me from such TV spin-offs as 'Son of Sanford and Son' and 'After Mannix.'"

Troy McClure, explaining the Spin-Off Showcase: "Not long ago, the Fox network approached the producers of "The Simpsons" with a simple request: thirty-five new shows to fill a few holes in their programming line-up. That's a pretty daunting task and the producers weren't up to it. Instead, they churned out three Simpsons spin-offs, transplanting already popular characters into new locales and situations."

The Simpsons' Obligatory Appearance:
Wiggum: *Well, if it isn't my old friends from Springfield, the Simpsons! What brings you folks to New Orleans?*
Bart: *Mardi Gras, man! When the Big Easy calls, you gotta accept the charges!*
Lisa: *Chief Wiggum, I can't wait to hear about all the exciting, sexy adventures you're sure to have against this colorful backdrop!*
Wiggum: *Well, golly, I'd love to chat, but my son's been kidnapped. You haven't seen him, have you? Caucasian male, between the ages of 6 and 10, thinning hair?*

"Love-Matic Grampa" Theme:
While shopping for some cans/An old man passed away/He floated up toward Heaven/But got lost along the way/Now he's the Love-matic Grampa!/The wise, Socratic Grampa!/And he'll fill our hearts with looove!

Homer's Obligatory Appearance:
Homer: *Dad, is that really you?*
Love-matic Grampa: *Darn tootin', you lousy fink! You buried me naked and sold my suit to buy a ping-pong table. What kind of a son—* (Homer unplugs the Love-matic Grampa.)
Homer: *Pffft. Call me when you get a karaoke machine.*

Moe: *Hey, I don't need no advice from no pinball machine. I'll have you know, I wrote the book on love.*
Grampa: *Yeah—All Quiet on the Western Front!*

Chief Wiggum, P.I., the Exposition:
Wiggum: *Ah, New Orleans. The Big Easy. Sweet Lady Gumbo. Old...Swampy.*
Skinner: *I still don't understand, Clancy. Why give up your job as a small-town police chief to set up a detective shop in New Orleans?*
Wiggum: *Oh, lotsa reasons, I suppose. Got kicked off the force, for one thing.*
Skinner: *For massive corruption.*
Wiggum: *For massive—exactly.*
Skinner: *As for me, I was born and bred here on the mean streets of N'Awlins. Oh, sure, I left briefly to take that principal job in Springfield, but in my heart I—I've always been a small-time hustler.*
Wiggum: *I know, that's precisely why I hired you as my leg man, Skinny Boy. I want you to put the word out: Chief Wiggum is here to clean up this crime dump!*

"Chief Wiggum, P.I. will return... right now." Voiceover announcer, explaining a brief pause.

"I might as well come clean with ya. I ain't too good at talkin' to women and—and I really wanted to do ya, so I brought along the 'Love Tester' to help me. As you may have guessed, it's inhabited by the ghost of my friend's dead father."

"Inflation, trade deficit, horrible war atrocities, how are we supposed to do our big musical number with so many problems in the world?"

THE STUFF YOU MAY HAVE MISSED

Actor Troy McClure hosts this showcase amidst a sea of framed pictures depicting such vintage TV show spin-offs as "Laverne & Shirley," "The Ropers," "Fish," "Rhoda" and "The Jeffersons."

The picture from "Rhoda" features Valerie Harper and Julie Kavner who is the voice of Marge.

The episode features another Homer/Ape reference; he wears a giant ape mask at Mardi Gras.

Skinny-Boy's line, "He's gradually getting away, Chief," resembles "They're very slowly getting away," Skinner's line in 1F05, "Bart's Inner Child."

When Kent Brockman introduces "The Simpson Family Smile-Time Variety Hour," he says it is "live." The clock behind him at the start of the show reads "8:20," the approximate time the segment is watched in the Pacific and Eastern time zones.

"LISA"

Identity:
Slim adolescent posing as Lisa Simpson in "The Simpson Family Smile-Time Variety Hour."

Energy level:
Peppy; occasionally bubbly.

Hair color:
Blonde.

Intellect:
Marginal.

Honors:
Sophomore prom queen five years running.

Enjoys:
Leading cheers in annoying fashion.

I WANT CANDY!

COMMANDANT

Occupation:
Head man, Rommelwood Military Academy.

Bearing:
Rigid.

Attitude:
Sexist and no-nonsense in the proper military way.

Believes:
A military academy is for boys and men, not girls.

> ALL RIGHT, LET'S GO OVER THIS ONE MORE TIME, JUST TO MAKE SURE I UNDERSTAND THE SITUATION...YOU'RE A GIRL?

Guest Voice:
Willem Dafoe as Commandant

THE SECRET WAR OF LISA SIMPSON

Episode 4F21   Original Airdate: 5/18/97   Writer: Rich Appel   Director: Mike Anderson

While Bart and his classmates are on a field trip to the Springfield Police Station, Bart sneaks away and discovers a large quantity of bullhorns. Grouping them together, he speaks into the powerful, single mega-bullhorn. A soundwave explosion rocks all of Springfield, shattering windows and temporarily deafening the populace. As punishment, Homer and Marge enroll Bart in a military academy.

After surveying the academy, Lisa decides that she, too, would like to enroll. However, the facility has never had a female cadet and the academy's commandant is taken aback. Nevertheless, he relocates a group of cadets, giving Lisa her own barracks. The move creates a wave of resentment and hazing activities. Even Bart refuses to speak to his sister.

Later, Bart secretly apologizes to Lisa and asks her to remain at the academy. Lisa is convinced that she will not pass a test in which the cadets must traverse a 150-foot rope over thornbushes. Bart covertly trains her but publicly continues the silent treatment. Lisa begins to climb but stops halfway across, exhausted. Bart breaks with his classmates and shouts words of encouragement to her. Her spirits lifted, Lisa continues to climb and passes the test.

SHOW HIGHLIGHTS

 "Aw, can't anybody in this town take the law into their own hands?"

"By 1964, experts say man will have established twelve colonies on the moon, ideal for family vacations." From the 1952 Monotone educational film, "Moon of Earth," screened in Miss Hoover's class.

"You dream about this day for so long, then when it comes, you don't know what to say." Mrs. Krabappel, drinking champagne with Skinner as Bart is taken away to military school.

"Please don't make me stay, Dad! I'll do anything you say! I'll find religion! I'll be good sometimes!"

"You thought I couldn't but I could, I did, and I could do it again, let's do it again!" Lisa, after conquering "the Eliminator."

Chief Wiggum: *You know, you do have options. For example, there are behavior-modifying drugs. How wedded are you to the Bart you know?*
Homer: *Not very.*

Lisa: *It's not my nature to complain, but so far today, we've had three movies, two filmstrips, and an hour and a half of "magazine-time." I just don't feel challenged.*
Skinner: *Of course we could make things more challenging, Lisa, but then the stupider students would be in here complaining, furrowing their brows in a vain attempt to understand the situation.*

"Since you attended public school, I'm going to assume you're already proficient with small arms, so we'll start you off with something a little more advanced." Firing range instructor, handing Bart a mini-rocket launcher.

"And that's everything that happened in my life right up to the time I got this phone call." Grampa, running out of things to say while talking on the phone to Lisa.

(The Simpsons stop at a classroom on their tour.)
Cadet Larsen: *Truth is beauty, beauty truth, sir!!*
Lisa: *They're discussing poetry! Oh! We never do that at my school!*
Teacher: *But the truth can be harsh and disturbing. How can that be considered beautiful?*
Marge: *Well, they sure sucked the fun out of that poem.*

Marge: *Well, it certainly was nice of you to accept Bart in the middle of the semester.*
Commandant: *Fortunately, we've had a couple of recent "freak-outs," so that freed up a couple of bunks.*
Bart: *"Freak-outs?"*

Lisa Calls Grampa from Military School:
Lisa: *Oh, Grampa, you're not busy are you?*
Grampa: *Well, you're really asking two questions there. The first one takes me back to 1934. Admiral Byrd had just reached the Pole, only hours ahead of the Three Stooges...*

(Cadets in raincoats stand around Bart and Lisa doing push-ups in the rain.)
Cadet Larsen: *What's the matter? Don't girls like doing push-ups in the mud?*
Lisa: *Is there any answer I can give that won't result in more push-ups?*
(The cadets huddle.)
Cadet Platt: *No.*

Bart: *But if you quit, it'd be like an expert knot-tier quitting a knot-tying contest right in the middle of tying a knot.*
Lisa: *Why'd you say that?*
Bart: *I don't know, I was just looking at my shoelaces.*

THE STUFF YOU MAY HAVE MISSED

Framed pictures hang on a row of electric chairs in the Springfield Police station's "Museum of Crime."

The "Earth/Moon Weight Conversion Chart" featured in the film "Moon of Earth" is (c) 1952, U.S. Department of Moon.

Banana stickers on the police radio that Wiggum does not mention include "Mr. Ripe," "Yellow Fellow," and "Peel King."

Bart uses 15 bullhorns in his bullhorn-chain.

The motto on Rommelwood's front gate reads, "A Tradition of Heritage."

In the English class at Rommelwood, the blackboard reads, "John Keats (Civilian)–'Ode on a Grecian Urn.'"

INDEX